A HISTORY OF
MATRIMONIAL INSTITUTIONS

A HISTORY OF
MATRIMONIAL INSTITUTIONS

CHIEFLY IN ENGLAND AND THE UNITED STATES WITH AN INTRO-
DUCTORY ANALYSIS OF THE LITERATURE AND THE
THEORIES OF PRIMITIVE MARRIAGE
AND THE FAMILY

BY

GEORGE ELLIOTT HOWARD Ph.D.

PROFESSORIAL LECTURER IN THE UNIVERSITY OF CHICAGO AUTHOR OF "LOCAL
CONSTITUTIONAL HISTORY OF THE UNITED STATES"

VOLUME THREE

HUMANITIES PRESS
New York
1964

First Published 1904 by
The University of Chicago Press

Reprinted 1964 by
HUMANITIES PRESS, INC.
303 Park Avenue South
New York, N.Y. 10010

Library of Congress Catalog Card Number: 63-21164

Printed in U.S.A. by
NOBLE OFFSET PRINTERS, INC.
NEW YORK 3, N. Y.

TO

Alice Frost Howard

HER HUSBAND DEDICATES THIS BOOK IN
GRATEFUL RECOGNITION OF HER
AID IN MAKING IT

ANALYTICAL TABLE OF CONTENTS

VOLUME ONE

PART I

ANALYSIS OF THE LITERATURE AND THE THEORIES OF PRIMITIVE MATRIMONIAL INSTITUTIONS

xi

PART II

MATRIMONIAL INSTITUTIONS IN ENGLAND

VOLUME TWO

PART II — *Continued*

PART III

MATRIMONIAL INSTITUTIONS IN THE UNITED STATES

VOLUME THREE

PART III — *Continued*

PART III

MATRIMONIAL INSTITUTIONS IN THE UNITED STATES

CONTINUED

CHAPTER XVII

A CENTURY AND A QUARTER OF DIVORCE LEGISLATION IN THE UNITED STATES, 1776–1903

[BIBLIOGRAPHICAL NOTE XVII.— The session laws and compilations used in the preparation of this chapter are the same as those mentioned in Bibliographical Note XVI; and they are listed in the Bibliographical Index, V. The entire body of divorce laws enacted in each of the states and territories since 1775 has been examined. Among the decisions cited the most important are West Cambridge v. Lexington (October, 1823), 1 Pickering, *Mass. Reports*, 507–12; Putnam v. Putnam (September, 1829), 8 Pickering, *Mass. Reports*, 433–35; Desaussure's comments on the case of Vaigneur v. Kirk (1808), 2 *South Carolina Equity Reports*, 644–46; Justice Pope's opinion in McCrery v. Davis (1894), 44 *South Carolina Reports*, 195–227; Justice Nisbet's opinion in Head v. Head, 2 *Georgia Reports* (1847), 191–211; Van Voorhis v. Brintnall, 86 *New York Reports* (1881), 18; Willey v. Willey, 22 *Washington Reports* (1900), 115–21; and Estate of Wood, 137 *California Reports* (1902), 129 ff.

For summaries of the divorce laws of the states at different periods see Lloyd, *Treatise on the Law of Divorce* (Boston and New York, 1887); Hirsh, *Tabulated Digest of the Divorce Laws of the U. S.* (New York, 1888; new ed., 1901); Stimson, *American Statute Law* (Boston, 1886), I, 682–715; Fairbanks, *The Divorce Laws of Mass.* (Boston, 1887); Neubauer, "Ehescheidung im Auslande," in *ZVR.*, VIII, 278–316; IX, 160–74 (Stuttgart, 1889–91); Woolsey, *Divorce and Divorce Legislation* (2d ed., New York, 1882); and compare the works of Vanness, Noble, Convers, Snyder, Ernst, and Whitney mentioned in Bibliographical Note XVI. Whitmore has a helpful article on "Statutory Restraints on the Marriage of Divorced Persons," in *Central Law Journal*, LVII, 444–49 (St. Louis, 1903). Consult the literature described in Bibliographical Note XVIII.]

I. THE NEW ENGLAND STATES

DURING the colonial era the broad outlines and essential principles of the American divorce law, as it still exists in the various states, had already taken form. Long before the Revolution it was predetermined that a free and tolerant policy in this regard must prevail in the United States. The

3

task of the legislator during the century following the birth
of the nation has, in general, consisted in effecting a further
liberalization in the causes of divorce; while at the same
time the details of the system have been gradually wrought
out.   At the close of the period one finds much more elaborate and careful provisions regarding causes, residence, notice, alimony and property than at the beginning.   An
attempt will be made in this chapter to sketch the course of
legislation in all of the states during a hundred and twenty-
five years.   Necessarily only the more salient features can
be brought out.   The beginning and the end, with some of
the more important intervening changes, may be dwelt upon.
The immense volume of laws, the constant stream of legislative enactments, the ceaseless tinkering of the statute-
maker, the wearisome repetitions, render anything more than
this very difficult and perhaps unnecessary.   The most that
one can hope for is to make the right impression; to disclose the true perspective by a judicious selection and grouping of the materials.

   a) *Jurisdiction; causes and kinds of divorce.*—Through
their silence on the subject nearly all of the first state
constitutions left the power of granting divorces in the
hands of the legislative bodies.   In Massachusetts, however,
the practice of the provincial period was temporarily continued.   "All causes of marriage, divorce, and alimony,"
declares the constitution of 1780, "shall be heard by the
Governor and Council, until the Legislature shall by law
make other provision."[1]   Such provision was made in 1786.
Yet six years thereafter Governor Hancock is obliged to return to the senate unsigned a bill "for dissolving the bond of
matrimony between Daniel Chickering and Abigail his wife,"
remarking that it is unconstitutional and the proposed divorce
is for a cause for which by law only a separation *a mensa et*

---

[1] *Const. of Mass.* (1780), chap. 3.

thoro may be granted.[1]   By the act of 1786 all questions of divorce and alimony are referred to the "Supreme Judicial Court holden for the County where the parties live," and its decrees are final.[2] Here the jurisdiction remained until 1887, when it was vested in the superior court with appeal to the first-named tribunal; and the power to hear petitions for separate maintenance and for the care, custody, education, and support of minor children was given to the courts of probate in the several counties.[3]

The statute of 1786 is reactionary with respect to the grounds of divorce. It is expressly declared that no divorce from the bond of matrimony, in the proper sense of the word, shall be allowed except for impotency or adultery in either of the parties. But in the outset it is necessary to be on one's guard against a confusion of terms caused by a retention of canonical usage. In this act, and for many years in the statutes of Massachusetts, as in those of some of the other states, the sentence of nullity of void or voidable wedlock, on the usual grounds of forbidden degrees, bigamy, or the like, is called "divorce."[4] For the first time in the revision of 1835 such unions, if solemnized within the state, are declared to be "absolutely void, without any decree of divorce, or other legal process;"[5] and this is typical of the

---

[1] For the document containing this veto see *Acts and Laws of the Commonwealth of Mass.* (1790-91: reprinted by the secretary of state, Boston, 1895), 575, 576.

[2] *Laws of the Commonwealth of Mass., 1780-1816* (1807-16), I, 303.

[3] Act of May 31, 1887: *Supp. to the Pub. Stat. of the Com. of Mass., 1882-88* (1890), 584, 585.

[4] The act provides "That divorces from the bond of matrimony shall be decreed, in case the parties are within the degrees aforesaid, or either of them had a former wife or husband, or for impotency or adultery in either of the parties."— *Laws of the Com. of Mass., 1780-1816*, I, 301.

[5] "All marriages which are prohibited by law on account of consanguinity or affinity between the parties, or on account of either of them having a former wife or husband then living; all marriages, solemnized when either of the parties was insane or an idiot, and all marriages, between a white person and a negro, Indian or mulatto," shall, if solemnized within the state, be absolutely void, "without any decree of divorce, or other legal process."— *Rev. Stat. of the Com. of Mass.* (1836), 479. The same is true when either of the parties is under the age of consent, "if they

tendency in other states[1] to adopt what is now the prevailing usage.[2]

The act under discussion was conservative in another important respect. Divorce from bed and board, which had crept into the judicial practice toward the close of the provincial era, was now allowed either partner by statute on the one ground of "extreme cruelty." Two new causes were added twenty-five years later. By the act of 1786, it will be observed, desertion and long absence, admitted during the earlier period as sufficient causes for dissolving the marriage bond, are not mentioned for either kind of divorce.[3] But in 1811 it was enacted that the wife may be divorced *a mensa et thoro*, whenever the husband "shall utterly desert" her, or whenever, "being of sufficient ability thereto," he shall "wantonly and cruelly neglect or refuse to provide suitable maintenance for her."[4] In all cases of separation from bed and board, as provided in 1829, the court may assign the wife all the personal estate which the husband received through the marriage, or such part of it as may seem just

shall separate during such nonage, and shall not cohabit together afterwards."— *Ibid.*, 479. The clause forbidding marriages between a white person and a negro, Indian, or mulatto was repealed Feb. 25, 1843: *Supp. to Rev. Stat., 1836-53* (1854), 248; *Acts and Resolves* (1843), 4.

[1] So in New Hampshire: compare the act of Feb. 17, 1791: *Laws of the State of N. H.* (1797), 295, with *Rev. Stat.* (1843), 293, when the modern usage was adopted. For Rhode Island see *Pub. Laws* (1798), 497, and later revisions; for Maine compare *Laws* (1821), I, 344, 345, with *Rev. Stat.* (1847), 364 (modern usage).

[2] On the confusing use of terms see BISHOP, *Marriage, Divorce, and Separation*, II, 214, who says: "Not unfrequently the judicial declaration of nullity is called a 'divorce.' It is properly so when the marriage it declares void was only voidable. For example, it is common and correct in law language to speak of impotence as cause for divorce;" but to prevent confusion he favors the term "sentence" or "decree of nullity" to indicate "the legal avoiding of a voidable marriage." On the other hand, SHELFORD, *Marriage and Divorce*, 365, holds that "divorce" cannot properly be applied to sentences for annulment of either void or voidable marriages. For the present state of the law this appears to be the right conclusion. BLACKSTONE, *Com.*, I, 440, retains the canonical usage.

[3] But an act of the preceding year "against adultery, polygamy, and lewdness" exempts from its penalties a person whose husband or wife has been absent seven years unheard of: Act of Feb. 17, 1785, *Laws of the Com. of Mass., 1780-1816*, I, 217, 218.

[4] Act of Feb. 28, 1811: *ibid.*, IV, 223.

under the circumstances; while "all promissory notes and other choses in action" belonging to her before the marriage, or made payable during the coverture to her alone, or jointly with the husband on account of property belonging to her or debts due to her before the marriage, and all legacies to her, and personal property, which may have descended to her, as heir, or be held for her in trust, or in any other way appertaining to her in her own right, none of which things enumerated have been reduced to possession by the husband before the libel was filed, shall be and remain her separate property; and she is empowered to bring suit to recover it "in the same manner as if she were a *feme sole*."[1] No further important change[2] in the law appears to have been made before 1870, when divorce from bed and board was abolished.[3]

Chief interest, therefore, centers in the history of divorce from the bond of wedlock. To the two grounds of dissolution originally permitted new causes were added from time to time. Thus in 1835 the confinement of either spouse at hard labor under penal sentence for a period of seven years or more is declared sufficient for such a divorce; and a pardon granted to the guilty person will not work a restoration of conjugal rights.[4] Utter and wilful desertion for a term of five years came next in 1838;[5] and in 1850 a fifth cause, probably relating to the Shakers, was added. If either partner, it is declared, shall leave the other without consent and join a "religious sect or society that believes, or professes to believe, the relation between husband and wife void

---

[1] Act of Feb. 18, 1829: *Laws of the Com. of Mass., 1828–31* (1831), 83, 84.

[2] The causes of divorce *a mensa et thoro* remain unaltered in *Rev. Stat. of the Com. of Mass., 1835* (1836), 480.

[3] *Supp. to Gen. Stat. of the Com. of Mass., 1860–72*, I (2d ed., Boston, 1873), 871 (act of June 23, 1870).

[4] *Rev. Stat.* (1836), 480. Impotency is also sanctioned; but this was already allowed by the act of 1786.

[5] Act of April 17, 1838: *Laws of the Com. of Mass.* (1838), 415.

or unlawful," and there remain for three years, such act shall be deemed in behalf of the injured person a "sufficient cause of divorce from the bond of matrimony."[1]

A measure of fundamental importance makes its appearance in 1867. By it the divorce system of Massachusetts is completely reorganized. Not only is the way opened for presently doing away with separation from bed and board, but provision is made for suspending final action in any suit for dissolution of marriage by a device similar to that adopted in the English statute of 1860. The distinction between the "decree *nisi*" and the "decree absolute" was then introduced. "Decrees for divorce from the bond of matrimony may in the first instance be decrees *nisi*, to become absolute after the expiration of such time, not being less than six months from the entry thereof, as the court shall, by general or special orders, direct. At the expiration of the time assigned, on motion of the party in whose favor the decree was rendered, which motion may be entertained by any judge in term or vacation, the decree shall be made absolute, if the party moving shall have complied with the orders of the court, and no sufficient cause to the contrary shall appear." The orders of the court referred to require the person in whose favor a decree *nisi* has been rendered to publish at his own cost, in one or more newspapers, designated by the court, the fact of granting of the decree together with its terms and such other notice as the court may direct.[2] It will be observed that there is no express provision for "intervention," as in England by a private citizen or the Queen's proctor.[3] The institution of the decree *nisi* gave the legislator thereafter a great deal of trouble. Statute after statute was enacted to alter, extend, or repeal its provisions. These

[1] Act of March 20, 1850: *Supp. to Rev. Stat., 1836-53*, I, 592.
[2] Act of May 9, 1867: *Supp. to Gen. Stat. of the Com. of Mass., 1860-72*, I, 565, 566. *Cf.* 98 *Mass. Reports*, 408; 104 *ibid.*, 567.
[3] See above chap. xi, sec. iii, *d*).

it would be useless to dwell upon, even if the import of some of them could readily be understood.[1] After thirty years of tinkering and experiment, the law now stands in substance about as it was first made. By the act of May 2, 1893, all decrees of divorce are in the first instance to be decrees *nisi*, without further proceedings "to become absolute after the expiration of six months;" unless the court on the application of some interested person otherwise orders.[2] The requirement of publication in the newspapers at the expense of the petitioner is not retained.

The introduction of the decree *nisi* in 1867, and the abrogation of the decree from bed and board in 1870, led at once to an extension of the causes of divorce from the bond of marriage. In addition to the five grounds already existing, a statute of the last-named year authorizes a full divorce for "extreme cruelty," "gross and confirmed habits of intoxication contracted after marriage," or "cruel or abusive treatment by either of the parties," and "on the libel of the wife, when the husband, being of sufficient ability, grossly or wantonly and cruelly refuses or neglects to provide suitable maintenance for her." Several of these causes, it will be noticed, had already existed as grounds for separation from bed and board, and were now merely transferred to full

---

[1] So by an act of 1870 the decree *nisi may* in three years and *shall* in five years be made absolute, upon proof of the parties living separate during the period; if they live together, the decree *nisi* becomes void: *Supp. to Gen. Stat.*, *1860-72*, I, 871. This act was repealed in 1873: *Supp. to Gen. Stat.*, *1873-77*, II, 104; but the interval in case of a decree for desertion was then fixed at three years: *ibid.*, 104. In the next year the act of 1867 was amended by adding, "but a decree of divorce when personal service is made on the libellee, or when the libel for divorce shall have been entered at a term prior to the term granting a decree of divorce, shall be a decree absolute, and not *nisi*": *ibid.*, II, 306 (June 30, 1874). On May 19, 1875, the interval fixed by the law of 1870 was restored: three years on petition of the libellant; five years on petition of either party: *ibid.*, II, 364. But in 1881 it was again made six months on the petition of either party: *Acts and Resolves* (1881), 563. The next year the law was slightly modified in the details of procedure, the six months' interval being retained: *ibid.* (1882), 178, 179; amending chap. 146, *Pub. Stat. of the Com. of Mass.* (1882), 813, 815.

[2] Act of May 2, 1893: *Acts and Resolves* (1893), 916, amending slightly another act of the same year: *ibid.*, 829, 830. *Cf. Rev. Laws* (1902), II, 1355.

divorce. "Utter desertion," first allowed in 1838, likewise
appears in this act as a new cause; but it is so only for the
reason that all limitation as to the term of desertion is now
omitted.[1]   But in 1873 the period was fixed at three years,[2]
and this term is retained in the present law.[3]   Finally in
1889 dissolution of wedlock is granted for "gross and confirmed drunkenness" caused "by the voluntary and excessive
use of opium or other drugs."[4]   By the omission of one, the
modification and combination of others, these ten causes have
now been reduced to seven.   By the present law a full
divorce, to be a decree *nisi* in the first instance, may be
granted for (1) adultery; (2) impotency; (3) utter desertion
for three years; (4) gross and confirmed habits of intoxication caused by the voluntary and excessive use of intoxicating
liquors, opium, or other drugs; (5) cruel and abusive treatment; (6) on the libel of the wife, if the husband, being of
sufficient ability, grossly or wantonly and cruelly refuses or
neglects to provide suitable maintenance for her; (7) when
either spouse has been sentenced to confinement at hard
labor for life or for five years or more.[5]

The century's legislation in the other New England states
regarding the causes of divorce shows important differences
in details and in the rate of progress; but the general tendency and the final result are much the same.   For a short
period previous to 1784 the legislature of New Hampshire
exercised the right of granting divorces from the marriage
bond.[6]   The constitution of that year, following the example

---

[1] *Supp. to Gen. Stat. of the Com. of Mass., 1860–72*, I, 871.

[2] Act of June 11, 1873: *Acts and Resolves* (1873), 908.

[3] *Pub. Stat. of the Com. of Mass.* (Boston, 1882), 813.

[4] Act of June 7, 1889: *Acts and Resolves* (1889), 1172.

[5] *Rev. Laws* (1902), II, 1352, 1353.   Divorce for joining a religious sect, under the
act of 1850, seems to have been dropped out in the revision.   It is still in *Pub. Stat.*
(1882), 813.

[6] See the *Index to the MSS. Laws of New Hampshire Recorded in the Office of the
Secretary of State, 1679–1883* (1886), 149, 150, where a list is given showing that legislative decrees were granted in 1766, 1771, 1773, 1778, 1779, 1780, 1781, 1782, and 1783.

of Massachusetts, put a stop to the practice.[1] So by the act
of February 17, 1791, which determined the general character of the divorce laws of that state for half a century,
jurisdiction is vested in the superior court of judicature,
where, under sanction of the constitution[2] of 1792, it
remained until 1855, when it was transferred to the supreme
court.[3] In the outset the laws of New Hampshire are more
liberal in this regard than those of Massachusetts, and the
development is more rapid. By the act of 1791, just mentioned, a divorce *a vinculo* may be granted for the impotency, adultery, extreme cruelty, or three years' absence of
either spouse; and to the wife when the husband wilfully
abandons her for three years, refusing to provide.[4] But, it
should be observed, separation from bed and board is not
recognized. This law stood unaltered until 1839, when,
in addition to the causes already assigned, a divorce is
authorized for three years' wilful desertion or refusal to
cohabit by either person, if the cause continues at the time
of petition.[5]

The next year a broad step in advance was taken. In
addition to the existing causes, five[6] new and important
grounds were at once introduced. A divorce may be granted
in favor of the "innocent party" when the other is convicted
and actually imprisoned for a felony; or becomes a habitual
drunkard and so continues for three years; or "so treats the

---

[1] See the provision in Poore, *Charters*, II, 1290.

[2] It is by that constitution left in the hands of the superior court until the legislature shall make provision: Poore, *Charters*, II, 1305; also in *Const. and Laws of
the State of N. H.* (1805), 18.

[3] See *Laws of N. H.* (1855), 1542; also *Gen. Stat.* (1867), 386; *Gen. Laws* (1878), 432,
433; *Pub. Stat.* (1891), 573.

[4] *Laws of the State of N. H.* (1797), 295.

[5] *Laws of N. H.* (1839, act of July 6), 400. This act was amended in 1840 so that
the divorce may be given within three months after passage of the act, provided the
whole time of desertion before and after shall not be less than three years: *Laws of
N. H.* (1840, June 19), 439, 440.

[6] Counting divorce for injury to health or endangering reason as two grounds, as
in the *Rev. Stat.* (1842), 293.

other, as seriously to injure health, or endanger reason;" or
"when the conduct of either party shall be so gross, wicked
and repugnant to the marriage covenant, as to occasion the
separation of the other for the space of three years."[1] This
last clause is omitted from the revised statutes of 1842.
But among the twelve grounds there enumerated two new
ones appear. As by the Massachusetts law of 1850, divorce
is now granted either person when the other joins and
remains three years with a religious sect or society "profess-
ing to believe the relation of husband and wife unlawful;"
or to the "wife of any alien or citizen of another state, living separate," when she has resided in the commonwealth
three years, the husband "having left the United States with
the intention of becoming a citizen of some foreign country,
and not having during that time" returned to "claim his
marital rights," nor having made suitable provision for her
support.[2] With the subsequent addition of two more causes
the tale is complete. Since 1854 any "citizen" may claim
a divorce when without his consent the wife willingly
absents herself "for three years together;" or when in like
manner she has "gone to reside beyond the limits" of the
state and there remained ten years together without returning to claim her marriage rights.[3] These fourteen general
grounds of divorce still appear in the statute-book;[4] but it
should be noted that not less than seven of them have to

---

[1] *Laws of N. H.* (1840, November), 488, 489. In the case of habitual drunkenness
and of gross and wicked conduct not more than two of the three years may precede
the passage of the act.

[2] *Rev. Stat. of the State of N. H.* (1843), 293. In these cases the time may be
counted before and after the act, or if the three years have already expired, then a
divorce may be granted in one month after it goes into force: *ibid.*, 293, 294. The
period for joining a religious sect was reduced to six months by the act of Jan. 4,
1849: *Laws of N. H.* (1848–49), 707; *Comp. Stat.* (1853), 377.

[3] *Laws of N. H.* (1854), 1424, 1425; also *Gen. Stat. of the State of N. H.* (1867), 335.

[4] They are still in force in *Pub. Stat.* (1900), 591. To constitute a cause there
must now be conviction for a "crime" punishable in the state by more than one
year's imprisonment; and there must be actual confinement under the sentence.

do with absence or desertion of one or the other of the
persons under various conditions.

At the close of the colonial era and until 1850, it will be
remembered,[1] the legislature of Connecticut continued to
grant divorces on various grounds; but jurisdiction in most
cases was exercised by the superior court,[2] where it still
remains.[3] Legislative divorce is not prohibited by the constitution; and it appears to be still permitted by the law. A
recent act provides that "whenever any petition for divorce
shall have been referred to any committee of the general
assembly, such committee may give to the attorney general
reasonable notice of all hearings on such petition, and he
shall thereupon take such action as he shall deem to be just
and equitable in the premises, and he shall appear before
such committee . . . . whenever in his opinion justice so
requires."[4] Since 1667, as elsewhere seen, divorce from
the bond of wedlock had been granted for adultery, fraudulent contract, wilful desertion for three years, and for seven
years' absence without word. To these grounds, in 1843,
"habitual intemperance" and "intolerable cruelty" were
added.[5] Three more new causes followed in 1849. Divorce
was then sanctioned for sentence to imprisonment for life;
"infamous crime involving a violation of conjugal duty;"
and for "any such misconduct . . . . as permanently
destroys the happiness of the petitioner, and defeats the
purpose of the marriage relation."[6] The remarkable
"omnibus" clause last quoted was not repealed until 1878.[7]

---

[1] See chap. xv, sec. i, c).

[2] So in the *Acts and Laws of his Majesty's Colony of Conn.* (1750), 43; in *Acts and Laws* (1784), 41; *ibid.* (1805), 457; the *Pub. Stat. Laws* (1821), 178, 179; *ibid.* (1835), 162, 163; *ibid.* (1838), 185, 186; *Pub. Acts* (1849), 17.

[3] *Gen. Stat. of Conn.* (1887), 612.   [4] Act of March 21, 1899: *Pub. Acts*, 996.

[5] *Pub. Acts* (1843), 20; *Rev. Stat.* (1849), 274. For a construction of "intolerable cruelty" see Shaw *v.* Shaw, 17 *Conn. Reports*, 189.

[6] *Pub. Acts* (1849), 17 (June 19). *Cf. Gen. Stat.* (1866), 305, 306, where the nine causes already existing in 1849 are enumerated; also *ibid.* (1875), 188.

[7] *Pub. Acts* (1878), 305.

The number of causes was thus reduced to eight, and thereafter no further changes seem to have been made.[1]

Throughout the century the supreme court of Rhode Island has exercised jurisdiction in cases of divorce and alimony,[2] although until 1851, as elsewhere explained, the legislature retained a share in this power. At the beginning of the period a marriage might be dissolved for (1) impotency, (2) adultery, (3) extreme cruelty, (4) wilful desertion for five years, (5) the husband's neglect or refusal to provide, or (6) for any other "gross misbehaviour and wickedness in either of the parties, repugnant to and in violation of the marriage covenant."[3] The last clause is surely broad enough, and no further ground of separation was found necessary until 1844. In that year (7) "continued drunkenness" is added.[4] Seven years later the court is given discretionary power to dispense with proof of full five years' desertion and to grant relief in less time.[5] Finally the extreme limit of modern legislation is reached in allowing (8) a decree when either spouse is guilty of "habitual, excessive, and intemperate use of opium, morphine, or chloral."[6] In 1902 the fifth cause in the above series was modified, a full divorce being then authorized for the husband's neglect *and* refusal to provide his wife with necessaries for at least one year.[7] So the century, which began with

---

[1] The eight causes already named appear in *Gen. Stat.* (1887), 612; and no later action seems to have been taken. *Cf. Gen. Stat.* (1902), 1090, 1091.

[2] So in 1798: *Pub. Laws of R. I.* (1798), 481. See also *Gen. Laws* (1896), 760, 761, where exclusive jurisdiction in such cases is vested in the appellate division of the supreme court.

[3] *Pub. Laws* (1798), 479.

[4] *Pub. Laws* (1844), 263. But this provision may be earlier; I have not been able to verify the date.

[5] *Laws of R. I.* (1851), 796.

[6] *Gen. Laws* (1896), 634. Eight causes are here formally enumerated; but the act further declares that when it is alleged in the petition that the parties have lived apart from each other for at least ten years, the court may in its discretion grant a divorce: *ibid.*, 634. This provision originated in 1893: *Acts and Resolves* (1892-93), 237.

[7] *Pub. Laws* (1902), 39-41.

six grounds, ends with but two new causes for the dissolution of wedlock.   In the meantime, however, we have a rare example of reactionary legislation.   In 1882 the policy of nearly two hundred and fifty years was reversed.[1]   It was then provided that in future "divorce from bed, board, and cohabitation, until the parties be reconciled, may be granted for any of the causes for which by law a divorce from the bond of marriage may be decreed, and for such other causes as may seem to require the same."[2]   This sweeping provision is still in force.[3]

The first word in the history of divorce legislation for Vermont appears in the records of the "assumption" period. In 1779 the "representatives of the freemen" authorize the superior court to grant dissolution of the bond of marriage for the same four causes allowed at that time by the Connecticut laws, but by implication only the aggrieved person is permitted to remarry.[4]   This restriction does not appear in the statutes enacted after the attainment of statehood. By these the supreme court may grant either spouse a decree for impotence, adultery, intolerable severity, three years' wilful desertion with total neglect of duty, or for the usual term of long absence unheard of.[5]   The same grounds are retained in 1805, but with one important modification.   In the case of "intolerable severity" it is left optional with the court whether the decree shall be from bed and board or from the marriage bond.[6]   This provision, however, was short-lived, for it seems to have been repealed in 1807.[7]   The

[1] For the rare cases of permission to live "apart" granted by the legislature cannot be regarded as historically important.

[2] *Pub. Stat.* (1882), 427.

[3] *Gen. Law* (1896), 634, 635; *Pub. Laws* (1902), 39.   This act of 1902 allows such separation, provided the petitioner has been a domiciled inhabitant of the state and has resided there for such length of time as the court shall deem sufficient.

[4] Slade, *Vermont State Papers*, including laws enacted 1779–86 (1823), 364.

[5] *Laws of the State of Vermont* (1798), 333.

[6] Act of Nov. 7, 1805: *Laws of the State of Vt.* (1808), I, 270–72.

[7] It appears to have been abrogated by sec. 3 of the act of Oct. 21, 1807: see *Laws of Vt.* (1825), 364, 365, note.

number of causes of divorce *a vinculo* in 1839 has increased to six, but one old ground—impotence has given place to two new ones—actual confinement on a criminal sentence for three years or more, and gross, wanton, and cruel neglect of the husband to provide when he is able.[1] By the existing law the same six causes are expressly recognized.[2] But the statute contemplates divorce on still other grounds; for it is provided that libels for causes other than those named shall be tried in the county where the persons or one of them resides.[3] The last word of the period is retrogressive, decrees from bed and board being restored after an interval of almost exactly one hundred years. By the act of November 24, 1896, such separations, "forever or for a limited time," are authorized, as in Rhode Island, "for any of the causes for which a divorce from the bond of matrimony may be declared."[4] Jurisdiction is now vested in the county courts, each held by an assigned judge of the supreme court, who may try questions of fact as well as of law.[5]

Very naturally the first divorce legislation of Maine is based largely upon the contemporary laws of Massachusetts; and her policy in this regard since the attainment of statehood in 1820 has developed on lines parallel to those followed by the parent commonwealth, although there are some interesting divergences in matters of detail. The statutes of 1821 embody the Massachusetts law of 1786, together with such subsequent legislation as was still in force. Jurisdiction is vested in the supreme judicial court. Divorce from the bond of marriage is allowed for the same two causes named in that act. Separation from bed and board for cruelty, utter desertion, and neglect to provide is authorized, just as in Massachusetts after 1811,[6] and this kind of divorce

---

[1] *Revision of the Stat.* (1840), 324.   [2] *Vermont Stat.* (1894), 507.   [3] *Ibid.*

[4] *Acts and Resolves* (1896), 43, 44.   [5] *Vermont Stat.* (1894), 508, 236.

[6] *Laws of the State of Maine* (1821), I, 344–47; also SMITH, *Laws of the State of Maine* (1834), I, 424 ff.

existed until 1883.   Three new grounds for dissolving marriage were allowed in 1830.   These were five years' wilful desertion, uniting with the society called Shakers, and sentence to
state's prison—in each of the latter two cases the term being
likewise five years.[1] To these were subsequently added fraudulent contract and three years' habitual drunkenness such as to
incapacitate either spouse from taking care of the family.[2]

A radical change was made in 1847.   All the foregoing
causes were at once superseded by a sweeping provision
which is without parallel in the previous history of New
England.   By an act of that year, amended in one particular
in 1849, any justice of the supreme judicial court, at any
term held in the county of the parties, may grant decrees of
divorce from the bond of wedlock, when "in the exercise of
a sound discretion" he may "deem the same reasonable and
proper, conducive to domestic harmony, and consistent with
the peace and morality of society."[3]   Moreover, to understand the full import of this law we must take into account
an enactment of 1850.   In no case is the libellant then to be
"restricted to the proof of causes happening within the
state," or where either of the persons is "residing within the
state," but he "may allege and prove any facts tending to
show that the divorce would be" just according to the provision of the law in question.[4]   The act of 1847 remained in
force until 1883,[5] when a new statute appeared which com-

[1] Act of March 6, 1830: *Pub. Acts* (1830), 1227, 1228. This statute merely changes
the terms of another of the preceding year: *ibid.* (1829), 1208, 1209.

[2] In 1835 a divorce is authorized "where the consent of one of the parties to the
marriage was obtained, by gross and deliberate fraud or false pretences . . . . provided the parties have not cohabited, as husband and wife, after such fraud was
known to the party, thus deceived."—*Pub. Acts* (1835), 177. Habitual drunkenness
was added in 1838: *Pub. Acts* (1838), 499, 500; *cf. Rev. Stat.* (2d ed., 1847), 364.

[3] The act of July 13, 1847, gave a "majority" of the justices this power: *Acts and
Resolves* (1847), 8; but this was amended in harmony with the text in 1849: *Acts and
Resolves* (1849), 104.

[4] *Ibid.* (1850), 150, 151.

[5] Except by an act of 1863, in addition to the "blanket" provision of 1847, three
years' wilful desertion is specified as a cause: *Laws* (1863), chap. 211, sec. 2; also in
Rev. Stat. (1871), 488.

pletely transformed the divorce system of Maine. Seven
causes of dissolution *a vinculo* are prescribed. These are
(1) adultery; (2) impotence; (3) extreme cruelty; (4) utter
desertion for three years; (5) gross and confirmed habits of
intoxication; (6) cruel and abusive treatment; and (7) gross,
cruel, and wanton neglect or refusal of the husband, being
able, to provide for the wife.[1] At the same time the decree
from bed and board is abolished; and the decree *nisi* is
instituted in practically the same form as in Massachusetts.[2]
In 1897 a modified provision as to residence was adopted,
and two years later the law took its present form. The
same seven causes sanctioned by the act of 1883 are retained,
except that under the fifth head the qualifying words are
added, "from the use of intoxicating liquors, opium, or other
drugs."[3]

  b) *Remarriage, residence, notice, and miscellaneous provisions.*—The character of a divorce law does not, of course,
depend wholly upon the number of causes for separation
allowed, but in large measure upon the conditions under
which the decree is granted and the safeguards provided to
prevent hasty or clandestine action. Whether or not either
or both of the divorced persons shall be allowed to contract
further marriage, and on what terms, has always been an
important question. The more general tendency of modern
legislation, in the United States and elsewhere, is to allow
entire freedom in this regard, except for a short period after
the decree. But in New England during the century the
matter has been dealt with in various ways. Thus in
Massachusetts, for more than fifty years after the Revolution, the guilty party to a complete divorce was absolutely

[1] *Acts and Resolves* (1883), chap. 212, secs. 1, 2, p. 175 (March 13); *Rev. Stat.*
(1884), 520–23.

[2] *Acts and Resolves* (1883), chap. 212, sec. 4, pp. 175, 176; *Rev. Stat.* (1884), 522.

[3] Compare the act of March 2, 1897: *Acts and Resolves* (1897), 232, 233, with that
of March 15, 1899: *ibid.* (1899), 89.

incapable of contracting a legal marriage. This doctrine is established by later judicial construction of the act of February 17, 1785, in connection with that of March 16, 1786. "We think it very clear," declares Chief Justice Parker, interpreting these laws in 1823, that "the marriage of the guilty party, after a divorce *a vinculo* for the cause of adultery, if contracted within this state, would be unlawful and void. The statutes which we think must have this construction are not expressed in very intelligible terms, but, on close examination, we think the intention of the legislature cannot be mistaken."[1] In this decision the court further raises one of the gravest difficulties of divorce legislation in the United States. The marriage in another state of the guilty party to a divorce in Massachusetts, under the laws just considered, is held to be valid, if such marriage is not forbidden in the state where the new marriage is contracted.[2] But will such a marriage be good in Massachusetts, should the persons at once return to that commonwealth? This important question, left in doubt by Chief Justice Parker, was settled in 1829. In the case of Putnam *v.* Putnam the court decided that if a man, "being a resident in this state for the sake of evading the law, goes into a

[1] Case of West Cambridge *v.* Lexington (Oct., 1823), 1 Pickering, 507-12. The act of 1785 provides that the penalties for "polygamy," which it prescribes, shall not extend "to any person that is or shall be at the time of such marriage divorced, by sentence of any Court . . . . unless such person is the guilty cause of such divorce." —*Acts and Laws* (Reprint, Boston, 1784), 118; also in *Perpetual Laws of the Com. of Mass.*, I, 217, 218. The act of 1786, chap. 69, provides that all "marriages where either of the parties :shall have a former wife or husband living at the time of such marriage, shall be absolutely void."—*Perpetual Laws of the Com.*, I, 301. This provision is ambiguous, and might of itself seem to make void the marriage even of the innocent party to a divorce; but, in the case just cited, the court held: "Supposing the legislature to have considered the parties to a marriage which had been dissolved as standing in the relation of husband and wife, so far as to bring them within the purview of the former statute [that of 1785], it will follow that a marriage of persons so situated would be void. It is true, that by this statute [that of 1786] standing by itself, the marriage of an innocent party to a divorce would not be protected; but the statutes, being *in pari materiâ*, must be construed together, and the exception in the first cited statute in favor of such persons, would avail." —1 Pickering, 509.

[2] See 1 Pickering, 510, 511.

neighboring state where such a marriage is valid, and is there married and immediately returns and continues to reside here, the marriage is valid here, and after his death his widow is entitled to dower in his estate."[1]

Gradually the stringency of the early Massachusetts rule was relaxed. An act of 1841 declares that whenever a divorce from the bond of matrimony "shall be decreed for any of the causes allowed by law, the guilty party shall be debarred from contracting marriage during the life-time" of the other, subject for disobedience to the penalty prescribed for "polygamy."[2] Twelve years later, by leave of the court, in case of divorce for desertion, the offending spouse is allowed to remarry.[3] A further step is taken in 1855. In all cases, except for adultery, the court is then empowered, on petition and proper notice, to allow the person against whom a decree has been granted to marry again.[4] In 1864 a new rule appears. Three years must now elapse in all cases, not excepting a decree for adultery, before such permission may be granted.[5] Still later all restriction as to time is removed,[6] but as the law now stands, the offending person, without petition to the Court, may again marry after an interval of two years from the date of the absolute decree.[7]

The early laws of Maine show no restraints upon remarriage after divorce, but since 1883 the Massachusetts precedent has been followed, with some interesting variations. In case of collusion, where both persons are guilty of

---

[1] Case of Putnam v. Putnam, 8 PICKERING, 433-35 (Sept., 1829).

[2] Act of March 13, 1841: *Acts and Resolves* (1841), 371; also in *Supp. to Rev. Stat.*, *1836-53*, I, 189.

[3] Act of May 19, 1853: *Supp. to Rev. Stat.*, *1836-53*, I, 976.

[4] Act of May 21, 1855, repealing the act of May 19, 1853: *Acts and Resolves* (1855), 823.

[5] Act of May 11, 1864: *Supp. to Gen. Stat.*, *1860-72*, I, 279. But there must be no collusion. See 10 ALLEN, 276.

[6] Act of June 11, 1873: *Supp. to Gen. Stat.*, *1873-77*, 104; Act of June 30, 1874: *ibid.*, 306.

[7] Act of May 6, 1881: *Acts and Resolves* (1881), 563; *Pub. Stat.* (1882), 815; *Rev. Laws* (1902), II, 1355.

adultery, no separation will be allowed.   After obtaining
the final decree, the person in whose favor it is granted may
not marry within two years without the court's permission.
Within that period the adverse party is absolutely forbidden
to remarry; nor may he do so thereafter without the court's
consent.[1]   There is also a unique provision for a new trial.
Within three years after a judgment has been rendered, a
rehearing as to divorce may be had in case the persons have
not cohabited nor either of them contracted a new marriage
during the period.   Moreover, if either has married again,
such new trial may be "granted as to alimony or specific
sum decreed" when "it appears that justice has not been
done through fraud, accident, mistake, or misfortune."[2]

During the "assumption" period the popular assembly
of Vermont followed the Connecticut rule as it then stood,
allowing only the innocent person to contract a new marriage.[3]
But from 1797 onward the laws of the state grant entire
freedom to either spouse in this regard.[4]   At present the
"libellee" is not permitted "to marry a person other than
the libellant for three years," unless the latter dies.[5]

The other states have been less conservative.   By the
New Hampshire law of 1840, already noticed, divorce from
the bond of marriage is allowed to the "innocent party" in
case of felony, drunkenness, and the other causes there
assigned.[6]   This provision is still retained;[7] but either person
may remarry.   So also by the Connecticut law previous to

---

[1] *Rev. Stat.* (1884), 520-22.

[2] *Rev. Stat. of the State of Maine* (1884), 522.   This provision originated in 1874: *Acts and Resolves* (1874), chap. 184, sec. 3, p. 130.

[3] Slade, *State Papers*, 364.

[4] By an act of 1797, both parties may at once remarry: *Laws of the State of Vt.* (1798), 364.

[5] Act of Nov. 27, 1878: *Acts and Resolves* (1878), 32, 33; also in *Stat. of Vt.* (1894), 511, 512.   The penalty for violation of this provision is imprisonment from one to five years.

[6] *Laws of N. H.* (1840), 488, 489.   See subsection *a*) above.

[7] *Pub. Stat. of N. H.* (1900), 591.

1849 it is the "aggrieved" who is to be counted as "single" and able to marry, while at present no such limitation appears. Rhode Island has been even more liberal. At no time during the century, apparently, has the legislature placed any conditions upon the remarriage of either party to a divorce decreed for any cause, except that in 1902 it was provided that no decree shall become final and operative until six months after trial and decision.[1]

Clandestine divorce is an evil as notorious, if not so harmful, as clandestine marriage. To prevent it the New England states have been fairly prudent in their regulation of "residence" and "notice." By the existing law of Massachusetts, a divorce will be granted for any lawful cause, occurring in the state or elsewhere, when the libellant has lived for five years in the commonwealth; or, when the parties were inhabitants of the state at the time of the marriage, if the libellant has been such an inhabitant for three years before the libel was filed, provided neither person came into the state for the purpose. With this exception, as expressly provided in the statute, a divorce will not be granted for any cause, if the parties have never lived together as man and wife in the commonwealth; nor for any cause occurring in another state or country, unless, before it occurred, they had so lived together in the commonwealth, and one of them was there living at the time it took place. A divorce lawfully decreed in another state or country is recognized as valid. On the other hand, when an inhabitant of the commonwealth goes outside the state to obtain a divorce for a cause which occurred in the state while the persons there resided, or for a cause which would not be recognized as lawful therein, the "divorce so obtained shall be of no force or effect" in the commonwealth.[2] Proceedings for a divorce

[1] *Pub. Laws of R. I.* (1902), 41.

[2] *Pub. Stat. of the Com. of Mass.* (1882), 813, 817; *Rev. Laws* (1902), II, 1353, 1357. The main features of the present law originated as early as 1835; *Rev. Stat.* (1836),

are not barred, however, when the "libellee has been continuously absent for such a period of time and under such circumstances as would raise a presumption of death."[1]

Similar provisions exist in the other states, although sometimes they are less severe. The New Hampshire court has jurisdiction in matters of divorce under three alternate conditions: (1) when both parties are domiciled in the state when the libel is filed; (2) when the plaintiff is so domiciled and the defendant is personally served with process in the state; and (3) when either of the parties is domiciled in the state at the commencement of the suit, and has actually resided there for the year preceding.[2] In Rhode Island the term of prior residence for the petitioner is two years.[3] As early as 1805 in Vermont a three-years' residence was required in order to obtain a divorce; and a decree would not be granted for any cause occurring before the applicant became a resident of the state.[4] The term was reduced to one year in 1807.[5] As the law stood in 1863, the requirement as to residence was still defective. "Such divorce for adultery, intolerable severity, and wilful desertion for three years may be granted when the causes happened while residing in another state or country if the libellant has resided in the state two years previous to the term of court to which the petition is preferred."[6] An attempt was made in 1878 to put a check upon the increasing number of

480, 484. By the act of May 2, 1877, the prior time of residence had been fixed at three years in all cases where the parties were inhabitants of the state at the time of the marriage: *Supp. to Gen. Stat.*, *1873-77*, II, 516.

[1] Act of May 8, 1884: *Acts and Resolves*, 181; *Supp. to Pub. Stat.*, chap. 219, p. 185; *Rev. Laws* (1902), II, 1353.

[2] *Pub. Stat. of the State of N. H.* (1891), 495; *ibid.* (1900), 590, 591.

[3] Raised from one year to two by *Pub. Laws* (1902), 40; but it is provided that if the defendant has for that time been a resident and domiciled inhabitant of the state, and has been actually served with process, the requirement of the act as to term of the petitioner's residence shall be satisfied.

[4] Act of Nov. 7, 1805: *Laws of State of Vt.* (1808), I, 270.

[5] *Laws of State of Vt.*, I, 272, 273, 274.   [6] *Gen. Stat.* (1863), chap. 70.

divorces by prescribing more careful conditions. No divorce is henceforth to "be decreed for any cause, if the parties have never lived together as husband and wife" in the state, nor unless the libellant shall have resided there "one full year next preceding the filing of the libel in court." Furthermore, no divorce may be granted for any cause "which shall have accrued in any other state or country, unless one of the parties was then living in the state, and unless before such cause accrued the parties had lived together in this state as husband and wife.[1] In substance this law is still in force, though the present provisions are more precise. A divorce may not be granted "for any cause which accrued in another state or country before the parties lived together in this state as husband and wife, and while neither party was a resident of this state, unless the libellant shall have resided in this state at least one year and in the county where the libel is preferred at least three months next before the term of the court to which the libel is preferred."[2] The statutes of Maine authorize divorce for any legal cause, if the persons were married in the state; or if they cohabited there after marriage; or if the libellant resided in the state when the cause of action occurred, or had so resided for one year prior to the commencement of the suit; or if the libellee is a resident of the state when suit is brought.[3] With regard to foreign divorces and divorces obtained outside the state by inhabitants thereof, the law of Maine is identical with that of Massachusetts.[4] Throughout the century Connecticut has maintained a high standard in this regard. With some qualifications, three years' prior residence has always been

---

[1] Act of Nov. 27, 1878: *Vermont Acts and Resolves* (1878), 32, 33.

[2] *Vermont Stat.* (1894), 507.

[3] Act of March 15, 1899: *Acts and Resolves*, 89. *Cf.* the act of 1897: *Acts and Resolves*, 232, 233, which in the residence clause contained the additional words "or if the libellee is a resident of the state" at the time. This clause was restored by *Acts and Resolves* (1903), 31.

[4] *Rev. Stat.* (1884), 522.

required of a petitioner coming into the state from abroad.[1] As the law now stands, a complaint will be dismissed unless the complainant has continuously resided in the state for the preceding three years, except when the cause of divorce arose subsequently to his removal into the same; or unless the defendant had in like manner there resided for three years, and actual service was made upon him; or "unless the alleged cause is habitual intemperance, or intolerable cruelty, and the plaintiff was domiciled in the state at the time of the marriage," and before bringing the complaint has returned with the intention of there remaining.[2]

Provision is likewise made by statute for proper notice to the defendant. Usually much freedom in this regard is left to the court. Thus in Maine, when the residence of the defendant can be ascertained, it must be named in the libel; and if the defendant lives out of the state, notice is to be made in such manner as the court may order. When the residence of the defendant is not known to the plaintiff and cannot be ascertained, the fact must be alleged under oath in the libel.[3] According to the Connecticut statute, the person aggrieved may make complaint to the court "in the form prescribed for civil actions, which shall be duly served on the other party, and whenever alimony is claimed, attachments to secure the same may be made by direction in the suit, or by an order pending suit in the same manner as in other civil actions." But when the adverse party resides out of the state or is absent from it, or his whereabouts is unknown to the plaintiff, "any judge or clerk of the supreme court of errors, or of the superior court, or any county commissioner, may make such order of notice to the adverse

---

[1] See *Acts and Laws* (1797), 457; also *Stat. of the State of Conn.* (1854), 380, where the term may be less for the plaintiff when the defendant has been three years in the state.

[2] *Gen. Stat. of Conn.* (1887), 613; *Gen. Stat.* (1902), 1091.

[3] *Rev. Stat. of Maine* (1884), 521.

party as he may deem reasonable." Then "such notice having been given and duly proved," if the court finds that the defendant has actually received it, the suit may go on; otherwise the court may either "hear the case, or, if it see cause, order such further notice to be given as it may deem reasonable, and continue the complaint until the order is complied with."[1] In no case may a complaint be heard or a decree rendered until after the expiration of ninety days; except when the defendant appears in person or by counsel, when the complaint is to be treated as "privileged" and assigned at once for trial.[2] By the Vermont act of November 26, 1884, designed to "diminish the frequency of divorces," it is provided that "at the term succeeding the term at which the cause is entered, or at any subsequent term to which the cause may be continued, the same shall not be heard unless the libellee is present, except in cases when it is proven to the court that the libellant has, in good faith, attempted to procure the attendance of the libellee and has been unable to do so." In this last event the court may in its discretion proceed to try the case, postpone the hearing in the hope of securing the presence of the libellee, or it may require the latter's deposition.[3] This provision was repealed in 1886.[4] By the present law, when the "libellee is without the state, the libellant may file his libel in the office of the clerk of the court in the county where the same is required to be brought, and such clerk shall issue an order stating the substance of the libel or petition, and requiring the adverse party to appear on the first day of the next stated term of the county court" and make answer. This order the libellant "shall cause to be published in such

[1] *Gen. Stat. of Conn.* (1887), 612; as modified by the act of May 11, 1899: *Pub. Acts,* 1042. For the earlier laws as to notice see *Acts and Laws* (1797), 457; *Pub. Stat.* (1821), 178; *Pub. Stat. Laws* (1835), 162, 163; *Rev. Stat.* (1849), 274, 275; *Stat. of the State* (1854), 379, 380. *Cf. Gen. Stat.* (1902), 1090.

[2] *Gen. Stat. of Conn.* (1887), 613.

[3] *Vermont Acts and Resolves* (1884), 86.   [4] *Acts and Resolves* (1886), 50.

newspaper as is directed by the order, three weeks successively, the last publication to be at least six weeks previous to the commencement of the term at which the libellee is required to appear." Should the libellee not appear, and "the notice of the pendency of the libel is considered by the court defective or insufficient, it may order further notice to be given."[1]

Massachusetts likewise has a recent provision as to notice. "When the adverse party does not appear," declares the act of 1898, "and the notice of the pendency of the libel is considered by the court to be defective or insufficient, it may order such further notice as it may consider proper." This statute further provides that "in all libels for divorce where the cause alleged is adultery, the person alleged to be *particeps criminis* with the libellee may appear and contest the libel."[2] Similar rules have been adopted by other states.[3]

Any serious attempt to go into the intricacies of divorce law and procedure would, of course, here be out of place. Every phase of the subject, as illustrated by the decisions and practice of the various state courts, is treated with sufficient fulness and remarkable clearness in Bishop's work on *Marriage, Divorce, and Separation*, but a few details of more general interest may be mentioned. As a rule, the legitimacy of the children, with the right of inheritance, is not affected by a divorce, even when it occurs for the adultery of the mother, but that question is left for separate deter-

---

[1] *Vermont Stat.* (1894), 508.

[2] Act of June 2, 1898: *Acts and Resolves*, 443; *cf. Rev. Laws* (1902), II, 1353, 1354.

[3] Rhode Island, in *Pub. Laws* (1902), 41, has provided that no divorce from the bond of marriage shall be granted "unless the defendant shall, in accordance with the rules adopted by the court, have been personally served with process, if within the state, or with personal notice duly authenticated, if out of the state, or unless the defendant shall have entered an appearance in the cause; or unless it shall appear to the satisfaction of the court that the petitioner does not know the address nor the residence of the defendant and has not been able to ascertain either after reasonable and due inquiry and search for six months," in which case the court may authorize publication. For the former law see *Pub. Stat.* (1882), 428; superseded by *Gen. Laws* (1896), 635. *Cf. Stat. of N. H.* (1891), 497.

mination by the courts in the usual way.[1] So also when a
supposed second marriage is dissolved, because entered into
by mistake while the former wife or husband was living, the
children are regarded as the legitimate issue of the parent
who at the time of the marriage was capable of contracting,
provided the union was made in good faith.[2] When the
validity of a marriage or the effect of any former decree of
divorce or nullity is doubted, the question may be tried by
the court on filing a libel, as in case of divorce.[3] Sometimes
the husband and wife are expressly allowed to be witnesses
in the suit;[4] or the statute may grant trial by jury at the
election of the parties.[5] Usually the court may authorize
the wife to resume her maiden name;[6] and occasionally it is
empowered to change the name of the minor children.[7]

c) *Alimony, property, and custody of children.*—During
the pendency of a suit for divorce the court is authorized to
make orders forbidding the husband to put any restraint upon
the personal liberty of the wife, and for the care and custody
of the minor children. At the same time it may require the
husband to deposit money to enable the wife to maintain or
defend the libel;[8] and just provision may also be made for her

---

[1] *Rev. Stat. of Mass.* (1835), 481: *Pub. Stat. of Mass.* (1882), 815: *Rev. Laws of Mass.* (1902), II, 1355; *Pub. Stat. of N. H.* (1900), 592; *Rev. Stat. of Maine* (1884), 522.

[2] *Rev. Stat. of Mass.* (1835), 482; *Pub. Stat. of Mass.* (1882), 810; *Rev. Laws of Mass.* (1902), II, 1347; *Rev. Stat. of Maine* (1884), 523.

[3] *Rev. Stat. of Maine* (1847), 367; *ibid.* (1883), 529; *Rev. Stat. of N. H.* (1843), 293; *Vermont Stat.* (1894), 505; *Rev. Laws of Mass.* (1902), II, 1346.

[4] As in Rhode Island: *Gen. Laws* (1896), 840; and Vermont: *Stat.* (1894), 273; Maine: *Acts and Resolves* (1899), 89. *Cf. Pub. Stat. of N. H.* (1891), 622.

[5] As in Maine: *Acts and Resolves* (1899), 89; *Rev. Stat.* (1884), 521; *ibid.* (1847), 368.

[6] *Vermont Stat.* (1894), 512; *Gen. Laws of R. I.* (1896), 636; *Gen. Stat. of Conn.* (1887), 613; *Pub. Stat. of Mass.* (1882), 815. In Maine the court may change the wife's name " at her request": *Acts and Resolves* (1901), 167.

[7] *Vermont Stat.* (1894), 512.

[8] By the Vermont act of Nov. 22, 1898: *Acts and Resolves*, 38, 39, when a married woman files a libel for divorce and prays for alimony, the husband is enjoined from conveying or removing from the state, during pendency of the libel, such portion of his estate as the judge may think necessary to secure alimony, and from concealing or interfering with the property or clothing of the wife and minor children, or such portion of his personal property as may be at the time in her possession.

temporary alimony or support.[1]   Vermont grants the county court authority, when the parents are living separate, though not divorced, to make orders for the "care, custody, maintenance, and education" of the minor children.   Similar orders relating to the children and for the support of the wife, in that state, may be made when without just cause a husband "fails to furnish suitable support to his wife, or has deserted her, or when the wife, for a justifiable cause, is actually living apart from her husband."[2]   In like manner, in all the states, the court may make proper orders for the care, custody, and education of the children after the divorce, and for permanent alimony to the wife.   In Vermont, New Hampshire, and Massachusetts alimony, or an allowance in the nature of alimony, may be decreed to the husband as well as to the wife.

A divorce for the cause of adultery committed by the woman, by the Massachusetts statute, does not affect her title to her separate real and personal estate during her life, except that the court may award the man a just share of it for the support of the minor children decreed to his custody. Should the divorced wife marry again, the former husband's interest in such separate estate, after her death, ceases, except as thus required for the children's alimony.   After divorce the wife is not entitled to dower; unless the cause be the husband's infidelity or his sentence to confinement at hard labor; and except when the husband dies before a decree *nisi*, granted on the wife's petition, has become absolute.[3]   The Massachusetts law, as thus broadly outlined, is typical of that which prevails throughout New England, although there are some important variations in matters of

---

[1] *Pub. Stat. of Mass.* (1882), 814; *Laws of Mass.* (1821), 508, 509; *Rev. Stat. of Mass.* (1835), 482; *Vermont Stat.* (1894), 509; *Rev. Stat. of Maine* (1884), 521; *Rev. Stat. of N. H.* (1843), 294.

[2] *Vermont Stat.* (1894), 510, 511.

[3] *Pub. Stat. of Mass.* (1882), 814–16; *Rev. Laws* (1902), II, 1355.

detail.[1] The Vermont statute, in particular, is very clear and elaborate in its provisions. "Upon the dissolution of a marriage, by a divorce or decree of nullity, for any cause except that of adultery committed by the wife," the latter is entitled to the immediate possession of her real estate. In all cases "the court may decree to the wife such part of the real and personal estate of her husband, as it deems just, having regard to the circumstances of the parties respectively; and it may require the husband to disclose on oath, what real and personal estate has come to him by reason of the marriage, and how the same has been disposed of, and what portion thereof remains in his hands." There is also provision for placing the property awarded the wife in the hands of trustees in her behalf.[2]

Finally, it may be noted, that only in recent years have any of these states made any adequate provision for gathering and publishing the statistics of divorce.[3]

[1] For New Hampshire, see *Pub. Stat.* (1900), 592, 593. The law of Connecticut is very general. For instance, the court may assign the woman as alimony any part of her late husband's estate not exceeding one-third thereof. If divorced for her misconduct, all property received from the husband in consideration of the marriage or of "love and affection" must be restored. A minor child must be supported by the parents; and upon complaint of either of them at any time, the court may inquire into their pecuniary ability, and pass a decree against either or both for its just maintenance: *Gen. Stat. of Conn.* (1888), 612-14. See also *Gen. Laws of R. I.* (1896), 633-36; *Rev. Stat. of Maine* (1884), 520-23, where it is provided that, when a divorce is decreed for the adultery of the wife, the husband "may hold her personal estate forever, and her real estate, of which she was seized during coverture, during his life, if they had a child born alive during marriage, otherwise during her life only, if he survives her; but the court may allow her so much of her real or personal estate as is necessary for her subsistence."—*Ibid.*, 522. But by an act of 1903 it is provided that where the wife is at fault the husband is "entitled to one-third, in common and undivided of all her real estate, except wild lands, which shall descend to him as if she were dead;" and the court in its discretion may grant him a part of her personal estate. In all cases the right, title, or interest of the libellee in the libellant's real estate is barred by the decree of divorce: *Acts and Resolves* (1903), 171.

[2] *Vermont Stat.* (1894), 509 ff.

[3] Massachusetts made such provision in 1882. Clerks of court are to submit annual reports to the secretary of the commonwealth who is to embody the facts in his own report to the legislature. The first report is to cover the period 1879-82: *Supp. to Pub. Stat.*, *1882-88*, 40, 41. In Connecticut and Rhode Island the clerks are to make a similar report to the secretary of the state board of health: *Gen. Stat. of Conn.* (1887), 566, 567: *Gen. Laws of R. I.* (1896), 768, 322. The same officer is made

II.   THE SOUTHERN AND SOUTHWESTERN STATES[1]

a) *Legislative divorce.*—In the South, as elsewhere[2] shown, divorces were at no time granted during the provincial era.   Even the provisions of the English ecclesiastical law were not in force, because tribunals competent to administer them were not created.   Separation by mutual consent, or some sort of separate maintenance, was the only kind of relief then obtainable.   Indeed, after independence was declared, it was more than half a century in Virginia and Maryland, and many years in North Carolina, before the courts were granted even partial jurisdiction in divorce causes.

The legislature, however, was not inactive.   Conservative as southern sentiment is supposed to have been regarding dissolution of the marriage bond, it is precisely in the South that legislative divorce was tried on the widest scale and where it bore its most evil fruit.   It seems probable that from the earliest times following the Revolution, in some of these states, marriages were dissolved by ordinary bills passed by the assemblies.   Of these a few examples have been discovered, although they are all of relatively late origin.   The earliest appear in the Maryland statutes. Thus, by the act of December 21, 1790, the marriage between John Sewall, of Talbot county, and Eve, his wife, was declared null and void, on the ground, set forth by

---

register of vital statistics in New Hampshire: *Pub. Stat.* (1891), 490; and that state has provided that the clerks of the supreme court shall report to the register the record of all divorces decreed since July 1, 1858: *Laws* (1901), 513.   Similar reports of decrees *nisi* are required in Maine: *Rev. Stat.* (1884), 522.   Vermont has provided for the registration of decrees under general direction of the secretary of the state board of health, who is to publish a biennial report, beginning in 1900: *Acts and Resolves* (1898), 41 ff.

[1] In this section are considered the laws of the District of Columbia and Porto Rico; the four territories, Arizona, Indian Territory, New Mexico, and Oklahoma; and the fifteen states, Alabama, Arkansas, Florida, Georgia, Kentucky, Louisiana, Maryland, Mississippi, Missouri, North Carolina, South Carolina, Tennessee, Texas, Virginia, and West Virginia.

[2] See chap. xv, sec. ii.

John in his petition, that, having been convicted of bearing a "mulatto child," his wife with the child had been condemned to servitude and sold, according to the cruel statute of 1715 "in such case made and provided."[1] Another instance of absolute divorce occurred in 1805. It seems that on account of his misconduct Archibald Alexander and his wife Susanna had "mutually agreed to live separate and apart from each other, and that articles of separation were entered into between them for that purpose." While they so lived apart the "said Susanna" took "upon herself the charge of six children, two of which were the children of the said Alexander." But, continues the petition, "in the month of July last there was a well founded report" that Archibald was dead; and "under this belief" Susanna formed a second marriage with John Musket. Accordingly, on their prayer, the legislature declared the former contract "absolutely and to all purposes null and void," and Archibald and Susanna "divorced *a vinculo matrimonii*," but without affecting the rights or legitimacy of the children of the first marriage.[2]

The session laws for 1806–7 afford five more examples of absolute divorce. On January 3, 1807, Pamela Sampson got herself released from her husband George, because they had long lived "on terms incompatible with the happiness of the conjugal union, which every day, if possible, increased, owing to intoxication which deranged his mind." On the next day Catherine Dimmett, finding herself in the same sad relation with James, her spouse, alleges that she "considers herself in hourly danger from his violence, as he not only attempted his own life, by cutting his own throat in the most barbarous and shocking manner," but has also repeatedly threatened hers, "thereby showing himself free from every moral restraint, and prepared for the commission

[1] *Laws of Md.* (1790), chap. xxv. *Cf.* BACON, *Laws of Md.* (1715), chap. 44, sec. 26.
[2] *Laws of Md.* (1805), chap. xxxiii.

of the most desperate and bloody deeds." Moreover, he remains in "one continuous state of intoxication, and freely indulges in every species of irregularity;" for all of which the worthy lawmakers felt justified in granting her prayer. On the same day, for cause not named, the nuptial tie of Benjamin and Ruth Fergusson was dissolved, but on condition that the act shall have no force unless the husband shall "give bond, with good and sufficient authority, to be approved by the orphan's court of Baltimore County, ... for the payment of the sum of thirty dollars *per annum* to the said Ruth during her life, so long as the said Benjamin shall live." In the other two cases no ground is assigned.[1]

During the following years the legislature was from time to time appealed to for relief.[2] In 1830 the first act regulating divorce appears in the statute-book. This law provides for judicial process in the initial stages, but leaves the final action to the assembly. It is made "lawful for any person who may intend to apply to the legislature for a divorce, to file a petition, stating the ground of his application, in the court of the county in which the person from whom he desires to be divorced resides." Upon the "filing of such petition, a subpoena shall issue to the party implicated, to appear and answer the same; and, upon such appearance, it shall be the duty of the court to issue a commission to a person or persons therein to be named, to take such testimony as the respective parties require." This testimony, taken after twenty days' notice, must be returned to the clerk of the court issuing the process, who is directed to forward it to the legislature together with "the petition, answer, and all other proceedings had under the application."[3]

---

[1] *Maryland Laws* (1806-7), chaps. xxxix, lxix, lxxvi, lxxvii, lxxx.

[2] Thus the *Laws* of 1807-8, chaps. xx (no cause given), xxx (no cause given), ciii (desertion and elopement of wife), clxvi (no cause given), yield four cases; and the *Laws* of 1809, chaps. xxiv, l, two cases more (no cause assigned).

[3] Act of Feb. 27, 1830: *Laws* (1829-30), chap. 202.

Still further precautions were taken in 1836. In no instance, it is declared, may a divorce be granted unless the persons shall have been *bona fide* residents of the state for at least twelve months before application. Furthermore, in the case of such residents the sanction of two-thirds of each branch of the legislature is required either for an absolute or for a limited divorce.[1] Five years later the preliminary procedure was changed, and some provision for notice to non-residents was introduced. Application is now to be made "to some justice of the peace, who shall thereupon issue a subpoena directed to some constable or other person, who shall serve the same on the person from whom the divorce is sought." After service and return of the subpœna, either party may, after the lapse of thirty days, proceed to take testimony before a justice of the peace, if they both reside in the same county or city, otherwise by deposition, and transmit it to the legislature at its next annual session. But when the libellee is a non-resident, or is absent from the state, the applicant must give at least three months' notice of his intention to ask the assembly for a divorce, in some newspaper published in the city of Baltimore. Such testimony shall be taken on oath before a justice and transmitted to the legislature as in the case of residents.[2]

The law of 1841 was the last attempt in Maryland to regulate legislative divorce. The efforts of the preceding twelve years to devise checks and provide safeguards were largely unavailing. Division of responsibility between the court and the legislature, whose effects are so well illustrated in the case of Georgia presently to be considered, is pretty sure to result in the removal of all real responsibility. Each successive year produced an increasing crop of divorces.

[1] Act of March 4, 1836: *Laws* (1835–36), chap. 128. Twelve months' residence is required by this act.

[2] Act of March 9, 1841: *Laws* (1840–41), chap. 238.

Thirty-one were granted in 1835, and thirty-six in 1837. Occasionally the decree is from bed and board; in most cases it is for absolute dissolution of the marriage bond. Usually it is curtly expressed in a few words of the statute-book. Often the cause is not mentioned; although, after 1830, the details in most instances are doubtless to be found in the judicial papers transmitted to the assembly.[1] In 1842, for the first time, full jurisdiction in divorce cases is bestowed upon the courts. Consequently there is a falling off in the number of legislative decrees; but they nevertheless continue to appear in the session laws until the constitution of 1851 forbids the general assembly to interfere in such matters.[2]

Virginia anticipated Maryland by fifteen years in granting to the superior court of chancery full power to hear and determine suits for absolute and partial divorce. The act of 1827 names the causes for which alone judicial divorces of either kind may be granted, and provides for alimony and custody of the children. But this statute also contemplates the obtaining of divorce *a vinculo* through resort to the legislature. It is provided that "every person intending to petition the general assembly for a divorce, shall file in the clerk's office of the superior court of laws, for the county in which he or she may reside, a statement of the causes on which the application is founded." At least two months before the next court, notice must be given to the adverse party "by personal service," when a resident in the state; otherwise, by publication for four weeks in "some newspaper printed in the city of Richmond." Thereupon, "without other pleadings in writing," the court "shall cause a jury to be impanelled to ascertain the facts set forth in the said

---

[1] For the numerous cases of legislative divorce see the *Index to the Laws of Maryland*, *1826–31; ibid., 1832–37; ibid., 1837–45*, 224–29.

[2] The constitution of 1851, Art. III, sec. 21, declares that "no divorces shall be granted by the General Assembly."

statement; and their verdict shall be recorded;" but the confession of the parties shall not be accepted as evidence at the trial. A certified copy of these proceedings must accompany every petition presented to the legislature; unless a divorce from bed and board shall have been previously granted by the court of chancery, in which case a copy of the record may be substituted.[1]

Under the law of 1827 resort was often made to the general assembly,[2] until in 1848 an act appeared which, after granting to Robert Moran a divorce from his wife Lydia, seeks to abrogate the practice so far as by statute it may be done. "Whereas," runs the preamble, "applications to the legislature for divorces *a vinculo matrimonii* are becoming frequent, and occupy much time in their consideration, and moreover involve investigations more properly judicial in their nature, and ought, so far as the legislature can do it, [to] be referred to the judicial tribunals of the state;" therefore the courts are granted the same full jurisdiction in absolute divorce which they already possessed in petition for separation from bed and board.[3] This law would not necessarily have put an end to the evil; for the acts of one legislature cannot bind those of another; but that was soon effected by the constitution of 1851, which deprived the assembly of all authority to hear divorce petitions.[4]

For a few years North Carolina tried a still different plan

---

[1] Act of Feb. 17, 1827: *Acts of the Gen. Assembly* (1826–27), 21, 22. The same act is repeated in *Supp. to Rev. Code* (1833), 222, 223. The law of 1827 appears to be the first legislation of Virginia on the subject of divorce, although "lawful divorce" — meaning doubtless that of the legislature — is incidentally mentioned in the act of 1792: *Acts* (1794), 205. The act of 1827 provides in all cases for an appeal to the court of appeals, but, apparently, not in divorces granted by the assembly.

[2] Thus, on Jan. 25, 1827, Macy, *alias* Amasa Gay (formerly Birdsong), got a divorce from her husband Charles. The cause is not mentioned, but he is not permitted to marry during her lifetime: *Acts* (1826–27), 126. On Jan. 27, 1827, David Parker, of the county of Nansemond, was released from his wife Jane, who likewise was not allowed to remarry: *ibid.*, 126.

[3] Act of March 18, 1848: *Acts of the Assembly* (1847–48), 165–67.

[4] Constitution of 1851, Art. IV, sec. 35: see *Code* (1860), 48.

for sharing responsibility between the courts and the legislature. By the act of 1814 full authority to grant separation from bed and board, for any of the causes therein named, with alimony to the wife, is conferred upon the superior court. The same tribunal may also try petitions for full divorce, dismissing the petition, dissolving the "nuptial ties or bonds of matrimony," or declaring the contract null and void, as the case demands; but it is especially provided that "no judgment, sentence, or decree of final or absolute divorce" shall be "valid until ratified by the general assembly."[1]   This condition was, however, removed in 1818;[2] and ten years thereafter legislative divorce was entirely abolished, so far as it was possible to accomplish it by statute. Because "the numerous applications for divorce and alimony, annually presented to the general assembly, consume a considerable portion of time in their examination, and consequently retard the investigation of more important (*sic*) subjects of legislation;" and because "such applications might be adjudicated by other tribunals with much less expenditure to the state, and more impartial justice to individuals;" it is therefore enacted that the superior courts of law shall have "sole and original jurisdiction" in both kinds of divorce. From this act it may be inferred that the legislature had granted divorces on petitions which had not gone through the courts and come up to it for ratification; and for causes other than those named in the statute.[3]   A few years later, by a constitutional amendment ratified in 1835, the assembly was deprived of the "power to grant a divorce or

---

[1] *Laws* (1814), chap. 5; also in *Haywood's Manual of the Laws of N. C.* (1819), 174-78.

[2] *Acts* (1818), chap. 968.

[3] This inference is justified by the words of the act as quoted, and from the clause declaring "that all applications for other causes than those specified"—in the act of 1814—"shall be subject to the rules and regulations provided in said act for the causes therein mentioned."—*Acts* (1827-28), 19, 20. The law of 1814, as to causes, appears unaltered in *Laws of the State* (1821), II, 1292-95.

secure alimony in any individual case;" and the same prohibition appears in the constitution of 1876.[1]

Until constitutionally prohibited in 1852-53, legislative
divorce also existed in Missouri.[2] The law of 1833 endeavors to restrict the action of the assembly to cases for
whose trial "before the judiciary" the law has not provided;
and it forbids entirely the hearing of any petition when the
causes for it "shall have accrued since the next two months
preceding the sitting of the legislature." At the same time
notice to the opposite party is made essential. In the case
of residents, two months' written notification is required,
service to be proved by affidavit. If the libellee is a non-
resident, publication in a newspaper for at least three weeks
successively will suffice.[3]

The government report shows several divorces in South
Carolina for the year 1869-70; and these were probably
granted by the legislature, for no divorce statute then existed.[4]

As early as 1803 the statutes of the Mississippi Territory
make provision for both kinds of divorce by judicial
sentence; but resort to the legislature is not prohibited.[5]
Later, by the constitution of 1817 and the laws thereunder
enacted, it is declared that "divorces from the bonds of
matrimony shall not be granted, but in cases provided for by
law, by suit in chancery;" but it is especially provided that
"no decree for such divorce shall have effect until the same
shall be sanctioned by two-thirds of both branches of the
general assembly."[6] This unwise condition—in substance so

[1] POORE, Charters, II, 1416 (1835), 1439 (1876).

[2] By the ninth amendment to the constitution of 1820, ratified at the session of
1852-53: Rev. Stat. (1856), I, 96; POORE, Charters, II, 1122. The prohibition is retained
in the constitution of 1875, Art. IV, sec. 53: POORE, Charters, II, 1175.

[3] Act of Jan. 31, 1833: Laws of a Public and General Nature (1842), II, 361.

[4] WRIGHT, Report, 388, 389, 155.

[5] Act of March 10, 1803: Stat. of Miss. Ter. (1816), 252-54.

[6] Constitution of 1817, Art. VI, sec. 17: POORE, Charters, II, 1064; carried out by
act of June 15, 1822: Code of Miss. (1848), 496.

often appearing in the enactments of the South—seems to
have lasted only until 1832, when it was omitted in the
constitution framed in that year.   In the meantime the
legislature had found plenty of work to do.   The session
laws of 1833, for example, contain nine divorce decrees,
passed probably just before the new constitution went into
effect.[1]

Alabama, as a part of the Mississippi Territory, was, of
course, affected by the act of 1803 above cited.[2]   Resort to
the legislature may have been practiced from the beginning.
At any rate, during the existence of the Alabama Territory—
from 1817 to 1819—ten divorces were thus obtained.[3]   The
people seem to have been so much in love with the custom
that it is sanctioned, on the usual co-operative plan, by the
constitution of 1819.   The sixth article of that instrument
requires that all decrees of the courts granting absolute
dissolution of wedlock shall be confirmed by two-thirds of
each house of the assembly, precisely in the same form as
by the constitution of Mississippi two years earlier.[4]   The
act of the next year, conferring jurisdiction in such cases on
the circuit courts and defining the causes of divorce, directs
that the record of evidence made by the court in each suit
shall be sent to the speaker of the house of representatives,
who is to open and have it read before the members.[5]

[1] *Laws* (1833), 235 ff.; Const. of 1832, Art. VII, sec. 15: POORE, *Charters*, II, 1077.
The omission of the clause expressly requiring legislative sanction in the constitution
of 1832 seems clearly to be intended to abolish legislative divorce.   Yet the act of 1840
makes the decrees of the courts "final and conclusive, as fully as though the same
had been confirmed by the legislature;" from which language one would naturally
infer that the legislature had continued to ratify divorces after the constitution
went into effect: *Laws* (1840), 51.

Legislative divorce is prohibited by the constitution of 1868, Art. IV, sec. 22:
POORE, *Charters*, II, 1084; and by Art. IV, secs. 87 and 90 of the constitution of 1890:
New York Convention Manual, Part II, Vol. I, 1067 (1894).

[2] The act also appears in *Digest of Laws of Ala.* (1823), 252.

[3] *Digest* (1823), 254.

[4] Art. VI, sec. 3, Const. of 1819: *Digest* (1823), 255: POORE, *Charters*, I, 42.

[5] Act. of Dec. 21, 1820: *Digest* (1823), 256.

It is not surprising that these "safeguards" proved as futile in Alabama as elsewhere. The obtaining of divorces was facilitated rather than hindered. The number annually granted mounts apace. In 1822 the record is not yet formidable, but the session laws show twenty-three cases in 1843, twenty-four in the next year, and not less than sixty-seven in 1849–50.[1] So it seemed necessary to appeal to organic law for a remedy. The constitution of 1865 therefore declares that absolute divorces shall only be granted by a suit in chancery; and that decrees in chancery "shall be final, unless appealed from in the manner prescribed by law, within three months" from the date of their enrolment. This section is repeated in the constitution of 1867; but in that of 1875 a different provision appears. "No special or local law," it is now declared, "shall be enacted for the benefit of individuals or corporations in cases which are or can be provided for by a general law, or where the relief sought can be given by any court" in the state.[2] From the terms of this section it may be inferred that in exceptional cases resort might still be had to the assembly. Accordingly, in 1883, by legislative decree, we find that Claudia Shaw, of Macon county, was released from the conjugal bond and constituted a *feme sole* for all purposes whatsoever.[3]

The history of American lawmaking in Louisiana opens with two divorce decrees passed by the legislative council of the Territory of Orleans. By the first of these acts, dated January 23, 1805, and signed by Governor Claiborne, the marriage of Captain James Stille and Lydia his wife is dissolved and each is "fully authorized" to "contract in

[1] For these examples see *Digest* (1823), 256–58 (those of 1821-22); *Acts* (1843), 143–47; *Acts* (1843–44), 210; *Acts* (1849–50), 517.

[2] *Cf.* Const. of 1865, Art. IV, sec. 30; that of 1867, Art. IV, sec. 30; and that of 1875, Art. IV, sec. 23: POORE, *Charters*, I, 53, 65, 81.

[3] *Acts* (1882–83), 587.

matrimony" again whenever to either it "may seem right."
This separation is allowed "in consequence of an unhappy
disagreement, resulting from circumstances of an afflicting
nature," which had prevented the couple from "enjoying
that harmony and domestic happiness which the conjugal
state was designed to produce," and leading them soon after
the marriage "to resolve upon and stipulate for a complete
and perpetual separation."[1]

This example found frequent imitation both before and
after the state of Louisiana was organized. By March 3,
1827, forty-six legislative divorces had been granted.[2] With
these, however, the history of such cases comes to an end;
for, a few days later, exclusive jurisdiction in all divorce
matters was bestowed upon the courts;[3] and the policy thus
adopted by statute was ratified by the constitution of 1845.[4]

A federal law in 1886 prohibits legislative divorce in any
of the territories of the United States. Previous to that
date, however, it had existed in Arizona. During the single
session of 1879 seventeen divorces were granted by legislative decree; and the practice may have continued until
stopped by congressional authority.[5]

Kentucky refrained from any divorce legislation until
1809, when jurisdiction was conferred upon the circuit

---

[1] *Acts Passed at the First Session of the Leg. Council of the Ter. of Orleans* (1805),
454–56. On May 1, 1805, a divorce was granted to James Elliot and Sophia his wife:
ibid., 456–58.

[2] LISLET, *Gen. Digest*, II, Appendix, 25, 26, gives the list, with dates. These
divorce acts, as usual, fill each but two or three lines in the statute-book, and usually
the cause is not assigned. For examples see *Acts* (1822), 12; *ibid.* (1826), 34, 58, 60, 62,
222; and *ibid.* (1827), 12, 18, 24.

[3] By the act of March 19, 1827: *Acts*, 130–35.

[4] Const. of 1845, Art. CXVII: POORE, *Charters*, I, 721; also Const. of 1852, Art.
CXIV: POORE, *op. cit.*, I, 735; *Civil Code* (1853), 19; Const. of 1864, Art. CXVII; and
Const. of 1868, Art. CXIII: POORE, *op. cit.*, I, 750, 767.

[5] Fifteen of these divorces were granted by the one act of Feb. 7, 1879: *Acts and
Resolutions* (1879), 5–8; for the others see *ibid.*, 46, 112; and compare the act of Congress of July 30, 1886: *Statutes at Large*, XXIV, 170. In the same year, 1879, twenty-
eight divorces were granted by the courts of Arizona, and five in the year before:
WRIGHT, *Report*, 151.

courts.[1]   But the jurisdiction was not exclusive; for year by
year until 1850, when the usual constitutional interdict appears,[2] the session laws show the assembly engaged in passing divorce decrees.[3]   In the meantime provision was made
for notice to the adverse party.   By the act of 1837, in case
of residents of the state, there must be one month's written
notice in which the ground of the intended application to
the legislature shall be set forth; while, if the defendant is
a non-resident, publication of the notice for four weeks in
some "authorized" newspaper "may supersede the necessity
of personal service."   When a divorce is granted on such
application, the wife shall receive back the estate which the
husband had with her at the marriage, unless she has been
guilty of conduct such as by the laws of the state would for-
feit her right of dower; and when the husband's conduct is
the cause of separation, she is entitled to the same share of
his real and personal property as if he were dead.[4]

A few years later the Kentucky assembly accomplished
a feat which surely "breaks the record" in the history of
social legislation.   On the 4th of March, 1843, in one short
act of less than two pages of type the hymeneal bonds of
thirty-seven couples were severed by one fatal clip of the
lawmakers' shears; while, in addition, room is found in the
bill to make provision for the children and to restore the
maiden names of some of the women, but not for any mention of the causes.[5]

It is in Georgia, however, that the divorce laws and judicial decisions reveal the strangest vicissitudes and the most
singular vagaries.   To understand the course of events it is
essential in the outset to observe two important facts.   The

[1] Act of Jan. 31, 1809: LITTELL, *Stat. Law* (1814), IV, 19, 20.

[2] Const. of 1850, Art. II, sec. 32: POORE, *op. cit.*, I, 671.

[3] See the Index to *Acts of the Gen. Assembly* for each year, 1809-50.

[4] Act of Feb. 23, 1837: *Acts* (1836-37), 323, 324.

[5] *Acts of the Gen. Assembly* (1842-43), 205, 206.

common law, it will be remembered,[1] was, with certain limitations, adopted by the state in 1784; and the constitution of 1798 permits "two-thirds of each branch of the legislature to pass acts of divorce," but only after the parties shall have had a fair trial before the superior court, and a "verdict shall have been obtained authorizing a divorce upon legal principles."[2] It would have been hard to select a phrase more ambiguous than the clause last quoted. Just what are the "legal principles" referred to? Are they the principles of the English ecclesiastical law, as constituting a part of the common law made binding in 1784? Are they perhaps to be sought in previous enactments of the state or province of Georgia? No such statutes have been discovered; and no divorce seems ever to have been granted, unless by the assembly after the Revolution. With this analysis of the problem before us, the course of legislation during the half-century following the adoption of the constitution of 1798 may now be traced.

The worthy lawmaker starts out valiantly. The act of 1802, giving the superior court primary and the legislature final jurisdiction in petitions for total divorce, as required by the constitution, is justified in language which seems grotesque in the light of later experience. Such a measure is needful, we are assured, not only because there are doubts as to the powers of the judges in divorce causes without a statute, but because "marriage being among the most solemn and important contracts in society, has been regulated in all civilized nations by positive systems;" and because "circumstances may require a dissolution of contracts founded on the most binding and sacred obligations which the human mind has been capable of devising, and such circumstances may combine to render necessary the dissolution of the con-

[1] See chap. xv, sec. ii.

[2] Const. of 1798, Art. III, sec. 9: *Digest of Laws of Ga.* (1801), 40; Poore, *op. cit.*, I, 394.

tract of marriage, which dissolution ought not to be dependent on private will, but should require legislative interference; inasmuch as the republic is deeply interested in the private business of its citizens."

The preliminary trial provided for by this act is before a jury whose verdict must take the following form: "We find that sufficient proofs have been referred to our consideration to authorize a total divorce, that is to say, a divorce *a vinculo matrimonii*, upon legal principles between the parties in this case"—which is an attempt, however awkward, to satisfy the demands of both law and constitution.[1] In 1806 a new statute appears, creating a most intricate procedure. As in 1802, no specific causes are named for either limited or complete divorce. All petitions coming before the superior court are to be referred to a "special jury, who shall enquire into the situation of the parties before their marriage and also at the time of the trial." They may grant either a conditional or a total divorce. In the former case their verdict shall make provision out of the husband's property for the separate maintenance of the wife and children; and the court shall cause the "verdict or decree to be carried into effect according to the rules of law, or according to the practice of chancery, as the nature of the case may require." The verdict for absolute divorce is, of course, placed before the legislature for approval. If the legislature "refuse to pass a law or to carry the same into effect," either person, on due notice to the other, may apply to the superior court of his county to appoint three commissioners who, after proper inquiry into the circumstances of the parties, by witnesses when necessary, may allow separate maintenance. The report of the commissioners to the court is to be entered as its judgment. Even now the matter is not ended. There is still a last chance for the discontented spouse. If dissatis-

[1] Act of Dec. 1, 1802: in *Compilation of Laws of Ga.* (1812), 98–100.

fied with the judgment, either person may apply for its modification to the next court, which shall refer the first report or decree to a commission comprising the original three members, with two others. The finding of this body is then entered as the definitive judgment of the court.[1]

Thus the law remained until 1833, except that a form of oath was prescribed in 1810.[2] In the meantime an ever-increasing number of divorce acts appears in the session laws.[3] Between 1798 and 1835 at least two hundred and ninety-one decrees for absolute dissolution of marriage were granted by the legislature. In the beginning of the period the average annual output was but four; at the close it had risen to not less than twenty-eight.[4] In one instance the previous finding of a jury seems to have been thought superfluous. John Cormick, having fled from Ireland to Georgia in 1798, before the constitution went into effect, and his family refusing to accompany him, the legislature, without a verdict, declared his person and property exempt from the claims of Eliza his wife as if they were never married, and John was fully authorized to do all things as if he had never entered into the matrimonial state.[5] Another case shows the Georgia lawmaker a close second in legal economics to his brother of Kentucky. On December 13, 1816, twenty-one pairs were set free and the offenders forbidden to remarry in thirteen lines of print, excluding the names.[6] In 1833 a rem-

---

[1] *Compilation of Laws of Ga.* (1812), 312-14.

[2] PRINCE, *Digest* (1837), 190; Head v. Head, 2 *Georgia*, 193.

[3] In the *Compilation of Laws* (1812), 61, 83, 113, 202-4, 264, 385, 408, 508, 509, 512, 569, are eighteen divorce acts; many appear in *Laws of Ga., 1810-19* (1821), 193-96, 252-63; and eighty-six cases, in DAWSON, *Compilation, 1819-29* (1831), 141-53.

[4] PRINCE, *Digest* (1837), 187, note, gives the following summary, which appears to be inconsistent: "The number of persons divorced by the legislature since the date of the present constitution up to the close of the annual session of 1835, is 291, averaging from 1800 to 1810, about 4; from 1810 to 1820, 8; from 1820 to 1830, 18, and since that time, 28 per annum." If his averages are correct, the total number for the entire period would be about 440.

[5] Nov. 27, 1807: *Compilation* (1812), 385, 386.

[6] *Laws of Ga., 1810-19* (1821), 262, 263.

edy was therefore sought through an amendment to the constitution. "Whereas," explains the preamble, whose redun-
dant adjectives may well be a sign of serious distress, "the
frequent, numerous, and repeated, applications to the legislature to grant divorces has (*sic*) become a great annoyance
to that body, and is (*sic*) well worth their attention," both on
account of the expense and the unnecessary "swelling" of
the laws and journals, and "believing that the public good
would be much promoted, and that the parties would receive
full and complete justice;" therefore it is enacted as a part
of the organic law that "divorces shall be final and conclusive when the parties shall have obtained the concurrent
verdicts of two special juries authorizing a divorce upon
legal principles."[1]

Unless it be assumed that there was no serious intention
to put a check upon the facility with which divorces could
be obtained, it is almost incredible that a provision so loose
and ambiguous should have been adopted. For the retention of the phrase "upon legal principles" still left a rich
field for speculation as to the proper grounds of divorce,
total or conditional; and it was equally uncertain whether
the juries could determine the law as well as the facts in
each case. So the courts, apparently, continued to grant as
many divorces without help of the assembly as were permitted before that body lost its power to interfere.

Affairs continued in this unsatisfactory condition until
1847, when suddenly what proved in the end to be a drastic
remedy was administered in the case of Head *v.* Head, tried
on appeal from the superior court of Monroe county. The
elaborate opinion of Justice Nisbet in this suit, reviewing as
it does the preceding legislation, is the best source of information for the history of divorce in Georgia. The case

---

[1] Const. 1798, Art. III, sec. 9, amendment of 1833, in force 1835: PRINCE, *Digest*
(1837), 911; POORE, *Charters*, I, 399.

arose in a petition for dissolution of the marriage bond on the sole ground of abandonment of the husband by the wife, which ground, "it is too plain to admit of question," is not "recognized as a cause of divorce *a vinculo*" by the common law. On the other hand, the counsel for the appellant argued that by "a fair construction of the constitution of Georgia, and of the laws enacted to carry it into effect, the question of a divorce or not, in its totality, is submitted to the special juries; that they are the sole and final judges in all cases of what shall be a good cause of divorce, irrespective of the common law principles." To determine, therefore, the relative powers of the judge and the jury, and to discover what are the "legal principles" mentioned in the constitution, became the dual problem which the court was called upon to solve. In the outset it is held by the court that the constitution of 1798 is in restraint of divorce in three ways: (1) by transferring full jurisdiction in the first instance from the legislature to the superior courts; for before that date the assembly had exercised "unlimited power over the subject;" (2) by restraining the legislative will through requiring a fair trial before a jury before that will could be exercised; (3) by "restricting both the courts and the legislature, as to their power to grant divorces, to such cases as were grantable upon *legal principles.*"

Disregard of these intended restrictions in the statutes and in judicial practice had led to most serious evils. The reasons assigned in the preamble to the amendment of 1835, Justice Nisbet urges, were not the true reasons which actuated its authors. That amendment arose "in a conviction upon the minds of prudent and discerning men, that divorces under the constitution of 1798 were alarmingly frequent;" and this was due to the fact that responsibility was divided between the courts and the legislature. "Under the old system, the courts but rarely seem to have felt, that they had

anything to do with the trial of the divorce cause, other than
to subserve the double purpose of an automaton agent in the
hands of lawyers to present their cases to the juries. Believing that the legislature, whether for good or evil, had made
the juries the sole arbiters of the law and facts, they could
of course feel no responsibility about the matter, and the
consequence was, as all men know who know anything of our
courts of justice, that divorces were had with flagrant facility;
that some were refused which ought to have been allowed,
and hundreds were granted which ought to have been
refused; and that the event of a divorce cause depended
more upon the fact whether it was defended or not, and if
defended, upon the zeal and ability of counsel, than upon
anything else. Nor was the case essentially different when
it came before the legislature. The legislature, taking it for
granted that the courts had settled all the *legal principles*
involved, in the majority of cases, with ready acquiescence
affirmed the judgment of the court and divorced the parties.
The wealth and standing of the parties, their political and
social relations, or, perhaps, the personal beauty and address
of a female libellant, controlled in many cases the action of
the legislature." Referring to the statistics of legislative
divorce, above quoted, the court continues: "How fearful
was the ratio of increase! Well might the patriot, the Christian, and the moralist look about him for some device to stay
this swelling tide of demoralization." But "it is said that
the new mode of granting divorces has not remedied the
evil; that divorces are as frequent under the new as under
the old constitution. This is, we admit, to a great extent
true, and the reason is obvious. It is owing to the wrong
construction of the constitution"—the submission to the
jury of the whole question of law as well as of fact. The
Georgia legislature was not checked, as in England, by the
record of two preceding trials;[1] "and although in France,

[1] See chap. xi, sec. 3, c).

divorces by the Napoleonic Code[1] may be granted without
cause, upon mutual consent merely, yet the application must
be made to a judicial tribunal, and the consent is subjected
to constraints, which create great and serious checks upon
its abuse."

Accordingly, it was held by the court that the sole causes
for "divorce in Georgia are those of the common law."   For
total divorce, or, more properly speaking, annulment of a
voidable marriage, these causes are "pre-contract, consanguinity, affinity, and corporal infirmity;" while for a partial
divorce adultery and cruelty are the only grounds recognized.

One cannot help admiring the stern moral courage which
enabled the court to render this decision.   At one stroke
and without warning the social standing of hundreds was
put in jeopardy.   Those who thought themselves single
found themselves married.   Many who may have taken new
partners became liable to actions for bigamy; and their children were bastards.   The justice was aware of his grave
responsibility.   "The judgment we have given in this case
is in repeal of the practice of the courts in a majority of the
circuits, and in disaffirmance of the opinion of eminent jurists
upon the bench and at the bar, and in conflict with that
public sentiment which, springing out of, and strengthened
by, the heretofore judicial facility which has characterized
the action of the courts, tolerates and expects divorces for
slight causes."   At the same time, however wise, and in the
event beneficent, may have been this judgment, one must
also confess that in its wider bearings it reveals the dangers
for society which may lurk in the unyielding logic of individual judicial opinion, should healthy public sentiment not
be allowed, at least in some measure, to direct and mold the
decrees of our courts of justice.[2]   The hardships arising from
the decision in question were redressed in 1849 by an act

---

[1] *Code Napoléon*, Nos. 233, 275-97.
[2] Case of Head *v.* Head, 2 *Georgia Reports*, 191-211.

validating all second marriages formed in consequence of
divorces granted for illegal causes by the courts or by the
legislature; and the same year this extraordinary episode in
social history was brought to a close by a constitutional
amendment declaring that "divorces shall be final and conclusive when the parties shall have obtained the concurrent
verdicts of two special juries authorized to divorce upon
such legal principles as the general assembly may by law
prescribe."[1]

b) *Judicial divorce: jurisdiction, kinds, and causes.* —
Although during the colonial period divorce laws had not
been enacted, after the birth of the nation the wheels of
legislation, in most cases, were slow in starting. Once set
going, however, they have moved swiftly enough, so that
now a great variety of grounds for dissolution of wedlock
are sanctioned. Under influence of ecclesiastical law and
tradition, conservatism is shown in the retention by nearly
all the older states of so-called divorce from bed and board.
Except in Arizona, Mississippi, Missouri, New Mexico, Oklahoma, Porto Rico, and Texas, partial divorce is still permitted in all of the commonwealths and territories under
review having any legislation on the general subject; for
South Carolina, except for a brief period, has never by
statute authorized any kind of divorce; and in Florida
separate alimony has the same effect as divorce from bed
and board.

By the Virginia law of 1827, as already seen, absolute
divorce, properly so called, can only be obtained from the
legislature, although the superior courts of chancery are
then authorized to annul voidable marriages.[2] The same
tribunals, however, are granted full "cognizance of matri-

[1] Const. of 1798, Art. III, sec. 9, amendment of 1849: COBB, *Digest* (1851), 1123;
POORE, *Charters*, I, 401.

[2] For natural and incurable impotency of body at the time of entering into the
matrimonial contract; as also for idiocy and bigamy.

monial causes on account of adultery, cruelty, and just cause of bodily fear; and in such cases may grant divorce *a mensa et thoro* in the usual method of proceeding in those courts." They may thus "decree perpetual separation and protection to the persons and property of the parties;" grant to "either, out of the property of the other, such maintenance as shall be proper;" restore "to the injured party, as far as practicable, the rights of property conferred by the marriage on the other;" and provide for the custody, guardianship, and support of the children.[1]

To the causes for which a limited divorce may be obtained "abandonment and desertion" was added in 1841, and the provision authorizing annulments was somewhat modified.[2] By the act of 1848, putting an end to legislative interference, the "circuit and superior courts of law and chancery" are given authority to grant absolute divorce on the single ground of adultery, with liberty to both parties to remarry, or only to the innocent or injured party, as may seem just.[3] A statute of the next year allows limited divorce for cruelty, reasonable apprehension of bodily hurt, abandonment, or desertion; and these four causes are still in force.[4]

By the present law, which, with a slight modification in 1872 and another in 1894, has remained unaltered since the act of 1853, eight causes for complete dissolution of wedlock are recognized; and jurisdiction in all suits for divorce, annulment, or separation is vested in the "circuit and cor-

[1] Act of Feb. 17, 1827: *Acts of Gen. Assembly* (1826–27), 21, 22. *Cf.* same law in *Supp. to Rev. Code* (1833), 222, 223.

[2] Act of March 17, 1841: *Acts of the Assembly* (1840–41), 78, 79. The court may declare contracts void on the grounds named in 1827, "or for any other cause for which marriage is annulled by the ecclesiastical law " (78).

[3] Act of March 18, 1848: *Acts of Assembly* (1847–48), 165–67.

[4] *Va. Code* (1849), 561. Probably the abandonment or desertion is for a time less than five years, as the latter period is sufficient for a divorce *a vinculo: Code* (1860), 530, and note. On joint application of the parties and due evidence of reconciliation, a decree of separation may be revoked by the same court granting it; and when three years have elapsed without reconciliation after such a decree, the court may grant a full divorce: *Acts* (1895–96), 103; modified by *ibid.* (1902–3), 87, 98.

poration courts on their chancery side." An absolute decree
may be obtained (1) for adultery; (2) natural or incurable
impotency of body existing at the time of entering into the
marriage contract; (3) where either party is sentenced to
confinement in the penitentiary; (4) where prior to the marriage either party, without the knowledge of the other, has
been convicted of an infamous offense; (5) "where either
party charged with an offence punishable by death or confinement in the penitentiary has been indicted, is a fugitive
from justice, and has been absent for two years;"[1] (6) where
either party wilfully deserts or abandons the other for three
years; (7) "where at the time of the marriage, the wife, without the knowledge of the husband, was *enceinte* by some
person other than the husband;" (8) or where prior to the
marriage she had been, without the husband's knowledge,
notoriously a prostitute. But it is especially provided that
for the last two causes no divorce shall be decreed if it
appears that the person applying has cohabited with the
other after gaining knowledge of the facts. The same is
true of "conviction of an infamous offence;" and under the
third cause, that of sentence to the penitentiary, a pardon
shall not restore the offender to conjugal rights.[2]

In West Virginia the circuit court on its chancery side
may grant total divorce for eight causes. Of these the first
four are identical with the corresponding numbers for Virginia. The rest are: (5) where either party wilfully abandons or deserts the other for three years; (6 and 7) the same
as the seventh and eighth for Virginia; (8) where the husband, prior to the marriage, has been, without knowledge of
the wife, notoriously a licentious person—thus dealing even
justice to each spouse. Furthermore, five grounds of limited

---

[1] This cause was added by the act of March 23, 1872: *Acts of the Assembly*
(1871–72), 418, 419.

[2] *Code of Va.* (1887), 561: *Acts of the Assembly* (1852–53), 47, 48. The term of desertion was reduced from five to three years by *Acts* (1893–94), 425.

divorce are there sanctioned. The first four are the same as those existing in Virginia since 1849; and in addition a fifth cause gives jurisdiction when either the husband or wife after marriage becomes a habitual drunkard.[1]

Kentucky anticipated by many years the mother-commonwealth of Virginia in defining the grounds for dissolving a marriage.[2]   Under the act of 1809 the several circuit courts are authorized to grant total divorce to either spouse (1) for abandonment and living in adultery, or (2) where the other has been condemned for a felony in any court of record in the United States; to the husband, when the wife has voluntarily left his bed and board for three years with the intention of abandonment; and to the wife, for treatment so cruel, barbarous, and inhuman as actually to endanger her life. To prevent too facile action of the courts, a check is devised similar to that later adopted by the English law. It is made the duty of the attorney prosecuting for the commonwealth to oppose the granting of any divorce warranted by this statute.[3]   A new cause of full divorce, analogous to that

[1] *Code of West Va.* (1891), 612, 613; *ibid.* (1900), 660-62. It is provided that "a charge of prostitution made by the husband against the wife falsely shall be deemed cruel treatment, within the meaning of this section."—*Code* (1900), 662. The penalties for bigamy do not extend to a person forming a new marriage when the husband or wife has been absent seven years and not heard from: *ibid.*, 971.

[2] As early as 1800 separate maintenance is secured to the wife in certain cases. It is enacted "that any court of quarter sessions or district court, shall be vested with jurisdiction to hear and determine applications from wives against their husbands for alimony, in cases where the husband has, or may hereafter desert or abandon his wife for the space of one year successively, or where he lives in open avowed adultery with another woman for the space of six months, and in cases of cruel, inhuman, and barbarous treatment."—*Digest of the Stat. Laws of Ky.* (1834), I, 121. Such cruel treatment warrants alimony even when life is not endangered: 2 J. J. MARSHALL, 324; but not divorce: *ibid.*, 322.

"Before the passage of the above act, the chancellor had power to grant alimony, and since the statute it may be decreed in cases not embraced by it."—*Digest* (1834), I, 121, note. "After a decree for alimony, the power of the husband over the wife shall cease;" and she may use such alimony, and acquire and dispose of any property, "without being subject to the control, molestation, or hindrance" of the husband, as if she were a *feme sole: ibid.*, I, 122. The two kinds of common-law divorce, in canonical sense, were originally recognized in Kentucky: HUMPHREY, *Compendium of the Common Law in Force in Ky.* (1822), 135.

[3] LITTELL, *Statute Law of Kentucky* (1814), IV, 19, 20.

allowed in some of the New England states, appears in 1812. When a man renounces the marriage agreement and refuses to live with his wife in conjugal relation "by uniting himself to any sect whose creed, rules, or doctrines require a renunciation of the marriage covenant, or forbid a man and wife to dwell and cohabit together," the aggrieved woman may have a full release; the offender is forbidden to remarry during the former's lifetime; or the wife may claim separate alimony and maintenance without divorce.[1]

No further legislation regarding the grounds of divorce appears until the foundation of the existing law of Kentucky was laid in the act of 1843. The present statute presents an exceedingly complex analysis of causes. "A jury shall not be impaneled in any action for divorce, alimony, or maintenance, but courts having general equity jurisdiction may grant a divorce for any of the following causes, to both husband and wife": I. To either party: (1) for "such impotency or malformation as prevents the conjugal relation;" (2) living apart without any cohabitation for two consecutive years. II. To the party not in fault: (1) for abandonment for one year; (2) living in adultery; (3) condemnation for felony within or without the state; (4) concealment of any loathsome disease existing at the time of the marriage, or contracting such afterwards; (5) force, duress, or fraud in obtaining the marriage; (6) uniting with any religious society whose creed and rules require renunciation of the marriage covenant, or forbid husband and wife to cohabit. III. To the wife, if not in like fault: (1) for confirmed habit of drunkenness on the part of the husband of not less than one year's duration, "accompanied with a wasting of his estate, and without any suitable provision for the maintenance of his wife and children;" (2) "habitually behaving toward her by the husband, for not less than six months, in

---

[1] Act of Feb. 8, 1812: LITTELL, *loc. cit.*, 407 ff. In case of divorce, the wife may not marry again within one year (409).

such cruel and inhuman manner as to indicate a settled aversion to her, or to destroy permanently her peace or happiness;" (3) "such cruel treatment or injury, or attempt at injury, of the wife by the husband, as indicates an outrageous temper in him, or probable danger to her life, or great bodily injury from remaining with him."   IV. To the husband: (1) when the wife is pregnant by another man without the husband's knowledge at the time of the marriage; (2) for habitual drunkenness on the part of the wife of not less than one year's duration, if he is not guilty of the same fault; (3) for adultery of the wife, or such lewd, lascivious behavior on her part as proves her to be unchaste, without actual proof of adultery committed.

A judgment of divorce in all cases "authorizes either party to marry again;" but, by a unique provision, "there shall not be granted to any person more than one divorce, except for living in adultery, to the party not in fault, and for the causes for which a divorce may be granted to both husband and wife." On joint application of the parties, every judgment for a divorce may be annulled by the court rendering it, they being restored to the condition of husband and wife; but thereafter a second divorce cannot be obtained for the same cause.

Separation from bed and board may originally have been obtainable in Kentucky under the common law:[1] but it does not seem to be noticed by any of the early statutes. For the first time, by the present code, it may be granted on any of the grounds which warrant a total divorce, or for "such other cause as the court in its discretion may judge sufficient."[2]

Previous to 1842 the function of the Maryland courts in divorce matters was restricted to the preparation of cases for

[1] HUMPHREY, *Compendium of the Common Law, in Force in Ky.*, 135, above cited.
[2] For the present law of divorce see *Ky. Stat.* (1903), 846-51; and compare the act of March 2, 1843: *Acts* (1842-43), 29, 30.

the legislature. By the act of that year full, though not exclusive, jurisdiction in both kinds of divorce is conferred upon the chancellor and upon the county courts sitting as equity tribunals. Divorce *a vinculo* is permitted (1) for impotence of either person at the time of the marriage; (2) "for any cause which by the laws of the state renders a marriage null and void *ab initio;*" (3) for adultery; (4) for abandonment with absence from the state for five years. The causes for which divorce *a mensa et thoro* is granted are (1) cruelty of treatment; (2) excessively vicious conduct; (3) abandonment and desertion; (4) in all cases where a total divorce is prayed for, if the causes proved be sufficient for such limited decree under the act.[1] In 1844 the term of absence as cause of complete divorce is reduced to three years.[2] Three years later a fifth cause appears. Complete dissolution of wedlock is now allowed when the female before marriage has been guilty of illicit carnal intercourse with another man without the husband's knowledge.[3] The five grounds of total divorce thus recognized are the only ones still sanctioned by the existing code; although under the fourth head it is provided, in more detail, that a decree shall be rendered only when the court is satisfied by competent testimony that there has been uninterrupted abandonment for at least three years, that such abandonment is deliberate and final, and that the separation of the parties is "beyond any reasonable expectation of reconciliation."[4] Likewise the same four causes of partial divorce, laid down in 1842, still appear in the statute-book, and in such cases the decree may be "forever" or "for a limited time," as shall seem just to the

---

[1] *Code of Md.* (1888), I, 143.

[2] Act of March 1, 1842: *Laws* (1841–42), chap. 262.

[3] *Laws* (1844), chap. 306.

[4] *Laws* (1846–47), chap. 340 (act of March 10, 1847); MACKALL, *Maryland Code* (1861), I, 74, 75. The causes of limited divorce and the other provisions of the act are the same as in that of 1842.

court. The equity tribunals now possess exclusive jurisdiction in all divorce matters.[1]

The North Carolina statute of 1814 allows the superior court to grant either kind of divorce (1) for bodily infirmity, or (2) for desertion and living in adultery. Separation from bed and board is likewise sanctioned when "any person shall either abandon his family or maliciously turn his wife out of doors, or by cruel or barbarous treatment endanger her life, or offer such indignities to her person as to render her condition intolerable or life burdensome."

Previous to 1827, as already noted, the judicial decree for partial divorce was final, while that for absolute dissolution of the marriage bond must be confirmed by the assembly. On the abolition of legislative divorce in that year a provision was inserted in the statute which seems to have had the effect of an "omnibus" clause. "All applications for other causes than those specified" in the act of 1814 for either kind of divorce "shall be subject to the rules and regulations provided in said act for the causes therein mentioned," thus giving the judiciary the full range which the assembly had hitherto possessed.[2] Later this clause took a simpler form, the courts being empowered to grant divorces on the grounds named in 1814 and for "any other just cause."[3] Six grounds subsequently added are retained in the present law. The superior courts are now authorized to decree absolute divorce (1) "if either party shall separate from the other and live in adultery;" (2) "if the wife shall commit adultery;" (3) "if either party at the time of the marriage was and still is naturally impotent;" (4) "if the wife at the time of the marriage be pregnant" by some other man and the husband be ignorant of the fact; (5) "if the

[1] *Laws* (1888), chap. 486, modifying an act of 1872, chap. 272, which is the basis of the present law in *Code of Md.* (1888), I, 142, 143.

[2] *North Carolina Acts* (1827-28), 20. *Cf.* the preceding section of the text.

[3] *Rev. Stat. of N. C.* (1837), 238-42.

husband shall be indicted for a felony and flee the state and does not return within one year from the time the indictment is found;" (6) "if after the marriage the wife shall wilfully and persistently refuse" marital duty for twelve months; (7) if either spouse shall abandon the other and live separate and apart for two years; and (8) in favor of the wife, being a citizen of the commonwealth at the time of the marriage, if the husband shall remove with her to another state, and while living with her there shall by cruel or barbarous treatment endanger her life or render her condition intolerable or burdensome, should she return to North Carolina and there reside separate and apart from the husband for the period of twelve months.[1] A divorce from bed and board may be granted (1) if either spouse shall abandon his or her family; (2) or shall maliciously turn the other out of doors; (3) or shall by cruel or barbarous treatment endanger the life of the other; (4) or shall offer such indignities to the person of the other as to render his or her condition intolerable and life burdensome; (5) or shall become a habitual drunkard.[2]

With the exception of one or two peculiar provisions, the law of Tennessee, enacted in 1799, is similar to that of the parent state North Carolina, adopted fifteen years later, although confirmation by the assembly is not required. A total divorce may be granted by the superior court (1) for bodily infirmity at the time of marriage; (2) bigamy; (3) when either consort "hath been guilty of acts and deeds inconsistent with the matrimonial vow, by adultery, or wil-

[1] The first three causes appear in *Public Laws* (1871-72), 339; the fourth is added by *ibid.* (1879), chap. 132, p. 240; the fifth by *ibid.* (1887), chap. 100, p. 190; the sixth by *ibid.* (1889), chap. 442, pp. 422, 423; the seventh by *ibid.* (1903), 846, amending an act in *ibid.* (1899), 337, which made the term of desertion one year; and the eighth by *ibid.* (1899), 124, 125. The seventh cause applies only to cases occurring before Jan. 1, 1903. The offender divorced for the seventh cause may not rewed in five years; and he must have been a resident of the state for the same period.

[2] The five causes of partial divorce are in *Public Laws* (1871-72), 339, 340. *Cf. Code of N. C.* (1883), I, 514.

ful and malicious desertion or absence without a reasonable cause, for the space of two years." In all cases the innocent person may remarry; but when the cause is long absence, he does so at his peril. For, as in Pennsylvania, should he contract a second marriage and thereafter the missing first spouse prove to be alive, a cruel Enoch Arden clause offers to the "party remaining single" at his return the option either of having his former wife restored or his marriage with her dissolved. By the same statute a divorce from bed and board may be allowed when (1) the husband "shall maliciously abandon, or (2) turn his wife out of doors; or (3) by cruel or barbarous treatment endanger her life; or (4) offer such indignities to her person as to render her condition intolerable, and thereby force her to withdraw." In such cases the court may grant the wife alimony, not exceeding one-third either of the husband's income or of his estate, as may seem just; and such alimony shall continue until a reconciliation takes place, or until the husband by his petition shall "offer to cohabit with her again, and use her as a good husband ought to do." Then the court may suspend the decree; or, if the wife refuse, may discharge and annul it at its discretion. Should the husband after reconciliation fail to keep his engagements, the decree of separation is to be renewed and the arrears of alimony paid.[1]

A new cause was added in 1819, the husband being allowed a total divorce when the woman at the time of the marriage was pregnant with a "child of color."[2] The act of 1835 recognizes practically the same causes for limited divorce as were prescribed in 1799, although they are differently expressed; and the separation may now be granted "forever" or for a "limited time," as shall seem just and reasonable to the court. By this statute likewise the

---

[1] Scott, *Laws of Tenn., Including those of North Carolina Now in Force* (1821), I, 645–48 (act of Oct. 26, 1799).

[2] *Laws* (1819), chap. 20; *Stat. Laws* (1831), I, 76.

grounds of total divorce are in substance identical with those of 1799, except that a new cause is added. Whenever a person has in good faith removed to the state and become a citizen thereof, and has resided there two years, he may secure a total divorce should his wife wilfully and without reasonable cause refuse to accompany him; provided he proves that he earnestly tried to get her to live with him after separation and that he did not come to the state for the sake of procuring the divorce.[1] So also in 1840 a female of good character who has resided in the state during the two years next preceding her petition, may be released from her husband for desertion during that period, or for any legal cause of divorce, although such cause may have accrued in another state.[2] Four years thereafter it is declared that a marriage may be dissolved when one party is "guilty of an attempt upon the life of the other," either by trying to poison, "or by any other means shewing malice."[3]

With some further important changes in 1858 and 1868, the law of Tennessee, as it now stands, was completed. Ten causes of absolute divorce are at present sanctioned: (1) natural and continued impotency of body; (2) knowingly entering into a second marriage in violation of a previous contract still existing; (3) adultery by either spouse; (4) "wilful or malicious desertion, or absence of either party without a reasonable cause for two whole years;" (5) conviction of any crime which by the laws of the state renders the offender infamous; or (6) which by the same law is declared to be a felony, with sentence to confinement in the penitentiary; (7) an attempt upon the life of husband or wife by poison or any other means showing malice; (8) refusal on the part of the wife to remove with her husband to the state,

---

[1] *Laws* (1835), cited in CARUTHERS AND NICHOLSON, *Compilation of the Stat. of Tenn.* (1836), 257–62.

[2] Act of Jan. 7, 1840: *Acts* (1839–40), chap. 54, p. 90.

[3] Act of Jan. 27, 1844: *Acts* (1843–44), chap. 176, pp. 200, 201.

wilfully thus absenting herself for two years; (9) pregnancy at the time of the marriage by another man without the husband's knowledge; (10) habitual drunkenness, when either spouse has contracted the habit after marriage.[1] A limited divorce, or a total divorce in the discretion of the court, may be granted to the wife (1) when the husband is guilty of cruel and inhuman treatment; or (2) of such conduct as renders it unsafe and improper for her to cohabit with him and be under his dominion and control; (3) when he has offered such indignities to her person as to render her condition intolerable and thereby forced her to withdraw; (4) when he has abandoned her; or (5) turned her out of doors and refused or neglected to provide for her support.[2] These causes, it will be noticed, are very nearly the same in substance as those named in 1799; and, as in 1819, separation may still be decreed for a limited time.

The history of divorce in Georgia has already been brought down to 1849, when resort to the assembly was finally forbidden. By the act of the next year specific causes for either kind of divorce are for the first time enumerated. After obtaining the concurrent verdict of two juries a total divorce may be decreed for (1) intermarriage within the Levitical degrees of consanguinity; (2) mental incapacity or (3) impotency at the time of the marriage; (4) force, menace, or duress in obtaining the marriage; (5) pregnancy of the woman at the time of the marriage by another man without the husband's knowledge; (6) adultery in either of the persons after marriage; (7) wilful and continued desertion for the term of three years; (8) conviction of either spouse of an offense involving moral turpitude, under which the offender is sentenced to imprisonment in

[1] Code of Tenn. (1884), 611; Shannon, Code (1896), 1042. The fifth and sixth causes appear in ibid. (1858), 483; the tenth, in Acts (1867–68), chap. 68.

[2] Code of Tenn. (1884), 611, 612. In Shannon, Code (1896), 1043, these are combined under three heads.

the penitentiary for two years or longer. Besides these, certain "discretionary" grounds are approved. In case of cruel treatment or habitual drunkenness on the part of either, the jury in its discretion may determine whether the divorce shall be absolute or limited. A general clause declares that all grounds other than those named in the act shall "only be cause for divorce from bed and board." In case of adultery, desertion, cruel treatment, or intoxication, a decree may not be granted when there is collusion or both parties are guilty of the same offense.[1] At the beginning of the century, the law of 1850, so far as the causes of full divorce and the discretionary grounds are concerned,[2] is still in force; while, in addition, the present statute simply anthorizes a separation from bed and board on "any ground which was held sufficient in the English courts prior to the fourth of May, 1784."[3] By the existing constitution the superior court still has jurisdiction; and for total dissolution of wedlock the concurrent verdicts of two juries at different terms of the court are essential to a decree.[4]

The grounds on which marriage may be annulled or dissolved were in 1803 first defined for the region of Alabama by the territorial assembly. The courts having equity jurisdiction were then authorized to grant total divorce for (1) intermarriage within the forbidden degrees; (2) natural impotency of body; (3) adultery; (4) "wilful, continued, and obstinate desertion, for the term of five years." Bigamous

---

[1] Act of Feb. 22, 1850: COBB, *Digest* (1851), 226; *Acts* (1849-50), 151, 152.

[2] Except that "fraud" is added to the fourth cause.

[3] *Code of Ga.* (1896), II, 224 ff. Instead of "Levitical," "prohibited" degrees is now used.

[4] Const. of 1877, Art. VI, secs. 4, 15, 16: *N. Y. Convention Manual*, Part II, Vol. I, 427, 431. *Cf.* Const. of 1865, Art. IV, sec. 2; 1868, Art. V, secs. 2, 3: POORE, *Charters*, I, 409, 420, 422.

In case of partial divorce one jury is sufficient: Const. of 1877, Art. VI, sec. 15; and such seems to have been the earlier practice: 16 *Ga.*, 81; *Code of Ga.* (1882), 394, note. A juror may be challenged for "conscientious scruples" regarding divorce: *Code* (1882), 397. This last-named provision appears in the act of Dec. 22, 1840: COBB, *Digest* (1851), 225, 226.

marriages were, of course, void from the beginning. Separation from bed and board was allowed on the sole ground of extreme cruelty in either of the parties; but in neither kind of divorce was a decree permitted where there was proof of collusion.[1] In 1820, the year after the admission of the state to the Union, the circuit courts gained jurisdiction ar,d were given power to render decrees of total divorce, subject to legislative appeal, on the following grounds: I. In favor of the husband: when the wife (1) is "taken in adultery;" (2) has voluntarily left his bed and board for the space of two years with the intention of abandonment; (3) has deserted him and lived in adultery with another man. II. In favor of the wife: when the husband (1) has left her during the space of two years with the intention of desertion; (2) has abandoned her to live in adultery with another woman; (3) when his treatment of her is "so cruel, barbarous, and inhuman as actually to endanger her life."[2] The provisions of this act were considerably modified in 1824;[3] but in 1832 they were restored, except that the period of abandonment for either partner was then fixed at three years.[4] A new cause was sanctioned in 1843, a total divorce being then allowed for pregnancy of the wife by another man at the time of the marriage, if without the husband's knowledge or consent;[5] and habitual drunkenness on the part of either was added to the list in 1870.[6]

The basis of the existing law of Alabama was laid in the act of 1852, although important additions to the causes were subsequently made. The court of chancery now has power to grant a divorce from the bond of wedlock according to the

[1] Act of March 10, 1803, passed by the Mississippi territorial legislature: *Digest of the Laws of Ala.* (1823), 252.

[2] Act of Dec. 21, 1820: *Digest* (1823), 256.

[3] Act of Dec. 23, 1824: *Acts* (1824), 61, 62.   [4] AIKIN, *Digest* (1833), 130–32.

[5] CLAY, *Digest of Laws of Alabama* (1843), 172; also in *Acts* (1843), 27.

[6] *Acts* (1869–70), 207, 208 (March 1).

following complex scheme: I. In favor of either spouse: (1) when at the time of the contract the other is "physically and incurably incapacitated from entering into the marriage state;" (2) for adultery; (3) for voluntary abandonment for two years; (4) for imprisonment in any state penitentiary for two years, the sentence being for seven years or longer; (5) for a crime against nature; (6) for "becoming addicted after marriage to habitual drunkenness."[1] II. In favor of the husband: for pregnancy of the wife, as provided in 1843. III. In favor of the wife: "when the husband has committed actual violence on her person, attended with danger to life or health, or when from his conduct there is reasonable apprehension of such violence." The chancellor is further authorized to decree a separation from bed and board for cruelty[2] in either of the consorts, or for any cause which will justify a decree from the bonds of matrimony, if the person applying therefor desires only a partial divorce.[3]

The law of March 10, 1803, beginning the history of divorce legislation for Alabama, applies also to Mississippi during the territorial stage; and, five years after the state was erected, its provisions, so far as they relate to the causes and kinds of divorce, were re-enacted in 1822.[4] In 1840 the time of desertion to warrant a total divorce was shortened from five to three years.[5] Ten years thereafter it was provided that any person already having a separation from bed and board may, by application to the chancery court of the

---

[1] *Code of Ala.* (1887), 253; *ibid.* (1897), 491–95. The first four of these causes appear in *Code* (1852), 378; the fifth and sixth in the act of 1870.

[2] For interpretation of " cruelty " see 23 *Alabama*, 785; 27 *Alabama*, 222; 28 *Alabama*, 315; 30 *Alabama*, 714; 44 *Alabama*, 670, 698.

[3] *Code of Ala.* (1887), 524–26; *ibid.* (1897), 492. The causes of full divorce mentioned under II and III appear in *Code* (1852), 378.

[4] *Stat. of Miss. Ter.* (1816), 252–54; and act of June 15, 1822, in *Code of Miss.* (1848), 495, 496.

[5] Act of Feb. 13: *Laws* (1840), 125.

district or the circuit court of the county where he resides, and producing a transcript of the decree, be divorced from the bond of matrimony. For the future the same privilege is extended to each of the parties to a partial divorce when they "have lived separate and apart from each other for the term of four years."[1] By a statute of 1858 this term is reduced to three years; and only those who have thus lived apart after partial separation are now allowed to petition for the entire dissolution of the marriage bond.[2] But in 1860, apparently to meet special cases, a law provides simply for a divorce *a vinculo* where the persons, prior to the act, have lived apart in the state four years without collusion.[3] A peculiar cause, a product of the Civil War, appears in 1862. The wife is then allowed a complete divorce when her husband is in the army or navy of the United States or resides in one of the United States in preference to one of the states of the Confederacy.[4] By a statute of 1863 a second marriage is valid when the first spouse has been five years absent; and such spouse is to be presumed dead in any question of alimony arising under the second marriage.[5] In 1867 any citizen marrying out of the state, whose spouse commits adultery before his return to the state, may after such return apply for a total divorce, provided he has not cohabited after discovery of the offense.[6] The causes of separation from bed and board, which had remained unaltered since 1803, were extended in 1857. A partial divorce is then allowed for habitual drunkenness, as well as for extreme cruelty in either person; while the wife is granted the same relief whenever the husband, being of sufficient ability, wantonly and cruelly fails to provide for her support; but a decree for partial separation shall in no case bar the right to full divorce from the

---

[1] Act of Feb. 14: *Laws* (1850), 122.   [2] Act of Nov. 29: *Laws* (1858), 166.
[3] Act of Feb. 9: *Laws* (1860), 202.   [4] Act of Jan. 29, 1862: *Laws* (1861-62), 246.
[5] Act of Dec. 1, 1863: *Laws* (1862-63), 125, 126.
[6] Act of Feb. 21, 1867: *Laws* (1866-67), 387.

bond of wedlock.[1]   A very important relaxation in the law takes place in 1871.   The two causes of partial divorce just mentioned—habitual drunkenness and cruel treatment— become grounds for total divorce; and the term of desertion is shortened from three to two years.[2]

By the present code of Mississippi, therefore, limited divorce is not authorized.   But courts having chancery jurisdiction may decree entire release from the marriage bond to the injured person (1) for natural impotency; (2) adultery, except by collusion or where there is cohabitation after knowledge of the offense; (3) sentence to the penitentiary when there is no pardon before imprisonment begins; (4) wilful, continued, and obstinate desertion for two years; (5) habitual drunkenness; (6) "habitual and excessive use of opium, morphine, or other like drug;" (7) habitual cruel and inhuman treatment;[3] (8) insanity or idiocy at the time of the marriage, if the party complaining did not then know of the infirmity; (9) previous marriage with some other person; (10) pregnancy of the wife by another man at the time of the marriage, the husband being ignorant of the fact; (11) intermarriage within the degrees of kindred prohibited by law.[4]

The first statute defining the grounds of divorce for Missouri was approved in 1807 by the legislature of Louisiana Territory.   Either a full or a partial divorce was then authorized when either person (1) is naturally impotent; (2) has entered into the marriage in violation of a "previous vow;" (3) has committed adultery; or (4) has been guilty of wilful and malicious desertion, without a reasonable cause, for four years.   The general court may likewise grant the

---

[1] *Rev. Code* (1858), 334.

[2] By the *Rev. Code* (1871): see WRIGHT, *Report*, 154; and WILLCOX, *The Divorce Problem*, 52.

[3] For interpretation of "cruel treatment" see Johns *v.* Johns, 57 *Miss.*, 530.

[4] *Ann. Code of Miss.* (1892), 419, 420.

wife a separation from bed and board when the husband shall either abandon his family or turn her "out of doors, or by cruel and barbarous treatment endanger her life, or offer such indignities to her person as to render her condition intolerable and thereby force her to withdraw from his house or family."[1] This law remained in force until 1833, when "extreme cruelty" and conviction of an "infamous crime" were added as causes warranting either the husband or wife to petition for absolute divorce.[2] The number is raised to seven by the revision of 1835, which is silent as to partial divorce; for "indignities" to the person of either such as already described are now made a legal ground for entire dissolution of marriage.[3] Vagrancy[4] of the husband and habitual drunkenness of either for the space of two years came next in 1845; and four years thereafter the introduction of two more causes completed the full quota of eleven grounds on which total divorce is still allowed by Missouri law. The act of 1849 authorizes a divorce to the man when the woman at the time of the marriage, or when it was solemnized, was pregnant by another person without the intended husband's knowledge; and to the wife, when the man prior to the marriage or its solemnization had been convicted of a felony or infamous crime without the woman's knowing it when the marriage took place. The benefits of this cause may now accrue to both persons; otherwise no

---

[1] Act of May 13, 1807: *Laws of a Pub. and Gen. Nature* (1842), 1, 90-92.

[2] *Ibid.*, II, 360.

[3] *Rev. Stat.* (1835), 225 (Jan. 24). The "indignities" need not be offered to the person: 5 *Missouri*, 278; 19 *Missouri*, 352; 16 *M. A.*, 422; 17 *M. A.*, 390; but one or two such acts are insufficient: 34 *Missouri*, 211.

[4] According to the code, a "vagrant" is "every person who may be found loitering around houses of ill-fame, gambling houses, or places where liquors are sold or drunk, without any visible means of support, or shall attend or operate any gambling device or apparatus;" and "every able-bodied married man who shall neglect or refuse to provide for the support of his family, and every person found tramping or wandering around from place to place without any visible means of support." Besides being liable to suit for divorce, such a husband may be sentenced to not less than twenty days in the county jail, or to pay a fine of 20 dollars, or both: *Rev. Stat.* (1889), I, 917; *ibid.* (1899), I, 621. On vagrancy as a cause see 26 *M. A.*, 647.

essential change in the statute has been made for half a century.[1]

In Florida, since 1828, divorce may be sought only by bill in chancery; and, since 1835, the equity courts have had exclusive jurisdiction, granting only complete dissolution of the marriage bond,[2] although in that state separate maintenance is equivalent to separation from bed and board. The causes now sanctioned are: (1) intermarriage within the forbidden degrees; (2) natural impotence of the defendant; (3) adultery in either party; (4) excessive cruelty; (5) habitual indulgence in violent and ungovernable temper;[3] (6) habitual intemperance; (7) wilful, obstinate, and continued desertion for one year; (8) a divorce obtained by the defendant in any other state or country; (9) having a husband or wife living at the time of the marriage; (10) incurable insanity.

The Louisiana code of 1808 provides for the annulment of marriage on legal grounds; and allows separation from bed and board (1) for adultery of the wife; or (2) for that of the husband "when he has kept his concubine in their common dwelling;" (3) when either has been guilty of excesses, cruel treatment, or outrages toward the other, if the ill-treatment is of such a nature as to render their living together insupportable; (4) on account of a public defamation by one of the married persons toward the other; (5) for abandonment; or (6) an attempt upon the life of the other by either spouse.[4]

---

[1] Act of March 12: *Laws* (1849), 49, 50; *Rev. Stat.* (1889), I, 1029–32; *ibid.* (1899), I, 741. The circuit courts have jurisdiction; and process is as in civil suits, except that the answer of the defendant need not be under oath.

[2] Acts of Oct. 31, 1828, and Feb. 4, 1835, in *Rev. Stat. of Fla.* (1892), 504; or THOMPSON, *Manual or Digest* (1847), 47, 222–24. Incurable insanity is made a legal ground of divorce by *Acts* (1901), 118–21.

[3] On the allegations necessary see Johnson *v.* Johnson, 23 *Florida*, 413; Burns *v.* Burns, 13 *Florida*, 369; and on what does not constitute a cause, Crawford *v.* Crawford, 17 *Florida*, 180.

[4] *Digest of Civil Laws Now in Force* (1808), 26, 28, 30; also *Code Civil* (1825), 80, 87–91; LISLET, *Gen. Digest*, II, 3 ff.; *Civil Code of La.* (1853), 19.

In 1827 the "district courts throughout the state and the parish court of New Orleans" were given "exclusive original jurisdiction in cases of divorce," with appeal to the supreme court. They were authorized to grant total divorce (1) for adultery of the wife; or (2) for that of the husband "when he has kept his concubine in the common dwelling, or openly and publicly in any other;" (3) for excesses, cruel treatment, or outrages, as conditioned for separation in 1808; (4) condemnation of either married person to an "ignominious punishment;" (5) abandonment for five years when the offender has "been summoned to return to the common dwelling," as is provided for in cases of separation from bed and board. It is, however, especially declared that, except when the cause is adultery or ignominious punishment, no full divorce shall be granted "unless a judgment of separation from bed and board shall have been previously rendered," and unless two years shall have thereafter expired without reconciliation. But in the two cases excepted above a "judgment of divorce may be granted in the same decree which pronounced the separation from bed and board."[1] The fifth cause approved in 1827 was supplemented by a new ground in 1832. Whenever either spouse is charged with an infamous crime and is a fugitive from justice beyond the state, a total divorce may be claimed by the other, without need of a previous decree of separation, on producing evidence of the actual guilt and flight of the accused.[2] "Habitual intemperance" on the part of either husband or wife was added to the list in 1855;[3] and in 1857 the time which must elapse between the decrees for partial and full divorce was reduced to one year.[4] An "omnibus"

---

[1] Act of March 19: *Acts* (1827), 130–35; also in *Civil Code* (1853), 19, 20. Such is still the law, except as to the term between the decrees.

[2] Act of April 2: *Acts* (1832), 152; also in *Civil Code* (1853), 20, 21.

[3] *Acts* (1855, March 14), 376.

[4] Act of March 16: *Acts* (1857), 137; Voorhies, *Rev. Stat. Laws* (1876), 313.

clause comes next in 1870, complete dissolution of wedlock being then permitted "for any such misconduct repugnant to the marriage covenant as permanently destroys the happiness of the petitioner;" but it was repealed in 1877.[1]

For the sake of convenience, the present law of Louisiana covering the grounds of divorce—whose evolution was thus completed in 1870—may now be summarized. Absolute divorce, without need of a previous decree of separation, is permitted where the husband or wife may have (1) been sentenced to an infamous punishment; or (2) been guilty of adultery.[2] A limited divorce, which may be followed in each case by a total divorce after one year, is authorized (1) for adultery on the part of either spouse; (2) when the other party has been condemned to an infamous punishment; (3) on account of the habitual intemperance of one of the married persons; (4) excesses, cruel treatment, or outrages of one of them toward the other; (5) for public defamation; (6) for abandonment on the part of one of the married persons; (7) for an attempt of one of them against the life of the other; (8) when the husband or wife has been charged with an infamous offense and shall have fled from justice, on producing proof of the actual guilt or flight.[3] An important modification was made in 1898. The person in whose favor a limited divorce has been rendered may apply and get a full divorce

---

[1] Compare the act of March 9: *Acts* (1870), 108; with *Acts* (1877), 192. VOORHIES, *op. cit.* (1884), 204–6, gives the law regarding the causes of divorce just as *ibid.* (1876), 312–14; and *ibid.* (1870), 18 ff.

[2] As in 1827, in these cases, a divorce may be "granted in the same decree which pronounces the separation from bed and board."

[3] *Rev. Civil Code* (1888), 68 ff.; *ibid.* (1897), 305, 306; *ibid.* (1870), 18 ff. *Cf.* WRIGHT, *Report*, 97, 98. The habitual intemperance (Cause 3) and cruel treatment (Cause 4) must still be of "such a nature as to render their living together insupportable."

"The abandonment (Cause 6) with which the husband or wife is charged must be made to appear by the three reiterated summonses made to him or her from month to month, directing him or her to return to the place of the matrimonial domicile and followed by a judgment which has sentenced him or her to comply with such request, together with a notification of the said judgment, given to him or her from month to month for three times successively."— *Rev. Civil Code* (1888), 70.

in one year, while the adverse party must wait two years before he can secure a similar decree, in the meantime the wife's right to alimony remaining unimpaired.[1]

The divorce legislation of the "Republic of Texas" has remained in force with little modification to the present hour. The district courts still have jurisdiction. By the act of January 6, 1841, a marriage may be declared null and void for impotency; and absolute divorce may be granted as follows: I. In favor of the husband: (1) when the wife is guilty of adultery; or (2) has left his bed and board for three years with the intention of abandonment. II. In favor of the wife: (1) when the husband has left her for three years with like intention; or (2) has abandoned her and lived in adultery with another woman. III. In favor of either spouse for excesses, cruel treatment, or outrages toward the other, if the ill-treatment is of such a nature as to render their living together insupportable.[2] These three groups appear unaltered in the present code; and there is added the following: IV. In favor of either husband or wife, "when the other shall have been convicted, after marriage, of a felony and imprisoned in the state prison; *provided*, that no suit for divorce shall be sustained" because of such conviction "until twelve months after final judgment," nor "then if the governor shall have pardoned the convict;" and provided also that the conviction has not been obtained on the testimony of either spouse.[3]

The grounds of divorce recognized in the statutes of Arkansas have been in force since 1838. The circuit courts may now grant total or limited divorce for the following causes: (1) when either spouse was at the time of the mar-

---

[1] Act of July 4, 1898: *Acts of the Assembly*, 34.

[2] *Laws of the Rep. of Texas*, V, 19–22; also in DALLAM, *Digest* (1845), 80, 81. *Cf.* the earlier act of 1837, in DALLAM, *op. cit.*, 79.

[3] *Rev. Civil Stat.* (1888), I, 885–88; *Ann. Civil Stat.* (1897), I, 1095, 1096. No. IV was added by act of May 27, 1876: *Laws*, 16.

riage and still is impotent of body; (2) when either deserts the other and remains absent one year without reasonable cause; (3) when a former spouse was living at the time of the marriage; (4) when either is convicted of felony or other infamous crime; or (5) shall be addicted to habitual drunkenness for the space of one year; or (6) shall be guilty of such cruel and barbarous treatment as to endanger the life of the other; or (7) shall offer such indignities to the person of the other as shall render his or her condition intolerable; (8) when subsequent to the marriage either person has committed adultery.[1]

By act of Congress,[2] certain general laws of Arkansas, including those of divorce, are extended to the Indian Territory; so the causes just enumerated are there in force.[3] Limited divorce does not exist in Oklahoma; but in that territory the district court may grant full dissolution of wedlock (1) when either person had a spouse living at the time of the marriage; (2) for abandonment during one year; (3) for adultery; (4) for impotency; (5) "when the wife at the time of the marriage was pregnant by another than her husband;" (6) for extreme cruelty; (7) for fraudulent contract; (8) for habitual drunkenness; (9) for gross neglect of duty; (10) for conviction and imprisonment in the penitentiary for a felony after marriage.[4]

"Arizona, from 1871–77, in addition to six ample reasons for divorce, had an 'omnibus clause' in operation which is a marvelous piece of legislation." "Whereas," we are told, "in the developments of future events, cases may be presented before the courts falling substantially within the limits of the law, as hereinbefore stated, yet not within

1 *Digest of Ark.* (1894), 680–83; *Rev. Stat.* (1838), 333. Incurable insanity appears as a ground in *Civil Code*, sec. 464, as amended in 1873; but it was dropped by *Acts* (1895), 76.

2 Act of May 2, 1890: *U. S. Stat. at Large*, XXVI, chap. 182, p. 81.

3 *Ann. Stat. of Ind. Ter.* (1899), 324.   4 WILSON, *Stat. of Okla.* (1903), II, 1119.

its terms, it is enacted, that whenever the judge who hears a cause for divorce deems the case to be within the reason of the law, within the general mischief the law is intended to remedy, or within what it may be presumed would have been provided against, by the legislature establishing the foregoing causes of divorce had it foreseen the specific case and found language to meet it without including cases not within the same reason, he shall grant the divorce." Well was this called, continues Richberg, "the 'seventh wonder' of Arizona's divorce code."[1]

A later statute, somewhat more cautiously, allows the district court to decree a total divorce (1) when the husband or wife is guilty of excesses, cruel treatment, or outrage toward the other, whether by the use of personal violence or any other means; (2) in favor of the husband when his wife shall have been taken in adultery; or (3) when she has voluntarily left his bed and board for the space of six months with the intention of abandonment; (4) in favor of the wife when the husband has left her for the same time with a like motive; (5) for his habitual intemperance; (6) for his wilful neglect to provide the necessaries or comforts of life during the same period, having sufficient ability, or failing to do so by reason of his idleness, profligacy, or dissipation; or (7) when he shall be taken in adultery; (8) in favor of either spouse when the other has been convicted after marriage of a felony and confined in any prison. Suit on the last-named ground cannot be sustained until six

[1] RICHBERG, "Incongruity of the Divorce Laws in the United States," *Publications of Mich. Pol. Sc. Association*, No. 4, p. 58.

For this act of Feb. 16, 1871, see *Comp. Laws of the Ter. of Ariz., 1864–71* (1871), 303, 304. The other six causes referred to in the text are (1) impotency; (2) marriage of a female under fourteen without parental consent and not ratified by her after reaching that age; (3) adultery in either without collusion or subsequent voluntary cohabiting; (4) extreme cruelty, or habitual intemperance, wilful desertion for one year, or neglect to provide for the wife; (5) force or fraud; (6) conviction of either of felony after marriage. For the earlier law see the *Howell Code*, 232 ff.; and the amendments of 1865, in *Comp. Laws* (1871), 297–303.

months after final judgment, nor when the husband or wife was convicted on the testimony of the other.[1] This law is superseded by the act of 1903. Absolute divorce may now be granted on complaint of the aggrieved for (1) adultery; (2) physical incapacity; (3) conviction and imprisonment for felony, provided that suit may not be sustained until one year after judgment and that conviction has not been had on the testimony of either spouse; (4) wilful desertion for one year, or for habitual intemperance; (5) excesses, cruel treatment, or outrages, whether by the use of personal violence or any other means; (6) to the wife for the husband's neglect for one year to provide her with common necessaries of life, having the ability, or his failure to do so because of idleness, profligacy, or dissipation; (7) to either for the other's conviction of felony before marriage without the innocent person's knowledge; (8) to the husband when without his knowledge the wife was pregnant by another man at the time of the marriage.[2]

In New Mexico the district courts may grant absolute divorce for (1) abandonment; (2) adultery; (3) impotency; (4) when without the husband's knowledge the wife at the time of the marriage was pregnant by another man; (5) cruel and inhuman treatment; (6) to the wife for the husband's neglect to support; (7) habitual drunkenness; (8) conviction and imprisonment for felony subsequent to the marriage.[3] Separation *a mensa et thoro* does not exist; but in the laws of 1884 there is a curious provision, which seems designed, in a truly patriarchal spirit, to soothe domestic ills and check matrimonial transgressions through intervention of

[1] *Rev. Stat. of Ariz.* (1887), 373, 374; *cf.* WRIGHT, *Report*, 90. By the act of 1871 the period of desertion is fixed at one year; and it is two years by the *Howell Code: Compiled Laws* (1871), 298, 304.

[2] *Rev. Stat. of Ariz.* (1901), 812-15; amended by *Acts* (1903), 52.

[3] *Acts of N. M.* (1901), 116 ff. For the earlier laws see *Acts of the Ass. of N. M.* (1886-87), 68; *Comp. Laws* (1897), 407. In case of permanent separation, without a dissolution of marriage, either spouse may institute a suit for division of property or disposal of the children; or the wife may bring suit for alimony alone: *ibid.*, 116.

the local magistrate.   One is left in little doubt as to the
right ideal of family life, being assured that "the duties and
relations that should exist between married persons are the
following, to wit: The husband is the head of the family;
he, nevertheless, owes fidelity, favor, support, and protection
to the wife; he should make her a participant in all the con-
veniences he enjoys; he should show her the utmost and
every attention in cases of sickness, misfortune or accident,
and provide for her the necessaries of life according to his
condition and ability; and the wife owes fidelity and
obedience to the husband; she is obliged to live with him
and accompany him to such place as he may deem proper
and advantageous to make his residence."   So when any
difficulty arises on account of failure in any of these things,
the injured person may go before the justice of the peace in
his "precinct and make complaint demanding judicial action."
Then the magistrate "shall forthwith dispatch his compulsory
writ directing the party defendant immediately to appear to
such complaint; both parties being present, it shall be the
duty of the justice to endeavor to effect a reconciliation, the
first of which endeavors he shall enter on record upon his
docket, affording the parties a reasonable opportunity; but
if after having so done, the person making the complaint
does not agree, the justice shall then proceed to try the
matter in a summary manner, provided always, that the
reasons for disagreement are simple, such as non-fulfillment"
of the duties above set forth.   In "case of conviction he
shall cause the delinquent to act as required by the laws of
the conjugal relation;" and when there is resistance he
"may order that such person be confined in the county jail,
there to remain until he comply with those duties by which
both the husband and wife were mutually bound."   Furthermore, it is especially provided, that when any persons are
thus put in jail "for an infraction of duty" and fail to

"furnish their own provision," the sheriff may "dispose of their services for their maintenance." Should, however, the trouble "arise from adultery, or cruelty, or ill temper, rendering the life of the consort insecure, the justice . . . . shall, after due investigation send the case up to the district court which shall take cognizance of and try the same;" and "whenever a temporary separation occurs between husband and wife in order to bring suit before the district court, the justice of the peace will provide how the family shall be cared for, and will immediately report to the probate judge of the county, so that the latter may provide for the care of the minors, their support and education, as also for the wife, in case she be the injured party, during the controversy or until otherwise provided for by the district court."[1]   It is not, perhaps, surprising that this whole subject is omitted from the compilation of 1897.

By the code of Porto Rico the district court has jurisdiction.   Partial divorce is not recognized; but marriage may be dissolved, on the petition of the aggrieved, for (1) adultery; (2) conviction of felony, which may involve the loss of civil rights; (3) "habitual drunkenness or the continued and excessive use of opium, morphine, or any other narcotic;" (4) cruel treatment or gross injury; (5) abandonment for one year; (6) "absolute, perpetual, and incurable impotence" occurring after marriage; (7) the "attempt of the husband or wife to corrupt their sons or to prostitute their daughters," or connivance of either in the same; (8) the proposal of the husband to prostitute the wife.[2]

The experience of South Carolina is peculiar.   After abstaining from any legislation on the subject for two hundred years, that state indulged in a conservative divorce statute in 1872.   Hitherto the courts were competent only

---

[1] *Compiled Laws of N. M.* (1885), 514, 516.

[2] *Rev. Stat. and Codes of Porto Rico* (1902), 813-17.

to grant separation from bed and board under the common
law. By the act in question they were empowered to pronounce decrees of absolute divorce in favor of either spouse
(1) for adultery and (2) for abandonment[1] during the space
of two years.[2] But this law was of short duration, being
repealed in 1878.[3] South Carolina legal sentiment on the
divorce problem is fairly revealed in connection with two
important decisions during the century. Commenting on
the case of Vaigneur *et al. v.* Kirk, decided in 1808, Editor
Desaussure contrasts the laxity of the marriage laws with
the stringency of the rule relating to divorce. "The subject of marriage, and consequently the legitimacy of children, is on the same loose footing in this state that it was
in England before" 1753[4] and as "it now is in Scotland.
We have no statute regulating marriages, or providing any
form for the celebration of them, or for recording them.
And they are usually celebrated in any form the parties
please, before a ,clergyman or magistrate." This "remarkable facility of contracting matrimony . . . . is strongly
contrasted with the impracticability of dissolving the contract. No divorce has ever taken place within the state.
The legislature has uniformly refused to grant divorces, on
the ground that it was improper for the legislative body to
exercise judicial powers. And it has as steadily refused to
enact any law to authorize the courts of justice to grant
divorces *a vinculo matrimonii*, on the broad principle that it
was a wise policy to shut the door to domestic discord, and
to gross immorality in the community."[5]

[1] " Provided, that, when the suit is instituted by the party deserting, it appears
that the desertion was caused by the extreme cruelty of the other party, or that the
desertion of the wife was caused by the gross or wanton and cruel neglect of the husband to provide suitable maintenance for her, he being of sufficient ability to do
so" (p. 30).

[2] Act of Jan. 31: *Acts and Joint Res.* (1872), 30 ff.

[3] Repealed by act of Dec. 20: *Acts and Joint Res.* (1878), 719.

[4] Previous to 26 Geo. II., chap. 33.

[5] H. W. DESAUSSURE, in 2 *S. C. Equity Reports*, 644 (revised edition).

With this view harmonizes the opinion of Justice Pope in McCreery *v.* Davis rendered in 1894. While separation from bed and board—the only form of divorce obtainable in the state—"is a judicial barrier to any attempt to exercise the rights or enforce the duties of the parties affected by the judgment, yet the courts are only too willing to have the parties restored to their original *status quo*, upon good cause shown. While the remedy is a hard one, and to a certain extent interferes with the operation of the laws of nature, still woman must be protected! After all, an unbending adhesion to the laws of right living has a healthy effect upon the lives of others. If self-denial is thus necessitated, it should not be forgotten that many natures are perfected through its beneficent influence. True philosophy would extract good from every condition. . . . . By art. IV, sec. 15, of our constitution, the courts of common pleas have exclusive jurisdiction in all cases of divorce, and by art. XIV, sec. 5, divorces from the bonds of matrimony shall not be allowed but by the judgment of a court as shall be prescribed by law. Thus the general assembly is denied the power to grant divorces directly, but is permitted to clothe the courts of common pleas with that power. This last they have refused to do by repealing the act of 1872;" and thus "we have the common law restored to us on this subject."[1]

Finally it may be noted that the supreme court of the District of Columbia has exclusive jurisdiction in all applications for either full or partial separation. Until recently a divorce from the bond of wedlock might be granted (1) when either spouse had a husband or wife living at the time of the contract, "unless the former marriage had been lawfully dissolved and no restraint imposed" on further marriage; (2) when the marriage was contracted during the

[1] Opinion of Justice Pope in McCreery *v.* Davis, 44 *S. C. Reports*, 195–227 (1894).

lunacy of either party; (3) when either was matrimonially
incapacitated at the time of the marriage; or (4) has since
committed adultery; (5) for habitual drunkenness for a
period of three years; (6) for cruel treatment endangering
the life or health of the complainant; or (7) for wilful
desertion and abandonment for two years.   A divorce from
bed and board was allowed (1) for cruel treatment endangering life or health; or (2) "reasonable apprehension, to the
satisfaction of the court, of bodily harm."[1]   A new and
drastic law was passed in 1901.   Hereafter absolute divorce
will be granted only for adultery, the guilty person not being
allowed to remarry.   Legal separation from bed and board
may be obtained for (1) drunkenness, (2) cruelty, or (3)
desertion.   Only residents may bring suit for divorce; and
unless the applicant has for three years been a *bona fide*
resident, no decree will be granted for a cause occurring
outside the District before such residence began.[2]

   c) *Remarriage, residence, notice, and miscellaneous
provisions.*— Throughout the century, and especially during
the first half, many of the southern states have been conservative, even severe, regarding the liberty of the person
offending to remarry after full separation; but in very
few cases is any restraint put upon the further marriage of
the person in whose favor the decree is granted.   The
divorce acts passed by the assembly of Virginia sometimes
expressly forbid the guilty person to contract further wedlock during the lifetime of the former spouse.[3]   The law of
1848, when the marriage bond is dissolved on account of
infidelity, authorizes the court in its discretion to allow both
parties to remarry or only the injured person, as may seem
just.[4]   Such substantially is the present law.   "In granting

---

[1] *Comp. Stat. of D. C.* (1894), 275, 276.   [2] Moore, *Code of D. C.* (1902), 199, 200.
[3] See the cases already cited, *Acts* (1826–27), 126.
[4] Act of March 18, 1848: *Acts of the Assembly* (1847–48), 165, 166.

a divorce for adultery, the court may decree that the guilty
party shall not marry again; in which case the bond of matrimony shall be deemed not to be dissolved as to any future
marriage of such party, or in any prosecution on account
thereof.   But for good cause shown, so much of any decree
as prohibits the guilty party from marrying again, may be
revoked and annulled at any time after such decree, by the
same court by which it was pronounced."[1]   No restraint
appears to be put upon the immediate remarriage of persons
separated for other causes.

The early statutes and the decrees for full divorce in
individual cases passed by the assembly of Maryland, by
their silence on the subject, appear to contemplate the further marriage of the persons at pleasure.   The law of 1872,
however, is somewhat conservative.   "In all cases where a
divorce *a vinculo matrimonii* is decreed for adultery or abandonment, the court may, in its discretion," forbid the guilty
party to "contract marriage with any other person during
the lifetime" of the injured spouse, the bond of marriage not
being dissolved, but remaining in full force with respect to
such offender.[2]   This restriction is now omitted from the
code.[3]   In the District of Columbia the guilty person may
not remarry except with the former spouse.[4]

Formerly the law of North Carolina was stringent in this
regard.   The act of 1814 permits the "complainant or innocent person" to "marry again as if he or she had never
been married;" leaving us to infer, perhaps, that the
defendant was not allowed such liberty.[5]   In 1828 it is

1 *Code of Va.* (1887), 562.

2 Act of April 1: *Laws* (1872), chap. 272, p. 445.

3 The *Code of Md.* (1888) seems to be entirely silent as to remarriage.

4 *Comp. Stat. of D. C.* (1894), 275 ff., allowing entire freedom; superseded by the
act of 1901: MOORE, *Code* (1902), 199, 200.

5 *Laws* (1814), chap. 5; and HAYWOOD, *Manual* (1819), 176.   The same provision
appears in *Laws of the State of N. C.* (1821), II, 1294.

squarely enacted that "no defendant or party offending, who shall be divorced from the bonds of matrimony . . . . shall ever be permitted to marry again."[1]   This rule stands in sharp contrast with the policy of the later law.   First the prohibition was restricted to the lifetime of the aggrieved.[2] Next, in 1869, the term was reduced to two years.[3]   From 1871 to 1895 no check whatever was put upon the further marriage of either spouse, whether guilty or innocent;[4] but now in case of wilful desertion the guilty defendant may not rewed in five years, or during the lifetime of the plaintiff, if divorced for the eighth cause above considered.

The Georgia statute approved in 1806 allows remarriage when a contract is nullified under the principles of ecclesiastical law; but denies the privilege to the person whose "improper or criminal conduct" is the cause of an absolute divorce, so long as the innocent consort lives.[5]   This rule long remained in force;[6] but under the existing code a rather peculiar procedure is adopted.   The jury according to whose final verdict a decree of absolute divorce is granted determines the rights and disabilities of the parties, including the question of remarriage, subject to the revision of the court; but provision is made for subsequent removal of the disabilities thus imposed.   On proper application, notice of which must be published in a newspaper for sixty days, with twenty days' personal notification to the other divorced person if still living and residing in the county, the question of granting relief is submitted to a new jury, "who shall hear all the

---

[1] *Acts* (1827–28), 20.   [2] *Rev. Code* (1855), chap. 39, sec. 17, p. 254.

[3] Act of April 7, 1869: *Pub. Laws*, 323.

[4] All restriction is removed by *Laws* (1870–71), chap. 193, sec. 46, p. 343; also in *Code of N. C.* (1883), I, 518.

[5] *Compilation of Laws of Ga.* (1812), 313.

[6] For instance, see Hotchkiss, *Codification* (1845), 331; Cobb, *Analysis* (1846), 294 ff.; Cobb, *Digest* (1851), 226 ff.

facts, and if, in their judgment, the interest of the applicant
or of society demands the removal of such disabilities," shall
so find; and the person relieved shall then be allowed to
form a second marriage as if no former contract had ever
existed.　At the trial the divorced person or any citizen of
the county may resist the application; but should no person
appear for this purpose, then "the solicitor-general shall
represent the state, with full power to resist the same, as in
ordinary divorce cases."[1]

By the Tennessee statute of 1799 no restraint is put upon
immediate remarriage in any case of divorce, except where
the cause is infidelity, when the guilty defendant may not
marry the person with whom the crime was committed during the lifetime of the former spouse.[2]　This provision still
appears unchanged in the code.[3]　The offender is dealt with
in precisely the same way by the Kentucky law of 1809; and
by it also the injured spouse is permitted to marry again
only after two years.[4]　In 1820 the innocent person is
relieved from all restraint;[5] both parties are treated as
"single" persons in 1843;[6] and likewise by the present statute, in all cases of divorce, no matter what the cause, guilty
and innocent alike are absolutely free to form new marriages whenever it shall please them so to do.[7]　The same
freedom exists in Arizona, New Mexico, Arkansas, Indian
Territory, Texas, West Virginia, and Missouri; although
in the last-named state until 1885 the guilty defendant was
not permitted to remarry for five years, "unless otherwise

---

[1] *Acts* (1872), 14; *ibid.* (1879), 51; also in *Code of Ga.* (1896), II, 29, 30.　A " verdict
of divorce in 1866 will not authorize the guilty party to marry again without proof of
a decree of court authorizing to marry."—62 *Ga.*, 408.

[2] Act of Oct. 26, 1799: SCOTT, *Laws of Tenn.* (1821), I, 647.

[3] *Code of Tenn.* (1884), 617; SHANNON, *Code* (1896), 1050.

[4] LITTELL, *Stat. Laws of Ky.* (1814), IV, 20.　This restriction upon the defendant
appears also in the act of 1812: *ibid.*, IV, 407-10.

[5] *Acts* (1819-20), 896.　　　　　　　　[6] Act of March 2, 1843: *Acts* (1842-43), 29, 30.

[7] *Kentucky Stat.* (1899), 827.

expressed in the decree of the court."[1]   Since 1857, in Mississippi, by a more stringent clause "the decree may provide, in the discretion of the court, that a party against whom a divorce is granted because of adultery shall not be at liberty to marry again;" but the freedom of the successful plaintiff is unrestrained.[2]   In 1824 the Alabama assembly in all cases forbade the guilty person to remarry; but this prohibition was removed by an act of February, 1870, which, however, lasted only until April, 1873, when it in turn was repealed.   By the existing code the chancellor in making his decree may, according to the evidence and nature of the case, direct whether the party, against whom the decree is rendered, shall be permitted to marry again; and in decrees now or hereafter rendered, when no order is made allowing or disallowing the divorced person to remarry, he may on petition and proper proof allow or disallow the petitioner to form a new marriage.[3]   It is constituted bigamy in Oklahoma for either divorced person to remarry within six months after the divorce, or until thirty days after final judgment, if appeal be taken.   Every decree of divorce shall recite that it "does not become absolute and take effect until the expiration of six months" from the day when it was rendered.[4] According to the Louisiana law, since 1808—at least until 1888—the wife cannot remarry until ten months after disso-

---

[1] *Rev. Stat. of Ariz.* (1887), 374; *Comp. Laws of N. M.* (1897), 407 ff.; *Digest of Ark.* (1894), 680 ff.; *Ann. Stat. of Ind. Ter.* (1899), 324–27; *Laws of the Rep. of Tex.* (act of Jan. 6, 1841), V, 20; also *Rev. Civil Stat. of Tex.* (1888), I, 887; *Ann. Civil Stat.* (1897), I, 1095–1100; *Code of W. Va.* (1899), 660 ff.; also Kelly, *Rev. Stat. of W. Va.* (1878), I, 495. The five-year limit for Missouri is fixed by the act of Jan. 24, 1835: *Rev. Stat.* (1835), 226; and is retained in *Rev. Stat.* (1845), 428; and *ibid.* (1879), I, 362; but it is struck out by *Laws* (1885), 159; and there is no restriction in *Rev. Stat.* (1899), I, 741–44. But by the act of Jan. 31, 1833, it was provided that "when one of the parties . . . . shall be divorced, it shall . . . . be lawful for the other party to marry again, after two years shall have expired."—*Laws of a Pub. and Gen. Nature* (1842), II, 361.

[2] *Ann. Code of Miss.* (1892), 420; *Rev. Code* (1857), 334.

[3] *Cf. Acts* (1824), 61, 62; *ibid.* (1869–70), 76, 77; *ibid.* (1872–73), 122; *Code of Ala.* (1897), 492, 493.

[4] *Stat. of Okla.* (1893), 876, 877; Wilson, *Statutes* (1903), II, 1122.

lution of the contract, whether by death, divorce, or decree
of nullity.[1] In case of divorce for infidelity the offender
may not marry his or her accomplice; and this last provision has been in force since 1827.[2] Under the same conditions as in Louisiana, the woman in Porto Rico may
not marry during a period of three hundred and one days
after dissolution of the marriage, or until a child is born if
she be pregnant at the time of the husband's death.[3] By
the criminal code of Florida, apparently, the guilty party
may not rewed.[4]

In all of the southern and southwestern states, except
Louisiana and, of course, South Carolina, a short term of residence is required to qualify the plaintiff to bring suit. Virginia began with a fairly cautious act in 1848. A definite
term is not fixed; but a petition for divorce must be brought
in the court of the county, city, or town where one of the
parties lives, and when the plaintiff has left the county or
other place where the married persons dwelt together, the
"suit shall be instituted and heard in the court" held for
that same county, if the defendant lives there still. The
benefits of the act do not extend to any save *bona fide* citizens
at the time of petition; nor to any case where the parties
have never lived together as citizens and as married persons
in the commonwealth; nor to any cause of adultery which
shall have occurred in any other state or country, unless the
parties at the time of such cause or before it took place were
citizens of the state and lived there together as husband and
wife.[5] By the present law no suit can be sustained unless
one of the persons has been domiciled in the state for at least
one year before; and it must be brought either in the county

[1] *Digest of Civil Laws* (1808), 28; *Rev. Civil Code* (1888), 68.
[2] *Rev. Laws* (1897), 306; *ibid.* (1870), 21; *Acts* (1827), 132, 134; *Acts* (1855), 376, 377.
[3] *Rev. Stat. and Codes of Porto Rico* (1902), 860.
[4] *Rev. Stat. of Fla.* (1892), 820.
[5] Act of March 18: *Acts of the Assembly* (1847-48), 165, 166.

or corporation where the parties last cohabited, or, at the option of the plaintiff, in that of the defendant, if still a resident of the state; otherwise in the place where the plaintiff dwells.[1]

The same rule as that of the parent state has existed in West Virginia since 1882, when a year's residence of one of the persons instead of mere residence at the time of the filing of the suit was introduced.[2] In Georgia twelve months in the state and six in the county for a divorce of either kind are required.[3] By the laws of Kentucky and Arkansas the term of previous residence for the plaintiff is also one year; and if the cause for divorce arose or existed without the state, he must have been a resident of the state at the time, unless it was also a ground of divorce where it existed or arose. In each of these states "an action for divorce must be brought within five years next after the doing of the act complained of."[4] In Alabama, when the defendant lives outside the state, the plaintiff must have been a *bona fide* resident for one year before bringing the action; or for three years when abandonment is the cause alleged.[5] Since 1822 in Mississippi the term of residence in the state for the applicant has been one year;[6] although, in 1857, a divorce shall be denied when the parties have never lived together as husband and wife in the state; as also for a cause occurring elsewhere, unless prior to its occurrence they have so dwelt together in the commonwealth. This last restriction does not apply to a *bona fide* citizen who marries abroad and does not discover the cause of divorce until after return to the state; but in case of desertion the term of *bona fide* residence must be three years.[7] An important change was introduced in 1863.

---

[1] *Code of Va.* (1887), 561.   [2] *Code of W. Va.* (1900), 662; *Acts* (1882), chap. 60.
[3] Act of Oct. 20, 1891: *Acts* (1890–91), 235.
[4] *Ky. Stat.* (1894), 769, 770; *Digest of Ark.* (1894), 681. *Cf.* Wright, *Report*, 80.
[5] *Code of Ala.* (1887), 525; *ibid.* (1897), 493.
[6] Act of June 15, 1822: *Code of Miss.* (1848), 495.   [7] *Rev. Code* (1857), 335.

It is then sufficient to be a citizen of the state or a resident of it for one year; but the applicant must make affidavit that he has not taken up residence to obtain a divorce.[1] By the existing code the courts of chancery may exercise jurisdiction only (1) when both persons are domiciled in the state when suit is commenced; or (2) when the complainant is so domiciled and the defendant is personally served with process in the state; or (3) when one of the consorts is thus domiciled and one or the other of them an actual resident for one year before action began.[2]

The time of residence for the petitioner is three years in the District of Columbia; and two years in Florida.[3] It is also two years in Tennessee, although the acts complained of were committed out of the state, or the petitioner lived out of the state at the time, and no matter where the defendant resides. A decree of divorce in a foreign state granted to a citizen of Tennessee who has merely temporarily transferred his residence there is void and will not be recognized.[4] In Maryland, since 1842, a divorce will not be granted when the cause occurs outside of the state, unless either the plaintiff or the defendant has resided in the state for the two preceding years.[5] By the North Carolina act of 1814 a stringent rule was adopted, only a citizen resident in the

---

[1] Act of Dec. 1, 1863: *Laws* (1862-63), 125, 126.

[2] *Ann. Code of Miss.* (1892), 421.

[3] *Rev. Stat. of Fla.* (1892), 504. But by the act of May 19, 1899, "when the defendant has been guilty of adultery in this state," then any citizen of the state, being the aggrieved, may get a divorce at any time, the two years' previous residence not being required: *Acts and Res.* (1899), 117. *Cf. Comp. Stat. of D. C.* (1894), 276, requiring two years; superseded by the act of 1901: MOORE, *Code* (1902), 200.

[4] *Code of Tenn.* (1884), 612; SHANNON, *Code* (1896), 1044 n. 2. Earlier the condition was citizenship and residence for one year: Act of Oct. 26, 1799: SCOTT, *Laws* (1821), I, 647; same in 1835, except the petitioner may have been absent on business or for health: CARUTHERS AND NICHOLSON, *Compilation* (1836), 260; also see 5 *Yerg.*, 203. A male citizen bringing suit for divorce must give bond and security for costs: *Acts* (1891), chap. 221, p. 433. On divorce in a foreign state see 3 *Lea*, 260.

[5] *Code of Md.* (1888), I, 144; *cf. Laws* (1841-42), chap. 262; *Laws* (1843), chap. 287; *Laws* (1886), chap. 10.

state for three years being allowed to sue.[1]   At present the plaintiff must show that the facts constituting the ground for divorce have existed for at least six months prior to filing the complaint, and that he has been a resident of the state for the preceding two years; and if the wife be plaintiff, she may set forth "that the husband is removing or about to remove his property and effects from the state, whereby she may be disappointed in her alimony."[2]   But in case of desertion the term of previous residence is five years. The period of previous residence for the plaintiff is six months in the state and county in Texas;[3] one year within the territory in New Mexico, Arizona, and Oklahoma;[4] while in Missouri it is one year, unless the offense or injury complained of was committed within the state, or when one or both of the persons resided there.   In all cases when the proceedings are *ex parte*, the court "shall, before granting the divorce, require proof of the good conduct of the petitioner and be satisfied that he or she. is an innocent or injured" person.[5]   In Arkansas and Indian Territory the plaintiff must "allege and prove" (1) "residence in the state for one year next before the commencement of the action:" (2) that the cause of divorce occurred or existed in the state, or, if out of the state, either that it was a legal cause there or that the applicant's residence was then in the state; (3) that the cause of divorce occurred or existed within five years before

[1] *Laws* (1814), chap. 5; Haywood, *Manual* (1819), 177; *Laws* (1821), II, 1294, 1295.

[2] *Code of N. C.* (1883), I, 575.   See Wright, *Report*, 83; *Pub. Laws* (1903), 846.

[3] The plaintiff must also be a *bona fide* resident of the state: *Rev. Civil Stat. of Tex.* (1888), I, 886; *Ann. Civil Stat.* (1897), I, 1097.

[4] By act of Congress, May 25, 1896: *Stat. at Large*, XXIX, 136, not less than one year's previous residence in any of the territories is required to entitle the plaintiff to bring suit for divorce. See *Rev. Stat. of Ariz.* (1901), 813; *Acts of N. M.* (1901), 117; Wilson, *Stat. of Okla.* (1903), II, 1119.

[5] *Rev. Stat. of Mo.* (1889), I, 1030; *ibid.* (1899), I, 742, 743.   This provision for residence appears in the statutes from 1835 onward: *Rev. Stat.* (1835), 225; *ibid.* (1845), 427; *ibid.* (1879), 361; and the period is one year by the act of May 13, 1807; *Laws of Pub. and Gen. Nature* (1842), I, 92.

the suit began.[1]   One year's residence is likewise required in Porto Rico, unless the act complained of was committed in the island or while one of the consorts resided there.[2]

A few of the states under consideration have adopted special provisions governing notice to the defendant.   Thus in Louisiana, "when the defendant is absent, or incapable of acting for any cause, an attorney shall be appointed to represent him, against whom, contradictorily, the suit shall be prosecuted."[3]   In North Carolina, if personal service cannot be made, the court may order service by publication, as in any other actions.[4]   By the law of Tennessee, process is authorized as in chancery cases.   If the wife is the petitioner, the suit may be heard and decided without service, either personal or by publication, if the bill was filed and the subpœna placed in the hands of the sheriff of the county in which the suit is instituted three months before the time when the subpœna is returnable; but the officer having the subpœna shall execute it if he can.[5]   In New Mexico service of process can be made by publication after obtaining an order from a judge of the supreme court, based on an affidavit showing the present residence of the defendant, if known, or last known place of residence, and efforts made to ascertain the present residence.   The order for publication shall direct that a copy of the summons be mailed to the present or last known residence of the defendant, and may direct such other means of bringing the action to the knowledge of the defendant as the judge shall deem proper.[6] Until recently Florida had a still different law.   If the

---

[1] *Digest of Ark.* (1894), 681; *Ann. Stat. of Ind. Ter.* (1899), 325.   The statute does not contemplate " constructive" residence; and applies to limited as well as absolute divorce: see Wood *v.* Wood, 54 *Ark.*, 172; 15 *S. W.*, 459.

[2] *Rev. Stat. and Codes of Porto Rico* (1902), 814.

[3] *Rev. Civil Code of La.* (1888), 69; *ibid.* (1870), 19.

[4] *Code of N. C.* (1883), I, 81, 82; WRIGHT, *Report*, 88.

[5] *Code of Tenn.* (1884), 613; WRIGHT, *Report*, 88.   [6] *Comp. Laws* (1897), 408.

defendant is absent from the state, so that ordinary process cannot be served, or, if served, he cannot be compelled to appear and answer or plead, the court may order a hearing on the bill, a copy of such order to be published in some public newspaper of the state, for the space of three months at least, or for a longer time, if the court shall so direct, or a copy of the bill and order for the hearing, certified by the clerk of the court, shall be actually served upon or delivered to the defendant at least three months before the day fixed for the hearing, or for a longer time, as the court may determine.   The present statute, however, directs simply that process be served as in other chancery suits.[1] This is the rule also in Virginia, West Virginia, Maryland, Mississippi, Arkansas, and Indian Territory; likewise in Georgia when the defendant is a non-resident; and in Alabama, where, if the defendant is a non-resident, publication is essential.[2]   In the District of Columbia process is according to the usual course of equity and the rules adopted by the court.   Missouri requires process as in other civil actions; and this is the law in the remaining states and territories of the group.[3]

The miscellaneous provisions are much the same as in the other parts of the United States.   Usually, in case of divorce, the legitimacy of the children is expressly ac-

---

[1] Compare *Rev. Stat. of Fla.* (1892), 505; WRIGHT, *Report*, 87.

[2] *Code of Va.* (1887), 561; *Code of W. Va.* (1900), 662; *Code of Md.* (1888), 142; *Ann. Code of Miss.* (1892), 421; *Code of Ga.* (1882), 395; *ibid.* (1896), II, 227; *Digest of Ark.* (1894), 681; *Ann. Stat. of Ind. Ter.* (1899), 325.   See WRIGHT, *Report*, 85–89.

By the Alabama Act of Dec. 14, 1898, in case of a decree *pro confesso* taken in the chancery court, the evidence having been taken and the cause being ready for decree, and no defense being interposed, if the complainant or his solicitor shall file a written request to the register or the clerk of the court to deliver the papers in the suit to the chancellor or judge, at the same time submitting his note of testimony in the case, then the chancellor shall render a decree in term time or in vacation: *Gen. Laws of Ala.* (1898–99), 118.

[3] *Rev. Stat. of Mo.* (1899), I, 742; *Rev. Stat. of Ariz.* (1887), 373 ff.; *ibid.* (1901), 439; *Rev. Civil Stat. of Tex.* (1888), I, 885 ff.; *Stat. of Okla.* (1893), 875; WILSON, *Stat. of Okla.* (1903), II, 1120; MOORE, *Code of D. C.* (1901), 21.

knowledged.[1] Sometimes provision is made for trial by jury, as in Georgia, Texas, and North Carolina;[2] or it is carefully forbidden, as in Kentucky;[3] and the law may permit the woman to resume her maiden name, as in Arkansas, Kentucky, Indian Territory, Oklahoma, Mississippi, and the District of Columbia.[4] Furthermore, in the District of Columbia, a disinterested attorney must be assigned to resist the decree in uncontested cases, or in any suit when the court sees fit;[5] and similar laws exist in Louisiana and Kentucky. Arbitration in place of judicial divorce is prohibited in Louisiana;[6] the married persons are allowed to be witnesses in Texas, Oklahoma, North Carolina,[7] and formerly in Florida; and occasionally provision is made for the annulment of the decree by further process before the courts.[8]

d) *Alimony, property, and custody of children.* — The statutes of these states contain the usual provisions for the protection and support of the wife and children during the suit for divorce; and sometimes the husband is required to furnish money to defray the wife's expenses in the same. The Virginia law authorizes the court in term or the judge in vacation to make an order compelling the "man to pay any sums necessary for the maintenance of the woman and

[1] For example, by *Code of Va.* (1887), 620; *Code of W. Va.* (1891), 666; *ibid.* (1900), 713; *Code of N. C.* (1883), I, 518; *Code of Ga.* (1896), II, 230; *Rev. Stat. of Fla.* (1892), 505; *Rev. Stat. of Ariz.* (1901), 814; *Rev. Civil Stat. of Tex.* (1888), I, 887; *Ann. Civil Stat. of Tex.* (1897), I, 1099; *Comp. Stat. of D. C.* (1894), 276, 277.

[2] *Code of Ga.* (1882), 396; *Rev. Civil Stat. of Tex.* (1888), I, 886; *Ann. Civil Stat. of Tex.* (1897), I, 1097; *Code of N. C.* (1883), I, 516.

[3] *Ky. Stat.* (1894), 767.

[4] *Digest of Ark.* (1894), 683; *Ann. Stat. of Ind. Ter.* (1899), 327; *Stat. of Ky.* (1894), 772; *Rev. Stat. of Mo.* (1899), I, 740; *Stat. of Okla.* (1893), 876; WILSON, *Stat. of Okla.* (1903), II, 1121; *Comp. Stat. of D. C.* (1894), 277; MOORE, *Code of D. C.* (1902), 200.

[5] MOORE, *Code of D. C.* (1902), 201.

[6] *Rev. Civil Code of La.* (1888), 69.

[7] *Laws of Tex.* (1897), 49; *Code of N. C.* (1883), I, 516; *Stat. of Okla.* (1893), 877, 878; WILSON, *Stat. of Okla.* (1903), II, 1123: *Acts and Res. of Fla.* (1885), 24.

[8] As by *Kentucky Stat.* (1894), 770, 771; *Digest of Ark.* (1894), 683; *Ann. Stat. of Ind. Ter.* (1899), 327; *Code of Va.* (1887), 562, 563; *Code of W. Va.* (1891), 614; *ibid.* (1900), 663.

to enable her to carry on the suit, or to prevent him from imposing any restraint on her personal liberty, or to provide for the custody and maintenance of the minor children" during the litigation. In the same way steps may be taken to preserve the estate of the husband, "so that it may be forthcoming to meet any decree," even compelling him to give security to abide by the decision.[1] North Carolina also grants the wife alimony *pendente lite;* but an order allowing it shall not be made "unless the husband shall have had five days' notice;" and in all cases of application for alimony it is admissible for him to be heard by affidavit in answer to the allegations made by the complainant. If he has abandoned his wife and left the state, or is in parts unknown, or is about to remove or dispose of his property for the purpose of defeating her claims, a notice is not required.[2] Arkansas and Indian Territory allow similar support during the suit, including attorney's fees.[3] By the Louisiana statute, "if the wife who sues for a separation" from bed and board, or for a divorce, "has left or declared her intention to leave the dwelling of her husband, the judge shall assign the house wherein she shall be obliged to dwell until the determination of the suit." She "shall be subject to prove her said residence as often as she may be required to do so, and in case she fails so to do, every proceeding on the separation shall be suspended." She is entitled to alimony *pendente lite*, if she constantly resides in the house assigned; and during the action, for the preservation of her rights, she may require an inventory and appraisement to be made of the property in the husband's possession and demand an injunction restraining him from disposing of any part thereof. After the commencement of the suit the husband

---

[1] *Code of Va.* (1887), 562; *cf. Code of W. Va.* (1900), 662.

[2] *Code of N. C.* (1883), I, 517.

[3] *Digest of Ark.* (1894), 681; *Ann. Stat. of Ind. Ter.* (1899), 326.

may not contract a debt on account of the community, nor sell the immovables belonging to the same; such alienation being void, if made "with the fraudulent view of injuring the rights of the wife." Custody of the children of the marriage, "whose provisional keeping is claimed by both husband and wife," belongs to the husband, whether plaintiff or defendant, "unless there shall be strong reasons to deprive him of it;" but when a separation from bed and board has been decreed, the "children shall be placed under the care of the party who shall have obtained the separation, unless the judge shall, for the greater advantage of the children and with the advice of the family meeting, order that some or all" of them be intrusted to the other spouse. In all cases of full divorce "the minor children shall be placed under the tutorship of the party who shall have obtained" the decree.[1]

Permanent alimony and the custody of the children after dissolution of marriage are generally provided for. Sometimes the wife is granted separate alimony without a decree of divorce, as in Virginia, Florida, Georgia, and Oklahoma.[2] From an early period the North Carolina statutes have been conspicuous for the relief granted to the wife after divorce, or, under certain circumstances, without formal separation. Thus by the act of 1814 the court may grant a woman having a limited divorce for cruelty or abandonment such alimony as the husband's means will admit, not exceeding either one-third of his real or personal estate or a like share of the annual profits of his estate, occupation, or labor.[3] The deserted wife gains still further protection in 1816.

---

[1] *Rev. Civil Stat. of La.* (1888), 70–72; *ibid.* (1870), 19–21; *ibid.* (1897), 306.

[2] *Code of Ga.* (1896), II, 236; *Rev. Stat. of Fla.* (1892), 505; *Stat. of Okla.* (1893), 877; WILSON, *Stat. of Okla.* (1903), II, 1123; *Code of Va.* (1887), 562. *Cf.*, for Virginia, 4 H. AND M., 507; 4 RAND., 662: 1 ROB., 608; 1 MINOR'S *Inst.*, 282.

[3] *Laws of N. C.* (1814), chap. 5; HAYWOOD, *Manual* (1819), 174 ff. It may be noted that the act of 1814 lays on the party "cast" in each divorce suit a tax of ten pounds payable to the state: *ibid.*, 177.

"Whereas," declares an act of that year, "cases of great hardship often occur, the husband being at liberty to return and squander away the estate of the wife, subsequently obtained;" to remedy the evil it is therefore enacted that in future the decree of separation from bed and board shall have the effect of securing to the wife "any property which she may subsequently obtain, either by her own labor, gift, devise, or operation of law, unless the court shall in their judgment otherwise order."[1]   Furthermore, in 1828–29 the courts were authorized to grant the wife separate alimony without divorce "whenever a man shall become an habitual drunkard or spendthrift, wasting his substance to the impoverishment of his family."[2]   The present law is conceived in the spirit of these early enactments.   In case of separation from bed and board, the amount of alimony is the same as in 1814.   Separate maintenance without a divorce is still allowed.   "When any husband shall separate himself from his wife and fail to provide her with the necessary subsistence according to his means and condition in life, or if he shall be a drunkard or spendthrift, the wife may apply for a special proceeding to the judge of the superior court for the county in which he resides, to have a reasonable subsistence secured to her and to the children of the marriage." Finally it may be noted that alimony may be decreed to the husband as well as the wife in Virginia and West Virginia.

Measures are taken in nearly every state for the division or other disposal of property after separation or divorce. The North Carolina law is very elaborate.   "Every woman who shall be living separate from her husband, either upon a judgment of divorce . . . . or under a deed of separation, executed by said husband and wife, and registered in the county in which she resides, or whose husband shall have been declared an idiot or a lunatic, shall be deemed and held

---

[1] *Acts* (1816), chap. 33: also in Haywood, *Manual*, 177, 178.   [2] *Acts* (1828–29), 25.

. . . . a free trader, and shall have power to convey her
personal estate and her real estate without the assent of the
husband." So also "every woman whose husband shall
abandon her, or shall maliciously turn her out of doors, shall
be deemed a free trader, so far as to be competent to contract and be contracted with, and to bind her separate property, but the liability of the husband for her reasonable
support shall not thereby be impaired, and she shall have
power to convey" her real and personal estate without her
husband's assent. When a marriage is dissolved *a vinculo*,
each of the parties loses all right to any estate by courtesy
or dower, and all right to a year's provision or a distribu-
tive share in the personal property of the other, or to
administer on the other's estate, and all rights whatsoever
in the other's estate gained by settlement in consideration
of the marriage. But if a "married woman shall elope with
an adulterer, or shall wilfully and without just cause abandon
her husband and refuse to live with him, and shall not be
living with" him at his death; or if a limited divorce be
granted on the husband's petition, "she shall thereby lose all
right to dower in the lands and tenements of her husband, and
also all right to a year's provision." In such cases the husband may convey his real estate as if he were unmarried, and
the wife is thereafter barred of all claims to dower. When
the husband is guilty of a similar offense, and his conduct is
not condoned by the wife, or in case a partial divorce has been
granted on her application, he shall suffer the like penalties.[1]

In Missouri a divorce obtained by the wife is considered
in law as the death of the husband, and she is looked upon

---

[1] *Code of N. C.* (1883), I, 696, 700; and *Laws* (1893), chap. 153, pp. 114–16, amending *Laws* (1871–72), chap. 193, sec. 44. By the law of the District of Columbia, "in
case of adultery of the wife, committed after . . . . divorce from bed and board, the
court may, on petition of the husband . . . . , deprive the wife of alimony from the
date of her said criminal act, and rescind her right of dower, as well as dispossess
her . . . . of the care, custody, and guardianship" of any child awarded to her by
the original judgment: *Comp. Stat.* (1894), 277. *Cf.* MOORE, *Code*, 201.

as his widow; but when at fault she is barred of dower.[1]
The guilty wife loses her right of dower also in Tennessee;
and there she cannot claim permanent alimony. In the
same state, when divorce is for the wife's infidelity, and the
woman afterwards cohabits with her paramour, she is made
"incapable of alienating, directly or indirectly, any of her
lands;" and after her death these are to be distributed
according to the rules of intestate inheritance.[2] Dower is
barred by grant of permanent alimony in Georgia;[3] and in
Louisiana, in case of separation from bed and board, the
defendant loses "all the advantages or donations" which the
plaintiff "may have conferred by the marriage contract or
since," while the latter preserves all those to which he or she
would otherwise have been entitled; and these dispositions
are to take place even when the advantages and donations
were "reciprocally made."[4]

Finally it must be noted as a matter of regret that in no
instance in these states has any provision been made for the
registration of divorces or the return and publication of
divorce statistics.

---

[1] *Rev. Civil Stat.* (1889), I, 1036. *Cf.* 61 *Mo.*, 148; and 57 *Mo.*, 200; 3 *M. A.*, 321.

[2] *Code of Tenn.* (1884), 616, 617. "If the wife, at the time of a decree dissolving
the marriage, be the owner of any lands, or have in her possession goods or chattels
or choses in action acquired by her own industry or given to her by devise or otherwise, or which may have come to her, or to which she may be entitled by the decease
of any relative intestate, she shall have entire and exclusive dominion and control
thereof, and may sue for and recover the same in her own name subject, however, to
the rights of creditors who became such before the decree was pronounced." When
"a marriage is dissolved at the suit of the husband, and the defendant is owner, in
her own right, of lands, his right to and interest therein and to the rents and profits
of the same, shall not be taken away or impaired by the dissolution."—*Ibid.*, 616, 617.
Cf. SHANNON, *Code* (1896), 1050.

[3] *Code of Ga.* (1896), II, 237; and 43 *Ga.*, 295. But in case of *bona-fide* separation
without divorce alimony may be granted: *Code* (1882), 401: *ibid.* (1896), II, 235.

[4] *Rev. Civil Code* (1888), 72, 73; *ibid.* (1870), 20.

In general, on all these provisions, see also *Code of Md.* (1888), I, 143, 144; *Rev.
Civil Stat. of Mo.* (1899), I, 742, 743; *Code of Ga.* (1896), II, 230 ff.; *Ann. Code of Miss.*
(1892), 420; *Digest of Ark.* (1894), 681 ff.; *Ann. Stat. of Ind. Ter.* (1899), 325–27; *Stat. of
Okla.* (1893), 875 ff.; WILSON, *Stat. of Okla.* (1903), II, 1119–23; *Kentucky Stat.* (1903),
846–51; *Rev. Stat. of Ariz.* (1887), 374, 375; *ibid.* (1901), 814, 815; *Rev. Stat. of Fla.* (1892),
505, 506; *Rev. Civil Stat. of Tex.* (1888), I, 886–88.

III.   THE MIDDLE AND WESTERN STATES[1]

a) Legislative divorce. — An examination of the session
laws reveals the fact that legislative divorce has at some time
existed in many western commonwealths.   During the territorial stage, in particular, and in some cases for a considerable period thereafter, the assemblies at each meeting were
called upon to hear and determine petitions for dissolution
of marriage which ought to have been relegated to the
courts.   Such, for example, was the practice in Michigan
until 1837, when it was forbidden by the first constitution of the state;[2] and in Illinois until a later time.   At the
session of 1817–18 the assembly of Illinois Territory
granted relief to Elizabeth Spriggs because she had been
"shamefully abandoned" by her husband, who, it is alleged,
is still guilty of "shameful" misconduct, and because she
must be "considerably injured if she cannot obtain a divorce sooner than in the ordinary way."[3]   Other cases
occurred from time to time;[4] and in 1831 the marital bonds
of twenty couples were dissolved by one act of a few lines.[5]
Indiana appears to have been nearly as indiscreet.   For
instance, in 1838 the marriage of John Duvall and Nancy
Duvall, *alias* Nancy Stack, was declared null and void.[6]
Two years later occurred a divorce from the bond of wedlock, the wife being permitted to resume her maiden name.
Thereafter it became the practice in this state for the
assembly to grant persons leave to file bills in the courts in

[1] In this section are analyzed the statutes of the following twenty-six states,
districts, and territories: Alaska, California, Colorado, Delaware, Hawaii, Idaho,
Illinois, Indiana, Iowa, Kansas, Michigan, Minnesota, Montana, Nebraska, Nevada,
New Jersey, New York, North Dakota, Ohio, Oregon, Pennsylvania, South Dakota,
Utah, Washington, Wisconsin, and Wyoming.

[2] Special divorce acts may be found in the *Ter. Laws of Mich.*, II, 655, 709, 710, 752,
753, 769; III, 840, 842, 847, 895, 901, 905 (three cases), 907 (two cases).

[3] *Laws of Ill.* (1817–18), 356.

[4] Thus on Jan. 15, 1825, two decrees were granted in one bill: *Laws* (1825), 120.

[5] Act of Feb. 15, 1831: *Laws*, 71, 72.   There is another example in *Laws* (1839), 79.

[6] *Laws of a Local Nature* (1838), 406.

cases where the prescribed causes for divorce by judicial process did not exist.   Thus in 1842 Mary Ann Bruner was allowed to file a petition because of "her disability by reason of her husband not having absented himself from her for two years," the full term necessary to constitute a valid ground according to the statute.[1]   Until 1851, when the constitution put a stop to this evil custom, many such applications were referred to the circuit courts, the full legal requirement being similarly waived.[2]   The early Minnesota lawmakers found plenty of business of the same kind.   "Be it enacted," runs a decree of the assembly in 1849, "that the marriage heretofore existing between Catherine Hathaway and her husband, Isaac Hathaway, ... is hereby dissolved; and the said parties are restored to all the rights and privileges of unmarried persons."[3]   Another example seems to show that a "pale-face" cannot always live happily with a "dusky mate."   It is solemnly declared "that Louis Laramie is hereby divorced from Wa-kan-ye-ke-win, his wife, as fully and effectually, as if the legal ceremony of marriage and its rites had never been solemnized."[4]   Similar decrees appear in the statute-book until in 1856 constitutional authority finally put a stop to legislative interference.[5]

During the first six years of territorial life many special divorce decrees may be found in the Nebraska laws; and they are invariably expressed in the curt and summary style peculiar to such legislation throughout the country, no reference usually being made to causes or to alimony.[6]   At the

[1] *Laws of a Local Nature* (1842), 117.

[2] *Cf. ibid.* (1842), 119, 120, 121; *ibid.* (1844), 148; *ibid.* (1849), 203, 300 (two cases); *ibid.* (1850), 105, 129, 194, 342, 344; *ibid.* (1851), 404, 441, 497.

[3] *Laws of Minn.* (1849), 89.   [4] *Ibid.*

[5] For examples see *Laws* (1851), 39, 40 (four cases); and *ibid.* (1852), 60, 61 (two cases).   Seven of the acts cited are also given or restated in *Collected Stat. of the Ter. of Minn. and Decis. of Supreme Court* (1853).

[6] Here is an example: "The bonds of matrimony between Obediah J. Niles and Hannah M. Niles shall be and the same are hereby dissolved."—*Laws and Resolu-*

same time Kansas was having a similar experience. One divorce petition was granted by the assembly in 1857, three in 1858, eight in 1859, while in 1860 the number suddenly rose to forty-three; for this was the "last chance" before the constitutional prohibition of 1859 went into effect.[1] Previous to 1847 Iowa was still more indulgent. Year after year appeals were made to the assembly for relief. Sometimes the intention appears to be to deny the defendant the privilege of further wedlock; as in 1840, when a decree was granted to dissolve the marriage contract, "so far as relates to the said Harriet Williams," who is allowed to change her name. Sometimes a partial divorce is sanctioned, as when the marital bond between John Philips and Nancy his wife was "so far dissolved as to permit the said parties to live separate and apart from each other." In this case the woman was given power to sue and be sued, and was allowed to retain the children. In 1841–42 eleven more legislative decrees were granted. The next year saw nineteen petitions combined in one bill, which was passed over the governor's veto by a two-thirds vote. The last examples occur in 1846, the year when Iowa was admitted to the Union as a state, and when the usual constitutional interdict appears.[2]

The practice existed also in Idaho,[3] Montana,[4] and Oregon.[5] On the Pacific coast, however, Washington is the

---

tions, I, 373 (act of Feb., 1857). For other cases see *ibid.*, 569, 570 (two cases, 1858), 653–55, 656 (three cases, 1860), 766, 767 (two cases, 1861). On Jan. 23, 1856, six petitions in one bill were referred to the judge of the district court for the first judicial district with power to dissolve marriage: *ibid.*, 300.

[1] *Private Laws of Kan.* (1860), 232–54. For other cases see *ibid.* (1858), 10–12 (three cases); and *ibid.* (1859), 41–45 (eight cases).

[2] *Cf. Laws of Ia.* (1840), 12; *ibid.* (1840–41), 7, 12; *ibid.* (1841–42), 3, 11, 13, 28, 30, 31, 66, 73, 94, 95 (eleven cases); *ibid.* (1842–43), 82–84 (nineteen cases); *ibid.* (1845–46), 42, 48, 51, 52, 61, 72, 79 (eleven cases).

[3] There are two cases in *Laws and Res.* (1871), 86, 91; others in *Gen. Laws* (1879), 54, 59–61; five in *ibid.* (1881), 439–41; and four in *ibid.* (1883), 164, 165.

[4] *The Private and Spec. Laws of Mont.* (1864–65), 554, 610, 685, 695, 699, 700, show nine cases of legislative divorce.

[5] For examples see *Spec. Laws* (1857), 12; *ibid.* (1857–58), 107, 108, 110, 111, 112 (twelve cases); *ibid.* (1858–59), 92–107 (thirty-one cases).

chief offender. Beginning with three cases in 1858 and one in 1859, the number mounts to fifteen in 1860, seventeen in 1861, fifteen in 1862, and sixteen in 1863; while after this date the session laws are silent on the subject.[1]

In some of the old middle states the custom was particularly tenacious. Of it the New York laws show scarcely a trace;[2] and in those of New Jersey no evidence at all has been discovered. The case is very different in Pennsylvania. Although in 1785 the courts were empowered to grant full or partial divorce for the causes specified, the habit of resorting to the assembly, especially when the offense complained of was not a cause recognized by the statute, survived from the provincial era. Thus in 1805 Rebecca Adkinson was released from her spouse Thomas, who for crimes committed had been sentenced to five years' imprisonment. "Whereas it appears that the conduct of the said Thomas, from the month of May, 1803, to the present time, has been one continued scene of vice, evincing a total dereliction of morality, and an entire neglect of his wife and tender infant," therefore, since the law has not provided for such emergency, the assembly sets Rebecca absolutely free from the wedding bond.[3] During the next year a case of somewhat unusual character arose. From the preamble to the bill it appears that as early as 1777 Jacob Sell and Eve, his wife, had divorced themselves by mutual consent, the woman by a written instrument relinquishing all her rights under the marriage. Thereafter, the man considering himself entirely

---

[1] See *Acts* (1858), 53, 54; *ibid.* (1859), 62; *ibid.* (1860: private laws), 473-79; *Session Laws* (1861: local laws), 71, 73, 74, 81, 83, 92, 93, 101-3, 110, 131, 132; *ibid.* (1862), Index; *ibid.* (1863), 138-44.

[2] But in *Laws* (1848), 94, 95, the following case of legislative interference may be found: "The right is hereby given to Ludwig Brunileu to apply to the supreme court of this state, in equity, for a divorce from his wife Bertha, ... with the same effect and on the same footing in every respect, as if they had been married in this state, and the offence or offences complained of had been committed in this state, and within five years prior to the time of such application."

[3] THOMPSON, *Laws of the Commonwealth of Pa.* (1804-6), VII, 73-75.

free from former obligations, took unto himself another wife, "by whom he now has living six children." Through "hard labor and honest industry" a considerable property was in due course acquired, some of which Sell had transferred. To this under the existing laws he could not give perfect title because of a claim to dower which "the aforesaid Eve may be supposed to possess." For this reason, and because he had grown old and was in a "delicate state of health," the assembly granted his petition for an absolute dissolution of the first marriage.[1] From this time onward many divorce decrees may be found in the session laws; and not until the adoption of the constitution of 1874 was the practice entirely abandoned.[2]

It was in Delaware, however, that legislative divorce died the hardest death. By the act of 1832 the superior court was given "sole cognizance of granting divorces" for cruelty, abandonment, and some other causes; and in 1852 it was enacted that no "petition for a divorce shall be received or acted on by the general assembly for any cause cognizable" by that court, "nor without proof of one month's public notice of the intention to prefer such petition, by advertisements in a newspaper published within the county of the petitioner's residence, if there be one," or, if not, then in some other newspaper in the state.[3] Although this declaration of the assembly restricting its jurisdiction to cases not provided for by law was subsequently more than once repeated,[4] there was still a wide range for interference, even if the will of one legislature could bind that of another. The number of petitions granted waxed apace. In 1887 it was forty-two;

---

[1] Thompson, *op. cit.*, 326-28.

[2] See, for example, *Acts* (1808), 138, 140, 146 (for cruelty, force at marriage, etc.); *ibid.* (1810), 82, 89, 194 (insanity before and after marriage, imprisonment for crime, abuse, and abandonment); *ibid.* (1811-12), 28, 34, 143, 195, 198, 228, 231, 237; *ibid.* (1820-21), 3, 29, 35, 48, 139.

[3] *Rev. Stat. of Del.* (1852), 78.   [4] *Ibid.* (1874), 150; *ibid.* (1893), 242.

in 1889, sixty-three; and two years later, forty-eight.[1] In the meantime a remedy was sought through appeal to constitutional interdict. Once the effort was almost successful. By an act of April 20, 1893, the assembly proposed an amendment to the constitution giving the supreme court exclusive jurisdiction in divorce suits, but only "for the causes and upon the conditions prescribed by the legislature.[2] This amendment failed of adoption; but its purpose was soon secured in the new constitution of 1897, which declares that "no divorce shall be granted, nor alimony allowed, except by the judgment of a court, as shall be prescribed by general and uniform law."[3]

b) *Judicial divorce: jurisdiction, kinds, and causes.*—
Regarding the causes of divorce the history of the middle and western states reveals little that is peculiar as compared with that of the southern or eastern group. On the whole, a medial course has been pursued. There is nothing very radical or very conservative. The statutes of these commonwealths are entitled to be looked upon as constituting the average American type.

The policy of New York has, indeed, seemed to be exceptional. Throughout the century absolute divorce has been allowed only on the scriptural ground. In 1787—for the first time since New Netherland came under English rule—a general divorce law was enacted. The preamble hints at the recent practice of special legislation. "Whereas," we are told, "the Laws at present in being within this state, respecting Adultery, are very defective, and Applications have, in Consequence, been made to the Legislature, praying their Interposition;" and since "it is thought more advisable . . . . to make some general Provision in such Cases, than to afford relief to Individuals, upon their partial representa-

---

[1] *Laws* (1887), 528–40; *ibid.* (1889), 1046–64; *ibid.* (1895), 300–308.

[2] *Laws* (1893), 617.   [3] *Const. of the State of Del.* (1897), Art. II, sec. 18, p. 141.

tions, without a just and Constitutional Trial of the Facts;" therefore for the offense named, when the persons are inhabitants of the state, a "Petition or Bill" may be presented to the chancellor. The latter is empowered to direct the trial of the case by a "special or common jury" before either the supreme or any circuit court; and in case of conviction may "pronounce the marriage between the said parties to be dissolved, and both of them freed" from its obligations. The guilty defendant is forbidden to "remarry any person whatsoever;" while the innocent plaintiff is fully authorized to "make and complete another marriage, in like manner as if the party convicted was actually dead." The divorce is not to affect the legitimacy of the children, and the chancellor is required to make proper orders for their care and maintenance and for the wife's alimony.[1]

No further legislation on the subject appears until 1813, when some important changes in the law were made. Now a petition for divorce, on the same grounds, may be brought only when the persons concerned were inhabitants of the state at the time the offense was committed; or when the marriage was solemnized or took place in the state, and the person injured was an actual resident of the state at the time of the offense and at the time of exhibiting the bill. The facts are to be tried by a "special or foreign" jury at some circuit court or sittings, to be held by a justice of the supreme court; and the person convicted is prohibited from further marriage only during the lifetime of the other spouse. But the most important innovation made by this act is the provision for partial divorce in favor of the wife. Under the same conditions as to residence, the court of chancery is empowered to grant a *feme covert* a decree of "separation from bed and board forever thereafter, or for a limited time,

---

[1] Act of March 30, 1787: *Laws of the State of N. Y.* (1789), II, 133, 134; and *ibid.* (1792), I, 428, 429.

as shall seem just and reasonable," when the husband has been guilty (1) of cruel and inhuman treatment; or (2) of such conduct "as may render it unsafe and improper for her to cohabit with him, and be under his dominion and control;" or (3) when he has abandoned her and neglected or refused to provide for her support. In all such cases, if the defendant prove the ill conduct of the complainant as a justification, he may be "dismissed with or without costs in the discretion of the court." On the other hand, whether a separation be decreed or not, the court is authorized "to make such orders and decree for the suitable support and maintenance" of the wife and children by the husband or out of his property, as the chancellor shall deem just.[1]

The *Revised Statutes* of 1827–28 make careful provision for the annulment of voidable marriages; and by the same enactment the divorce law is recast. Through sentence of nullity the chancellor may declare void a marriage for the following causes existing at the time of the contract: when (1) either husband or wife was below the age of consent; or (2) had a spouse living under a marriage still in force; or (3) was an idiot or lunatic; or (4) when consent of either was obtained by force or fraud; or (5) when either was physically incompetent to enter the matrimonial state. All these grounds of nullity, with one slight change and some modification of the conditions on which suit may be brought, are sanctioned by the present code.[2] Divorce from the bond

[1] Act of April 13, 1813: Van Ness and Woodworth, *Laws of N. Y.* (1813), II, 197–201.

[2] *Rev. Stat. of 1827-28* (Albany, 1829), II, 141-44. This law provides that no bill for annulment may be brought by the party who was of lawful age of consent, nor by the other if there is voluntary cohabitation after age of consent. Suit on the ground of force or fraud is likewise barred, if there has at any time been voluntary cohabitation; and in case of physical disability, it must be brought within two years after solemnization of the marriage: *ibid.*, II, 142, 143. *Cf.* Stover, *Code of Civil Procedure* (1902), II, 1832-33, where the last-named provision is retained. By this *Code*, II, 1626, 1627, the fourth ground of annulment is broadened by adding the word "duress;" and a woman is authorized to bring action (1) when she had not reached the age of sixteen at the time of the marriage; (2) when the marriage took place without the

of wedlock according to the revision of 1827–28 may be granted on the same conditions regarding residence as those prescribed in 1813, except that it allows the injured person, if an actual inhabitant at the time of exhibiting the bill, to bring suit whenever the offense complained of has been committed in the state. As in 1803, the guilty defendant is forbidden to remarry until after the death of the complainant. The three grounds of separation from bed and board in favor of the wife allowed in that year remain unaltered, save that under the second head the phrase referring to her being under the husband's "dominion and control" is omitted; and now, when the marriage takes place out of the state, the parties must have "become and remained inhabitants" of it for at least one year, and in order to warrant a decree the woman must be an actual resident thereof at the time of bringing complaint.[1]

Under the existing law of New York, for adultery, absolute divorce may be granted to either the husband or wife (1) when both were residents of the state at the time of the offense; (2) when the marriage took place within the state; (3) when the plaintiff was a resident of the state when the offense was committed, and so remains at the commencement of the suit; (4) where the offense was committed in the state and the person injured is a resident thereof when the action is brought. In the first instance the judgment is "interlocutory;" and three months must elapse before it can be made final.[2] Remarriage is allowed only under the same conditions as in 1813 and 1827, except that now the law does not "prevent the remarriage of the parties to the

consent of parent or guardian; or (3) "when it was not followed by consummation or cohabitation, and was not ratified by any mutual assent of the parties after the plaintiff attained the age of sixteen years." *Cf. Laws* (1887), chap. 22, p. 25, for the origin of these clauses.

[1] *Rev. Stat. of 1827–28*, II, 144–47.

[2] So required by *Laws* (1902), II, chap. 364; STOVER, *Code of Civil Proced.* (1902), II, sec. 1774, p. 1863.

action." At present suit for partial divorce may be brought by either spouse, and not by the wife only, as under the earlier laws. The grounds allowed are (1) cruel and inhuman treatment; (2) conduct rendering it unsafe and improper for the plaintiff to cohabit with the defendant; (3) abandonment; (4) where the wife is plaintiff, the neglect or refusal of the husband to provide for her.[1] When the marriage takes place out of the state the provision of 1827–28 requiring one year's previous residence of the parties and actual residence of the plaintiff at the commencement of the action is still maintained.[2]

New Jersey, whose early history ran so closely parallel to that of New York, has during the century pursued a policy regarding divorce more liberal than that of the neighboring commonwealth. As so often happens, the act of 1794 confuses the grounds of annulment with those of divorce proper. The court of chancery is authorized to decree "divorces from the bond of matrimony" (1) when the husband and wife are within the prohibited degrees of kinship; (2) for adultery; (3) for "wilful, continued, and obstinate desertion for the term of seven years;" or (4) when either person had a lawful spouse living at the time of the later marriage, although the statute inconsistently declares such unions "invalid from the beginning" and "absolutely void." This last-named provision is still in force.[3] By the law of 1794,

---

[1] It has been decided in Kennedy v. Kennedy, 73 N. Y., 363, affirming 47 N. Y. Supr., 56, that "threats of violence of such a character as to induce a reasonable apprehension of bodily injury, and charges of infidelity, made in bad faith, as auxiliary to and in aggravation of the threatened violence, are sufficient to constitute 'cruel and inhuman treatment.'" Cf. STOVER, Code of Civil Proced. (1892), II, 1639, 1640, note.

A "groundless and malicious charge against a wife's chastity, and spitting upon her are gross acts of cruelty, and words of menace accompanied by the probability of bodily violence, if they inflict indignity and threaten pain, are sufficient." See Whispell v. Whispell, 4 BARB., 217; and cf. Lutz v. Lutz, 31 N. Y. St. Rep., 718; Waltermire v. Waltermire, 110 N. Y., 183; Uhlmann v. Uhlmann, 17 Abb. N. C., 236; Mason v. Mason, 1 EDW., Ch., 278; Perry v. Perry, 2 BARB., Ch., 311.

[2] STOVER, Code of Civil Proced. (1902), II, 1846.

[3] Gen. Stat. of N. J. (1896), II, 1267.

moreover, separation from bed and board is sanctioned for "extreme cruelty" in either spouse.[1]

A new statute appears in 1820. The conditions as to residence are now defined; the court of chancery may grant absolute dissolution of wedlock for the same causes as in 1794; and separation from bed and board is still permitted for extreme cruelty, but now it may be decreed, "forever, or for a limited time."[2] In the revision of the divorce laws approved April 15, 1846, the term of wilful and continued desertion is reduced to five years;[3] in 1857 two years more are lopped off;[4] and finally a statute of 1890 declares a period of two years' such desertion sufficient to constitute a ground of full divorce.[5]

Accordingly, by the present law of New Jersey dissolution of wedlock may be decreed by the court of chancery (1) when the marriage is bigamous; (2) when it is within the forbidden degrees of kinship;[6] (3) for adultery; (4) for "wilful, continued, and obstinate desertion during the term of two years;" and (5) when at the time of the marriage either spouse was "physically and incurably impotent," in which case the contract is declared "invalid from the beginning and absolutely void."[7] But it is important to observe that in certain cases the term of desertion is subject to a peculiar statutory definition. It is declared that "wilful and obstinate desertion shall be . . . . construed as 'continued' . . . . notwithstanding that after such desertion

[1] Act of Dec. 2, 1794: PATERSON, Laws of N. J. (1800), 143, 144.

[2] Act of Feb. 16, 1820: Laws of N. J. (1821), 667-69.   [3] Stat. of N. J. (1847), 923.

[4] Act of March 20: Acts (1857), 399. The law of 1846 is retained in ELMER, Digest (2d ed. by NIXON, Philadelphia, 1855), 205-8.

[5] Act of March 5: Pub. Laws (1890), 34; Gen. Stat. (1896), II, 1274.

[6] A marriage within the forbidden degrees is not void but voidable, and until so pronounced must be treated as valid: Boylan v. Deinzer, 18 STEWART, N. J. Equity Reports, 485.

[7] Impotence as a ground of divorce appears in Rev. Stat. (1874), 255. Cf. also Gen. Stat. (1896), II, 1267. Before this enactment a marriage could not be annulled for impotence: Anonymous, 9 C. E. GREEN, N. J. Equity Reports, 19.

has . . . . begun, the deserting party has . . . . been imprisoned in this or any other state or country upon conviction by due process of law for a crime, misdemeanor or
offence, not political," anywhere committed; provided, however, that such desertion has continued without interruption
a sufficient length of time after discharge from prison to
make up when added to the term of desertion prior to the
confinement the full term of three [two] years.[1] Since 1891
three causes of separation from bed and board have been
allowed. For desertion, adultery, or extreme cruelty, in
either spouse, the court of chancery may now decree such
partial divorce "forever thereafter, or in the case of extreme
cruelty, for a limited time, as shall seem just and reasonable;" but in every case except for extreme cruelty the
petitioner "shall prove that he or she has conscientious
scruples against applying for a divorce from the bond of
matrimony."[2]

The framers of the Pennsylvania statute of 1785 saw fit
to indulge in an apologetic preamble. "Whereas," we are
assured, "it is the design of marriage, and the wish of the
parties entering into that state, that it should continue during their joint lives, yet where the one party is under natural
or legal incapacities of faithfully discharging the matrimonial vow, or is guilty of acts and deeds inconsistent with the
nature thereof, the laws of every well-regulated society ought
to give relief to the innocent and injured person;" therefore
it is enacted that the justices of the supreme court may grant
divorce, "not only from bed and board, but also from matrimony," (1) when either person at the time of the contract
was and still is physically incompetent; (2) has knowingly

---

[1] Act of Apr. 1: *Pub. Laws* (1887), 132; also in *Gen. Stat.* (1896), II, 1273. This
provision thus seems to be in force; if so, since the act of 1890 already cited, the term
must be two years.

[2] Act of March 4: *Pub. Laws* (1891), 76. In general, for the present law regulating both kinds of divorce in New Jersey, see *Gen. Stat.* (1896), II, 1267-75.

entered into a bigamous marriage; (3) has committed adultery; or (4) has been guilty of "wilful and malicious desertion, without a reasonable cause," for the space of four years. The court is empowered to grant a divorce from bed and board, but not from the bond of wedlock, "if any husband shall, maliciously, either (1) abandon his family, or (2) turn his wife out of doors, or (3) by cruel and barbarous treatment endanger her life, or (4) offer such indignities to her person, as to render her condition intolerable, or life burdensome, and thereby force her to withdraw from his house and family." In these cases the wife is allowed "such alimony as her husband's circumstances will admit of so as the same do not exceed the third part of the annual profits or income of his estate, or of his occupation or labour," or the court may decree "but one of them" as justice may require. She shall continue to enjoy this alimony "until a reconciliation shall take place, or until the husband shall by his petition or libel, offer to receive or cohabit with her again, and to use her as a good husband ought to do." Then the court is authorized either to suspend the decree; or, if the wife refuse "to return and cohabit under the protection of the court," it may discharge and annul the same. But if he fail to make good his offers and engagement, the "former sentence and decree may be revived and enforced;" and the arrears of alimony may be ordered paid.[1]

By the first statute of the period, it thus appears, a liberal divorce policy was adopted by Pennsylvania, and besides, it should be remembered, the courts were not the only source of relief. For many years, as already seen, the assembly exercised jurisdiction in divorce matters. After 1785 the first step in the practical relaxation of the law was taken in 1804, when jurisdiction, hitherto vested exclusively in the supreme court, was extended to the county courts of common

[1] Act of Sept. 19, 1785: *Laws of the Com. of Pa.* (1803), III, 102-6. Repealed March 13, 1815: *Laws of Gen. Assem.* (1822), VI, 286; PURDON, *Digest* (1818), 130.

pleas, where it still remains.[1] Since that date the progress
of legislation has been rapid enough.   Under the existing
law, as the result of a century's growth, not less than eleven
grounds of complete divorce are recognized.   By the statute
of 1815, repealing the law of 1785, the four causes sanctioned by the latter are re-enacted, the term of "malicious
desertion and absence from the habitation of the other"
—as the clause is now phrased—being reduced to two
years; and it is further provided that full dissolution of
marriage may be decreed (5) when any husband, by cruel
and barbarous treatment, shall have endangered the life of
his wife; or (6) offered such indignities to her person as to
render her condition intolerable and life burdensome, thereby
forcing her to withdraw from his house and family.[2]   Marriage within the forbidden degrees of affinity or consanguinity
(7) was made a ground in the same year;[3] lunacy of the
wife (8) came next in 1843;[4] and in 1854 divorce was sanctioned (9) when the alleged marriage was procured by
fraud, force, or coercion, and has not been later confirmed
by the acts of the person injured; (10) when the wife, by
cruel and barbarous treatment, has rendered the condition
of her husband intolerable or life burdensome; or (11) when
either spouse has been convicted for felony with imprisonment for more than two years.[5]   These eleven causes are

[1] *Laws of the Com.*, VII, 375.

[2] Act of March 13, 1815: in *Laws of Com.* (1822), VI, 286; and Pepper and Lewis,
Digest (1896), I, 1633.

[3] *Laws of the Com.* (1822), VI, 288; Pepper and Lewis, *Digest*, I, 1634. But when
marriages within such degrees "shall not have been dissolved during the lifetime of
the parties, the unlawfulness of the same shall not be enquired into after the death
of either husband or wife."

[4] By the act of April 13, 1843: *Laws* (1843), 233; Pepper and Lewis, *Digest*, I,
1636, "where the wife is lunatic or *non compos mentis*" a petition for divorce may be
"exhibited by any relative or next friend" who shall make the affidavit provided
for in other cases of divorce.

[5] Act of May 8: *Laws* (1854), 644; Pepper and Lewis, *Digest* (1896), I, 1635.
When divorce is granted the husband for the tenth cause, the wife may be allowed
alimony according to his circumstances.

By an act of March 9, 1855 (*Pub. Laws*, 68; Pepper and Lewis, *Digest*, I, 1636),
the courts of common pleas are given jurisdiction in all cases of divorce "from the

still in force, although in 1903 a new law regarding the
crimes of either spouse to constitute a cause was adopted.[1]

On the other hand, the century has produced but one
change in the special grounds of partial divorce. Petitions
for separation from bed and board are still allowed only in
favor of the wife. The four causes sanctioned in 1785,
re-enacted in 1815 and 1817, are yet in force;[2] while, since
1862, adultery on the part of the husband is admitted as a
fifth ground of complaint.[3]

An important innovation appears in 1893. A new group
of discretionary causes is then created. The courts are
empowered to grant the wife a divorce, either from bed and
board or from the bond of wedlock, on four several grounds.
Three of these are identical with the third, fourth, and fifth
causes of partial divorce just enumerated. In addition, two
years' "wilful and malicious desertion" by the husband is
admitted. These same four causes are declared valid "where
it shall be shown to the court by any wife that she was
formerly a citizen of this commonwealth, and that having
intermarried with a citizen of any other state or any foreign
country, she has been compelled to abandon the habitation
and domicile of her husband" in such place, thereby being
"forced to return to this commonwealth in which she had
her former domicile." In any such case, if personal service
by subpœna cannot be made upon the husband by reason of

bonds of matrimony for the cause of personal abuse, or for such conduct on the part
of either the husband or the wife as to render the condition of the other party
intolerable and life burdensome, notwithstanding the parties were at the time of
the occurring of said causes domiciled in another state;" but the applicant must be
a citizen and have been a resident of the state for one year. This act, according to
judicial interpretation, does not establish new causes for divorce, but only enlarges
the jurisdiction of the court in reference to the parties under causes already recognized: Schlichter v. Schlichter, 10 *Phila. Reports*, 11 (1873). Cruel and barbarous
treatment must be alleged in the libel: Pennington v. Pennington, *ibid.*, 22.

[1] *Laws of Pa.* (1903), 19; repealing the act of June 1, 1891: *ibid.* (1891), 142.

[2] PEPPER AND LEWIS, *Digest* (1896), I, 1637. *Cf.* the act of March 13, 1815: *Laws
of the Com.* (1822), VI, 286; and *Laws* (1817), 405.

[3] *Laws* (1862), 430; PEPPER AND LEWIS, *Digest*, I, 1637, 1638.

his non-residence, the court before entering a decree shall require proof that, in addition to the publication required by law, actual or constructive notice of the proceedings has been given him, either "by personal service or by registered letter to his last known place of residence, and that a reasonable time has thereby been afforded to him to appear" and make defense. The wife, however, is only entitled to the benefits of this act when she has been a citizen and resident of the state for one year previous to bringing suit.[1]

It must further be observed, in connection with the present laws of Pennsylvania regarding absolute divorce, that the principle of the colonial statute touching cases of long absence has unfortunately been perpetuated. The snare is still set for the feet of the unwary. "If any husband or wife, upon false rumor, in appearance well founded, of the death of the other (when such other has been absent for the space of two whole years), hath married . . . . again, he or she shall not be liable to the pains of adultery;" but on return the person remaining unmarried may elect either to have the former spouse restored or to have the former contract dissolved, leaving the second marriage undisturbed.[2]

By the Delaware statute of February 3, 1832, the superior court is authorized to grant absolute divorce, or, in its discretion, partial divorce or merely alimony, where either spouse (1) had a lawful husband or wife living at the time of the marriage; (2) has been wilfully absent from the other for three years with the intention of abandonment; (3) has committed adultery; or (4) extreme cruelty; or (5) where

---

[1] Act of June 20: *Laws* (1893), 471; PEPPER AND LEWIS, *Digest*, I, 1638, 1639.

[2] Act of 1815: *Laws of the Commonwealth* (1822), VI, 288; PEPPER AND LEWIS, *Digest* (1896), I, 1634.

"While a well-founded belief in the death of her first husband will relieve a woman marrying a second time from the pains of adultery, it cannot validate her second marriage, if, in fact, her first husband was living when it was solemnized."— Thomas *v.* Thomas, 124 *Pa.*, 646; s. c., 23 *W. N. C.*, 410 (1889). *Cf.* PEPPER AND LEWIS, *Digest*, I, 1634, ed. note.

the male was actually impotent when the marriage took place.[1] Just twenty years later an entirely new grouping of causes and kinds of separation was introduced. The superior court is empowered to grant a full divorce (1) for adultery of the wife; and (2) for impotency of either person at the time of marriage; while separation from bed and board is allowed (1) for adultery of the husband; (2) for extreme cruelty; or (3) for wilful absence of either for three years with intent to abandon. At the same time a distinction was made between divorce and annulment. The court is authorized to declare null and void a marriage (1) within the prohibited degrees of affinity or consanguinity; (2) between a white person and a negro or mulatto; (3) where either person was insane; or (4) had a spouse living at the time of the contract.[2] At present the annulment of voidable contracts is still governed by the enactment of 1852.[3]

In 1859 a revised scheme was substituted. Absolute divorce is authorized on the same two grounds as in 1852, the unjust discrimination regarding the husband's infidelity being still maintained. On the other hand, "a divorce from the bond of matrimony, or from bed and board, at the discretion of the court," may now be decreed for (1) adultery of the husband; (2) extreme cruelty; (3) procurement of the marriage by force or fraud; (4) want of legal age—sixteen for males and fourteen for females—if after that age the marriage has not been voluntarily ratified; (5) wilful abandonment for three years; (6) conviction in any place, before or after marriage, of a crime deemed felony by the laws of the state; (7) habitual gross drunkenness for three years, contracted after marriage; or (8) three years' wilful neglect by the husband to provide his wife with the common necessaries of life.[4]

[1] Laws of Del. (1832), 148–50.   [2] Rev. Stat. of Del. (1852), 238.
[3] Rev. Stat. (1893), 596.
[4] Act of Feb. 24, 1859, amending the act of 1852: Laws (1859), 730, 731.

By the present law of Delaware, which has existed since 1873, the superior court may decree absolute divorce for (1) adultery in either spouse; (2) desertion for three years; (3) habitual drunkenness; (4) impotency at the time of marriage; (5) extreme cruelty; or (6) conviction of felony, as in 1859. The discretionary grounds on which the court may grant either full or limited divorce are now reduced to two, these in substance being nearly identical with the fourth and eighth causes sanctioned by the statute of 1859.[1]

The history of judicial divorce in the West begins with the statute adopted for the Northwest Territory in 1795. Jurisdiction is vested in the general court and the circuit courts, which are empowered to grant absolute divorce (1) for adultery; (2) impotency; (3) where either person had a husband or wife alive at the time of the second marriage; or to grant partial divorce for extreme cruelty in either spouse.[2] This law was repealed in 1804 by an act of the legislature of Ohio—that portion of the Northwest Territory having been made a state in 1802—giving the supreme court sole cognizance of divorce suits. By it no provision for partial divorce is made; but full dissolution of marriage is sanctioned (1) for bigamy, as in 1795; (2) for wilful absence for five years; (3) for adultery; and (4) for extreme cruelty.[3] After eighteen years' trial, the plan of 1804 was in its turn superseded. Six grounds of absolute divorce were then provided. Of these four are identical with those just mentioned, except that the term of wilful absence is reduced to three years. In addition there are recognized (5) physical incompetence

---

[1] *Cf.* Act of March 12: *Laws of Del.* (1873), 633–35; or the same in *Rev. Stat.* (1874), 475; with *Rev. Stat.* (1893), 595.

The discretionary grounds are now (1) " procurement of the marriage by fraud for want of age, the husband being under the age of eighteen years or the wife being under the age of sixteen years at the time of the marriage, and such marriage not being after those ages voluntarily ratified;" (2) "wilful neglect on the part of the husband for three years to provide for his wife the necessaries of life suitable to her condition."

[2] CHASE, *Stat.*, I, 192, 193 (act of July 15, 1795).   [3] *Ibid.*, 493, 494.

at the time of the marriage; and (6) sentence with actual imprisonment for violation of the criminal laws of the state, provided application be made during the term of confinement.[1] Two years later a new plan was adopted. Absolute divorce was permitted for the six causes allowed in 1822; and partial divorce, which had not existed by statute for twenty years, was revived; the courts, on the same six grounds, being authorized, instead of full dissolution of wedlock, to decree separation from bed and board, or merely alimony, according to justice and the circumstances in each case.[2] This provision, however, was short-lived; for in 1833 partial divorce was a second time abolished.[3]

Thus matters stood until 1853, when a measure appeared by which the law was much relaxed in several important respects. Jurisdiction, which since 1804 had remained solely in the supreme tribunal of the state, was now vested in the several courts of common pleas. In addition to the six grounds for full divorce already created, four new causes were recognized. These were (7) fraudulent contract; (8) gross neglect of duty; (9) habitual drunkenness for three years; and (10) a decree of divorce in another state "by virtue of which the party who shall have obtained such decree shall have been released from the obligations of the marriage contract, while the same remains binding upon the other."[4]

These ten causes of absolute divorce are still sanctioned by Ohio law. No provision is made for limited divorce; but there is an "action for alimony, which is in effect a limited divorce, and which may be brought by the wife for any of the following causes," also sanctioned by the act of 1853:

1 Act of Jan. 11, 1822: CHASE, Stat., II, 1210, 1211.

2 Act of Jan. 7, 1824: CHASE, Stat., II, 1408, 1409.

3 Act of Feb. 22, 1833: CHASE, Stat., III, 1934.

4 Act of March 11, 1853: SWAN, Stat. of Ohio (1854), 324-28. But the provision regarding sentence and imprisonment is differently worded. At present (BATES, Ann. Rev. Stat. (1900), II, 2948) the paragraph reads: "The imprisonment of either party in a penitentiary under sentence thereto; but the petition for divorce under this clause shall be filed during the imprisonment of the adverse party."

(1) adultery; (2) any gross neglect of duty; (3) abandonment without good cause; (4) separation in consequence of the husband's ill-treatment, whether the wife is maintained by him or not; (5) habitual drunkenness; and (6) sentence to imprisonment in a penitentiary, if application be made while the husband is so confined.[1]

Indiana, in 1816, is the next portion of the Northwest Territory to be admitted to the Union. Two years after the attainment of statehood her legislature passed the first divorce statute, granting jurisdiction to the circuit courts. By the enactment full divorce in favor of either spouse when aggrieved is allowed for (1) adultery; (2) matrimonial incapacity; (3) bigamous contract; (4) two years' absence with intent to abandon; (5) desertion and living in adultery; (6) conviction for felony; and (7) in favor of the wife when the husband's treatment of her is extremely barbarous and inhuman.[2] In 1824 an "omnibus" clause was introduced, a full divorce being then allowed on petition of the injured person (8) "in all cases where the court in its discretion" shall deem the same "just and reasonable."[3] These grounds are all sanctioned by the act of 1831.[4] Still another cause was admitted in 1836. The circuit courts are empowered to grant the wife absolute divorce (9) when the husband for two years has been a habitual drunkard, and has failed for "any unreasonable length of time to make provision for his family." By the same act, moreover, a marriage may be dissolved "in all cases where the parties have been guilty of murder, manslaughter, burglary, robbery, grand or petty larceny, forgery, counterfeiting, arson, bribery, perjury, or any other crime" the penalty for which on conviction is

[1] For the present law of Ohio see Bates, *Ann. Rev. Stat.* (1897), II, 2804-10. *Cf.* Wright, *Report*, 106. Jurisdiction is still vested in the courts of common pleas, although in certain counties the probate courts have cognizance: Bates, *op. cit.*, II, 2804.

[2] Act of Jan. 26, 1818: *Laws of the State of Ind.* (1818), 226-29.

[3] *Rev. Laws* (1824), 156, 157; same in *ibid.* (1831), 213-15.

[4] Act of Jan. 17, 1831: *Rev. Laws* (1831), 213.

"imprisonment at hard labor in the penitentiary."[1] But, apparently, this is meant to be a restatement of the sixth cause above given.[2]

Only two years elapsed before a new general statute was adopted, authorizing full divorce on eight grounds. Six of these correspond to the first, second, sixth, seventh, eighth, and ninth causes already sanctioned. Bigamous marriage and desertion with adultery no longer appear as causes; while the fourth ground, as above enumerated, is so modified as to require a separate statement for the husband and wife respectively. The husband (7) is allowed a full divorce for two years' absence of the wife with intent to abandon; and the wife is granted the same relief (8) for like absence of the husband, "and also for any other cause or causes"—a most singular legislative freak.[3] In 1843 this vicious clause was dropped. Abandonment for two years is now made a cause of divorce in favor of either person, thus reducing the number of legal grounds to seven. At the same time, in modification of a cause already existing, the wife is allowed a petition on account of "cruel and inhuman treatment" by the husband, "or when his conduct towards her has been such as may render it unsafe and improper for her to live with him." The other five causes sanctioned by the statute of 1838 are re-enacted without change.[4] A relaxation of the law takes place in 1849. One year's abandonment is declared sufficient to constitute a cause; but in such case the court is especially empowered, in its discretion, to grant a divorce, waiving all objections in regard to time of separation, if it deems a reconciliation "hopeless."[5]

[1] Laws of a Gen. Nature (1836), 69.

[2] Nevertheless, the act of 1836 provides for causes in addition to those sanctioned by the act of 1831, which includes conviction for felony as in 1818.

[3] Rev. Stat. (1838), 242–44. The sixth ground, as enumerated in the text, the first of this act, is "any crime" committed in the United States or the territories, the punishment for which is deemed "infamous."

[4] Rev. Stat. (1843), 598 ff.   [5] Act of June 1: Gen. Laws (1849), 62, 63.

A pause of three years next ensues before the lawmaker resumes his tinkering with the causes of divorce. The act of 1852 admits the seven general grounds, as these had existed since the change in 1849; but with two important modifications. For now "habitual drunkenness," without reference to the term during which it has existed, and cruel treatment, each on the part of either husband or wife, are constituted reasons for dissolving the marriage bond. By the same law a divorce for adultery is denied when there has been (1) connivance; (2) voluntary cohabitation after knowledge of the offense; (3) neglect to petition within two years; or (4) when the petitioner is guilty of the same crime.[1] Seven years later the time of abandonment, to constitute a cause, was reduced to one year, the court being thus deprived of its discretionary power to grant a divorce for desertion during a shorter period.[2]

Finally the long series of enactments defining the grounds of absolute divorces came to a halt in 1873, when the law of Indiana in this regard took its present form. The superior and circuit courts, on petition of either spouse, are granted jurisdiction. Three very important and beneficial amendments, producing a marked decrease in the number of divorces annually granted, are now made. The term of abandonment is increased from one year to two years; "failure of the husband to make reasonable provision for his family" is changed to such failure for a "period of two years;" and, most significant of all, the omnibus clause, existing since 1824 and rephrased in 1838, providing that divorces may be granted "for any other cause" which the court shall deem "reasonable and proper," is stricken out.[3] As a result, the marriage tie may now be dissolved for (1) adultery; (2) impotence existing at the time of the mar-

---

[1] Rev. Stat. (1852), II, 233–38.   [2] Laws of Ind. (1859), 108.
[3] For construction of the omnibus clause, see Ritter v. Ritter, 5 Blackf., 81.

riage; (3) abandonment for two years; (4) cruel and inhuman treatment; (5) habitual drunkenness; (6) failure of the husband to make reasonable provision for his family for two years; (7) the conviction of either person, in any country, subsequent to the marriage, of an infamous crime. Until very recently limited divorce was not recognized in Indiana; but a married woman might bring action for the support of herself and infant children in the following cases, being analogous to those sanctioned by the Ohio law: (1) when the husband shall have deserted his wife, or wife and children, without leaving sufficient provision for support; (2) when he shall have been convicted of felony and imprisoned in the state prison, not leaving his wife, or wife and children, the same provision; (3) when he is a habitual drunkard and by reason thereof becomes incapacitated or neglects to provide for his family; or (4) when he renounces the marriage covenant, or refuses to live with his wife in the conjugal relation, by joining himself to a sect or denomination the rules and doctrines of which require such renunciation or forbid a man and woman to dwell and cohabit together in the conjugal relation according to the true intent and meaning of the institution of marriage.[1] A statute of 1903 authorizes separation from bed and board "for a limited time" in case of (1) adultery; (2) "desertion, or where the wife is plaintiff, neglect or refusal to suitably provide for her, covering a period of six months;" (3) habitual cruelty of one party, "or such constant strifes of both parties as render their living together intolerable;" (4) habitual drunkenness, "or the confirmed and excessive use of morphine, cocaine, or any other drug;" (5) gross and wanton neglect of conjugal duty for six months.[2]

[1] Act of March 10: *Laws of Ind.* (1873), 107–12; also HORNER, *Rev. Stat.* (1896), I, secs. 1024–49; II, sec. 5132; BURNS, *Ann. Stat.* (1901), I, 443, 444; III, 559.

[2] *Laws of Ind.* (1903), 114, 115.

In 1818, closely following Indiana, Illinois was carved from the bountiful region northwest of the Ohio River. After a year's delay, a divorce law was enacted in 1819; and this, as amended in 1825, authorizes both kinds of separation. Full dissolution of wedlock may be granted for (1) physical incapacity at the time of solemnization; (2) adultery; (3) two years' voluntary and continued absence. Partial divorce is likewise sanctioned for (1) extreme and repeated cruelty in either spouse: or (2) constant and habitual intemperance in either for two years. "But in the latter case it shall be incumbent on the complaining party to show that he or she had performed all the duties of a faithful and affectionate husband or wife."[1]

The act of 1827 is silent as to limited divorce, which has not since been recognized in Illinois. Full divorce may now be granted by the circuit courts, sitting as courts of equity, when either person (1) was at the time of the marriage and still is naturally impotent; (2) had a husband or wife living at the time of the marriage; (3) has since been guilty of adultery; or (4) wilful desertion for two years; or (5) extreme and repeated cruelty; or (6) habitual drunkenness for two years.[2] A step backward was taken in 1832 through the adoption of a kind of omnibus clause. By proceedings in chancery full dissolution of marriage is authorized (7) for all causes of divorce not provided for by any law of the state.[3] Next, after an interval of thirteen years, on the petition of the aggrieved, comes (8) conviction for felony or other infamous crime.[4] This is followed after the lapse of thirty years more by the sanction (9) of absolute divorce

[1] Act of Jan. 17, 1825, to amend an act of Feb. 22, 1819: *Laws of Ill.* (1825), 169.

[2] *Rev. Code* (1827), 180, 181.

[3] Act of Dec. 4, 1832: *Rev. Laws* (1833), 234, 235. In the statutes this is not enumerated as a cause; but it surely is one in effect.

[4] *Rev. Stat.* (1845), 196; also in Purple, *Comp.* (1856), I, 493, 494; and in *Stat. of Ill.* (1864), 150, 152.

when either person "has attempted the life of the other by poison or other means showing malice."[1]

The tale of causes allowed by the present law of Illinois is thus complete. Separation from bed and board is not provided for by statute. In general, chancery process is required. The circuit courts of the respective counties and the superior court of Cook county (Chicago) are clothed with jurisdiction in divorce controversies.[2]

Michigan became a separate territory in 1805, and seven years thereafter the supreme court was granted jurisdiction in both kinds of divorce.[3] By the act of 1819 marriage may be dissolved for adultery in either spouse, when the husband and wife are inhabitants of the territory, or when the marriage was solemnized therein; as also when the injured person was an actual resident of the territory at the time of the offense, and so remains when the bill is filed. When guilty, the wife forfeits her right of dower. On the other hand, the court may grant her a divorce *a mensa*, forever or for a limited time, (1) for "cruel and inhuman treatment;" (2) for such conduct on the part of the husband "as may render it unsafe and improper for her to cohabit with him and be under his dominion and control;" or (3) when "he has abandoned her and refuses or neglects to provide" for her support.[4]

A different plan appears in 1832. A divorce from the bond of wedlock is now permitted (1) for impotency, and (2) for adultery. Furthermore, the court, in its discretion, is empowered to grant either person a full or a partial divorce (1) for extreme cruelty, or (2) for five years' wilful deser-

---

[1] Act of March 10, 1874: Gross, *Stat. of Ill., 1818-74* (3d ed., 1872-74), III, 176.

[2] Hurd, *Rev. Stat.* (1898), 631-34. *Cf. Rev. Stat.* (1845), 196, 197; and Starr and Curtis, *Ann. Stat.* (1896), II, 1435-55.

[3] Act of 1812: *Territorial Laws of Mich.*, I, 183.

[4] Act of Nov. 13, 1819: *Territorial Laws of Mich.*, I, 495-98; *cf.* the act of Apr. 12, 1827: *ibid.*. II, 363-66, repeating the provisions given in the text from the act of 1816.

tion. By this act jurisdiction is vested in the supreme court and either of the circuit courts of the territory.[1] A statute of the next year retains all these provisions of 1832, except that the term of wilful desertion, to constitute a discretionary ground, is reduced to three years.[2] Five years later, after Michigan became a state, a divorce is made unnecessary when a marriage is void or when the persons contracting it are below the age of consent. At the same time the grounds of separation are reconsidered. Absolute divorce is now authorized (1) for adultery; (2) for impotence; (3) for five years' desertion; (4) for sentence to imprisonment at hard labor for three years or more; and either a full or a partial divorce, on the petition of either spouse, (1) for extreme cruelty; (2) for three years' "utter desertion;" or (3) on application of the wife, when the husband, being of sufficient ability to provide a suitable maintenance for her, "shall grossly or wantonly and cruelly refuse or neglect to do so."[3] In 1844 extreme cruelty, "whether practiced by using personal violence, or by any other means," was substituted for the corresponding clause in the act of 1838.[4] Next, in 1846 and 1847 came swift changes in the law of desertion, but only in their turn to be swept away in 1848.[5] So in 1851 we reach an act by which the grounds of divorce in Michigan have been determined for half a century.

By the existing law, as then enacted, on application of the aggrieved, a full divorce may be decreed by the court of chancery, or by the circuit court of the county where the parties or one of them resides, for (1) adultery; (2) physical incompetency; (3) sentence to imprisonment for three years

---

[1] Act of June 28, 1832: *Ter. Laws of Mich.*, III, 931, 932.

[2] Act of Apr. 4, 1833: *Ter. Laws of Mich.*, III, 1005-7.

[3] *Rev. Stat.* (1838), 336, 337.   [4] *Acts* (1844), 74.

[5] The *Rev. Stat.* (1846), 333, make the term of desertion two years for either absolute or limited divorce. The *Acts* (1847), 168, 169, lengthen the period to five years for absolute divorce and three years for partial divorce. But these changes are repealed by *Acts* (1848), 194.

or more, no pardon to affect the status of the divorced persons; (4) two years' desertion; (5) when the husband or wife shall have become a habitual drunkard; "and (6) the circuit courts may, in their discretion, upon application as in other cases, divorce from the bonds of matrimony any party who is a resident of this state, and whose husband or wife shall have obtained a divorce in any other state." The same tribunals are authorized, in their discretion, to grant either a limited or a full divorce in favor of the aggrieved for (1) extreme cruelty, "whether practiced by using personal violence, or by any other means;" (2) utter desertion for two years; or (3) on complaint of the wife for the husband's neglect to provide, as by the law of 1838.[1]

Wisconsin, the remaining[2] portion of the region originally governed by the ordinance of 1787, was erected into a separate territory in 1836. Its divorce legislation, which in its general outline is similar to that of Michigan, began in 1838–39, when the district court of each county was given jurisdiction in both kinds of separation. The causes of absolute divorce then recognized are (1) impotence; (2) adultery. Those of partial divorces are (1) extreme cruelty; (2) two years' wilful desertion; (3) habitual drunkenness; (4) abandonment of the wife by the husband, or "his refusal or neglect to provide for her."[3]

In 1849, the year following the attainment of statehood, was adopted a new statute by which the foundation of the present system was laid. By it, as under the present law, a marriage is declared absolutely dissolved without any decree of divorce or legal process whenever either spouse is sentenced to imprisonment for life; and a pardon is not to effect a restoration of conjugal rights. The circuit courts

---

[1] Howell, *Gen. Stat.* (1882-83), II, 1621-30; Miller, *Comp. Laws* (1899), III, 2653–66; *cf. Acts* (1851), 71, 72. The partial divorce may, as originally, be "forever or for a limited time."

[2] Except a part of Minnesota.

[3] *Stat. of the Ter. of Wis.* (1838–39), 140, 141.

are granted jurisdiction.   Both full and partial divorce are provided for.   Absolute divorce is allowed for (1) adultery; (2) impotence; (3) sentence of either spouse to imprisonment for a period of three years or more, no pardon working a restoration of conjugal rights; (4) wilful desertion for one year next preceding the commencement of the action; (5) when the treatment of the wife by the husband has been "cruel and inhuman, whether practiced by using personal violence, or by any other means," or "when the wife shall be guilty of like cruelty to her husband or shall be given to intoxication;" (6) when the husband or wife shall have been a habitual drunkard for the space of one year immediately preceding the filing of the bill.   To these grounds was added as a cause in 1866: (7) voluntarily living entirely separate for the five years next preceding the commencement of the action.[1]   So the law of absolute divorce remains at the present time, all attempts to make insanity a permanent ground having thus far failed.[2]

The history of partial divorce in Wisconsin is soon told. The provisions of the act of 1849 are still in force.   The causes of separation from bed and board, forever or for a limited time, there recognized are (1) the fourth, fifth, and sixth grounds of full divorce above specified; (2) extreme cruelty of either spouse; (3) on complaint of the wife when the husband, being of sufficient ability, shall refuse or neglect to provide for her; or (4) when his conduct toward her is such as may render it unsafe and improper

[1] Act of March 31, *Gen. Laws* (1866), 40.

[2] In 1856 the court in its discretion was authorized to decree a divorce when either spouse shall become incurably insane and "shall have so remained for the term of seven years continuously," the husband being required to give bond with security for the maintenance of the wife during her life: Act of March 31, *Gen. Acts* (1856), 96.   After two years this act was repealed: *Gen. Laws* (1858), 82.   A second attempt was made in 1881.   A full divorce was then authorized when either husband or wife shall have been insane for the space of five years immediately preceding the commencement of the action, and the court shall be satisfied that the insanity is incurable: Act of April 2, *Laws* (1881), 376-78.   This statute was repealed the next year: *Laws* (1882), 798.

for her to live with him. It is expressly declared that a
divorce from the bond of matrimony may be decreed for
either of the three causes last named, "whenever, in the
opinion of the court, the circumstances of the case are such
that it will be discreet and proper to do so." From the
somewhat awkward arrangement of its provisions, therefore,
the general effect of this statute appears to be that a full
divorce *may* be granted for any ground recognized by it,
provided the court deems it prudent to exercise its discretionary authority. Furthermore, it must be noted that by
the existing law, just as in 1849, the circuit court is empowered to allow separate maintenance when a partial divorce is
denied.[1]

We may next pass to the long list of new states in the
West and Northwest whose generous boundaries spread over
the Mississippi valley, the vast regions of the Rocky Moun-
tains, and the Pacific slope. The course of legislation in
Minnesota has run closely parallel to that of Wisconsin,
though it is divergent in some important details. In 1851,
seven years before the admission of that state to the Union,
a statute logically declared bigamous marriages and those
within the forbidden degrees, if solemnized in the territory,
void without a decree. At the same time, as causes of absolute divorce in favor of the aggrieved were sanctioned (1)
adultery; (2) impotency; (3) sentence to imprisonment in
the penitentiary after the marriage, no subsequent pardon
effecting a restoration of conjugal rights; (4) wilful desertion for one year next preceding the commencement of the
suit; (5) cruel and inhuman treatment, whether practiced
by using personal violence or by any other means; (6)
habitual drunkenness for one year immediately preceding
the filing of the complaint. By this act no provision is

---

[1] *Cf. Rev. Stat.* (1849), 393–98; *ibid.* (1858), 623–28; *ibid.* (1872), II, 1269–76; *Ann.
Stat.* (1889), I, 1362–75; and SANBORN AND BERRYMAN, *Wis. Stat.* (1899), I, 1702–20.

made for partial divorce.[1] The term of wilful desertion
was increased from one year to three years in 1866;[2] but
in 1895 the shorter period was restored, so that under
the existing law the six grounds of absolute divorce as
sanctioned in 1851 are recognized, except that "cruel and
inhuman treatment" is constituted a cause, the original
explanatory clause being omitted.[3] On the other hand,
limited divorce is now provided for. Since 1876, on complaint of a married woman, separation from bed and board
is authorized (1) for cruel and inhuman treatment by the
husband; (2) for such conduct on his part as may render it
unsafe and improper for her to cohabit with him; or (3) for
abandonment and refusal or neglect by him to provide for
her. The district court of the county where the persons or
one of them resides is now vested with jurisdiction in all
actions for divorce or for the annulment of marriage.[4]

One of the worst and most characteristic features of American state legislation is seen in the session laws of Iowa,
where the statute-maker is perennially engaged in adopting,
changing, abrogating, or re-enacting plans of divorce and
alimony. The first step was taken in 1838, when the district court of the county where the persons or one of them
resides was given jurisdiction on the petition of the aggrieved.
The grounds of absolute divorce then allowed are (1) impotence; and (2) adultery. Those of divorce *a mensa* or of
divorce from the bond of wedlock, in the discretion of the
court, are (1) extreme cruelty; or (2) wilful desertion for
one year.[5] This law was repealed and a new one adopted in

[1] *Rev. Stat. of Minn.* (1851), 272-76.

[2] *Gen. Stat. of Minn.* (1866), 408-12. "The revisers repeated this chapter under
two titles, the second being entitled ' Limited Divorces,' but the legislature rejected
Title II and did not change or amend Title I."—*Ibid.*, 408, note.

[3] Act of April 22, *Session Laws* (1895), 158. *Cf. Gen. Stat.* (1894), I, 1267, for the law
modified in 1866.

[4] *Cf. Laws* (1876), chap. 118; *Gen. Stat. of Minn.* (1894), I, 1273, 1267; *Session Laws*
(1895), 158.

[5] Act of Dec. 29, 1838: *Laws of Ia.* (1838-39), 179, 180.

the next year.　Nothing is now said of separation from bed and board; but a full divorce may be had by the injured spouse for (1) impotency; (2) bigamous marriage; (3) adultery; (4) one year's desertion; (5) felony; (6) habitual drunkenness; (7) cruel treatment; (8) indignities.[1]　Three years later this statute in turn gave place to another by which the same causes are sanctioned, except, under the sixth head, it is provided that "said habitual drunkenness shall be contracted after marriage."[2]　In 1846, however, this proviso was dropped; and at the same time an "omnibus" clause was sanctioned.　A full divorce may now be granted (9) "when it shall be made fully apparent to the satisfaction of the court, that the parties cannot live in peace and happiness together, and that their welfare requires a separation."[3]　The eighth ground was dropped in 1851, and at the same time it was again specified under the sixth head that drunkenness shall have become habitual after marriage.[4]

Thus matters stood until 1855, when the worthy legislators managed to put the law in a curiously awkward shape. It was then decreed that "hereafter no divorce otherwise than from bed and board shall be granted except" (1) where either spouse shall commit adultery; (2) be convicted of felony; (3) was impotent at the time of the marriage; or (4) wilfully deserts the other for the space of three years.　"In all other enumerated causes heretofore deemed sufficient"—continues the statute—"no divorce otherwise than a divorce from bed and board shall be granted."[5]　This scheme was short-lived.　An act of 1858 revives the law as it stood in 1851, except that the term of wilful desertion was extended

---

[1] Act of Jan. 17, 1840: *Laws of Ia.* (1839–40), 120–22.

[2] Act of Jan. 20, 1843: *Rev. Stat. of Ia.* (1843), 237–41.

[3] Act of Jan. 17, 1846: *Laws of Ia.* (1845–46), 23.　　　　[4] *Code of Ia.* (1851), 223.

[5] Act of Jan. 24, 1855: *Laws of Ia.* (1854–55), 112, 113.

to two years and the omnibus clause was omitted, thus leaving seven grounds of petition in force.[1]

The present law of Iowa governing the causes of divorce took its rise in the code of 1873. The district court in the county where the plaintiff or defendant resides still has jurisdiction. Limited divorce is not recognized, but "it appears that courts of equity will grant alimony without divorce to a wife where she is separated from her husband because of his misconduct, though no express statutory provision is found authorizing such proceeding."[2] A full divorce may be decreed against the husband (1) when he has committed adultery subsequent to the marriage; (2) when he wilfully deserts his wife and absents himself without reasonable cause for the space of two years; (3) when after marriage he is convicted of felony; or (4) becomes addicted to habitual drunkenness; or (5) when he is guilty of such inhuman treatment as to endanger the life of his wife; and against the wife, for the five causes just enumerated, and also (6) when at the time of the marriage she was pregnant by a man other than her husband, unless the husband then had an illegitimate child or children living and the fact was unknown to her.[3]

The divorce legislation of Kansas begins in 1855, the next year after the territory was erected. The grounds on which the aggrieved may secure a complete dissolution of the matrimonial bond are (1) impotence continuing from the time of the marriage; (2) bigamous marriage; (3) adultery; (4) wilful desertion and absence for two years without reasonable cause; (5) conviction of felony or infamous crime; (6) habitual drunkenness for two years; (7) cruel and bar-

[1] Act of March 15: *Laws of Ia.* (1858), 97, 98.

[2] Wright, *Report*, 96. *Cf.* Graves *v.* Graves, 36 *Ia.*, 310; Whitcomb *v.* Whitcomb, 46 *Ia.*, 437.

[3] *Cf. Ann. Code of Ia.* (1897), 1135-47; and *Code of Ia.* (1873), 399-401; also *Laws of Ia.* (1870), 429 (jurisdiction).

barous treatment endangering life; (8) intolerable indignities offered to the person; (9) vagrancy of the husband.[1] In
1859 this law gave place to another, by which the fifth,
eighth, and ninth causes above enumerated were omitted;
the term of wilful absence, under the fourth head, was reduced to one year; and habitual drunkenness became a
cause, without specification of the time during which it must
have existed.[2] The very next year this plan was in its turn
superseded. A new act allowed separate alimony without
dissolution of marriage, and sanctioned eleven grounds of
total divorce. The first four of these are identical with the
corresponding numbers in 1855, as modified in 1859. In
addition are approved (5) pregnancy of the wife at the time
of the marriage by a man other than the husband; (6) extreme cruelty; (7) fraudulent contract; (8) gross neglect of
duty; (9) habitual drunkenness; (10) sentence for crime and
imprisonment therefor in a penitentiary, provided complaint
be filed during the term of confinement; (11) when one person has secured a divorce in another state or territory, leaving the obligation binding on the other.[3]

The eleventh cause just specified was dropped in 1868.
The remaining ten were then re-enacted;[4] and these grounds,
without addition or essential change, constitute the law of
Kansas at the present time. In this state there is no separation from bed and board. But "the wife may obtain alimony alone from the husband without a divorce . . . . for
any of the causes for which a divorce may be granted."[5] By

---

[1] *Stat. of Kan.* (1855), 310, 311.   [2] Act of Feb. 7: *Gen. Laws of Kan.* (1859), 385.

[3] Act of Feb. 27: *Gen. Laws of Kan.* (1860), 105-10. An Act of June 4, 1861, provides that a person presenting a copy of an act of the Territory of Kansas by which
he has been divorced "shall be entitled to a decree of divorce without issuing summons thereon."— *Gen. Laws* (1861), 146.

[4] "Code of Civil Procedure," approved Feb. 25, 1868, Art. XXVIII: in PRICE,
RIGGS, AND MCCAHON, *Gen. Stat. of Kan.*, 757-59. The law of 1868 reappears in
DASSLER, *Laws of Kan.* (1876), II, 761-63; *ibid.* (1879), 690-92.

[5] *Laws of Kan.* (1897), II, 273-77; DASSLER, *Gen. Stat.* (1901), 1055.

the constitution, jurisdiction in all divorce actions is vested
in the district courts;[1] and the supreme court has authority
when suits are brought up on error.[2]

Both kinds of separation are provided for by the Nebraska
law of 1856; and a marriage is then declared to be completely dissolved without decree in case of conviction and
imprisonment for life. The district court of the county
where the married persons or one of them resides is empowered to grant absolute divorce on complaint of the aggrieved
for (1) adultery; (2) physical incompetency at the time of
the marriage; (3) sentence to imprisonment for three years
or more, no pardon effecting a restoration of conjugal rights;
(4) two years' wilful abandonment without good cause; (5)
habitual drunkenness. The same tribunal may decree either
a limited or a full divorce for (1) extreme cruelty; or (2) two
years' utter desertion by either spouse; and (3) in favor of
the wife, when the husband, being of sufficient ability, shall
grossly or wantonly and cruelly refuse or neglect to provide
for her.[3] No essential change appears in the statutes until
1875, when imprisonment for life was made a sixth ground
of absolute divorce;[4] and so the law of Nebraska remains at
the present hour.[5]

Separation from bed and board has at no time been
authorized by the laws of Colorado. The district courts
have jurisdiction. Full divorce may now be granted in favor
of the aggrieved on eight grounds; and in this regard there
have been few changes since the first statute of 1861. The
present causes are (1) impotence continuing from the time

---

[1] Art. II, sec. 18, Const. of 1859.

[2] See Ulrich v. Ulrich, 8 Kan., 402. Cf. Wesner v. O'Brien, 1 Ct. App., 416; and
McPherson v. the State, 56 Kan., 140 ff.

[3] Act of Jan. 26: Laws (1856), 154–59.

[4] Act of Feb. 19: Laws (1875), 80. Cf. Gen. Stat. of Neb. (1873), 344–51; and Stat. of
Neb., in force Aug. 1, 1867, 128–35, where the causes approved in 1856 appear without
essential change.

[5] Compiled Stat. (1901), 577. The law regarding jurisdiction is the same as in 1856.

of the marriage or originating thereafter in consequence of immoral or criminal conduct; (2) bigamous contract; (3) adultery; (4) one years' wilful desertion and absence without reasonable cause (5) extreme or repeated acts of cruelty, consisting as well in the infliction of mental suffering as of bodily violence; (6) failure on the part of the husband, being in good bodily health, to make reasonable provision for his family for the space of one year; (7) habitual drunkenness of either spouse for the same period; (8) conviction of felony.[1]

Since the original statute of 1870, in Wyoming, a bigamous contract or a marriage where the persons are related within the forbidden degrees, or where either is insane or an idiot, is void without judicial decree.[2]   In that state separation from bed and board has never been sanctioned.   Under the existing law, as it has stood since 1882, absolute divorce is allowed either person when aggrieved for (1) adultery; (2) physical incompetence continuing from the time of the marriage; (3) conviction of a felony and imprisonment therefor in any prison, no subsequent pardon effecting a restitution of conjugal rights; (4) wilful desertion for one year; (5) when either husband or wife has become a habitual drunkard; (6) extreme cruelty; (7) neglect of the husband for the period of one year to provide the common necessaries of life, unless such neglect is the result of poverty which he could not have avoided by ordinary industry; (8) indignities rendering the condition of either spouse intolerable; (9) conduct on the part of the husband constituting him a vagrant within the

---

[1] Act of April 3, 1893: *Laws of Col.*, 236, 237; also in MILLS, *Ann. Stat.* (1897), III, 434.   The sixth cause was added in 1881.   At the same time the term of habitual drunkenness was reduced to one year, instead of two years, as by the law of 1861; while desertion and departure from the territory " without intention of returning," until then a ground for divorce when committed by the husband, was made a ground when committed by either party: *Laws of Col.* (1881), 112; also in *Gen. Stat.* (1883), 397 ff.   The first cause, in its present form, arose in *Laws of Col.* (1885), 189, and it differs somewhat from the original provision in *ibid.* (1861-62), 360.

[2] Act in force Jan. 1, 1870: *Laws* (1869), 274; VAN ORSDEL AND CHATTERTON, *Rev. Stat.* (1899), 794.

meaning of the law; (10) when before the marriage or its solemnization either person shall have been convicted of a felony or infamous crime in any state, territory, or count[r]y without knowledge of the fact by the other at the time of the marriage; (11) when the intended wife at the time of contracting the marriage or its solemnization is pregnant by any man other than her intended husband, and without the latter's knowledge at the time of the solemnization.

Although there is no limited divorce in Wyoming, the law in certain cases allows separate alimony to be granted to the wife without a formal decree of separation.[1]

The legislation of Utah begins in 1852 with an act so faulty that its consequences have become notorious in the divorce annals of the United States.   A vicious residence clause, coupled with a loose requirement regarding notice and an "omnibus" provision among the enumerated grounds of complaint, became in effect a standing temptation to clandestine divorce seekers from outside the territory.   It is formally declared that the court of probate of the county of the plaintiff shall have jurisdiction in all petitions, and these are to be made in writing upon oath or affirmation setting forth the grounds of action.   "If the court is satisfied," continues the statute, "that the person so applying is a resident of the Territory, or wishes to become one; and that the application is made in sincerity and of" the plaintiff's "own free will and choice, and for the purpose set forth in the petition; then the court may decree a divorce from the bonds of matrimony" against the defendant "for any of the following causes, to wit": (1) impotence at the time of the mar-

[1] Act of March 8: *Laws* (1882), 73–81; *Rev. Stat.* (1887), sec. 1571, pp. 419–24; also Van Orsdel and Chatterton, *Rev. Stat.* (1899), 794–800. The first six of the causes above enumerated were introduced by the act which came into force Jan. 1, 1870: *Laws* (1869), 274–81; but then under the third head, conviction and imprisonment for three years or more were necessary to constitute a ground; and by the sixth cause it was required that one of the parties should be "repeatedly guilty of such unhuman treatment as shall endanger the life of the other." The remaining five causes first appeared in 1882.

riage; (2) adultery; (3) wilful desertion or absence without reasonable cause for more than one year; (4) habitual drunkenness subsequent to the marriage; (5) inhuman treatment endangering life; (6) "when it shall be made to appear to the satisfaction and conviction of the court, that the parties cannot live in peace and union together, and that their welfare requires a separation." Nevertheless, the courts are encouraged to adopt a cautious and conservative policy. They are allowed to defer "their decree of divorce, when the same is applied for, to any specified time, not exceeding one year, when it appears" that a compromise may be made; and "during the time of such deference . . . . , the bonds and engagements of matrimony may not be violated by the parties." Furthermore, the court is empowered to punish by fine or imprisonment or both any person "who shall stir up unwarrantable litigation between husband and wife, or seek to bring about a separation between them."

This statute was doubtless made in good faith. For, although it remained in force without change for a quarter of a century, it does not appear that the Latter Day Saints showed any strong tendency to take advantage of its glaring defects. But it is not surprising that evil should come of it. The petitioner in a divorce suit need not be a "*bona fide* resident of the territory. The formal expression of an intention to become a resident was all that was required. The plea of a citizen of any part of the United States that he intended to become a citizen of Utah was entertained equally with that of a regularly domiciled resident."[1] Besides, under the "blanket" provision anything might be alleged in the petition as a ground for action. The natural result was that certain sharp lawyers in eastern cities seized the opportunity to promote clandestine divorce on a large scale. Through their skilful plans and the connivance of local judges, the

[1] WRIGHT, *Report*, 203-6, 156.

courts of several counties were converted into veritable "divorce bureaus," so that between 1875 and 1877 there was a surprising increase in the annual crop of divorce decrees. Accordingly, in 1878 the assembly passed a statute which effectually put an end to this anomalous state of affairs. One year's *bona fide* residence was now required; a decree was forbidden in case of default of the defendant except on legal testimony; better provisions for notice were made; and the "omnibus" clause was abandoned.   By this act, separation from bed and board is not provided for; but an absolute divorce, in favor of the aggrieved, may be granted for (1) impotence at the time of marriage; (2) adultery; (3) wilful desertion for more than one year; (4) wilful neglect of the husband to provide for the wife the common necessaries of life; (5) habitual drunkenness; (6) conviction of felony; (7) cruel treatment, to the extent of causing great bodily injury or great mental distress.[1]   To these grounds in 1903 was added (8) permanent insanity, when the defendant has been duly declared insane five years before.[2]   Furthermore, by an act of 1896 separate maintenance without a decree of divorce is allowed the wife for desertion by the husband or when, without her fault, she is living separate from him.[3]

By an act of 1853 the legislature of Oregon Territory allows divorce petitions presented under oath to be determined by the district court of the county in which the cause occurs, or in which the defendant resides or is found, or in which the plaintiff resides, if in this last case it be either the county in which the parties last cohabited or that in which the plaintiff has resided for six months next preceding the action.   Absolute divorce in favor of the aggrieved is permitted on ten grounds.   These are (1) impotence continuing since marriage; (2) adultery committed since marriage and

---

[1] Act of Feb. 2: *Laws* (1878), 1, 2; also *Rev. Stat. of Utah* (1898), 333, 334.
[2] *Laws of Utah* (1903), 39, 40.   [3] *Laws* (1896), 111.

remaining unforgiven; (3) bigamous contract; (4) compulsion or gross fraud in procuring the marriage, if a rescission be sought in a reasonable time after removal of the restraint or discovery of the fraud; (5) wilful desertion for two years without reasonable cause; (6) conviction of felony or infamous crime; (7) habitual gross drunkenness contracted since marriage; (8) harsh and cruel treatment; (9) personal indignities rendering life burdensome; (10) six months' voluntary neglect of the husband to provide the wife with a home and the common necessaries of life.[1]   This statute was, however, of short duration.   In 1854 the third and fourth causes were dropped; bigamous contracts and those entered into through compulsion or fraud being now properly treated as grounds for annulment of void or voidable marriages.   The remaining eight causes recognized in 1853 were retained, except that the term of wilful desertion was reduced to one year; and a period of one year was likewise fixed in case of voluntary neglect to provide.[2]   Eight years later neglect to provide ceased to be a legal ground of complaint.   At the same time it was enacted that "habitual gross drunkenness" to constitute a cause must exist for two years immediately before the commencement of the suit; and the period of wilful desertion was extended to three years.[3]

The law governing the grounds of action, as it still exists in Oregon, took its present form in 1887; and, with the exception of the one clause omitted in 1862, it is practically the same as it was established in 1854.   Separation from bed and board is not recognized.   The circuit courts, sitting at least twice a year in each county, have jurisdiction.   A full divorce may be obtained on petition of the aggrieved

[1] Act of Feb. 1, 1853: *Gen. Laws of Ore.* (1852-53), 49-51.

[2] Act of Jan. 17, 1854: *Stat. of Ore.* (1853-54), 494-97.   *Cf.* also the same, *ibid.* (1854-55), 536-41.

[3] Act of Oct. 11, 1862: *Laws*, secs. 485 ff.; and the same in DEADY AND LANE, *Organic and Other Gen. Laws of Ore., 1843-1872* (1874), 208-12.

for (1) impotence; (2) adultery; (3) conviction of felony; (4) habitual gross drunkenness contracted since marriage and continuing for one year prior to the commencement of the suit; (5) wilful desertion for the period of one year; (6) cruel and inhuman treatment or personal indignities rendering life burdensome.[1]

The divorce laws of Washington have been remarkably free from violent changes. The current of legislation has run smoothly along. Separation from bed and board has never been provided for; but eight causes of absolute divorce were recognized by the first territorial act on the subject in 1854. These are (1) force or fraud in procuring the marriage, provided there be no subsequent voluntary cohabitation; (2) adultery unforgiven, if application be made within one year after knowledge of the offense; (3) impotence; (4) abandonment for one year; (5) cruel treatment; (6) habitual drunkenness; (7) neglect or refusal of the husband to make suitable provision for his family; (8) imprisonment in the penitentiary, if complaint be filed during the term of such confinement.[2] In 1860 was added a new ground in the form of an "omnibus" provision. A divorce was then permitted on application of either spouse (9) "for any other cause deemed by the court sufficient, or when the court shall be satisfied that the parties can no longer live together."[3] Thus the law remained without change for twenty-five years; but in 1885 it was provided (10) that in "case of incurable, chronic mania or dementia of either party, having existed for ten years or more, the court may in its discretion grant a divorce."[4] Finally in 1891 the list of grounds for full dissolution of wedlock sanctioned by the present code of Washington was completed. A full divorce is now allowed, in

[1] Act of Feb. 27: *Laws* (1887), 52, 53; same in *Codes and Stat. of Ore.* (1902), I, 275. On cruelty as a cause see Morris v. Morris, 73 *Am. Dec.*, 619–31.

[2] *Stat. for the Ter. of Wash.* (1854), 405–7.

[3] Act of Jan. 23: *Acts* (1860), 318–20.   [4] Act of Dec. 22, 1885: *Laws* (1885–86), 120.

modification of the fifth cause above enumerated, (11) for "personal indignities rendering life burdensome."[1] Originally the district courts were vested with jurisdiction, but since 1889 the superior courts in the separate counties have had authority in all cases of divorce, alimony, and annulment.[2]

In 1851, at the second session of the state legislature, California granted the district courts "within their respective districts" jurisdiction in divorce questions. Nine causes of "divorces from bed and board, or from the bonds of matrimony," were then recognized. But in 1874 three of these—natural impotence, force or fraud, and the marriage of a female under the age of fourteen years without consent of parent or guardian or without ratification by her after reaching that age—were dropped, and thereafter they were rightly treated as grounds for annulment of voidable contracts. The remaining six causes were then re-enacted, with some changes in the prescribed conditions, but only as grounds of absolute divorce. The statute of 1874 is still in force, full dissolution of wedlock, but not separation from bed and board, being sanctioned for (1) adultery; (2) extreme cruelty; (3) wilful desertion; (4) wilful neglect; (5) habitual intemperance; (6) conviction of felony.

After this formal enumeration of the grounds of petition, the first code of California carefully defines the terms employed and prescribes the conditions under which the law shall take effect. Thus "wilful desertion, wilful neglect, or habitual intemperance must continue for one year before either is a ground for divorce." By the original act of 1851, it may be noted, a period of three years was prescribed for both wilful desertion and wilful neglect to provide. In 1853, however, the term of wilful desertion was reduced to two years; and the same time was fixed for wilful neglect in

[1] Act of Feb. 24: *Laws* (1891), 42; also in *Ann. Codes and Stat. of Wash.* (1897), II, 1595-1600.

[2] *Const. of 1889*, Art. IV, secs. 5, 6.

1870. A period during which habitual intemperance must exist to constitute a cause of divorce was not mentioned until the statute of 1874, by which, in this case as well as in the two others above named, the one-year term was required. By the existing code extreme cruelty is defined as the "infliction of grievous bodily injury or grievous mental suffering."[1] "Wilful desertion is the voluntary separation of one of the married parties from the other with the intent to desert." But when one person is induced by the stratagem or fraud of the other "to leave the family dwelling-place, or to be absent, and during such absence the offending party departs with intent to desert the other, it is desertion by the party committing the stratagem or fraud, and not by the other." In like manner "departure or absence of one party from the dwelling-place, caused by cruelty or by threats of bodily harm from which danger would be reasonably apprehended from the other, is not desertion by the absent party but it is desertion by the other." Separation by consent, with or without the understanding that one of the married persons will apply for a divorce, is not desertion. Moreover, "absence or separation, proper in itself, becomes desertion whenever the intent to desert is fixed during such absence or separation."[2] Wilful neglect is defined as the neglect of the husband to provide for his wife the common necessaries of life, he having the ability to do so; or his failure to pro-

---

[1] On cruelty see Powelson v. Powelson, 22 *Cal.*, 358; Morris v. Morris, 14 *Cal.*, 76; Kelly v. Kelly, 1 *West Coast Rep.*, 143; Eidenmuller v. Eidenmuller, 37 *Cal.*, 394; Johnson v. Johnson, 14 *Cal.*, 459; Pierce v. Pierce, 15 *Am. Dec.*, 210, note. In general Poore v. Poore, 29 *Am. Dec.*, 664.

[2] Sec. 96 of the "Civil Code" also declares that "persistent refusal to have reasonable matrimonial intercourse as husband and wife, when health or physical condition does not make such refusal reasonably necessary, or the refusal of either party to dwell in the same house with the other party, when there is no just cause for such refusal, is desertion."— Deering, *Codes and Stat.* (1886), II, 34; Pomeroy, *Civil Code* (1901), 48.

On desertion see especially Hardenberg v. Hardenberg, 14 *Cal.*, 654; Benkert v. Benkert, 32 *Cal.*, 467; Morrison v. Morrison, 20 *Cal.*, 431; Christie v. Christie, 53 *Cal.*, 26; also Stein v. Stein, 5 *Col.*, 55; Pilgrim v. Pilgrim, 57 *Iowa*, 370.

vide as the result of "idleness, profligacy, or dissipation."[1] Finally, habitual intemperance is described as "that degree of intemperance from the use of intoxicating drinks which disqualifies the person a great portion of the time from properly attending to business, or which would reasonably inflict a cause of great mental anguish" upon the innocent person.[2] In like spirit the reasons for denying a decree are minutely specified by the law. Original jurisdiction in all questions of divorce and annulment of marriage is now vested in the superior courts in their respective counties or other districts.[3]

The California codes and decisions, as is well understood, have been freely adopted or followed by a number of western states. This is especially true regarding divorce legislation. The causes and conditions of action recognized by California law have often been accepted outright.[4] Such, for example, is the case in Montana. By the code of 1895 the same six causes sanctioned by the law of California since 1874 are recognized; while the prescribed definitions, already in part summarized from that law, are almost exactly reproduced. The grounds for dissolution of wedlock are identical, except in their phraseology, with those authorized by the original Montana act of 1865, save that in addition impotence and bigamous contract were then enumerated among the legal causes of divorce. There is no separation from bed and board in Montana; but the wife may be allowed separate maintenance, although a decree of divorce is denied. Since

[1] For interpretation of the law regarding neglect to provide see Devoe v. Devoe, 51 *Cal.*, 543; Washburn v. Washburn, 9 *Cal.*, 475; Rycraft v. Rycraft, 42 *Cal.*, 444.

[2] On habitual intemperance consult Mahone v. Mahone, 19 *Cal.*, 626, 629; Haskell v. Haskell, 54 *Cal.*, 262.

[3] DEERING, *Codes and Stat. of Cal.* (1886), III, 31. The development of the law of California regarding divorce, as given in the text, may be traced in *Stat.* (1851), 186, 187; *ibid.* (1853), 70; *Comp. Laws* (1853), 371, 372; act of March 12, 1870: in *Stat.* (1869-70), 291; act of March 30, 1874: in *Acts Amendatory of the Codes*, 181-91; POMEROY, *Civil Code* (1901), 40-62.

[4] For some account of the influence of the California Codes see HEPBURN, *Hist. Dev. of Code Pleading in America and Eng.* (Cincinnati, 1897), especially 93 ff., 104 ff., 160.

1865 the respective district courts, on the chancery side, have had jurisdiction in absolute divorce and in all questions of alimony and annulment of voidable contracts.[1]

What has just been said of Montana may be repeated for Idaho, where the California system was adopted in 1887.[2] By an act of 1895, however, incurable insanity was admitted as a seventh cause of full divorce.[3] In this case, as in all the others since 1864, the district court in the county of the plaintiff has jurisdiction. Earlier the laws relating to the causes were somewhat less closely patterned upon the California statutes. The act of 1864 allows a full divorce for (1) impotence at the time of the marriage; (2) adultery committed since marriage and remaining unforgiven; (3) wilful desertion for two years; (4) conviction of felony or infamous crime; (5) habitual gross drunkenness, contracted since marriage, incapacitating the offender from contributing his or her share to the support of the family; (6) extreme cruelty; (7) neglect of the husband for two years to provide the common necessaries of life, unless such neglect is the result of poverty which could not be avoided by ordinary industry.[4] Three years later the California law, as it then stood, allowing nine causes of full divorce, was adopted, except that the terms of habitual intemperance and wilful neglect were each fixed at two years, and a period of one year was made sufficient for wilful desertion. It should also be noted that this Idaho statute, unlike the contemporary law

[1] Compare the act of Feb. 7, 1865: in *Acts* (1864–65), 430, 431; and *Comp. Codes and Stat. of Mont.* (1895), 478–80.

[2] *Rev. Stat. of Idaho* (1887), 303–7.

[3] But a divorce is not allowed, under this provision, unless the insane person shall have been regularly and duly confined in an insane asylum of the state for at least six years immediately before the action: act of Feb. 4: *Gen. Laws* (1895), 11, 12. By an act of Feb. 14: *Gen. Laws* (1899), 232, 233, were added the words, "nor unless it shall appear to the court that such insanity is permanent and incurable;" and now it is sufficient if the previous confinement has been in an asylum "of a sister state," provided the plaintiff has been an actual resident for one year: *ibid.*, (1903), 332, 333.

[4] Act of Jan. 16, 1864: in *Laws of the Ter. of Idaho* (1863–64), 615–18.

of California, made no provision for partial divorce.[1] It
was superseded in 1875 by a new act[2] which is identical in
its provision regarding the grounds of action with that of
1867; and no further change was made until the present
California plan was sanctioned in 1887.

The experience of the Dakotas has been very similar to
that of Idaho and Montana, so far as the final results are
concerned; but the early territorial legislation was often
clumsy in form, vicious in character, and subject to frequent
and violent changes. The original act of 1864 grants the
several district courts jurisdiction in petitions for absolute
dissolution of marriage on suit brought in the county where
the persons or one of them resides, for (1) adultery; (2) impotence; (3) imprisonment in a penitentiary subsequently
to the marriage, no pardon effecting a restoration of conjugal rights; (4) cruel and inhuman treatment, "whether
practised by using personal violence, or by any other
means"; (5) habitual drunkenness for one year next before
filing the complaint; (6) "when it shall be made fully to
appear that from any other reason or cause existing, the
parties cannot live in peace and happiness together, and
that their welfare requires a separation."[3] Separation from
bed and board is not contemplated by the law of 1864; but
in 1866 a new statute appears by which both kinds of
divorce are provided for. A full divorce is permitted only
on the scriptural ground; but a partial divorce "for life or
for a limited time" may be decreed in favor of the
aggrieved for (1) cruel treatment; (2) conduct rendering
cohabitation unsafe or improper; (3) abandonment, accompanied by refusal to fulfil the matrimonial obligations sanctioned by the statute. If in any case a decree of separa-

[1] Act of Jan. 9: *Laws* (1867), 69–71.

[2] Act of Jan. 13, 1875: *Comp. and Rev. Laws of Idaho* (1875), 639–41.

[3] Act of Jan. 15: in *Gen. and Private Laws* (1864), 19–26.

tion be denied, the court may provide for the separate maintenance of the wife and children by the husband or out of his property.[1] The very next year this act was replaced by another which allows the aggrieved spouse absolute divorce for (1) bigamous contract; (2) wilful absence for five years; (3) adultery; (4) impotency; (5) pregnancy of the wife at the time of the marriage by a man other than the husband without the latter's knowledge; (6) extreme cruelty; (7) habitual drunkenness; (8) imprisonment in a penitentiary anywhere in the United States for violation of the criminal laws;[2] (9) whenever it shall be made to appear that the husband or wife of the applicant "has obtained a decree of divorce in any of the courts of any other territory or state, by virtue of which the party who shall have obtained such decree shall have been released from the obligation of the marriage contract, while the same remains binding upon the other party." Limited divorce is not mentioned by this statute; but, in place of it, a wife may obtain separate alimony for (1) the husband's adultery; (2) his gross neglect of duty; (3) abandonment by him without good cause; (4) where there is a separation in consequence of his ill-treatment; (5) his habitual drunkenness; or (6) his confinement in any prison in the country, or for any crime warranting such punishment in the territory.[3]

Only four years elapsed before the restless lawmaker was again at work. By an act of 1871 a divorce from bed and board or from the bonds of matrimony may be granted (1) for impotence at the time of marriage; (2) "when the female at the time of the alleged marriage was under the age of fourteen years, and the alleged marriage was without the consent of her parents, or guardians, or other persons having

---

[1] Act of Jan. 12, 1866: *Laws, Memorials, and Resolutions* (1865–66), 13–16.

[2] If for a crime of the same grade as warrants such imprisonment in the territory, and if application be made during the term of confinement.

[3] Act of Jan. 10, 1867; in *Gen. Laws* (1866–67), 45–52.

the legal custody or charge of her person; and when such marriage was not voluntarily ratified on her part" after the attainment of that age; (3) for adultery; (4) for extreme cruelty by the infliction of grievous bodily or mental suffering; (5) for habitual intemperance; (6) for two years' wilful desertion; (7) for having the ability to provide and failure so to do on account of idleness, profligacy, or dissipation; (8) "when from threatening words or acts, the weaker party feels in danger of bodily injury;" (9) when the consent was obtained by "force, fraud, intimidation, deception, or influence of stronger minds;" (10) for conviction of felony after marriage.[1] Here matters rested until 1877, when the California system, including the six causes and the careful definitions of the code, was adopted.[2] This plan without change is retained in the existing laws of South Dakota;[3] as also in those of North Dakota, except that between 1899 and 1901, following the lead of Idaho, incurable insanity for two years was admitted as a seventh ground of absolute divorce.[4] In neither of these states is partial divorce recognized. The district courts in North Dakota still have original jurisdiction; while in South Dakota authority is vested in the circuit courts within the respective circuits or their subdivisions.[5]

Nevada has likewise closely followed the example of California. Separation from bed and board has at no time been

[1] Act of Jan. 13, 1871: in *Gen. Laws* (1870–71), 414. In the same volume, curiously enough, the civil code of Jan. 12, 1866, including the divorce law of that year, as given in the text, is re-enacted; and so the act of Jan. 10, 1867, is entirely ignored. But the early legislation of Dakota is exceptionally bungling and confusing.

[2] *Rev. Codes of the Ter. of Dak.* (1877), 215, 216; also in LEVISSEE, *Ann. Codes* (1883), II, 747–52. By the code of 1877 the term of wilful desertion, wilful neglect, and habitual intemperance was fixed at two years; but the one-year period was substituted in 1881: Act of March 1, *Laws* (1881), 66.

[3] *Stat. of S. D.* (1899), II, 1025–30; *Rev. Codes* (1903), 598–603.

[4] Act of March 6: *Acts* (1899), 95; but insanity as a ground is omitted in *Laws* (1901), 81, 82. There is no partial divorce in North Dakota; but, though a decree be denied, the court may provide for the maintenance of the wife and children by the husband: *Rev. Codes* (1895), 614. *Cf.* McFarland *v.* McFarland, 2 *N. W. Rep.*, 269; Ross *v.* Ross, 10 *N. W. Rep.*, 193.

[5] *Rev. Codes of N. D.* (1895), 611–15, 929; *Stat. of S. D.* (1899), II, 1489; I, 237.

provided for. Bigamous marriages and those within the forbidden degrees of consanguinity are void without decree or other legal proceedings.[1] But since 1875, with one exception, the grounds of absolute divorce have been practically the same as those prescribed by the California code, although they are differently expressed, and there are not the same minute provisions regarding the application of the law and the conditions of action. On complaint of the aggrieved the courts are now authorized to dissolve the bonds of wedlock for (1) impotence at the time of the marriage continuing to the time of divorce; (2) adultery since marriage, remaining unforgiven; (3) wilful desertion for one year; (4) conviction of felony or infamous crime; (5) habitual gross drunkenness, contracted since marriage and incapacitating the offender from contributing his or her share toward the support of the family; (6) extreme cruelty; (7) neglect of the husband for the period of one year to provide the common necessaries of life, unless such neglect is the result of poverty which could not have been avoided by ordinary industry. Thus the laws of Nevada regarding the causes of divorce have been remarkably free from change; for the statute of 1875 in this regard is identical with the original act of 1861, except that by the latter the terms of wilful desertion and wilful neglect to provide are each fixed at two years.[2]

For Alaska the act of Congress does not authorize partial

[1] Since 1861 these marriages have thus been void without judicial proceedings; while those below the age of consent, or when there was want of understanding, or when obtained by fraud with no subsequent voluntary cohabitation, are void from the time a decree of nullity is pronounced. But a marriage shall in no case be adjudged a nullity, on the ground of being under age of consent, if the parties cohabited freely after reaching that age; nor the marriage of an insane person, if there be similar cohabitation after restoration to reason: act of March 28: *Laws* (1861), 96, 97; same in *Comp. Laws* (1900), 115.

[2] *Cf.* the act of Nov. 28: *Laws* (1861), 96–99; that of Feb. 15: *Laws* (1875), 63; and *Comp. Laws* (1900), 115–18. Partial divorce is not recognized; but the common law, as administered by the ecclesiastical courts, is a part of the law of Nevada, so far as not superseded by statute: Wuest *v.* Wuest, 17 *Nev.*, 216. For the interpretation of extreme cruelty see Reed *v.* Reed, 4 *Nev.*, 395; Gardner *v.* Gardner, 23 *Nev.*, 207; Kelley *v.* Kelley, 18 *Nev.*, 48.

divorce; but marriage may be dissolved for (1) impotency; (2) adultery; (3) conviction of felony; (4) two years' wilful desertion; (5) "cruel and inhuman treatment, calculated to impair health or endanger life;" or (6) habitual gross drunkenness contracted since marriage and continuing one year before the suit.[1]

By the law of Hawaii both kinds of divorce are provided for. Separation from bed and board forever or for a limited time will be granted when either spouse has been guilty of (1) excessive and habitual ill-treatment; or (2) habitual drunkenness; and (3) to the wife for the husband's neglect or refusal to provide her with the necessaries of life. At any time, on joint application of the persons, with satisfactory evidence of reconciliation, the decree of separation may be revoked by the court. According to a unique scheme, the grounds of absolute divorce are arranged in two groups: (1) A marriage will be dissolved, on petition of the aggrieved, when either consort has (a) committed adultery; (b) is guilty of three years' wilful and utter desertion; (c) has been sentenced to imprisonment for life, or for seven years or more, no pardon effecting a restitution of conjugal rights; or (d) has contracted "the disease known as Chinese leprosy, and is incapable of cure." (2) When one of the married persons has been guilty of (a) extreme cruelty; or (b) habitual drunkenness; and (c) when the husband, being of sufficient ability to provide suitable maintenance for his wife, neglects or refuses so to do. But it is especially enacted that if the person applying for a decree "shall not insist upon a divorce from the bond of matrimony, a divorce only from bed and board shall be granted." Jurisdiction is vested in the circuit courts of the circuit where the persons last cohabited as husband and wife; but no divorce for any cause will be allowed if they have never so lived together in the territory.[2]

<hr>

[1] *U. S. Stat. at Large*, XXXI, 408–10; *Laws of Alaska* (1900), 243–46.

[2] *Civil Laws of the Hawaiian Islands* (1897), 715–21.

c) Remarriage, residence, notice, and miscellaneous provisions.—It has been found convenient in the preceding section to trace throughout the period the development of the New York law regarding the remarriage of divorced persons. By the original statute of 1787, it thus appears, the guilty defendant is forever prohibited from marrying again. Under the acts of 1813 and 1827–28 the restriction is limited to the lifetime of the innocent former spouse; and this rule is retained in the present law, although in harmony with the practice elsewhere widely prevailing, the parties to the action are at liberty to renew their matrimonial vows. The defendant, however, may marry again in case the court in which the judgment is given "shall in that respect modify such judgment, which modification shall only be made upon satisfactory proof that the complainant has remarried, that five years have elapsed since the decree of divorce was rendered, and that the conduct of the defendant since the dissolution of said marriage has been uniformly good."[1] At no time, apparently, has any legal check been put upon the immediate remarriage of the successful plaintiff after final decree; and a way has been found by which the guilty defendant may at once contract further wedlock through evasion of the statute. In 1881 the precedent established by Massachusetts in 1829 was followed by the New York court of appeals. It was then decided that when a husband who has been divorced in New York for his adultery "goes into another state for the purpose of evading our law, and there contracts a second marriage during the lifetime of his former wife, and immediately returns to and resides within this state, such second marriage is, nevertheless, valid, and the issue thereof legitimate."[2]

[1] *Rev. Stat.* (1889), IV, 2599; Stover, *Code of Civil Proced.* (1902), II, 1843. *Cf.* 5 Barbour, *Chancery Reports*, 117; 11 *N. Y.*, 228; 34 *N. Y.*, 643; 42 *N. Y.*, 546; 2 Hun, *N. Y. Supreme Court Reports*, 241; 92 *N. Y.*, 146.

[2] Van Voorhis *v.* Brintnall, 86 *N. Y.*, 18; reversing s.c. 23 Hun, *N. Y. Supreme Court Reports*, 260; as summarized in Brightly, *Digest of the Decis. of all the Courts of N. Y.*, II, 2531, 2532, where the later cases are cited. *Cf.* especially Thorp *v.* Thorp (1882), 90 *N. Y.*, 602; and Moore *v.* Hegeman (1883), 92 *N. Y.*, 521.

On the other hand, it is held that the restraint applies to the remarriage of divorced persons even when the divorce was granted in another state. Thus dower was "denied on a showing that the deceased husband, while a resident of Massachusetts, had been divorced from his wife for his fault and later had removed to New York and married the plaintiff while his former wife was living. It was held that the New York statutes governed whether the divorce was granted in that state or not, so long as the marriage was celebrated in New York."[1] But elsewhere the courts have taken the opposite position, holding that the restraint on remarriage applies only to divorces granted in the state where it is imposed.[2]

During the century the statutes of New Jersey have in effect, though not expressly, allowed either person absolute freedom of remarriage after divorce.[3] A different rule has been followed in Pennsylvania and Delaware. By a law of the former state in 1785, "he or she, who hath been guilty of the adultery, may not marry the person with whom the said crime was committed, during the life of the former husband or wife."[4] This provision is still in force; and, except in the single case specified, the law of that state puts no restriction whatever upon the remarriage of either person after a decree dissolving the marriage tie. Since 1832 with respect to remarriage the law of Delaware has in substance been identical with that of the sister-commonwealth, except that the prohibition of marriage with the paramour is not confined to the lifetime of the former spouse.[5]

[1] H. J. WHITMORE, "Statutory Restraints on the Marriage of Divorced Persons," *Central Law Journal*, LVII, 447; Smith *v.* Woodworth, 44 BARBOUR, *Chancery Reports*, 198.

[2] Bullock *v.* Bullock, 122 *Mass. Reports*, 3; Clark *v.* Clark, 8 CUSHING, *Mass. Reports*, 385; Succession of Hernandez, 46 *La. Ann.*, 962; 15 *So. Rep.*, 461.

[3] The law provides that the penalties for "polygamy" shall not extend to persons marrying after having been lawfully divorced from the bonds of matrimony: *Gen. Stat. of N. J.*, I, 1057. *Cf. ibid.*, II, 1267 ff.

[4] *Cf.* the act of 1785: CAREY AND BIOREN, *Laws of the Com.*, III, 105; PEPPER AND LEWIS, *Digest*, I, 1646, 1647.

[5] *Cf.* the act of February 3, 1832: *Laws*, 150, with *Rev. Stat. of Del.* (1893), 598.

By their complete silence on the subject the statutes of Ohio appear always to have allowed either person entire freedom of remarriage after divorce. Since 1831 the same liberty has been expressly granted by the laws of Indiana;[1] except that when the defendant has been "constructively" summoned without other notice than publication in a newspaper, the person obtaining a decree of divorce is not permitted to marry again until the expiration of two years, during which period the judgment may be opened at the instance of the defendant.[2] But by the original act of 1818 the offender is not released from the bonds of matrimony while his former spouse is living.[3] This restriction is maintained by the statute of 1824, unless the court in its discretion, "judging from the circumstances of the case," shall expressly grant a release.[4] In 1825 the legislature of Illinois required the court in a decree of absolute divorce to prohibit the offender from remarrying within two years.[5] After 1827 this provision was dropped;[6] and at present Illinois, like New Jersey, through the remission of the penalty for bigamy allows entire freedom in this regard.[7] Michigan began with a severe rule. The territorial enactment of 1819 forbids the defendant adulterer to wed again until the complainant be actually dead.[8] This provision was not long

[1] *Rev. Laws of Ind.* (1831), 214; *Rev. Stat.* (1838), 243; *ibid.* (1843), 606; *ibid.* (1852), II, 237; *ibid.* (1896), I, sec. 1048; Burns, *Ann. Stat.* (1901), I, 1059.

[2] *Laws of Ind.* (1873), 108, 109; *Rev. Stat.* (1896), I, sec. 1030. This section applies only to parties "constructively" summoned: Sullivan *v.* Learned, 49 *Ind.*, 252. The general policy of the law is against disturbing divorces granted: McJunkin *v.* McJunkin, 3 *Ind.*, 30; McQuigg *v.* McQuigg, 13 *Ind.*, 294.

[3] Act of Jan. 26, 1818: *Laws of Ind.* (1818), 228.

[4] *Rev. Laws of Ind.* (1824), 157.   [5] Act of Jan. 17: *Laws of Ill.* (1825), 169.

[6] The act of June 1, 1827: *Rev. Code* (1827), 181, allows the injured person to obtain a dissolution of the marriage contract; but neither this nor any subsequent statute seems expressly to forbid the defendant to remarry.

[7] Hurd, *Rev. Stat.* (1899), 565.

[8] *Ter. Laws of Mich.*, I, 496; see also act of April 12, 1827: *ibid.*, II, 363-66. An act of this last date (*ibid.*, II, 543), for the punishment of crime, exempts persons marrying again after divorce from the pains of bigamy, provided they may do so by the terms of the decree or by those of the law where the divorce was granted. The act of June 28, 1832 (*ibid.*, III, 931, 932), is silent as to remarriage.

retained; and the existing statute permits the court to decree
that the person against whom any divorce is granted shall
not marry again within any period not exceeding two years.[1]

The legislation of the newer states of the Mississippi valley and the Pacific slope discloses the same lack of harmony
in dealing with the question in hand. By the laws of Wyoming, Utah, and Nevada either spouse, whether guilty or
innocent, is left absolutely free to contract further wedlock
as soon as he likes after divorce. At present the same is
true of Iowa, although under the early enactments the guilty
defendant was forbidden to remarry.[2] In Kansas, by a statute of 1855, the guilty person is restrained from marrying
again during five years unless so permitted by the terms of
the decree.[3] Between 1859 and 1881 entire freedom was
allowed.[4] Subsequently in that state it has been "unlawful
for either party . . . . to marry any other person within six
months from the date of the decree of divorcement," or, if
appeal be taken, "until the expiration of thirty days from
the day on which final judgment shall be rendered by the
appellate court." Marriage in violation of this statute is declared bigamy and void.[5] Nebraska since 1885, Oregon
since 1862, Washington since 1893, and Minnesota since
1901, have each interdicted remarriage within the same
period of six months after a decree of divorce.[6] In Idaho

[1] HOWELL, Gen. Stat. (1890), III, 3605; MILLER, Comp. Laws (1899), III, 2666.

[2] By the act of Jan. 24, 1855, the guilty party is prohibited from remarrying:
Laws of Ia. (1854–55), 112. The restriction was dropped in 1858: Laws (1858), 97, 98,
236: Ann. Code (1897), 1135–47.

[3] Stat. of Kan. (1855), 312.

[4] Gen. Laws of Kan. (1859), 385. This and the later acts to 1881 are silent as to
remarriage.

[5] Laws of Kan. (1889), 145; same in Comp. Laws of Kan. (1897), II, 276: "Every
decree of divorce shall recite the day and date when judgment was rendered in the
cause, and that the decree does not become absolute and take effect until the expiration of six months from said time." Cf. the act of March 5: Laws of Kan. (1881),
229–31, where the six-months' prohibition first appears.

[6] The Nebraska law is peculiar in that, in addition to the general prohibition of
marriage in six months, it especially forbids the defendant in error or appellee to

since 1903 the term is "more than six months;" while in North Dakota since 1901 it is but three.[1] Since 1893 Colorado has gone farther, requiring in such a case a delay of one year.[2] The same delay is required in Wisconsin since 1901;[3] while in Montana, since 1895, the innocent person must needs wait two years and the guilty person three years before renewing the marital bond with anyone save the former spouse.[4] South Dakota, when the cause is adultery, still refuses, as in the territorial stage, to permit the guilty defendant to rewed during the lifetime of the innocent plaintiff, unless, indeed, with the latter.[5] In Alaska neither party may marry a third person until proceedings on appeal are ended, or if no appeal be taken, during one year, the statutory term for bringing such action.[6]

Until very recently in California no clear restraint was put upon further wedlock after full separation. In 1897, following the example of Colorado, the legislature provided that in case of dissolution a new marriage may validly be contracted by either person only when the decree of divorce

marry again during the pendency of proceedings in error or on appeal under the penalties prescribed for bigamy: *Laws of Neb.* (1885), chap. 49, pp. 248, 249; *Comp. Stat. of Neb.* (1901), 582. See *Codes and Stat. of Ore.* (1902), I, 280, 296; *Codes and Gen. Laws* (1892), I, 458; being the same as act of Oct. 11, 1862: *Organic and Other Gen. Laws of Ore., 1843-72*, 211, 218; *Ann. Codes and Stat. of Wash.* (1897), II, 1599; *Laws* (1893), 225.

[1] *Laws of N. D.* (1901), 81, 82; *Laws of Idaho* (1903), 10, 11.

[2] *Laws of Col.* (1893), 240, 241; MILLS, *Ann. Stat.* (1897), III, 441, 442.

[3] "But upon application of such divorced person, any court of record or presiding judge thereof, who granted the divorce, ... may authorize" marriage within the year: *Acts of Wis.* (1901), 369.

[4] *Complete Codes and Stat. of Mont.* (1895), 480.

[5] *Stat. of S. D.* (1899), II, 1025, 1028; *Rev. Codes* (1903), 602. This principle was adopted by the territorial assembly: LEVISSEE, *Ann. Codes* (1884), II, 750. Except for a brief term in 1866, the earlier territorial laws allow entire freedom of remarriage: see act of Jan. 12, 1866: *Laws, Memorials, and Resolutions* (1865-66), 14, forbidding the guilty adulterer to remarry during the lifetime of the innocent spouse; but in the next year this was replaced by a new law allowing full liberty: Act of Jan. 10, 1867: *Gen. Laws, Memorials, and Resolutions* (1866-67), 45-52.

[6] *U. S. Stat. at Large*, XXXI, 408-10, 415.

has been rendered at least one year before.[1]   This amendment, it seems, was designed primarily to remedy an abuse
arising in the uncertainties of California law—one often encouraged by careless legislation in the United States.   Its
purpose, says Judge Belcher in the opinion below cited,
"was to correct a great public evil which had become too
rife—to put a stop to marriages within the period allowed
for the appeal from the decree of divorce, which might be
and sometimes had been reversed, with great scandal to the
parties who had married again."   In the meantime this new
and stringent provision has given occasion for still more
serious evils originating in the inharmonious laws of adja-
cent states.   The statutes of Nevada, whose borders are
within easy reach of San Francisco, have not fixed a period
within which divorced persons may not contract further wedlock.   As a result, Reno has become the Gretna Green of
California couples who there seek to evade the interdict of
their own law.   Whether a person who retains his domicile
in California may contract a valid marriage in Nevada within
less than one year after having been divorced in the former
state is a question regarding which the decisions of the superior courts long contradicted one another.[2]   But the supreme

---

[1] " Sec. 61.   A subsequent marriage contracted by any person during the life of
a former husband or wife . . . . , with any person other than such former husband
or wife, is illegal and void from the beginning unless:
    "1.   the former marriage has been annulled or dissolved; provided, that in case
it be dissolved, the decree of divorce must have been rendered and made at least one
year prior to such subsequent marriage."—Act of Feb. 25: *Stat. and Amend. to the
Codes* (1897), 34.
    " Sec. 91.   The effect of a judgment decreeing a divorce is to restore the parties
to the state of unmarried persons." — Act of March 30, 1874: *Amendments to the Codes*
(1873-74), 189; also in Deering, *Codes and Stat. of Cal.* (1886), II, 31; Pomeroy, *Civil
Code* (1901), 44.

[2] In Abbie Rose Wood *v.* Estate of Joseph M. Wood, filed in the superior court of
San Francisco, June 14, 1900, Judge Belcher decided that the marriage on Jan. 1,
1898, in Reno, Nev., of a person divorced in California, Aug. 19, 1897, the former husband still living, was not valid.   He relies upon the words of nullity in the amendment of 1897; and the fact that the person went to another state solely for the purpose of getting married while still retaining her domicile in California.   " Section 61,
Civil Code, contains no penal clause, as stated; but it does contain words of nullity,

tribunal has just determined[1] that California in this regard is to take her place by the side of New York and Massachusetts, whose example Washington had already followed.[2] To overcome the effect of this decision, the legislature has enacted that if in any case the court "determines that a divorce ought to be granted an interlocutory judgment must be entered, declaring that the party in whose favor the court decides is entitled to a divorce." After one year has expired, on its own motion or the motion of either person, the court "may enter final judgment granting the divorce," unless action on appeal or on a motion for a new trial is pending.

and words which suspend, as to third persons, the operation of the decree . . . . ; and these cannot be avoided by merely invoking another jurisdiction for that purpose. The two sections (61 and 91, C. C.) are to be read together, and, so read, their interpretation and meaning are free from either uncertainty or ambiguity. The law of the domicile is invoked, and the law of the domicile controls. No other jurisdiction can relieve against it."—See *San Fran. Law Journal* (July 2, 1900), 1.

In a case decided on Dec. 10, 1900, Judge Trout, of the superior court of San Francisco, takes the same position as Judge Belcher.

On the other hand, on Dec. 4, 1900, Judge Hebbard, of the same court, in Adler *v.* Adler, maintains the validity of a similar Reno marriage. He holds that the California law "is in restraint of marriage," since it fixes an arbitrary prohibitory period. "We may imagine the reason which induced the passage of the section, by an examination of the law of the State of Oregon upon the same subject. In that state there is no fixed prohibitory period, but the law is to the effect that, pending an appeal from a decree of divorce, if one be taken, and, if not, during the time in which it may be taken, the parties shall be incapable of contracting marriage with a third person. In California an appeal from a final judgment must be taken in six months; an appeal from an order granting or refusing a new trial in sixty days. The great majority of divorce cases go to judgment upon the default of the defendants, and in such cases there can be no appeal upon the merits of the cause. When no appeal can be taken, or when the time for appeal has gone by and none taken, why compel the parties in the case to abstain from matrimony for the remainder of the year thereafter? The proportion of divorce decrees appealed from is infinitely small, and therefore the prohibition in section 61 discriminates against the many, for the protection of the few; it is an arbitrary law." He relies upon Pearson *v.* Pearson, 51 *Cal.*, 120 (1875), construing sec. 63 of the Civil Code to the effect that "all marriages contracted without this state, which would be valid by the laws of the country in which the same were contracted, are valid in this state."—*San Fran. Law Journal* (July 16, 1900), 1.

[1] See the Estate of Wood, 137 *Cal.* (1902), 129 ff., where Reno marriages are held valid, three justices dissenting.

[2] In Willey *v.* Willey, 22 *Wash.* (Jan. 27, 1900), 115-21. The courts of Oregon have taken the opposite view, holding such marriages of residents of Oregon contracted in another state absolutely void under the statute: McLennan *v.* McLennan, 31 *Ore.* (1897), 480.

"In no case can a marriage of either of the parties during the life of the other be valid in this state, if contracted within one year after the entry of an interlocutory decree." But this legislation,[1] it is believed, will be declared unconstitutional by the supreme court.[2]

Expressly or by implication the divorced couple are excepted from the restraint, and permitted to rewed in Alaska, California, Colorado, Idaho, Kansas, Montana, New York, Oklahoma, Oregon, South Dakota, Vermont, and Washington. On the question whether, in the absence of statutory authority, such remarriage of the divorced persons comes within the restraint, the decisions of the courts are conflicting.[3]

All of the twenty-six states under consideration have prescribed rules or conditions regarding the residence of the plaintiff in divorce suits. In nearly every instance a definite term of previous residence in the state, or in the state and in the county, of the action is fixed. This term varies from six months to three years, one year being the prevailing period. In the West the requirements in this regard are not in general so rigid as in some eastern and southern states; but during the past two decades encouraging progress has been made.

The law of New York governing residence has in the preceding subsection already been presented. A fixed term is not prescribed, except that in cases of partial divorce, when the marriage was solemnized outside the state, the persons must have "continued to be residents" of the state for at least one year, and the plaintiff must be resident at

---

[1] Acts of March 2 and 16, 1903, *Stat. and Amend. to the Codes*, chaps. lxvii, clviii.

[2] It has already been so declared by Judge Rhodes in the superior court of Santa Clara county.

[3] Compare Moore v. Moore, 8 ABB., *N. C.*, 171-73; Colvin v. Colvin, 2 PAIGE, 385-87, denying the right of remarriage in such cases; with Moore v. Hegeman, 92 *N. Y.*, 521-29, where the question is left undecided.

the time the action is commenced.[1]   Delaware has not fixed
a definite period of residence; but no divorce from the bond
of matrimony will be decreed when the cause assigned
therefor in the petition occurred out of the state and the
"petitioner was a non-resident thereof at the time of its
occurrence, unless for the same or like cause such divorce
would be allowed by the laws of the state or country in
which it is alleged to have occurred."[2]   Delaware, like Maine
and Massachusetts, has attempted to prevent clandestine
divorce through evasion of the laws.   "When any inhabitant
. . . . shall go into any other jurisdiction to obtain a divorce
for any cause occurring here; or for any cause which would
not authorize a divorce by the laws of this state; a divorce
so obtained shall be of no force or effect in this state."[3]   The
statute of New Jersey gives the court of chancery jurisdiction in actions for divorce when either the complainant or
defendant is an inhabitant of the state "at the time of the
injury, desertion, or neglect;" when the marriage took place
within the state, and the complainant is an actual resident at
the time the injury arose, and at the time of exhibiting the
bill; when the adultery occurred within the state and either
spouse is a resident thereof at the commencement of the
suit; or when one of the persons, at the time of filing the
bill and for the term of two years during which the desertion shall have continued, is a resident of the commonwealth.[4]   When the cause is adultery committed outside the
state, three years' previous residence on the part of either
the complainant or the defendant is always required.[5]

[1] STOVER, *Code of Civil Proced.* (1892), II, 1640.

[2] *Rev. Stat. of Del.* (1893), 598; being the act of 1891: *Laws*, XIX, chap. 243, p. 480.

[3] *Rev. Stat. of Del.* (1893), 598.   "In all other cases a divorce decreed in any other
state or country " is valid: *ibid.*, 598.

[4] *Gen. Stat. of N. J.* (1896), II, 1273; being act of March 7, 1889: *Pub. Laws*, 48.
This law has existed in nearly the same form since 1820: see act of Feb. 16, 1820:
Laws of the State (1821), 667.

[5] *Gen. Stat. of N. J.* (1896), II, 1273; being act of May 11, 1886: *Pub. Laws*, 345.

A term of twelve months' previous residence was established by Indiana in 1831.[1] This was increased to two years in 1838, regardless of the place where the alleged cause of divorce occurred.[2] A period of one year was again adopted in 1849.[3] Three years later the law was still further relaxed by making *bona fide* residence in the county of the action sufficient to warrant a petition.[4] In 1859 the one-year term was once more restored,[5] only to yield in 1873 to a *bona fide* residence of two years in the state and six months in the county; and this provision is still in force.[6] The legislation of Michigan shows similar vicissitudes. The act of 1819 allows an absolute divorce for adultery when the parties are "inhabitants" of the territory, or when the marriage was solemnized therein, and the injured person is an actual resident at the time of the offense and at the time the complaint is filed.[7] In 1832 a residence of three years was fixed for the plaintiff in both full and partial divorce;[8] but in 1838 the term was reduced to two years, and to half that time in 1844.[9] The period of one year is still sanctioned when the cause of action occurs within the state. By the careful act of May 26, 1899, no decree of divorce will be granted in any case unless (1) the plaintiff has resided in the state for one year preceding; or (2) the marriage sought to be dissolved was solemnized in the state and the plaintiff has since resided therein to the time of the petition. Furthermore, in no case will a decree be granted unless (1) the defendant is domiciled in the state when the petition is filed; or (2) was so domiciled when the alleged cause for the action

---

[1] *Rev. Laws of Ind.* (1831), 213.   [2] *Ibid.* (1838), 243.   [3] *Gen. Laws* (1849), 62.

[4] *Rev. Stat.* (1852), 234: of "which *bona fide* residence the affidavit of the petitioner shall be *prima facie* evidence."

[5] *Laws of the State* (1859), 108.

[6] Act of March 10: *Laws* (1873), 109; same in *Rev. Stat.* (1896), I, sec. 1031.

[7] *Ter. Laws of Mich.*, I, 495.   [8] *Ter. Laws of Mich.*, III, 931.

[9] *Rev. Stat.* (1838), 337; *Acts* (1844), 74.

arose; or (3) when he voluntarily appears at the trial, or is brought in by publication, or has been personally served with process or notice. On the other hand, when the cause of action occurs outside the state, a divorce will not be allowed unless the complainant or the defendant shall have resided in the commonwealth for two years immediately before the filing of the petition. If the defendant is not domiciled in the state at the time of commencing the suit, or when the alleged cause arose, before a decree will be granted the complainant must prove that the parties have actually lived and cohabited together as husband and wife within the state, or that the complainant has there resided in good faith for the two preceding years.[1]

Since 1785 Pennsylvania has required that the plaintiff in a suit for absolute divorce must be a citizen of the state and a resident therein at least one whole year before the action is begun.[2] The one-year term is prescribed likewise in Ohio, except when the action is for alimony alone;[3] in Illinois since 1827, unless the offense or injury complained of was committed in the state, or while one or both of the persons resided there;[4] in Minnesota since 1851, except when the suit is on the ground of adultery committed while the plaintiff was a resident of the state;[5] in Wisconsin since 1838–39, except when the cause is adultery similarly committed, or when the marriage was solemnized in the state

---

[1] *Pub. Acts* (1899), 326, 327. When the order for appearance is served outside the state, the law requires that the fact of service be proved by affidavit before a justice or notary whose legal character and signature must be attested by the certificate of a court of record. See the earlier act of 1895: *Pub. Acts* (1895), 371; and *cf.* Howell, *Gen. Stat.*, II, 1624; Miller, *Comp. Laws* (1899), III, 2657.

[2] *Cf.* the act of June 20: *Laws of Pa.* (1893), 471; also in Pepper and Lewis, *Digest* (1896), I, 1638, 1639; and the act of Sept. 19, 1785: *Laws of the Com. of Pa.* (1803), III, 105.

[3] Bates, *Ann. Stat. of Ohio* (1897), II, 2805. The law of 1827 requires two years' residence on the part of the plaintiff: Chase, *Stat.*, III, 1581.

[4] *Cf.* act of June 1, 1827: *Rev. Code of Ill.* (1827), 182; Hurd, *Rev. Stat. of Ill.* (1898), 632: being the same as *ibid.* (1845), 196.

[5] *Cf. Rev. Stat. of Minn.* (1851), 274; *Gen. Stat.* (1894), I, 1268, 1269.

and the plaintiff resided there from the time of such marriage to the time of bringing suit, or when the wife is plaintiff and the husband has resided in the state for one year
preceding the commencement of the action;[1] in Iowa since
1838, "except when the defendant is a resident of the state
served by personal service;"[2] in Colorado since 1861, unless
the application is made upon "grounds of adultery or extreme
cruelty when the offence was committed within the state;"[3]
in Kansas since 1855;[4] in Utah since 1878;[5] in Montana
since 1865;[6] in Washington since 1854;[7] in Oregon since
1862;[8] in California since 1891;[9] in North Dakota since

[1] The development of the Wisconsin law of residence may be traced in *Stat. of the
Ter.* (1838–39), 140; *Rev. Stat.* (1849), 395; *ibid.* (1858), 623–28 (in which the clause
referring to the wife as plaintiff first appears); *Ann. Stat.* (1889), I, 1368.

[2] The petition for divorce "must state that the plaintiff has been for the last
year a resident of the state, specifying the township and county in which he or
she has resided, and the length of such residence therein after deducting all absences
from the state; that it has been in good faith and not for the purpose of obtaining
a divorce only"; and "in all cases it must be alleged that the application is made
in good faith and for the purpose set forth in the petition."—*Ann. Code of Ia.* (1897),
1137; same in *Code* (1873), 339. See also act of Dec. 29, 1838: *Laws* (1838–39), 179, 180,
first fixing the period of one year's previous residence.

[3] "Provided, further, that such suit shall only be brought in the county in which
such plaintiff or defendant resides, or where such defendant last resided."— MILLS,
Ann. Stat. of Col. (1897), III, 437, 438; being the act of 1893: *Laws*, 239. *Cf.* the original act in *Laws of Col.* (1861–62), 360, 361, fixing the one-year term.

[4] *Laws of Kan.* (1897), II, 273; being same as *Gen. Stat.* (1868), 757. *Cf.* original
act of 1855: *Stat.* (1855), 311. In 1859 the term of residence was reduced to six months,
but the one-year period was restored the next year: *Laws of Kan.* (1859), 385; *ibid.*
(1860), 108. Now the petitioner must be a resident of the county of the action.

[5] See the preceding subsection.

[6] *Comp. Codes and Stat. of Mont.* (1895), 482. See *Acts* (1864–65), 430.

[7] *Ann. Codes and Stat. of Wash.* (1897), II. 1596; *Stat.* (1854), 405–7. The term was
reduced to three months in 1864, but restored to one year in 1866: *Stat.* (1864), 13;
Stat. (1865–66), 89, 90.

[8] When the marriage was solemnized in the state, it is sufficient if the plaintiff
be an inhabitant thereof at the commencement of the suit. If not solemnized in the
state, both parties must be inhabitants at the commencement of the suit, and the
plaintiff for one year before (act of 1862). The plaintiff must be an inhabitant of the
state at the commencement of the suit and for one year before; "which residence
shall be sufficient to give the court jurisdiction, without regard to the place where
the marriage was solemnized, or the cause jof suit arose" (act of 1865): *Codes and
Gen. Laws* (1902), I, 277. By the act of 1853, in force till 1862, the term of residence
was fixed at six months: *Gen. Laws.* (1852–53), 49–51.

[9] *Stat. and Amend. to Codes of Cal.* (1891), 52. The plaintiff must be a resident
of the state one year and of the county three months. Between 1851 and 1891 the
term was six months: Act of March 25: *Stat. of Cal.* (1851), 186, 187.

1899;[1] and in Wyoming since 1901.[2]   In Alaska by the federal law of 1903, the plaintiff must be an inhabitant of the district for two years before suit is brought; and the same term had already been prescribed for Hawaii.[3]

Four states are less stringent in their requirements.   In Nebraska, since 1856, petition will not be granted unless the plaintiff has resided in the state for six months, except when the marriage was solemnized in the state and the plaintiff has there dwelt since the marriage to the time when the suit is commenced.[4]   The same term has been required in Idaho since 1864;[5] while in Nevada, since 1861, the plaintiff must have resided six months in the county where suit is brought, unless the action is begun "in the county in which the cause thereof shall have accrued, or in which the defendant shall reside, or be found, or in which the plaintiff shall reside if the latter be the county in which the parties last cohabited."[6]   Until 1899, as in the territorial stage, South Dakota required only ninety days' *bona fide* residence on the part of the plaintiff.   In that year the term was increased to six months; but in no case will a divorce be granted without personal service within the state, or, when the defendant is non-resident, personal service and order of publication "until the plaintiff shall have a *bona fide* residence in the state for one year" next before the granting of a decree.[7]

---

[1] *Acts* (1899, Feb. 3), 94: The plaintiff must have been a resident of the state in good faith for twelve months, and be a citizen of the United States or have declared his intention to become such citizen. By the earlier law, as at the close of the territorial period, the term of residence was ninety days: *Rev. Codes of N. D.* (1895), 614.

[2] *Laws of Wyo.* (1901), 4.

[3] *U. S. Stat. at Large*, XXXIII, 944. The period is two years in Hawaii: *ibid.*, XXXI, 150.

[4] *Comp. Stat. of Neb.* (1901), 577; *Laws* (1856), 155.

[5] *Rev. Stat. of Idaho* (1887), 305; *Laws* (1867), 69. The law of residence took its present form in 1867: but the provision of 1864, *Laws* (1863-64), 615, 616, is identical with that of Nevada quoted in the text.

[6] *Comp. Laws of Nev.* (1900), 115. *Cf. Laws* (1861), 96, 97; and *Laws* (1875), 63.

[7] *Stat. of S. D.* (1899), II, 1029; *Rev. Codes* (1903), 602. The territorial law of 1883: LEVISSEE, *Ann. Codes of Ter. of Dak.* (1884), 751, requires a residence of ninety days.

The laws of every state in this group contain some provision requiring notice to the defendant when personal service cannot be had. Such notice is given as in equity suits in Illinois and Nebraska; as in ordinary civil actions in California,[1] Idaho, Montana, Oregon, Utah, Washington, Wisconsin,[2] and Wyoming; and in the remaining commonwealths special rules regarding publication, usually in the newspapers, are in force.[3]

The miscellaneous provisions regarding divorce and divorce actions are in character similar to those already mentioned for other states. In California, Hawaii, Illinois, Michigan, Montana, Nebraska, New Jersey, New York, North Dakota, Ohio, South Dakota, and Wyoming the legitimacy of the children of the marriage is expressly recognized in case of divorce. Trial by jury in the finding of facts is allowed in Illinois, Nevada, New York,[4] Pennsylvania, and Wisconsin; while in Washington it is expressly denied; and in Colorado the guilt or innocence of the defendant must be determined by the

[1] In California and Montana summons and publication in divorce suits are given under the general provisions for civil actions: POMEROY, *Codes and Stat.: Civil Proced.* (1901), secs. 410 ff.; *Codes and Stat. of Mont.* (1895), 782, 796, 797. This is, of course, not inconsistent with Sharon *v.* Sharon (1885), 67 *Cal.*, 185, ruling that an action for divorce is a case in equity under the clause in the constitution conferring appellate jurisdiction on the supreme court.

[2] The statute of Wisconsin requires the proceedings to be as in "courts of record " so far as practicable: *Ann. Stat.* (1889), I, 1362.

[3] In New York, for instance, the order for publication must direct that the summons be published "in two newspapers, designated in the order as most likely to give notice to the defendant, for a specified time, which the judge deems reasonable, not less than once a week for six successive weeks; " and unless the judge is satisfied from affidavits presented that the defendant's residence is unknown, it must also require that copies of the summons, complaint, and order be mailed to him at a specified place: BIRDSEYE, *Rev. Stat.* (1896), I, 18. The laws of Ohio and Kansas are similar: BATES, *Ann. Rev. Stat. of Ohio* (1897), II, 2805; *Laws of Kan.* (1897), II, 273. By the statute of Pennsylvania, if the adverse party is not found, the court may issue an alias subpœna, and trial may be set for a later term. If a second time personal service cannot be had, notice must be "published in one or more newspapers printed within or nearest to the said county for four weeks successively " prior to the first day of the next term: PEPPER AND LEWIS, *Digest* (1896), I, 1642. Colorado has a careful provision. See also *Civil Laws of the Hawaiian Islands* (1897), 716-18; and the new law of New Jersey: *Acts* (1903), 122, 123.

[4] By *Laws* (1899), 1471, 1472, on application of either party, when the assigned cause is adultery, a jury must be called; and in other cases it may be empaneled.

verdict in every case.[1]   The statutes of Kansas, Nebraska,
Ohio, Wisconsin, and Wyoming permit either consort to be a
witness in the case; and by those of Illinois, Kansas, Minnesota, Nevada, Ohio, Oregon, Wisconsin, and Washington
the court may authorize the woman to change her name.
She is granted this privilege in Alaska only when not the
person in fault.   In several instances special provision is
made for defending the action.   According to the Indiana
law, "when a petition for divorce remains undefended, it
shall be the duty of the prosecuting attorney to appear and
resist" the same.[2]   In Colorado, when the defendant fails
to appear, the court must appoint an attorney who shall
secure a fair and impartial hearing of the case.[3]   By the
law of Oregon the state is constituted a party in such suits,
and it is the duty of the district attorney, "so far as may
be necessary to prevent fraud or collusion," to control the
proceedings for the defense.[4]   Washington has a similar
law;[5] and in special cases the prosecuting attorney in Idaho
and Michigan is likewise required to oppose the granting of
a decree.[6]   Soliciting divorce business by advertising or

[1] MILLS, *Ann. Stat. of Col.* (1897), III, 438; *Ann. Codes and Stat. of Wash.* (1897),
II, 1600.

[2] *Rev. Stat. of Ind.* (1896), I, sec. 1038.   An emergency act of 1901 makes provision
for counties of 100,000 inhabitants; that is, for Marion county, containing Indianapolis.   Where no *bona fide* counsel for the defendant is entered in the appearance
docket, the prosecuting attorney is to enter his name therein, and to resist the
petition on behalf of the state.   Any attorney, other than the prosecuting attorney,
appearing for the defendant, if so ordered by the court, must file a written authority
executed by the defendant: *Laws* (1901), chap. 151, pp. 336, 337.   In substance this
requirement as regards the prosecuting attorney is made general for the state by an
act of 1903: *Laws*, 393, 394.

[3] MILLS, *Ann. Stat.*, III, 438; *Laws* (1893), 238, 239.

[4] *Codes and Gen. Stat.* (1892), I, 664 (act of Oct. 11, 1862); *Codes and Stat.* (1902),
I, 456.

[5] *Ann. Codes and Stat.* (1897), II, 1600.

[6] This is the duty of the district attorney in Idaho, and of the county attorney
in Utah, when the ground of the petition is the alleged insanity of the defendant:
Gen. Laws of Id. (1895), 12; *Laws of Utah* (1903), 39, 40; and of the prosecuting
attorney in Michigan, when there are children under fourteen years of age whose
interests require his intervention: HOWELL, *Gen. Stat.*, III, 3605; MILLER, *Comp.
Laws* (1899), III, 2665.

otherwise is sometimes prohibited under severe penalty, such being the case in California, Illinois, Indiana, Minnesota, Montana, New York, Ohio, and Washington.[1] Indiana has a unique enactment expressly declaring that a divorce legally granted in any other state shall have full effect in that commonwealth.[2] Everywhere due provision is made for alimony, care of the children, and the adjustment of property rights. There is great variation in matters of detail; but in general the laws of the middle and western states relating to these subjects are very similar to those of New England. For the purpose of the present chapter further notice may therefore be dispensed with. Only in Michigan,[3] Ohio, Illinois, and Indiana, it may be mentioned in conclusion, has any adequate provision been made for the collection and publication of divorce statistics.

[1] *Cal. Stat. and Amend. to the Codes* (1891), 279; *ibid.* (1893), 48; *ibid.* (1900–1901), 444; *Rev. Stat. of Ill.* (1898), 633, 634; *Rev. Stat. of Ind.* (1896), I, sec. 2129; BATES, *Ann. Rev. Stat. of Ohio* (1897), II, 3218; *Ann. Codes and Stat. of Wash.* (1897), II, 1987, 1988; *Gen. Laws of Minn.* (1901), 286. By *Laws of N. Y.* (1902), I, 536, this offense is made a misdemeanor. *Cf. Laws of Montana* (1903), 146.

[2] *Rev. Stat.* (1896), I, 1049.

[3] Act of Feb. 11, 1897: *Pub. Acts of Mich.*, 12; *ibid.* (1899), 69.

CHAPTER XVIII

PROBLEMS OF MARRIAGE AND THE FAMILY

[BIBLIOGRAPHICAL NOTE XVIII.— Materials for a more extended study of the questions touched upon in this chapter are set forth in Part IV of the Bibliographical Index. Wright's *Report on Marriage and Divorce* is, of course, indispensable. It may be supplemented from the *Eleventh Census, U. S.*, I; the *Census of Massachusetts*, 1875, 1885, 1895; the *Registration Reports* of the New England states, of which the forty-first for Massachusetts is most important; and from those of Indiana, Illinois, Michigan, and Ohio. Useful summaries of statistics may also be found in Secretary Dike's *Reports of the National Divorce Reform League*, and its successor, the *National League for the Protection of the Family* (Montpelier and Boston, 1886–1903). An important statistical monograph is Willcox's *Divorce Problem* (2d ed., New York, 1897). This should be read in connection with his "Study in Vital Statistics," in *Pol. Science Quarterly*, VIII (New York, 1893); his "Marriage Rate in Michigan," in *Pub. of Am. Stat. Association*, IV (Boston, 1895); Crum's "Marriage Rate in Massachusetts," in the same volume; and Kuczynski's article in *Quart. Jour. of Economics*, XVI (Boston, 1902). See also Dike, "Statistics of Marriage and Divorce," in *Pol. Science Quarterly*, IV (New York, 1889), a study of the government report; *idem*, "Facts as to Divorce in New England," in *Christ and Modern Thought* (Boston, 1881); Wells, *Divorce in Mass.*, extract from the *41st Registration Report* (Boston, 1882); Abbott, "Vital Statistics," in *28th Rep. Mass. State Board of Health* (Boston, 1897); Wright, *Practical Sociology* (New York and London, 1899); Mayo-Smith, *Statistics and Sociology* (New York and London, 1895); Loomis, "Divorce Legislation in Conn.," in *New Englander*, XXV (New Haven, 1866); and Allen, "Divorces in New England," in *North Am. Rev.*, CXXX (New York, 1880). Important foreign statistical works are Bertillon, "Note pour l'étude stat. de divorce," in *Annales de démographie internat.*, IV (Paris, 1880); *idem*, *Étude démographique du divorce* (Paris, 1883); *idem*, "Du sort des divorcés," in *Jour. de la soc. de statistique* (Paris, 1884); Oettingen, *Die Moralstatistik* (2d ed., Erlangen, 1874); Rubin and Westergaard, *Statistik der Ehen* (Jena, 1890); Bertheau, *Lois de la population* (Paris, 1892); Molinari, "Decline of the French Population," in *Jour. of Royal Stat. Soc.*, L (London, 1887); Ogle, "Marriage-Rates and Marriage-Ages," *ibid.*, LIII (London, 1890); Farr, "Influence of Marriage on the Mortality of the French People," in *Trans. Nat. Assoc. for Promotion of Soc. Science*, LVIII (London,

1859); *idem, Vital Statistics*, Parts I, II (London, 1885); Newsholme, *Vital Statistics* (3d led., London, 1892); Cauderlier, *Les lois de population* (Brussels, 1900); Lindner, *Die unehelichen Geburten als Sozialphänomen* (Naumburg, 1899); *Statistik der Ehescheidungen in der Stadt Berlin, 1885–94* (Berlin, n. d.); the parliamentary *Return of the Number of Divorces in Foreign Countries, Misc.*, No. 4 (London, 1895), Part II, being for British Colonies; and *Reports of the Laws of Marriage and Divorce*, Parts I, II (London, 1894).

On the divorce problem see *An Essay on Marriage; or, the Lawfulness of Divorce* (Philadelphia, 1788), presenting the principal arguments in its favor; Westbrook, *Marriage and Divorce* (Philadelphia, 1883); *idem, The Clerical Combination to Influence Civil Legislation on Marriage and Divorce* (Philadelphia, 1887); Fisher, *The Causes of the Increase of Divorce* (Boston, 1883); Richard, *Marriage and Divorce* (London, 1888); Robinson, "The Diagnostics of Divorce," in *Jour. of Soc. Science*, No. 14 (Boston and New York, 1881); Janes, "Divorce: Sociologically Considered," in *New Englander and Yale Review*, LIV (New Haven, 1891); Phillips, "The Divorce Question," in *International Review*, XI (New York, 1881); Savage, "Matrimony and the State," in *Forum*, X (New York, 1890); Adler, "The Ethics of Divorce," in *Ethical Record*, II, III (Philadelphia, 1889–90); Wright, "Marriage and Divorce," in *Christian Register*, LXX, 655–58 (Boston, 1891); Lecky, *Democracy and Liberty*, I, chap. vii (New York and London, 1896); and Bryce, "Marriage and Divorce," in his *Studies in Hist. and Jur.* (New York and London, 1901). The following are very conservative: David Hume, "Of Polygamy and Divorces," in his *Essays*, I (London, 1875); Little, "Marriage and Divorce: the Doctrine of the Church of England," in *Contemporary Review*, LXVIII (London, 1895); Hurd, "Scriptural Ground of Divorce," in the *New Englander and Yale Review*, XLV (New Haven, 1886); Phelps, "Divorce in the United States," in *Forum*, VIII (New York, 1889); Caverno, *Treatise on Divorce* (Madison, 1899); Gladstone, symposium ̦with Bradley and Dolph on "The Question of Divorce," in *North Am. Review*, CXLIX (New York, 1889); Greeley, "Marriage and Divorce: a Discussion with Robert Dale Owen," in *Recollections of a Busy Life*, 571 ff. (New York, 1869); *idem, Love, Marriage, and Divorce, and the Sovereignty of the Individual* (New York, 1853), a discussion with James and Andrews; Convers, *Marriage and Divorce* (Philadelphia, 1889), presenting the Catholic view; Dike, "Some Aspects of the Divorce Question," in *Princeton Review*, N. S., XIII (New York, 1884); and Woolsey, *Divorce and Divorce Legislation* (2d ed., New York, 1882).

In Italy divorce is favored by Gioja, *Teoria civile e penale del divorzio* (Milan, 1803); Mazzoleni, *La famiglia nei rapporti coll individuo e colla società* (Milan, 1870); Bianchi, *Il divorzio* (Pisa, 1879);

Bernardo, *Il divorzio nella teoria e nella pratica* (Palermo, 1875); Marescalchi, *Il divorzio e la instituzione sua in Italia* (Rome, 1889); and opposed by Giudici, *Memoria sul divorzio* (Milan, 1798); Rosmini, *Des lois civiles concernant le mariage des chrétiens* (trans., Paris, 1853); Zamperini, *Il divorzio considerato nella teoria e nella pratica di D. di Bernardo* (Verona, 1876); and Gabba, "The Introduction of Divorce in Italy," in *Am. Church Review*, XXXIII (New York, 1881). In France the rise of a sentiment favoring divorce may be traced in *Cri d'une honnête femme qui reclame le divorce* (London, 1770); *Contrat conjugal* (Paris, 1781; Neuchatel, 1783); Bouchotte, *Observations sur le divorce* (Paris, 1790); Hennet, *Du divorce* (Paris, 1792); Tissot, *Le mariage, la séparation, et le divorce* (Paris, 1868), giving an account of the principal French and Italian writers; Naquet, *Le divorce* (Paris, 1877); Bertillon, in the works above cited; Cavilly, *La séparation de corps et le divorce* (Paris, 1882); Fiaux, *La femme, le mariage, et le divorce* (Paris, 1880); and Dumas, *La question du divorce* (Paris, 1879; 5th ed., 1880). Divorce is opposed by Madame Necker, *Réflexions sur le divorce* (Paris, 1792; or Lausanne, 1794); Bonald, *Du divorce* (Paris, 1801); Malleville, *Du divorce* (Paris, 1801); Chrestien, *Dissertation historique* (Paris, 1804); Hennequin, *Du divorce* (Paris, 1832); Ozanam, "Du divorce," in his *Mélanges*, I (Paris, 1859); Daniel, *Le mariage chrétien et le Code Napoléon* (Paris, 1870); Durrieux, *Du divorce* (Paris, 1881); Vidieu, *Famille et divorce* (Paris, 1879). This book was answered by Dumas in the work just cited; and he in turn was replied to by Féval, *Pas de divorce* (11th ed., Paris, 1880); and Hornstein, *Le divorce* (Paris, 1880). Kellen, *Was ist die Frau?* (Leipzig, 1892) gives an account, with extracts, of Dumas's utterances on social questions.

Problems of the family are discussed by Allen, "The New England Family," *New Englander*, XLI (New Haven, 1882); Dike, *Perils to the Family* (Auburndale, 1887); *idem, The Family in the History of Christianity* (New York, 1886); *idem*, "Problems of the Family," in *Century*, XXXIX (New York, 1890); *idem*, "The Religious Problem of the Country Town," in *Andover Review*, II, III, IV (Boston, 1884–85); Mathews, "Christian Sociology: the Family," in *Amer. Jour. of Sociology*, I (Chicago, 1896); Blaikie, *The Family: Its Scriptural Ideal and its Modern Assailants* (London, 1889); Mulford, *The Nation*, chap. xv (New York, 1871); Bushnell, "The Organic Unity of the Family," in his *Christian Nurture* (New York, 1861); Potter, "The Message of Christ to the Family," in his *Message of Christ to Manhood* (Boston, 1899); Peabody, "Teachings of Jesus Concerning the Family," in his *Jesus Christ and the Social Question* (New York, 1900); Buckham, "The Relation of the Family to the State," in *International Review*, XIII (New York, 1882); Pearson, "Decline of the Family," in his *National Life and Character* (London, 1893); answered by Muirhead,

"Is the Family Declining?" in *Internat. Jour. of Ethics*, VII (Philadelphia, 1896); Commons, "The Family," chap. 10 of his "Sociological View of Sovereignty," in *Am. Jour. of Sociology*, V (Chicago, 1900); Stewart, *Disintegration of the Families of the Workingmen* (Chicago, 1893); Salter, *The Future of the Family* (Chicago, 1885); Devas, *Studies of Family Life* (London and New York, 1886); Henderson, *Social Elements* (New York, 1898); Small and Vincent, *Study of Society* (New York, Cincinnati, and Chicago, 1894); Ward, *Dynamic Sociology*, I, chap. vii (New York, 1883); Thwing, *The Family* (Boston, 1887); Planta, *Reconstruction der Familie* (Chur, 1886); Hermann, *Die Familie vom Standpunkte der Gesammtwirthschaft* (Berlin, 1889); Thiersch, *Ueber Christliches Familienleben* (8th ed., Augsburg, 1889); Naumann, *Christenthum und die Familie* (Berlin, 1892); Riehl, *Die Familie* (11th ed., Stuttgart, 1897); Gasparin, *Die Familie* (Gütersloh, 1870); Koenigswarter, *Hist. de l'org. de la famille en France* (Paris, 1851); Godelle, *Des principes fond. de la famille* (Metz, 1869); Grevin, *L'égalité dans la famille* (Douai, 1876); Bobbio, *Sulle origini e sul fond. della famiglia* (Turin, 1891); Assirelli, *La famiglia e la società* (Milan, 1887); Janet, *La famille* (10th ed., Paris, 1877); Le Play, *L'organisation de la famille* (4th ed., Tours and Paris, 1895); Durkheim, *Int. à la sociologie de la famille* (Bordeaux, 1888); Bonjean, *Enfants révoltés et parents coupables* (Paris, 1895); Baudrillart, *La famille et l'éducation en France* (Paris, 1874); Morillot, *Condition des enfants nés hors mariage* (Paris, 1865); Lallemand, *Hist. des enfants abandonnés* (Paris, 1885); *idem*, *La question des enfants abandonnés* (Paris, 1885); Milhaud, *Protection des enfants sans famille* (Paris, 1896); Gaume, *Hist. de la société domestique* (Paris, 1844), presenting the strong Catholic view; Pelletan, *La famille: la mère* (Paris, n. d.). For Germany and England see Biographical Note XI.

Marriage problems are discussed by Giles, *Treatise on Marriage* (London, 1771); Ryan, *Philosophy of Marriage* (3d ed., London, 1839); Amat, *Treatise on Matrimony* (San Francisco, 1864); Watkins, *Holy Matrimony* (London, 1895); Potwin, "Should Marriage be Indissoluble?" in *New Englander and Yale Review*, LVI (New Haven, 1892); Malcome, *The Christian Rule of Marriage* (Philadelphia, 1870); Pomeroy, *Ethics of Marriage* (New York, 1889); Gray, *Husband and Wife* (2d ed., Boston, 1886); Lea, *Christian Marriage* (London, 1881); Harte, *Laws and Customs of Marriage* (London, 1870); Quilter, *Is Marriage a Failure?* (Chicago, 1889); Colfavru, *Du mariage . . . . en Angleterre et aux États-Unis* (Paris, 1868); Carlier, *Le mariage aux États-Unis* (Paris, 1860); Cook, "Marriage Celebration in the U. S.," and "Reform of the Marriage Celebration," both in *Atlantic*, LXI (Boston, 1888); Snyder, *The Geography of Marriage* (2d ed., New York and London, 1889); Chavassé, *Traité de l'excellence du mariage* (Paris, 1685);

Gasparin, *Le mariage au point de vue chrétien* (2d ed., Paris, 1844); Picot, *Le mariage* (Paris, 1849); Cadet, *Le mariage en France* (Paris, 1870); Acollas, *Trois leçons . . . . du mariage* (Geneva and Berne, 1871); *idem*, *Le mariage* (Paris, 1880); Sincholle, *Le mariage civil et le mariage religieux* (Poitiers, 1876); Legrand, *Le mariage et les mœurs en France* (Paris, 1879); Hayem, *Le mariage* (Paris, 1872); Schoelcher, *La famille, la propriété, et le christianisme* (Paris, 1875); Hippel, *Ueber die Ehe* (4th ed., Frankfort and Leipzig, 1794); Volkmar, *Philosophie der Ehe* (Halle, 1794); Krug, *Philosophie der Ehe* (Reutlingen, 1801); Jörg and Tzschirner, *Die Ehe aus dem Gesichtspunkte der Natur, der Moral, und der Kirche* (Leipzig, 1819); Stäudlin, *Geschichte der Vorstellungen und Lehren von der Ehe* (Göttingen, 1826); Liebetrut, *Die Ehe nach ihrer Idee und nach ihrer geschichtlichen Entwicklung* (Berlin, 1834); Marr, *Der Mensch und die Ehe* (Leipzig, 1848); Hoffmann, *Die christliche Ehe* (Berlin, 1860); Glock, *Die christliche Ehe und ihre modernen Gegner* (Karlsruhe and Leipzig, 1881). Socialistic writers on the subject are Robert Owen, *Marriages of the Priesthood of the Old Immoral World* (4th ed., Leeds, 1840); Robert Dale Owen, "Marriage and Placement," in *Free Inquirer*, May 28 (New York, 1831); Pearson, *Ethic of Free Thought* (London, 1888); Besant, *Marriage; As It Was, As It Is, and As It Should Be;* Gronlund, *The Co-operative Commonwealth* (3d ed., London, 1891); Morris and Bax, *Socialism* (London and New York, 1893); Carpenter, *Love's Coming of Age;* Stürmer, *Moderner Eheschacher* (Leipzig, 1894); Proudhon, *Amour et mariage* (Brussels and Leipzig, n. d.); and Bebel, *Die Frau und der Sozialismus* (31st ed., Stuttgart, 1900), whose book is discussed by Oettingen, *Zur Theorie und Praxis des Heiratens* (Leipzig, n. d.). See also Oettingen's *Obligatorische und fakultative Civilehe nach den Ergebnissen der Moralstatistik* (Leipzig, 1881); Coulon, *De la réforme du mariage* (Paris, 1900); Kuhlenbeck, *Reform der Ehe* (Leipzig, 1891); Ewart, *Die Emancipation in der Ehe* (Hamburg and Leipzig, 1895); Vortmann, *Die Reform der Ehe* (Zürich, 1894); Lacombe, *Le mariage libre* (Paris, 1867); Löwenherz, *Prostitution oder Production, Eigentum oder Ehe* (Neuwied, n. d.); especially the able and radical works of Caird, *The Morality of Marriage* (London, 1897); Stetson, *Women and Economics* (Boston, 1900); and Schreiner, "The Woman Question," in *Cosmopolitan*, XXVIII (Irvington, 1899); *idem*, "The Woman's Movement of Our Day," in *Harper's Bazar*, XXXVI (New York, 1902). Swedenborg's system is set forth in his *Conjugal Love and its Chaste Delights* (new ed., London, 1862); it is summarized by Hayden, *Ten Chapters on Marriage* (2d ed., Boston, 1863); and expounded by Mann, *Five Sermons on Marriage* (New York, 1882).

On questions of heredity and selection consult Nisbet, *Marriage and Heredity* (London, 1890); Laurent, *Mariages consanguins et dégé-*

nérescences (Paris, 1895); Féré, *La famille névropathique* (Paris, 1894); Strahan, *Marriage and Disease* (London, 1892); Reibmayr, *Die Ehe Tuberculoser* (Leipzig and Vienna, 1894); Fournier, *Syphilis und Ehe* (Berlin, 1881); Stanley, "Artificial Selection and the Marriage Problem," in *Monist*, II (Chicago, 1891); *idem*, "Our Civilization and the Marriage Problem," in *Arena*, II (Boston, 1890); criticised by Wallace, "Human Selection," in *Fortnightly Review*, XLVIII (London, 1890); Wertheimer, "Homiculture," in *Nineteenth Century*, XXIV (London, 1898); and especially Wood, *Some Controlling Ideals of the Family Life of the Future* (New York, 1902).

Sex problems are treated by Clarke, *Sex in Education* (Boston, 1873), who is criticised in the works of Brackett, Howe, and Greene; Geddes, *Evolution of Sex and Sex in Education* (1899–1900); Maudsley, *Sex in Mind and Education* (New York, 1884); Ames, *Sex in Industry* (Boston, 1875); Lyttelton, *Training of the Young in the Laws of Sex* (London and New York, 1900); Blackwell, *The Human Element in Sex* (new ed., London, 1894); Brown, *Gunethics* (New York and London, 1887); Trall, *Sexual Physiology and Hygiene* (Glasgow and London, 1897); Gardner, *The Conjugal Relations* (Glasgow and London, 1898); Walker, *Intermarriage* (Birmingham, 1897); Heinzen, *The Rights of Women and the Sexual Relations* (Chicago, 1898); Tait, *Magdalenism* (2d ed., Edinburgh, 1842); Lecour, *La prostitution à Paris et à Londres, 1789–1877* (Paris, 1882); Guyot, *La prostitution* (Paris, 1882); Parents-Duchatelet, *De la prostitution dans la ville de Paris* (Paris, 1837); Dühren, *Das Geschlechtsleben in England* (Charlottenburg and Berlin, 1901–3); Klebs, *Verhältniss des männ. und weib. Geschlechts in der Natur* (Jena, 1894); Herman, *Sexualismus und Aetiologie* (Leipzig, 1899); Lindwurm, *Geschlechtsliebe* (Leipzig, 1879); Debay, *Philosophie des Ehelebens* (Berlin, 1895); Mantegazza, *Hygiene der Liebe* (3d ed., n. p., n. d.); Nemmersdorf, *Der Kampf der Geschlechter* (Leipzig, 1891); Daalen, *Die Ehe und die geschlecht. Stellung der Frau* (Berlin, 1896); Gardener, "A Battle for Sound Morality, or the Hist. of Recent Age-of-Consent Legislation in the U. S.," in *Arena*, XIII, XIV (Boston, 1895); Flower, "Wellsprings of Immorality," *ibid.*, XI, XII (Boston, 1894–95); *idem*, "Social Conditions as Feeders of Immorality," *ibid.*, XII (Boston, 1895); *idem*, "Prostitution within the Marriage Bond," *ibid.*, XIII (Boston, 1895); Pearson, "Socialism and Sex," in his *Ethic of Free Thought* (London, 1888).   Early German works of interest are *Der rechte Gebrauch und Missbrauch des Ehe-Bettes* (Leipzig, 1734); being a translation of Defoe's *Use and Abuse of the Marriage Bed* (London, 1727); Hencke, *Volles entdecktes Geheimniss der Natur* (Braunschweig, 1786); Josephi, *Ueber die Ehe und physische Erziehung* (Göttingen, 1788); Heydenreich, *Mann und Weib: ein Beytrag zur Philosophie über die Geschlechter* (Leipzig, 1798); Butte, *Die Biotomie des Menschen*

(Bonn, 1829). See also the works of Stetson, Caird, Bebel, and Schreiner above mentioned.

In the text an account is given of the early literature of the movement for woman's emancipation in its relation to marriage. For further study may be consulted Stanton, Anthony, and Gage, *History of Woman Suffrage* (New York and Rochester, 1881–87); Fawcett, Hirsch, *et al.*, in Theodore Stanton's *Woman Question in Europe* (New York, London, and Paris, 1884); Ostrogorski, *Rights of Women* (London, 1893); Johnson, *Woman and the Republic* (New York, 1897), strongly anti-suffrage; Legouvé, *Hist. morale des femmes* (8th ed., Paris, n. d.); Cohn, *Die deutsche Frauenbewegung* (Berlin, 1896), containing a select bibliography; Duboc, *Fünfzig Jahre Frauenfrage in Deutschland;* Sybel, *Ueber die Emancipation der Frauen* (Bonn, 1870); Richter, *Das Recht der Frauen auf Arbeit* (2d ed., Vienna, 1869); Büchner, *Ueber weibliche Berufsarten* (Darmstadt, 1872); Morgenstern, *Frauenarbeit in Deutschland* (Berlin, 1893); Hertzberg, *Der Beruf der Frau* (Leipzig, 1892); Jastrow, *Das Recht der Frau* (Berlin, 1897); Bridel, *Le droit des femmes* (Paris, 1893); Günther (R.), *Weib und Sittlichkeit* (Berlin, 1898); Günther (C.), *Das Recht der Frau auf Arbeit* (Berlin, 1899); Mont, *Das Weib* (2d ed., Leipzig, 1880); Gamble, *Evolution of Woman* (New York, 1894); Bücher, *Die Frauenfrage in dem Mittelalter* (Tübingen, 1882); and Mary Roberts Smith's able study of the "Statistics of College and Non-College Women," in *Pubs. of Am. Stat. Assoc.*, VII (Boston, 1901).   For further material see Bibliographical Notes IX, X, XI.]

I.   THE FUNCTION OF LEGISLATION

In the United States, not less clearly than elsewhere in countries of western civilization, marriage and the family are emerging as purely social institutions.   Liberated in large measure from the cloud of mediæval tradition, their problems are seen to be identical in kind with those which have everywhere concerned men and women from the infancy of the human race.   Accordingly, the extension of the sphere of secular legislation practically to the entire province of these institutions is a phenomenon of surpassing interest. Consciously or unconsciously, it is a recognition of the fact that matrimonial forms and family types are the products of human experience, of human habits, and are therefore to be dealt with by society according to human needs.   In this regard the Reformation marks the beginning of a social revolution.   From the days of Luther, however concealed in theological garb or forced under theological sanctions, however opposed by reactionary dogma, public opinion has more and more decidedly recognized the right of the temporal lawmaker in this field.   In the seventeenth century the New England Puritan gave the state, in its assemblies and in its courts, complete jurisdiction in questions of marriage and divorce, to the entire exclusion of the ecclesiastical authority.   Even the Council of Trent, by adjusting the dogma regarding the minister of the sacrament, had already left to Catholic states the way open for the civil regulation of matrimony—a way, as already seen, on which France did not hesitate to enter.[1]   Later the French Revolution wrested from the church judicial and legislative authority in matrimonial law and administration, and placed it in the hands of the state.   In 1792, by a wise and tolerant enactment, civil marriage and civil registration were established; but at the same time the revolt against the old ecclesiastical régime led to the sanction of free divorce.   Absolute dissolution of wedlock was then authorized at the mutual desire of both husband and wife, for incompatibility of temper on the petition of either spouse, and for seven other specified causes.[2]

[1] See chap. viii, sec. i; and consult GLASSON, Le mar. civil et le divorce, 210 ff., 232-51.

[2] On the revolutionary legislation regarding marriage and divorce (1792-1816) see NAQUET, Le divorce (Paris, 1877), 37-56, 153-353, containing extracts from the debates, text of the laws, reports, and other documents; Archives parlementaires, XXVI, 166-86, giving the report on the proposed civil marriage law; WRIGHT, Report, 1004-6, presenting summaries of the laws; CHAMPION, "La révolution et la réforme de l'état civil," La révolution française, June 14, 1887; COLFAVRU, "La question du divorce devant les législateurs de la révolution," ibid., March 14, 1884; KOENIGSWARTER, Histoire de l'organisation de la famille en France, 268 ff.; GLASSON, Le mar. civil et le divorce, 252-75; LEGRAND, Le mariage et les mœurs en France, 196-99; DURRIEUX, Du divorce, 99 ff.; FÉVAL, Pas de divorce, 74 ff.; FIAUX, La femme, le mariage, et le divorce, 25 ff.; VRAYE AND GODE, Le divorce et la séparation du corps, I, 7-26; BERTILLON, Étude démographique du divorce, 89 ff.; and in general LASAULX, Uebereinstimmung der französischen Ehetrennungsgesetze mit Gotteswort (Koblenz and Hadamar, 1816).

A powerful influence on revolutionary opinion must have been exerted by the

The natural result was a vast number of decrees.[1] Accordingly, in 1803 the Code Napoléon, while retaining civil marriage, adopted a more conservative policy regarding divorce. Incompatibility was no longer recognized; mutual consent was admitted under limitations; and the whole number of specified causes was reduced to five. The divorce law of 1803 was abrogated in 1816, and only restored in its essential features in 1884; but the liberal policy of France, as expressed in the Code Napoléon, has undoubtedly had a powerful influence in the extension of civil marriage and divorce throughout Europe, where, as in America, the modern statute-maker has recovered and passed beyond the point gained by the Roman imperial constitutions between Augustus and Justinian.

The right of society to deal freely with the whole province of marriage, divorce, and the family may be conceded. To determine the proper character and sphere of legislation

remarkable *Contrat conjugal*, published in 1781, again in 1783, and in German translation in 1784, which advocated civil marriage and free divorce, while attacking the ecclesiastical system of impediments and dispensations. The revolutionary ideas regarding divorce are also vigorously presented by HENNET, *Du divorce* (3d ed., Paris, 1792); and by BOUCHOTTE, *Observations sur le divorce* (Paris, 1790). On the other hand, the divorce law of 1792 is criticised and divorce opposed by MADAME NECKER, *Réflexions sur le divorce* (Paris, 1792; Lausanne, 1794); as in *Du divorce* (Paris, 1801), 1 ff., by BONALD, who opposed the law of 1803 and secured its repeal in 1816. See PÈRE DANIEL'S *Le mariage chrétien et le Code Napoléon* (Paris, 1870); and for an examination of the literature of the period, TISSOT, *Le mariage, la séparation, et le divorce*, 174 ff., 180 ff., 196 ff., 211 ff., 222 ff.

[1] In Paris alone during the first twenty-seven months after the passage of the act 5,994 divorces were granted; while in 1797 the divorce decrees in that city actually outnumbered the marriages: GLASSON, *Le mar. civil et le divorce*, 261, 262. Accordingly, in 1798, the law was amended so as to make divorce for "incompatibility" allowable only six months after final failure of attempts at reconciliation;" and this law also required all municipal authorities to proceed, and all teachers of public and private schools to take their pupils, "to the usual meeting places of the community every ten years in person and in state, there to make stern proclamation of the parties divorced during the previous decade, with the view of thus checking divorces."—WRIGHT, *Report*, 1005; NAQUET, *Le divorce*, 212-37, giving documents; BRUN, "Divorce Made Easy," *North Am. Rev.*, CLVII (July, 1893), 12, 13; citing DUVAL, *Souvenirs thermidoriens*, I, 60, 61. See also the *Rapport* (27 thermidor, an. V) of Portalis, who was the chief advocate of the amendment. In 1800, it is alleged, there were about 4,000 marriages and 700 divorces in Paris, To what extent the relative decrease was due to the change in the law can only be conjectured.

is a very different matter. What is the quality of the existing laws under the interpretation given to them by the courts? Are they adequate to secure proper social control? What is the legitimate aim, and what are the needful limits of future legislation? Should the laws be uniform for the fifty-three states and territories; and, if so, how is uniformity to be attained? These are practical questions with whose solution it is high time that society should more earnestly concern itself.

a) The statutes and the common-law marriage.—The defects in the matrimonial laws of the United States are many and grave; but perhaps the chief obstacle in the way of securing a proper social control is the general recognition of the validity of the so-called "common-law marriage." Almost everywhere the public celebration of wedlock is intended by the statute; and in nearly all the states a license or certificate is required before the solemnization may take place. Yet, according to the prevailing doctrine, as expressed in judicial decisions or in the statutes themselves, these provisions are interpreted as merely "directory," not "mandatory;" and marriage contracts made in total disregard of them, by words of mutual present consent, are sustained as valid, although the prescribed penalties may be enforced for violation of the written law. In short, the vicious mediæval distinction between validity and legality is retained as an element of common matrimonial law in the United States.[1]

The doctrine that an informal marriage *per verba de praesenti* is valid unless expressly declared void by "words of nullity" in the statute is not an invention of the American courts. It is the doctrine maintained by the English judges previous to the decision in the case of the Queen *v.* Millis in

[1] On this doctrine, with the leading cases, see KENT, *Commentaries* (14th ed., Boston, 1896), II, secs. 87 ff., pp. 119 ff.; REEVE, *The Law of Husband and Wife* ("Domestic Relations"), 250–58; GREENLEAF, *Law of Evidence* (16th ed., Boston, 1899), II, secs. 460–64, pp. 441–47; and especially BISHOP, *Mar., Div., and Sep.*, I, secs. 409 ff., pp. 176 ff.

1844; and from the evidence already presented[1] it seems
almost certain, if indeed it be not demonstrated, that it was
the accepted doctrine in the English colonies. According
to an able writer, the colonial statutory "system" entirely
superseded the common law; and this system has been "destroyed" by a revolution, effected through the decisions of
the American courts, "which has introduced into our law
much of the insecurity, the irreverence, the license, of the
Middle Ages," our common law today being "the canon law
that existed prior to the Council of Trent."[2] No doubt our
common-law marriage is thoroughly bad, involving social
evils of the most dangerous character; and no doubt the
colonial legislative system was a remarkable advance upon
anything which had elsewhere appeared. But the common-
law marriage was not introduced by the American judges;
nor is it historically correct to say that in the English
colonies it had been entirely supplanted by legislation, however admirable in its intent and quality that legislation may
have been. For the colonial period, as elsewhere shown, the
relation of the statutes governing marriage to the common
law can only partially be determined from the court records.
In the southern colonies the judicial history of the subject is
almost a complete blank.[3] Other evidence, however, is available. Only during the thirty-five years between 1661 and
1696 does any statute of Virginia expressly declare a marriage void if not contracted according to its provisions. The
new law of 1696, enacted in place of the statute of 1661/2,
which was then repealed, declares that "many great and

---

[1] See chaps. xii-xv, inclusive.

[2] Cook, "The Marriage Celebration in the United States," *Atlantic*, LXI, 521.
"But in the early part of this century there arose in the courts a discussion regarding the nature of our common law, and the relation of that law to our statute law in
governing the celebration of marriage—a discussion which since then has constantly increased, and has gradually brought about a revolution unparalleled in the
history of our subject."—*Ibid.*

[3] Chap. xv, sec. ii; chap. xiii, sec. iv.

grievous mischeifes . . . . dayly doe arise by clandestine and secret marriages to the utter ruin of many heirs and heiresses;" and yet it is significant that the words of nullity contained in the earlier act are omitted. Indeed, by the terms of this law the validity of an irregular marriage thereafter contracted by a female between the ages of twelve and sixteen is clearly implied, although she is to be severely punished.[1] Dissenters had refused to marry according to the statute which they regarded as oppressive; and their resistance, perhaps with a feeling that the act of 1661/2 was itself invalid as being in conflict with the English common law, may have led to the omission of the words of nullity in all subsequent statutes of Virginia. After 1696 irregular marriages were probably regarded as valid, as they certainly were previous to 1661/2; for an act of 1642/3, while prescribing severe penalties for the secret marriage of indented servants, shows beyond question that such a contract, or one between a freeman and an indented maid servant, is looked upon as binding.[2] The facts are much the same for the other southern colonies. After 1692 the invalidating clause disappears from the statutes of Maryland. Only between 1766 and 1778, in North Carolina, is a marriage contracted without previous license expressly declared to be null and void; and it is enlightening that even during this short period of twelve years the penalty of invalidity is not extended to illegal celebration. It was mainly a device of the lawmaker to secure the governor in his revenue from the license fees. The South Carolina act of 1706 merely prescribes penalties for its violation; and, besides, its provisions relating to the celebration were entirely disregarded in the western country, where the various religious sects made use of civil forms or practiced their own peculiar rites. In both the Carolinas as well as in Georgia, since marriages illegally

---

[1] Chap. xiii, sec. i.   [2] HENING, *Statutes*, I, 252, 253. See chap. xiii, sec. i.

celebrated before unauthorized laymen or ministers seem to have been valid, there is little reason to doubt that clandestine and other informal contracts by present consent of the parties were likewise good; but regarding this point we have no positive information.[1]

The history of marriage in the middle and the New England colonies leads us to a similar result. From the facts brought to light in the Lauderdale Peerage case, backed by the testimony of Rev. John Rodgers in 1773, it is almost certainly established that the common-law marriage was valid in New York province, and that for eighty-four years preceding the Revolution no other law relating to the subject was in force.[2] In New England the formalities prescribed by the statutes were doubtless usually observed. Yet there were many clandestine and other irregular marriages, and in some instances we know that these were treated as valid.[3] Such was the case in the Plymouth jurisdiction, where "self-marriage" was punished only by a fine. In Massachusetts similar cases of "hand-fasting" and "self-gifta" appear. In one case, that of Governor Bellingham in 1641, the contract was not declared void by the court, although the grand jury had presented his excellency for his offense. Fifteen years later Joseph Hills, "being presented by the grand jury for marrying of himself contrary to the law of the colony," confessed his fault and was merely "admonished by the court."[4] Moreover, at no time during the colonial and provincial periods did the statutes of Massachusetts expressly declare marriages void for disregard of the celebration or other formalities prescribed;[5] and the

[1] For these colonies see chap. xiii, secs. iii, iv.

[2] Chap. xiv, sec. i, c). [3] Chap. xii, sec. vi.

[4] *MSS. Records of the County Court of Middlesex* (Apr. 1, 1656), I, 80.

[5] See the case of Usher *v.* Troop (Throop), 1724–29, in which is raised the question as to whether the "constitutions and canons ecclesiastical of the Church of England" are binding in Massachusetts: *MSS. Records of the Superior Court of Judicature*, 1725–30, fol. 236. *Cf.* chap. xii, secs. i, ii.

same is true of the daughter-colony of Connecticut. By the
Rhode Island acts of 1647 and 1665 the issue of a union not
formed by the "due and orderly course of law" is pronounced illegitimate; but it is very suggestive that the
words of nullity do not appear in any of the later statutes
of that province. Occasionally in the colonies statutes were
enacted to validate irregular marriages previously contracted.
Such were the acts of Rhode Island, 1698; of North Carolina, 1766; and of Virginia, 1780. But it would clearly be
rash to infer that the marriages concerned were in fact void
without such special intervention. Notoriously this is but a
speedy and simple way of quieting doubt as to the status of
the children or their rights of property and inheritance.
Whether a court would nullify the contracts in question is a
different matter. On the whole, the evidence seems clearly
to show that the colonial statutes sustained the same relation
to the English common law as did the constitutions of the
English church requiring the solemnization of wedlock
before a clergyman. The colonial statute, like the ecclesiastical constitution, might determine the legal forms which
must be observed to escape a penalty; but the common-law
marriage was nevertheless valid unless expressly declared
null and void in the act itself. Furthermore, it is by no
means certain that the colonial assemblies were generally
competent, even in this way, to set aside the common law.

After the beginning of independent national life the English common law as a whole in its various branches was
retained as a part of the law of the land, unless superseded
by constitutional or statutory legislation. It was therefore
inevitable that the state and federal courts, as cases arose,
should declare whether it had been so superseded. There
could no longer be any question, as in the colonial period,
regarding the competency of the legislator to define the conditions of a valid matrimonial contract. A brief history of

the acceptance or rejection of the common-law marriage in the United States, whether by statute or by judicial decree, may now be presented.[1]

The leading case came before the supreme court of New York in 1809, when Chief Justice Kent accepted as binding a common-law marriage, declaring that no solemnization was requisite; that "a contract of marriage made *per verba de praesenti* amounts to an actual marriage, and is as valid as if made in *facie ecclesiae;*" and that the existence of such a contract may be proved "from cohabitation, reputation, acknowledgment of the parties, acceptance in the family, and other circumstances from which a marriage may be inferred."[2] This decision determined the policy of New York for nearly a century, until the common-law marriage was at last superseded by the statute of 1901; and its influence upon the tribunals of other states has been increased through the sanction of its doctrine by the leading authorities upon matrimonial law.[3] The contract by mere present consent

---

[1] Cook, "The Mar. Cel. in the U.S.," *Atlantic*, LXI, 520–32, has given a systematic account of the subject to the year 1888. To this article, and to his " Reform in the Celebration of Marriage," *ibid.*, 680–90, I am indebted; as also to Bennett, " Uniformity in Marriage and Divorce Laws," *Am. Law Register*, N. S., XXXV, 221–31. *Cf.* Convers, *Mar. and Divorce*, 15–119; Stewart, *Mar. and Divorce*, 78 ff.

[2] In the case of Fenton *v.* Reed (1809), 4 Johns., 52; 4 *Am. D.*, 244; Ewell, *Cases on Domestic Relations*, 397–99. Following are the essential facts in this celebrated case. In 1785 John Guest "left the state for foreign parts." During his absence, in 1792, his wife Elizabeth married Reed. Subsequently in the same year her first husband, Guest, returned to the state and there resided until his death in June, 1800. He professed to have no marital claim upon Elizabeth; so she lived with Reed as a wife continuously from 1792 until the latter's death in 1806. Was she the lawful wife of Reed from 1792 to 1800 during the lifetime of Guest? If not, was she, without the observance of any formalities, his lawful wife from 1800 to 1806 after Guest's demise? To the first question the court answered "no," holding that "the statute concerning bigamy does not render the second marriage legal, notwithstanding the former husband or wife may have been absent above five years, and not heard of. It only declares that the party who marries again in consequence of such absence . . . . , shall be exempted from the operation of the statute, and leaves the question of the validity of the second marriage just where it found it." To the second question the court answered "yes," as explained in the text. *Cf.* Starr *v.* Peck, 1 Hill, *N. Y.*, 270.

[3] The doctrine of his own decision was formulated in 1826 by Kent in the first edition of his *Commentaries*. Ten years earlier, in 1816, it had been accepted by Reeve, former chief justice of Connecticut, in his treatise on the *Law of Husband and Wife*. It was followed in 1842 by Greenleaf in his work on *Evidence;* and

of the parties, regardless of the statutory requirements, has been widely accepted as valid in the group of southern and southwestern states and territories. It was so judicially accepted in South Carolina[1] at least as early as 1832; in Louisiana[2] in 1833; Georgia[3] in 1860; District of Columbia[4] in 1865; Alabama[5] in 1869; Arkansas[6] in 1872; Missouri[7] in 1877; and Florida[8] in 1880. By the earlier decisions of Tennessee a strict compliance with the statute was required, the court even declaring in 1829[9] that a marriage solemnized before a justice of the peace out of his own county was "absolutely null and void." This opinion was sustained by a decree of 1831; but later judgments favor the common-law agreement. Texas has had a similar experience. In 1883 and again in 1894 the common-law contract was repudiated, the court deciding that license and parental consent according to the statute were essential;[10] but more recently

later by BISHOP in his well-known book on *Marriage and Divorce*. On the other hand, the younger PARSONS, the first edition of whose *Contracts* appeared in 1853, is inclined to reject the Kent doctrine: see the 8th ed., II, 78 ff.; and compare COOK, "The Mar. Cel. in the U. S.," *Atlantic*, XLI, 521, 522.

[1] See Fryer *v.* Fryer (1832), RICHARDSON'S *Equity Cases*, 92 ff. *Cf.* the case of Vaigneur *v.* Kirk (1808), 2 *S. C. Equity Reports*, 640–46; and 10 McCORD'S *Statutes*, 357, ed. note; *ibid.*, II, 733, ed. note.

[2] Holmes *v.* Holmes (1833), 6 *La.*, 463. In this state, under influence of French and Spanish law, the common-law contract appears always to have been regarded as valid.

[3] Askew *v.* Dupree (1860), 30 *Ga.*, 173; *cf.* Clark *v.* Cassidy, 64 *Ga.*, 662.

[4] Blackburn *v.* Crawfords (1865), 3 WALL., 175; Diggs *v.* Wormley (1893), 21 *D. C.*, 477, 485; Jennings *v.* Webb (1896), 8 *App. D. C.*, 43, 56. *Cf.* Green *v.* Norment (1886), 5 MACKEY, 80–92.

[5] In Campbell *v.* Gullatt (1869), 43 *Ala.*, 57. But see the earlier decisions in S. *v.* Murphy (1844), 6 *Ala.*, 765–72; 41 *Am. D.*, 79; and Robertson *v.* S. (1868), 42 *Ala.*, 509; being conflicting and indecisive as to whether the statute is merely "directory."

[6] Jones *v.* Jones (1872), 28 *Ark.*, 19–26. According to S. *v.* Willis (1848), 9 *Ark.*, 196–98, consent of the parent is not essential.

[7] Dyer *v.* Brannock (1877), 66 *Mo.*, 391; 27 *Am. R.*, 359. The license required by statute is not essential to a valid marriage: S. *v.* Bittick (1890), 103 *Mo.*, 183.

[8] Daniel *v.* Sams (1880), 17 *Fla.*, 487–97.

[9] In Bashaw *v.* S. (1829), 1 YERG., 177; affirmed in Grisham *v.* S. (1831), 2 YERG., 589; opposed in Andrews *v.* Page (1871), 3 HEISK., 653–71; and apparently questioned in Johnson *v.* Johnson (1860), 1 COLDW., 626.

[10] Dumas *v.* S. (1883), 14 *Tex. Cr. App.*, 464–74; Tel. Co. *v.* Procter (1894), 6 *T. C. A.*, 300, 303.

the highest tribunal has held the opposite view.[1] Among the states of the middle and western group Pennsylvania in 1814 was first to follow the New York precedent.[2] Ohio[3] came next in 1861; and Illinois[4] in 1873. By the law of Michigan, declares Judge Cooley decisively in 1875—in an opinion accepted as authority by the federal courts—a marriage may be good, although the statutory regulations have not been complied with. "Whatever the form of ceremony, or even if all ceremony was dispensed with, if the parties agreed presently to take each other for husband and wife, and from that time lived together professedly in that relation, proof of these facts would be sufficient to constitute proof" of a binding marriage; and "this," he adds, "has become the settled doctrine of the American courts."[5] This view has been accepted in Iowa[6] in 1876; Minnesota[7] in 1877; Wisconsin[8] in 1879; Indiana[9] in 1884; Kansas[10] in 1887; Nebraska[11] and Colorado[12] in 1893; Nevada[13] in 1896; and favored by the decisions of New Jersey[14] since 1824.

[1] Cumby v. Henderson (1894), 6 T. C. A., 519–23; 25 S. W., 673; Ingersol v. McWillie (1895), 9 T. C. A., 543, 553; 30 S. W., 56; Chapman v. Chapman (1897), 16 T. C. A., 384; and especially Railway Co. v. Cody (1899), 20 T. C. A., 520–24.

[2] Hantz v. Sealey (1814), 6 BINN., 405; also Rodebaugh v. Sanks (1833), 2 WATTS, 9–12; and Commonwealth v. Stump (1866), 53 Pa., 132–38.

[3] Carmichael v. S. (1861), 12 Ohio, 553–61.

[4] Port v. Port (1873), 70 Ill., 484; Bowman v. Bowman (1887), 24 Ill. App., 165–78.

[5] Hutchins v. Kimmel (1875), 31 Mich., 126–35; 18 Am. R., 164–69.

[6] Blanchard v. Lambert (1876), 43 Iowa, 228–32. Since 1851 the statutes of Iowa have clearly accepted the common-law marriage: Code of Iowa (1851), secs. 1474, 1475; ibid. (1897), 1124.

[7] S. v. Worthington (1877), 23 Minn., 528.

[8] Williams v. Williams (1879), 46 Wis., 464–80; Spencer v. Pollock (1892), 83 Wis., 215–22.

[9] Teter v. Teter (1884), 101 Ind., 129; 51 Am. R., 742. In Roche v. Washington (1862), 19 Ind., 53, the opposite position is taken.

[10] S. v. Walker (1887), 36 Kan., 297; 59 Am. R., 556.

[11] Bailey v. S. (1893), 36 Neb., 808–14.

[12] Israel v. Arthur (1893), 18 Col., 158, 164; Taylor v. Taylor (1897), 10 C. A., 303, 304.

[13] S. v. Zichefield (1896), 23 Nev., 304–18.

[14] Wyckoff v. Boggs (1824), 2 HALST., 138–40; and especially Pearson v. Howey (1829), 6 HALST., 12, 18, 20.

Moreover, the Supreme Court of the United States has sanctioned the same doctrine. In Jewell v. Jewell,[1] considered in 1843, opinions on the question were evenly balanced, just as they were in the Queen v. Millis which came before the Lords during the next year; but in 1877, in the case of Meister v. Moore,[2] involving a marriage contracted under the law of Michigan, Justice Strong adopted "as authoritative" Judge Cooley's interpretation rendered two years before.

On the other hand, in a number of states the courts have decided that the common-law marriage is entirely superseded by the statutes, even when these do not contain words of nullity, and sometimes when they are expressed in terms far less "mandatory" than in some instances where the opposite doctrine prevails.[3] In the words of a writer who believes the courts are historically and logically justified in this view, "they affirm that when from a comparative study of the whole course of legislation as well as of the terms of the various statutes, it is the plain intent to make conformity to any statutory formality indispensable to the constitution of marriage, such common law is *ipso facto* repealed, and a marriage celebrated by mere consent, without this formality, has no validity whatever in law. One such indispensable formality, at least, they find in the intent of the statutes, namely, the presence at the celebration of an authorized third person."[4] First to take this position was Massachusetts in 1810, the year after Kent's opposite decision already cited, when Chief Justice Parsons, in an opinion which has

---

[1] Jewell v. Jewell (1843), 1 HOWARD, 219–34.

[2] Meister v. Moore (1877), 96 *U. S.*, 76–83.

[3] See BENNETT, "Uniformity in Mar. and Div. Laws," *Am. Law Register*, N. S., XXXV, 223 ff., who points out that the statutes of Alabama, Pennsylvania, and Missouri, where the common-law marriage is valid, are far more prohibitory than those of Massachusetts, Maryland, or West Virginia, where it is void. The statute of Alabama says positively that "no marriage shall be solemnized without a license issued by the judge of probate of the county where the female resides;" but a marriage so solemnized is nevertheless valid.

[4] COOK, "The Mar. Cel. in the U. S.," *Atlantic*, LXI, 523.

been steadily sustained ever since, but which is not remarkable for historical knowledge, held that "when our ancestors left England, and ever since, it is well known that a lawful [valid?] marriage there must be celebrated before a clergyman in orders;" and hence in Massachusetts, although "not declared void by any statute," a "marriage merely the effect of a mutual engagement between the parties, or solemnized by any one not a justice of the peace or an ordained minister, is not a legal marriage, entitled to the incidents of a marriage duly solemnized."[1] Since 1848 the Massachusetts doctrine has been followed by Vermont.[2] In the same year it was adopted in New Hampshire;[3] but in the absence of more recent decisions the law of that state cannot be regarded as absolutely settled. It was favored in Maine[4] by a decision of 1841, although the informal contract was not then positively rejected by a direct decree. The courts of Connecticut are silent on the question; but the statute declares that all marriages "attempted to be solemnized by any other person" than those authorized by it "shall be void."[5]

---

[1] Milford v. Worcester (1810), 7 *Mass.*, 48–58. See also, to the same effect, Commonwealth v. Munson (1879), 127 *Mass.*, 459–71; 34 *Am. R.*, 411. In this case it is correctly held that Justice Bigelow's decision in Parton v. Hervey (1854), 1 GRAY, 119, that the statute is merely "directory," relates to banns and parental consent, and not to solemnization; for Milford v. Worcester is cited as authority.

[2] See the opinion of Judge Redfield in Northfield v. Plymouth (1848), 20 *Vt.*, 582, holding that a common-law marriage could not be regarded as valid without "virtually repealing our statutes," thus reversing the doctrine of Newbury v. Brunswick (1829), 2 *Vt.* 151; 19 *Am. D.*, 703; and consult especially Morrill v. Palmer (1895), 68 *Vt.*, 1–23, holding "that what . . . . Kent calls the 'loose doctrine of the common law,' in relation to marriage, was never in force in this state."

[3] See the opinion of Chief Justice Gilchrist in Dumbarton v. Franklin (1848), 19 *N. H.*, 257, rejecting as irrelevant Judge Woodbury's *obiter dictum* in Londonderry v. Chester (1820), 2 *N. H.*, 268–81, usually cited to sustain the common-law marriage; but this objection to it is scarcely valid.

[4] S. v. Hodskins (1841), 19 *Me.*, 155–60; 36 *Am. D.*, 743. *Cf.* Ligonia v. Buxton, 2 *Me.*, 95. According to Hiram v. Pierce, 45 *Me.*, 367, the statute of Maine, like that of Massachusetts, is only directory regarding parental consent in case of minors.

[5] *Gen. Stat. of Ct.* (1902), 1086. According to REEVE, *Law of Husband and Wife*, 252 ff.; followed by KENT, *Commentaries*, II, secs. 87 ff., the common-law marriage was formerly good in Connecticut.

Several states of the South have taken a similar stand. Maryland[1] and North Carolina[2] have thus repudiated the common-law agreement, a formal celebration being made essential to a valid marriage. The supreme court of West Virginia has gone farther, holding that not only solemnization, but also license and other prescribed formalities, are requisite. "Our statute," runs a decision of 1887, "has wholly superseded the common law, and in effect, if not in express terms, renders invalid all attempted marriages contracted in this state, which have not been solemnized in compliance with its provisions. . . . . When the terms of the statute are such that they cannot be made effective, to the extent of giving each and all of them some reasonable operation, without interpreting the statutes as mandatory, then such interpretation should be given them."[3] In 1821 the common-law contract was judicially accepted in Kentucky;[4] but by the model statute of 1852—remarkable for clearness and terseness—a "marriage is prohibited and declared void when not solemnized or contracted in the presence of an authorized person or society."[5] Likewise in Mississippi until recently the informal agreement was held sufficient to constitute the parties husband and wife;[6] but

[1] The common-law marriage was sustained in Cheseldine v. Brewer (1739), 1 HAR. AND McH., 152; overruled and the opposite doctrine supported in Denison v. Denison (1871), 35 Md., 361. In Jackson v. Jackson (1894), 80 Md., 176–96, it is held that the "fact that the marriage was performed by a clergyman may be inferred from the evidence." Cf. BISHOP, Mar., Div., and Sep., I, sec. 416, p. 179.

[2] S. v. Samuel (1836), 2 DEV. AND BAT., 177–85; followed in S. v. Patterson (1842), 2 IREDELL, N. C., 346–60; left undecided in S. v. Ta-cha-na-tah (1870), 64 N. C., 614. Cf. S. v. Robbins (1845), 6 IREDELL, N. C., 23–27, where apparently a celebration, but not a license, is held essential to a valid marriage (25); and especially S. v. Wilson (1897), 121 N. C., 657, where it is declared that a marriage "pretendedly celebrated before a person not authorized would be a nullity."

[3] Beverlin v. Beverlin (1887), 29 W. Va., 732–40.

[4] Dumaresly v. Fishly (1821), 3 A. K. MARSHALL, 368–77. See also Commonwealth v. Jackson, 11 BUSH., Ky., 679.

[5] Acts (1850–51), 212–16 (law in force July 1, 1852); sustained in Estill v. Rogers (1866), 1 BUSH., Ky., 62; Stewart v. Munchandler, 2 BUSH., Ky., 278.

[6] Hargroves v. Thompson (1856), 31 Miss., 211; Dickerson v. Brown (1873), 49 Miss., 357; Floyd v. Calvert (1876), 53 Miss., 37; Rundle v. Pegram (1874), 49 Miss., 751.

since 1892 the statute renders a marriage invalid if contracted or solemnized without a previous license.[1] Moreover, in Porto Rico, by the code of 1902, the authorization and celebration of the contract "according to the forms and solemnities prescribed by law" are requisite for a valid marriage.[2] With these six southern and the four New England commonwealths must be classed five states of the middle and western division. Two of these—Oregon[3] since 1870 and Washington[4] since 1892—have proceeded by judicial decree; and three—California[5] in 1895, Utah[6] in 1898, and New York[7] in 1901—have superseded the common-law agreement by statutes containing the nullifying clause.

All the other states and territories have enacted laws governing the celebration and other preliminaries of marriage; but whether these laws are to be regarded as mandatory or merely directory has not yet been judicially determined. The courts are thus silent in Connecticut and Rhode Island,[8] of the New England group; in Arizona, Indian Territory, New Mexico, Oklahoma, and Virginia, of

---

[1] *Ann. Code of Miss.* (1892), 679.

[2] *Rev. Stat. and Codes of Porto Rico* (1902), 805.

[3] Holmes v. Holmes (1870), 1 ABB., *Cir. Ct.* (U. S.), 525, declaring the statute regarding the solemnization of marriage mandatory.

[4] *In re* McLaughlin's Estate (1892), 4 *Wash.*, 570; 30 *Pac. R.*, 651; *in re* Wilbur's Estate (1894), 8 *Wash.*, 35.

[5] It may require judicial interpretation to determine the law of California. Sec. 55 of the *Civil Code*, since the act of 1895, does not contain the *usual* words of nullity; but sec. 68 declares that a marriage is not invalidated by violation of the provisions governing solemnization, license, authentication, and record "*by other than the parties themselves.*" One or two of the superior court judges have already decided that the statutory formalities are mandatory.

[6] The *Rev. Stat. of Utah* (1898) rendered marriage void when not celebrated before an authorized person. Before this date a common-law contract was binding: U. S. v. Simpson, 4 *Utah*, 227; 7 *Pac.*, 257.

[7] See chap. xvi, sec. iii, a).

[8] In Peck v. Peck (1880), 12 *R. I.*, 485–89, the court declined to decide whether a common-law contract is valid, there being no prohibitory language in the statute. *Cf.* also S. v. Boyle (1882), 13 *R. I.*, 537; and Ben. Association v. Carpenter (1892), 17 *R. I.*, 720. In Williams v. Herrick (1899), 21 *R. I.*, 401–3, the court appears to favor the validity of a marriage without a formal ceremony, if begun with "matrimonial intent."

the southern and southwestern group; in Alaska, Delaware, Hawaii, Idaho, Montana, North Dakota, South Dakota, and Wyoming,[1] of the middle and western division.   Of these Delaware, Virginia,[2] and Connecticut would probably reject the common-law doctrine, were the question brought to a judicial test; while it would almost certainly be accepted by the courts of the other twelve states and territories, should the statutes remain as they are.   Indeed, in a number of the last-named states, notably in Idaho, Montana, and South Dakota, it is virtually sanctioned by the terms of the statutes themselves.

It appears, then — to summarize the details presented in the foregoing discussion — that twenty-three states and territories have already sanctioned or favored the common-law marriage; while twelve others are soon likely to do so, unless the statutes shall be changed.   On the contrary, eighteen commonwealths have repudiated or are inclined to repudiate the informal agreement.   Six of these, it should be noted, have liberated themselves by statute; five — Mississippi, California, Utah, New York, and Porto Rico[3] — having done so within the last ten years.   This is a fact of vast social importance. From it the reformer may gather new courage.   In such legislation, in response to a better-educated popular sentiment, lies the hope of the future: to free American society from the manifold evils which lurk in the doctrine of the common-law marriage.   It is, indeed, marvelous that a progressive people with respect to an institution which is the

[1] According to Connors v. Connors (1895), 40 Pac., 966, a license is not essential in Wyoming.

[2] In Beverlin v. Beverlin, 29 W. Va., 736, the judge says, "I have been unable to find any case in which the courts of Virginia or this state have ever held that a common-law marriage was held valid; " and this, he adds, is "persuasive evidence " that it is not.   In Colston v. Quander (1877), 1 Va. Decisions (not officially reported), license is declared not essential; but in this case there was a formal celebration. On the probable position of the states which have not decided see COOK, The Mar. Cel. in the U. S., 525, 526.

[3] Of course the statute of Porto Rico must be regarded as preventing, not abolishing, the common-law marriage.

very basis of the social order should so long neglect the function of proper public control.   For what, according to its nature, is the common-law marriage?   Its possibilities for anarchy are realistically described by Chief Justice Folger, of New York, in 1880, when that state was still exposed to them.   "A man and a woman," he declares, "who are competent to marry each other, without going before a minister or magistrate, without the presence of any person as a witness, with no previous public notice given, with no form or ceremony, civil or religious, and with no record or written evidence of the act kept, and merely by words of present contract between them, may take upon themselves the relation of husband and wife, and be bound to themselves, to the state, and to society."[1]   Verily this is individualism absolutely unrestrained!   It is the simple truth, as already suggested, that in principle the canon law as it existed in Catholic lands before the Council of Trent, and in England until the marriage act of 1753, with a possibility of all of its attendant scandals and hardships, still survives in the United States.[2]   The apology of the Middle Ages was found in the sacramental dogma.   Matrimony as such, under whatever conditions contracted, was too "holy" to be dissolved or effectively hindered for the ordinary prudential reasons which appeal to the statesman or legislator.   Today there is doubtless a lingering tradition of the same false

[1] Quoted by Cook, "The Mar. Cel. in the U. S.," *Atlantic*, LXI, 526. On the frauds perpetrated under the guise of the common-law marriage see also the opinion of Judge Pryor of New York: quoted by Richberg, *Incongruities of the Divorce Laws*, 61, 62. "It is singular," said Chief Justice Gilchrist in 1848, "that the most important of all human contracts, on which the rights and duties of the whole community depend, requires less formality for its validity than the conveyance of an acre of land, a policy of insurance, or the agreements which the statute of frauds requires should be in writing."— Dumbarton v. Franklin, 19 *N. H.*, 264, 265.

[2] Except, perhaps, in practically getting rid of the subtle doctrine of marriage *per verba de futuro cum copula:* see the decision in Starr v. Peck (1841), 1 Hill, *N. Y.*, 270; Ewell, *Cases*, 403. *Cf*. Cheney v. Arnold (1857), 15 *N. Y.*, 345; Ewell, 407-13; this being followed in Duncan v. Duncan, 10 *Ohio*, 181; but discarded in Port v. Port, 70 *Ill.*, 484; and Peck v. Peck, 12 *R. I.*, 484; 34 *Am. R.*, 702. *Cf*. Bishop, *Mar., Div., and Sep.*, I, secs. 353-77, pp. 147-62; Kent, *Commentaries*, II, sec. 87 ff., pp. 119 ff.

sentiment.   Yet the common-law marriage is now supported
on two principal grounds.   The innocent offspring, we are
told, ought not to suffer because the parents have neglected
the formalities prescribed by a mere statute.   Moreover, to
declare an irregular, perhaps a clandestine, union void is to
invade the most sacred right of the individual.   There is
urgent need that the American people should realize the
fallacy of such arguments.   Far better that the children of
a delinquent minority should bear the stain of illegitimacy
than that the welfare of the whole social body should be
endangered.   For the same reason the supposed right of the
individual must yield to the higher claims of society.   In no
part of the whole range of human activity is there such
imperative need of state interference and control as in the
sphere of the matrimonial relations.   In this field as in
others we are beginning to see more clearly that the highest
individual liberty can be secured only when it is subordi-
nated to the highest social good.   It is, however, not merely
the public which suffers.   "Our common-law marriage fails
to protect not only the contracting parties, but also the
families to which they belong.   Indeed to protect the latter
it makes not the least attempt, and in this respect it is far
behind the law of Western Europe."[1]   As a preliminary to
a general reform of our marriage laws as a whole it is earnestly to be desired that every state or territory not already
emancipated should enact a statute as clear and decisive as
that of Kentucky, Utah, or New York, absolutely repudiat-
ing the common-law contract.   It is only through legislation
that this revolution can be effected.   It is not the proper
function of the courts to attempt it.   It may be that those
states which have superseded the common law through judicial interpretation of their statutes have done well.   The
end has perhaps justified the means.   It is quite possible

[1] COOK, "The Mar. Cel. in the U. S.," *Atlantic*, LXI, 528.

that in those cases it was the intent of the lawmaker to render the statute mandatory. Nevertheless he did not express his intent in the form which has itself become a part of the common law. Chief Justice Parsons and his followers may have been enforcing a "higher law;" but it was a "judge-made" law. History is on the side of Chief Justice Kent and the great number of jurists who have followed him. Moreover, it is evident from the trend of recent decisions that not much more can be expected from the courts. According to the overwhelming weight of juridical opinion, to go farther in this way would be to legislate consciously through the bench. Besides "bench-made" law is always *ex post facto*. The only practical course is to create or further develop a sound popular sentiment in favor of proper social control of the marital relation; and then to express that sentiment in statutes whose terms are mandatory beyond the possibility of evasion.

b) Resulting character of matrimonial legislation.—The absurd and demoralizing conflict between common-law validity and statutory legality ought first to be abolished, because in large measure it hinders, even frustrates, the effort to develop a thorough and uniform system of matrimonial administration in the United States. This once effected, there will remain plenty of hard work to do. If we consider the details of our legislation, as already analyzed in the sixteenth chapter, we perceive in nearly every department urgent need of reform, often of radical innovation. Almost everywhere there is a want of clearness, certainty, and simplicity; and this defect is all the more harmful because of the lack of uniformity among the different states. Diversity, even conflict, in every branch of state legislation is a burdensome incident of the federal system; and in no branch is the evil more formidable than in the field of marriage and divorce. As hereafter suggested, we need not despair of eventually overcoming it; but from the very nature of the case it may be many years before an effective remedy can generally be applied. In the meantime it is all the more necessary that the laws of each individual state should be made as clear, simple, and efficient as possible, and that every opportunity should be seized to prepare the way for a common matrimonial code for the whole country.

First of all, the statutes relating to the preliminaries of marriage ought to be overhauled. Already during the past century progress has been made. Within the last two decades in particular many reforms in matters of detail have been carried out in various states. Furthermore, in the broad features or outlines of the law throughout the country an approximation to a uniform system has been attained; and this fact may be of great significance when the task of securing absolutely the same law for all the states is earnestly taken in hand. Thus there is practical agreement among the states and territories in requiring a license from a local civil officer before a marriage may be legally celebrated. The dual system of banns or license survives only in Maryland, Georgia, Delaware, and Ohio. All the other states and territories, except Alaska, New Mexico, and South Carolina, where there is no statute governing the subject, with New York and New Jersey, where there is a substitute plan, have each adopted a system of civil license or certificate, the same in its purpose, though varying widely in the forms and procedure prescribed. This is a stride in the direction at once of simplicity and harmony; and besides, for its own sake, it is well to get rid of the ancient device of oral banns, which has proved as unsatisfactory in America as in the Old World. Again, we have developed substantially a common statutory law regarding the manner of entering into the marital relation. Everywhere, except in Maryland and West Virginia, where a religious ceremony is essential to a valid union, the optional civil or religious ceremony, at the pleasure of the persons contracting, is sanctioned by the law. As already seen, this dual system has its roots planted deeply in the history of two centuries. It is clearly entitled to be regarded as the American plan; although since 1836, with important modifications, it has also been accepted in the British Isles. It does not follow, however, that it is the ideal plan. It is too complex; and it is an obstacle in the way of developing the most efficient system of matrimonial administration. It is inconsistent with a proper social control. It will prevent the attainment of the "maximum of simplicity and the maximum of certainty" in matrimonial legislation. It is awkward, thoroughly illogical, to intrust the execution of that part of the law on which publicity and security so much depend to two different classes of persons: the one consisting of civil officers created and wholly under control of the state; the other in its origin, its personnel, and its character completely beyond such control, and only subject to administrative rules and restraints. With this system it will be very difficult to establish a proper standard of special fitness, of special knowledge, such as is highly needful to exact from public servants intrusted with functions of vast social importance. European peoples have reached a wiser solution of the problem in prescribing in all cases without exception, as the prerequisite of a valid marriage, the obligatory celebration before an authorized civil officer, leaving the wedded pair to decide, as wholly a private matter, whether a religious ceremony shall be added.

It is, however, highly probable that the optional system of celebration is too firmly grounded in popular sentiment to be soon discarded. The practical reformer must perforce content himself with striving to make it as effective as possible. At present the law is very lax in providing proper safeguards for the religious solemnization. In the first place, the qualified minister should be authorized to act only within the local district of his permanent residence, the limits thereof to be defined by statute.   By the early laws of New England, as we have already seen, the clergyman's functions were carefully confined to his own town, district, or county; and similar requirements appear elsewhere in some of the older statutes.   This wise policy has been gradually abandoned, so that now in no instance is there such a restriction.   Only in a very few cases, as in Massachusetts, Rhode Island, and Vermont, is authority conferred only upon ministers dwelling within the state.   Apparently in the great majority of states and territories, although the statutes are often far from clear, all qualified ministers, residing anywhere in the United States, may act.   Indeed, Louisiana is still more generous, granting full privilege to celebrate wedlock to any clergyman or priest "whether a citizen of the United States or not."   Another useful lesson may be learned from the early laws.   Proofs of ordination by the filing of credentials were often demanded.   Some of the southern states went farther, exacting from the minister a bond for the faithful performance of his trust, in addition to credentials of ordination and good standing.   Both these conditions are still enforced by the statutes of Kentucky,[1] Virginia, and West Virginia.   Some other states have contented themselves with less severe requirements.   Rhode Island has thus a careful system of local registration; in Maine and New Hampshire the clerical celebrant must secure a "commission" from the governor; in Minnesota, Wisconsin, Nevada, and Arkansas he must file his credentials with the proper county officer and receive a certificate; Ohio requires a license from the county judge of probate; a license from the proper authority is also demanded in Hawaii;[2] but

[1] *Kentucky Stat.* (1903), 843, 844.

[2] *Civil Laws of the Hawaiian Islands* (1897), 700.

in the majority of cases no such precautions are specified in the statutes. Here is need of reform. Under present social conditions, and considering the vast multiplication and subdivision of religious sects, the Virginia system is not too rigorous to justify its adoption throughout the land. Furthermore, the future lawmaker may perhaps get a suggestion from English legislation, which has had to deal with the same problem. The ministers of every religious sect are authorized to celebrate marriages according to its own rites; but, aside from Jews, Quakers, and the Church of England, otherwise provided for in the statute, they may do so only in a "registered building" and in the presence of the civil registrar of the district and two witnesses.

The laws regarding the civil ceremony are also seriously defective, if not in all respects equally lax. The magistrate in the exercise of his functions is not usually restricted to a local district sufficiently small to guarantee safe administration. In this regard the colonial and early state legislation was superior. At present in twenty-two states and territories the justice of the peace, or the corresponding local officer, is confined to his own county or district. Elsewhere he may act anywhere within the commonwealth; and this is almost universally the rule with the higher judges and officials who are granted the same authority. In no case, except in Virginia, and in Massachusetts under the act of 1899, is there any provision for the appointment of a person to celebrate wedlock for an area of less extent than the county. Nor are the persons to whom is confided this important social trust possessed of the needful qualifications. They are not selected because of special fitness. In no instance, unless in Virginia, does the law provide for the separate office of marriage celebrant. The duties of such a post are conferred, *ex officio*, in a haphazard fashion, upon a great variety of functionaries, who are either incompetent or else too busy with other matters to discharge them properly. As a rule, the justice of the peace is thus notoriously unfit; and there is something grotesque in giving authority to solemnize marriages to aldermen and police justices, as in New York; to speakers of the house and senate, as in Tennessee; or to the county supervisors, as in Mississippi. In this regard we have much to learn from European states, some of which have created special local officers for this branch of administration. Thus in France[1] all marriages are regularly celebrated before the mayor of the commune; in Germany,[2] before the registrar of the district in which one of the betrothed persons resides, or before some civil officer designated by him in writing; while in England the legal celebrant in case of civil procedure is also the district registrar, whose presence is likewise requisite at the religious ceremony when conducted according to the rites of the nonconformist sects. Massachusetts alone has taken a step in the right direction. The act of 1899, already summarized, not only provides that no justice of the peace—except when the holder of a specified clerical office —shall solemnize marriage unless specially designated therefor by the governor's certificate, but it also limits the number of justices who may be thus licensed. Touching another point in this connection the American lawmaker is at fault. Often there is no direct provision to secure evidence of the contract. Only nineteen of the fifty-three[3] states and territories expressly require the presence at the ceremony of even one witness; while in two or three other cases the statute appears to take their presence for granted.

The license system is uncertain and complex in many of its features. To guard against the clandestine marriage of

[1] Bodington's Kelly, *French Law of Marriage*, 12.

[2] By the law of 1875 marriages are thus celebrated before the local *Standesbeamten:* Kohler, *Das Eherecht des bürg. Gesetzbuches*, 16, 17, 55 ff.

[3] Counting Hawaii which was not included in chap. xvi.

minors, an affidavit from either the bride or bridegroom ought to be made obligatory in all cases, instead of leaving its requirement to the discretion of the officer, as is now usually the practice where there is any provision at all regarding the matter. In several instances the age below which parental consent is required is still too low; and the laws of some states are entirely silent on the subject. Throughout the country the limit for each sex ought to coincide with the attainment of legal majority.[1] More care should be taken to prevent deception when consent of parent or guardian is produced in writing. At the very least, in harmony with the requirement of many states, the affidavit of one witness to the signature should always be made obligatory; and in every such case it might be well as a guaranty to exact a license bond.[2] There is a still graver fault in the license laws of nearly the whole country. Nowhere, except in Porto Rico, is there any adequate provision regarding notice or the filing and trial of objections to a proposed marriage. Maine and Wisconsin have each made a start in requiring the certificate or license to be procured five days before the celebration. No other state, except New Hamp-

---

[1] In "Diagnostics of Divorce," *Jour. of Soc. Sci.* (Am. Assoc.), XIV, 136, PROFESSOR ROBERTSON takes the extreme view that "no person should be marriageable under the age of 21, and a marriage ceremony celebrated between persons either of whom is under age should be *ipso facto* void."

[2] Neither in England nor anywhere in the United States is a marriage declared void for want of parental consent. The leading case on the point is Parton *v.* Hervey, 1 GRAY, 119. "Some years ago a young girl, only thirteen years of age, named Sarah Hervey, was enticed away from her widowed mother's house by a young fellow, named Parton, of bad character and dissolute habits, who by false representations as to the age of the girl, procured a marriage license, and persuaded a magistrate to formally marry them. She returned to the house of her mother who forbade the young man to see her. Upon his petition against the mother for writ of habeas corpus, the Supreme Court of the Commonwealth, after full consideration, ordered the young wife to be surrendered to the husband, and he bore her away in triumph. . . . . The mother then brought suit against a confederate of the husband, who had aided in enticing away the girl and in practising the fraud upon the magistrate; but the mother again failed in her efforts to vindicate her rights to protect her daughter, since it distinctly appeared that the marriage was with the daughter's full and free consent."—Hervey *v.* Moseley (1856), 7 GRAY, 449; as summarized by BENNETT, "Uniformity in Mar. and Div. Laws," *Am. Law Register*, N. S., XXXV, 222.

shire[1] and New Jersey in the case of non-residents, seems to have provided for such a delay; and in all cases apparently, except Porto Rico, the license is issued at the time the notice of intention to marry is filed.[2] All this is contrary to sound public policy. The notice of intention should be recorded for a reasonable period, say ten days, before issuance of the license; and during this term it should be officially posted, and also published in the newspapers —not merely concealed in the register or published at the discretion of the official, as is now the usual course. Objections might then be filed, and in case of need tried in a court clothed with proper jurisdiction, before the celebration were allowed to proceed. Under the existing state legislation it would be difficult, certainly awkward, to stop a proposed marriage on the ground of alleged legal impediments. To make an objection effective, it might be necessary either to "anticipate the notice" or to interrupt the nuptial ceremony.[3] There is also much confusion, and uncertainty regarding the place of obtaining the license and that of making return. In no instance is a definite term of residence for either the man or the woman prescribed; and this is a fruitful source of clandestine marriage.[4] A glance

---

[1] *Laws of N. H.* (1903), 79.

[2] Louisiana formerly had a law requiring notice of intention to be filed fifteen days before issue of license; but it appears to have been repealed. In Porto Rico the period of delay is ten days.

[3] As suggested by COOK, "The Mar. Cel. in the U. S.," *Atlantic*, LXI, 687.

[4] The laxity of the law in this respect, coupled with that of permitting the license to be issued without delay, is the most fruitful source of clandestine marriages. There are many so-called "Gretna Greens" in the United States. One is (or was) at Aberdeen, O.: WHITNEY, *Marriage and Divorce*, 43; another at Greenwich, Conn. Oct. 2, 1900, the San Francisco *Chronicle* had the following telegram: "Greenwich's reputation as a Gretna Green and that of Judge Burns of Greenwich of the Borough court as one who marries all who come, appears to have extended to the Pacific Slope. On Saturday there arrived in town —— —— of Alameda, California, and —— —— of Los Angeles, California. They went to Judge Burns' office, arranged for the marriage ceremony, and then secured a marriage license from the town clerk. . . . . Immediately after the ceremony" they "left town, maintaining the greatest secrecy as is the usual custom." Another wedding resort, for the benefit of Chicago, is the little town of St. Joseph, Mich., where in the four years, 1897-1900, 1,594 licenses

at the facts collected in the sixteenth chapter will show that in some states the license must be secured in the place of the bride's residence; in others, in that of the marriage; while in a third group it may be issued in the place where either dwells. Indeed, Pennsylvania, more liberal still, allows a choice among all three places. The same laxity exists regarding the place of return; and sometimes the place of return is not the same as that of issue. A reasonable term of residence ought always to be required; and, unless in cases of emergency, the license should be issued by, and return made to, the same official in the district where the woman dwells. Even the lack of uniformity in license fees is sometimes the cause of migration to neighboring districts for the sake of cheaper weddings.[1] Finally, a marriage entered into without license, just as without authorized celebration, should be declared null and void by the statute.

During the last fifteen years considerable progress has been made in the state systems of registration; but in most cases the laws are still exceedingly lax; and too frequently they are badly executed, or remain a "dead letter" on the statute book.[2]

The radical reform of the administrative division of our matrimonial laws on some such lines as those suggested will be a worthy task for the future legislator. As a necessary antecedent of more detailed action the official system should be entirely reconstructed. The simplest mechanism is likely to prove the best. Its elements are close at hand in the local constitution. Every county should be divided into districts, for each of which a registrar should be authorized to

are said to have been issued to persons residing outside the state, the ceremony being performed by ministers. In 1903 an attempt to adopt the Wisconsin plan, requiring an interval of five days between the issue of the license and the celebration, failed by a very few votes.

[1] Examples are given by DIKE, "Statistics of Marriage and Divorce," *Pol. Sci. Quart.*, IV, 597.

[2] On the faults of the registration laws see *ibid.*, 594, 595.

license, solemnize, and register all marriages civilly contracted therein;[1] and to license, register, and attend religious
celebrations. His authority should be carefully restricted
to the district and no other person should be permitted to
share his functions. The district registrars should report at
short intervals to the county registrar, who in turn should
annually submit a summary of statistics to the registrar-
general for the state, by whom the local registrars should be
commissioned. If desirable for the sake of economy, especially in states of sparse population, the collection and registry of all vital statistics might be intrusted to the same
series of officials.[2] The moral influence of the creation of
a distinct system, such as that outlined, would itself be of
great value. It would effectively accent the high relative
importance to society of matrimonial law and of intelligent
service in its administration.

Aside from its public features, just considered, the future
matrimonial code of the United States will have to remedy
numerous defects in the substance of the law. These may
be seen by reference to the detailed examination elsewhere
presented. In particular, it will be necessary to get rid of
the appalling chaos of state regulations regarding void and
voidable contracts. The absurd conflicts touching the forbidden degrees of relationship are a positive social menace.
The most serious complications may arise. For instance, a
man and a woman who may be legally wed in the place
where they dwell might, should they move a mile across the
state line and then marry, be guilty of incestuous union and

---

[1] In his enlightening criticism of our matrimonial laws COOK, "The Mar. Cel. in
the U. S.," *Atlantic*, LXI, 688, has suggested the division of the county into districts
for the appointment of registrars.

[2] In England the registration of births and deaths in the district is intrusted to
a separate registrar: Compare the details of the British system as presented in
chap. x, sec. iii.

By the law of Massachusetts towns of more than 2,000 inhabitants may choose a
separate registrar to record and license, but not to celebrate, marriages: see chap. xvi,
sec. i, c).

their children become bastards.   Surely it ought to be possible for an enlightened people to agree upon a common rule
in a matter of such vital concern.[1]

In many of the states the laws governing the "age of
consent"—that is, the age below which a person may not
legally consent to carnal union[2]—are still very defective,
although distinct progress has been made since 1885.   In
that year Mr. W. T. Stead's exposure of the frightful traffic
in young girls then tolerated in London aroused the social
conscience on both sides of the sea.   The "old common
law period of ten, sometimes twelve, years" was then "the
basis of the age of consent legislation of most of the states,
and also of the law of congress pertaining to rape in the
District of Columbia and other territory under the immediate jurisdiction of the national government. . . . . It was
not until after the astounding revelations made by Mr.
Stead . . . . that the age of consent laws in the United
States began to attract attention. . . . . Even then the age
of consent in England was thirteen years.   One outcome
of Mr. Stead's shocking exposures was the speedy raising
of the age by the British parliament from thirteen to sixteen
years, Mr. Gladstone and others advocating eighteen."   The
New York Committee for the Prevention of State Regulation of Vice was already engaged in its long struggle to
"thwart the periodical efforts[3] made to introduce in New

[1] Cf. RICHBERG, Incongruity of the Divorce Laws, 65 ff.

[2] "Age of consent laws, in their usual acceptation, refer to the crime of rape,
and designate the age at which a young girl may legally consent to carnal relations
with the other sex.   Statutes pertaining to rape provide, in varying phrase, for the
punishment of 'whoever ravishes and carnally knows a female by force and against
her will,' at any age; and also penalties for whoever unlawfully and carnally knows
a female child, with or without consent, under a given age."—POWELL, in Arena,
XI, 192.

[3] "In the New York senate, in 1890, a bill was introduced to lower the age of
consent from sixteen to fourteen years.   It was reported favorably by the senate
judiciary committee, but vigorous protests against the proposed retrograde legislation were promptly sent to Albany by the friends of purity, and the disreputable
scheme was defeated.   It was understood to have originated with Rochester attorneys

York and other American cities the odious old-world system
of licensed and state-regulated vice; but its members were
quite unaware, until Mr. Stead's startling London revelations suggested the inquiry here, that, by the age of consent
laws of New York and of most of the states, young girls of
ten years were made legally capable of consenting to their
own ruin, and that at that time in one state, Delaware, the
age was at the shockingly low period of seven years! Bad
as English law had been shown to be in its inadequate protection of girlhood our own legal position . . . . was found
to be still worse. The New York committee, as soon as the
facts were known, inaugurated a campaign of petitions to
sundry state legislatures and to the congress of the United
States, asking that the age be raised to at least eighteen
years, and the work was also entered into earnestly and
effectively by the Woman's Christian Temperance Unions
and the White Cross societies."[1] Under the leadership of
Helen H. Gardener, Frances E. Willard, and others, the
women of the country conducted a veritable "crusade" of
education against the existing state laws, which for zeal,
ability, and effective method may well serve as a model for
future united efforts in favor of social reforms. It was
pointed out as a notorious fact "that brothels and vice-
factories get their recruits from the ranks of childhood—

who sought thus to provide a way of escape for a client, a well-to-do debauchee guilty
of despoiling a young girl under the legally protected age of sixteen." A similar
attempt, in the house, in 1892, in the interest of the New York brothel-keepers, was
barely defeated by calling for the yeas and nays. "In the Kansas senate, in 1889, a
bill was introduced and passed to lower the age . . . . from eighteen to twelve years.
The house was flooded with earnest protests, and its judiciary committee reported
adversely the disgraceful senate bill."—Powell, loc. cit., 194, 195.

[1] Aaron M. Powell, editor of the *Philanthropist*, in the *Arena* (1895), XI, 192-
94. The *Arena* was the principal medium of publication for the reformers: see the
symposium by Powell, Gardener, and others, "The Shame of America," *Arena*,
XI, 192-215; the symposium by Gardener, Robinson, and others, *ibid.*, XIII, 209-25;
the symposium by Leach and Campbell, *ibid.*, XII, 282-88; Smith, "Age of Consent
in Canada," *ibid.*, XIII, 81-91; and especially Gardener, "A Battle for Sound
Morality," *ibid.*, XIII, 353-71; XIV, 1-32, 205-20, 401-19. *Cf.* Flower, "Wellsprings
of Immorality," *ibid.*, XII, 337-52.

from the ignorance which is unprotected by the law;" that "children's lives are thus wrecked, and the state is burdened with disease and vice and crime and insanity, which is transmitted and retransmitted until its proportions appall those who understand;" and that it is absurd to make the legal age for consent to a valid marriage higher than that for consent to prostitution. It was urged that the age of consent ought to be advanced to that of legal majority; that girls "have a right to legal protection of their persons, which is more imperative by far than is the protection which every state has recognized as a matter beyond controversy when applied to a girl's property or her ability to make contracts, deeds, and wills, or to her control of herself in any matters which are of importance to her as an individual, and to the state, because she is one of its citizens whose future welfare is a matter of moment to the commonwealth;" and that in respect to her person, as well as regarding property or marriage, she should be protected even against her own will.[1] As a result of the campaign of 1895 alone the age of consent was raised in no less than fifteen states and territories; and in the outset it was significantly pointed out that the "two states in which the age of legal protection for girlhood has been raised to eighteen years are states in which women vote — Wyoming, upon equal terms with men, and Kansas, in municipal elections."[2] A brief summary of the laws of the states and territories regarding the subject under consideration may now be presented.

Encouraging progress has been made in New England, although, in comparison with some of the new commonwealths of the West, the facts are not very creditable. By the Rhode Island statute the age of consent is sixteen.[3] In

---

[1] GARDENER, "A Battle for Sound Morality," *Arena*, XIII, 354, 355.

[2] POWELL, in *Arena*, XI, 195; *cf.* GARDENER, *ibid.*, XIII, 358.

[3] *Gen. Laws of R. I.* (1896), 999.

New Hampshire it was raised from thirteen to sixteen in 1897;[1] in Vermont, from fourteen to sixteen in 1898;[2] and in Connecticut, from fourteen to sixteen in 1895, while in 1901 the maximum term of imprisonment for abusing a girl under sixteen was increased from three to thirty years.[3] The age limit was only ten in Maine until 1887. It was then raised to thirteen, and in 1889 to fourteen years.[4] In Massachusetts likewise the disgracefully low age of ten years for a girl was sanctioned by statute from 1852 until 1886, when thirteen was substituted. Two years later it was increased to fourteen; and by an act of 1893 an offense against a female under sixteen may be punished by imprisonment for life or for any shorter term of years.[5] The results are even less satisfactory in the southern and southwestern group of states. Florida now heads the list, but with a rather inadequate penalty, the age of consent being raised from sixteen to eighteen years in 1901.[6] Missouri in 1889 increased the age from twelve to fourteen, and in 1895 advanced it nominally to eighteen; but the provisions of the law are such as practically to leave the limit of protection at fourteen years.[7] Previous to 1895 in Arizona the age of consent was fourteen. In that year it was raised to

---

[1] *Laws of N. H.* (1897), 30, 31; *Pub. Stat.* (1900), 832.

[2] *Vermont Stat.* (1895), 877; *Acts and Resolves* (1898), 90, 91.

[3] *Gen. Stat. of Conn.* (1887), 325; *Pub. Acts* (1887), 669; *ibid.* (1895), 580; *ibid.* (1901), 1208; *Gen. Stat.* (1902), 350.

[4] *Rev. Stat. of Me.* (1884), 883; *Acts and Resolves* (1887), 110; *ibid.* (1889), 170.

[5] *Mass. Acts and Resolves* (1886), 270; *ibid.* (1888), 40; *ibid.* (1893), 1381; *Rev. Laws* (1902), II, 1745.

[6] *Laws of Fla.* (1901), 111; penalty, not less than ten years' imprisonment, or a fine not exceeding $2,000, or both.

[7] Up to fourteen carnally knowing a girl is rape, punishable by death or imprisonment for not less than five years, at the discretion of the jury: *Rev. Stat.* (1899), I, 547. Between fourteen and eighteen, not only must the girl be "of previously chaste character"—which begs the whole question—but the penalty is ridiculously light: imprisonment in the penitentiary for two years; *or* a fine of not less than $100 nor more than $500; *or* confinement in the county jail not less than one month nor more than six months or both such fine and confinement: *Laws* (1895), 149; also in *Rev. Stat.* (1899), I, 547. *Cf. Rev. Stat.* (1889), I, 850; GARDENER, in *Arena*, XIV, 31.

eighteen; but unfortunately it was reduced to seventeen in 1899.[1] In Arkansas[2] it was raised from twelve to sixteen years in 1893; in Louisiana,[3] from twelve to sixteen in 1896; in the District of Columbia[4] and in Indian Territory[5] it has been sixteen since 1889; in Oklahoma[6] it was increased from fourteen to sixteen in 1895; in Maryland,[7] from ten to fourteen in 1890, and to sixteen in 1898; in Tennessee,[8] from ten to sixteen years and one day in 1893; but the statutes of the three states last named are so lax as really to leave the age of consent at twelve in Tennessee and at fourteen in Maryland and Oklahoma. Texas advanced the limit from ten to twelve in 1891, and to fifteen in

[1] *Laws of Arizona* (1895), 48; *ibid.* (1899), 29; the same in *Rev. Stat.* (1901), 1226: penalty, imprisonment for life or for not less than five years.

[2] Act of April 1, 1893: *Digest* (1894), 572: penalty, not less than five nor more than twenty-one years in prison. In Arkansas rape is punished by death, and, by exception, the execution is to be public; but this does not apply in case of conviction under the consent law.

[3] Act 115 (1896), 165; also in *Rev. Laws* (1897), 196: "if any person over the age of 18 years shall have carnal knowledge of any unmarried female between the ages of 12 and 16 with her consent he shall be deemed guilty of felony," and be imprisoned with hard labor not exceeding five years.

[4] Act of Feb. 9, 1889: 1 *Supp. to U. S. Stat.*, c. 120, p. 641; also *Code of D. C.* (1902), 170: penalty not less than five nor more than thirty years' imprisonment, or death when the jury so determines.

[5] Act of Feb. 9, 1889, applying to all territory in exclusive jurisdiction of the U. S.: 1 *Supp. to U. S. Stat.*, c. 120, p. 641; *Ann. Stat. Ind. Ter.* (1899), 845: first offense, not more than fifteen years in prison; each later offense, not more than thirty years.

[6] When the girl is under fourteen the offense is rape punishable by not less than ten years in the territorial prison; between fourteen and sixteen the penalty is not less than five years' such imprisonment, if she be of "previous chaste and virtuous character": *cf. Stat. of Okla.* (1893), 467; and *Laws* (1895), 104, 105.

[7] Up to fourteen for the girl the penalty is death or imprisonment for life or for any definite term from eighteen months to twenty-one years: *cf. Pub. Gen. Laws of Md.* (1888), I, 533, 534; with *Laws* (1890), c. 410, p. 447. By the act of 1898, c. 218, abuse of a girl between fourteen and sixteen is only a misdemeanor punishable by not *more* than two years in the house of correction *or* by a fine not to *exceed* $500: PRENTISS'S *Supp. to Code* (1898), 195.

[8] In Tennessee the offense against a girl below twelve years of age is punishable, as in case of rape, by death or, if the jury please, by imprisonment for life or not less than ten years; from twelve to sixteen, it is a felony, with three to ten years in prison, if the child be of previous chaste character, and if she can bring witnesses to support her statements. The one day was added by way of a joke! See the interesting account of the passage of the act by DROMGOOLE, in *Arena*, XI, 209–12; and for the act consult *Laws* (1893), c. 129, § 1, 273, 274; *Code* (1896), 1593, 1594.

1895;[1] South Carolina,[2] from ten to fourteen, and Virginia,[3] from twelve to fourteen, in 1896; West Virginia,[4] from twelve to fourteen in 1901; North Carolina,[5] from ten to fourteen in 1895; Alabama,[6] from ten to fourteen in 1897; while fourteen is likewise the age in New Mexico[7] and possibly also in Georgia;[8] but because of vicious clauses in their statutes a girl is in fact only given effectual protection below the age of ten in Alabama and North Carolina, and by common law at the same age in Georgia. Twelve is the limit in Kentucky;[9] and Mississippi[10] still retains the shamefully low age of ten years.

The most enlightened legislation regarding the age of consent is found among the states of the middle and west-

[1] *Laws of Tex.* (1891), 96; *ibid.* (1895), 79, 104: not less than two years in the penitentiary.

[2] *Acts of S. C.* (1896), 223: a felony; penalty, death or imprisonment for life, unless the jury recommends the offender to mercy, when the court shall reduce the punishment to imprisonment for a term not exceeding fourteen years.

[3] Act of March 3, 1896: *Acts* (1895–96), 673: penalty, death or imprisonment from five to twenty-one years, as the jury may determine.

[4] *Acts of W. Va.* (1901), 218: penalty, death or imprisonment from seven to twenty years, as the jury may decide; but the penalty does not apply to a boy under fourteen ravishing a girl over twelve " with her free consent."

[5] By the *Code of N. C.* (1883), 444, the age is ten; raised to fourteen by *Pub. Laws* (1895), 374; but the crime is only " punished by fine *or* imprisonment at the discretion of the court, provided she has never previously had sexual intercourse with any male person."

[6] The *Code of Ala.* (1897), 460, punishes the abuse of a girl below fourteen, at the discretion of the jury, either by death or by not less than ten years in prison; but an act of 1897, also in the *Code*, punishes carnal knowledge of a female between ten and fourteen only by a fine of $50 to $500, and the offender " may be imprisoned in the county jail for six months." This provision appears to reduce the protection of a child above ten to little more than a pretense: *Acts* (1897), 944.

[7] *Comp. Laws of N. M.* (1897), 344: penalty, five to ten years' imprisonment.

[8] For Georgia, in 1895, the age of consent was reported as fourteen, or any younger age if the jury finds that " by reason of her intelligence she knows good from evil ": see GARDENER, in *Arena*, XIV, 415, 416; but I have not been able to find this provision in the present *Code*. The penalty for rape is death, unless the jury recommend to mercy, when it is one to twenty years' imprisonment at hard labor: *Code* (1896), III, 36, 39. This penalty applies when the girl is under ten: 11 *Ga.*, 227.

[9] *Ky. Stat.* (1899), 516: penalty, ten to twenty years in prison.

[10] *Ann. Code* (1892), 372: penalty, death, unless the jury fix the punishment at life imprisonment. There is in Mississippi an abduction law to protect girls below sixteen: but the age-of-consent law stops at ten. *Cf.* GARDENER, *loc. cit.*, 416.

ern group. Kansas[1] in 1887, and Wyoming[2] in 1890, set a good example by raising it to eighteen years. The same limit was adopted by Nebraska,[3] Colorado,[4] Idaho,[5] and New York[6] in 1895; by Utah[7] in 1896; by Washington[8] in 1897; and by North Dakota in 1903.[9] Until 1889 Delaware sanctioned the barbarous age of seven years. It was then advanced to fifteen, and in 1895 to eighteen, for both sexes; but the penalties prescribed by the statute are far too lenient to guarantee entire protection beyond the age of seven.[10] Next come ten states and districts in which the age is actually or nominally placed at sixteen years. Minnesota[11] in

[1] *Laws of Kan.* (1887), c. 150, § 1: *Gen. Stat.* (1901), 437: penalty, five to twenty years in prison.

[2] Act of Dec. 18, 1890, amending an act of March 14, 1890, which fixed the age at fourteen: *Laws of Wyo.* (1890), 130: *ibid.* (1890–91), 85, 86; *Rev. Stat.* (1899), 1236; penalty, rape, with imprisonment "not less than one year or during life."

[3] Raised from fourteen: *Laws of Neb.* (1895), 314, 315; *Comp. Stat.* (1901), 1409: penalty three to twenty years in prison. But the value of the law is lessened by the provision that it shall not apply in case of a girl over fifteen if "previously unchaste."

[4] *Laws of Col.* (1895), 155: penalty, one to twenty years in prison; raised from sixteen to eighteen.

[5] Raised from ten to fourteen in 1893, and advanced to eighteen in 1895: penalty, imprisonment for life or not less than five years. Compare *Rev. Stat. of Idaho* (1887), 733; *Laws* (1893), 10, 11; *Laws* (1895), 19; and *Penal Code* (1901), 134, 139.

[6] Raised from sixteen: *Laws of N. Y.* (1895), c. 460; BIRDSEYE's *Rev. Stat.* (1901), III, 3012: rape in second degree; penalty, not more than ten years in prison; rape in first degree, with not less than twenty years in prison, when an imbecile, etc.

[7] *Laws of Utah* (1896), 87; *Rev. Stat.* (1898), 902, 877: felony, penalty, not more than five years in prison.

[8] From 1881 to 1897 the age in Washington was twelve: *cf. Laws* (1897), 19; BALLINGER's *Codes and Stat.* (1897), II, 1951, note. Present penalty, imprisonment for life or any term of years.

[9] Abuse of a female below eighteen is now made rape in the first degree: *Laws of N. D.* (1903), 200.

[10] *Laws of Del.* (1889), 951; *ibid.* (1895), 192; *Rev. Stat.* (1893), 924: when below seven, rape, with death penalty: when between seven and eighteen, misdemeanor, punished by not more than seven years in prison or a fine of not exceeding $1,000 or both, at the discretion of the court. *Cf.* GARDENER, in *Arena*, XIV, 411, 412.

[11] *Gen. Laws of Minn.* (1891), c. 90, § 1, p. 162; *Stat.* (1894), II, 1747: penalty, confinement in the state prison for life, when the girl is under ten; when between ten and fourteen, seven to thirty years; between fourteen and sixteen, one to seven years in state prison, or in county jail three months to one year.

1891, South Dakota[1] in 1893, Michigan,[2] Montana,[3] and Oregon[4] in 1895, Ohio[5] in 1896, and California[6] in 1897, each advanced to this limit from fourteen. Sixteen is also the age in Alaska.[7] But in 1902 Ohio took a backward step, so lowering the penalty for the offense as nearly to destroy the force of her law. Pennsylvania[8] and New Jersey[9] each raised the age from ten to sixteen in 1887; but in Pennsylvania the girl must prove previous good character, and in both states the penalties are too lax to secure adequate protection beyond the age of ten. Since 1896 the age of consent has been fifteen in Iowa.[10] In Illinois[11] since 1887, Nevada[12] since 1889, Indiana[13] since

[1] *Laws of S. D.* (1893), c. 138; *Ann. Stat.* (1901), II, 1916, 1917: rape in second degree; penalty, not less than five years in the state prison.

[2] *Pub. Acts of Mich.* (1895), 170: penalty, imprisonment for life or any term of years.

[3] *Codes and Stat. of Mont.* (1895), 1062, 1063: penalty, imprisonment for life or not less than five years.

[4] From 1864 to 1895 the age was fourteen : HILL's *Codes* (1892), I, 897; *Laws of Ore.* (1895), 67: penalty, three to twenty years in prison.

[5] Ohio raised the age from ten to fourteen in 1887, and advanced it to sixteen by the act of March 3, 1896: *Acts* (1875), 93 (age made ten years) ; *ibid.* (1887), 65; *ibid.* (1896), 54: BATES's *Ann. Stat.* (1897), II, 3144, 3145: rape if the boy is over eighteen; penalty, three to twenty years in prison; lowered by *Acts* (1902), 344, to one to twenty years. "or 6 months in the county jail or workhouse at the discretion of the court, which is hereby authorized to near testimony in mitigation or aggravation of sentence." *Cf.* BATES, *Ann. Rev. Stat.* (1903), III, 3307-8.

[6] Compare *Stat. and Amend. to Codes* (1889), 223, and *ibid.* (1897), 201: penalty, not less than five years in prison.

[7] *Laws of Alaska* (1900), 4.

[8] *Pub. Laws of Pa.* (1887), 128; PEPPER AND LEWIS, *Digest* (1896), I, 1318, 1319: penalty, when the woman child is between ten and sixteen, fine not exceeding $1,000 and imprisonment not exceeding fifteen years, if she "was of good repute;" below ten, without this condition. Thus there is no sure protection beyond ten. No conviction when boy is under sixteen.

[9] *Laws of N. J.* (1887), 230; *Gen. Stat.* (1896), I, 1096: penalty, not exceeding $1,000, or imprisonment at hard labor not more than fifteen years, or both. There is also an abduction law to protect a female under fifteen: *Gen. Stat.* (1896), I, 1064. The age is ten in *Rev. Stat.* (1874), 148.

[10] Raised from thirteen; *Acts of Ia.* (1896), 71; *Ann. Code* (1897), 1888: penalty, imprisonment for life or any term of years.

[11] *Laws of Ill.* (1887), 171; HURD's *Rev. Stat.* (1901), 634: penalty, when male is above sixteen, imprisonment for life or not less than one year.

[12] Raised from twelve: *Stat. of Nev.* (1889), 74 ; *Comp. Laws* (1900), 914, 915: rape when the boy is fifteen or more; penalty, imprisonment for life or not less than five years.

[13] Raised from twelve: *Acts of Ind.* (1893), 22; BURNS's *Ann. Stat.* (1901), I, 790: penalty, one to twenty-one years in prison.

1893, Wisconsin[1] since 1895, and in Porto Rico by the code of 1902,[2] it is fourteen; while in Hawaii it is but ten years.[3]

It appears, then, although in many cases the statutes are very imperfect, that of the fifty-three states and territories twelve have actually or nominally advanced the age of consent to eighteen; one to seventeen; twenty-two to sixteen; two to fifteen; thirteen to fourteen; while two still retain the low age of twelve and one that of ten years. It should everywhere be raised to eighteen or twenty-one—the age of legal majority for a woman in her business or political relations—by a statute as rigorous as that of Idaho or Kansas. A wide field for beneficent legislation therefore remains; and, although morality "can not be legislated into a people," it is precisely by wise measures of this character that the lawmaker can render powerful aid in the creation of an environment favorable to moral and social progress.

c) *Resulting character of divorce legislation.*—What has just been said regarding the function of social legislation applies with special force to the laws relating to divorce. Here, as in the case of marriage, there is a wide sphere of useful activity for the lawmaker. He cannot, it is true, reach the root of the matter: the fundamental causes of divorce which are planted deeply in the imperfections of the social system—particularly in false sentiments regarding marriage and the family—and which, as will presently appear, can only be removed through more rational principles and methods of education. He can, however, by carefully drawn and uniform statutes render the external conditions—the legal environment—favorable for the operation of the proper remedy. In this sense it is possible to have "good divorce laws," just as we may have good charity laws, good laws for

---

[1] Raised from twelve: *Laws of Wis.* (1895), c. 370, sec. 1; *Wis. Stat.* (1898), 2668: penalty, five to thirty-five years in prison.

[2] *Rev. Stat. and Codes of Porto Rico* (1902), 532, 533: penalty, not less than five years in the penitentiary.   [3] *Penal Laws of Hawaiian Islands* (1897), 73.

the check of contagious diseases, or good laws in any department of remedial social legislation.[1] So far as their ethical content is concerned, good divorce laws, like any other, will not lead, but must follow at some distance, the highest moral sentiment of the community. They should, however, follow as closely as practicable in order to secure the obedience of all. In this field it is highly essential that the laws should be simple, certain, and uniform. They should not from their very nature become a dead letter, or even an encouragement to domestic discord, by offering opportunity for evasion, collusion, or lax interpretation. Statutes which are not in good faith executed, like those of France under the old *régime*, are always a fruitful source of social disorder. They tend to destroy the reverence for law itself. In this respect the divorce laws of many of the states are still defective, although decided progress has been made during the last twenty years. Within this period the foundation of what may some time become a common and effective divorce code for the whole Union has slowly been laid. Little by little, as the detailed discussion already presented in the seventeenth chapter reveals, more stringent provisions for notice have been made, longer terms of previous residence for the plaintiff required, and more satisfactory conditions of remarriage after the decree prescribed; while some of the "omnibus" clauses in the list of statutory causes have been repealed. Much of the best of this work has been accomplished, it is but just to record, through the activity of the National Divorce Reform League and its successor, the National League for the Protection of the Family, under the able guidance of its alert

---

[1] "When the question is asked, 'What is the best divorce law?' the only answer can be, 'There is no good divorce law.' There are some faults in human nature which always have existed and apparently always will exist; and there is no satisfactory method of dealing with them."—BRYCE, *Studies in Hist. and Jurisprudence*, 853. This assertion would apply equally well to the whole body of laws dealing with questions arising in human conduct or social relations. It is misleading, and instead of helping to a solution tends to befog the issue.

and zealous corresponding secretary, Rev. Samuel Dike, of Auburndale.[1] By this league was suggested the compilation of the elaborate report of Hon. Carroll D. Wright, commissioner of labor, published in 1889; and this has had a powerful influence for good, providing the body of facts needful for the wise direction of legal reform. But in many ways in various states lax legislation is still a demoralizing social factor. Thus, until the statute of 1902 has perhaps put a stop to the traffic, Rhode Island was a favorite resort of persons from New York who were able to escape the marital bond through the institution of "fake suits" for nonsupport. Reno, Nev., has continued to be the Mecca of newly divorced people from California and elsewhere, seeking to evade their own laws by flight to a place where there are no legal obstacles to immediate remarriage.[2] Greenwich, Conn., sustains a similar relation to New York. Sioux Falls, S. D.—to produce one more from the many examples which might be mentioned—appears still to have a flourishing "divorce colony;" yet it may be true, as strongly urged, that the laws of this state, though liberal, are honestly and strictly interpreted.[3] Nor must it be inferred in such cases that those who seek relief in a foreign jurisdiction are for that reason unworthy people. There are sometimes wrongs committed under shelter of the marriage bond so monstrous as to warrant any legal means of gaining relief. Indeed, the evil of clandestine divorce in the United States has been much exaggerated. "A vital question con-

[1] See the *Reports* of the league and the numerous papers of Mr. Dike mentioned in the fourth division of the "Bibliographical Index."

[2] The evils which may result from conflicts of this kind in the divorce laws are discussed in a lively way by Richberg, *Incongruity of the Divorce Laws*, 69, 70. But the California act of 1903, if constitutional, may check the abuse: see pp. 150, 151, above.

[3] See Realf, "The Sioux Falls Divorce Colony and Some Noted Colonists," *Arena*, IV, Nov., 1891, 696–703, and compare the remarks of Dike, in *Rep. of Nat. Div. Ref. League* (1891), 12, who has taken pains to correct the exaggerated accounts of the newspapers; those of Hare, *Marriage and Divorce*, 16 ff.; and see the articles of A. R. Kimball and R. Ogden mentioned in Part IV of the Bibliographical Index.

nected with divorce," declares Commissioner Wright in
1891, "relates to the real or supposed migration of parties
from one state to another for the purpose of seeking divorce.
The popular idea is that a great deal of migration takes
place for the purpose named. This idea is dispelled in some
degree by the statistics that are available upon this point,
and getting at the truth as nearly as possible, it is found
that but little less than 20 per cent. of all the couples in the
country were divorced in other states than those in which
they were married. But the ordinary migration of parties
for legitimate purposes, especially from the older to the newer
states, which in 1870 showed that 23+ per cent. of the
native born population, and for 1880 22+ per cent. of such
population were living in states other than the ones in which
they were born, would apparently reduce the percentage of
persons migrating for the purpose of divorce to a point even
less than that stated."[1]   In fact, for the reason assigned by
Mr. Wright, it seems highly probable that the number of
such persons must be placed at considerably less than 10 per
cent. of the whole number of persons divorced in the United
States.[2]   Accordingly, it has been inferred that uniformity
of law throughout the country would do little to lower the
divorce rate.   "The establishment of uniform laws," con-

[1] Extract from an address delivered by HON. CARROLL D. WRIGHT before the
fourteenth National Conference of the Unitarian Society, Saratoga, N. Y., 1891: in
Arena, V, 143; printed entire in the *Christian Register*, Oct. 8, 1891; based on the
statistics collected in his *Report*, 193–206. Commenting on the passage quoted the
editor of the *Arena* says (142):

"Another charge made against our divorce laws is that, not being uniform, certain states are being overrun with persons of loose moral character, who seek release
from marriage ties. Those who make this charge seem to overlook the fact that
persons of loose moral character would not be liable to go to the trouble of leaving
their home and state in order to gratify guilty passions. But those who find the
marriage tie too galling for endurance and yet who wish to be law-abiding citizens
presumably, will take advantage of liberal, enlightened, and humane laws, framed
with a view to increase the happiness of the people rather than made in such a way
as to foster immorality and enforced prostitution."

[2] According to the method of determining the amount of interstate migration
for the purpose of securing divorce suggested by WILLCOX, "A Study in Vital Statistics," *Pol. Sci. Quart.*, VIII, 90–92.

cludes Mr. Dike, "is not the central point of the problem."[1] Furthermore, there is another important fact bearing on the evil of clandestine divorce. In a number of cases arising in various states the courts have declared null and void decrees secured in jurisdictions where the plaintiffs were not *bona fide* residents, even when they had dwelt in such jurisdictions for the statutory term prescribed as a condition for obtaining a divorce.[2]

To some extent the evil of lax administration of the divorce laws is exaggerated by popular opinion. In the main the courts are careful and conscientious in the trial of suits. According to the report of Commissioner Wright, in seventy counties scattered over twelve states but 67.8 per cent. of the petitions for divorce were granted. From this fact it is inferred that "judges exercise a reasonable care before issuing a decree." For the counties investigated "it is certain that in about 30 per cent. of the cases of petition a decree has been denied. The number of cases involved is sufficiently large and the localities sufficiently different to lead one to the conclusion that the same state of affairs exists throughout the country, and that our courts, instead of being careless in the matter of granting decrees, weigh well the causes alleged, and do not grant decrees unless the allegations of the libellants are fairly sustained."[3] Still, under the laws as they exist there is plenty of opportunity for

[1] DIKE, "Statistics of Marriage and Divorce," *Pol. Sci. Quart.*, IV, 608-12.

[2] See Streitwolf *v.* Streitwolf (1900), *Opinions of U. S. Supreme Court*, No. 13, p. 553, involving a decree of divorce granted in North Dakota to a resident of New Jersey; Bell *v.* Bell (1900), *ibid.*, 551, voiding a similar judgment secured in Pennsylvania by a resident of New York; and S. *v.* Armington (1878), 25 *Minn.*, 29-39, in which a divorce granted in Utah to a resident of Minnesota in 1876 was declared void for want of jurisdiction. Similar decisions, involving the notorious fraudulent divorces obtained in Utah before the change of the law in 1878, "have been reached in criminal trials in New York, Indiana, and Iowa, and in civil suits in Massachusetts, Kansas, and Tennessee"—the earliest in 1877: WILLCOX, "A Study in Vital Statistics," *Pol. Sci. Quart.*, VIII, 86 n. 1.

[3] WRIGHT, *Report*, 162-64. In the whole country, during the years 1867-86, 328,716 decrees were granted, representing probably 484,683 petitions.

abuse, even when the court is cautious. The service of notice on the absent defendant through the mails or through publication in the newspapers, allowed in many states, and the fact that only in a few instances is there any provision requiring the prosecuting attorney to resist an undefended libel, afford occasions for fraud.[1] Some of the usual statutory causes of divorce, under the refinement of judicial interpretation, seem virtually to invite divorce.[2] This is to some extent true of "nonsupport," "wilful absence," "desertion," and "gross neglect of duty;" while "cruelty" has become almost an "omnibus clause." Under plea of "constructive cruelty" or "mental anguish" the grievances admitted as valid grounds for dissolution of wedlock are often trivial or even absurd, although it is likely that they are sometimes put forward as a shield or substitute for graver wrongs which the plaintiff is reluctant to disclose.[3] The general introduction of the decree *nisi*, giving opportunity for reflection, might prove a wholesome correction of the almost necessarily liberal policy of the courts in such cases. Divorce suits are sometimes too hastily disposed of by the judges because of the pressure of other litigation. The creation of a limited number of special divorce courts in each of the states might prove a remedy, if care were taken not to so increase the cost of actions as virtually to discriminate against the poor.

[1] In forty-five counties in twelve states, for the period 1867-86, notice was served by publication in 9,944 cases; in 17,040 cases personal service was made; and in 2,681 cases no evidence on the point was obtainable: WRIGHT, *Report*, 201, 202.

[2] For a good discussion of the scope of various statutory grounds of divorce, with the defenses, as actually interpreted by the courts, see WHITNEY, *Marriage and Divorce*, 108-56; and compare BISHOP, *Mar., Div., and Sep.*, I, 610 ff., II, 1 ff.; STEWART, *Law of Mar. and Div.*, 203 ff.; LLOYD, *Law of Div.*, 147 ff., 180 ff.; CONVERS, *Mar. and Divorce*, 180 ff.

[3] The ninety-nine illustrations of the allegations of the plaintiff presented in WRIGHT'S *Report*, 172-78, constitute very interesting reading. Some of them are quoted by BRYCE, *Studies in Hist. and Jurisp.*, 835, 836. The frauds arising in the procedure are forcibly described by JUDGE JAMESON, "Divorce," *North Am. Rev.*, CXXXVI, 323, 324; and the conflicts in laws by PHILLIPS, "Divorce Question," *Internat. Rev.*, XI, 139-52.

The appearance of the government report in 1889 revealed for the first time something like the real facts regarding divorce in the United States. In the entire country during the period of twenty years (1867–86) covered by the report, 328,716 petitions for full or partial divorce were granted. From 9,937 decrees in 1867, the number rose to 11,586 in 1871, 14,800 in 1876, 20,762 in 1881, and to 25,535 in 1886, showing an increase in twenty years of 157 per cent., while there was a gain in population of but 60 per cent. during the same period. Comparing the last year with the first, only four states in the Union — Delaware, Connecticut, Maine, and Vermont — show a decrease in the divorce rate; while, more fairly, comparing the fourth quinquennium with the first, only the three states last named show such a "decrease in their divorce movement." [1] Of the whole number of divorces during the twenty years, 112,540 were granted to the husband and 216,176 to the wife. Among the principal causes, at each stage of the wedded life, only for adultery were more decrees granted on the husband's petition than on the wife's. [2] "As regards the ratio of divorces to marriages, six states report marriages fully enough for a trustworthy comparison. Of these, Connecticut has for the entire period a divorce to 11.32 marriages and for the worst year, 1875, one to 8.81; Rhode Island gives one to 11.11 for the period and one to 9.36 in 1884, closely approaching that for the preceding years; Vermont one to 16.96 for the period and at its worst, in 1871, one to 13; Massachusetts gives one to 31.28 for the period, its worst being one to 22.54 in 1878; Ohio averages one to 20.65, with an almost unvarying progress downward to one to 15.16

---

[1] Wright, *Report*, 139–42.

[2] According to the table by classified causes: Wright, *Report*, 181–83. However, the relative number of divorces granted on the wife's petition varies greatly among the states: from 39.3 per cent. in North Carolina to 77.9 in Nevada: compare the table in Willcox, *The Divorce Problem*, 34–37.

in 1886;" and in the District of Columbia the rate for the
period is 31.28, while at the best it is 74.65 in 1868 and at
the worst 20.82 in 1877. "In some other states where marriages are less fully reported, the ratios are as follows:
Illinois one to 14.76 for the period, while Cook county gives
one to 13.6; Michigan one to 12.92; Minnesota one to 30.05;
New Hampshire one to 9.74 (its lowest, one to 7.6 in 1880,
being evidently due to very imperfect returns of marriages);
New Jersey shows one to 49.39; Kansas one to 17.42; Wisconsin one to 21.07; and Delaware one to 36.99. These
last, it should be noted, are some of them for shorter periods
than twenty years."[1] This method of comparing the number of divorces granted with the number of marriages celebrated is not very satisfactory. "It is vicious in this, that
the marriages celebrated each year cannot be compared
scientifically with the divorces drawn from the whole volume
of marriages celebrated in the past thirty or forty years,
many of which even took place in foreign countries."[2] The
commissioner has therefore adopted another method of comparison, not entirely free from error, based on the estimated
number of existing married couples. From this it appears
that in 1870, for the entire country, there were 664 married
couples to one divorce granted, while in 1880 the number of
such couples to one decree had fallen to 481.[3] Estimated
another way, on the basis of the eleventh census, in 1867
there were 173 divorces to 100,000 couples and 250 in 1886.[4]

The divorce rate in the United States is higher than in
any other country for which statistics are collected and
published, with the single exception of Japan,[5] being lowest

---

[1] DIKE, "Statistics of Marriage and Divorce," *Pol. Sci. Quart.*, IV, 607, sum-
marizing the tables and figures in WRIGHT, *Report*, 135-39.

[2] WRIGHT, *Report*, 137.   [3] *Ibid.*, 147-49.

[4] WILLCOX, *The Divorce Problem* (2d ed.), 16-19, and Appendix.

[5] According to WILLCOX, "A Study in Vital Statistics," *Pol. Sci. Quart.*, VIII, 78,
the "number of persons divorced (not the number of divorces) to every 100,000 of the
population" is as follows for various countries, the date being 1886 unless otherwise

in the southeastern and highest in the western and southwestern states.[1]   As in Europe the divorce rate is higher
and the marriage rate lower in the cities than in the country.[2]
Again, while the marriage rate per capita of population is
steadily descending, the divorce rate is on the average rising,
although the "North Atlantic group of states, from Maine to
Pennsylvania inclusive, shows no increase" in the twenty
years, the growth of divorce just keeping pace "with the
population."[3]   For some of the western states the more
recent statistics are sufficiently startling.   "Divorces in Ohio
increased from 2,270 in 1889 to 3,217 in 1899, and the ratio
to marriages has become 1 to 10.9.   There were 2,418
divorces in Michigan in the year 1900, or 1 to 9.6 marriages.
Here about two-thirds of the applications are granted.   In
some states three-fourths of the suits are successful.   In
Michigan the statistics show that nearly all the divorces are
granted to residents of the state.   Indiana shows a remarkable
change for the worse.   Almost a generation ago Indiana was
notoriously bad.   Then the laws were improved and her
divorce rate was no worse than that of some states in the
east; but for some unexplained reason divorces of late have
increased rapidly.   In 1899 there were granted no less than
4,031 divorces, and 4,699 in the year 1900.   In the last

stated: Ireland, 0.28; Italy (1885), 3.75; England and Wales, 3.79; Canada, 4.81; Australia (including New Zealand and Tasmania), 11.14; German Empire, 25.97; France,
32.51; Switzerland, 64.49; United States, 88.71; Japan, 608.45. "In the year 1886," he
adds, "there were in Japan 315,311 marriages and 117,964 divorces, more than one
divorce to every three marriages and more than four and a half times as many
divorces as there were in the United States, although the population of Japan was
only about two-thirds as great."

1 WILLCOX, op. cit., 92–96.

2 WRIGHT, Report, 158–63: WILLCOX, op. cit., 74, 75; BERTILLON, Étude démographique du divorce, 54–57; and Statistik der Ehescheidungen der Stadt Berlin, vi,
vii, showing that for each 10,000 married persons living in Berlin in 1867 29.85 divorces
were granted, while in 1894 the rate had risen to 37.93.

3 WILLCOX, op. cit., 73 ff., 93 ff. Cf. WRIGHT, Report, 145, 146. Within this group
the New England states show a small decrease in the divorce rate; "while in New
York, New Jersey, and Pennsylvania as a whole it has slightly increased, the two
offsetting each other."

year the ratio of divorces to marriages of the same year became **1** to 5.7 for the entire state," and 1 to 3.8 in the county of Marion containing Indianapolis.[1] In Europe likewise the marriage rate is decreasing and the divorce rate increasing, each in some countries with even greater rapidity than on the average in the United States. Moreover, the growth of divorce in recent years is a remarkable phenomenon in Catholic as well as Protestant lands. Thus in the entire German Empire divorces rose from 5,342 in 1882 to 6,677 in 1891, the population during the same decade rising from 45,719,000 to 49,767,000. In Holland there were together 271 divorces and separations in 1883 and 474 in 1892, the population at the same time advancing from 4,225,065 to 4,669,576. During the same ten years divorces in Sweden rose from 218 to 316, the population being 4,603,595 at the beginning and 4,806,865 at the end of the period. In this decade, the population making but slight advance, the aggregate number of divorces and separations in Switzerland decreased from 1,013 to 953. In France for each 1,000 marriages celebrated 14 divorces were decreed in 1885 and 24 in 1891, the population showing a very small increase. For the decennium beginning in 1884 and closing in 1893 the number of divorces decreed in Belgium mounted from 221 to 497, while the population grew from 5,784,958 to 6,262,272. During the same period in Greece the number rose from 88 to 103. In Bavaria—like Greece or Belgium a Catholic state—there is also a rapid growth of

---

[1] DIKE, in *Rep. of Nat. League for Protection of the Family* (1901), 6, 11. But in 1902, for the state, the ratio was 1 divorce to 7.6 marriages; *ibid.* (1903), 10.

In 1896 the number of marriages celebrated to one divorce granted was 19.2 in Massachusetts, 15.7 in Vermont, 14.9 in Connecticut, 9.2 in Rhode Island, and only 8.3 in Maine. In 1901 the ratio in Rhode Island had fallen to 8.2; while it had risen in Connecticut to 15.8 and in Massachusetts to 20.2: *Registration Report* (Me., 1896), 91; *ibid.* (Vt., 1896), 96; DIKE in *Report* (1901), 11. In 1902 the number of marriages to one divorce was sixteen in Massachusetts; 8.4 in Rhode Island; 10 in Vermont; and only about six in Maine; while in 1901 it was 8.3 in New Hampshire: DIKE, *op. cit.* (1903), 9, 10.

divorce, the number of decrees advancing from 218 in 1882
to 308 in 1891, thus giving a rate of one divorce for 24,490
of the population at the commencement as compared with
18,279 at the close of the decade.[1] "In England divorces
rose from 127 in 1860 to 390 in 1887, an increase much
more rapid than that of population or of marriages. Judicial separations rose between the same years from 11 to 50.
In Scotland divorces which in 1867 numbered 32 had, in
1886, grown to 96, a still more rapid rise, as it covers only
twenty instead of twenty-seven years. It is worth noting
that in England it is usually the husband who petitions for
a divorce, and almost always the wife who seeks a judicial
separation."[2]

It has long been observed that in Europe the marriage
rate falls in hard times and rises again on the return of prosperity. "According to all experience," declares Mill, "a
great increase invariably takes place in the number of marriages in seasons of cheap food and full employment."[3] The
middle and upper classes, says Fawcett, "do not often marry
unless they have reasonable prospect of being able to bring
up a family in a state of social comfort. . . . . But the
laborers, who form the majority of the population, are but
slightly influenced by such cautious foresight. Even a tri-
fling temporary improvement in their material prosperity

[1] For these facts see the parliamentary *Return of the Number of Divorces in
Foreign Countries* (Part I, being Misc. No. 4, 1895), 3–5, 8, 9, 10, 12, 15, 16. See also
Bertillon, *Étude démographique du divorce*, 58 ff., 74 ff.; the table in *Statistik der
Ehescheidungen der Stadt Berlin*, vi, vii, giving figures (1867–94) for German and other
lands as well as for the city; Oettingen, *Die Moralstatistik*, 134–62, *passim;* Rubin
and Westergaard, *Statistik der Ehen* (relating chiefly to Denmark and particularly
to Copenhagen); Cadet, *Le mariage en France* (containing many statistical tables
for marriage and divorce); Naquet, *Le divorce* (giving two tables for marriage and
divorce, 1840–74); Woolsey, *Divorce and Divorce Legislation*, 181–93; Muirhead, "Is
the Family Declining?" *Internat. Jour. of Eth.*, Oct., 1896, 33 ff.; Mayo-Smith, *Statistics and Sociology*, 101 ff., 124; Wright, *Report*, 981 ff.; and the mass of marriage
statistics in Cauderlier, *Les lois de la population et leur application à la Belgique.*

[2] Bryce, *Studies in Hist. and Jurisp.*, 841.

[3] Mill, *Prin. of Pol. Econ.* (Boston, 1848), I, 413.

acts as a powerful impulse to induce them to marry; for it is a demonstrated statistical fact that the number of marriages invariably increases with the decline in the price of bread."[1] Farr and Bodio reach the same conclusion.[2] Ogle on the other hand, while agreeing entirely with these writers as to the favoring influence of prosperity and the depressing effect of hard times on the number of marriages, finds in England, so far as the price of bread alone is concerned, that the reverse is true, more marriages there taking place among the laboring class when bread is dear. In this case, he urges, the higher cost of bread may itself be an incident of increased industrial activity, depending in part on the rise of freight charges on imported wheat. So he concludes that "the marriage rate rises and falls with the amount of industrial employment, which in its turn is determined by the briskness of trade, as measured by the values of exports, which also rise and fall concomitantly, and produce by their effect upon freights a simultaneous rise or fall in the price of wheat."[3] The researches of Oettingen, Bertillon, and especially those of Cauderlier, have also disclosed a general variation in the marriage rate corresponding with the rise or fall in the price of the necessaries of life.[4] War in particular has a powerful influence in lowering the marriage rate, while on the restoration of peace the loss may be largely or entirely recovered. "In 1864 Denmark was at war with

---

[1] FAWCETT, *Manual of Pol. Econ.* (4th ed., London, 1874), 143.

[2] BODIO, *Del Movimento della populazione in Italia e in altri stati d'Europa* (1876), 136, 137; FARR, *Vital Statistics*, 68–75; and *idem*, in *Report of the Registrar General:* quoted by OGLE, "On Marriage Rates," etc., *Jour. of the Royal Statistical Society*, LIII, 254 ff. *Cf.* NEWSHOLME, *Vital Statistics*, 45, 46.

[3] OGLE, *op. cit.*, 256–63. CAUDERLIER, *Les lois de la population*, 71–74, 113, 114, has also shown in the case of England that foreign commercial relations must be considered in determining the condition of material well-being.

[4] OETTINGEN, *Die Moralstatistik*, 89–94, and authorities there cited; BERTILLON, *Annales de démographie internationale*, I, 24; CAUDERLIER, *op. cit.*, 61–78, 102 ff., giving statistics for Germany, Belgium, England, and France. *Cf.* MAYO-SMITH, *Statistics and Sociology*, 100, 101.

Prussia, and its marriage rate fell from 15.0 to 11.13" for each 1,000 inhabitants, "the lowest point it has ever yet reached, but in the next year, the war being over, rose to 17.8, and was higher than it has ever been again. In 1866 Austria was at war with Prussia, and, while the Prussian rate fell from 18.2 to 15.6, the Austrian rate fell from 15.5 to 13.0, but on the cessation of hostilities rose in 1867 to 19.3, a higher level than in any earlier year."[1] According to Willcox,[2] the same rule appears to hold good in the United States. In Massachusetts for the period 1850–90 the marriage rate was low in the years of industrial depression and during the Civil War. Furthermore, the same writer has for the first time demonstrated that the average divorce rate for the whole country is affected in the same way, sinking in hard times and rising again on the restoration of business. Represented graphically, the curve for the Massachusetts marriages and the curve for United States divorces (1867–86), with slight exceptions, "uniformly ascend and descend together and reach their maxima and minima in the same years. Depressions in trade have had a tendency to decrease divorces as well as marriages;" whereas in England, while the marriage rate falls the divorce rate rises in hard times. But in that country divorce is notoriously very expensive and hence mainly a luxury for the rich. So it is concluded that "this difference between the effect of hard times in England and in the United States, together with the very rapid increase of divorce among the southern negroes, and the fact that only about one wife in six of those obtaining divorces receives any alimony, are among the indications that divorce has become very frequent and perhaps most frequent among our lower middle classes, and has

[1] OGLE, op. cit., 255; cf. OETTINGEN, op. cit., 93, 94.

[2] WILLCOX, "A Study in Vital Statistics," Pol. Sci. Quart., VIII, 76, 77. Cf. idem, "The Marriage Rate in Michigan," Pub. Am. Stat. Assoc., IV, 7; and CRUM, "The Marriage Rate in Massachusetts," ibid., 328, 329.

reached for weal or woe a lower stratum than perhaps anywhere in Europe." [1]

Whether the number of divorces is directly influenced by legislation is a question which has given rise to decided difference of opinion. Bertillon, writing in 1883 in favor of the new divorce law of France then under consideration, took the position that statutes extending the number of causes of divorce or relaxing the procedure in divorce suits have little influence "upon the increase in the number of decrees." [2] Yet, for obvious reasons, he predicted that the first, though not the lasting, result of a change in the law allowing absolute divorce instead of mere separation would be the opposite of this conclusion. Such, in fact, was the case. In 1883 there were 3,010 separations; while, after the new code took effect, 4,478 divorces and separations were granted in 1884, 6,245 in 1885, and 6,211 in the following year. [3] Only a part of this can be accounted for by the change in law, for there had been a rapid increase during the preceding fifty years. [4] For the United States this point has been examined by Professor Willcox, and his results go to show that the difference in the divorce rate existing among the states cannot very largely be accounted for by the difference in the number of grounds of petition sanctioned by the respective statutes. Thus in 1880 New York admitted one cause, New

---

[1] WILLCOX, loc. cit., 76, 77, 79–82. On the increase of divorce among the southern negroes see idem, The Divorce Problem, 21–23, 29–32.

[2] BERTILLON, op. cit., 20–28, 88–102; WRIGHT, Report, 150.

[3] See table in WRIGHT, Report, 145.

[4] See the table in BOTTET, La famille, 47 ff. His figures do not agree with those quoted from WRIGHT's Report: According to his table, 3,010 separations were granted in 1883; 3,790 separations and divorces in 1884; 4,640 in 1885; 6,270 in 1886; 7,983 in 1887; and 7,430 in 1888. Compare KELLER, "Divorces in France," Procds. of the Am. Stat. Assoc., I, 469 ff., who summarizes TURQUAN, Résultats statistiques de cinq années de divorce. See also "Divorce: from a French Point of View," North Am. Rev., CLV, 721–30, by NAQUET, author of the law of 1884; and the vigorous criticism of BRUN, "Divorce Made Easy," ibid., CLVII, 11–17. In 1897, 7,460 divorces were decreed; while in 1900 there were only 7,157; DIKE, Rep. of the Nat. League for Protection of the Family (1903), 11.

Jersey two causes, and Pennsylvania four; yet on the average in that year for each 100,000 married couples New York was granting 81 divorces, New Jersey 68, and Pennsylvania 111.[1] "This means that more divorces for adultery are granted in New York, relatively to population, than for adultery and desertion in New Jersey, and almost as many as for adultery, desertion, cruelty, and imprisonment in Pennsylvania. Assume the number of married couples in the three states in 1875 to be a mean between the estimates for 1870 and 1880, and compare with this mean the total number of divorces for adultery in the three states for the twenty years. Pennsylvania had annually 16 such divorces to 100,000 couples, New Jersey had 26, and New York 78. Judging from the court records, one would say that adultery was about three times as frequent in New York as in New Jersey, and about five times as frequent as in Pennsylvania. No such inference is warranted. The true conclusion is that limiting the causes increases the number of divorces in those which remain, but without materially affecting the total number. A certain proportion of the married couples in the three states desired divorce, and was willing to offer the evidence required in order to obtain the decree. The number of causes, then, seems to have affected the grounds urged for divorce, but in no large degree the total number."[2] It is possible that this conclusion is somewhat too emphatic. The problem is very complex, and it is hard to make allowance for all its conditions. For example, it should not be forgotten that New Jersey has but one tribunal, the court of chancery, authorized to grant divorce, whereas New York has many; and if states sanctioning a wider range of causes were selected for comparison, the result might be changed, though scarcely to any wide extent.

[1] WILLCOX, *The Divorce Problem*, 37, 38.

[2] *Ibid.* (2d ed.), 45, 46; WRIGHT, *Report*, 148, 169.

Commissioner Wright has attempted to discover the general influence of legislation by examining every change in the laws during twenty years in connection with the divorce statistics. Often a sudden increase, and occasionally a slight decrease, in the rate is observed without any alteration in the statutes. In fourteen instances, however, he believes it "quite apparent that the lines of statistics are curved in accordance with laws enacted just previous to the curves."[1] The changes effected by these laws are of many kinds, including the addition and repeal of causes and various alterations in the procedure, some of them complex. But under careful scrutiny in some instances the statistics reveal no certain causal relation between the change in the divorce rate and the antecedent change in the statute. Indeed, in the light of Professor Willcox's detailed criticism of the figures, four of Mr. Wright's test cases must be rejected, so far as evidence afforded by the statistics is concerned;[2] four or five others show considerable influence of legislation; while in the rest that influence is slight, temporary, or questionable.[3] Contrary to the popular opinion, restrictions upon the remarriage of divorced persons would

[1] Wright, *Report*, 150 ff.

[2] Including the repeal in 1878 of the celebrated Connecticut "omnibus clause" introduced in 1849. On the alleged influence of this clause see Dike, "Facts as to Divorce in New England," in *Christ and Modern Thought*, 197-202; *idem*, "Some Aspects of the Divorce Problem," *Princeton Review*, March, 1884, 170, 171; and especially Loomis, "Divorce Legislation in Conn.," *New Englander*, XXV, 436 ff., 441, 442, giving a table of Connecticut divorces by counties, 1849-65; and Allen, "Divorce in New England," *North Am. Rev.*, CXXX, 547 ff., giving statistics for the period 1860-78.

[3] For example, Massachusetts created four new causes of divorce in 1870; and in 1873 reduced the time of desertion necessary to constitute a ground of divorce from five to three years. Divorces increased from 337 in 1872 to 611 in 1874. A part of this gain was probably due to the change in law, although in all the entire group of north Atlantic states there was at the same time a large increase which cannot be thus accounted for. The lax law of residence in Utah previous to 1878, and the reduction of the term of desertion from two years to one by the Dakota legislature in 1881, were each responsible for an increase in the divorce rate: compare Wright, *Report*, 152 ff., 156, 203 ff.; Willcox, *A Study in Vital Statistics*, 85-90; *idem, The Divorce Problem*, 41-61; with the criticism of Dike, "Legislation and Divorce," *New York Eve. Post*, July 2, 1891.

not affect in a large degree the divorce rate, although only foreign statistics are available to test the point.   These show that within the first two or three years after dissolution of marriage divorced men are not much more inclined to re-marry than are widowers, while during the same period a considerably greater number of divorced women than widows renew the nuptial ties.[1]   With an increasing rate, which does not advance uniformly, it is perhaps impossible to measure exactly the effects of lax or restrictive legislation.   The divorce movement is dependent upon social forces which lie far beyond the reach of the statute-maker.   Yet it seems almost certain that there is a margin, very important though narrow, within which he may wisely exert a restraining influ-ence.   Good laws may, at any rate, check hasty impulse and force individuals to take proper time for reflection.   They may also by securing publicity prevent manifold injustice in the granting of decrees.

After all, in this fact do we not catch a glimpse of the proper sphere of divorce legislation?   Divorce is a remedy and not the disease.   It is not a virtue in a divorce law, as appears to be often assumed, to restrict the application of the remedy at all hazards, regardless of the sufferings of the social body.   If it were always the essential purpose of a

---

[1] See BERTILLON, *Note pour l'étude statistique du divorce*, 464 ff., 471-73, giving Berlin statistics for 1878 which show that divorced men remarry within the first three years at about the same rate as widowers, while divorced women remarry more rapidly than widows.   The results obtained from Swiss statistics are nearly the same: see the table in BERTILLON, "Du sort des divorcés," *Jour. de la société de sta-tistique de Paris*, June, 1884; reproduced by WILLCOX, *The Divorce Problem*, 27.   On the other hand, OETTINGEN, *Die Moralstatistik*, 153-62, on the basis of statistics for Saxony (1834-49) and the Netherlands (1850-54), shows a strong tendency to remarry on the part of divorced persons of either sex, as compared with widows and widow-ers, the divorced women remarrying much more frequently than the men.   DIKE, *Rep. of the Nat. Div. Ref. League* (1891), 18, gives some facts for Connecticut. . In 1889, 286 divorced persons were married, "135 men and 151 women, which is a little above one-third of the number divorced in the year.   In 1890 there were 477 divorces granted, or 954 individuals divorced: and there were 350 divorced persons" — 143 men and 207 women — "who married again."   To be of much value these figures should be compared with the number of marriages of widowers and widows for the same period.

good law to diminish directly the number of *bona fide* divorces, the more rational course would be to imitate South Carolina and prohibit divorce entirely. Divorce is not immoral. It is quite probable, on the contrary, that drastic, like negligent, legislation is sometimes immoral. It is not necessarily a merit, and it may be a grave social wrong, to reduce the legal causes for a decree to the one "scriptural" ground. The most enlightened judgment of the age heartily approves of the policy of some states in extending the causes so as to include intoxication from the habitual use of strong drinks or narcotics as being equally destructive of connubial happiness and family well-being. Indeed, considering the needs of each particular society, the promotion of happiness is the only safe criterion to guide the lawmaker in either widening or narrowing the door of escape from the marriage bond. The divorce movement is a portentous and almost universal incident of modern civilization. Doubtless it signifies underlying social evils vast and perilous. Yet to the student of history it is perfectly clear that this is but a part of the mighty movement for social liberation which has been gaining in volume and strength ever since the Reformation. According to the sixteenth-century reformer, divorce is the "medicine" for the disease of marriage. It is so today in a sense more real than Smith or Bullinger ever dreamed of; for the principal fountain of divorce is bad matrimonial laws and bad marriages. Certain it is that one rises from a detailed study of American legislation with the conviction that, faulty as are our divorce laws, our marriage laws are far worse; while our apathy, our carelessness and levity, regarding the safeguards of the matrimonial institution are well-nigh incredible. Indeed, there has been a great deal of misdirected and hasty criticism of American divorce legislation. Even thoughtful scholars sometimes indulge in the traditional arraignment. The laws of the American states produced since 1789, declares Bryce, present "the largest and the strangest, and perhaps the saddest, body of legislative experiments in the sphere of family law which free self-governing communities have ever tried."[1] Such sweeping assertions are in many ways misleading and fail to advance the solution of the divorce problem. There is, of course, in the aggregate a "large" body of statutes; for each of the fifty-three commonwealths, on this subject as on all others, has a separate code; but the harm resulting either from the bulk or the perplexity of the laws, while needing a remedy, is not so serious as is commonly assumed. More and more in their essential features the divorce laws of the states are duplicating each other; and there is already ground for hope that in reasonable time they may attain to practical uniformity. Furthermore, it may well be questioned whether the complexity or the conflict in the American codes is so pronounced as in the numerous systems of divorce law maintained in the states of the German Empire until the enactment of the imperial code of 1900. In some cases in German lands the law was obscure and well-nigh past finding out. Prussia alone had three different systems; and Bavaria was in the same plight.[2] If American legislation is on the average more liberal in extending the enumerated grounds of divorce, it would surely be rash to assume that it is the "sadder" on that account. The question is: Has American social liberalism, in this regard as in so many other respects, increased the sum of human happiness? Besides, "laxity" in this connection is not exclusively a feature of American legislation. It may be reasonably doubted whether any "omnibus clause" in the country gives wider discretion to the court than the fourth of the five causes sanctioned by the new uniform law of Germany,

[1] BRYCE, *Studies in Hist. and Jur.*, 830.

[2] See WRIGHT, *Report*, 1030, 1033 ff.

allowing divorce when "either spouse has been guilty of grave violation of the obligations based on the marrriage or of so deeply disturbing the marital relation through dishonorable or immoral behavior that the continuance of the marriage cannot be expected from the other."[1]   Even broader provisions formerly existed in the codes of some of the separate German states, and may still be found elsewhere in Europe.

The achievement of a wisely conceived and carefully drafted uniform law for the entire country, would be of great advantage, although it might not directly cause a very great decrease in the average divorce rate, and certainly would not produce the same rate for the individual states.[2]   How may such a uniform law be secured?   The method of procuring the enactment of a federal law under a constitutional amendment—once much in favor[3]—has for the present been almost

[1] "Wenn der andere Ehegatte durch schwere Verletzung der durch die Ehe begründeten Pflichten oder durch ehrloses oder unsittliches Verhalten eine so tiefe Zerrüttung des ehelichen Verhältnisses verschuldet hat, dass dem Ehegatten die Fortsetzung der Ehe nicht zugemuthet werden kann."— *Reichsgesetzbuch*, Tit. 7, § 1568.   For discussion see KOHLER, *Das Eherecht des bürg, Gesetzbuchs*, 42–46.

But the statistics seem to show that the law is conservatively administered. The number of divorces is decreasing.   "For the years 1891-95, inclusive, the annual average was 7,258.   In 1896 there were 8,601; in 1897 there were 9,005; in 1898 there were 9,143; and in 1899 they had become 9,563.   But under the new law in 1900 they dropped to 8,934, and in 1901 they were 8,037."—DIKE, *Report* (1903), 8, 9, on the authority of the Chief of the Statistical Bureau of Berlin.

The other grounds of divorce allowed by the imperial statute are adultery, attempt on the life of either spouse by the other, malicious desertion, and insanity (Geisteskrankheit) of three years' standing.   Divorce for malicious desertion is decreed only after a preliminary suit for the re-establishment of marital relations and a year's delay to allow the deserter to return to conjugal duty: *Reichsgesetzbuch*, Tit. 7, § 1567.

[2] The uniform divorce law for the Swiss cantons, which went into effect in 1876, has not tended to produce a uniform rate.   In 1885, for instance, Appenzell, Outer Rhodes, " has forty-nine times as much divorce as Unterwalden o. d. W., while with all the divergences of law in this country the differences of rate are much less."— WILLCOX, *The Divorce Problem*, 59, giving a table of the decrees granted in the twenty-six cantons, 1876-85; compiled from *Die Bewegung der Bevölkerung in der Schweiz im Jahre 1885* (Beilage I).

[3] DIKE, "Uniform Marriage and Divorce Laws," *Arena*, II, 399-408, gives a valuable discussion of the two methods of procedure.   See also BENNETT, "National Divorce Legislation," *Forum*, II, 429-38; STEWART, "Our Mar. and Div. Laws," *Pop. Sci. Monthly*, XXIII, 232, 233; and JAMESON, "Divorce," *North Am. Rev.*,

abandoned by active workers.   Instead, it is preferred, through the state commissions on uniform legislation, to urge the adoption of a model statute by the separate commonwealths.   These commissions, now thirty-five in number, have prepared a bill for a law governing divorce procedure; and its temperate and practical provisions ought to gain its general adoption.[1]   All this is well; but it is still more needful to strive for a common marriage law.   In the end it may be found necessary, under a constitutional amendment, to appeal to the federal power.   What service could a national legislature render more beneficent than the creation of a code embracing every division of the intricate law of marriage and divorce?   Aside from its educational value as a moral force, such a code in material ways would prove a powerful guaranty of social order and stability.

In the meantime it is essential to fix the attention upon causes rather than effects.   For the wise reformer, who would elevate and protect the family, the center of the problem is marriage and not divorce.

II.   THE FUNCTION OF EDUCATION

It is needful in the outset, as already suggested, frankly to accept marriage and the family as social institutions whose problems must be studied in connection with the actual conditions of modern social life.   It is vain to appeal to ideals born of old and very different conditions.   The guiding light will come, not from authority, but from a rational under-

---

CXXXVI, 325, all favoring a constitutional amendment; also NORTH, "Uniform Mar. and Div. Laws," *ibid.*, CXLIV, 429–31; LLOYD, *Law of Divorce*, 269 ff.; JOHNSON, *Remarks upon Uniformity of State Legislation;* SNYDER, *Problem of Uniform Legislation*, 3 ff., favoring state action.   In his *Geography of Marriage*, 182 ff., SNYDER favors concert of action among the states and a prohibitory amendment restricting or defining the maximum number of causes for divorce which a state might sanction. See also the articles by STANWOOD AND STANTON mentioned in the Bibliographical Index, IV; and consult the *Reports of the Conferences of the State Boards of Commissioners for Promoting Uniformity of Legislation in the U. S.*

[1] See *Reports of the Nat. League for the Protection of the Family* (1900), 7; (1901), 8.

standing of the existing facts. Small progress can be
expected while leaning upon tradition. The appeal to theological criteria is, no doubt, matter of conscience on the part
of many earnest men. Nevertheless the vast literature which
seeks to solve social questions through the juggling with
ancient texts seems in reality to be largely a monument of
wasted energy. Much of it is sterile, or but serves to retard
progress or to befog the issue. Witness the perennial discussion of the "scriptural" grounds of divorce, or of the
Levitical sanction or condemnation of marriage with a deceased wife's sister! Witness the vapid homilies and treatises
on the wedded life! There is, in truth, urgent need that the
moral leaders of men should preach actual instead of conventional social righteousness. It is high time that the
family and its related institutions should be as freely and
openly and unsparingly subjected to scientific examination
as are the facts of modern political or industrial life.

From the infancy of the human race, we have already
seen, the monogamic family has been the *prevailing* type.
There have been, it is true, many variations, many aberra-
tions, from this type under diverse conditions, religious,
economic, or social. Under changing influences the inter-
relations of the members of the group—of husband and wife,
of parent and child—and their relations individually and
collectively to the state, have varied from age to age or from
people to people. There have been wife-capture, wife-
purchase, and the *patria potestas*. But in essential character—at first for biological, later for ethical or spiritual
reasons—the general tendency has always been toward a
higher, more clearly differentiated type of the single pairing
family. Moreover, setting aside all question of special
priestly sanctions, the healthiest social sentiment has more
and more demanded that the "pairing" should be lasting.
Whether of Jew or gentile, the highest ideal of marriage

has become that of a lifelong partnership. Are these tendencies to remain unbroken? Is the stream of evolution to proceed, gaining in purity and strength? Are marriage and the family doomed; or are they capaple of adaptation, of reform and development, so as to satisfy the higher material and ethical requirements of the advancing generations? Seemingly they are now menaced by serious dangers. Some of them have their origin in the new conditions of a society which is undergoing a swift transition, a mighty transformation, industrially, intellectually, and spiritually; while others, perhaps the more imminent, are incident to the institutions themselves as they have been shaped or warped by bad laws and false sentiments. Apparently, if there is to be salvation, it must come through the vitalizing, regenerative power of a more efficient moral, physical, and social training of the young. The home and the family must enter into the educational curriculum. Before an adequate sociological program can be devised the facts must be squarely faced and honestly studied. In the sphere of domestic institutions, even more imperatively than in that of politics or economics, there is need of light and publicity.

The family, it is alleged, is in danger of disintegration through the tendency to individualism which in many ways is so striking a characteristic of the age.[1] Within the family itself there are, indeed, signs that a rapid transition from status to contract is taking place in a way which Maine

---

[1] PEABODY, "The Teaching of Jesus Concerning the Family," in his *Jesus Christ and the Social Question*, 129 ff.; DIKE, "Problems of the Family," *Century*, XXXIX, 392, 393; *idem*, *Some Aspects of the Divorce Question*, 177 ff.; *idem*, *Perils of the Family*; MULFORD, *The Nation*, 276-83; BUSHNELL, "The Organic Unity of the Family," in his *Christian Nurture*, 90-122; HENDERSON, *Social Elements*, 71 ff.; ALLEN, "Divorces in New England," *North Am. Rev.*, CXXX, 559 ff.; POTTER, "The Message of Christ to the Family," in his *Message of Christ to Manhood*; SALTER, *The Future of the Family*; MATHEWS, "The Family," *Am. Journal of Sociology*, I, 457-72; PEARSON, "The Decline of the Family," in his *National Life and Character*, 227 ff.; and the reply of MUIRHEAD, "Is the Family Declining?" *Int. Jour. of Ethics*, Oct., 1896, 33 ff.; ROSS, *Social Control*, 405, 433. The ablest appreciation of the value of individualism is that of MILL, *On Liberty* (2d ed.), 100 ff.

scarcely contemplated; for he appears to have imagined that precisely in this sphere the process was already virtually complete. The bonds of paternal authority are becoming looser and looser. In America in particular young men and even young women earlier than elsewhere tend to cut their parental moorings and to embark in independent business careers. So also more and more clearly the wife is showing a determination to escape entirely from *manu viri*—still sustained by the relics of mediæval law and sentiment—and to become in reality as well as in name an equal partner under the nuptial contract. The state also has intervened to abridge the parental authority. Minor children are no longer looked upon as the absolute property of the father. For the purpose of education, society removes them for a considerable part of the period of nonage from home and immediate parental control; and, on the other hand, it forbids their employment in mines, factories, or other injurious vocations during their tender years. Under child-saving laws they may even be removed from home, when they are cruelly treated or exposed to vicious influences, and placed under the protection of the state. Thus, little by little, to use the phrase of a thoughtful writer, the original "coercive" powers of the family under the patriarchal *régime* have been "extracted" and appropriated by society. In the education of the young the family retains the lesser part. "The state has here interfered in the private ordering of the household by taking the child from its parents for one-third of its waking hours, and has introduced order and system into the training of children, together with the assertion of rights on their part. The family becomes therefore less a coercive institution, where the children serve their parents, and more a spiritual and psychic association of parent and child based on persuasion. A more searching interference on the part of the state, together with a new set of governmental organizations for its enforcement, is found in the boards of children's guardians, the societies for the prevention of cruelty to children, orphans' asylums, state public schools, with their investigating and placing-out agents, empowered under supervision of the courts to take children away from parents and to place them in new homes. A large part of the unlimited coercion of the *patria potestas* is here extracted from the family and annexed to the peculiar coercive institution where it is guided by notions of children's rights, and all families are thereby toned up to a stronger emphasis on persuasion as the justification of their continuance."[1]   Here we catch a glimpse of the direction of future evolution in the family.   At the same time it appears that the disintegration of paternal and marital coercive power is not a serious menace to the family.   It has cleared the way for a higher and nobler spiritual domestic life.   The real danger is that the family and the home will surrender an undue share of their duty and privilege to participate in the culture and training of the young.   This function for the good of society may be vastly developed, though mainly on new lines bearing directly on the nature of marriage and the family.   Of this function some further mention will presently be made.

More threatening to the solidarity of the family is believed to be the individualistic tendencies arising in existing urban and economic life.[2]   With the rise of corporate and associated industry comes a weakening of the intimacy of home ties. Through the division of labor the "family hearth-stone" is fast becoming a mere temporary meeting-

[1] COMMONS, "The Family," in his "Sociological View of Sovereignty," in *Am. Jour. of Sociology*, V, 683 ff., 688, 689. On the future of the family compare SPENCER, *Principles of Sociology*, I, 737 ff., 788; LETOURNEAU, *L'évolution du mariage*, 444 ff.; PEARSON, "The Decline of the Family," in his *National Life and Character*, 255, 256; MUIRHEAD, "Is the Family Declining?" *Int. Jour. of Ethics*, Oct., 1896, 53-55; TILLIER, *Le mariage*, 283 ff., 316.

[2] *Cf.* PEABODY, *Jesus Christ and the Social Question*, 162-79; MUIRHEAD, *Is the Family Declining?* 35.

place of individual wage-earners. The congestion of population in cities is forcing into being new and lower modes of life. The tenement and the "sweating system" are destructive of the home. Neither the lodging-house, the "flat," nor the "apartment" affords an ideal environment for domestic joys. In the vast hives of Paris, London, or New York even families of the relatively well-to-do have small opportunity to flourish—for self-culture and self-enjoyment. To the children of the slum the street is a perilous nursery. For them squalor, disease, and sordid vice have supplanted the traditional blessings of the family sanctuary. The cramped, artificial, and transient associations of the boarding-house are a wretched substitute for the privacy of the separate household.[1] For very many men club life has stronger allurements than the connubial partnership. Prostitution advances with alarming speed. For the poor, sometimes for the rich, the great city has many interests and many places more attractive than the home circle. The love of selfish indulgence and the spirit of commercial greed, not less than grinding penury, restrain men and women from wedlock. Yet the urban environment has also the opposite effect. In the crowded, heterogeneous, and shifting population of the great towns marriages are often lightly made and as lightly dissolved. Indeed, the remarkable mobility of the American people, the habit of frequent migration, under the powerful incentives of industrial enterprise, gold-hunting, or other adventure, and under favor of the marvelously developed means of swift transportation, will account in no small degree for the laxity of matrimonial and family ties in the United

---

[1] In the great centers of Germany, we are assured, the family of the blood-kindred has yielded to the family composed of kindred and strangers. For lack of space in the closely packed districts people are forced to live almost in common: Göhre, *Drei Monate Fabrikarbeiter*, 12 ff., 37 ff. *Cf.* Bebel, *Die Frau und der Sozialismus*, 123, 124; and Rade, *Die sittlich-religiöse Gedankenwelt unserer Industriearbeiter*, 117 ff.; Stewart, *Disintegration of the Families of the Workingmen;* Henderson, *Social Elements*, 73.

States. May not one gather courage even from this untoward circumstance? Assuredly the present thus clearly appears to be an age of transition to a more stable condition of social life. Furthermore, the perils to the family of the kind under review need not be fatal. They are inherent mainly in economic institutions which may be scientifically studied and intelligently brought into harmony with the requirements of the social order. Already in great municipal centers, through improved facilities for rapid transit, the evils resulting from dense population are being somewhat ameliorated. Of a truth, every penny's reduction in streetrailway fares means for the family of small means a better chance for pure air, sound health, and a separate home in the suburbs. The dispersion of the city over a broader area at once cheapens and raises the standard of living. Every hour's reduction in the period of daily toil potentially gives more leisure for building, adorning, and enjoying the home.

To the socialist the monogamic family in its present form is decidedly a failure. "To those who would substitute common ownership for industrial liberty, the institution of the family presents one of the most persistent obstacles. Domestic unity is inconsistent with the absolute social unity vested in the state."[1] The larger social body must be composed of individual members, free and equal; and it will not tolerate within itself a smaller body with special groupinterests of its own, much less with any vestige of coercive authority over its constituent parts. There must be no *imperium in imperio*. Writers like Engels[2] seek consolation and support in Bachofen's theory of a universal stage of mother-right before the monogamic family with the institution of private property had brought domestic slavery into

---

[1] Peabody, *op. cit.*, 140.

[2] See Engels, *Der Ursprung der Familie*, 4 ff.; and his follower, Bebel, *Die Frau und der Sozialismus*, 1 ff., 93 ff.

the world. They "hold that the monogamic family is a relic of decaying civilization. All ideas on which it rests, the subordination and dependence of women, the ownership of children, the belief in the sacredness of marriage as a divine institution, above all respect for the individual ownership of property and the rights of inheritance as permanent elements in our social organization — have been undermined. The foundations are sapped and the superstructure is ready to topple in."[1]

Woman in particular has been the devoted victim of the greed of individual possession upon which the monogamic family rests. "Far back in history," according to Edward Carpenter, "at a time when in the early societies the thought of inequality had hardly arisen, it would appear that the female, in her own way — as sole authenticator of birth and parentage, as guardian of the household, as inventress of agriculture and the peaceful arts, as priestess and prophetess or sharer in the councils of the tribe — was as powerful as man in his, and sometimes even more so. But from thence down to today what centuries of repression, of slavehood, of dumbness, of obscurity have been her lot!"[2]

Under socialism, declare Morris and Bax, marriage and the family will be affected "firstly in economics and secondly in ethics. The present marriage system is based on the general supposition of economic dependence of the woman on the man, and the consequent necessity of his making provision for her." In the new social order this degrading condition must disappear. "Property in children would cease to exist, and every infant that came into the world would be born into full citizenship, and would enjoy all its advantages, whatever the conduct of its parents might be. Thus a new

---

[1] MUIRHEAD, *Is the Family Declining?* 37.

[2] CARPENTER, *Love's Coming of Age;* quoted from MUIRHEAD, *op. cit.*, 37. The views of various socialists regarding woman and marriage are criticised by HERTZBERG, *Der Beruf der Frau*, 43-57.

development of the family would take place, on the basis, not
of a predominant life-long business arrangement, to be formally and nominally held to, irrespective of circumstances,
but on mutual inclination and affection, an association ter-
minable at the will of either party." Thus a higher morality
would be sanctioned. There would be no "vestige of repro-
bation for dissolving one tie and forming another."[1]

A similar demand for liberty is made by Laurence Gronlund. Economically "the coming commonwealth" will place
woman "on an equal footing with man." But she will be
"equal," not "alike;" for in the new society the sexes will
no longer be free industrial competitors, but each will have
its special vocation. Physiological differences will not be
ignored. "Woman will become a functionary, she will have
suitable employment given her, and be rewarded according
to results, just the same as men." Like men she will have
suffrage, not as a right or a privilege, but as a trust. "The
new order will necessarily, by the mere working of its economic principles, considerably modify" the marriage relation; and "is that relation such an ideal one now, that it
would be a sacrilege to touch it? Is marriage not now, at
bottom, an establishment for the support of woman? Is not
maintenance the price which the husband pays for the
appendage to himself? And because the supply generally
exceeds the demand—that is, the effective demand—has
woman not often to accept the offer of the first man who
seems able to perform this pecuniary obligation?" If it be
objected that this is taking "rather a commercial view" of
the "holy" relation, is not, "as a matter of fact, marriage
regarded by altogether too many as a commercial institution?
Do not, in fact, the total of young women form a matrimonial
market, regulated by demand and supply?" "Now the Co-
operative Commonwealth will dissipate this horror," enabling

[1] MORRIS AND BAX, *Socialism: Its Growth and Outcome*, 299, 300.

every healthy adult man and woman to find a mate.   Thus, contrary to false charges, socialists are not trying to destroy the family: "they want to enable every man and woman to form a happy family!"·   Modern democracy revolts against the patriarchal constitution of the family, upon whose model all feudal and ancient societies were organized.   In the "very nature of things family-supremacy will be absolutely incompatible with an interdependent, a solidaric, common-wealth; for in such a state the first object of education must be to establish in the minds of the children an indissoluble association between their individual happiness and the good of all."[1]

The manifold social evils which take their rise directly or indirectly in marriage as it is—be the actual causes what they may—have always justly aroused the unsparing criti-cism of socialistic writers.   Thus to Robert Owen—whose pure life was unreservedly and courageously devoted to the social good, as he understood it—marriage was a member of his "trinity of causes of crime and immorality among man-kind."[2]   With almost the fanatical zeal of an apostle of a new religion, he railed at the "single" family.[3]   He pro-claimed the glad tidings of the swift approach of the new moral order.   Then "the imaginative laws of the marriages of the priesthood must be among the first to be abolished, by reason of their extended injurious influence upon human nature, poisoning all the sources of the most valuable quali-ties which Nature has given to infant man.   These marriages have dried up the fountain of truth in human nature; they

[1] GRONLUND, The Co-operative Commonwealth, 193-206.

[2] OWEN, Marriages of the Priesthood of the Old Immoral World, 54: "I resume the subject of marriage because it is the source of more demoralization, crime, and misery, than any other single cause, with the exception of religion and private prop-erty; and these three together form the great trinity of causes of crime and immo-rality among mankind."   For examples of the bitter denunciations which Owen's doctrines naturally provoked see the tract of BRINDLEY, The Marriage System of Socialism (Chester, 1840); and that of BOWES, The 'Social Beasts' (Liverpool, 1840).

[3] For examples see Marriages of the Priesthood, 41, 43, 44, 81.

perpetually insinuate that man can love and hate at his pleasure, and that to be virtuous he must live according to the dictates of the laws and ceremonies devised by the priesthood, that he must hate according to the same dictation, and that if he does not thus love and hate, he is vicious, and he will be eternally punished in another world," while on earth he will suffer from the human laws and by the public opinion which priests have inspired.[1] Under the new moral order all this will be changed. Marriages will be more lasting than now. "Every individual will be trained and educated, to have all his powers cultivated in the most superior manner known; cultivated too under a new combination of external objects, purposely formed, to bring into constant exercise the best and most lovely qualities only of human nature." Wealth for all will be "produced in superfluity." Therefore all will be "equal in their education and condition," and without any distinction except as to age. "There will be then no motive or inducement for any parties to unite, except from pure affection arising from the most unreserved knowledge of each other's character. . . . . There will be no artificial obstacles in the way of permanent happy unions of the sexes; for . . . . the affections will receive every aid which can be devised to induce them to be permanent;" and the wedded pair "will be placed as far as possible in the condition of lovers during their lives." In "some partial instances," however, happiness might not even thus be secured. In such event, "without any severance of friendship between the parties, a separation may be made, the least injurious to them and the most beneficial to the interests of society."[2] In fine, Robert Owen's book, although often vague in expression and violent in tone, contains in its state-

[1] OWEN, *op. cit.*, 81.

[2] *Ibid.*, 86, 87, giving an extract from his six lectures delivered at Manchester in 1837.

ments, and still more in its suggestions, practically the whole
program of later socialistic writings on the subject of marriage and the family, except the argument based on historical
evolution.[1]

Robert Dale Owen followed in his father's footsteps.   He
finds even the Haytian institution of "placement"—an informal union made and dissolved at the pleasure of the contracting persons—far superior in its morality and its stability
to the sacramental marriage which exists by its side.[2]

August Bebel, in his able book on *Woman and Socialism*,
draws a powerful indictment of matrimonial relations under
the existing order.   To this source, in his view, may be
traced the prevalence of sexual crimes and the most dangerous tendencies now threatening the integrity of society.   Infanticide, abortion, and prostitution; the decline in the birth
and marriage rates; the increase in the number of divorces;
the subjection of woman—all these, he says, are due mainly
to the influence of the present "coercive marriage."   This is
so because that "marriage is an institution bound up in the
closest way with the existing social order and with it must
stand or fall."   Coercive marriage is the creature of economic
conditions, the "normal marriage" of the present bourgeois
society; and with that society it is already in process of dis-
ruption.   "Since all these unnatural conditions, being especially harmful to woman, are grounded in the nature of the

---

[1] Owen's book was written in 1835, just before the passage of the new civil-mar-
riage law; and the violence of its tone may in part have been provoked by the injustice and intolerance sanctioned by the Hardwicke act of 1753, at that time in force.
In 1840 he declared, as regards the *form* of marriage, that the law of 1836 had "exactly " met his "ideas and wishes;" and that all which he then desired was " to see
another law enacted, by which *Divorces*, under wise arrangements, and on principles
of common sense, may be obtained equally for rich and poor."—*Op. cit.*, 90.   He himself outlines marriage and divorce laws which possess some excellent features: *ibid.*,
88–90.

[2] ROBERT DALE OWEN, " Marriage and Placement," *Free Inquirer*, May 28, 1831;
and his letter to Thomas Whittemore, editor of the Boston *Trumpet*, May, 1831; both
quoted by BESANT, *Marriage*, 23, 24, 26, 27.   The *Free Inquirer* was founded in New
York city by Robert Dale Owen and Frances Wright in 1829: JOHNSON, *Woman and
the Republic*, 121.

bourgeois society and are growing with its duration, that society is proving itself incapable of remedying the evil and of emancipating woman. Another social order is therefore needful for this purpose." In the new state, economically and socially, woman will be entirely independent. She will no longer be the subject of authority and of exploitation; but, free and equal by man's side she will become "mistress of her own destiny."[1]

Whatever may be thought of the remedy suggested by socialistic writers, whether or not our only hope lies in the co-operative commonwealth, it is certain that they have rendered an important public service. They have earnestly studied and set forth the actual facts. With unsparing hand they have laid bare the flaws in our domestic institutions as they really exist. They have clearly proved that the problems of marriage and the family can be solved only by grasping their relations to the economic system. They have shown that progress lies along the line of the complete emancipation of woman and the absolute equality of the sexes in marriage. In accomplishing all this they have in effect done much to arouse in the popular mind a loftier ideal of wedded life.

The liberation of woman in every one of its aspects profoundly involves the destiny of the family. It signifies in all the larger activities of life the relative individualization of one-half of human kind. This means, of course, a weakening of the solidarity of the family group, so far as its cohesion is dependent on the remnants of mediæval marital authority. Will the ultimate dissolution of the family thus become the price of equality and freedom? Or rather, is it not almost certain that in the more salubrious air of freedom

---

[1] BEBEL, *Die Frau und der Sozialismus*, 93 ff., 175, 176, 427 ff., 431; or the same in WALTHER's translation, 43 ff., 229 ff. Compare KARL PEARSON's discussion of "Socialism and Sex" in his *Ethic of Free Thought*, 427–46; and CAIRD, *Morality of Marriage*, 123–27.

and equality there is being evolved a higher type of the family, knit together by ties—sexual, moral, and spiritual—far more tenacious than those fostered by the régime of subjection?   How remarkable, in England as well as in America, is the revolution already accomplished!   Few facts in social history are more instructive than the change which has taken place in the tone of the literature dealing with woman and her relations to marriage and the family.   In the eighteenth century and until far down into the nineteenth it is for the most part utterly frivolous or sentimental.   Vapid satire abounds.   Erotic or facetious verse at the expense of the "fair sex" or "wedded love" finds ready popular response.   Even in what is meant for earnest discussion woman is treated as a helpless being, to be petted, cajoled, or corrected, not too harshly, by her superior lord; or else she is edified with endless lectures on the sacred duty of guarding her virtue—a fact which throws a lurid and unintentional light on the moral standards of the age.   Imagine an *Essay on Old Maids*,[1] tediously spun out in three volumes; or a book like Eliza Haywood's *Female Spectator*,[2] which,

---

[1] *A Philosophical, Historical, and Moral Essay on Old Maids, by a Friend of the Sisterhood* (London, 1785). Some of the gleanings from history in the second and third volumes are not entirely devoid of permanent interest.

[2] HAYWOOD, *The Female Spectator* (7th ed., London, 1771). This is a fairly representative compilation of gossip and literary anecdote regarding woman, but without a trace of sociological perception.

For examples of the lighter productions referred to see *An Essay on Marriage, in a cautionary Epistle to a Young Gentleman, wherein the Artifices and Foibles of the Fair*, etc. (London, 1750); *The Deportment of a Married Life: Laid down in a Series of Letters . . . . to a Young Lady . . . . lately Married* (2d ed., London, 1798; 3d ed., 1821); BOONE, *The Marriage Looking-Glass: written as a Manual for the Married and a Beacon to the Single* (London, 1848); GUTHRIE, *Wedded Love* (London, 1859), a volume of sentimental verse. Some of them have a pious or theological tone: *The Advantages and Disadvantages of the Married State . . . . under the Similitude of a Dream* (5th ed., London, 1760); *Conjugal Love and Duty* (4th ed., Dublin and London, 1758); *Reflections on Celibacy and Marriage, in Four Letters to a Friend* (London, 1771); SANDEMAN, *The Honour of Marriage opposed to all Impurities* (London, 1777); BEAN, *The Christian Minister's Affectionate Advice to a New Married Couple* (4th ed., London, 1809). Others contain valuable passages, while vividly reflecting the contemporary view regarding woman's inferior position: "Philogamus," *The Present State of Matrimony* (London, 1739); *The Art of Governing a Wife; with Rules for Batchelors* (London, 1747).

although in four volumes, had already reached its seventh edition in 1771.

Nevertheless, the beginning of an efficient agitation for woman's rights was then made. As early as 1696 appeared Mary Astell's vigorous *Defense of the Female Sex*, further developing views which she had expressed two years earlier.[1] The next year Defoe, advocating an "academy for women," made a strong plea for the equal education of the sexes.[2] A singularly clear and incisive exposure of the *Hardships of the English Laws in relation to Wives* was published in 1735. The writer, apparently a woman, while protesting that her adversaries for want of arguments resort to "points of wit, smart jests, and all-confounding laughter," presents many striking proofs from judicial annals and elsewhere to show that in England the "estate of wives is more disadvantageous than slavery itself;" that they "may be made prisoners for life at the discretion of their domestick governors;" and that they "have no property, neither in their own persons, children, or fortunes."[3] In 1739 an anonymous writer, signing herself "Sophia," produced a forceful *Vindication of the natural Right of the Fair-Sex to a perfect Equality of Power, Dignity, and Esteem with the Men*, in which, appealing to "rectified reason," she urged that difference in sex relates to the "propagation of human nature," whereas in "soul there is no sex," and diversity must therefore come from education and environment.[4] Mary Wollstonecraft's better known and much more elabo-

---

[1] ASTELL, *An Essay in Defense of the Female Sex* (London, 1696; 3d ed., 1697). *Cf.* her *Serious Proposal to the Ladies* (London, 1694; 3d ed., 1697); and her *Reflections upon Marriage* (London, 1700; 4th ed., 1730).

[2] DEFOE, *An Essay upon Projects* (London, 1697).

[3] *The Hardships of the English Laws in relation to Wives* (London, 1735), 4 ff.

[4] "SOPHIA," *Woman not Inferior to Man; or, A short and modest Vindication of the natural Right of the Fair-Sex to a perfect Equality of Power, Dignity, and Esteem with the Men* (London, 1739; 2d ed., 1740). This tract was answered by a "GENTLEMAN," *Man Superior to Woman; or, a Vindication of Man's Natural Right of Sovereign Authority over the Woman* (London, 1739), insisting that woman was not

rate *Vindication of the Rights of Woman*,[1] published in 1792, was therefore not without helpful predecessors. But it is immensely superior to them in its literary power and its intellectual grasp. The fearless, direct, and unaffected way in which the subject is handled, especially the questions of sex and education, discloses the dawn of a new era of discussion. More clearly than ever before the liberation of woman appears as a sociological problem of the greatest moment to mankind. True, much space is devoted to combating objections which may now seem trivial; but to the average mind of Mary Wollstonecraft's day they were by no means trivial, and they had to be cleared away before the full light could come in.

The foundations were thus laid upon which, chiefly during the last half-century,[2] a vast literary superstructure—

created at all, but is "a sort of after-produced being" who must not "presume to call in question the great duty of vassalage" to man, under penalty of the withdrawal of his heart from her power. To this "SOPHIA" rejoined in *Woman's Superior Excellence over Man* (London, 1740).

[1] A new edition of this book, with an introduction by MRS. FAWCETT, appeared in London in 1890. *Cf.* PENNELL, "A Century of Women's Rights," *Fort. Rev.*, XLVIII, 408 ff.; RAUSCHENBUSCH-CLOUGH, *A Study of Mary Wollstonecraft and the Rights of Woman;* OSTROGORSKI, *The Rights of Women*, 40; RICHTER, *Mary Wollstonecraft die Verfechterin der "Rechte der Frau."*

[2] In Germany DOROTHEA CHRISTINE ERXLEBEN, in her *Gründliche Untersuchung der Ursachen, die das weibliche Geschlecht vom Studium abhalten* (Berlin, 1742); *Vernünftige Gedanken vom Studiren des schönen Geschlechts* (Frankfort and Leipzig, 1749); and HIPPEL, *Bürgerliche Verbesserung der Weiber* (Berlin, 1792); followed by his *Nachlass über weibliche Bildung* (Berlin, 1801), were already beginning the agitation for woman's liberation. A remarkably clear and incisive essay in defense of woman, entitled *De l'égalité des deux sexes*, appeared in Paris in 1673. CONDORCET, *Lettres d'un bourgeois de New Haven à un citoyen de Virginie* (1787) compressed into a few sentences the basic arguments for the movement. In the same year appeared MARY WOLLSTONECRAFT'S *Thoughts on the Education of Daughters*, a forerunner of her *Vindication* five years later. During the next fifty years a few earnest champions of woman's freedom came forward. First was MARY ANNE RADCLIFFE, *Female Advocate, or an attempt to recover the Rights of Women from Male Usurpation* (London, 1799); followed by HANNAH MATHER CROCKER, *Observations on the Real Rights of Women* (Boston, 1818); WILLIAM THOMPSON AND MRS. WHEELER, *Appeal . . . . of Women* (London, 1825), a book written in reply to a statement in JAMES MILL'S article on *Government*, and possibly influencing John Stuart Mill's later thoughts on the subject; SARAH M. GRIMKE, *Letters on Equality of the Sexes* (Boston, 1838); LADY SYDNEY MORGAN, *Woman and her Master* (London, 1840); MRS. ELLIS, *Woman's Rights and Duties* (London, 1840). The movement took organic form in

controversial, historical, and scientific — has been erected; a many-sided literature worthily embodying the thought of a great transitional stage in social progress. The opponents of woman's liberation have been forced to choose new weapons. Satire and mockery are no longer in vogue. Both sides are very much in earnest. The tone of present discussion is nothing if not serious. Moreover, while the battle for sexual equality in the family and in the state is very far from being yet fought out, the ultimate victory seems already assured.

It would, indeed, be very strange if some incidental harm should not result from the veritable revolution in the condition of American women which little more than a generation has produced. This is the inevitable penalty which social progress has always to pay. Yet in the present case the transitional loss to the family or to the larger social body is exceedingly slight compared even with the immediate gain. This is especially true of woman's new intellectual life with all its manifold activities. It matters not whether she is showing herself mentally man's equal. If any justification of her new rôle were needed it might suffice to affirm that she has precisely the same right as man to free and unhampered self-development in whatever direction and in whatever manner she herself shall find most conducive to her happiness. But it is amply justified by its social results. It cannot be seriously doubted that woman's admission to equal privilege of higher education is enabling her better to share with man in doing the world's work. Besides, in spite of the vain imaginings of misogynistic

1848, when the first convention was held at Seneca Falls, New York. This was followed in 1850 by conventions in Ohio and Massachusetts. In 1851 MRS. JOHN STUART MILL'S powerful article in the July number of the *Westminster Review* on the "Enfranchisement of Women" supplied the agitation with a definite program. See FAWCETT, *The Woman Question in Europe*, 273, note; STANTON, ANTHONY, AND GAGE, *Hist. of Woman Suffrage*, I, 70 ff.; OSTROGORSKI, *Rights of Women*, 54 ff.; JOHNSON, *Woman and the Republic*, 39 ff.; WADE, *Women, Past and Present*, 247.

philosophers,[1] the problem of special sexual function in its relation to mental capacity is being settled in woman's favor. "Science," declares Lourbet, in completing his valuable survey, "is incapable of demonstrating the 'irremediable' mental inferiority of woman. . . . . The pretended antagonism between mental power and sexual power, which does not withstand rigorous analysis, appears definitively to be destroyed by experience, by the tangible facts which incessantly strike the eye."[2]   Herbert Spencer reaches the conclusion that "were liberties to be adjusted to abilities, the adjustment, even could we make it, would have to be made irrespective of sex."[3]

It is singular what acute anxiety is felt by adherents of the old régime[4] lest woman's new intellectual life should prove disastrous to her physical constitution, unmindful of the fact that even now for the majority of married women the burdens of the orthodox "natural sphere" are far more

[1] According to HARTMANN, *The Sexes Compared*, 3, 6 ff., there is between man and woman a fundamental and irremovable distinction: The woman rules sexually and therefore "we must, by way of compensation, uphold the legal superiority of man." In establishing sexual equality the progress of culture receives a severe blow.   More wonderful is the teaching of SCHOPENHAUER. "Women," he says, "are directly adapted to act as the nurses and educators of our childhood, for the simple reason that they themselves are childish, foolish, and short-sighted—in a word are big children all their lives, something intermediate between the child and the man, who is a man in the strict sense of the word."—*On Women:* in DIRCKS'S *Essays of Schopenhauer*, 65; or his *Sämmtliche Werke*, III, 649 ff.

[2] LOURBET, *La femme devant la science contemporaine*, 157, 161. See especially BEBEL, *Die Frau und der Sozialismus*, 233 ff.

[3] SPENCER, *Justice*, 186. For an elaborate discussion of woman's mental capacity see MILL, *Subjection of Women*, 91–146.

[4] For example, see DR. STRAHAN, "The Struggle of the Sexes: its Effect upon the Race," *Humanitarian*, III (Nov., 1893), 349–57; replying to an article entitled "Sex Bias" in the same journal for July of that year; EDSON, "Women of Today," *North Am. Rev.*, CLVII, 440–51; who is criticised by ICHENHAEUSER, *Die Ausnahmestellung Deutschlands in Sachen des Frauenstudiums*, 8 ff.; an article entitled "'Woman's Rights' Question Considered from a Biological Point of View," *Quart. Jour. of Sci.*, XV, 469–84; which is effectually disposed of by WARD, "Our Better Halves," *Forum*, VI, 266–75. Ward is attacked by ALLEN, "Woman's Place in Nature," *Forum*, VII, 258–63. ROMANES, "Mental Differences of Men and Women," in *Pop. Sci. Monthly*, XXXI, 383–401, takes a conservative or intermediate position. A liberal view is held by BROOKS, "The Condition of Women Zoölogically," *ibid.*, XV, 145 ff., 347 ff.; and by WHITE, "Woman's Place in Nature," *ibid.*, VI, 292–301.

harmful. The tables are decidedly turned by a radical writer who with truth declares that "evidence is rapidly accumulating which makes it almost impossible to deny that the feminine constitution has been disastrously injured during the long ages of patriarchal rule, and that this beloved 'sphere' of woman, where she was thought so safe and happy, has, in fact, been a very seed-bed of disease and misery and wrong;" that "through these ages of overstrain of every kind—physical, emotional, nervous—one set of faculties being in perpetual activity while the others lay dormant, woman has fallen into a state that is more or less ailing and diseased; that upon her shoulders has been laid the penalty of the injustice and selfishness of men."[1] Even if the participation of woman in the mental activities and the public vocations which men have hitherto monopolized should prove harmful to her, has she not a right to discover the fact by experience? "I consider it presumptuous," said John Stuart Mill in the outset of the organized emancipation movement, "in anyone to pretend to decide what women are or are not, can or cannot be by natural constitution. They have always hitherto been kept, as far as regards spontaneous development, in so unnatural a state that their nature cannot but have been greatly distorted and disguised, and no one can safely pronounce that if woman's nature were left to choose its direction as freely as men's, and if no artificial bent were attempted to be given to it except that required by the conditions of human society, and given to both sexes alike, there would be any material difference, or perhaps any difference at all, in the character and capacities which would unfold themselves."[2]

It is vain for "scientific optimism" to seek in "nature" a justification for woman's sexual subjection. "Independ-

---

[1] CAIRD, *Morality of Marriage*, 13, 174, 175.

[2] Quoted by CAIRD, *op. cit.*, 14. For a trenchant discussion of this point compare MILL, *Subjection of Women*, 38-52, 111 ff., *passim*.

ently . . . . of its false facts and false premises, this pretended scientific defense of the undue inequality of the sexes in man is fundamentally unsound in resting upon a thoroughly false assumption, which is only the more pernicious because widely prevalent. It assumes that whatever exists in nature must be the best possible state. . . . . The only practical use to which we put science is to *improve upon nature*, to control all classes of forces, social forces included, to the end of bettering the conditions under which we inhabit the earth. This is true civilization, and all of it."[1]

The fear that the education of woman, in connection with her growing economic independence, will prove harmful to society through her refusal of matrimony or maternity appears equally groundless. According to Dike, "the demand for her enfranchisement, either as a right or on the ground of expediency, grows out of this way of treating her as an individual whose relations to society are less a matter of condition and more of personal choice. And this principle is carried into a sphere entirely her own. A partial loss of capacity for maternity has, it is said, already befallen American women; and the voluntary refusal of its responsibilities is the lament of the physician and the moralist."[2] It is true that the birth-rate is falling.[3] So far as this depends upon male sensuality, a prevalent cause of sterility; upon selfish love of ease and luxury—of which men even more than women are guilty; or upon the disastrous influence of the

---

[1] WARD, *Dynamic Sociology*, I, 662.

[2] DIKE, "Some Aspects of the Divorce Question," *Princeton Rev.*, March, 1884, 180. Compare ALLEN, "The New England Family," *New Englander*, March, 1882, 146 ff.; CREPAZ, *Die Gefahren der Frauen-Emancipation*, 24 ff.

[3] KUCZYNSKI, "Fecundity of the Native and Foreign Born Pop. of Mass.," *Quart. Jour. of Economics*, XVI, 1-36; CRUM, "The Birth-Rate in Mass.," *ibid.*, XI, 248-65; DUMONT, "Essai sur le natalité en Mass.," *Jour. de la soc. stat. de Paris*, XXXVIII (1897), 332-53, 385-95; XXXIX (1898), 64-99; MOLINARI, "Decline of the French Population," *Jour. of the Royal Stat. Soc.*, LIII, 183-97; MAYO-SMITH, *Statistics and Sociology*, 67 ff.; USSHER, *Neo-Malthusianism*, 137-64; EDSON, "Women of Today," *North Am. Rev.*, CLVII, 446 ff.

present extremes of wealth and poverty—of which women as well as men are the victims—it is a serious evil which may well cause us anxiety; but so far as it is the result of the desire for fewer but better-born children—for which, let us hope, the advancing culture of woman may in part be responsible—it is in fact a positive social good.[1] It is true also that, while fewer and fewer marriages in proportion to the population are taking place, men as well as women are marrying later and later in life.[2] Here again, for the reasons just mentioned, the results are both good and bad. Certain it is that early marriages and excessive child-bearing have been the twin causes of much injury to the human race. "To the superficial observer," declares a writer very conservative as to the effects of woman's emancipation, "it may appear that every marriage must enrich the state, and that early marriages must lessen the amount of sexual immorality, but inquiry will prove conclusively how fallacious are those views. Early marriages certainly tend to the production of large families, but then a family, to be a source of wealth to the state, must at least be self-supporting, which is exactly what the feeble, degenerate children of the great mass of our early marriages are not. They are brought forth ill-developed and unhealthy; their immature, improvident parents are unable to either feed or educate them as they ought to be fed and educated; hence, instead of being a source of wealth to the state, they prove a serious drain upon her resources. A large percentage of these miserable children succumb during infancy, but a great number drag out a pitiful existence,

---

[1] Sometime, it is to be hoped, society may seriously take in hand the problem of restraining the propagation of criminals, dependents, and the other unfit: see WARNER, *American Charities*, 132, 133.

[2] WILLCOX, "A Study of Vital Statistics," in *Pol. Sci. Quart.*, VIII, 76, 77; OGLE, "On Marriage-Rates and Marriage-Ages," *Jour. of the Royal Stat. Soc.*, LIII, 272 ff.; KUCZYNSKI, "Fecundity of the Native and Foreign Born Pop. in Mass.," *Quart. Jour. of Economics*, XVI, 1-36; MAYO-SMITH, *Statistics and Sociology*, 103 ff., 124; CRUM, "The Marriage Rate in Mass.," *Pub. of Am. Stat. Assoc.*, IV, 331 ff.; WALLACE, "Human Selection," *Fort. Rev.*, XLVIII, 335 ff.

only to become inmates of our workhouses and infirmaries, our asylums and prisons, and, after being supported at the public expense for a longer or shorter period, to die prematurely, leaving the state poorer than they found it and no better. It is indeed a small percentage of the children of the immature that ever become robust useful, self-supporting citizens."[1]

It is not marriage or maternity which educated women are shunning; but they are declining to view marriage as their sole vocation or to become merely child-bearing animals. Let us not worry about the destiny of college women.[2] It is simply wrong wedlock which they are avoiding. They have, suggests Muirhead, a careful regard for the "kind" of marriage. They are determined to have only "the genuine article." They "look in marriage not only for the old fashioned 'union of hearts,' but for the union of heart and head in some serious interest which will survive the mere attractions of sex and form a solid bond of union even in the absence of others which, like the birth of children, depend on fortune." So "far from being hostile" to the family, "they are only preparing the way for a purer and more beneficent form of family life." The "maternal instinct is happily not confined to the uneducated."[3] The rise of a

---

[1] Strahan, *Marriage and Disease*, 245 ff., giving statistics. *Cf.* Edson, "The Evils of Early Marriages," *North Am. Rev.*, CLVIII, 230–34; Ussher, *Neo-Malthusianism*, 213 ff.; Wallace, "Human Selection," *Fort. Rev.*, XLVIII, 333 ff.; Legouvé, *Hist. morale des femmes*, 74–84.

[2] See especially the excellent paper of Mary Roberts Smith, "Statistics of College and Non-College Women," *Pub. of the Am. Stat. Assoc.*, VII, 1–26, whose conclusions support the view taken in the text; and Sidgwick, *Health Statistics of Women Students of Cambridge and Oxford and Their Sisters* (Cambridge, 1890), who reaches similar general results. *Cf.* Thwing, "What Becomes of College Women?" *North Am. Rev.*, CLXI, 546–53, taking a very favorable view of the influence of higher education on woman in her domestic relations; and Shinn, "The Marriage Rate of College Women," *Century*, L, 946–48. Consult also the articles of F. M. Abbott, C. S. Angstman, G. E. Gardner, and F. Franklin mentioned in the Bibliographical Index, IV; and read Clara E. Collet's "Prospects of Marriage for Women," *Nineteenth Century*, XXXI, 537–52.

[3] Muirhead, "Is the Family Declining?" *Int. Jour. of Ethics*, Oct., 1896, 47–50.

more refined sentiment of love has become at once a check and an incentive to marriage.[1]

Long ago Mrs. John Stuart Mill explained how essential are knowledge and equality to render woman the real companion of man in the struggle for existence; how the subjection and ignorance of the wife degrade not only her own character, but that of the husband as well. "There is hardly any situation more unfavorable to the maintenance of elevation of character, or force of intellect, than to live in the society, and seek by preference the sympathy, of inferiors in mental endowments."[2]

If woman's even partnership with man in the nurture of the family and in facing the exigencies of external life depends mainly on equal education, never was such education more urgently required than at the present hour. Social and industrial problems are constantly demanding higher and higher mental training for their solution. The same is true of the problem of the family. It is very largely a question of reform and development in home education. Clearly, then, husband and wife have great need of intelligent sympathy and counsel in the discharge of their joint, yet partially differentiated, tasks. Hence, it should be the high

---

[1] There are many reasons why all persons do not marry. Among these is a loftier ideal of love. "Persons often live single a whole life-time because they are unable to obtain the only one in the world for whom they can ever experience a throb of pure passion. . . . . We see then that this more diffused and elevated form of love becomes at once the greatest incentive and the greatest barrier to marriage. It differs wholly from the localized passion in being *selective*. While it is less selfish, it must be called out by, and exclusively directed toward, one definite object. From this circumstance it may be called the *objective* form of love."—WARD, *Dynamic Sociology*, I, 626.

[2] MRS. MILL, "Enfranchisement of Women," *Westminster Review*, July 1851; or *Dissertations and Discussions*, III, 117, 118. " While far from being expedient, we are firmly convinced, that the division of mankind into castes, one born to rule over the other, is in this case, as in all cases, an unqualified mischief; a source of perversion and demoralization, both to the favored class and to those at whose expense they are favored; producing none of the good which it is the custom to ascribe to it, and forming a bar, almost insuperable while it lasts, to any really vital improvement, either in the character or in the social condition of the human race."—*Ibid.*, 101. *Cf.* MR. MILL's masterly discussion of the relative effects of equality and inequality in marriage, in *Subjection of Women*, 53-90, 146 ff.

function of public education to promote this healthy companionship in social duty. Furthermore, American experience appears to show that it can best do so by training young men and women together. Indeed, in this regard the sociological value of coeducation is very important. Theoretically it seems reasonable to assume that those who are to work together in later life may gain some advantage by spending the years of study side by side. The practical result of coeducation in the western states, where it has been given the freest opportunity, appears to demonstrate that such is actually the case. The majority of those who have had extended experience, after making all due allowance for special difficulties to be surmounted, are emphatic in their opinion that mentally and morally both sexes are the gainers by it, as compared with training in separate institutions.[1] It is true that eventually marriages very often result from such associations. That is precisely the gist of the matter. Are not the conditions entirely favorable to the fostering of happy unions? Under what better auspices can attachments be formed than when young men and women are learning to gauge each other's character through the varied social and intellectual rivalries of the years of scholastic life?

Educational equality, however, is but one aspect of the movement for woman's liberation. There are other factors of the ideal partnership of the sexes in the uplifting of society. Intellectual emancipation is proceeding, and necessarily must proceed, hand in hand with political and economic emancipation. The three movements are in large

[1] "Yet coeducation wisely managed is almost indispensable to the training of noble men and women; for education in its broadest sense takes account of all the influences that go to form character. It is not wholly intellectual, but is moral and social, and can best be carried forward, under a proper régime, where young men and women are educated and trained together."—LIVERMORE, *What Shall We Do with Our Daughters?* 44 ff. Cf. KUHNOW, *Frauenbildung und Frauenberuf,* 7 ff.; and especially WOLLSTONECRAFT, *Vindication of the Rights of Woman,* 361 ff., 381-413.

measure blended and interdependent. The participation of woman in the new vocations—industrial, artistic, professional, or administrative—implies a great advance in mental training. It means a distinct unfoldment of faculties and character. "No sociological change equal in importance to this clearly marked improvement of an entire sex has ever taken place in one century."[1] It is a revolution in which one-half of the human race is becoming an equal factor with the other in intellectual and economic production. At last woman is gaining a share in the social consciousness; she is entering into the social organization as a new and regenerative force. Doubtless, in the process of readjusting new functions and conditions to the old some temporary harm may ensue. Yet happily the alarm is subsiding lest by her entrance on the new vocations woman should permanently wreck her physical constitution, refuse to marry, or cause industrial disaster through over-competition.[2] With far

---

[1] STETSON, *Women and Economics*, 151. On the woman labor question see the very enlightening discussion of OLIVE SCHREINER, "The Woman's Movement of Our Day," *Harper's Bazar*, XXXVI (1902), 3-8, 103-7, 222-27; and her "Woman Question," *Cosmopolitan*, XXVIII (1899-1900), 45-54, 182-92, emphasizing the danger of woman's "sex-parasitism," through her economic dependence. Compare GÜNTHER, *Das Recht der Frau auf Arbeit*, 6 ff.

[2] The hardships which women as well as men endure under the present industrial conditions have little connection with their economic emancipation. "What some call a woman's movement for industrial liberty is not quite what it is claimed to be. It is largely an incident in the movement of property, which is seeking its own ends, caring very little for either sex or age. In order to find an easier place under the common industrial yoke that rests upon the neck of every individual, women seek more and more employments. But it is not so much womanhood as it is property that is the real impelling cause."—DIKE, "Problems of the Family," *Century*, XXXIX, 392. *Cf.* LEGOUVÉ, *Hist. morale des femmes*, 366-90; GRAFFENRIED, "The Condition of Wage-Earning Women," *Forum*, XV, 68 ff.; EDSON, "American Life and Physical Deterioration," *North Am. Rev.*, CLVII, 440 ff., referring to the alleged evil effects of woman's new activities; DILKE, "Industrial Position of Women," *Fort. Rev.*, LIV, 499 ff., discussing the condition of factory workers; PHILLIPPS, "The Working Lady in London," *ibid.*, LII, 193 ff.; BREMNER, "The Financial Dependence of Women," *North Am. Rev.*, CLVIII, 382 ff., protesting against regarding the economic "dependence of the wife as degradation;" and COLLET, "Official Statistics on the Employment of Women," *Jour. of the Stat. Soc.*, LXI, 216-60. MRS. MILL, "Enfranchisement of Women," *Dissertation*, III, 109 ff., effectually disposes of the objection based on the alleged effects of woman's industrial competition with men. *Cf.* the elaborate discussion of BEBEL, *Die Frau und der Sozialismus*, 202 ff.

greater justice a century ago it was complained that the
"intrusion of men-traders" into woman's work was driving
her to destitution and thus fostering the "social evil."[1] The
callings into which women are charged with "intruding"
were, many of them, women's callings before they were men's.

It is within the family itself that the growing economic
independence of woman is producing the highest sociological
results.   Under the old domestic régime on both sides of
the sea the woman who married entered legally, potentially,
upon a life of financial bondage.   In the theory of the common law the wife, with her children, her goods, and the
fruits of her toil, was the sole property of the husband.
Only in 1886 did the mother in England gain legal capacity
for the partial custody of her offspring;[2] and in but few of
the American states has she been placed on equal footing with the father in this regard.[3]   Even now the "husband
in England can claim damage from the man who has ruined
his family life, but the woman can claim none from the rival
who has supplanted her."[4]   In both England and the United
States notable progress has already been made in equalizing
the property rights of the sexes; but the process is yet far
from complete.   The prevailing conception of marriage as a
status in which the wife is "supported" by the husband is
degrading in its influence on the woman's character.   It
tends to deaden her moral perceptions and to paralyze her
mental powers.   Girls are trained, or they are forced by

[1] MARY ANNE RADCLIFFE, *The Female Advocate* (London, 1799).   A petition of
women to Louis XVI. in 1789 prays "that men may not ply the trades belonging to
women, whether dressmaking, embroidery, or haberdashery.   Let them leave us, at
least the needle and the spindle, and we will engage not to wield the compass or the
square."— OSTROGORSKI, *The Rights of Women*, 26, 27; following LEFAURE, *Le socia-
lisme pendant la révolution*, 122.

[2] By the Custody of Infants Act, 1886: see the discussion of CAIRD, *Morality of
Marriage*, 49, 55 ff.

[3] BISHOP, *Marriage, Div., and Sep.*, II, 452 ff.

[4] PEARSON, "The Decline of the Family," in his *National Life and Character*,
240, 234, 235.   In many of the American states the wife may bring action against the
seducer of her husband: BISHOP, *Mar., Div., and Sep.*, I, 568.

poverty, to look upon wedlock as an economic vocation, as a means of getting a living.   The result is that under the old order marriage tends to become a species of purchase-contract in which the woman barters her sex-capital to the man in exchange for a life-support.   The man—not the woman as originally—has become the chooser in sex-selection.   In the family, therefore, the sex-motive has become excessively pronounced, thrusting into the background higher social and spiritual ideals.[1]   The liberation movement thus means in a high degree the socialization of one-half of the human race.   Woman declines longer to be restricted to the

[1] This fact is seized upon in one of the most powerful books produced in recent sociological discussion.   According to Mrs. Stetson "we are the only animal species in which the female depends on the male for food, the only animal species in which the sex-relation is also an economic relation.   With us an entire sex lives in a relation of economic dependence upon the other sex."   The wife may toil unceasingly; but the labor which she "performs in the household is given as a part of her functional duty, not as employment."   She is therefore not her husband's "business partner;" for as an intended equivalent for what she gets she contributes neither labor nor capital nor experience nor even motherhood.   She contributes her sex-attractions.   Sex-distinctions are therefore excessively developed; and the "sexuo-economic relation" becomes inevitable.   "By the economic dependence of the human female upon the male, the balance of forces is altered.   Natural selection no longer checks the action of sexual selection, but coöperates with it;" for "man, in supporting woman, has become her economic environment."   Under "sexual selection the human creature is of course modified to its mate," as with all creatures.   When the mate becomes also the master, when economic necessity is added to sex-attraction, we have the two great evolutionary forces acting together to the same end; namely, to develop sex-distinction in the human female.   For, in her position of economic dependence in the sexual relation, sex-distinction is with her not only a means of attracting a mate, as with all creatures, but a means of getting a livelihood, as is the case with no other creature under heaven.   Because of the economic dependence of the human female on her mate she is modified to sex to an excessive degree.   This excessive modification she transmits to her children; and so is steadily implanted in the human constitution the morbid tendency to excess in this relation, which has acted so universally upon us in all ages, in spite of our best efforts to restrain it."   While in man the immediate dominating force of sexual passion may be more conspicuous, in woman it holds more universal sway.   "For the man has other powers and faculties in full use, whereby to break loose from the force of this; and the woman, specially modified to sex and denied racial activity, pours her whole life into love."   Useful to the race as was this evolution originally, its influence for good has long since reached its limit.   Excessive sex-energy has threatened to "destroy both individual and race."   Hence woman is declining longer to be confined to her highly specialized sexual function and is demanding an equal place in the social organization.   She is gaining a social consciousness: STETSON, *Women and Economics*, 5, 12 ff., 37 ff., 48, 122-45.   *Cf.* SCHREINER, "The Woman Question," *Cosmopolitan*, XXVIII, 183 ff., on "sex-parasitism."

dwarfing environment of sexual seclusion; and demands the means and the privilege of engaging in the larger activities of self-conscious society.[1]

We are thus confronted by still another phase of the emancipation movement—the divorce problem. In this problem woman has a peculiar interest. The wife more frequently than the husband is seeking in divorce a release from marital ills; for in her case it often involves an escape from sexual slavery. The divorce movement, therefore, is in part an expression of woman's growing independence. In this instance as in others it does not, of course, follow that the individualistic tendency is vicious. Nowhere in the field of social ethics, perhaps, is there more confusion of thought than in dealing with the divorce question. Divorce is not favored by anyone for its own sake. Probably in every healthy society the ideal of right marriage is a life-long union. But what if it is not right, if the marriage is a failure? Is there no relief? Here a sharp difference of opinion has arisen. Some persons look upon divorce as an evil in itself; others as a "remedy" for, or a "symptom" of, social disease. The one class regard it as a cause; the other as an effect. To the Roman Catholic, and to those who believe with him, divorce is a sin, the sanction of "successive polygamy,"[2] of "polygamy on the instalment plan."[3]

---

[1] Cf. STETSON, op. cit., 156 ff. "The woman's club movement is one of the most important sociological phenomena of the century—indeed, of all centuries—marking as it does the first timid steps toward social organization of these so long unsocialized members of our race;" for "social life is absolutely conditioned upon organization."—Ibid., 164. On woman's clubs see CROLY, Hist. of the Woman's Club Movement in America; HENROTIN, Attitude of Women's Clubs Toward Social Economics; LIVERMORE, North Am. Rev., CL, 115; ANSTRUTHER, Nineteenth Century, XLV, 598-611; and a symposium in Arena, VI, 362-88. The financial dependence of the wife is discussed by COOKE, "Real Rights of Women," North Am. Rev., CXLIX, 353, 354; and by IVES, "Domestic Purse Strings," Forum, X, 106-14, showing the hardships and temptations of wives dependent upon the husband for current supplies of money.

[2] According to CARDINAL GIBBONS there are "two species of polygamy—simultaneous and successive ": " Is Divorce Wrong?" in North Am. Rev., CXLIX, 520.

[3] The epigram of Father Yorke, of San Francisco.

At the other extreme are those who, like Milton and Humboldt,[1] would allow marriage to be dissolved freely by mutual consent, or even at the desire of either spouse. Nay, there are earnest souls, shocked by the intolerable hardships which wives may suffer under the marital yoke, who, pending a reform in the marriage law, would, like the Quakers of earlier days, ignore the present statutory requirements and resort to private contract.[2] According to the prevailing opinion, however, as expressed in modern legislation, divorce should be allowed, with more or less freedom, under careful state regulation. Whatever degree of liberty may be just or expedient in a more advanced state of moral development, it is felt that now a reasonable conservatism is the safer course. Yet divorce is sanctioned by the state as an individual right; and there may be occasions when the exercise of the right becomes a social duty. The right is, of course, capable of serious abuse. Loose divorce laws may even invite crime. Nevertheless, it is fallacious to represent the institution of divorce as in itself a menace to social morality. It is not helpful to allege, as is often done, that with the increase of divorce certain crimes wax more frequent, thus

[1] WILHELM V. HUMBOLDT, *Sphere and Duties of Government*: cited by MILL, *On Liberty*, 185, 186.

[2] For examples see SEWELL, in *Westminster Review*, CXLV, 182 ff., suggesting a form of private contract; and BESANT, *Marriage*, 19, 20, who asks: "Why should not we take a leaf out of the Quakers' book, and substitute for the present legal forms of marriage a simple declaration publicly made? . . . . but as soon as the laws are moralized, and wives are regarded as self-possessing human beings, instead of as property, then the declaration may, with advantage, seek the sanction of the law." She mentions the well-known cases of Mary Wollstonecraft, her daughter and Shelley, Richard Carlile, and that of George Henry Lewes and George Eliot. Mrs. Caird would not go so far. The state, she concludes, has no right to interfere in the marriage contract. "How can it withdraw its interference without causing social confusion? The answer seems plain. By a gradual widening of the limitations within which individuals might be allowed to draw up their private contracts, until, finally, moral standards had risen sufficiently high to enable the state to cease from interfering in private concerns altogether."—*The Morality of Marriage*, 126. DONISTHORPE, "The Future of Marriage," *Fort. Rev.*, LI, 263, recommends a system of free private contract for one year, renewable at the pleasure of the parties. He is criticised by MALMSBURY, *ibid.*, 272-82. *Cf.* also "Marriage and Free Thought," *ibid.*, L, 275 ff.

insinuating the effect for the cause.   It is just as illogical
to assume that the prevalence of divorce in the United
States is a proof of moral decadence as compared with other
countries in which divorce is prohibited or more restricted.
To forbid the use of a remedy does not prove that there is
no disease.   Is there any good reason for believing that
what Tocqueville said fifty years ago is not true today?
"Assuredly," he declares, "America is the country in the
world where the marriage tie is most respected and where
the highest and justest idea of conjugal happiness has been
conceived."[1]   It is remarkable, says Lecky, "that this great
facility of divorce should exist in a country which has long
been conspicuous for its high standard of sexual morality
and for its deep sense of the sanctity of marriage."[2]   Bryce
passes a similar judgment: "So far as my own information
goes, the practical level of sexual morality is at least as high
in the United States as in any part of northern or western
Europe (except possibly among the Roman Catholic peas-
antry of Ireland)."   There "seems no ground for conclud-
ing that the increase of divorce in America necessarily
points to a decline in the standard of domestic morality,
except perhaps in a small section of the wealthy class,
though it must be admitted that if this increase should
continue, it may tend to induce such a decline."[3]   Even
more emphatic is Commissioner Wright.   After eloquently
describing the relatively high place which woman has
reached in our land, he continues: "I do not believe that
divorce is a menace to the purity and sacredness of the
family; but I do believe that it is a menace to the infernal
brutality, of whatever name, and be it crude or refined, which
at times makes a hell of the holiest human relations.   I

---

[1] Tocqueville, *La démocratie en Amérique*, II, 215.

[2] Lecky, *Dem. and Liberty*, II, 208.

[3] Bryce, *Studies in Hist. and Jur.*, 850.

believe the divorce movement finds its impetus outside of laws, outside of our institutions, outside of our theology; that it finds its impetus in the rebellion of the human heart against that slavery which binds in the cruelest bonds of the cruelest prostitution human beings who have, by their foolishness, by their want of wisdom, or by the intervention of friends, missed the divine purpose, as well as the civil purpose of marriage.   I believe the result will be an enhanced purity, a sublimer sacredness, a more beautiful embodiment of Lamartine's trinity,—the trinity of the father, the mother, and the child"—to preserve which "in all its sacredness, society must take the bitter medicine labelled 'Divorce.'"[1]

This brings us to the root of the matter: the need of a loftier popular ideal of the marriage relation.   "An ounce of prevention is worth a pound of cure."   While bad legislation and a low standard of social ethics continue to throw recklessly wide the door which opens to wedlock, there must of necessity be a broad way out.   How ignorantly, with what utter levity,[2] are marriages often contracted; how many thousands of parents fail to give their children any serious warning against yielding to transient impulse in choosing a mate;

[1] WRIGHT, in *Arena*, V, 141, 143. See also his *Practical Sociology*, 170 ff.; and compare the article of SAVAGE, "Matrimony and the State," *Forum*, X, 117 ff.; that of JANES, "Divorce Sociologically Considered," *New Englander*, May, 1891, 395–402; and that of ADLER, "The Ethics of Divorce," in *Ethical Record*, II, 200–209; III, 1–7.

[2] The following newspaper paragraph relating to a notorious wedding resort in Michigan illustrates the schocking frivolity with which the most important of human relations is sometimes treated: "It is estimated that fully 20,000 people will visit this city tomorrow to attend the third annual Maccabees' county picnic. . . . . It is thought tomorrow will prove to be the greatest day in the history of St. Joseph as the Gretna Green of Chicago. . . . . Fully forty-four bridal couples will arrive from Chicago to take advantage of being married free, as is offered by the Maccabees in a part of their program. The parties with matrimonial intentions, upon calling at Marriage Temple, will be furnished by County Clerk Needham with their license and a handsome marriage certificate, free of charge, provided they consent to be married in public from the verandah of the hotels. Any clergyman in the city, upon request . . . . , will officiate. Hundreds of excursionists from Indiana will come for the express purpose of witnessing the ceremonies." On this point read the interesting article of DENDY, "Marriage in East London," *Cont. Rev.*, LXV, 427–32.

how few have received any real training with respect to the duties and responsibilities of conjugal life! What proper check is society placing upon the marriage of the unfit? Is there any boy or girl so immature if only the legal age of consent has been reached; is there any "delinquent" so dangerous through inherited tendencies to disease or crime; is there any worn out debauchee, who cannot somewhere find a magistrate or a priest to tie the "sacred" knot? It is a very low moral sentiment which tolerates modern wife-purchase or husband-purchase for bread, title, or social position. "As our laws stare us in the face," exclaims an eloquent writer, "there is no man so drunken, so immoral, so brutal, so cruel, that he may not take to himself the purest, the most refined, the most sensitive of women to wife, if he can get her. There is no woman so paltry, so petty, so vain, so inane, so enfeebled in body and mind by corsets or chloral, flirtation, or worse, that she may not become the wife of an intellectual, honorable man, and the mother of his doomed children. There is no pauper who may not wed a pauper and beget paupers to the end of his story. There is no felon returned from his prison, or loose upon society un-condemned, who may not make a base play at wedlock, and perpetuate his diseased soul and body in those of his de-scendants, without restraint. There is no member of what we call our 'respectable' classes who may not, if he choose, make a mock of the awful name of marriage, in sacrilege to which we are so used that we scarcely lift an eyelid to suppress surprise or aversion at the sickening variety of the offence."[1]

It is vain to conceal from ourselves the fact that here is a real menace to society. Marriages thus formed are almost sure to be miserable failures from the start. It is the

[1] Elizabeth Stuart Phelps, "Women's Views of Divorce," *North Am. Rev.*, CL, 130, 131.

simple truth, as earnest writers have insisted, that often under such conditions the nuptial ceremony is but a legal sanction of "prostitution within the marriage bond," whose fruit is wrecked motherhood and the feeble, base-born children of unbridled lust.   The command to "be fruitful and multiply," under the selfish and thoughtless interpretation which has been given it, has become a heavy curse to womanhood and a peril to the human race.[1]   On the face of it, is it not grotesque to call such unions holy or to demand that they shall be indissoluble?   What chance is there under such circumstances for a happy family life or for worthy home-building?   In sanctioning divorce the welfare of the children may well cause the state anxiety; but are there not thousands of so-called "homes" from whose corrupting and blighting shadow the sooner a child escapes the better for both it and society?

How shall the needed reform be accomplished?   The raising of ideals is a slow process.   It will not come through the statute-maker, though he can do something to provide a legal environment favorable for the change.   It must come through an earnest and persistent educational effort which

[1] *Cf.* Flower, "Prostitution Within the Marriage Bond," *Arena*, XIII, 59–73; *idem*, "Wellsprings of Immorality," *ibid.*, XI, 56–70; Heinzen, *The Rights of Women and the Sexual Relations*, 44 ff.; Stetson, *Women and Economics*, 63 ff.; Caird, *Morality of Marriage*, 73–91, 134 ff., discussing the influence of the Reformation upon sensuality; Karl Pearson, "Socialism and Sex," in his *Ethic of Free Thought*, 427–46, on the alleged evil influence of Luther on the sex-relations; Bebel, *Die Frau und der Sozialismus*, 93 ff., taking the opposite view as to Luther, and considering the causes of the decline in the birth and marriage rates.

The traditional opinion is represented by Naumann, *Christenthum und Familie*, 21, 22, who believes in getting children at all hazards, relying on God to take care of them: "Es gibt auch Christen," he says, "welche sich vor Entfaltung des vollen Gottessegens in den Ehen fürchten, ganz als ob es nicht wahr wäre: was unser Gott erschaffen hat, das will er auch erhalten. In unsern Augen ist es Glaubensschwäche, wenn ein christliches Volk sich vor dem Gottessegen reicher, blühender Kinderschaaren fürchtet." On the same side see Hartmann, *The Sexes Compared*, 28 ff.; Pomeroy, *The Ethics of Marriage*, 45 ff., 94 ff. For an antidote read the able discussion of the diminishing need of child-bearing under modern conditions, by Olive Schreiner, "The Woman Question," *Cosmopolitan*, XXVIII, 51 ff.; and Lady Somerset, "The Welcome Child," *Arena*, XII, 42–49; criticised by Ussher, *Neo-Malthusianism*, 101 ff., 201. *Cf.* Wright, *Practical Sociology*, 68 ff.; Bertheau, *Lois de la population*, 299 ff., 342 ff.

shall fundamentally grapple with the whole group of problems which concern the related, though distinct, institutions of marriage, the home, and the family. In this work every grade in the educational structure, from the university to the kindergarten and the home circle, must have its appropriate share. Already a few of our higher institutions have made a worthy beginning. Departments of physical culture, economics, history, and sociology are providing instruction of real value. But the movement should become universal; and the curriculum should be broadened and deepened. The actual concrete problems must be dealt with frankly and without flinching. To gain the right perspective it is highly important that a thorough historical basis should be laid through the study of ethnology, comparative religion, and the evolution of cultural, economic, and matrimonial institutions. Moreover, the elements of such a training in domestic sociology should find a place in the public school program. If need be, a little more arithmetic or a little more Latin may be sacrificed. Where now, except perhaps in an indirect or perfunctory way, does the school boy or girl get any practical suggestion as to home-building, the right social relations of parent and child, much less regarding marriage and the fundamental questions of the sexual life? In this field the home, as the complement or coadjutor of the school and the state, has a precious opportunity. Indeed, our inspiring hope lies in the fact that, in spite of unfavorable conditions, many homes, presided over by enlightened parents, are discharging worthily, if not yet ideally, the high function of social training. Here father, mother, and child are equal members of the "trinity." Here it is held as binding an obligation and as joyous a privilege for the parents to honor their children as for the children to honor their parents. Of a truth, is there anything on earth more beautiful and inspiring than the real companionship of parent and child; than a home life in which the characters of the young are molded and their faculties drawn out by free and frank discussion with their elders; where mutual love is based on mutual respect?   But what shall be said of the opposite picture—of the countless families in which mother and child still cower before the paternal despot; where authority and not reason prevails; where, as in the good old colonial days, the child is harshly thrust into the background and his insistent individualism is insulted and repressed?   Before the home can become a healthful school for social education, parents must themselves be trained; they must become aware of their real place in the social order.

In the future educational program sex questions must hold an honorable place.   Progress in this direction may be slow, because of the false shame, the prurient delicacy, now widely prevalent touching everything connected with the sexual life.   Nor is it a light matter to brave orthodox sentiment in this regard.   It is not always safe for the teacher, even in institutions deeming themselves modern, to deal frankly with the organic facts which are of vital concern to the human race.   The folly of parents in leaving their children in ignorance of the laws of sex is notorious.   Yet how much safer than ignorance is knowledge as a shield for innocence.   The daughter will face the vicissitudes of life more securely if she has been told of the destiny that awaits her as wife and mother; if she has been warned of the snares with which lust has beset the path of womanhood.   The son is likely to live a nobler life if he has learned to repudiate the dual standard of sexual morality which a spurious philosophy has set up; if he understands that "instincts" may be safely controlled; if he has been warned that selfish excesses within or without the marriage bond must be dearly paid for by the coming generations.   Indeed, it is of the greatest moment to society that the young should be trained in the general laws of heredity. Everywhere men and women are marrying in utter contempt of the warnings of science. Domestic animals are literally better bred than human beings. Through ignorance and defiance of the rules of health, we are destroying our physical constitutions. Under the plea of "romantic love" we blindly yield to sexual attractions in choosing our mates, selfishly ignoring the welfare of the race. Is there not a higher ideal of conjugal choice? Experience shows that in wedlock natural and sexual selection should play a smaller and artificial selection a larger rôle.[1] The safety of the social body requires that a check be put upon the propagation of the unfit. Here the state has a function to perform. In the future much more than now, let us hope, the marriage of persons mentally delinquent or tainted by hereditary disease or crime will be legally restrained. Yet law can do relatively little. A reform of this kind must of necessity depend mainly upon a better educated popular sentiment; upon a higher altruism which shall be capable of present sacrifice for the permanent good of the race. "When human beings and families rationally subordinate their own interests as perfectly to the welfare of future generations as do animals under the control of instinct the world will have a more enduring type of family life than exists at present. This can only be accomplished by the development of controlling ideals which are supported not only by reason and intelligence but by ethical impulse and religious motive. This larger altruism which protects the permanent interests of the future against the more

[1] For a radical discussion of this topic, see STANLEY, "Artificial Selection and the Marriage Problem," *Monist*, II, 51 ff.; *idem*, "Our Civilization and the Marriage Problem," *Arena*, II, 94-100. He is criticised by WALLACE, "Human Selection," *Fort. Rev.*, XLVIII, 325 ff. An extreme position is taken by GRANT ALLEN, "The Girl of the Future," *Universal Rev.*, May, 1890; and "Plain Words on the Woman Question," *Fort. Rev.*, Oct., 1889. *Cf.* WERTHEIMER, "Homiculture," *Nineteenth Century*, XXIV, 390-92.

temporary values of the present must be of the heart as much as of the head. . . . . In the mating of men and women, money, social position, worldly expediency, the conventional and fictitious values so influential in these days, will count for much less, while organic health and efficiency, character, unselfish devotion to high ideals, to the great world interests will count for far more. In this obedience to ideals so farsighted, romantic love will not be lost in any way, as some seem to fear. Men and women will not choose one another in cold blood simply because intelligence and reason point the way, but human sentiment and every romantic quality will be enhanced when permanent and future interests are furthered by a saner and finer human choice."[1]

There is then no need to despair of the future. It is vain to turn back the hand on the dial. The problem of individual liberty has become the problem of social liberty. Individualization for the sake of socialization must continue its beneficent work. There must be growth, constant readjustment. Marriage will in truth be holy if it rests on the free trothplight of equals whose love is deep enough to embrace a rational regard for the rights of posterity. The home will not have less sanctity when through it flows the stream of the larger human life. The family will, indeed, survive; but it will be a family of a higher type. Its evolution is not yet complete. Coercive ties will still further yield to voluntary spiritual ties; for individual liberty appears to be the essential condition of social progress.

[1] See Dr. Thomas D. Wood's able paper, *Some Controlling Ideals of the Family Life of the Future*, 27.

BIBLIOGRAPHICAL INDEX

BIBLIOGRAPHICAL INDEX

APPARENTLY no successful attempt has ever been made to prepare a complete and systematic bibliography of matrimonial institutions. Indeed, to do so would be a formidable undertaking; but that such a book would be of vast service to social history no one can doubt. Useful lists of authorities, however, are appended to the works of various writers, notably to Lubbock's *Origin of Civilization;* Starcke's *Primitive Family;* Chamberlain's *Child and Childhood;* Lehr's *Le mariage;* and especially Westermarck's *Human Marriage.* For marriage with kindred, including the deceased wife's sister, there is a good, though not exhaustive, bibliography by A. H. Huth in the *Report of the First Annual Meeting of the Index Society* (London, 1879), 25–47; greatly enlarged in his *Marriage of Near Kin* (2d ed., London, 1887), 394–465. Ethbin Heinrich Costa's *Bibliographie der deutschen Rechtsgeschichte* (Braunschweig, 1858) is helpful, particularly for the earlier monographic literature. For supplementary materials, especially the curiosities of the subject, consult Hugo Hayn's *Bibliotheca Germanorum erotica: Verzeichniss der gesammten deutschen erotischen Literatur mit Einschluss der Uebersetzungen, nebst Angabe der fremden Originale* (2d ed., Leipzig, 1885); the same writer's *Bibliotheca Germanorum nuptialis* (Cologne, 1890); and the well-known *Bibliographie des ouvrages relatifs à l'amour, aux femmes, au mariage,* etc. (3d ed., 6 vols., San Remo, London, Nice, and Turin, 1871–73). Legal works on marriage and related institutions are included in Martin Lipenius's *Bibliotheca realis juridica omnium materiarum, rerum, et titulorum, in universo universi juris ambitu occurrentium, post F. G. Struvii et G. A. Jenichenii curas emendata . . . . et locupletata* (2 vols., folio, Leipzig, 1757); but of much more service for the present purpose is the great work of J. F. von Schulte, *Die Geschichte der Quellen und Literatur des canonischen Rechts von Gratian bis auf die Gegenwart* (3 vols., bound in 4, Stuttgart, 1875–80). Many recent publications are entered in George K. Fortescue's *Subject Index of the Modern Works Added to the Library of the British Museum in the Years 1880–1895* (3 vols., London, 1886–97); while Poole's *Index* contains the titles of more than 1,200 articles on various phases of the subject, including woman in her family relations.

For topical analysis of the literature presented in this Bibliographical Index consult the critical and descriptive notes at the heads of the respective chapters.

I. EARLY HISTORY OF MATRIMONIAL INSTITUTIONS

Abercromby, John. "Marriage Customs of the Mordvins." *Folk-Lore*, I, 417–62. London, 1890.

Achelis, A. "Die Geschlechtsgenossenschaft und die Entwickelung der Ehe." *Zeitschrift der Gesellschaft für Erdkunde zu Berlin*, XXV, Heft 4. Berlin, 1890.

Achelis, T. "Die Entwicklung der Ehe." *Beiträge zur Volks- und Völkerkunde*, II. Berlin, 1893.

——— "The Historical Development of the Family." *Open Court*, II, 806, 807. Chicago, 1888–89.

Adam, Lucien. Du parler des hommes et du parler des femmes dans la langue caraibe. Paris, 1879.

Adams, Henry. Historical Essays. New York, 1891.

Alabaster, Ernest. Notes and Commentaries on Chinese Criminal Law. London, 1899.

American Anthropologist. 11 vols. Washington, 1888–98.

American Antiquarian. 20 vols. Chicago, 1879–98.

American Association for the Advancement of Science. *Proceedings*. 47 vols. Philadelphia, Cambridge, and Salem, 1849–98.

Amram, D. W. "Divorces on Condition [Hebrew]." *Green Bag*, III, 381–83. Boston, 1891.

——— "Chapters from the Ancient Jewish Law: Divorce." *Ibid.*, IV, 36 ff., 493 ff. Boston, 1892.

——— The Jewish Law of Divorce. Philadelphia, 1896.

Anchieta, Padre José d'. "Informação dos casamentos dos Indios do Brazil." *Revista trimensal de historia e geographia*, VIII (1846), 254–62. Rio de Janeiro, 1867.

Annales de l'Institut international de sociologie. Publiées sous la direction de René Worms. II, "Travaux du second congrès, septembre–octobre 1895." Paris, 1896.

Anthropological Institute of Great Britain and Ireland, Journal of. 26 vols. London, 1872–97.

Araki, Toratoro. Japanisches Ehoschliessungsrecht: eine historisch-kritische Studie. Inaugural-Dissertation. Göttingen, 1893.

Atkinson, J. J. Primal Law. London, New York, and Bombay, 1903.

Avery, J. "Polyandry in India and Thibet." *American Antiquarian and Oriental Journal*, IV, 48–53.

——— "The Races of the Indo-Pacific Oceans: Polynesians." *American Antiquarian*, VI, 361–69. Chicago, 1884.

Ayrer, Georg Heinrich. De jure connubiorum apud Romanos quam sub divini numinis tutela, etc. Göttingen, 1736.

Backer, Louis de. Le droit de la femme dans l'antiquité: son devoir au moyen âge. A. Claudin, éditeur. Paris, 1880.

Bachofen, J. J. Das Mutterrecht: eine Untersuchung über die Gynaikokratie der alten Welt nach ihrer religiösen und rechtlichen Natur. Stuttgart, 1861.

——— Die Sage von Tanaquil. Heidelberg, 1870.

——— Antiquarische Briefe. Strassburg, 1886.

Bader, Clarisse. La femme dans l'Inde antique: études morales et littéraires. 2d ed. Paris, 1867.

——— La femme biblique, son influence religieuse, sa vie morale et sociale. New ed., revised and corrected. Paris, 1873.

——— La femme grecque: étude de la vie antique. 2 vols. 2d ed. Paris, 1873.

——— La femme romaine: étude de la vie antique. 2d ed. Paris, 1877.

Baegert, Jacob. "An Account of the Aboriginal Inhabitants of the Californian Peninsula." Trans. by Charles Rau. *Report of the Smithsonian Institution* for 1864, 378–99. Washington, 1865.

Bagehot, Walter. Physics and Politics. London, 1872.

Ball, B. W. "The Rights of Women in Ancient Athens." *Atlantic Monthly*, XXVII, 273–86. Boston, 1871.

Bandelier, A. F. "On the Social Organization and Mode of Government of the Ancient Mexicans." *Report of the Peabody Museum*, II, 557–699. Cambridge, 1880.

Bardesan (*ca.* 250 A. D.). Book of the Laws of Countries. (Identical with his De Fato.) Trans. in William Cureton's Spicilegium syriacum. London, 1855.

Baring-Gould, S. "Marriage." In his Germany, Present and Past, 96–126. New York, n. d.

Baron, J. "Das Heirathen in alten und neuen Gesetzen." In R. Virchow and I. von Holtzendorff's *Sammlung gemeinverständlicher wissenschaftlicher Vorträge.* Berlin, 1874.

Barthélemy, Anatole de. "Le droit du seigneur." *Revue des questions historiques*, I, 95–123. Paris, 1866.

Bastian, A. "Ueber die Eheverhältnisse." *ZFE.*, VI.

——— "Matriarchat und Patriarchat." *Ibid., Verhandlungen*, 331–41. Berlin, 1886.

Bastian, A.　Die Rechtsverhältnisse bei verschiedenen Völkern der Erde.　Berlin, 1872.

Baway, Ahamadu.　"The Marriage Customs of the Moors of Ceylon."　*Journal of the Royal Asiatic Society*, Ceylon Branch, X, 219–33.　Colombo, 1888.

Beauchamp, W. M.　"Permanence of Early Iroquois Clans and Sachemships."　*Proceedings of the American Association for the Advancement of Science*, XXXIV, 381–92.　Salem, 1886.

——　"Aboriginal Communal Life in America."　*American Antiquarian*, IX, 343–50.　Chicago, 1887.

Beckwith, Paul.　"Notes on Customs of the Dakotahs."　*Report of the Smithsonian Institution* for 1886, Part I, 245–57.　Washington, 1889.

Bergel, J.　Die Eheverhältnisse der alten Juden im Vergleiche mit den griechischen und römischen.　Leipzig, 1881.

Bernhöft, F.　Staat und Recht der römischen Königszeit im Verhältniss zu verwandten Rechten.　Stuttgart, 1882.

——　Verwandtschaftsnamen und Eheformen der nordamerikanischen Volksstämme.　Rostock, 1888.

——　"Ueber die Grundlagen der Rechtsentwicklung bei den indogermanischen Völkern."　*ZVR.*, II.　Stuttgart, 1880.

——　"Das Gesetz von Gortyn."　*Ibid.*, VI.　Stuttgart, 1886.

——　"Zur Geschichte des europäischen Familienrechts."　*Ibid.*, VIII.　Stuttgart, 1888.

——　"Die Principien des europäischen Familienrechts."　*Ibid.*, IX.　Stuttgart, 1891.

——　"Altindische Familienorganisation."　*Ibid.*, IX.　Stuttgart, 1891.

——　"Ehe und Erbrecht der griechischen Heroenzeit."　*Ibid.*, XI.　Stuttgart, 1895.

Bertholon, M.　"Les formes de la famille chez les premiers habitants de l'Afrique du nord d'après les écrivains de l'antiquité et des coutumes modernes."　*Archives de l'anthropologie criminelle*, VIII (1893), 581–614.

"Bibliophile" (pseud.).　Les nuits d'épreuve des villageoises allemandes avant le mariage.　Brussels, 1877.

Billington, Mary Frances.　Women in India.　London, 1895.

Blumentritt, Ferdinand.　Versuch einer Ethnographie der Philippinen.　Gotha, 1882.

Boaz, Franz.　"The Social Organization and the Secret Societies of the Kwakiutl Indians: Based on the Personal Observations and the Notes Made by Mr. George Hunt."　*Report of the Smithsonian Institution* for 1895, 311–738, *Report of the U. S. National Museum*.　Washington, 1897.

Bogišić, V. De la forme dite "Inokosna" de la famille rurale chez les Serbes et les Croates. Paris, 1884.

Botsford, G. W. "The Athenian Constitution." *Cornell University Studies in Classical Philology*, IV. Boston, 1893.

Bourdin, Albert. De la condition de la mère en droit romain et en droit français. Paris, 1881.

Brehm, A. C. Thierleben. 10 vols. 3d ed. Leipzig and Vienna, 1891.

Brinton, D. S. "Religions of Primitive Peoples." *American Lectures on the History of Religion.* 2d series. New York and London, 1897.

Brissonius, Barnabe. De ritu nuptiarum. Paris, 1564.

—— De jure connubiorum. Paris, 1564. (Published and bound with the preceding.)

Brooks, W. K. The Law of Heredity. 2d ed. Baltimore and New York, 1883.

Brouardel, P. L'infanticide. Paris, 1897.

Buch, Max. Die Wotjäken, eine ethnologische Studie. From *Acta societatis scientiarum Fennicae,* XII. Helsingfors, 1882.

Buchner, Max. Kamerun. Leipzig, 1887.

Burnell, A. C., and Hopkins, E. W. The Ordinances of Manu. London, 1891.

Carr, Lucien. The Social and Political Position of Women among the Huron-Iroquois Tribes. From the *XVI. Report of the Peabody Museum.* Cambridge, 1883.

Cassel, Paulus. Gesammelte Schriften. I. Berlin, 1893.

Catlin, George. Indian Tribes. 2 vols. London, 1857.

Chamberlain, Alexander Francis. The Child and Childhood in Folk-Thought. New York, 1896.

Chamblain, L. J. De la puissance paternelle chez les Romains: dissertation présentée à la faculté de droit de Paris. Paris, 1829.

Chaplin, J. "The Position of Women among the Ancient Romans." *Baptist Review,* III, 466 ff.

Chinese Marriage. Mariage impérial chinois: un cérémonial. Traduit par G. Devéria. Paris, 1887.

Ciccotti, Ettore. Donne e politica negli ultimi anni della republica romana. Milan, 1895.

Codrington, R. H. "Social Regulations in Melanesia." *Journal of the Anthropological Institute,* XVIII, 300–313. London, 1889.

—— The Melanesians: Studies in Their Anthropology and Folk-Lore. Oxford, 1891.

Combier, Émilien. Du divorce en droit romain: de la séparation du corps en droit français. Paris, 1880.

Corbusier, W. M. "The Apache-Yumas and Apache-Mojaves." *American Antiquarian*, VIII, 276–84, 325–39. Chicago, 1886.

Cornil, Georges. "Contribution à l'étude de la patria potestas." *Nouvelle revue historique de droit*, XXI, 416–85. Paris, 1897.

Corre, A. La mère et l'enfant dans les races humaines. Paris, 1882.

Couch, John Andrew. "Woman in Early Roman Law." *Harvard Law Review*, VIII, 39–50. Cambridge, 1895.

Crawley, Ernest. "Sexual Taboo: A Study of the Relations of the Sexes." *Journal of the Anthropological Institute*, XXIV, 116–25, 219–35, 430–46. London, 1895.

—— The Mystic Rose: A Study of Primitive Marriage. New York, 1902.

Cunow, H. "Die ökonomischen Grundlagen der Mutterherrschaft." *Neue Zeit*, XVI. Jahrgang, I, No. 4. Stuttgart, 1897–98.

—— Die Verwandtschafts-Organisationen der Australneger: ein Beitrag zur Entwicklungsgeschichte der Familie. Stuttgart, 1894.

Curr, E. C. The Australian Race. 4 vols. Melbourne, 1886.

Daigoro, Goh. "The Family Relations in Japan." *Transactions of the Japan Society*, II.

Danks, B. "Marriage Customs of the New Britain Group." *Journal of the Anthropological Institute*, XVIII, 281–94. London, 1889.

Darab Dastur. Next-of-Kin Marriages in Old Iran. London, 1888.

Dargun, L. "Mutterrecht und Raubehe und ihre Reste im germanischen Recht und Leben." In Gierke's *Untersuchungen*, XVI. Breslau, 1883.

—— Mutterrecht und Vaterrecht. Leipzig, 1892.

—— "Ursprung und Entwicklungs-Geschichte des Eigenthums." *ZVR.*, V. Stuttgart, 1884.

Darinsky, A. "Die Familie bei den kaukasischen Völkern." *Ibid.*, XIV, 149–210. Stuttgart, 1900.

Darwin, C. The Variation of Animals and Plants under Domestication. 2 vols. New York, 1890.

—— The Descent of Man and Selection in Relation to Sex. New York, 1890.

Davoud-Oghlou, Garabed Artin. Histoire de la législation des anciens Germains. 2 vols. Berlin, 1845.

Dawson, James. Australian Aborigines: The Language and Customs of Several Tribes of Aborigines in the Western District of Victoria. Melbourne, Sydney, and Adelaide, 1881.

Delbrück, Berthold. Altindisches Tempuslehre. Halle, 1876.

—— Die indogermanischen Verwandtschaftsnamen. Leipzig, 1885.

Delbrück, Berthold. "Das Mutterrecht bei den Indogermanen." *Preussische Jahrbücher*, XCVII, Heft 1. Berlin, 1895.

Delpit, Jules. Réponse d'un Campagnard à un Parisien ou réfutation du livre de M. Veuillot sur le droit du seigneur. Paris, 1857.

D'Évreux, Père Yves. Voyage dans le nord du Brésil fait durant les années 1613 et 1614; avec une introduction et des notes par Ferdinand Denis. Leipzig and Paris, 1864.

Dobrizhoffer, Martin. Of the Weddings, and Of the Marriages of the Abipones, an Equestrian People of Paraguay (II, 207–15). 3 vols. Trans. from the original Latin. London, 1822.

Donaldson, James. "Women in Ancient Greece." *Contemporary Review*, XXXII, 647 ff. London, 1878.

—— "Women in Ancient Athens." *Ibid.*, XXXIV, 700–716. London, 1879.

—— "The Position of Women in Ancient Rome." *Ibid.*, LIII, LIV. London, 1888.

Doolittle, J. Social Life of the Chinese. 2 vols. New York, 1867.

Dorsey, James Owen. "Omaha Sociology." *III. Report of Bureau of Ethnology*, 205–370. Washington, 1884.

—— "Siouan Sociology: A Posthumous Paper." *XV. Report of Bureau of Ethnology*, 205–44. Washington, 1897.

Drummond, H. The Ascent of Man. New York, 1894.

Dubief, Disseruit L. Qualis fuerit familia romana, tempore Plauti, ex ejus Fabulis. Molini, 1859.

Duboc, Karl Julius. Die Psychologie der Liebe. Hanover, 1874.

Düringsfeld, Ida von, and Reinsberg-Düringsfeld, Otto Freiherr von. Hochzeitsbuch: Brauch und Glaube der Hochzeit bei den christlichen Völkern Europas. Leipzig, 1871.

Duschak, M. Das mosaisch-talmudische Eherecht. Vienna, 1864.

Düsing, Carl. Die Regulierung des Geschlechtsverhältnisses. Jena, 1884.

Eells, Myron. "The Twana, Chemakum, and Klallam Indians of Washington Territory." *Report of the Smithsonian Institution* for 1887, 605–81. Washington, 1889.

Eggers, F. W. Th. Ueber das Wesen und die Eigenthümlichkeiten der alt-römischen Ehe mit Manus. Altona, 1833.

Ellis, A. B. The Tshi-Speaking Peoples of the Gold Coast of West Africa. London, 1887.

—— The Ewe-Speaking Peoples of the Slave Coast of West Africa. London, 1890.

—— "Survivals from Marriage by Capture." *Popular Science Monthly*, XXXIX, 207–22. New York, 1891.

—— "On Polyandry." *Ibid.*, 801–9. New York, 1891.

Ellis, A. B. "Marriage and Kinship among the Ancient Israelites." *Ibid.*, XLII, 325–37. New York, 1892–93.

Ellis, Havelock. Man and Woman: A Study of Human Secondary Characters. London, 1896.

—— Studies in the Psychology of Sex. Vol. I, "Sexual Inversion." London, 1897.

Engels, Friedrich. Der Ursprung der Familie, des Privateigenthums, und des Staats. 5th ed. Stuttgart, 1892.

Esmein, A. Mélanges d'histoire du droit et de critique: droit romain. Paris, 1886.

Espinas, Alfred. Des sociétés animales. 2d ed. Paris, 1878.

Farrar, J. A. "Early Wedding Customs." In his Primitive Manners and Customs, 188–238. London, 1879. The same in *Gentleman's Magazine*, new series, XXI, 321–45. London, 1878.

—— "Marriage by Capture." *Gentleman's Magazine*, new series, XL, 267–73. London, 1888.

Fawcett, F. "On Basivis: Women, Who, through Dedication to a Deity, Assume Masculine Privileges." *Journal of the Anthropological Society* (Bombay), II (1891), 322–54.

Featherman, A. Social History of the Races of Mankind. 6 vols. London, 1881–91.

Fielde, Adele M. "Chinese Marriage Customs." *Popular Science Monthly*, XXXIV, 241–46. New York, 1888.

Finck, H. T. Romantic Love and Personal Beauty: Their Development, Causal Relations, and Historical and Natural Peculiarities. 2 vols. London, 1887.

—— Primitive Love and Love-Stories. New York, 1899.

Fischer, Chr. J. Ueber die Probenächte der teutschen Bauernmädchen. Wortgetreues Abdruck der Original-Ausgabe, Berlin and Leipzig, 1780. Leipzig, 1898.

Fison, Lorimer. "Views of Primitive Marriage." *Popular Science Monthly*, XXVII, 203–15. New York, 1880.

Fison, Lorimer, and Howitt, A. W. Kamilaroi and Kurnai. Melbourne, 1880.

Fletcher, Alice C. "The Emblematic Use of the Tree in the Dakotan Group." *Proceedings of the American Association for the Advancement of Science*, XLV, 191–209. Salem, 1897.

—— "A Study from the Omaha Tribe: The Import of the Totem." (An abstract.) *Ibid.*, XLVI, 325–34. Salem, 1898.

Flittner, C. G. Die Feyer der Liebe, oder Beschreibung der Verlobungs- und Hochzeits-Ceremonien aller Nationen. Berlin, 1795.

Foras, Amédée, Comte de. Le droit du seigneur au moyen âge: étude critique et historique. Chambéry, 1886.

Fraser, J. G. The Golden Bough: A Study in Comparative Religion. 2d ed. 3 vols. London, 1900.

—— Totemism. Edinburgh, 1887.

—— "Kinship and Marriage in Early Arabia." *Academy*, XXIX, 220, 221. London, 1886.

Frerichs, H. Zur Naturgeschichte des Menschen. 2d ed. Norden, 1891.

Friedlaender, Ludwig. Darstellungen aus der Sittengeschichte Roms. 6th ed. 3 vols. Leipzig, 1888–90.

Friedrich, J. B. Ueber die jüdische Beschneidung in historischer, operativer und sanitätspolizeilicher Beziehung. Ansbach, 1844.

Friedrichs, Karl. "Zur Matriarchatsfrage." *ZFE.*, XX. Berlin 1880.

—— "Das Eherecht des Islams." *ZVR.*, VII. Stuttgart, 1887.

—— "Ueber den Ursprung des Matriarchats." *Ibid.*, VIII. Stuttgart, 1888.

—— "Familienstufen und Eheformen." *Ibid.*, X. Stuttgart, 1892.

—— "Zum japanischen Recht." *Ibid.*

Fritsch, G. Die Eingeborenen Südafrikas ethnographisch und anatomisch. Breslau, 1873.

Fustel de Coulanges. The Ancient City. Trans. by Small. 3d ed. Boston and New York, 1877; also Boston, 1896.

Galton, F. "Marriage Systems of Australian Aborigines." *Journal of the Anthropological Institute* XVIII, 70–72. London, 1889.

Gaya, Louis de. Cérémonies nuptiales de toutes les nations. Original ed. Paris, 1680. (There are various summaries, and also a later edition, Paris, 1852.)

Geddes, Patrick, and Thompson, J. Arthur. The Evolution of Sex. New York, n. d.

Gerlach, Fridericus de. De Romanorum connubio commentatio. Hallis Saxonum, 1851.

Gessert, F. A. Ad legem Juliam de adulteriis coercendis. G. A. Kleuschrod, *Praes.* Wirceburgi, 1795.

Giddings, Franklin H. Principles of Sociology. New York and London, 1896.

Gide, P. Étude sur la condition de la femme dans le droit ancien et moderne, et en particulier sur le sénatus-consulte velléien. 2d ed. by A. Esmein. Paris, 1885.

Giraud-Teulon, A. La mère chez certains peuples de l'antiquité: études sur les sociétés anciennes. Paris and Leipzig, 1867.

—— Les origines du mariage et de la famille. Geneva and Paris, 1884.

Gomme, G. L. "On the Evidence for Mr. McLennan's Theory of the Primitive Human Horde." *Journal of the Anthropological Institute*, XVII, 118–33. London, 1888.

Gooroodass, Banerjee. "The Hindu Law of Marriage and Stridahn." *Tagore Law Lectures*, 1878. Calcutta, 1879.

Gramont, Le Comte F. de. Comment on se marie. Brussels, 1858.

Gray, John Henry. China: A History of the Laws, Manners, and Customs of the People. Ed. by William Gow Gregor. 2 vols. London, 1878.

Greenwood, J. The Wild Man at Home. London, n. d.

Grinnell, G. B. "Marriage among the Pawnees." *American Anthropologist*, IV, 275–81. Washington, 1891.

Groos, Karl. Die Spiele der Thiere. Jena, 1896.

——— The Play of Animals. Trans. by Eliz. L. Baldwin. New York, 1898.

Grosier, L'Abbé. Extracts from his De la Chine, 1819. (1) "De la piété filiale," Liv. X, chap. ix; (2) "Mariages chinois," Liv. XI, chap. i.

Grosse, Ernst. Die Formen der Familie und die Formen der Wirthschaft. Freiburg and Leipzig, 1896.

Grossmann, F. E. "The Pima Indians of Arizona." *Report of the Smithsonian Institution* for 1871, 407–19. Washington, 1873.

Grupen, Christian Ulrich. Tractatio de vxore romana cum ea, quae in manvm convenit, farre, coemtione et vsu, tum illa, quae vxor tantummodo habebatur. Hanoverae, 1727.

Gumarães, José da Silva. "Memoria: Sobre os usos, costumes e linguagem dos Appiaacás, e descobrimento de novas minas na Provincia de Mato Grosso." *Revista trimensal de historia e geographia*, etc., VI. 2d ed. Rio de Janeiro, 1865.

Haas, E. "Die Heirathsgebräuche der alten Inder nach den Grihyasûtra." In Weber's *Indische Studien*, V, 267–412. Berlin, 1862.

Halbert, H. C. "Courtship and Marriage among the Choctaws of Mississippi." *American Naturalist*, XVI, 222, 223. Philadelphia, 1882.

Hanoteau, A., and Letourneaux, A. La Kabylie et les coutumes kabyles. 3 vols. Paris, 1893.

Harper, Robert Francis (editor). The Code of Hammurabi, King of Babylon about 2250 B. C. University of Chicago Press Chicago, 1904.

Harrison, Charles. "Religion and Family among the Haidas (Queen Charlotte Islands)." *Journal of the Anthropological Institute*, XXI, 14–29. London, 1892.

Hartland, E. S. "Marriage Ceremonies among the Aborigines of Bengal." *Imperial and Asiatic Quarterly Review*, new series, V, 183–211. Moking, [1893].

Hase, E. De manu juris romani antiquioris contentio. Hallis, 1847.

Hasse, Johann Christian. Das Güterrecht der Ehegatten nach römischem Recht. Berlin, 1824.

Haupt, Ernest Frederick. De poena adulterii ex lege Julia coercendis adulteriis. Lipsiae, 1797.

Haupt, Paul. Die sumerischen Familiengesetze in Keilschrift; Transcription und Übersetzung, nebst ausführlichem Commentar und zahlreichen Excursen: eine assyriologische Studie. Leipzig, 1879.

Hearn, W. E. The Aryan Household. London and Melbourne 1879.

Hellwald, Friedrich von. Kulturgeschichte in ihrer natürlichen Entwicklung bis zur Gegenwart. 3d ed. Augsburg, 1883.

—— Die menschliche Familie. Leipzig, 1889.

Henrici, E. "Das Volksrecht der Epheneger und sein Verhältnis zur deutschen Colonisation im Togogebiete." *ZVR.*, XI. Stuttgart, 1895.

Hermann, Emanuel. "Die Familie vom Standpunkte der Gesammtwirthschaft." *Volkswirthschaftliche Zeitfragen*, Jahrgang 10, Heft 8. Berlin, 1889.

Hildebrand, Richard. Über das Problem einer allgemeinen Entwicklungsgeschichte des Rechts und der Sitte. Graz, 1894.

—— Recht und Sitte auf den verschiedenen wirthschaftlichen Kulturstufen. I. Theil. Jena, 1896.

Hitchcock, Romyn. "The Ainos of Yezo, Japan." *Report of the Smithsonian Institution* for 1890, 429–502, *Report of U. S. National Museum*. Washington, 1891.

Hoffman, Walter James. "The Menomini Indians." *XIV. Report of the Bureau of Ethnology*, Part I. Washington, 1896.

Hölder, E. Die römische Ehe. Zurich, 1874.

Honegger, J. J. Grundsteine einer allgemeinen Culturgeschichte der neuesten Zeit. 5 vols. Leipzig, 1868–74.

Hotman, Antoine. De veteri ritu nuptiarum. (Published and bound with Brissonius's two works.) Lugduni Batavorum, 1641.

Hotman, François. De sponsalibus. (Published and bound with the preceding.)

—— De ritu nuptiarum et jure matrimoniorum. (Published and bound with the preceding.)

Houzeau, J. C. Études sur les facultés mentales des animaux. Mons, 1872.

Howard, Clifford. Sex Worship. 2d ed. Washington, 1898.

Howitt, A. W. "Australian Group Relations." *Report of the Smithsonian Institution* for 1883, 797–824. Washington, 1885.

Howitt, A. W. "Remarks on the Class Systems Collected by Mr. Palmer." *Journal of the Anthropological Institute*, XIII, 335–46. London, 1884.

—— "Further Notes on the Australian Class Systems." *Ibid.*, XVIII, 31–66. London, 1889.

Howitt, A. W., and Fison, Lorimer. "From Mother-Right to Father-Right." *Ibid.*, XII, 30–44. London, 1882.

—— "On the Deme and the Horde." *Ibid.*, XIV, 142–68. London, 1885.

Hozumi, N. Ancestor-Worship and Japanese Law. Tokio, 1902.

Hruza, Ernst. Beiträge zur Geschichte des griechischen und römischen Familienrechts. I, "Ehebegründung nach attischem Rechte." Erlangen and Leipzig, 1892. II, "Polygamie und Pellikat nach griechischem Rechte." *Ibid.*, 1894.

Huc, M. The Chinese Empire. 2 vols. London, 1855.

Humboldt, Alexandre de. Vues de Cordillères, et monuments des peuples indigènes de l'Amérique. Large folio. Paris, 1810.

[Hurtant, P. T. N.]. Coup d'œil anglois sur les cérémonies du mariage. Geneva, 1750. (Compiled from Louis de Gaya's Cérémonies nuptiales de toutes les nations.)

Hutchinson, Henry Neville. Marriage Customs in Many Lands. London, 1897.

Jacolliot, Louis. La femme dans l'Inde. (La femme aux temps védiques, aux temps brahmaniques, et dans l'Inde de la décadence.) Paris, 1877.

Jardine, J., and Forchhammer, E. Notes on Buddhist Law. (Nine papers on marriage, etc.) Rangoon, 1883.

Jolly, Julius. Ueber die rechtliche Stellung der Frauen bei den alten Indern nach den Dharmaçâstra. Munich, 1876.

—— "Ueber die Systematik des indischen Rechts." *ZVR.*, I. Stuttgart, 1878.

—— "Die juristischen Abschnitte aus dem Gesetzbuch des Manu." *Ibid.*, III, IV. Stuttgart, 1882–83.

Jörs, Paul. Die Ehegesetze des Augustus. Marburg, 1894.

Jubainville, H. D'Arbois de. "Le droit du roi dans l'épopée islandaise." *Revue archéologique*. Paris, 1881.

Jung, K. E. Der Welttheil Australien. Leipzig, 1882.

Junius, F. A. De annulo Romanorum sponsalitio commentatio. Leipzig, [1744?].

[Kantemir, Dmitri.]. Coutumes du pays roumain. Trans. by J. E. Voinesco. In Vasili Aleksandri's Les Doïnas, 121–27. 2d ed. Paris, 1855.

Karlowa, O. Die Formen der römischen Ehe und Manus. Bonn, 1868.

Katscher, Leopold. Bilder aus dem chinesischen Leben, mit besonderer Rücksicht auf Sitten und Gebräuche. Leipzig and Heidelberg, 1881.

—— Aus China: Skizzen und Bilder. I. Leipzig, [1877].

Kautsky, Carl. "Die Entstehung der Ehe und Familie." *Kosmos*, XII. Stuttgart, 1882.

Klemm, Gustav. Allgemeine Cultur-Geschichte der Menschheit. 10 vols. Leipzig, 1842–52.

Keane, A. H. Ethnology. 2d ed. Cambridge, 1896.

—— Man: Past and Present. Cambridge, 1899.

Kingsley, Mary. Travels in West Africa. London, 1897.

Koehne, K. "Das Recht der Kalmücken." *ZVR.*, IX. Stuttgart, 1891.

Kohler, J. "Rechtshistorische und rechtsvergleichende Forschungen." (Part III, on "Indisches Ehe- und Familienrecht.") *Ibid.*, III. Stuttgart, 1882.

—— "Studien über Frauengemeinschaft, Frauenraub und Frauenkauf." *Ibid.*, V. Stuttgart, 1884.

—— "Studien über zwei babylonische Rechtsurkunden aus der Zeit Nabonids." *Ibid.*, V. Stuttgart, 1884.

—— "Die Ionsage und Vaterrecht." *Ibid.*, V. Stuttgart, 1884.

—— "Studien über künstliche Verwandtschaft." *Ibid.*, V. Stuttgart, 1884.

—— "Aus dem chinesischen Civilrecht." *Ibid.*, VI. Stuttgart, 1886.

—— "Das Recht der Birmanen." *Ibid.*, VI. Stuttgart, 1886.

—— "Das Recht der Chins." *Ibid.*, VI. Stuttgart, 1886.

—— "Die Ehe mit und ohne Mundium." *Ibid.*, VI. Stuttgart, 1886.

—— "Ueber das Recht der Australneger." *Ibid.*, VII. Stuttgart, 1887.

—— "Ueber das Recht der Papuas auf Neu Guinea." *Ibid.*, VII. Stuttgart, 1887.

—— "Das Recht der Armenier." *Ibid.*, VII. Stuttgart, 1887.

—— "Ueber das vorislamitische Recht der Araber." *Ibid.*, VIII. Stuttgart, 1888.

—— "Studien aus dem japanischen Recht." *Ibid.*, X. Stuttgart, 1892.

—— "Das Recht der Azteken." *Ibid.*, XI. Stuttgart, 1895.

—— "Ueber das Negerrecht, namentlich in Kamerun." *Ibid.*, XI. Stuttgart, 1895.

—— Zur Urgeschichte der Ehe: Totemismus, Gruppenehe, Mutterrecht. Separat-Abdruck aus *ibid.*, XII. Stuttgart, 1897.

Kohler, J. "Rechte der deutschen Schutzgebiete." *Ibid.*, XIV, 294–319, 321–94, 409–55. Stuttgart, 1900.

——— "Rechtsverhältnisse auf dem ostindischen Archipel und den westlichen Karolinen," *ibid.*, VI. "Aus dem Praxis des buddhistischen Rechts in Birma," *ibid.*, VI. "Die Gewohnheitsrechte des Pendschabs," *ibid.*, VII. "Ueber das Recht der Goajiroindianer," *ibid.*, VII. "Indische Gewohnheitsrechte," *ibid.*, VIII. "Ueber die Gewohnheitsrechte von Bengalen," *ibid.*, IX. "Die Gewohnheitsrechte der Provinz Bombay," *ibid.*, X. "Gewohnheitsrechte der indischen Nordwestprovinzen mit Einschluss von Audh," *ibid.*, XI.

Kovalevsky, Maxime. Tableau des origines et de l'évolution de la famille et de la propriété. Stockholm, 1890.

——— Gesetz und Gewohnheit im Kaukass. (Russian text.) Moskow, 1890.

——— "Matrimonial Customs and Usages of the Russian People, and the Light They Throw on the Evolution of Marriage." In his Modern Customs and Ancient Laws of Russia. London, 1891.

——— "Marriage among Early Slavs." *Folk-Lore*, I, 463–80. London, 1890.

Krafft-Ebing, R. von. Psychopathia Sexualis, with Especial Reference to Contrary Sexual Instinct. 7th ed. Trans. by Charles Gilbert Chaddock. Philadelphia and London, 1894.

Kranz, M. Natur- und Kulturleben der Zulus. Wiesbaden, 1880.

Krause, Aurel. Die Tlinkit-Indianer: Ergebnisse einer Reise nach der Nordwestküste von Amerika und der Beringstrasse ausgeführt im Auftrage der Bremer geographischen Gesellschaft, 1880–81. Jena, 1885.

Krauss, Friedrich S. Sitte und Brauch der Südslaven. Vienna, 1885.

——— "Das Mundschaftsrecht des Mannes über die Ehefrau bei den Südslaven." *Mittheilungen der anthropologischen Gesellschaft*, XV, 101–10. Vienna, 1885.

Kremer, Alfred von. Kulturgeschichte des Orients unter den Chalifen. Vienna, 1875.

Kubary, J. S. "Aus dem samoanischen Familienleben." *Globus*, XLVII, 70–72, 86–88. Braunschweig, 1885.

Kulischer, M. "Die geschlechtliche Zuchtwahl bei den Menschen in der Urzeit." *ZFE.*, VIII. Stuttgart, 1888.

——— "Intercommunale Ehe durch Raub und Kauf." *Ibid.*, X.

——— "Die communale 'Zeitehe' und ihre Ueberreste." *Archiv für Anthropologie*, XI, 215–29. Braunschweig, 1879.

Kuntze, Johannes Emil. Excurse über römisches Recht. 2d ed. Leipzig, 1880.

Kurtz, Joh. Heinrich. Die Ehen der Söhne Gottes mit den Töchtern der Menschen. Berlin, New York, and Adelaide, 1857.

—— Die Ehe des Propheten Hosea. Dorpat, 1859.

Laband, P. "Rechtliche Stellung der Frauen im altrömischen und germanischen Recht." *Zeitschrift für Völkerpsychologie und Sprachwissenschaft*, III. Berlin, 1865.

Lacombe, P. La famille dans la société romaine: étude de moralité comparée. Paris, 1889.

Labessade, Léon de. Le droit du seigneur et la Rosière de Salency. Paris, 1878.

Lafitau, J. F. Mœurs des sauvages Amériquains, comparées aus mœurs des premiers temps. 2 vols. Paris, 1724.

Lallier, R. De la condition de la femme dans la famille athénienne au Ve et au IVe siècle. Paris, 1875.

Lang, Andrew. "Early History of the Family." In his Custom and Myth. London, 1884.

—— Social Origins. (Published with Atkinson's Primal Law.) London, New York, and Bombay, 1903.

Langeron, Louis. Du divorce en droit romain: droits des enfants naturels sur les biens de leur père ou mère en droit français. Paris, 1857.

Lasaulx, Ernst von. Zur Geschichte und Philosophie der Ehe bei den Griechen. Munich, 1852.

Laumier, Charles Lazare. Cérémonies nuptiales des peuples anciens et modernes. Paris, 1829.

Lawlace, W. M. The Japanese Wedding. New York, 1889.

Legge, J. The Life and Teachings of Confucius. 3d ed. London, 1872.

Leist, B. W. Graeco-italische Rechtsgeschichte. Jena, 1884.

—— Alt-arisches Jus Gentium. Jena, 1889.

Léry, Jean de. "Du mariage, polygamie & degrez de consanguinité observez par les sauvages: & du traittement de leurs petits enfans." In his Histoire d'un voyage faict en la terre du Bresil, autrement dite Amerique, 301–11. 3d ed. Geneva, 1585.

Letourneau, Charles. Sociology Based upon Ethnography. Trans. by H. M. Trollope. New ed. London, 1893.

—— "L'évolution du mariage et de la famille." Vol. VI of *Bibliothèque anthropologique*. Paris, 1888.

—— "The Evolution of Marriage and of the Family." *Contemporary Science* series. New York, n. d.

Lewis, H. The Ancient Laws of Wales. Ed. by Lloyd. London 1889.

Lichtschein, L. Die Ehe nach mosaisch-talmudischer Auffassung und das mosaisch-talmudische Eherecht. Leipzig, 1879.

Linton, E. Lynn. "Womanhood in Old Greece." *Fortnightly Review*, XLVII, 105–123, 715–31. London, 1887.

—— "The Roman Matron and the Roman Lady." *Ibid.*, XLVIII, 237–58. London, 1887.

Lippert, Julius. Die Geschichte der Familie. Stuttgart, 1884.

—— Kulturgeschichte der Menschheit in ihrer organischen Aufbau. 2 vols. Stuttgart, 1886–87.

Lockhart, J. H. S. "Marriage Customs of the Manchus." *Folk-Lore*, I, 481–92. London, 1890.

Loring, W. W. "Marriage." In his A Confederate Soldier in Egypt, 105–13. New York, [1884, copyright].

Louïse, Paul. Du sénatus-consulte velléien et de l'incapacité de la femme mariée: thèse, faculté de droit de Douai. Chateau-Thierry, 1873.

Lubbock, Sir John. "The Social and Religious Condition of the Lower Races of Man: An Address to the Workingmen of Liverpool." *Report of the Smithsonian Institution* for 1869, 341–62. Washington, 1872.

—— "On the Development of Relationships." *Journal of the Anthropological Institute*, I, 1–29. London, 1872.

—— The Origin of Civilization and the Primitive Condition of Man. 5th ed. New York, 1889.

Lushington, J. S. "On the Marriage Rites and Usages of the Jâts of Bharatpur." *Journal of the Asiatic Society of Bengal*, II, 273–97. Calcutta, 1833.

Lyall, A. C. Asiatic Studies: Religious and Social. 2d ed. London, 1884.

Maanen, Janus Maria von. Dissertatio juridica inauguralis: de muliere in manu et in tutela. Lugduni Batavorum, 1823.

MacCauley, Clay. "The Seminole Indians of Florida." *V. Report of Bureau of Ethnology*, 469–531. Washington, 1887.

Macfarlane, A. "Analysis of Relationships of Consanguinity and Affinity." *Journal of the Anthropological Institute*, XII, 46–63. London, 1883.

McGee, W. J. "The Beginning of Marriage." *American Anthropologist*, IX, 371–83. Washington, 1896.

—— "The Siouan Indians: A Preliminary Sketch." *XV. Report of Bureau of Ethnology*, 153–204. Washington, 1897.

—— "The Seri Indians." *XVII. Report of the Bureau of Ethnology*, Part I. Washington, 1898.

Mackenzie, Collin. "An Account of the Marriage Ceremonies of the Hindus and Mahommedans, as Practised in the Southern Peninsula of India." *Transactions of the Royal Asiatic Society*, III. London, 1835.

McLennan, Donald. "Ancient Marriage Customs." *Nature*, XIII, 585.

McLennan, J. F. "The Levirate and Polyandry." *Fortnightly Review*, XXVII, 694–707. London, 1877.

—— "Exogamy and Endogamy." *Ibid.*, XXVII, 884–95. London, 1877.

—— "Bride-Catching." *Argosy*, II, 31–42. London, 1866.

—— and Donald. The Patriarchal Theory. London, 1885.

—— Studies in Ancient History, Comprising a Reprint of Primitive Marriage. New ed. London, 1886.

—— Studies. 2d ser. Ed. by Eleanora A. McLennan and Arthur Platt. London, 1896.

Magalhães, Jose Vieira de. "Familia e religião selvagem." In his "Ensais de anthropologia: região e raças selvagens." *Revista trimensal do Instituto historico, geographico e ethnographico do Brasil*, XXXVI. Rio de Janeiro, 1873. 2d ed., separately published, Rio de Janeiro, 1876.

Mahlmann, Theodor. De matrimonio veterum Romanorum ineundi et maxime dissolvendi. Halle, 1845.

Maine, Sir Henry. Lectures on the Early History of Institutions. New York, 1875.

—— Ancient Law. New York, 1878.

—— Dissertations on Early Law and Custom. New York, 1883.

Mallen, Pierre-Gaspard Justus. De la puissance paternelle en droit romain dans l'ancien droit français et sous le code Napoléon: thèse, faculté de droit de Paris. Paris, 1858.

Mallery, Garrick. "Israelite and Indian: A Parallel in Planes of Culture." *Proceedings of the American Association for the Advancement of Science*, XXXVIII, 287–331. Salem, 1890.

Mantegazza, Paul. Anthropologisch-kulturhistorische Studien über die Gesellschaftsverhältnisse des Menschen. Trans. from the Italian. 3d ed. Jena, [1888].

—— Die Physiologie der Liebe. Trans. from the Italian by Karl Kolberg. 30th ed. Berlin, 1897.

Marche, G. A. Historia juris civilis de divortiis. Leipzig, 1764.

Marquardt, Joachim, and Mommsen, Theodor. Handbuch der römischen Alterthümer. 7 vols. Leipzig, 1876–88.

Marshall, W. E. A Phrenologist amongst the Todas or The Study of a Primitive Tribe in South India: History, Character, Customs, Religion, Infanticide, Polyandry, Language. London, 1873.

Martius, C. F. Ph. von. Von dem Rechtszustande unter den Ureinwohnern Braziliens. Munich, 1832.

Martius, C. F. Ph. von. "Zur Ethnographie Amerika's zumal Brasiliens." Vol. I of his Beiträge zur Ethnographie und Sprachenkunde Amerika's. Leipzig, 1867.

Mason, O. T. Woman's Share in Primitive Culture. New York, 1894.

Mathew, John. "The Australian Aborigines." Journal of the Royal Society of New South Wales, XXIII, 335–449. Sydney, [1889].

Mathews, R. H. "Australian Class Systems." American Anthropologist, IX, 411–16; X, 345–47. Washington, 1896–97.

—— The Victorian Aborigines: Their Initiation, Ceremonies, and Divisional Systems. Ibid., XI, 325–43. Washington, 1898.

Mayne, J. D. A Treatise on Hindu Law and Usage. 4th ed. Madras and London, 1888.

Medhurst, W. H. "Marriage, Affinity, and Inheritance in China." Transactions of the Royal Asiatic Society, China Branch, IV, 1–49. Hongkong, 1855.

Mégavorian, A. Étude ethnographique et juridique sur la famille et le mariage arméniens. Lausanne, 1894.

Meier, H. E., and Schömann, G. F. Der attische Process. Berlin, 1883–87.

Meyer, ——. Die Rechte der Israeliten, Athener, und Römer. Leipzig, 1862–63.

Meyer, Paul Martin. Der römische Konkubinat nach den Rechtsquellen und den Inschriften. Leipzig, 1895.

Michaelis, Johann David. Abhandlung von den Ehegesetzen Mosis, welche die Heyrathen in die nahe Freundschaft untersagen. Göttingen, 1768.

Mielziner, M. The Jewish Law of Marriage and Divorce. Cincinnati, 1884.

Millar, John. Observations Concerning the Distinction of Ranks in Society. London, 1771; 4th ed., Edinburgh, 1806.

Miln, Louise Jordan. Wooings and Weddings. Chicago, 1900.

Mitchell, Arthur. "Blood-Relationship in Marriage Considered in its Influence upon the Offspring." Memoirs of the London Anthropological Society, II, 402–56. London, 1866.

Möllendorff, P. G. von. Das chinesische Familienrecht. Shanghai, 1895.

Moore, Theophilus. Marriage Customs and Modes of Courtship of the Various Nations of the Universe. 2d ed. New York, 1820.

Morael, G. L. M. Droit romain: du divorce; Droit français: de la conversion de la séparation de corps en divorce. Paris, 1888.

Morgan, Lewis H. A Conjectural Solution of the Origin of the Classificatory System of Relationship. From the *Proceedings of the American Academy of Arts and Sciences*, VII (February 11, 1868). Cambridge, 1868.

—— Laws of Descent of the Iroquois. N. p., n. d.

—— "Systems of Consanguinity and Affinity of the Human Family." *Smithsonian Contributions to Knowledge*, XVII. Washington, 1871.

—— Ancient Society. New York, 1878.

—— "Houses and House-Life of the American Aborigines." *Contributions to North American Ethnology*, IV. Washington, 1881.

Mooney, James. The Siouan Tribes of the East. Bureau of Ethnology, Washington, 1894.

Morrison, W. D. The Jews under the Roman Rule. 2d ed. London, 1892.

Moure, Amédée. "Les Indiens de la province de Matto-Grosso (Brésil)." *Nouvelles annales des voyages* . . . . *rédigées par V. A. Malte-Brun*, II, 5–19. Paris, 1862.

Moy, M. L. "La famille dans Homère: soirées littéraires de la Sorbonne." *Revue des cours littéraires de la France et de l'étranger*. 6th year, No. 23 (May 8, 1869), 359–64.

Mucke, J. R. Horde und Familie in ihrer urgeschichtlichen Entwickelung. Stuttgart, 1895.

Muirhead, J. Historical Introduction to the Private Law of Rome. Edinburgh, 1886.

Müller, F. Max. Biographies of Words and the Home of the Aryas. London, 1888.

Müller, Herrmann. Am Neste. Berlin, 1881.

Munzinger, W. Ostafrikanische Studien. Schaffhausen, 1864.

Murdoch, John. "Ethnological Results of the Point Barrow Expedition (1881–3)." *IX. Report of Bureau of Ethnology*, 3–441. Washington, 1892.

Nadaillac, J. F. A. du P. L'évolution du mariage. Paris, 1893.

Nelson, Edward William. "The Eskimo about Bering Strait." *XVIII. Report of Bureau of Ethnology*, Part I. Washington, 1899.

Newman, R. Report of the Committee of the New York State Medical Society on the Result of Consanguineous Marriages. Albany, 1869.

Niblack, Albert P. "The Coast Indians of Southern Alaska and Northern British Columbia." *Report of Smithsonian Institution* for 1888, 225–386, "Report of U. S. Museum." Washington, 1890.

Nicolaÿ, Fernand.   Histoire des croyances, superstitions, mœurs, usages, et coutumes. (Book IX, 233–351.) 3 vols, Paris, 1901.

Nuptials.   Dei riti delle antiche nozze romane: ai nobilissimi sponsi Signor Conte Giulio Cesarei e Signora Donna Maria de' Conti di Marsciano. Perugia, 1791.

Ouvré, Henri.   "Observations sur le régime matrimonial au temps d'Homère." *Annales de la faculté des lettres de Bordeaux*, 2d series, VII, 285–304. Paris, 1886.

Pagés, M. J. P.   "La famille romaine." *Mémoires de l'Académie des sciences de Toulouse*, 1882, 324–34.

Palmer, Edward.   "Notes on Some Australian Tribes." *Journal of the Anthropological Institute*, XIII, 266–334. London, 1884.

Parker, E. H.   "Comparative Chinese Family Law." *China Review*, VIII, 67–107. Hongkong, 1879–80.

Paulhan, Fr.   "L'origine du mariage." *Revue scientifique*, 4th series, IV, 78–83. Paris, 1895.

Peal, S. E.   "On the 'Morong,' as Possibly a Relic of Pre-Marriage Communism." *Journal of the Anthropological Institute*, XXII, 244–60. London, 1893.

Peet, S. D.   "Village Life and Clan Residences among the Emblematic Mounds." *American Antiquarian*, IX, 10–34. Chicago, 1887.

—— "Houses and House-Life among the Prehistoric Races." *Ibid.*, X, 333–57. Chicago, 1888.

—— "The Earliest Abodes of Man." *Ibid.*, XV, 1–14. Chicago, 1893.

—— "The Tribal Records in the Effigies." *Ibid.*, XV, 90–113. Chicago, 1893.

—— "Ethnographic Religions and Ancestor Worship." *Ibid.*, XV, 230–45. Chicago, 1893.

—— "Personal Divinities and Culture Heroes." *Ibid.*, XV, 348–72. Chicago, 1893.

Peritz, Ismar J.   "Woman in the Ancient Hebrew Cult." *Journal of Biblical Literature*, XVII, Part II. [Boston, 1898.]

Peschel, Oscar.   The Races of Man and Their Geographical Distribution. From the German. London, 1889.

Picot, J. B. C.   Du mariage romain, chrétien et français. Paris, 1849.

Pischon, K. N.   Der Einfluss des Islâms auf das häusliche, soziale, und politische Leben seiner Bekenner. Leipzig, 1881.

Pizzi, I.   "Les coutumes nuptiales aux temps heroïques de l'Iran." *Muséon*, II, 3. Louvain, 1883.

Ploss, H.   Ueber das Geschlechtsverhältniss der Kinder bedingenden Ursachen. Berlin, 1859.

Ploss, H. "Ueber das Heirathsalter der Frauen bei verschiedenen Völkern." *Mittheilungen des Vereins für Erdkunde zu Leipzig*, 1872. Leipzig, 1873.

—— Das Kind in Brauch und Sitte der Völker. 2 vols. New ed. Leipzig, 1884.

—— Das Weib. 4th ed. 2 vols. Leipzig, 1895.

Plutarch. Lives. 6 vols. Ed. Langhorne. 4th ed. London, 1826.

Posada, Adolpho. Théories modernes sur les origines de la famille, de la société, et de l'état. Trans. from the Spanish by Frantz de Zeltner. Paris, 1896.

Post, Albert Hermann. Die Geschlechtsgenossenschaft der Urzeit und die Entstehung der Ehe. Oldenburg, 1875.

—— Der Ursprung des Rechts. Oldenburg, 1876.

—— Die Anfänge des Staats- und Rechtslebens. Oldenburg, 1878.

—— Die Grundlagen des Rechts und die Grundzüge seiner Entwickelungsgeschichte. Oldenburg, 1884.

—— Einleitung in das Studium der ethnologischen Jurisprudenz. Oldenburg, 1886.

—— Afrikanische Jurisprudenz. 2 vols. Oldenburg and Leipzig, 1887.

—— Studien zur Entwickelungsgeschichte des Familienrechts. Oldenburg and Leipzig, 1890.

—— "Die Kodifikation des Rechts der Amaxosa." *ZVR.*, XI.

Poste, E. (editor). Gaii institutionum juris civilis commentarii quatuor. 3d ed. Oxford, 1890.

Poulton, E. B. The Colours of Animals. New York, 1890.

Powell, J. W. "Wyandotte Society: A Short Study of Tribal Society." *Proceedings of the American Association for the Advancement of Science*, XXIX, 675–88. Salem, 1880.

—— (director). Reports of the Bureau of Ethnology to the Secretary of the Smithsonian Institution, 1881–95, 18 vols., 4to. Washington, 1879–99.

—— (in charge). Contributions to North American Ethnology. 9 vols. Washington, 1877–93. In *U. S. Geographical and Geological Survey of the Rocky Mountain Region*.

Pratz, Le Page du. "Des Mœurs & Coutumes des Peuples de la Louisiane, & particulièrement de celles des Natchez & de leur Langue." In his Histoire de la Louisiane, II, 307 ff., 385–406. Paris, 1758.

Puchta, O. F. Cursus der Institutionen. 2 vols. Leipzig, 1875.

Quaterfages, A. de. The Human Species. New York, 1890.

Raepsaet, J. J. Recherches sur l'origine et la nature des droits connus anciennement sous les noms de droits des premières nuits, de markette, d'afforage, marcheta, maritagium et Bumede. Gand, 1817.

Ramsay, W. M. The Cities and Bishoprics of Phrygia. Vols. I, II. Oxford, 1895–97.

Ratzel, Friedrich. "Der Staat und sein Boden geographisch betrachtet." Bd. XVII der *Abhandlungen der philologisch-historischen Classe der königlichen Sächsischen Gesellschaft der Wissenschaften*, No. 4. Leipzig, 1896.

—— The History of Mankind. Trans. from 2d German ed. by A. J. Butler. 3 vols. London, 1896–98.

Rawlinson, George. The History of Herodotus. 4 vols. New York, 1889.

Redhouse, J. W. Notes on Prof. E. B. Tylor's "Arabian Matriarchate." N. p., 1884.

Redslob, Gustav Moritz. Die Levirats-Ehe bei den Hebräern. Leipzig, 1836.

Rehme, P. "Ueber das Recht der Amaxosa." *ZVR.*, X. Stuttgart, 1892.

Rein, W. Das römische Privatrecht und das Civilprocess. Leipzig, 1836.

Riggs, Stephen Return. "Dakota Grammar, Texts, and Ethnography." Ed. by James Owen Dorsey. *Contributions to North American Ethnology*, IX. Washington, 1893.

Rink, H. J. Tales and Traditions of the Eskimos. Edinburgh and London, 1875.

—— The Eskimo Tribes. Copenhagen and London, 1887.

Risley, H. H. "Primitive Marriage in Bengal." *Asiatic Quarterly Review*, II, 71–96. London, 1886.

Rockhill, William Woodville. "Notes on the Ethnology of Tibet. Based on the Collections in the U. S. National Museum." *Report of the Smithsonian Institution* for 1893, 665–747. "Report of U. S. National Museum." Washington, 1895.

Rogers, E. V. "The Legal Position of Women in Ancient Greece." *Green Bag*, XI, 209–19. Boston, 1899.

Rosenbaum, Julius. Geschichte der Lustseuche im Alterthume, etc. 6th ed. Halle, 1893.

Rossbach, August. Untersuchungen über die römische Ehe. Stuttgart, 1853.

—— Römische Hochzeits- und Ehedenkmäler. Leipzig, 1871.

Roth, Henry Ling. "On the Significance of the Couvade." *Journal of the Anthropological Institute*, XXII, 204–44. London, 1893.

Roth, Henry Ling. The Natives of Sarawak and British North Borneo. 2 vols. London, 1896.

Roth, Walter Edmund. Ethnological Studies among the North-West-Central Queensland Aborigines. Brisbane and London, 1897.

Ryan, A. W. "The Family in Roman Civil Law." *Church Review*, LXIII, 113–39. New York and London, 1891.

Saalschuetz, J. L. Das mosaische Recht. 2 Theile. Berlin, 1846. 2d ed. 1853.

Salomon, Charles. Du mariage du droit des gens et en général des mariages sans connubium. Paris, 1889.

Salt, H. S. Animals' Rights Considered in Relation to Social Progress; with a Bibliographical Appendix. Also an Essay on Vivisection in America by Alfred Leffingwell. New York, 1894.

Sarasin, Paul and Fritz. Die Weddas von Ceylon und die umgebenden Völkerschaften: ein Versuch, die in der Phylogenie des Menschen ruhenden Räthsel der Lösung näher zu bringen. I, Text; II, Atlas. 2 vols. Wiesbaden, 1892–93.

Saravasti, Pundita Ramabai. The High-Caste Hindu Woman. With Introduction by Rachel L. Bodley. 3d ed. Philadelphia, 1888.

Savigny, F. R. von. "Ueber die erste Ehescheidung in Rom." *Abhandlungen der königlichen Akademie der Wissenschaften in Berlin*, 1814–16. Berlin, 1818.

Sayce, A. H. Social Life among the Assyrians and Babylonians. London, 1893.

——— Babylonians and Assyrians: Life and Customs. New York, 1899.

Schäffle, G. F. Bau und Leben des socialen Körpers. 2d ed. 4 vols. Tübingen, 1881.

Schellong, O. "Ueber Familienleben und Gebräuche der Papuas der Umgebung von Finschhafen." *ZFE.*, XXI., 10–25. Berlin, 1889.

Schenk, Leopold. Einfluss auf das Geschlechtsverhältniss. 3d ed. Magdeburg and Vienna, 1898.

Scherzer, Ferrand. La puissance paternelle en Chine: étude de droit chinois. Paris, 1878.

Schlagintweit, E. "Die Hindu-Wittwe in Indien." *Globus*, XLIII, 246–48. Braunschweig, 1883.

Schmoller, G. "Die Urgeschichte der Familie." In his *Jahrbücher*, I (1899).

Schmidt, Franz. Sitten und Gebräuche bei Hochzeiten, Taufen, und Begräbnissen in Thüringen. Weimar, 1863.

Schmidt, Karl. Jus primae noctis. Freiburg, 1881.

Schmidt, Karl. Slavische Geschichtsquellen zur Streitfrage über das Jus Primae Noctis. Posen, 1886.

Schmidt R. De hymenaeo et talasio dis veterum nuptialibus. Kiliae, 1886.

Schneider, Wilhelm. Die Naturvölker: Missverständnisse, Missdeutungen, und Misshandlungen. 2 Theile. Paderborn and Münster, 1885–86.

Schrader, O. Sprachvergleichung und Urgeschichte. Jena, 1883.

—— Prehistoric Antiquities of the Aryan Peoples. Trans. by F. B. Jevons from the 2d ed. London, 1890.

Schrenck-Notzing, A. von. Therapeutic Suggestion in Psychopathia Sexualis, with Special Reference to Contrary Sexual Instinct. Trans. by Charles Gilbert Chaddock. Philadelphia and London, 1895.

Schroeder, L. von. Die Hochzeitsgebräuche der Esten. Berlin, 1888.

Schultz, Hermann. De jure succedendi feminarum apud Romanos, ejusque mutati caussis. Trajecti ad Rhenum, 1826.

Schurman, J. G. The Ethical Import of Darwinism. New York, 1888.

Seebohm, Frederic. The Tribal System in Wales. London and New York, 1895.

Seebohm, Hugh E. On the Structure of Greek Tribal Society. London and New York, 1895.

Selden, J. Uxor ebraica, seu de nuptiis et divortiis ex jure civile, id est, divino et talmudico, veterum Hebraeorum, libri tres. Editio nova, 4to. Francofurte ad Oderam, 1673. Or the same in Opera omnia, II (III, as bound).

—— Opera omnia, tam edita quam inedita. Folio. 3 vols., bound in 6. London, 1726.

Sharp, Elizabeth A. "Papyri and Antiquities from Oxyrhynchus." Independent, LI, 2043, 2044. New York, 1899.

Simcox, Edith J. Primitive Civilization. 2 vols. London and New York, 1894.

—— "The Native Australian Family." Nineteenth Century, XLVI, 51–64. London, 1899.

Smith, Arthur H. Chinese Characteristics. London, 1899.

—— Village Life in China: A Study in Sociology. New York, Chicago, and Toronto, [1899].

Smith, Mrs. James, and Stewart D. The Booandik Tribe of South Australian Aborigines. 1880.

Smith, W. R. Kinship and Marriage in Early Arabia. Cambridge, 1885.

Smithsonian Institution. *Annual Reports of the Board of Regents.* With the *Reports of the U. S. National Museum.* Washington, 1855–97.

Smyth, Brough R. The Aborigines of Victoria. Melbourne and London, 1878.

Sohm, Rudolph. The Institutes of the Roman Law. Trans. by Ledlie. Introductory Essay by Erwin Grueber. Oxford, 1892.

Solotaroff, H. "On the Origin of the Family." *American Anthropologist*, XI, 229–42. Washington, 1898.

Souza, Gabriel Soares de. "Tratado descriptivo do Brazil em 1587." *Revista do Instituto historico e geographico do Brazil,* XIV. Rio de Janeiro, 1851.

Spencer, Baldwin, and Gillen, F. G. The Native Tribes of Central Australia. London and New York, 1895.

Spencer, Herbert. Principles of Sociology. 2 vols. New York, 1879–86.

—— "A Rejoinder to Mr. McLennan." In his Various Fragments. New York, 1898. The same in *Fortnightly Review,* XXVII, 895–902. London, 1877.

—— "The Status of Women and Children." *Popular Science Monthly,* XI, 433–55. New York, 1877.

—— "The Evolution of the Family." *Ibid.,* XI, 129–42, 257–71. New York, 1877.

Stade, Hans. The Captivity of Hans Stade of Hesse, in A. D. 1547–1555, among the Wild Tribes of Eastern Brasil. Trans. by Albert Tootal, of Rio de Janeiro, and annotated by Richard Burton. Hakluyt Society, London, 1874.

Starcke, C. N. The Primitive Family. New York, 1889.

—— "On Human Marriage [Westermarck's]." *International Journal of Ethics,* III, 452–65. Philadelphia, 1893.

Stegeren, D. De conditione civili feminarum atheniensium. Zwallae, 1839.

Steinen, Karl von den. Durch Centralbrasiliens: Expedition zur Erforschung der Schingú im Jahre 1884. Leipzig, 1886.

—— Unter den Naturvölkern Brasiliens: Reiseschilderung und Ergebnisse der zweiten Schingú-Expedition, 1887–8. Berlin, 1894.

Stephen, A. M. "The Navajo." *American Anthropologist,* VI, 345–62. Washington, 1893.

Stevenson, Matilda Coxe. "The Sia." *XI. Report of the Bureau of Ethnology,* 3–157. Washington, 1894.

Stillé, C. J. "Women in Ancient Greece and Rome." *Lippincott's Magazine,* XXXII, 107–17. Philadelphia, 1883.

Stricker, Wilhelm. Die Amazonen in Sage und Geschichte. Berlin, 1868.

Stricker, Wilhelm. "Ethnologische Untersuchungen über die kriegerischen Weiber (Amazonen) der alten und neuen Welt." *Archiv für Anthropologie*, V, 220–25. Braunschweig, 1872.

Stuart-Glennie, John S. "The Origin of Matriarchy." In Garrett's Women of Turkey, II, 547–619. London, 1891.

Stubbe, Chr. Die Ehe im Alten Testament. Jena, 1886.

Szymansky, Maximil. De natura familiae graecae. Berlin, 1840.

Tamuri, Naomi. "The Japanese Bride." In Harper's *Black and White* series. New York, 1893.

Tardieu, Ambroise. De la puissance paternelle en droit romain et en droit français. Paris, 1875.

Tscheng-ki-Tong. The Chinese Painted by Themselves. Trans. from the French by James Millington. London, [1885?].

Tegg, W. The Knot Tied: Marriage Ceremonies of All Nations. London, 1877.

Thomas, William I. "The Relation of Sex to Primitive Social Control." *American Journal of Sociology*, III, 754–76. Chicago, 1898.

—— "On a Difference in the Metabolism of the Sexes." *Ibid.*, III. Chicago, 1898.

—— "Sex in Primitive Morality." *Ibid.*, IV, 774–87. Chicago, 1899.

Thwaites, R. G. "The Wisconsin Winnebagoes." *Wisconsin Historical Collections*, XII. Madison, 1892.

Tillier, L. Le mariage: sa genèse, son évolution. Paris, 1898.

Tillinghast, Joseph Alexander. "The Negro in Africa and America." *Publications of the American Economic Association*, III. New York, 1902.

Titsingh. Cérémonies usitées au Japon pour les mariages, les funérailles, et les principales fêtes de l'année. Trans. from the Japanese. 3 vols. Paris, 1822.

Tornauw, N. von. "Das Eherecht nach den Verordnungen des Islams." *ZVR.*, V. Stuttgart, 1884.

Trumbull, H. L. The Blood-Covenant: A Primitive Rite and its Bearing on Scripture. New York, 1885.

—— "Betrothals and Weddings in the East." In his Studies in Oriental Social Life, 7–72. Philadelphia, 1894.

—— The Threshold Covenant. 2d ed. New York, 1896.

Tupper, C. L. Punjab Customary Law. 3 vols. Calcutta, 1881.

Turner, Lucien M. "Ethnology of the Ungava District, Hudson Bay Territory." *XI. Report of the Bureau of Ethnology*, 159–350. Washington, 1894.

Turner, Paul. Slavisches Familienrecht. Strassburg, 1874.

Tylor, E. B.   Researches into the Early History of Mankind. New York, 1878.

———— "On a Method of Investigating the Development of Institutions; Applied to Laws of Marriage and Descent." *Journal of the Anthropological Institution*, XVIII, 245–72. London, 1889.

———— "The Matriarchal Family System." *Nineteenth Century*, XL, 81–96. London, 1896.

Unger, J.   Die Ehe in ihrer welthistorischen Entwicklung. Vienna, 1850.

Vambéry, Hermann.   Der Islam im neunzehnten Jahrhundert Leipzig, 1875.

———— Das Türkenvolk. Leipzig, 1885.

Veblen, Thorstein.   "The Instinct of Workmanship and the Irksomeness of Labor." *American Journal of Sociology*, IV, 187–201.   Chicago, 1898–99.

———— "The Beginnings of Ownership." *Ibid.*, IV, 352–65. Chicago, 1898–99.

———— "The Barbarian Status of Woman." *Ibid.*, IV, 503–14. Chicago, 1898–99.

Veuillot, Louis.   Le droit du seigneur au moyen âge. 3d ed. Paris, 1878.

Vidyasagar, E. C.   Widow Marriage among Hindus.   Calcutta, 1855.

Vignoli, Tito.   Ueber das Fundamentalgesetz der Intelligenz im Tierreiche.   Leipzig, 1879.

Vincenti, Ch. von.   Die Ehe im Islam.   Vienna, 1876.

Volkov, Théodore.   "Rites et usages nuptiaux en Ukräine." *L'Anthropologie*, II, 160–84, 407–37, 537–87; III, 541–63. Paris, 1891–92.

Wächter, K.   Ueber die Ehescheidung bei den Römern.   Stuttgart, 1822.

Wagner, Moriz.   "Die Kulturzüchtung des Menschen gegenüber der Naturzüchtung im Tierreich." *Kosmos*, 1886, I.

Waitz, Theodor.   Anthropologie der Naturvölker.   6 vols.   Leipzig, 1858–77.   Vol. I, 2d ed.;   and Vols. V and VI, 1st ed., ed. by George Gerland.

Wake, C. Staniland.   Le mariage communal.   Paris, 1875.   (A reply to M. Barbier.)

———— "The Origin of the Classificatory System of Relationship Used among Primitive Peoples." *Journal of the Anthropological Institute*, VIII, 144–80.   London, 1879.

———— "The Primitive Human Family." *Ibid.*, IX, 1–17.   London, 1880.

Wake, C. Staniland. "The Nature and Origin of Group Marriage." *Ibid.*, XIII, 151–61. London, 1884.

—— The Primitive Human Horde. London, 1888. Reprinted from *ibid.*, February, 1888.

—— Serpent-Worship, and Other Essays. London, 1888.

—— The Development of Marriage and Kinship. London, 1889.

—— "The Growth of the Marriage Relation." In Sociology, Popular Lectures and Discussions before the Brooklyn Ethical Association, 69–87. Boston, 1890.

Wallace, A. R. Tropical Nature, and Other Essays. London, 1878.

—— Darwinism: An Exposition of ⸢the Theory of Natural Selection. London, 1891.

Weber, A. F. "Vedische Hochzeitssprüche." In his Indische Studien, V, 177–266. Berlin, 1862.

Wessely, Karl. "Ein griechischer Heiratscontract vom Jahre 136 n. Chr." *Xenia Austriaca*, I, 59–77. Vienna, 1893.

Westermarck, Edward. The History of Human Marriage. London and New York, 1891; 2d ed., practically unchanged, 1894.

—— "A Reply to Starcke's 'Westermarck on Marriage.'" *International Journal of Ethics*, IV, 94–101. Philadelphia, 1893. (See Starcke.)

Wilken, G. A. Das Matriarchat (das Mutterrecht) bei den alten Arabern. Leipzig, 1884.

Willoughby, C. "Indians of the Quinaielt Agency, Washington Territory." *Report of the Smithsonian Institution* for 1886, Part I, 267–82. Washington, 1889.

Winternitz, M. "On a Comparative Study of Indo-European Customs, with Special Reference to the Marriage Customs." *Transactions of the International Folk-Lore Congress.* London, 1891.

—— "Das altindische Hochzeitsrituell nach dem Apastambiya-Grihyasūtra, und einigen anderen verwandten Werken." *Denkschriften der kaiserlichen Akademie der Wissenschaften*, philologisch-historische Classe, XL, 1–113. Vienna, 1892.

Wlislocki, H. von. "Die Stamm- und Familienverhältnisse der transsilvanischen Zeltzigeuner." *Globus*, LIII, 183 ff. Braunschweig, 1888.

Wood, Edward J. The Wedding Day in All Ages and Countries. New York, 1869.

Wundt, Wilhelm. Vorlesungen über die Menschen- und Thierseele. Hamburg and Leipzig, 1892.

ZFE.=Zeitschrift für Ethnologie. Berlin, 1869 ff.

ZVR.=Zeitschrift für vergleichende Rechtswissenschaft. Ed. by Bernhöft, Cohn, and Kohler. 14 vols. Stuttgart, 1878–1900.

Zimmer, Heinrich. Altindisches Leben. Berlin, 1879.

Zmigrodzki, Michael von. Die Mutter bei den Völkern des arischen Stammes. Munich, 1886.

Zöller, Hugo. Forschungsreisen in der deutschen Kolonie Kamerun. Berlin and Stuttgart, 1886.

II. MATRIMONIAL INSTITUTIONS IN ENGLAND AND UNDER GERMANIC AND CANON LAW

Abbot, Archbishop George. The Case of Impotency as debated in England in that remarkable tryal, *An.* 1613. between Robert, Earl of Essex, and the Lady Frances Howard. 2 vols. (bound in one). London, 1715. (Vol II. is a collection of similar cases by the editor.)

Acidalius, Valens. Disputatio nova contra mulieres, qua probatur eas homines non esse. 1695. (See Gediccus.)

Agrippa, Henry Cornelius. De nobilitate & praecellentia foeminei sexus, libellus, cum orationibus epistolis, etc. [Coloniae], 1567. 1st ed., Coloniae, 1532. (There is an English translation by Henry Care, London, 1670.)

—— De sacramento matrimonij declamatio. (Published with the preceding.)

—— Sermo de vita monastica. (Published with the preceding.)

Alethaeus, Theophilus (Johann Lyser). Discursus politicus de polygamia. 2d ed. Freiburg, 1676. (See Warmund.)

—— Polygamia triumphatrix, id est discursus politicus de polygamia. Cum notis Athanasii Vincenti [Johann Lyser]. Londini Scanorum, 1682.

Allen, T. Paynter (compiler). Opinions of the Hebrew and Greek Professors of the European Universities on the Spiritual Aspect of the Question Regarding the Legalization of Marriage with a Deceased Wife's Sister. London, 1882.

Alleyne, John. The Legal Degrees of Marriage Stated and Considered. 2d ed., corrected and enlarged. With an Appendix containing letters from several divines and others. London, 1774; 2d ed., 1775.

Altenrath, Siegmund. Zur Beurtheilung und Würdigung Martin Luthers. Frankfort, 1889.

Amalfi, Gaetano. Come si sposano in Tegiano; uso populare. Naples, 1888.

Amira, Karl von. Erbenfolge und Verwandtschafts-Gliederung nach den altniederdeutschen Rechten. Munich, 1874.

Amys, J. De matrimonio. Zutphaniae, 1741.

Ancona, Alessandro d'. Usi nuziali dei contadini della Romagna. Pisa, 1878.

Andreae, Karl. Ueber den Einfluss des Irrtums auf die Gültigkeit der Ehe nach katholischem und protestantischem Kirchenrecht. Göttingen, 1893.

Andrews, W. History of the Dunmow Flitch of Bacon Custom. London, 1877.

Arcuarius, Daphnaeus (Laurentius Beger). Kurtze . . . . Betrachtung des in der Natur- und göttlichen Recht begründeten heiligen Ehestandes. [Heidelberg?], 1679.

Armytage, George John (compiler). "Allegations for Marriage Licences Issued by the Vicar-General of the Archbishop of Canterbury, 1660–1679." *Publications of the Harleian Society*, XXXIII, XXXIV. London, 1892.

Asgill, John. A Question upon Divorce. London, 1717.

Ashton, J. Social Life in the Reign of Queen Anne. 2 vols. London, 1882.

—— The Fleet: Its River, Prison, and Marriages. London, 1889.

Ashworth, Philip. Das Witthum (Dower) im englischen Recht. Frankfort a. M., 1899.

Astell, Mary. A Serious Proposal to the Ladies by a Lover of Their Sex. London, 1694; 3d ed., 2 vols., 1697.

—— An Essay in Defence of the Female Sex. London, 1696(?); 3d ed., 1697.

—— Some Reflections upon Marriage. London, 1700; 3d ed., 1706; 4th ed., 1730.

Atherley, E. G. A Practical Treatise of the Laws of Marriage and Other Family Settlements. London, 1813.

Attkins, W. A. Law of Marriage: The Speech of his Grace the Archbishop of Canterbury, in the House of Lords, Feb. 25, 1851, on the Marriages in Affinity Bill, Examined by the Word of God and Common Sense. With an Appendix containing his Grace's speech. Salford, 1851.

Ayrer, Georg Heinrich. De jure connubiorum apud veteres Germanos. 2 parts. Göttingen, 1738.

Baker, Charles E. Husband and Wife, and Married Women's Property Act of 1882. New ed. London, [1882].

Barazetti, Caesar. Das Eherecht mit Ausschluss des ehelichen Vermögensrechts nach dem Code Napoléon und dem badischen Landrecht. Hanover, 1895.

—— Das Eltern- und Kindesrecht nach dem Code Napoléon und dem badischen Landrecht. Hanover, 1896.

Barrett-Lennard, Thomas. The Position in Law of Woman . . . . at Common Law as Modified by . . . . Equity and by Recent Legislation [in England]. London, 1883.

Barrington, D. Observations upon the Statutes, chiefly the more ancient from Magna Charta to the Twenty-first of James the First, c. XXVII. 2d ed., 4to. London, 1766; 3d ed., 1769; 5th ed., 1796.

"Barrister, A." Divorce a vinculo matrimonii, in connection with Holy Scripture. London, 1857.

Baumgart, Bernhard. De concubinatu, a Christo et apostolis prohibito. *Praes.*, J. J. Breithaupt. Halle, 1713.

Beal, W. An Analysis of Palmer's Origines Liturgicae. Cambridge, 1850.

Beames, John. A Translation of Glanville. London, 1812.

Beard, J. R. Notes on Lord John Russell's Marriage Bill. London, 1834.

Beauchet, Ludovic. Étude historique sur le forme du mariage. *Nouvelle Revue Historique*, 1882, 351–93, 631–83. Paris, 1882.

—— Étude historique sur les formes de la célébration du mariage dans l'ancien droit français. Paris, 1883.

—— Formation et dissolution du mariage dans le droit islandais du moyen-âge. Paris, 1887.

Beck, J. J. De conjugalis debiti praestantione, von Leistung der ehelichen Pflicht. N. p., 1706.

Beckman, Johannes Philippus. Specimen juridicum inaugurale de connubiis protestantium cum catholicis secundum leges germanicas. Lugduni Batavorum, 1777.

Behrend, J. Fr. Lex salica. Berlin. 1874.

Belleau, Eusèbe. Des empêchements dirimants de mariage. Lévis, 1889.

Bendeleben, H. De diverso sponsalium et matrimonii iure. *Praes.*, J. H. Boehmer. Halle, 1718, 1738.

Benemann, J. C. De natura matrimonii. *Praes.*, J. S. Stryck. Halle, 1708.

Bennecke, Hans. Die strafrechtliche Lehre vom Ehebruch. I, "Das römische, canonische, und das deutsche Recht bis zur Mitte des XV. Jahrhunderts." Marburg, 1884.

Bérenger-Feraud, L. J. B. "Mariage et progéniture." In his Superstitions et survivances étudiées au point de vue de leur origine et de leurs transformations, II, 175–234. Paris, 1896.

Berg, G. D. Ueber die Verbindlichkeit der kanonischen Ehehindernisse in Betreff der Ehen der Evangelischen: Eine kirchenrechtliche Abhandlung. Breslau, 1836.

Berger, F. L. De praescriptione sponsaliorum. Wittenberg, 1724.

Bernhöft, F. Frauenleben in der Vorzeit. Wismar, 1893.

Bertin, Ernest. Les mariages dans l'ancienne société française. Paris, 1879.

Bessel [Landgerichts-Präsident zu Saarbrücken]. Ueber die gemischten Ehen in kirchlicher und legislativer Hinsicht. Frankfort a. M., 1839.

Besserer, Carl. Versuch einer systematischen Entwickelung des Rechtsverhältnisses der beyden Geschlechter. Part I. Giessen, 1800.

Beust, Joachim. Tractatus de sponsalibus et matrimoniis ad praxim forensem accommodatus. Wittenberg, 1586.

Beza, Theodore. Tractatio de polygamia. Geneva, 1568.

——— Tractatio de repudiis et divortiis. Geneva, 1569.

Bidembach, Felix. De causis matrimonialibus tractatus. Frankfort, 1608.

Biener, F. A. "Beiträge zu der Geschichte der Civilehe." *Zeitschrift für deutsches Recht und Rechtswissenschaft*, XX, 119–47. Tübingen, 1861.

Bierling, E. R. "Kleine Beiträge zur Lehre über Eheschliessung und Trauung." *ZKR.*, XVI, 288–316. Freiburg and Tübingen, 1881.

Bigelow, M. M. Placita Anglo-Normannica: Law Cases from William I. to Richard I. Boston, 1881.

Binder, Matthäus Joseph. Praktisches Handbuch des katholischen Eherechtes. 4th enlarged ed., by Joseph Scheicher. Freiburg, 1891.

Bingham, J. Origines Ecclesiasticae; or, The Antiquities of the Christian Church, and Other Works. 9 vols. London, 1840 ff.

Bingham, J. Foote. The Christian Marriage Ceremony: Its History, Significance, and Curiosities. New York, 1871.

Binney, T. The Men of Glasgow and the Women of Scotland: Reason for Differing from the Rev. Dr. Symington's View on the Levitical Marriage Law. London, n. d.

Binterim, A. J. An matrimonio mixto, cujus ante conjunctionem cautiones sunt pollicitae ecclesiasticae, parochus catholicus (salva conscientia) benedicere possit etiam tunc, quando nupturientes modo coram ministro protestantico matrimonialiter contraxerunt? Düsseldorf, 1847.

Blackstone, William. Commentaries on the Laws of England. By Sharswood. 2 vols. Philadelphia, 1869.

Blount, C. "To justifie the marrying of two sisters, the one after the other." In his Miscellaneous Works, 137–53. N. p., 1695.

Blumstengel, K. G. Die Trauung in evangelischem Deutschland nach Recht und Ritus. Weimar, 1879.

Boeli, F. A. De conjugio nec non consanguinitatis et affinitatis gradibus. Helmstadt, 1699.

Böhmer, J. H. De matrimonio coacto. *Resp.*, B. F. Reichenbach. Presented 1717; published, Halle, 1735.

Böhmer, G. L. De copulae sacerdotalis a deposito clerico furtim impetratae injusto favore. Göttingen, 1745.

Böhmer, G. W. Ueber die Ehegesetze im Zeitalter Karl des Grossen und seiner nächsten Regierungsnachfolger. Göttingen, 1826; Register, Göttingen, 1827.

Bohn, The Standard Library Cyclopaedia of Political, Constitutional, and Forensic Knowledge. 4 vols. London, 1860. (Cited as Bohn, Political Cyclopaedia.)

Born, J. F. De bannis nuptialibus. Leipzig, 1716.

Bouvet, Francisque. De la confession et du célibat des prêtres ou la politique du Pape. Paris, 1845.

Brace, Charles Loring. Gesta Christi; or, A History of Humane Progress under Christianity. 3d ed. New York, 1883.

Bracton, H. de. De legibus et consuetudinibus Angliae. Ed. by Twiss in "Rolls Series." 6 vols. London, 1878–83.

Bracton's Note Book. A collection of cases decided in the king's courts during the reign of Henry the Third, annotated by a lawyer of that time, seemingly by Henry Bratton. Ed. by F. W. Maitland. 3 vols. London, 1887.

Brand, J. Popular Antiquities. Ed. by Ellis. New ed. 3 vols. London, 1873–77.

Bräunig, Karl Ferdinand. Das Recht der Ehescheidung auf Grund der Schrift und Geschichte. Zwickau, 1861.

Breitenbach, G. Chr. Dissertatio de matrimonio allophylorum, sive personarum diversae religionis. Giessen, 1740.

Brentano, Franz. Zur eherechtlichen Frage in Österreich: Krasnopolski's Rettungsversuch einer verlorenen Sache. Berlin, 1896.

Brenz, Johann. Wie yn Ehesachen . . . . zu handeln (1530). In Sarcerius's collections.

Brereton, William. "Travels in Holland, 1634–35." *Chetham Society Publications*, I.

Brett, Thomas. Commentaries on the Present Laws of England. 2d ed. 2 vols. London, 1891.

Briefe über die Civilehe: den Liberalen Oesterreichs gewidmet: "Keine Halbheit." Vienna, 1869.

Bright, J. E. A Treatise on the Law of Husband and Wife, as Respects Property. 2 vols. New York, 1849.

Bright, W. Chapters on Early English Church History. Oxford, 1888.

Britton. The French Text with an English Translation, Introduction, and Notes, by F. M. Nichol. 2 vols. Oxford, 1865.

Brougham, H. "Speech on the Scotch Marriage and Divorce Bill, Sept. 3, 1835." In his Speeches, III, 457–71. London, 1838.

―――― "Discourse on the Law of Marriage, Divorce, and Legitimacy (1835)." *Ibid.*, III, 429–56. London, 1838.

Brouwer, Henry. De jure connubiorum apud Batavos recepto, Libri duo. In quibus jura naturae, divinum, civile, canonicum, prout de nuptiis agunt, referuntur, expenduntur, explicantur. Amsterdam, 1665.

Browne, G. F. The Marriage of Divorced Persons in Church. London, 1896.

Browning, Ernst. An Exposition of the Laws of Marriage and Divorce . . . . in the Court for Divorce and Matrimonial Causes. London, 1872.

Browning, W. E. The Practice and Procedure of the Court for Divorce and Matrimonial Causes. London, 1862.

Bruckner, Hieronymus. Decisiones juris matrimonialis. Gotha, 1724.

Brunner, H. Das anglonormannische Erbfolgesystem. Leipzig, 1869.

——— Deutsche Rechtsgeschichte. 2 vols. Leipzig, 1887; 2d ed., 1892.

——— "Die fränkisch-romanische Dos." *Berliner Sitzungsberichte*, XXIV, 545 ff. Berlin, 1894.

Bucer, Martin. De regno Christi servatoris nostri libri II: Ad Eduardum VI. Angliae regem scripti. Basel, 1557.

——— Argumenti Buceri pro et contra. Original-Manuscript Bucers, "die Gründe für und gegen die Doppelehe des Landgrafen Philipp des Grossmüthigen de anno 1539," veröffentlicht durch v. L. Cassel, 1878.

Buchen, Adam Colbius von. Christliche Predigten über das Buch Tobie | Darinnen | als in einem lustigen Ehespiegel | . . . . fast alles | was vom heyligen Ehestandt und der Haushaltung zu wissen von nöten | ganz kurtz | doch gründlich | erkläret wirdt. Frankfort, 1592.

Bücher, Carl. Die Frauenfrage im Mittelalter. Tübingen, 1882.

Buchka, G. "Die Bedeutung der kirchlichen Trauung im geltenden Rechte." *ZKR.*, XVII. Freiburg and Tübingen, 1882.

——— Das mecklenburgische Ehescheidungsrecht in seinem Verhältniss zur protestantischen Eherechtswissenschaft, und zur Judikatur des Reichsgerichts. Wismar, 1885.

Bucksisch, F. G. De apostolis uxoratis. Die Apostel unseres Herrn Jesu Christi haben alle, ausgenommen Johannes und Paulus, Weiber gehabt. *Praes.*, J. A. Schmid. Wittenberg, 1734.

Buckstaff, Florence G. "Married Women's Property in Anglo-Saxon and Anglo-Norman Law." *Annals of the American Academy of Political and Social Science*, IV. Philadelphia, 1893.

Buddeus, Johann Karl. "Ehebruch." In Ersch and Gruber's Encyclopädie. I. Sect., T. 31, 394–403. Leipzig, 1838.

Buddeus, Johann Karl. Richter, Aemilius Ludwig, and others. "Ehe." *Ibid.*, I. Sect., T. 31, 280 ff., 309 ff. Leipzig, 1838.

Bugenhagen, Johann. De conjugio episcoporum et diaconorum ad venerandum doctorem Wolfgangum Reissenbusch. Wittenberg, 1525.

—— Von Ehebruch und Weglaufen (1539). In Sarcerius's collections.

[Bullinger, Heinrich]. The Christen | State of matrimonye | The orygenall of holy wedlok: whan | where, how, and of whom it was instituted & | ordeyned: what it is: how it ought to proceade: what be the occasions, frute and commodities | thereof. Contrary wise, how shamefull & hor | rible a thinge whordome & aduoutry is: How | one oughte also to chose hym a mete and conue | nient spouse to kepe and increase the mutuall | loue, trouth and dewtie of wedloke: and | how married folkes shulde bring up | their children in the feare | of god | Translated by Myles Couerdale | [1541]. There were a 12mo edition and also an 8vo edition in 1543.

—— Der christlich Ehestand. Zürich, 1579.

Bulwer, Edward (compiler). The Parish Registers of St. Martin-cum-Gregory in the City of York. I and II, 1539–1734: Part IV. York, 1895.

Bunny, Edmund. Of Divorce for Advlterie, and Marrying again: that there is no sufficient warrant so to do. Oxford, 1610.

Burckhardus, Adolph Carl. Dissertatio de poenis secundarum nuptiarum. Marburg, 1717.

Burn, J. S. History of the Fleet Marriages. 2d ed. London, 1834.

—— Registrum ecclesiae parochialis. The History of Parish Registers in England. 2d ed. London, 1862.

Burn, Richard. The Ecclesiastical Law. 4 vols. London, 1842.

Burnet, Gilbert. History of the Divorce of Henry VIII. and Katherine of Aragon. 1690?

—— The History of the Reformation of the Church of England. New ed. 2 vols. London, 1850.

Butler, Charles. On the Marriage of Cousin Germans. Oxford, 1619. (For the Latin edition see Florens.)

Buxtorf, Johann (the younger). Dissertatio de sponsalibus et divortiis. Basel, 1652.

Calixtus, Georg. De conjugio clericorum tractatus. Frankfort, 1653.

Campbell, J. Lives of the Lord Chancellors and Keepers of the Great Seal. 4th ed. 10 vols. London, 1856–57.

Cardwell, E. Documentary Annals of the Reformed Church of England, 1546–1716. Oxford, 1839; the same, 2 vols., 1844.

Carpzov, F. B.   Circa nuptiis personarum diversae religionis. *Praes.*, J. G. Krausius.   Wittenberg, 1735.

Carrance, Évariste.   Le mariage chez nos pères.   Récits et légendes. Bordeaux and Paris, 1872.

Cavilly, Georges de.   La séparation de corps et le divorce à l'usage des gens du monde et la manière de s'en servir.   Manuel des époux mal assortis.   Paris, 1882.

Celibacy.   Recherches philosophiques et historiques sur le célibat. Geneva, 1781.

—— Reflections on Communities of Women and Monastic Institutes.   Taunton, 1815.

—— Letters on the Constrained Celibacy of the Clergy of the Church of Rome.   London, 1816.

—— Aufruf an das aufgeklärte Europa zur Aufhebung des Cölibatgesetzes von einem Priester Ungarns.   Ofen, 1848.

—— Du mariage et du célibat.   Par un chrétien.   Paris, 1863.

—— Der Cölibat in seiner Entstehung, seinen Gründen und Folgen.   Eine Zeitfrage für das bevorstehende Concil.   Von einem katholischen Geistlichen.   Munich, 1869.

Cetty, H.   Die altelsässische Familie.   From the French.   Freiburg, 1891.

Chester, Joseph Lemuel (general editor).   "Allegations for Marriage Licences Issued from the Faculty Office of the Archbishop of Canterbury at London, 1543–1869."   Ed. by G. J. Armytage.   *Publications of the Harleian Society*, XXIV. London, 1886.

—— (general editor).   "Allegations for Marriage Licences Issued by the Bishop of London, 1520–1828."   Ed. by G. J. Armytage.   *Ibid.*, XXV, XXVI.   London, 1887.

—— (general editor).   "Allegations for Marriages Issued by the Dean and Chapter of Westminster, 1558–1699; also, for Those Issued by the Vicar-General of the Archbishop of Canterbury, 1660–1679.   Ed. by G. J. Armytage.   *Ibid.*, XXIII.   London, 1886.

—— (general editor).   London Marriage Licences, 1521–1869. Ed. by Joseph Foster.   London, 1887.

Chronicles of the Divorce Court.   Part I, April, 1861.   London, n. d.

Chronicles of Breaches of Promise.   London, n. d.

Cigoi, Aloys.   Die Unauflösbarkeit der christlichen Ehe und die Ehescheidung nach Schrift und Tradition.   Paderborn, 1895.

Civilehe und Kirchenzucht.   Von einem sächsischen Geistlichen. Meissen, [1875].

Clark, C., and Finnelly, W. (compilers).   Reports of Cases Decided in the House of Lords, X (containing The Queen *v.* Millis). London, 1845.

Cri d'une honnête femme qui réclame le divorce, conformément aux loix de la primitive Église, à l'usage actuel du royaume catholique de Pologne, etc. London, 1770.

Crim. Con. Actions and Trials and other Legal Proceedings relating to Marriage before the passing of the present divorce act. London, n. d.

Croke, Alexander. A Report of the Case of Horner against Liddiard, upon the question of what consent is necessary to the marriage of illegitimate minors (Consistorial Court of London, 1799) . . . . with an Introductory Essay upon . . . . the laws relating to illegitimate children. London, 1800.

Croly, George. The Divine Origin, Appointment, and Obligation of Marriage. London, 1836.

—— Marriage with the sister of a deceased Wife. Injurious to morals, and unauthorized by Holy Scriptures. London, 1849.

Crowder, G. A. Letters of several distinguished members of the Bench of Bishops on . . . . marriage with a deceased wife's sister. 2d ed. London, 1846.

Culmann, F. W. Morganatische Ehe und Ursprung des Feudalwesens. Strassburg, 1880.

Cumming, C. F. Gordon. In the Hebrides. New ed. London, 1886.

Curiöse Rechts-Sache, von Trennung einer durch der Eltern Zwang vollenzogenen Ehe. Frankfort and Leipzig, 1727.

Dahn Felix. Bausteine. Gesammelte kleine Schriften. 6 vols. Berlin, 1879–84.

—— "Das Weib im altgermanischen Recht und Leben." In Sammlung gemeinnütziger Vorträge, No. 7. Prague, n. d.

Daniel, E. The Prayer Book; Its History, Language, and Contents. London, [1877].

Davies, J. L. "Marriage with a Deceased Wife's Sister." In his Social Questions from the Point of View of Christian Theology, 309–26. London, 1885.

Dedekind, Adolf. Das protestantische Ehescheidungsrecht und Verwandtes. Braunschweig, 1872.

[Defoe, Daniel]. A Treatise concerning the Use and Abuse of the Marriage Bed. London, 1727.

—— Religious Courtship: being historical discourses on the necessity of marrying religious wives only. London, 1729.

—— Der rechte Gebrauch des Ehe-Bettes, etc. 2d ed. Leipzig, 1734.

[Delany, Patrick]. Reflections upon Polygamy and the Encouragement given to that Practice in the Scriptures of the Old Testament. By Phileleutherus Dubliniensis. London, 1737.

Delphinus, Hieronymus. Eunuchi Conjugium. Die Capaunen-Heyrath. Hoc est scripta et judicia varia de conjugio inter eunuchum et virginem juvenculam. Halle, 1697.

Denham, J. F. Marriage with a deceased wife's sister not forbidden by the Law of Nature; not dissuaded by Expediency; not prohibited by the Scriptures. London, 1847.

Denton, W. England in the Fifteenth Century. London, 1888.

Desminis, Demosthenes D. Die Eheschenkung nach römischem und insbesondere byzantinischem Recht. Athens, 1897.

Dezert, G. Desdevises du. Les unions irrégulières en Navarre sous le régime du Fuero Général. Caen, 1892.

Didon, P. Indissolubilité et divorce. Conférences de Saint-Philippe du Roule. 4th ed. Paris, 1880. Also a German translation. Regensburg, 1893.

Dieckhoff, A. W. Die kirchliche Trauung, ihre Geschichte im Zusammenhange mit der Entwickelung des Eheschliessungsrechts und ihr Verhältniss zur Civilehe. Rostock, 1878.

—— Civilehe und kirchliche Trauung. Das Gegensatzverhältniss zwischen beiden dargelegt. Rostock, 1880.

Dietrick, Hans C. Evangelisches Ehescheidungsrecht nach den Bestimmungen der deutschen Kirchenordnungen des 16. Jahrhunderts. Erlangen, 1892.

"Divorce." *Law Review*, I. London, 1845.

Divorce. Essay upon Divorcement writ for the good of both sexes. London, 1715.

—— Treatise concerning Adultery and Divorce. London, 1700.

—— Cases of, for several Causes. London, 1715.

—— Ueber den einzig wahren Ehescheidungsgrund in der christlichen Kirche so wie in christlichen Staaten. Von einem Fürsten. Bayreuth, 1838.

Divorce Cases. Die interessantesten Ehescheidungsprocesse der älteren und neueren Zeit. Leipzig, n. d.

Divorce controversy. Controversiae circa jura divortiorum editis opusculis agitatae et boni publici causa collectae atque coniunctim editae. 2d ed. Halle, 1729. Comprising:
1. Kayser, J. F. De jure principis evangelici circa divortia.
2. Lange, J. M. Gründlicher Beweiss, dass die Divortia, oder Ehescheidungen, jurae naturae verbothen seyn, etc.
3. Kayser, J. F. Gegen-Beweiss, Dass die Ehescheidungen dem natürlichen und geoffenbarten göttlichen Recht nicht gänzlich verboten, etc. Halle, 1716.
4. Lange, J. M. Göttlich-triumphirende Wahrheit seines gründlichen Beweises, etc., anno 1717.
5. Michaelis, K. F. Sanam de jure principis evangelici circa divortia doctrinam, 1730.

6. Kayser, J. F.   Fundamenta doctrina de divortiis [against Michaelis].   Halle, 1730.

Dodd, J. A.   History of the Canon Law.   London, 1884.

Dodson, John.   A report of the judgment . . . . of Sir William Scott . . . . in the cause of Dalrymple the wife, against Dalrymple the husband.   With an Appendix containing papers, etc. London, 1811.

Döllinger, J. J. I.   Ueber gemischte Ehen.   5th ed.   Regensburg, 1838.

——— Lehrbuch der Kirchengeschichte.   2d ed.   2 vols.   Regensburg, 1843.

——— Heidenthum und Judenthum.   Vorhalle zur Geschichte des Christenthums.   Regensburg, 1857.

Douce, Francis.   Illustrations of Shakespeare.   2 vols.   London, 1807.

[Dugard, Samuel].   The Marriage of Cousin Germans, vindicated from the censures of Unlawfullnesse, and Inexpediency.   Oxford, 1673.

Duke, Henry H.   The Question of Incest.   London, 1883.

Du Plessis de Grenédan.   Histoire de l'autorité paternelle dans l'ancien droit français.   Paris, 1900.

Dwight, Sereno Edwards.   The Hebrew Wife: or, The law of marriage, examined in relation to the lawfulness of polygamy, and to the extent of the law of incest.   With Introductory recommendation by Ralph Wardlaw.   Glasgow, 1837.

Early English Text Society.   Original series, CVIII.   London, 1897.

Eckestein, P. H.   De divortio ex causa desertionis.   *Praes.*, B. Bardili.   Tübingen, 1675.

Eckenstein, Lina.   Woman under Monasticism.   Cambridge, 1896.

Eckhardt, F. W.   "Das Witthum oder Dotalitium und Vidualitium in ihrer historischen Entwickelung."   *Zeitschrift für deutsches Recht*, X, 437 ff.   Tübingen, 1846.

Edelmann, C. G.   De legitimis impedimentis ex jure germanico. *Praes.*, Wilhelm Hoffmann.   Frankfort, 1736.

Edgar, A.   "Marriage in Olden Times."   In his Old Church Life in Scotland, 134–203.   2d series.   London, 1886.

Ehebund, der, im Bereich der Kirche und des Staates . . . . von einem protestantischen Geistlichen beym Königl. Sächs. Appellations-Gerichte.   Zwickau, 1839.

Eichborn, Hermann.   Das Ehehinderniss der Blutsverwandtschaft nach kanonischem Rechte.   Breslau, 1872.

Eliot, E. G.   Marriage Bill.   Speeches of the Earl of St. Germans and Viscount Gage in the House of Lords, Feb. 25, 1851. London, 1851.

Ellendorf, J. Welchen Sinn hat das Breve vom 25. März 1830 in Betreff der gemischten Ehen, und wie verhält sich zu selbem die bekannte Instruktion? Berlin, 1838.

Ellough (Suffolk), The Parish Registers of. Privately printed, 1886.

Elphinstone, Howard W. "Notes on the English Law of Marriage." *Law Quarterly Review*, V. London, 1889.

Erasmus, Desiderius. "Christiani matrimonii institutio." In Opera Omnia, V, 615–723. Folio. Lugduni Batavorum, 1704. (First separate ed., Basel, 1526.)

——— De matrimonio christiano. Lugduni Batavorum, 1650.

Erler, Julius. Ehescheidungsrecht und Ehescheidungsprozess. 2d ed. Berlin, 1900.

Ernst, W. A Treatise of Marriage and Divorce. London, 1879.

Esmein, A. Le mariage en droit canonique. 2 vols. Paris, 1891.

Essays in Anglo-Saxon Law. Boston, 1876.

Essich, J. P. De clericis maritis dissertatio historica. Augusta Vindelicorum, 1747.

Evans, Sir W. D. (compiler). A Collection of Statutes. 8 vols. London, 1823.

Ewald, E. C. "The Fleet Marriages." In his Paper and Parchment, 227–48. London, 1890.

Exeter, Lord Bishop of. Marriage with Deceased Wife's Sister. Exeter, 1882.

Facts and Opinions Tending to Show the Scriptural Lawfulness of Marriage with a Deceased Wife's Sister. London, 1872.

Ferguson, R. S. A Boke of Recorde or Register of the Burgh of Kirby Kendal. Kendal and Carlisle, 1892.

Fergusson, J. Report of some Decisions by the Consistorial Court of Scotland, in actions of Divorce, 1811–17. Edinburgh, 1817.

Feyerabend, J. D. De privilegiis mulierum. *Praes.*, J. V. Bechmann. Presented, 1667; published, Jena, 1672.

Ficker, Julius. Untersuchungen zur Rechtsgeschichte. 4 vols. Innsbruck, 1891–99.

Filarete, Prodicogine. Difesa delle donne contra la falsa narratione di Onofrio Filiriaco intorno l'operationi loro. Padua, 1588.

Fischell, E. De conjugum jure germanico debitis. Berlin, n. d.

Fischer, A. "Die älteste evangelische Kirchenordnung und die frühesten Kirchenvisitationen in Hohenlohe." *ZKR.*, XV, 1–48. Freiburg and Tübingen, 1880.

Fitzherbert, A. The new Natura Brevium. Dublin, 1793.

Fleiner, Fritz. Obligatorische Civilehe und katholische Kirche. Eine kirchenrechtliche Abhandlung. Leipzig, 1890.

Fleiner, Fritz. Die tridentinische Ehevorschrift. Leipzig, 1892.

Fleta seu commentarius juris Anglicani sic nuncupatus sub Eduardo rege primo. With Selden's Ad Fletam dissertatio. 2d ed. London, 1685.

Florens, Francis. Tractatus de nuptiis consobrinarum prohibitis aut permissis. Et Caroli Butleri Magd. Suggenia sive de propinquitate matrimonium impediente regula. Frankfort, 1643.

Forbes, Lord. Marriage with a Deceased Wife's Sister. Aberdeen and London, 1883.

Forbidden Degrees. The Relationships Which Bar Marriage Considered Scripturally and Socially. London, 1873.

Forster, V. G. De nuptiis. Wittenberg, 1617.

Foster, T. Campbell. A review of the law relating to marriages within the prohibited degrees of affinity and of the canons and social considerations by which the law is supposed to be justified. London, 1847.

Fraenkel, Arnold. Das Familienrecht des bürgerlichen Gesetzbuchs für das deutsche Reich. Hanover, 1898.

Fraser, Patrick. Conflict of Laws in Cases of Divorce. Edinburgh, 1860.

Frati, L. "Costumanzi e pompe nuziali bolognesi nel medio evo." In Nozze Cian-Sappa-Flandinet. Bergamo, 1894.

Fredegarius (Scholasticus). Ex Sancti Georgii Florentii Gregorii, Episcopi Turonensis, Historia Francorum Epitomata. Excerpta. In Guadet and Turanne's trans. of Gregory, IV, 159–86. Paris, 1838.

Freeman, Edward A. Comparative Politics. London, 1873.

Freisen, Joseph. Geschichte des canonischen Eherechts bis zum Verfall der Glossenlitteratur. Tübingen, 1888; 2d ed., Paderborn, 1893.

Frensdorff, F. "Ein Urtheilsbuch des geistlichen Gerichts zu Augsburg aus dem 14. Jahrhundert." ZKR., X. Tübingen, 1871.

Freybe, Albert. Altdeutsches Frauenlob. Züge deutscher Sitte und Gesinnung aus dem Frauenleben. Leipzig, 1873.

—— Das deutsche Haus und seine Sitte. Gütersloh, 1892.

Friedberg, Emil. "Zur Geschichte der Eheschliessung." 2 articles. ZKR., I, III. Berlin and Tübingen, 1861–63.

—— Aus der protestantischen Eherechtspflege des sechszehnten Jahrhunderts. Mit ungedruckten Briefen und Bedenken Melanchthons. Ibid., IV. Tübingen, 1864.

—— Das Recht der Eheschliessung. Leipzig, 1865.

—— "Beiträge zur Geschichte des brandenburgisch-preussischen Eherechts." ZKR., VI, VII. Tübingen, 1866–67.

Friedberg, Emil. Verlobung und Trauung. Leipzig, 1876.

—— Die Geschichte der Civilehe. Berlin, 1877.

—— Lehrbuch des katholischen und evangelischen Kirchenrechts. 2d ed. Leipzig, 1884.

—— and Dr. Wasserschleben. "Zwei Gutachten erstattet dem deutschen Juristentag über das Connubium zwischen Christen und Nichtchristen." *ZKR.*, IX. Tübingen, 1870.

Friedericus, Georgius. De divortio meditationes. Leipzig, 1842.

Friedericus, Philipp. De adulterio desponsatorum. Vulgo vom Ehebruch der Verlobten. New ed. Jena, 1743.

Fritsche, Johann. Unvorgreiffliche Erörterung der Frage: Was von der Polygamie oder Viel-Weiberey zu halten sey? Hamburg, 1677.

Fröböse, J. C. W. Dr. Martin Luther's ernste, kräftige Worte über Ehe und eheliche Verhältnisse. Hanover, 1829.

Froude, James. The Divorce of Catherine of Aragon. New York, 1891.

Fry, John. Some considerations on the act to prevent clandestine marriages in a letter from a gentleman of the Temple to the Lord B—p of L—. London, 1754.

—— The case of marriages between near kindred. London, 1756; 2d ed., 1773.

Furnivall, F. J. Child-Marriages, Divorces, and Ratifications, etc., in the Diocese of Chester, A. D. 1561–66. Also Entries in the Mayors' Books, Chester, 1558–1600. Edited from the MS. written in court while the witnesses made their depositions, and from the Mayors' Books. Being Vol. CVIII, original ser., *Early English Text Society Publications.* London, 1897.

Gage, Matilda Joslyn. Woman, Church, and State. A Historical Account of the Status of Woman through the Christian Ages. With Reminiscences of the Matriarchate. Chicago, 1893.

Gairdner, James. "New Lights on the Divorce of Henry VIII.," in *English Historical Review*, XI, XII. London, 1896–97.

Gally, Henry. Some Considerations upon Clandestine Marriages. London, 1730; 2d ed., 1750.

Galy, Charles. La famille à l'époque mérovingienne. Étude faite principalement d'après les Récits de Grégoire de Tours. Paris, 1901.

Garreau, L. L'état social de la France au temps des croisades. Paris, 1899.

Gataker, Thos. A marriage prayer or succinct meditations . . . . London, printed by Anne Griffin for Fulke Clifton, 1637.

Gautier, Léon. La chevalerie. Paris, 1884.

Geary, N. The Law of Marriage and the Family Relations. London, 1892.

Gediccus, Simon. Disputatio perjucunda, qua anonymus probare nititur mulieres homines non esse [per Valentem Acidalium]: cui opposita est Sim. Gedicci defensio sexus muliebris. Hagae-Comitis, 1644; 1st ed., 1595.

Gee, H., and Hardy, W. J. Documents Illustrative of English Church History. London, 1896.

Geffcken, Heinrich. Zur Geschichte der Ehescheidung vor Gratian. Leipzig, 1894.

—— "Zur ältesten Geschichte und ehegerichtlichen Praxis des Leipziger Konsistoriums." ZKR., 3. Folge, IV, 7–67. Freiburg and Leipzig, 1894.

Gennari, Ab. Giuseppe. Degli usi de' Padovani de' tempi di mezzo ne' loro matrimonj memoria. Letta . . . . e pubblicata nel giorno delle faustissime nozze del N. H. E. Gio: Antonio Baglioni e della N. D. Foscarina Papafava. Venice, 1800.

Gengler, H. G. De morgengaba secundum leges antiquissimas Germanorum. Bamberg, 1843.

Gentleman's Magazine. London, 1731–.

Gentleman's Magazine Library. "Manners and Customs." Ed. by George Lawrence Gomme. Boston, n. d.

Gerigk, Hubert. Irrtum und Betrug als Ehehindernnisse nach kirchlichem und staatlichem Rechte. Breslau, 1898.

—— Das Ehehinderniss des Irrtums im kanonischen Rechte. Breslau, 1898.

Gerlach, Otto von. Kirchenrechtliche Untersuchung der Frage: Welches ist die Lehre und das Recht der evangelischen Kirche, zunächst in Preussen, in Bezug auf die Ehescheidungen und die Wiederverheirathung geschiedener Personen? Abdruck aus der Zeitschrift für Protestantismus und Kirche. Erlangen, 1839.

Giachi, V. Amori e costumi latini. Città di Castella, 1885.

Gibson, James. Marriage Affinity Question: or, Marriage with the Sister of a Deceased Wife Fully Discussed. Edinburgh, 1854.

Giesebrecht, Wilhelm von. "Sagen aus Fredegar und der Chronik der Frankenkönige." In his translation of Gregory, II., 363–81. Leipzig, n. d.

Giles, W. A Treatise on Marriage. London, 1771.

Gilman, Herbert Webb. Index to the Marriage Licence Bonds of the Diocese of Cork and Ross, Ireland, from 1623 to 1750. Cork, 1896–97.

Girault, Ch. De la prohibition du mariage entre le beau-frère et la belle-sœur, l'oncle et la nièce, la tante et le neveu. Observations sur la proposition de loi tendant à modifier la rédaction des art. 331 et 335 du Code Civil sur la légitimation des enfants nés hors mariage. Extrait de la *Revue pratique de droit français*. Paris, 1874.

Gladstone, W. E. "The Bill for Divorce (1857)." In his Gleanings of Past Years, II, 47–106. London, 1879.

Glasson, E. Le mariage civil et le divorce dans l'antiquité et dans les principales législations modernes de l'Europe. 2d ed. Paris, 1880.

―――― Histoire du droit et des institutions politiques, civiles et judiciaires de l'Angleterre. 6 vols. Paris, 1882–83.

―――― Observations sur la famille et la propriété chez les Germains. Orléans, 1885.

―――― Le droit de succession dans les lois barbares. Paris, 1886.

―――― "Décadence du mariage religieux et origine du mariage civil au XVIIIᵉ siècle." *Académie des sciences morales et politiques*, December, 1899.

Godolphin, J. Repartorium canonicum; or, an Abridgment of the Ecclesiastical Laws of the Realm, consistent with the Temporal. 3d ed. London, 1687.

Goeze, J. M. Die geretete Ehre der Ehe mit der verstorbenen Frauen Schwester. Halberstadt, 1707.

Golz, H. De morgengaba Germanorum. Halle, *ca*. 1860.

Göschel, Jacob Marian. Versuch einer historischen Darstellung der kirchlich-christlichen Ehegesetze von Christus bis auf die neuesten Zeiten in vier Perioden. Nebst einem Anhange: Über die alten Gebräuche bei der kirchlichen Ehe-Einsegnung. Aschaffenburg, 1832.

Göschen, O. Doctrina de matrimonio ex ordinationibus ecclesiae evangelicae saeculi decimi sexti adumbrata. Halle, 1848.

―――― "Ehe," in Herzog's *Encyclopœdie*, III, 666–707. Stuttgart and Hamburg, 1855.

Gramberg, D. De jure patrum-familias. Leipzig, 1677.

Graunt, John. Natural and Political Observations mentioned in the following Index, and made upon the Bills of Mortality. Reprint of 3d ed. Oxford, 1665.

Great Britain. "First Report of the Commissioners appointed to inquire into . . . . the . . . . law of . . . . the Prohibited Degrees of Affinity, and . . . . Marriages Solemnized Abroad or in the British Colonies, etc." *British Documents*, XXVIII. Folio. London. 1848.

―――― "First Report of the Commissioners appointed . . . . to inquire into the Law of Divorce, etc." *Ibid.*, XL. Folio. London, 1853.

―――― "Divorce. Evidence before the Select Committee of the House of Lords, appointed to consider Lord Brougham's

Bill, presented in 1844, to amend the jurisdiction of Committee of the Privy Council." Reprinted, *ibid.*, XL. Folio. London, 1853.

Great Britain. "Report of the Royal Commission on the Laws of Marriage, 1868." *Ibid.*, XXXII. London, 1868.

Gregorovius, J. A. De matrimonio personarum diversae religionis. *Praes.*, Theodor Paul. Regiomonti, 1712.

Gregory's Pastoral Care. King Alfred's West-Saxon Version. Ed. by Henry Sweet. Early English Text Society, XLV. London, 1871.

Greiff, J. E. De pactis futurorum sponsaliorum, von Ja-Wort. *Praes.*, Ch. Thomassius. Halle, 1712.

Greve, August. Wer hat bei Christen das Recht von Gott die Ehe zu schliessen, der Staat oder die Kirche? Hermannsburg, 1878.

[Greve, T.]. Die Ehescheidung nach der Lehre des Neuen Testamentes. Leipzig, 1873.

Griffin-Stonestreet, Geo. Stonestreet. Nuptiae sacrae: Objections to the amended Unitarian Marriage Bill of 1827. London, 1828.

Grimm, Jacob. Deutsche Rechtsalterthümer. 2d ed. Göttingen, 1854.

—— "Nothzucht der Frauen." *Zeitschrift für deutsches Recht*, V, 1–29; IX, 330–36. Leipzig, 1841; Tübingen, 1845.

Grohman, W. A. B. Gaddings with a Primitive People: Being a Series of Sketches of Tyrolese Life and Customs. New York, 1878.

Grünwald, A. Die Eheschliessung . . . . nebst einem Anhange: Die Ehehindernisse und ihre rechtliche Eintheilung. Vienna, 1881.

Grupen, Christian Ulrich. De virgine prae vidua ducenda. Oder: Dass es besser sey, ein jung Mädgen zu heirathen, als eine junge Wittwe. 3d ed. Lemgoviae, 1740.

—— De uxore theotisca, von der teutschen Frau. Insbesondere de virginum praegustatoribus, jure deflorationis, jure primae noctis, Maiden-Rents, Marcheta, etc., etc. Göttingen, 1748.

Gubernatis, Angelo de. Storia comparata degli usi nuziali in Italia e presso gli altri popoli Indo-Europei. 2d ed. Milan, 1878.

Gundling, N. H. De emtione uxorum, dote et morgengaba. Leipzig, 1731.

Güpner, J. B. Dissertatio inauguralis juridica, De jure thalami, vom Rechte des Ehe-Bettes. Jena, 1703.

H. J. S. Des mariages entre parents. Paris, 1821.

Habicht, H. Die altdeutsche Verlobung in ihrem Verhältniss zu dem Mundium und der Eheschliessung. Jena, 1879.

Haddan and Stubbs. Councils and Ecclesiastical Documents. Ed. after Spelman and Wilkins. 3 vols. Clarendon Press, 1869–78.

Haggard, John (compiler). Reports of Cases argued and determined in the Consistory Court of London; containing the judgments of the Right Hon. Sir William Scott. 2 vols. London, 1822. (Containing Dalrymple v. Dalrymple.)

Hahn, G. L. Die Lehre von den Sacramenten in ihrer geschichtlichen Entwicklung innerhalb der abendländischen Kirche bis zum Concil von Trident. Berlin, 1864.

Hale, W. H. A Series of Precedents and Proceedings in Criminal Causes extending from the year 1475 to 1640, extracted from the Act-Books of Ecclesiastical Courts in the Diocese of London. London, 1847.

Hallam, Henry. The Constitutional History of England. 3 vols. New York, 1870.

Hamilton, J. E. A Treatise on Polygamy proving it to be the Will of God: and that Christ was the giver of no New Law, in which are also considered the Just Grounds of Divorce, and what constitutes a Lawful Marriage in the Sight of God. Dublin, 1786.

Hammick, J. T. The Marriage Law of England. 2d ed. London, 1887.

Hanauer, L'Abbé. "Coutumes matrimoniales au moyen âge." Mémoires de l'Académie Stanislas. Nancy, 1892.

Hansard, T. C. (publisher and compiler). The Parliamentary Debates from the Year 1803 to the Present Time. London, 1812 ff.
    First series, 1803–20. 41 vols.
    Second series, 1820–30. 25 vols.
    Third series, 1830–91. 356 vols.

Hanus, J. J. "Erklärung des Wortes 'Morgengaba.'" Abhandlungen der böhmischen Académie. V. Folge, 8. Theil.

Nar, C. von. Erläuterungen zu dem bayerischen Gesetze über Heimat, Verehlichung und Aufenthalt vom 16. April, 1868. Erlangen, 1869.

Hardships of the English Laws in Relation to Wives, The. With an Explanation of the Original Curse of Subjection passed upon the Woman. London, 1735.

Hare, J. C. Vindication of Luther against his Recent English Assailants. 2d ed. Cambridge, 1855.

Harless, G. C. A. Die Ehescheidungsfrage. Eine erneute Untersuchung der neutestamentlichen Schriftstellen. Stuttgart, 1861.

Harpprecht, F. C. De jure liberorum, a desponsatis, ante benedictionem sacerdotalem, nec ex post subsecutam, procreatorum. Presented, 1696. Halle, 1730.

Harpsfield, Nicholas.   Treatise on the Pretended Divorce between Henry VIII. and Catherine of Aragon.   Ed. by Pocock.   Camden Society, new series, 1878.

Harrison, J. Carter.   An Epitome of the Laws of Probate and Divorce.   4th ed.   London, 1891.

Hartmann, J. P.   De secundis nuptiis.   *Praes.*, J. J. Helfferich.   Tübingen, 1745.

Heinlein, Max Ritter Hassarek von.   Die bedingte Eheschliessung. Eine canonistische Studie.   Vienna, 1892.

[Heller, G. W.].   Ueber die Strafe des Ehebruchs nach den Begrifen und Gesetzen der alten und neuen Deutschen.   Ulm, 1773.

Hengham, R.   Summae.   Folio.   London, 1737.   Appended to and bound with Fortescue's De laudibus legum Angliae.   London, 1737.

Hennig, F. E.   De poena bigamiae ordinaria.   *Praes.*, A. F. Schott, Leipzig, 1771.

Hergenhahn, Theodor.   Eheschliessungs- und Ehescheidungs-Recht nach der Rechtsprechung des deutschen Reichsgerichts. 2 vols. (I, 2d ed.).   Hanover, 1890–93.

Hergenröther, P.   Die Civilehe, 1870.

Hermann, Eugen.   Eintracht gibt Macht, oder die dringende Nothwendigkeit für die evangelische Kirche unserer Zeit zu einem gleichmässigen Verfahren in Hinsicht auf die gemischten Ehen sich zu vereinigen, etc.   Düsseldorf, 1844.

Herold, J. B.   Dissertatio juridica de fato matrimonii, vulgo, die Ehen werden im Himmel gemacht.   Frankfort, 1704.

Heusler, Andreas.   Institutionen des deutschen Privatrechts.   2 vols.   Leipzig, 1885–86.

Hildebrand, Joachim.   De nuptiis veterum christianorum libellus. Helmstadt, 1701.

Hildebrand, K.   Untersuchungen über die germanischen Poenitentialbücher.   Würzburg, 1851.

Hill, Richard.   Blessings of Polygamy displayed in an affectionate address to the Rev. Martin Madan occasioned by his work . . . . Thelyphthora.   London, 1781.

Hilse, Karl.   Civil- und Misch-Ehe.   Eine Untersuchung der Fragen wegen Einführung der Civilehe und Freigabe der Mischehen zwischen Christen und Juden.   Nebst eines Eheschliessungsgesetzes.   Berlin, 1869.

Hinschius, Paul.   "Das Ehescheidungsrecht nach den angelsächsischen und fränkischen Bussordnungen."   *Zeitschrift für deutsches Recht und deutsche Rechtswissenschaft*, XX, 66–87. Tübingen, 1861.

——— "Beiträge zur Geschichte des Desertionsprocesses nach evangelischem Kirchenrecht."   *ZKR.*, II.   Berlin, 1862.

Hirschfeld, J. "The Law of Divorce in England and in Germany." *Law Quarterly Review*, XIII. London, 1897.

Hochzeitsgebräuche aller Nationen der Welt. From the French. Schwabach, 1781, 1783.

Hodgetts, J. F. Older England, Illustrated by the Anglo-Saxon Antiquities in the British Museum. London, 1884.

Hoffer, J. B. De secundis nuptiis ad Germanorum mores caute applicanda. Altdorf, 1759.

Hofmann, F. Ueber den Verlobungs- und den Trauring. Vienna, 1870.

Hofmann, Johann Andreas. Handbuch des teutschen Eherechts, nach den allgemeinen Grundsätzen des teutschen Rechts sowohl, als der besondern Landes- Stadt- und Orts-Rechte. Jena, 1789.

Hoffmann, C. P. De die ac nocte nuptiali. Regiomonti and Lipsiae, 1743

—— De aetate juvenili contrahendis sponsalibus ac matrimoniis idonea. Regiomonti and Lipsiae, 1743.

Hoffmann, W. Die christliche Ehe. Berlin, 1860.

Höltzl von Sternstein, J. F. F. Positiones selectae de matrimonio ad morganaticam, Vulgo Vermählung zur linken Hand. Altorffii, 1684.

Holtzmüller, G. S. De mysogynia eruditorum. *Praes.*, M. G. Schroeder. Leipzig, 1717.

Homeyer, G. Ueber die Heimath nach altdeutschem Recht, insbesondere über das Hantgemal. Berlin, 1852.

Homilies, The Old English. Ed. by Richard Morris. Early English Text Society. London, 1868.

Hope, Alex. J. Beresford. The Report of Her Majesty's Commission on the Laws of Marriage, relative to Marriage with a deceased Wife's Sister, examined. 3d ed. London, 1849.

Horne, Andrew. The Mirrour of Justices. Trans. (*ca.* 1646–47) by W. H[ughes]. London, 1768.

—— The Mirror of Justices. Ed. for the Selden Society by W. J. Whittaker. With an Introduction by F. W. Maitland. London, 1895.

Horoy. Du mariage civil du prêtre catholique en France. Paris, 1890.

Hoveden, Robert (editor). The Register Booke of Christenings, Marriages, and Burialls within the Precincts of the Cathedrall and Metropoliticall Church of Christe of Canterburie. London, 1878.

Hovey, A. The Scriptural Law of Divorce. Philadelphia, 1866.

Howell, T. B., and Howell, T. J. A Complete Collection of State Trials, to 1783. 34 vols. London, 1816–28.

Howlett, E. "Marriage Customs." In Andrews's (William) Curious Church Customs, 99–125. 2d ed. London, 1898.

Hoyer, Hermann. Die Ehescheidungsfrage. Ein Versuch zur Ausgleichung der Differenzen zwischen Staat und Kirche. Berlin, 1859.

Hübler, Bernhard. Eheschliessung und gemischte Ehen in Preussen nach Recht und Brauch der Katholiken. Berlin, 1883.

Hubrich, Eduard. Das Recht der Ehescheidung in Deutschland. Berlin, 1891.

Humphrey, William. Christian Marriage. London, 1886.

Hundrich L. Ehen und Scheidungen in älterer und neuerer Zeit, mit Hinsicht auf die neue preussiche Gesetzgebung. Breslau, 1855.

Huschke, C. Was lehrt Gottes Wort über die Ehescheidung? Leipzig, 1860.

——— Beleuchtung der Einwürfe gegen meine Schrift "Was lehrt Gottes Wort über die Ehescheidung?" Leipzig, 1861.

Hutchinson, Peter Orlando. Chronicles of Gretna Green. 2 vols. London, 1844.

Huth, A. H. "Index to Books and Papers on Marriage between Near Kin." *Report of First Annual Meeting of the Index Society*, 25–47. London, 1879.

——— The Marriage of Near Kin. 2d ed. London, 1887.

Inderwick, F. A. The Interregnum. London, 1891.

Ireland, J. Nuptiae sacrae; or an Inquiry into the Scriptural Doctrine of Marriage and Divorce. Addressed to the Two Houses of Parliament. London, 1801; reprinted 1821, 1830.

James I. The workes of the most High And Mightie Prince James. Folio. London, 1616.

Jastrow, Ignaz. "Zur strafrechtlichen Stellung der Sklaven bei Deutschen und Angelsachsen." In Gierke's *Untersuchungen*, 2. Breslau, 1878.

Jeaffreson, John Cordy. Brides and Bridals. 2 vols. London, 1872.

——— (editor). Middlesex County Records. 3 vols. Published by the Middlesex County Record Society. London, n. d.

Jenks, E. Constitutional Experiments of the Commonwealth. Cambridge, 1890.

Jessopp, A. The Coming of the Friars. 5th ed. New York, 1892.

Johnson, J. A Collection of all the Ecclesiastical Laws, Canons, etc., concerning the Church of England. With Notes by Baron. 2 vols. Oxford, 1850–51.

Johnstoun, James. A juridical dissertation concerning the Scripture doctrine of marriage contracts, and the marriages of Cousin-Germans. Illustrated from the canon, civil, and statute-law. London, 1734.

Jones, W. Finger-Ring Lore, Historical, Legendary, Anecdotal. 2d ed. London, 1890.

Jordan, S. Programma observationes quasdam in doctrinam de morgengaba germanica continens. Heidelberg, 1721.

Kahl, W. "Civilehe und kirchliches Gewissen." *ZKR.*, XVIII, 295–367. Freiburg and Tübingen, 1883.

Kawerau, W. "Die Reformation und die Ehe." *Schriften des Vereins für Reformationsgeschichte*, X. Halle, 1892.

Keble, John. Against profane dealing with holy matrimony in regard of a man and his wife's sister. Oxford, 1849.

—— Sequel of the Argument against immediately repealing the laws which treat the nuptial bond as indissoluble. Oxford and London, 1857.

Kelham, Robert Britton. Containing the antient Pleas of the Crown. London, 1762.

Kemble, J. M. The Saxons in England. New ed. 2 vols. London, 1876.

Kenny, Courtney Stanhope. The History of the Law of England as to the Effects of Marriage on the Wife's Legal Capacity. London, 1879.

Kettner, F. G. Judicia und Responsa von der Ehe mit des Weibes Schwester. Quedlingburg, n. d.

Kettner, Johann J. "Welche Person von meinen Anverwandten darf ich nicht zur Ehe nehmen?" In his Zwei Abhandlungen. Leipzig, 1780.

Klee, H. Die Ehe. 2d ed. Mayence, 1853.

Klein, August. Das heutige Eherecht im Herzogthum Sachsen-Altenburg. Strassburg, 1881.

—— Das Eheverlöbniss nach gemeinem, sowie nach dem Rechte, wie es auf Grund der Reichsgesetzgebung im Königreich Sachsen und in den zu dem Bezirke des gemeinschaftlichen thüringischen Oberlandesgerichtes zu Jena gehörigen rechtsverwandten Staaten heute gilt. Strassburg, 1881.

Klein, O. Beiträge zur Lehre von der morganatischen Ehe. Erlangen, 1897.

Kling, Melchior. Tractatus matrimonialium causarum. 3d ed. Frankfort, 1577; 1st ed., 1553.

Klitsche, Th. F. Geschichte des Cölibats der katholischen Geistlichen . . . . zum Tode Gregor VII. Augsburg, 1830.

Koehne, C. "Die Geschlechtsverbindung der Unfreien im fränkischen Recht." In Gierke's *Untersuchungen*, XXII. Breslau, 1888.

Koenigswarter, L. J. Histoire de l'organisation de la famille en France. Paris, 1851.

Kohler, F. Das Eherecht des bürgerlichen Gesetzbuchs einschliesslich des ehelichen Güterrechts. Stuttgart, 1898.

Krabbes, Theodor. Die Frau im altfranzösischen Karlsepos. Marburg, 1884.

Kraut, W. T. Die Vormundschaft nach den Grundsätzen des deutschen Rechts. 3 vols. Göttingen, 1835–59.

Krueger, P., and Mommsen, T. Corpus juris civilis. Ed. stereotypa. Berlin, 1872.

Krull, J. De nuptiis. Praes., T. Mevius. Wittenberg, 1632.

Kunstmann, Friedrich. Die lateinischen Poenitentialbücher der Angelsachsen. Mayence, 1844.

Kutschker, Johann B. Die gemischten Ehen von dem katholischkirchlichen Standpuncte aus betrachtet. 2d ed. Vienna, 1838.

Laboulaye, E. Recherches sur la condition civile et politique des femmes. Paris, 1843.

Lagneau, Gustave. Remarques démographiques sur le célibat en France. Paris, 1885.

Lamprecht, Karl. Deutsche Geschichte. I. Berlin, 1891.

Laspeyres, E. A. T. Dissertatio canon. computationis et nuptiarum propter sanguinis propinquitatem ab ecclesia prohibitarum sistens historiam. Berlin, 1825.

Laspeyres, E. H R. De debitis coniugum ex liberarum Germaniae civitatum hanseaticarum jure commentatio. Halle, 1857.

Lathbury, T. A History of the Book of Common Prayer. 2d ed. Oxford and London, 1859.

Lauenstein, Rudolph. Hannoverisches Eherecht. Hanover, 1869.

Lauginger, J. G. De consensu parentum ad nuptias liberorum. Praes., Theodor Paul. Regiomonti, 1699.

Lavves Resolvtions of Womens Rights, The: or, The Lavves Provision for Woemen. A methodicall Collection of such Statutes and Customes, with the Cases, Opinions, Arguments and points of Learning in the Lavv, as doe properly concerne Women. London, 1632.

Lawrence, Basil Edwin. The History of the Laws Affecting the Property of Married Women in England. London, 1884.

Lawton, George. The Marriage Act (4 Geo. IV., cap. 76). London, 1823.

Lea, Henry C. A History of Sacerdotal Celibacy. 2d ed. Boston, 1884.

Leber, C. "Des coutumes et usages anciens relatifs aux mariages." In his Collection des meilleurs dissertations, XI. Paris, 1838.

Lecky, W. E. H. History of European Morals from Augustus to Charlemagne. 3d ed. 2 vols. New York, 1881.

Lecky, W. E. H. A History of England in the Eighteenth Century. 8 vols. New York, 1888–90.

––––––– Democracy and Liberty. 2 vols. New York, 1896.

Le Geyt, Philip. Observations on the bill now before Parliament, for regulating the marriages of dissenters, who deny the doctrine of the Trinity. London, 1827.

Lehman, C. Florilegium politicum auctum. Das ist erneuerter politischer Blumen-Garten. In 4 Theilen. Frankfort, 1662.

Lehmann, K. Verlobung und Hochzeit nach den nordgermanischen Rechten des früheren Mittelalters. Munich, 1882.

Leinz, A. Der Ehevorschrift des Concils von Trient Ausdehnung und heutige Geltung. Eine canonistische Studie. Freiburg im Breisgau, 1888.

Leland, J. Antiquarii de rebus britannicis collectanea. Editio altera. 6 vols. London, 1770.

Lettres écrites au R. P. Lamy, prestre de l'oratoire, sur le sujet de la femme pécheresse de l'Évangile. Rouen, 1699.

Lewis, Randle. Reflections on the Causes of unhappy Marriages. London, 1805.

Lewis, W. Die Succession des Erben in die Obligationen des Erblassers nach deutschem Recht. Berlin, 1864.

Liebermann, F. (editor). Die Gesetze der Angelsachsen. Halle, 1898 f.

Liebetrut, Friedrich. Die Ehe nach ihrer Idee, und nach ihrer geschichtlichen Entwickelung. Berlin, 1834.

Lincken, H. De matrimonio lege salica contracto, Germanice von der Vermählung zur lincken Hand. *Resp.*, A. C. Hübner. Altdorf, 1676.

Lind, P. E. De coelibatu christianorum per tria priora secula. Havniae, 1839.

Lindeborn, Johann. In matrimonii sacramentum. Coloniae, 1675.

Lingard, John. The History and Antiquities of the Anglo-Saxon Church. 2 vols. London, 1845. (There is a recent 2d ed., n. p., n. d.)

Lipold, J. C. Arbor consanguinitatis et affinitatis. N. p., n. d.

Livingston, J. H. A Dissertation on the Marriage of a Man with his Sister in Law. New Brunswick, 1816.

Lobethan, F. G. A. Einleitung zur theoretischen Ehe-Rechts-Gelahrtheit. Zwote verbesserte Auflage. Halle, 1785.

Locke, J. "Two Treatises on Civil Government." Preceded by Sir Robert Filmer's "Patriarchia." 2d ed. Morley's *Universal Library*, IX. London, 1887.

Lods, Armand. Le mariage des prêtres devant la loi civile. Paris, 1888. (Bound with Horoy.)

Loening, E. Geschichte des deutschen Kirchenrechts. 2 vols. Strassburg, 1878.

Loersch, Hugo. "Ein eherechtliches Urtheil von 1448." *ZKR.*, XV, 407–10. Freiburg and Tübingen, 1880.

Lohen, Christopher von. De parentum ad nuptias a liberis contrahendas consensu. *Praes.*, J. C. Boltz. Regiomonti, 1685.

Lombard, Peter. Textus sententiarum. N. p., 1488. (Sutro Library, San Francisco.)

Loy, Johann Wilhelm. Das protestantische Eherecht. In einer Reihe theologischer und juristischer Bedenken. Erster Theil. Nürnberg and Altdorf, 1793.

Lubliner, O. Louis. Essai critique sur la nouvelle législation concernant le mariage en Pologne. Promulgée en 1836. Dans ses rapports avec l'histoire et le droit canonique; suivi du texte traduit en français. Brussels and Leipzig, 1840.

Luchaire, Achille. Manuel des institutions françaises. Période des Capétiens directs. Paris, 1892.

Luckock, Herbert M. The History of Marriage Jewish and Christian, in Relation to Divorce and Certain Forbidden Degrees. London, 1894.

Ludlow, J. M. Articles "Arrhae," "Betrothal," "Bigamy," "Bridal-Ring," "Consent to Marriage," and "Contract of Marriage." In Smith and Cheetham's Dictionary of Christian Antiquities, I.

Luther, Martin. An die herrn Deutschs Ordens. Wittenberg, 1523.

—— Bücher und Schriften des theuren seligen Mans Gottes Doct. Mart. Lutheri. 8 vols., folio. Jena, 1564 (I), 1555 (II), 1560 (III), 1556 (IV), 1561 (V), 1561 (VI), 1562 (VII), 1580 (VIII).

—— Colloquia oder Tischreden. Folio. Frankfort, 1571.

—— "Vom heyligen Ehestandt und Oeconomia oder Haushaltung." In Tischreden, cap. 36, folios 349*b*–374*a*.

—— "Sermon vom Ehelichen Stande." In Bücher und Schriften, I (1564), folios 169*b*–172*a*.

—— "Predigten über das erste Buch Mose." *Ibid.*, IV (1556), folios 2*a*–247*b*.

—— "Von Ehesachen." *Ibid.*, V (1561), folios 237*a*–257*b*.

—— Kleinere Schriften, II. "Von Ehe- und Klostersachen." Zwölf Stücke. Ausgabe der Bücherfreunde. Bielefeld and Leipzig, 1877.

—— See Strampff, Fröböse, and Niess.

Lutherophilus (pseud.). Das sechste Gebot und Luthers Leben. Halle, 1893.

Lyndwood (Lindewode), G. Provinciale seu constitutiones Angliae. Folio. Completed, 1433. 1st ed., Oxford, 1470–80. (Editions here used: that of 1505; and that of Oxford, 1679.)

M. . . . . De l'institution du célibat dans ses rapports avec la re-ligion, les mœurs, et la politique; suivi de l'histoire de tout ce qui s'est passé au Concile de Trente, relativement à la ques-tion du mariage des prêtres. Paris, 1808.

McAnnally, D. R. "About the Wedding-Ring." *Popular Science Monthly*, XXXII, 71–76. New York, 1887.

M'Caul, A. A letter to Vice-Chancellor Sir W. Page Wood, in vindication of the ancient interpretation of Leviticus xviii, 18. London, 1859.

Mack, Martin Joseph. Ueber die Einsegnung der gemischten Ehen. Tübingen, 1840.

Macrae, John. The Scripture Law of Marriage with Reference to the Prohibited Degrees. 2d ed. London and Edinburgh. 1862.

Macqueen, John. A Practical Treatise on the Appellate Jurisdic-tion of the House of Lords and Privy Council; together with the Practice on Parliamentary Divorce. London, 1842.

Madan, M. Thelyphthora; or a Treatise on Female Ruin, in its Causes, Effects, Consequences, Prevention, and Remedy; con-sidered on the basis of divine Law. 2d ed. London, 1781; 1st ed., London, 1780. (See Hill, Cookson, and Towers.)

Magee, W. C. "Marriage with a Deceased Wife's Sister (House of Lords, May 19, 1870)." In his Speeches, 80–92. London, 1892.

Maitland, F. W. "Magistri Vacarii Summa de matrimonio." *Law Quarterly Review*, XIII. London, 1897.

Majer, E. T. De separatione cohabitationis. *Praes.*, B. Bardili. Tübingen, 1675.

Makower, F. The Constitutional History and Constitution of the Church of England. London, 1895.

Man, Thomas, and Welby, William. A Treatise on Salomons Mariage or a Congratulation for the Happie & Hopefull Mar-iage between the most illustrious & Noble Prince Frederike the V Countie Palatine of Rhine, Elector of the Sacred Roman Empire etc and the Most Gracious & Excellent Princess the Ladie Elizabeth sole daughter unto the High & Mighty Prince James by the grace of God King of great Britain France & Ire-land, Joyfully solemnized upon the 14. day of Fevuarie 1612, In the Kings Palace of White Hall in London. Imprinted by F. K. for Thomas Man the elder, & William Welby, and are to be sold at the Suanne in Pauls Church-Yard. London, 1612.

Margerison, Samuel (editor). The Registers of the Parish Church of Calverley, in the West-Riding of County of York, I–III. Bradford, 1880–87.

Marriage and divorce. Ueber Ehe und Ehescheidung, Staat und Kirche, und deren Verhältniss zu und untereinander. Votum eines Theologen. Nürnberg, 1838.

"Marriage de jure and de facto." *Law Review*, II. London, 1845.

Marriage Law Defence Union. Addresses Delivered at a Public Meeting. Edinburgh, 1884.

—— Tracts Issued by the. 2 vols. London, 1889.

Marriage of priests. Underricht auss Göttlichen vnd Gaystlichen Rechten | Auch auss den flayschlichen Bepstischen vnrechten | ob ain Priester ain Eeweyb | oder Concubin | das ist | ain bey-schlaff haben möge. Von aynem Ainsidel etc. N. p., 1526.

Marriage of an Uncle with his Niece, Defence of. London, 1686.

Marriage ordinance. Des Herzogthums Wirtemberg erneuerte Ehe- und Ehe-Gerichts-Ordnung. Stuttgart, 1687.

"Marriage Relation, The." *London Quarterly Review*, July, 1849. (On Report of the Commissioners.)

Marriage, A Treatise of; with a defence of the 32nd article of the Church of England. 1673.

Marriage with wife's sister. Unterschiedliche Streit Schrifften | . . . . samt den Actis eines . . . . Coloquii, uber die Frage: Ob Gott verbotten | oder zugelassen habe | dass einer seines ver-storbenen Weibs Schwester heyraten möge? Oettingen, [*ca.* 1687].

Marriage with a deceased wife's sister. Opinions of Eminent Di-vines, shewing that Marriage with a Deceased Wife's Sister is permitted in Scripture, and ought to be legalized in England. N. p., n. d.

—— Opinions of Eminent Statesmen, and others; shewing that Marriage with a Deceased Wife's Sister is permitted in Scrip-ture, and, consequently, ought to be legalized in England. N. p., n. d.

—— The Opinions of a Layman on the Method . . . . of some Modern Divines. New York, 1827.

—— Supplement to reasons assigned by an elder of the free church for declining to sign a petition to Parliament against a bill for legalizing. Glasgow, Edinburgh, and London, 1854.

—— Facts and Opinions tending to shew the Scriptural Law-fulness of a marriage with a deceased wife's sister, and the consequent necessity for its legalization in England. London, 1864.

Martene, E. De antiquis ecclesiae ritibus. 4 vols. Folio. Ant-werpiae, 1763–64.

Martin, Alfred. Exposé de l'ancienne législation genévoise sur le mariage. Geneva, 1891.

Martitz, F. von. Das eheliche Güterrecht des Sachenspiegels und der verwandten Rechtsquellen. Leipzig, 1867.

Maskell, W. The Ancient Liturgy of the Church of England. 3d ed. Oxford, 1882.

—— Monumenta ritualia ecclesiae anglicanae. 3 vols. 2d ed. Oxford, 1882.

Maulde La Clavière, R. de. Les femmes de la Renaissance. Paris, 1898.

Meier, Ludov. Arn. Ernestus. Jus, quod de forma matrimonii ineundi valet, quomodo ex pristina juris condicione profectum sit, disquiritur. Berolini, 1856.

Mejer, Otto. "Anfänge des Wittenberger Consistoriums." *ZKR.*, XIII. Tübingen, 1876.

—— "Zur Geschichte des ältesten protestantischen Eherechts." *Ibid.*, XVI, 35–106. Freiburg and Tübingen, 1881.

—— Zum Kirchenrecht des Reformationsjahrhunderts. Drei Abhandlungen. Hanover, 1891.

Melanchthon, Philip. "De conjugio (1551)." In Opera omnia, I. Pars Post. Erlangen, 1828.

—— " De arbore consanguinitatis et affinitatis, sive de gradibus." In Sarcerius's Collections.

Memminger, E. P. De divortio propter insidias vitae structas. *Praes.*, S. Stryck. Halle, 1738.

Mentzer, Balthassar. De conjugio tractatus. Wittenberg, 1612.

—— Num sponsis, ante solennemine ecclesiae copulationem et benedictionem, concumbentibus, publica poenitentia iuste imponatur ? 6th reprint. Wittenberg, 1728.

Méril, M. Édélestand du. "Des formes du mariage et des usages populaires qui s'y rattachaient surtout en France pendant le moyen âge." In Étude sur quelques points d'archéologie. Paris and Leipzig, 1862.

Merrick, M. M. Marriage a Divine Institution. London, 1754.

Meurer, C. "Die rechtliche Natur des tridentiner Matrimonial-Decrets." *ZKR.*, XXII, 97–126. Freiburg, 1889.

—— Das landesherrliche Ehescheidungsrecht. Freiburg, 1891.

Meyer, Johann. Uxor christiana sive de conjugio inter duos deque incestu et divortiis, dissertationes tres. Amsterdam, 1688.

Meyer, Lucian. Der Einspruch wider die Ehe nach französischem Recht. Strassburg, 1884.

Meyern, W. Fr. Hinterlassene kleine Schriften. 3 vols. Vienna, 1842.

Meynial, E. "Le mariage après les invasions." *Nouvelle revue historique de droit*, XX, 514–31, 737–62 ; XXI, 117–48. Paris, 1896–97.

Meyrick, F. "Marriage." In Dictionary of Christian Antiquities, II.

Michaelis, David. Paralipomena contra polygamiam, et oratio de felicibus connubiis aliarum scientiarum cum philologia orientali. Göttingen, 1757.

Michelet, M. Origines du droit français. Paris, 1837.

Milton, John. Prose Works. Bohn ed. 5 vols. London, 1889–90.

Mixed marriages. Ueber die gemischten Ehen. Oder: Ist es ein allgemeines katholisches Kirchengesetz, dass by gemischten Ehen die Kinder katholish werden müssen? Verneinend bewiesen, etc. Stuttgart, 1827.

—— Nationaler und historischer Standpunkt zur Beurtheilung des Verhältnisses zwischen Staats-Regierungen und dem römischen Stuhle in Beziehung auf gemischte Ehen, etc. Cologne, 1839.

—— Entwurf des Gesetzes über gemischte Ehen. Mit den betreffenden Bestimmungen einheimischer und fremder Gesetze. Gedrucktes Manuscript. Berlin, 1839.

—— Die gemischten Ehen in der Erzdiöcese Freiburg. Nach den Aktenstücken dargestellt. Zugleich ein Beitrag zur Beleuchtung der katholischen Zustände in Baden. Regensburg, 1846.

—— Der Streit über gemischte Ehen und das Kirchenhoheitsrecht im Grossherzogthum Baden. Karlsruhe, 1847.

—— Beleuchtung und actenmässige Ergänzung der Karlsruher Schrift: "Der Streit über gemischte Ehen und das Kirchenhoheitsrecht im Grossherzogthum Baden." Schaffhausen, 1847.

Moens, W. J. C. O. (editor). "Hampshire Allegations for Marriage Licences Granted by the Bishop of Winchester, 1689–1837." Publications of Harleian Society, XXXV, XXXVI. London, 1893.

Molesworth, W. Nassau. History of England. 3 vols. London, 1877.

Mone, Bader, and Dambacher. "Eherecht der Hörigen im 13.–16. Jahrhunderte." Zeitschrift für Geschichte des Oberrheins, VII, 129–256. Karlsruhe, 1856.

Monthly Review. London, 1749 ff.

Montmorency J. E. G. de. "The Changing Status of a Married Woman." Law Quarterly Review, XIII. London, 1897.

Montz, F. J. J. De jure connubiorum. Praes., J. F. Hertling. Heidelberg, 1729.

Monumenta Germaniae historica.

Moodie, J. Principles, Changes, and Improvements in the Law of Marriage. London, 1849.

Moore, C. G. (editor). Registers of Broad Chalke, Co. Wilts, from 1538–1780. London, 1880.

Moore, T. How to be Married in All Ways and Everywhere. London, 1890.

Morer, Thomas. Two Cases: the first of Adultery and Divorce . . . . The second of Baptism. London, 1702.

Morgan, Hector Davies. The Doctrine and Law of Marriage, Adultery, and Divorce. 2 vols. Oxford, 1826.

Morganatic marriage. Geschichte morganatischer und legitimirter Fürsten- und Grafen-Ehen in Deutschland. Halle, 1874.

Mosheim, J. L. von. Commentatio de divortio, oder von den in dem Neuen Testament gegründeten Ursachen der Ehescheidung. Jena, 1773.

Moy, E. von. Das Eherecht der Christen in der morgenländischen und abendländischen Kirche bis zur Zeit Karls des Grossen nach den Quellen dargestellt. Regensburg, 1833.

Muirhead, James. Notes on the Marriage Laws of England, Scotland, and Ireland, with Suggestions for Their Amendment and Assimilation. Edinburgh and London, 1862.

Müller, H. Der grosse Einfluss der fürstlichen Heiraten, und der Frauen im Allgemeinen, im Mittelalter; besonders während des "Hundertjährigen Krieges" zwischen Frankreich und England (1337–1453). Heidelberg, 1897.

Müller, J. Ueber Ehescheidung und Wiederverehlichung geschiedener Gatten. Zwei Vorträge. Berlin, 1855.

Müller, P. De annulo pronubo, vulgo vom Jaworts- oder Trauring, de modo computationis graduum, de osculo sancto. Jena, 1734.

Münter, Friedrich. Die Christin im heidnischen Hause, von den Zeiten Constantins des Grossen. Copenhagen, 1828.

Muther, Theodor. "Drei Urkunden zur Reformationsgeschichte." Niedner's Zeitschrift für historische Theologie, XXX. Gotha 1860.

Nachet. "Liberté du mariage des prêtres." In Mémoire produit à la Cour de Cassation pour M. Dumonteil, fils. Paris, 1833.

Napiersky, Leonhard. Die Morgengabe des rigischen Rechts. Dorpat, 1848.

Nevizano, Joanne. Sylvae nuptialis libri sex. Lugduni, 1556; 1st ed., Parrhisiis, 1521.

Nichols, John. The Progresses, Processions and Magnificent Festivities of King James the First. 4 vols. London, 1828.

Nicolai, J. G. De repudiis et divortiis, ex jure divino, canonico, civili, etc. 2 parts. Dresden, 1685.

Niemeier, J. B. De conjugiis prohibitis dissertationes junctim editae. Accesserunt supplementa cum indice rerum. Helmstadt, 1705.

Niess, Ernst. Ehestands-Buch. Eine Sammlung von Bibelstellen, Liederversen und Aussprüchen Dr. Martin Luthers, etc. Eisleben and Leipzig, 1858.

Noordkerk, H. De matrimoniis, ob peccatum sodomiticum jure solvendis. Amsterdam, 1733.

Norton, Hon. Mrs. (Caroline Elizabeth). A letter to the Queen on Lord Chancellor Cranworth's Marriage and Divorce Bill. 3d ed. London, 1855.

Notes and Queries. London, 1850 ff.

Notes on Cases in the Ecclesiastical and Maritime Courts, II (1842–43). London, 1844.

Nunziante, E. Un divorzio ai tempi di Leone X. da XL lettere inedite di Jacopo Sannazaro. Rome, 1887.

Nurra, P. "Usi e costumi nuziali di Sardegna." In Nozze of Cian-Sappa-Flandinet. Bergamo, 1894.

Observations on the Marriage Laws. London, 1815.

Ochino, Bernardino. A Dialogue of Polygamy. Trans. from the Italian, by John Garfeild. London, 1657. First published at Zurich, 1563.

Oettinger, M. Johann. Warhaffte historische Beschreibung der fürstlichen Hochzeit, und dess Hochansehnlichen Beylagers, so der durchleuchtig Hochgeborn Fürst vnnd Herr, Herr Johann Friderich Hertzog zu Würtemberg vnd Teck . . . . mit der auch durchleuchtigen hochgebornen Fürstin vnnd Frewlin, Frewlin Barbara Sophia Marggrävin zu Brandenburg, etc. Stuttgart, 1610.

Opet, O. "Die erbrechtliche Stellung der Weiber in der Zeit der Volksrechte." In Gierke's *Untersuchungen zur deutschen Staats- und Rechtsgeschichte*, XXV. Breslau, 1888.

Oppenheim, O. G. "Die Verhandlungen des englischen Parlaments über die Einführung der Civil-Ehe." *ZKR.,* I. Berlin, 1861.

Ormulum, The. Ed. by Robert Holt. Oxford, 1878.

Ortloff, H. "Die Confession der Kinder aus gemischten Ehen zwischen Evangelischen und Katholischen und deren Confessionswechsel, in Besonderen nach dem Landesrecht des Grossherzogtums Sachsen-Weimar-Eisenach." *ZKR.,* 3d ser., VI, 51–105. Freiburg and Leipzig, 1896.

Oswald, J. H. Die dogmatische Lehre von den heiligen Sakramenten der katholischen Kirche. 5th ed. 2 vols. Münster, 1894.

Oxford University, members of. Epithalamia sive Lusus Palatini in Nuptias Celsissimi Principis Domini Friderici Comitis Palatini ad Rhenum &c. et Serenissimae Elisibethae Iocobi Potentissimi Britanniae Regis Filiae Primogenitae. Oxford, 1613.

Pallavicino, Sforza. Istoria del Concilio di Trento. Ove insieme rifutasi con auctorevoli testimonianze una storia falsa divulgata nello stresso argomento sotto nome di Pietro Soave Polano. Folio. 4 vols. Rome, 1833; see also the Latin ed., Antwerp, 1673.

Palmer, W. Origines liturgicae, or Antiquities of the English Ritual, and a Dissertation on Primitive Liturgies. 2 vols. 3d ed. Oxford, 1839; 4th ed., 2 vols., London, 1845.

Pannella, G. Usi nuziali dell' Abruzzo Teramano e pasquino di Teramo. Teramo, 1894.

Parker, M. De antiquitate britannicae ecclesiae. Folio. London, 1729. Earlier eds., Lambeth, 1572; Hanoveriae, 1605.

Parker Society, Publications of the. Cambridge, 1841-55:
  Becon. Early Works, 1843; Catechism, 1844; Prayers, 1844.
  Bradford. Writings, 2 vols., 1848-53.
  Bullinger. Decades, 4 vols., 1849-52.
  Calfhill. Answer to John Martiall's Treatise of the Cross, 1846.
  Cooper. Answer in Defence of the Truth, 1850.
  Coverdale. Writings and Translations, 1844; Remains, 1846.
  Cranmer. Works. 2 vols. 1844-46.
  Fulke. Defence against Gregory Martin, 1843; Stapleton's Fortress, 1848.
  Grindal. Remains, 1843.
  Hooper. Early Writings, 1843; Later Writings, 1852.
  Hutchinson. Works, 1842.
  Jewell. Works, 4 vols., 1845-50.
  Latimer. Sermons and Remains, 1845.
  Liturgies of 1549 and 1552 of Edward VI., 1844; Liturgies of Elizabeth, 1847.
  Parker. Correspondence, 1853.
  Philpot. Examinations and Writings, 1842.
  Pilkington. Works, 1842.
  Ridley. Works, 1841.
  Rogers. Exposition of Thirty-nine Articles, 1854.
  Sandys. Sermons, 1841.
  Tyndale. Doctrinal Treatises, 1848; Expositions and Notes, 1849: Answer to Sir Thomas More's Dialogue, 1850.
  Whitaker. Disputation, 1849.
  Whitgift. Works, 3 vols., 1851-53.
  Zurich Letters, 2 vols., 1842: Original Letters from the Zurich Archives, 1847.

Paton, Chalmers Izett. Marriage with a Deceased Brother's Wife, Condemned by the Laws of Nature, Scripture, and the Testimony of Churches and Nations. London, 1869.

Penka, Josef. Beantwortung einer eherechtlichen Frage der heiligen Schrift, den Zeugnissen der heiligen Väter und dem Ausspruche der heiligen allgemeinen Kirchenversammlung zu Trident gemäss. Olmütz, 1855.

Peronne, J.   Über die gemischten Ehen.   Aus dem Lateinischen übersezt durch Joseph Maria Aringer.   Augsburg, 1840.

——— De matrimonio christiano.   3 vols.   Leodii, 1861.

Peters, J. L. L.   Commentatio ad Tit. 47, legis salicae, qui inscribitur "de reipus."   Berlin, 1830.

Peters, W.   Die Ehescheidung und die Ungültigkeits- oder Nichtig-keits-Erklärung der Ehe im Geltungsbereiche des preussischen allgemeinen Landrechts.   Berlin, 1881.

Phillimore, Joseph.   Substance of the speech of Joseph Phillimore, LL.D., in the House of Commons, Mar. 27, 1822, on moving for leave to bring in a bill to amend the marriage act.   2d ed. London, 1822.

Phillimore, W. P. W. (editor).   Gloucestershire Parish Registers.   I, II.   London, 1896.

Phillips, George.   Englische Reichs- und Rechtsgeschichte seit der Ankunft der Normannen im Jahre 1066 nach Christi Geburt. 2 vols.   Berlin, 1828.

——— Lehrbuch des Kirchenrechts.   3d ed.   Regensburg, 1881.

Phillips, G. J.   "Das Ehehinderniss der beigefügten Bedingung." ZKR., V, VI.   Tübingen, 1865–66.

Philogamus (pseud.).   The present State of Matrimony, or the real Causes of Conjugal Infidelity, with Reflexions on the State of Matrimony among the Ancient Greeks and Romans, and a view of their manner of Educating their Young Ladies, compared by the Modern.   London, 1739.

Pitré, Giuseppe.   Usi nuziali del popolo Siciliano.   Palermo, 1878.

——— Usi natalizi, nuziali e funebri del popolo Siciliano.   Palermo, 1879.

——— Antichi usi nuziali in Sicilia.   Palermo, 1880.

Plea for an Alteration of the Divorce Laws.   London, 1831.

Pleadings for the Marquis de Gesvres against the Marchioness. 2 vols.   London, 1714.

Pocock, Nicholas.   Records of the Reformation: The Divorce, 1527– 1533.   2 vols.   Oxford, 1870.

Poggi, F.   Usi nuziali nel centro della Sardegna.   Sassari, 1894.

Pollen, Thomas.   The Fatal Consequences of Adultery, to Monarchies as well as to Private Families . . . . and an Historical Account of Marriage.   London, 1772.

Pollock, Sir F., and Maitland, F. W.   The History of English Law.   2 vols.   Cambridge, 1895.

Pollock, Sir F.   A First Book of Jurisprudence for Students of the Common Law.   London, 1896.

Polwhele, R.   An Essay on Marriage, Adultery and Divorce, etc. London, 1823.

Pompen, J. Tractatus de dispensationibus et de revalidatione matrimonii. 2d ed. Amsterdam, 1897.

Popp, Friedrich. Über Ehescheidung. Amberg, 1800.

Pothier, R. J. Traité du contrat de mariage. 2 vols. Paris, 1772.

Poubelle, E. R. Discours sur la condition privée de la femme. Toulouse, 1868.

Powles, L. D. Browne and Powles' Law and Practice in Divorce and Matrimonial Causes. 6th ed. London, 1897.

Poynter, Thomas. A concise view of the doctrine and practice of the Ecclesiastical Courts in Doctors' Commons, on various points relative to the subject of marriage and divorce. London, 1822.

Prémontval, M. de. La monogamie ou l'unité dans le mariage. 3 vols. La Haye, 1751–52.

Preussische Eherechts-Reform, Die. Berlin, 1842.

Prothero, G. W. Select Statutes and other Constitutional Documents Illustrative of the Reigns of Elizabeth and James I. Oxford, 1894.

Pusey, E. B. A Letter on the Proposed Change in the Laws prohibiting Marriage between those near of Kin. Reprinted from *British Magazine*, November, 1840. Oxford, 1842.

——— (editor). Evidence given before the Commission Appointed to inquire into the State and Operation of the Law of Marriage. Oxford, 1849.

——— God's Prohibition on the Marriage with a Deceased Wife's Sister, Leviticus xviii, 6, not to be set aside by an Inference from a Restriction of Polygamy among the Jews, Leviticus xviii, 18. Oxford and London, 1860.

R . . . . , A. F. Betrachtungen über den Klerikal- und Mönchsgeist, im neunzehnten Jahrhundert, mit besonderer Rücksicht auf die Ehelosigkeit der Geistlichkeit. N. p., 1805.

Radcliffe, John (editor). The Parish Registers of St. Chad, Saddlworth in County of York: Marriages, Births, and Burials from 1613–1751. Uppermill, 1887.

Rady, J. B. Die Reformatoren in ihrer Beziehung zur Doppelehe des Landgrafen Philipp. Frankfort and Luzern, 1890.

Rambaud, Alfred. Histoire de la civilisation française. Paris, 1898.

Rantzow, Louis, Comte de. Discussion si la polygamie est contre la lois naturelle ou divine. St. Petersburg, 1774.

Raynolds, John. A defence of the judgment of the reformed churches. That a man may lawfullie not onelie put awaie his wife for her adulterie, but also marrie another. [London], 1609; 2d ed., 1610.

Rees, J. D. "Meddling with Hindu Marriages." *Nineteenth Century*, October, 1890. London, 1890.

Reeves, John. History of the English Law. Ed. by W. F. Finlason. 5 vols. Philadelphia, 1880.

Reformationsgeschichte, Schriften des Vereins für. 14 vols. Halle, 1883–96.

Register Booke of Inglebye iuxta Grenhow. As much as is extant in the old booke for Christnings, Weddings and Burials since the yeare of our Lord 1539. By me John Blackburne, Curate. Canterbury, 1889.

Register, The Annual, or a View of the History, Politics and Literature. London, 1758 ff.

Reinsberg-Düringsfeld, Ida, Baroness von. "Lieben und Freien in Piemont." *Illustrierte Frauen-Zeitung*, June 7, 1875. Berlin, 1875.

Reinsch, Gustav. Stellung und Leben der deutschen Frau im Mittelalter. Berlin, 1882.

Report of the Cases of Regina v. Millis et Regina v. Carroll, in the Queen's Bench in Ireland, in Easter and Trinity terms, 1842. Dublin, 1842.

Riccius, P. M. De matrimonio ad morganaticam contracto. 1717.

Richard, Ap. Marriage and Divorce. London, 1888.

Richardus, J. F. De conditionibus sponsaliorum impossibilibus. *Praes.*, J. F. Ludovicus. Presented, 1701; published, Halle, 1741.

Richecour, A. de. Essai sur l'histoire et la législation des formes requises pour la validité du mariage. Paris, 1856.

Richter, A. C. De secundis nuptiis praecipue illustrium personarum. Presented, 1723; printed, Halle, 1734.

Richter, Aemilius Ludwig. Die evangelischen Kirchenordnungen des sechszehnten Jahrhunderts. Urkunden und Regesten zur Geschichte des Rechts und der Verfassung der evangelischen Kirche in Deutschland. 2 vols. Weimar, 1846.

—— Beiträge zur Geschichte des Ehescheidungsrechts in der evangelischen Kirche. Berlin, 1858.

—— Lehrbuch des katholischen und evangelischen Kirchenrechts. . . . In achter Auflage bearbeitet von Dr. Richard Dove und Dr. Wilhelm Kahl. Leipzig, 1886.

—— and Schulte, J. F. (editors). Canones et decreti concilii tridentini. Leipzig, 1853.

—— and Friedberg, Emil (editors). Corpus juris canonici. 2d ed. Leipzig, 1881 f.

Riedler, Franz Jos. Bedingte Eheschliessung. Eine kanonistische Untersuchung. Kempten, 1892.

Riehl, F. Westfälisches Bauernrecht (Erb- und Familienrecht) im Geltungsbereiche des Gesetzes betreffend das eheliche Güterrecht in der Provinz Westfalen. Minden, 1896.

"Rights and Liabilities of Husband and Wife." *Edinburgh Review*, January, 1857.

Rituale Romanum. Pauli Quinti pontificis maximi . . . . editum inde vero à Benedicto XIV. P. M. Auctum, et castigatum. Romae, 1816.

Rive, Friedrich. Geschichte der deutschen Vormundschaft. I. Braunschweig, 1862.

Roberts, A., and Donaldson, J. (editors). The Ante-Nicene Fathers. American reprint. Revised by A. C. Coxe. 9 vols. Buffalo, 1885–87.

Robertson, Edmund. "Marriage." In Encyclopædia Britannica. XV. London, 1883.

Robertson, Erasmus. The Law of Legitimation by Subsequent Marriage. London, 1829.

Roeder, Fritz. Die Familie bei den Angelsachsen. Eine kultur- und litterarhistorische Studie auf Grund gleichzeitiger Quellen. Erster Hauptteil: "Mann und Frau." Halle, 1899.

Rogers, Thomas. The Catholic Doctrine of the Church of England; an Exposition of the Thirty-Nine Articles. Ed. for the Parker Society by J. J. S. Peronne. Cambridge, 1854.

Roldanus, Johannes. Disputatio theologica de mente Pauli, volentis episcopum esse unius uxoris maritum. *Praes.*, Johann von Marck. Lugduni Batavorum, 1710.

Rosenmüller, Johann Georg (editor and translator). Julians eines pelagianischen Bischoffs zu Eclanum Widerlegung der Bücher Augustins über den Ehestand und die Lust. Leipzig, 1796.

Rosenthal, Eduard. Die Rechtsfolgen des Ehebruchs nach kanonischem und deutschem Recht. Würzburg, 1880.

Roskovány, Augustine de. De matrimonio in ecclesia catholica. Augustae Vindelicorum, 1837.

Roth, P. "Das deutsche eheliche Güterrecht." *ZVR.*, I. Stuttgart, 1878.

Royal Commission on Historical Manuscripts. Fifteen Reports with Appendices; Calendar of the Manuscripts of the Marquis of Salisbury, Parts I–VI; Reports on Manuscripts in the Welsh Language, I. In all 78 vols. London, 1870–98.

Rullkoetter, William. The Legal Protection of Women among the Ancient Germans. Chicago, 1900.

Sachsse, C. R. Sachsenspiegel oder sächsisches Landrecht. Heidelberg, 1848.

Sack, K. H. Die katholische Kirche innerhalb des Protestantismus und ihr Recht, vorzüglich in den gemischten Ehen. Cologne, 1838.

Saettler, J. C. In sextum decalogi praeceptum, in conjugum obligationes, et quaedam matrimonium spectantia, praelectiones. 2d ed. Gratianopoli, 1844.

Sahme, R. F.   De matrimonio legitimo absque benedictione sacerdotali.   Halle, 1722.

Sakellarios, Ph.   Die Sitten und Gebräuche der Hochzeit bei den Neugriechen verglichen mit denen der alten Griechen.   Halle, 1880.

Salis, L. R. von.   Die Publikation des tridentinischen Rechts der Eheschliessung.   Basel, 1888.

Salkeld, William.   Reports of cases adjudged in the Court of King's Bench.   3 vols.   From the 6th London ed.   Philadelphia, 1822.

[Salmon Thomas].   A critical Essay concerning Marriage.   London, 1724.

Salomone-Marino, Salvatore.   Come si prepari la sposa; uso nuziali dei contadini di Sicilia.   Palermo, 1890.

Sanchez, T.   Disputationum de s^{to} matrimonii sacramento.   2 vols.   Folio.   Venice, 1625.

Sanders, Francis (editor).   The Parish Registers of Eastham, Cheshire, from 1598 to 1700.   London, 1891.

Sanders, Francis, and Irwine, N. F. (editors).   The Parish Registers of Bebington, Co. Chester, from 1558–1701.   Liverpool, 1897.

Sandhaas, Georg.   Fränkisches eheliches Güterrecht.   Giessen, 1866.

Sarcerius, Erasmus.   Ein Buch vom heiligen Ehestande/ und von Ehesachen/ mit allen vmbstendigkeiten/ zu diesen Dingen gehörig/ darinnen zugleich natürlich/ Göttlich/ Keiserlich/ vnd Bepstlich Recht angezogen wird/ zum Teil aus vieler gelerter Theologen Bücher gezogen/ zum Teil vom zusamenzieher selbst geschrieben.   Item/ werden in diesem Buch auch viel felle in Ehesachen gesetzt/ sampt gelerter Theologen rathschlege darüber.   [Leipzig], 1553.

——   Corpus Jvris Matrimonialis.   Vom Ursprung, Anfang vnd herkhomen des heyligen Ehestandts.   Frankfort, 1569.

Savigny, Friedrich Carl von.   "Darstellung der in den preussischen Gesetzen über die Ehescheidung unternommenen Reform.'   In Vermischte Schriften, V.   Berlin, 1850.

Saxons.   "Among the Transylvanian Saxons": I, "Marriage Customs;" II, "Births and Deaths."   *Popular Science Monthly*, XXI.   New York, 1887.

Saxsen, Michael.   Arcana annuli pronubi, Das ist Geheimnis und bedeutung des Ehelichen Traw Ringes.   Leipzig, 1594.

Sayer, Joseph.   A Vindication of the Power of Society to annull the Marriages of Minors, entered into without Consent of Parents or Guardians.   London, 1755.

Schelhas, J. E.   Dissertatio de clandestinis sponsalibus juratis, Vulgo von heimlichen Verlöbnüssen.   *Praes.*, W. H. Brückner.   Jena, 1716.

Schellenberg, C. O. Ueber die Einführung der Civilehe. Vortrag gehalten auf dem siebenten deutschen Protestantentage zu Leipzig am 13. August, 1873. Leipzig, 1873.

Scherer, R. von. Ueber das Eherecht bei Benedict Levita und Pseudo-Isidor. Graz, 1879.

Scherr, J. Deutsche Kultur- und Sittengeschichte. 2d ed. Leipzig, 1858.

――― Geschichte der deutschen Frauenwelt. 2 vols. 3d ed. Leipzig, 1873. (1st ed. was entitled Geschichte der deutschen Frauen. Leipzig, 1860.)

Scheurl, Adolf von. Zur praktischen Lösung der Ehescheidungsfrage. Nuremberg, 1861.

――― "Eheform in Baiern." *ZKR.*, VI. Tübingen, 1866.

――― "Die Ablösung des Eherechts von dem Kirchenrecht." *Ibid.*, XIII. Tübingen, 1876.

――― Die Entwicklung des kirchlichen Eheschliessungsrechts. Erlangen, 1877.

――― "Zur Lehre von dem Ehehindernisse der Verwandtschaft." *ZKR.*, XVI. Freiburg and Tübingen, 1881.

――― Das gemeine deutsche Eherecht und seine Umbildung durch das Reichsgesetz vom 6. Februar, 1875. Erlangen, 1882.

――― "Consensus facit nuptias." *ZKR.*, XXII. Freiburg, 1889.

Schilling, Ernst Moritz. Der Ehescheidungsprocess in den Sächsischen Gerichten. Leipzig, 1831.

Schincke. "Hochzeit und Hochzeitsgebräuche." In Ersch und Gruber's Encyklopädie, Sec. II, T. 9, pp. 166–96. Leipzig, 1832.

Schleusner, G. "Zu den Aufängen protestantischen Eherechts im 16. Jahrhundert." *ZKG.*, VI, 1884; XII, 1891; XIII, 1892. Gotha, 1884–92.

Schmalian, J. H. De ambitu connubiali, Vom Frey-Werben. *Praes.*, P. Müller. Wittenberg, 1745.

Schmid, Reinhold. Die Gesetze der Angelsachsen. Leipzig, 1858.

Schmidt, Karl. The Social Results of Early Christianity. Trans. by Mrs. Thorpe. London, 1889.

Schmitt, Georg. Die Schlüsselgewalt der Ehefrau nach deutschem Recht. Munich, 1893.

Schmitz, Herm. Jos. Die Bussbücher und die Bussdisciplin der Kirche. Mayence, 1883.

Schneidewin, Johann. De nuptiis. Jena, 1585.

Schoepsius, C. G. De serto virginum, Vom Jungfer-Crantz. *Praes.*, J. H. Mejer. Presented, 1693; published, Halle, 1746.

Schönwerth, Fr. Aus der Oberpfalz. Sitten und Sagen, I ("Ehe, Hexen," etc.). Augsburg, 1857.

Schott, August Ludwig. Einleitung in das Eherecht zu akademischem und gemeinnüzlichem Gebrauch. Nuremberg, 1802.

Schroeder, Richard. Geschichte des ehelichen Güterrechts in Deutschland. 2 vols. Stettin, Danzig, and Elbing, 1864–74.

—— "Das eheliche Güterrecht Deutschlands in Vergangenheit, Gegenwart und Zukunft." *Deutsche Zeit- und Streit-Fragen*, Jahrg. 4, Heft 59. Berlin, 1875.

—— Lehrbuch der deutschen Rechtsgeschichte. 2d ed. Leipzig, 1894.

Schubarth, F. M. Das Eherecht des Entwurfs eines bürgerlichen Gesetzbuchs für das Königreich Sachsen in landeskirchlicher Beziehung. Predigerconvents-Vortrag vom 9. April, 1861. Leipzig, 1861.

Schubert, H. von. Die evangelische Trauung, ihre geschichtliche Entwicklung und gegenwärtige Bedeutung. Berlin, 1890.

Schulenburg, Emil. Die Spuren des Brautraubes, Brautkaufes und ähnlicher Verhältnisse in den französischen Epen des Mittelalters. Rostock, 1894.

Schulte, J. F. von. Handbuch des katholischen Eherechts. Giessen, 1855.

—— "Die Statthaftigkeit der Civilehe nach katholischen Grundsätzen." *ZKR.*, XI. Tübingen, 1873.

—— Der Cölibatszwang und dessen Aufhebung. Bonn, 1876.

—— Die Geschichte der Quellen und Litteratur des canonischen Rechts von Gratian bis auf die Gegenwart. 3 vols., bound in 4. Stuttgart, 1875–80.

—— Lehrbuch des katholischen und evangelischen Kirchenrechts. 4. Aufl. des katholischen, 1. des evangelischen. Giessen, 1886.

Schultz, Alwin. Das höfische Leben zur Zeit der Minnesänger. Leipzig, 1879–80.

Schütze, Gottfried. Lobschrift aug die Weiber der alten deutschen und nordischen Völker. New ed. Hamburg, 1776.

Scobell, H. A Collection of Acts and Ordinances of general Use made in Parliament, 1640–1656, formerly published, etc. Being a continuation of that work, from the end of Mr. Pulton's Collection. Folio. London, 1658.

Scopp, J. G. De jure divortiorum. Frankfort and Leipzig, 1756.

Sehling, E. Die Wirkungen der Geschlechtsgemeinschaft auf die Ehe. Eine kirchenrechtliche Abhandlung. Leipzig, 1885.

—— "Die Ehescheidung Napoleons I." *ZKR.*, XX. Freiburg, 1885.

—— Unterscheidung der Verlöbnisse in kanonischem Recht. Leipzig, 1887.

Seidler, C. H. Beiträge für Reform der preussischen Ehegesetzgebung. Nordhausen, 1861.

Seiff, J. C. De divortio totali, seu quoad vinculum, lege evangelii licito. Giessen, 1740.

Senckenberg, H. C. Jura egressus e potestate parentum germanica ac romana. *Resp.*, S. J. Hoffmann. Giessen, 1743.

Several Proceedings of Parliament, 1650–53. Newspaper. Sutro Library, San Francisco.

Shelford, Leonard. A Practical Treatise of the Law of Marriage and Divorce, as altered by the Recent Statutes. London, 1841.

Sicherer, Hermann von. Ueber Eherecht und Ehegerichtsbarkeit in Bayern. Munich, 1875.

Sick, C. F. Dissertatio de consanguinitatis ratione ac indole ad eruendas notiones vocum juris germanici: Sippe, Sippzahl, Sippzahlrecht. Tübingen, 1802.

Sickel, Th. (editor). Zur Geschichte des Concils von Trient. 3 Abtheilungen. Vienna, 1870–72.

Siegel, H. Das deutsche Erbrecht. Heidelberg, 1853.

—— Deutsche Rechtsgeschichte. 3d ed. Berlin, 1895.

Sie oder du, oder Erörterung der Frage: in wie weit die Sprache des gefälligen Umgangs auch in der Ehe beizubehalten sey? Frankfort and Leipzig, 1786.

Simplicius Christianus. Summarische Widerlegung des politischen Discurs von der Viel-Weiberey | So ein Atheistischer Huren-Teuffel J. L. Boshafftiglich aussgestreuet | enthalten ist. [Leipzig], 1677.

Siricius, Michael. Uxor una ex jure naturae et divino, moribus antiquis et constitutionibus imperatorum et regum. Giessen, 1669.

Slevogt, Gottlieb. De vocatione ad pastoratum sub conditione matrimonii cum defuncti pastoris vidua aut filia ineundi. Jena, 1748.

Smith, S. B. Elements of Ecclesiastical Law. New York, 1887–88.

Smith, Valentin. "De la famille chez les Burgondes." In Mémoires lus à la Sorbonne, 1864.

Smith, W., and Cheetham, S. A Dictionary of Christian Antiquities. 2 vols. London, 1875–80.

Sohm, Rudolph. "Die geistliche Gerichtsbarkeit im fränkischen Reich." *ZKR.*, IX. Tübingen, 1870.

—— Das Recht der Eheschliessung. Weimar, 1875.

—— Trauung und Verlobung. Weimar, 1876.

—— Zur Trauungsfrage. Heilbronn, 1879.

—— Die obligatorische Civilehe und ihre Aufhebung. Weimar, 1880.

Sohm, Rudolph.   Kirchenrecht.   Bd. I, "Die geschichtlichen Grundlagen." Leipzig, 1892.

Spangenberg, G. A.   Exercitatio antiqua doni Germanorum matutini quod vulgo morgengabam appellant. Göttingen, 1767.

Spangenberg, E. P. J.   Die Minnehöfe des Mittelalters und ihre Entscheidungen oder Aussprüche. Leipzig, 1821.

Spence, George.   The Equitable Jurisdiction of the Court of Chancery. 2 vols. Philadelphia, 1846.

Spener, J. C.   De repudiorum jure imprimis ex implacabilis odii causa. *Praes.*, J. C. Richter. Wittenberg, 1737.

Spirgatis, Eugen.   "Verlobung und Vermählung im altfranzösischen volkstümlichen Epos." *Wissenschaftliche Beiträge zum Jahresbericht des Leibniz-Gymnasiums zu Berlin, Ostern, 1894.* Berlin, 1894.

Stälin, P. F.   "Die Form der Eheschliessung nach der neueren Gesetzgebung." *ZKR.*, IV, V, VI. Tübingen, 1864–66.

Statutes of the United Kingdom, LXXVI.   London, 1836. (Containing the acts of 6 and 7 William IV.)

Statutes at Large of England and of Great Britain: from Magna Charta to the Union of the Kingdoms of Great Britain and Ireland. 10 vols. Ed. by John Raithby. London, 1811.

Stäudlin, C. F.   Geschichte der Vorstellungen und Lehren von der Ehe. Göttingen, 1826.

Stavert, W. J. (editor).   The Parish Register of Burnsall-in-Craven, 1559–1700. Skipton, 1893.

Stebbing, Henry.   An Enquiry into the force and operation of the annulling clauses in the late Act for the better preventing of clandestine marriages. London, 1754.

——— A dissertation on the power of States to deny civil protection to the marriages of minors, made without the consent of their parents or guardians. London, 1755.

Stephens, A. J.   Laws Relating to the Clergy. 2 vols. London, 1848.

Sticinsky, Friedrich.   Von der Ungültigkeitserklärung als Aufhebungsart der Ehe zwischen Gliedern der evangelisch-lutherischen Kirche nach livländischem Recht. Dorpat, 1851.

Stobbe, O.   Beiträge zur Geschichte des deutschen Rechts. Braunschweig, 1865.

Stoddart, Sir J.   A Letter to . . . . Lord Brougham, on the Opinions of the Judges in the Irish Marriage Cases. London, 1844.

——— Irish Marriage Question. Observations on the Opinion delivered by the Right Honourable the Lord Cottenham, 23d of February, 1844, on the writ of error in the case of the Queen *v.* Millis. London, 1844.

Stölzel, Adolf. Deutsches Eheschliessungsrecht. 3d ed. Berlin, 1876.

────── "Umgestaltung der Vorschriften des preussischen allgemeinen Landrechts über ungültige Ehen durch die neuere Gesetzgebung." *Zeitschrift für Rechtsgeschichte*, XVII. Freiburg and Tübingen, 1882.

────── "Zur Geschichte des Ehescheidungsrechtes." *ZKR.*, XVIII. Freiburg and Tübingen, 1883.

────── Ueber das landesherrliche Ehescheidungsrecht. Ein Beitrag zur Geschichte des Ehescheidungsrechtes und zu Interpretation der neuern Reichsgesetzgebung. Berlin, 1891.

Stone, Emily Baily. "Marrying in the Fifteenth Century." *Lippincott's Magazine*, LIX, 107–12. Philadelphia, 1897.

Strack, K. Aus dem deutschen Frauenleben. 2 vols. Leipzig, 1873–74.

Strampff, H. L. von (editor). Dr. Martin Luther: Ueber die Ehe. Aus Dr. Martin Luthers Schriften zusammengetragen, geordnet und mit Bemerkungen versehen. Berlin, 1857.

Stravinski, David. De conjugio illegitimo indulgentia principis confirmato. *Resp.*, G. F. Günther. Presented, 1697; published, Leipzig, 1707.

Strippelmann, F. G. L. Das Ehescheidungsrecht nach gemeinem und insbesondere nach hessischem Rechte. Cassel, 1854.

Struvvius, G. A. De jure divortiorum. Von dem Recht und Ursachen der Ehescheidung. Jena, 1745.

Stryck, E. A. De ioco, Vom Schertz und dessen Rechtsgebrauch bey Verlöbnissen, etc. *Praes.*, J. Hoppius. Halle, 1740.

Stubbs, William. Select Charters and Other Illustrations of English Constitutional History. Oxford, 1881.

────── Seventeen Lectures on the Study of Mediæval and Modern History. Oxford, 1886.

────── The Constitutional History of England. 3d ed. 3 vols. Oxford, 1887.

Surtees Society, Publications of the. LXIII: Manuale et processionale ad usum insignis ecclesiae Eboracensis. Ed. by William George Henderson. London, 1875.

Süsskind, M. Die Stellung der Civilehe in Staat und Kirche. Philosophisch und rechtsgeschichtlich entwickelt mit Folgerungen für die Gesetzgebung. N. p., 1849.

Swabey, M. C. M., and Tristram, T. H. Reports of Cases Decided in the Court of Probate and in the Court of Divorce and Matrimonial Causes. II, 1858–60; III, 1862–64.

Swinburne, Henry. A Treatise of Spousals, or Matrimonial Contracts. London, 1686.

Swinderen, Oncko van. Disputatio iuridica inauguralis, de poly-
gynia. Groningae, 1795.

Swinderen, O. Q. van. "Ueber das Güterrecht der Ehefrau in
England." *ZVR.*, V. Stuttgart, 1884.

Swiss Marriage Jurisdiction. Ehegerichts-Ordnung für den Kan-
ton Basel-Stadttheile. Basel, 1837.

Sydow, Rudolf von. Darstellung des Erbrechts nach den Grundsätzen des Sachsenspiegels. Berlin, 1828.

Szlávik, M. "Zur Frage der Civilehe in Ungarn." *ZKR.*, 3d
series, IV, 190–203. Freiburg and Leipzig, 1894.

Tancred. Summa de matrimonio. Ed. by Agathon Wunderlich
Göttingen, 1841.

Tarducci, F. "Usi nuziali." *Rasegna Emiliana*, I, 148–62. Mo-
dena, 1888.

Tebbs, H. V. Essay on the "Scripture Doctrines of Adultery and
Divorce." London, 1822.

Theiner, A. (editor). Acta genuina SS. Œcumenici Concilii Tridentini sub Paulo III. Julio III. et Pio IV. PP. MM. ab Angelo
Massarello Episcopo Thelesino ejusdem concilii secretario con-
scripta. Folio, 2 vols. Zagabrae Croatiae, [1874].

Theiner, T. A. and A. Die Einführung der erzwungenen Ehelosigkeit bei den christlichen Geistlichen und ihre Folge. Bearbeitet von Fr. Nippold. 3d ed., 3 vols. Barmen, [1891–98].

Thiersch, H. W. J. Das Verbot der Ehe innerhalb der nahen Verwandtschaft und der heiligen Schrift. 1869.

Thomasius, Christian. De concubinatu. *Resp.*, E. J. Kiechel.
Halle, 1713.

———— De crimine bigamiae. Vom Laster der zwiefachen Ehe.
Leipzig and Halle, 1721.

———— Tractatio de validitate coniugii, invitis parentibus con-
tracti et per benedictionem sacerdotis depositi consummati,
oder: Von der Gültigkeit der Ehe, welche wider der Eltern
Willen geschlossen und durch Einsegnung eines abgesetzten
Predigers vollzogen worden. Halle and Leipzig, 1722.

Thorpe, B. Ancient Laws and Institutes of England. Record Commission. Folio, London, 1840.

Thrupp, John. The Anglo-Saxon Home: A History of the Domestic Institutions and Customs of England from the Fifth to the
Eleventh Century. London, 1862.

Thwing, C. F. and C. F. B. The Family: An Historical and Social
Study. Boston, 1887.

Towers, John. Polygamy Unscriptural; or two Dialogues between
Philalethes and Monogamus, in which some of the principal
errors of the Rev. Mr. M—D—N's Thelyphthora are detected.
London, 1780.

Traill, H. D. (editor). Social England. 6 vols. New York and London, 1898.

Tschornio, A. W. De poena concubitus à personis per divortium solutis commissi. *Praes.*, F. L. Stoltze. Leipzig, 1736.

Tunstall, J. A. Vindication of the Power of States to prohibit Clandestine Marriages .... in answer to .... Dr. Stebbing's Dissertation. 1755.

Turner, J. A. Discourse on Fornication, with an appendix concerning Concubinage. London, 1698.

Turner, J. Horsefall (editor). The Non-Conformist Register of Baptisms, Marriages, and Deaths compiled by the Rev. Oliver Heywood and T. Dickenson, 1644–1702, 1702–1752. Brighouse, 1881.

Turner, Sharon. History of the Manners, Landed Property .... of the Anglo-Saxons. London, 1805.

Unitarian Marriage Bill, A Letter to the .... Earl of Liverpool, on the; in which is considered the expediency, as well as the justice, of redressing the grievance complained of by dissenters. London, 1827.

Vacarius, Magister. "Summa de matrimonio." Ed. by F. W. Maitland. *Law Quarterly Review*, XIII. London, 1897.

Vaux, J. E. "Marriage Customs." In his Church Folklore, 90–118. London, 1894.

Vazeille, M. F. A. Traité du mariage, de la puissance maritale, et de la puissance paternelle. 2 vols. Paris, 1825.

Velthuysen, L. V. Tractatus de naturali pudore et dignitate hominis in quo agitur, de incestu, etc. Trajecti ad Rhenum, 1686.

Vives [Vivus], J. L. Opera. 2 vols. Folio. Basel, 1555.

Vives, J. L. A very | frvtefvl and | pleasant booke cal | ed the Instruction of a Chris | ten Woman, made first in | latyne, by the right fa | mous clerke mayster | Lewes Viues, and | tourned out of latyne into | Englische | by Ry | charde Hyrde | . London, 1557.

——— "Die Erziehung der Christin. Seiner aller-gnädigsten Herrin, Katharina von Spanien, Königin von England, u. s. w., gewidmet." In his Ausgewählte pädagogische Schriften. Uebersetzt und mit Einleitung und Anmerkungen versehen von Dr. Rudolph Heine. Bd. XVI of Richter's Pädagogische Bibliothek. Leipzig, n. d.

Voigt, Moritz. Ueber das Vadimonium. Leipzig, 1881.

Vogt, P. J. (editor). Kirchen- und Eherecht der Katholiken und Evangelischen in den preussischen Staaten. 2 Theile. Breslau, 1856.

Voisin, A. Contribution à l'histoire des mariages entre consanguins. Paris, 1863.

Vorthusianus, Leonhardus Jacobus. Von Vneinigkeit der Concilien der Priester Ehe, etc. Leipzig, 1546.

Wachsmuth, J. N. Dissertatio de exceptione sponsaliorum clandestinorum ab ipso contrahente opposita. *Praes.*, C. A. Tittel. Jena, 1754.

Wachter, Ferdinand. "Frauen." In Ersch und Gruber's Encyclopädie, Sect. I., T. 48, pp. 324 ff. Leipzig, 1848.

Wächter, Carl Georg von. Abhandlungen aus dem Strafrecht. I, Entführung und Nothzucht, 1. Abschnitt, "Aelteres Recht." Leipzig, 1835.

Wackernagel, W. "Familienrecht und Familienleben der Germanen." *Taschenbuch für Geschichte und Alterthum in Süddeutschland*, 257 ff. Freiburg, 1846.

Wagner, J. G. De divortio, et convictus conjugalis separatione, Vulgo: Von der Ehescheidung zu Tisch und Bett. Halle, 1723.

Wagner, T. Siebenfältiger Ehehalten = Teuffel | Das ist: Ein Ernsthaffte Sermon | von vberhandnemmender Bossheit der Ehehalten vnd Dienstbotten jetziger Zeit. Ulm, 1651.

Waitz, Georg. Deutsche Verfassungsgeschichte. 8 vols. Kiel, 1865–78.

——— "Über die Bedeutung des Mundium im deutschen Recht." *Sitzungsberichte der königlichen preussischen Akademie der Wissenschaften, 1886*, No. XIX. Berlin, 1886.

Walpole, Horace. Memoirs of the Reign of George the Second. 3 vols. Ed. by the late Lord Holland. London, 1847.

——— Letters. Ed. by Cunningham. 9 vols. London, 1880.

Walpole, Spencer. A History of England. 6 vols. London, 1890.

Walter, F. Deutsche Rechtsgeschichte. 2d ed. 2 vols. Bonn, 1875.

——— Corpus juris germanici antiqui. 3 vols. Berlin, 1824.

Walton, Frederick Parker. Scotch Marriages, Regular and Irregular. Edinburgh, 1893.

——— A Handbook of Husband and Wife According to the Law of Scotland. Edinburgh, 1893.

Warmund, Gottlieb [Johann Lyser?]. Gewissenhafte Gedancken vom Ehestande. Freiburg, 1679. (After six introductory pages, this is apparently a reprint of the German edition of Lyser's book (Freiburg, 1675) under title of "Gespräch zwischen Polygamo und Monogamo." "Gottlieb Warmund" is probably Johann Lyser, although this is the usual pseudonym of Gottlieb Hosemann.)

Warnkoenig, L. A., and Stein, L. Französische Staats- und Rechtsgeschichte. 3 vols. Basel, 1875.

Wasserschleben, F. W. H. Die Bussordnungen der abendländischen Kirche, nebst einer rechtsgeschichtlicher Einleitung. Halle, 1851.

Wasserschleben, F. W. H. Das Prinzip der Successionsordnung nach deutschem insbesondere sächsischem Rechte. Gotha, 1860.

—— Die germanische Verwandtschaftsberechnung und das Prinzip der Erbfolge nach deutschem insbesondere sächsischem Rechte. Giessen, 1864.

—— Das Ehescheidungsrecht kraft landesherrlicher Machtvollkommenheit. Giessen, 1877.

—— Das Ehescheidungsrecht kraft landesherrlicher Machtvollkommenheit. Zweiter Beitrag. Berlin, 1880.

Waters, Henry Fitz Gilbert. Genealogical Gleanings in England. Extracts from marriage licenses granted by the bishop of London, 1598–1639. From *Historical Collections of the Essex Institute*, XXVIII. Salem, 1892.

Waters, R. E. Chester. Parish Registers in England. Their History and Contents. New ed. London, 1883.

Waterworth, J. The Canons and Decrees of the Sacred Œcumenical Council of Trent. New York, 1848.

Watkins, O. D. Holy Matrimony: A Treatise on the Divine Laws of Marriage. London, 1895.

Weber, H. F. De vera inter sponsalia de praesenti et nuptias differentia. Parchimi, 1825.

Wege, A. De odio secundarum nuptiarum. *Praes.*, P. Müller. 3d ed. Wittenberg, 1737.

Weickhmann, Joachim. Apologie Anderer Thiel | oder, abgenöthigte Rettung der göttlichen Warheit: dass Gott in seinem Wort die vielweibige Ehe verbothen; Als auch [III. Theil] seiner beleidigten Unschuld | wider . . . . Willenbergen | . . . . in Deutscher Sprache verfertiget | Auf Veranlassung einer Deutschen von J. A. L. entworffenen Schrifft. Leipzig, 1717.

Weinhold, Karl. Altnordisches Leben. Berlin, 1856.

—— Die deutschen Frauen in dem Mittelalter. 2d ed. 2 vols. Vienna, 1882.

—— "Reipus und Achasius." Haupt's *Zeitschrift*, VII, 539.

Weinrich, Dr. von. "Die Reichsgesetzgebung und das materielle Ehescheidungsrecht." *ZKR.*, XX, 297–333. Freiburg, 1885.

Werner, J. G. De pactis dotalibus, sub formula: Hut bey Schleyer und Schleyer bey Hut conspectis. Submitted, 1714; published, Wittenberg, 1742.

Weydmann, L. Luther, ein Charakter- und Spiegelbild für unsere Zeit. Hamburg and Gotha, 1850.

Weyhe-Eimke, Arnold Freiherr von. Die Rechtmässigen Ehen des hohen Adels des Heiligen Römischen Reiches deutscher Nation. Prague, 1895.

Wharton, J. J. S. An Exposition of the Laws Relating to the Women of England. London, 1853.

Whately, Richard.   Extract from a Letter on the Marriage Laws addressed . . . . to the late Bishop of Norwich (Dr. Hinds). Dublin, 1851.

Whispers for the Ear of the Author of Thelyphthora. London, 1781.

Whitforde, Richard.   A Werke for housholders, or for them yt | haue the gydynge or gouernaunce of any | company.   Gadred & set forth by a professed | brother of Syon Richarde Whitforde. and | newly corrected & prynted agayne wᵗ an ad | dicion of policy for hous holdynge, set forth | also by the same brother. | [2d ed., London, 1537; 1st ed., 1530.]

Wilda, W. E.   Das Strafrecht der Germanen.   Halle, 1842.

Wildvogel, Ch.   De jure thalami.   Vom Rechte dēs Ehebettes.   N. p., 1757.

Wilisch, Fr. G.   Dissertatio de arrha a sponsae heredibus restituenda: Von Erstattung des Mahlschatzes nach der Braut Tode. *Praes.*, C. L. Crellius.   Wittenberg, 1753.

Wilkins, David.   Concilia Magnae Britanniae et Hiberniae, 446–1717. 4 vols.   London, 1736–37.

Wilks, S. C.   Present Law of Banns a Railroad to Marriage. London, 1864.

Willenberg, S. F.   De matrimonio imparium, Von ungleicher Ehe. Defensa a D. F. Hoheiselius.   Halle, 1727.

——— Commentatio de matrimonio conscientiae, Gallis mariage de conscience.   Jena, 1741.

Windheim, Augustus Dorothea von (translator).   Des Herrn Premontvals Monogamie. 3 Theile.   Nuremberg, 1753.

Wing, John.   The Crowne Conjugall, or the Spouse Royall, a discovery of the True Honour and Happines of Christian Matrimony, published for their consolation who are married, and their encouragement who are not, intending the benefit of both. Middleburgh, 1620.

Wittmann, G. M.   Katholische Grundsätze über die Ehen welche zwischen Katholiken und Protestanten geschlossen werden. Aus dem Lateinischen übersetzt von einem Katholischen Geistlichen.   Stadtamhof, 1831.

Wolff, Martin.   " Zur Geschichte der Witwenehe im alt deutschen Recht."   *Mittheilungen des Instituts für österreichische Geschichte*, 369–88.

[Wolseley, Sir C. W., and Barlow, Bishop Thomas].   The Case of Divorce and Re-Marriage thereupon discussed.   By a Reverend Prelate of the Church of England and a private Gentleman. Occasioned by the late act of Parliament for the Divorce of the Lord Rosse.   London, 1673.

Women.   The Laws respecting women, as they regard their natural Rights, or their Connections and Conduct.   London, 1777.

Womens Rights, the Lavves Resolutions of. See Lavves Resolutions.

Wordsworth, C., Bishop of Lincoln. "On Marriage with a Deceased Wife's Sister." In his Miscellanies, III, 237–56. London, 1889.

——— "On Marriage and Divorce." In his Miscellanies, III, 202–36. London, 1889.

Wright, T. A. History of Domestic Manners and Sentiments in England during the Middle Ages. London, 1862.

Wunderlich, H. D. De separatione à thoro et mensa. *Praes.*, D. D. Hasentien. Jena, 1774.

Young, Ernest. "The Anglo-Saxon Family Law." In Essays in Anglo-Saxon Law. Boston, 1876.

Zeidler, Melchior. De polygamia ut & de matrimonio cum defunctae uxoris sorore disquisitio. Ed. Wartmann. Helmstadt, 1698.

ZKG.=Zeitschrift für Kirchengeschichte, 1876–98. 18 vols. Gotha, 1877–98.

ZKR.=Zeitschrift für Kirchenrecht. Herausgegeben von R. Dove und E. Friedberg. 29 vols. Berlin, Tübingen, and Freiburg, 1861–97.

Zetzkius, Jacob. Dissertatio juridica de matrimonio ad morganaticam contracto, vulgo: Von Vermählung zur linken Hand. Regiomonti, 1692.

Zhishman, Jos. Das Eherecht der orientalischen Kirche. Vienna, 1864.

Zimmermann, D. B. Der Priester-Cölibat und seine Bedeutung für Kirche und Gesellschaft. Kempten, 1899.

Zimmermann, F. "Ueber die Gerichtsbarkeit in Ehesachen der Katholiken im Grossherzogthume Hessen." *ZKR.*, VII. Tübingen, 1867.

Zoepfl, Heinrich. De tutela mulierum Germanica. Heidelberg, 1828.

——— Deutsche Rechtsgeschichte. 4th ed. 3 vols. Braunschweig, 1871–72.

Zum=Bach, C. A. [Landgerichtsrath]. Ueber die Ehen zwischen Katholiken und Protestanten. Historische Beiträge und Bemerkungen. Cologne, 1820.

III. MATRIMONIAL INSTITUTIONS IN THE UNITED STATES

A. MANUSCRIPTS

In the office of the Clerk of Courts, Middlesex County, Mass.:
Files of the County Court for Middlesex County, 1655–91.
Records of the County Court for Middlesex County, 1649–86. 4 vols. Vol. II (1664–70) missing.

Records of the Court of General Sessions of the Peace for Middlesex County, 1692–1822. 9 vols., folio. Vol. I contains court records for the period October, 1686, to March, 1688/89.

In the office of the Clerk of the Supreme Judicial Court for the County of Suffolk, Mass.:

Early Court Files of Suffolk, 1629–1800. A collection of files of colonial and provincial courts, of the Superior Court of Judicature held in the several counties, and of the Supreme Judicial Court. Several hundred volumes for the colonial and provincial periods.

Records of the Court of General Sessions of the Peace for the County of Suffolk, 1702–32. 4 vols., folio; and a volume of fragments, 1738–80.

Minute Books of the Court of General Sessions for the County of Suffolk, 1743–73. Fragments. 5 vols., folio.

Records of the Superior Court of Judicature, Court of Assizes and General Goal Delivery in the Province of Massachusetts Bay, 1692–1780. 33 vols., folio. Vol. II also contains records of various courts, 1686–87.

Records of the Governor and Council, or of the Council, relating to Divorces, 1760–86. 1 vol., folio, marked " Divorce."

In the Boston Athenæum:

Records of the County Court of Suffolk County, October, 1671, to April, 1680.

In the New York State Library, Albany:

New York Colonial Manuscripts: Dutch, 1630–64; English, 1664–1776.

Marriage License Bonds, for the Provincial Period. *Ca.* 40 vols.

B. BOOKS AND ARTICLES

Adams, Charles Francis. Some Phases of Sexual Morality and Church Discipline in Colonial New England. Reprinted from *Proceedings of the Massachusetts Historical Society*, June, 1891. Cambridge, 1891.

——— Three Episodes of Massachusetts History. 2 vols. Boston, 1893.

Adams, Marion. Courtship and Marriage in Colonial New England. A Thesis in the History Department, Stanford University, 1897.

Albany, Annals of. Joel Munsell, compiler. 10 vols. Albany, 1850–59.

Albany, Collections on the History of, from its Discovery to the Present Time, with Notices of its Public Institutions and Biographical Sketches of Citizens Deceased. Joel Munsell, compiler. 4 vols. Albany, 1865–71.

Andrews, Andrela Lilian. Studies in Sewall's Diary. A Thesis in the History Department, Stanford University, 1897.

Andros Tracts. A Collection of Pamphlets and Official Papers, issued during the period between the overthrow of the Andros Government and the establishment of the Second Charter of Massachusetts. *Publications of the Prince Society.* 3 vols. Boston, 1868–74.

Applegarth, A. C. "Quakers in Pennsylvania." *Johns Hopkins University Studies*, X. Baltimore, 1892.

Arnold, S. G. History of the State of Rhode Island. 2 vols. New York, 1874.

Atwater, E. E. A History of the Colony of New Haven. New Haven, 1881.

Bacon, Leonard. The Genesis of the New England Churches. New York, 1874.

Bailey, Frederick W. Early Connecticut Marriages as Found on Ancient Church Records Prior to 1800. New Haven, [1896].

——— Early Massachusetts Marriages Prior to 1800 as Found on the Official Records of Worcester County. First Book. New Haven, [1897].

Bailey, Sarah Loring. Historical Sketches of Andover, Massachusetts. Boston, 1880.

Ballard, E. A. (editor). The Act Relating to Marriage Licenses, etc., in Pennsylvania. 2d ed. Philadelphia, 1885.

Bancroft, George. History of the United States of America. 6 vols. New York, 1886.

Bancroft, H. H. The Native Races of the Pacific States. 5 vols. New York, 1875–82.

Bartlett, Jonathan. Remarks on the Question, Is it lawful to marry the sister of a deceased wife? Bridgeport, 1814.

Belknap, Jeremy. The History of New Hampshire. Dover, 1812.

——— "Queries respecting the Slavery and Emancipation of Negroes in Massachusetts, proposed by the Hon. Judge Tucker of Virginia, and answered by the Rev. Dr. Belknap (1795)." 1 *Massachusetts Historical Collections*, IV, 191–211. Reprinted, Boston, 1835.

Bishop, J. P. New Commentaries on Marriage, Divorce, and Separation. 2 vols. Chicago, 1891.

Bliss, W. R. Colonial Times on Buzzard's Bay. Boston, 1888.

——— Side Glimpses from the Colonial Meeting-House. Boston, 1896.

Booth, Mary L. History of the City of New York from its Earliest Settlement to the Present Time. New York, 1859.

Boston, Town Records of, 1634–1777. 7 vols. In 2d, 7th, 8th, 12th, 14th, 16th, and 18th *Reports of the Boston Record Commission.* Boston, 1876–1900.

Bradford, William. History of Plymouth Plantation. Boston, 1856.

Brigham, William (editor). The Compact with the Charter and Laws of New Plymouth, etc. Boston, 1836.

Brodhead, J. R. History of the State of New York. 2 vols. New York, 1853–71.

Brooks, H. M. The Olden Time Series. The Days of the Spinning-Wheel in New England. Boston, 1886.

Browne, William Hand. "Maryland. The History of a Palatinate." In American Commonwealths. 4th ed. Boston, 1888.

Browne, W. Hardcastle. A Digest of Statutes, Decisions, and Cases throughout the United States upon the Subjects of Divorce and Alimony. Philadelphia, 1872.

——— A Commentary on the Law of Divorce and Alimony. Philadelphia, 1890.

Bruce, P. A. Economic History of Virginia in the Seventeenth Century. 2 vols. New York and London, 1896.

Buford, H. M. The Rights of Property of Married Women under the Laws of Kentucky. Read before the Lexington Bar Association. Cincinnati, 1871.

Burnaby, Andrew. Travels through the Middle Settlements in North America in the Years 1759–60. London, 1798.

Butler, J. D. "British Convicts Shipped to American Colonies." *American Historical Review,* II. New York, 1897.

Campbell, Douglas. The Puritan in Holland, England, and America. 2 vols. New York, 1892.

Carlier, Auguste. Le mariage aux États-Unis. Paris, 1860.

——— Histoire du peuple américain. 2 vols. Paris, 1864.

——— Marriage in the United States. Trans. by B. Joy Jeffries. Boston, 1867.

Carroll, B. R. Historical Collections of South Carolina. 2 vols. New York, 1836.

Chalmers, George. Political Annals of the Present United Colonies. Book I. London, 1780.

——— "Christian Marriage." *Church Quarterly Review,* XII, 1–35. London, 1881.

Clericus (pseud.). Reasons in favor of the erasure of the law which forbids a man to marry his deceased wife's sister. New York, 1827.

——— The argument of Domesticus [pseud. of Alexander McClelland] on the question whether a man may marry his deceased wife's sister. New York, 1827.

Colden, Cadwallader. "Letters on Smith's History of New York." *Collections of the New York Historical Society*, Fund Series, I. 1868.

Connecticut. Acts and Laws of his Majesty's English Colony of Connecticut in New England, in America. Folio. Revisions of New London, 1715, 1750, and New Haven, 1769.

—— Acts and Laws of the State of Connecticut in America. Folio. New London, 1784.

—— General Court. Code of 1650, to which are added Extracts from Laws and Judicial Proceedings of New Haven Colony commonly called Blue Laws. Hartford, 1822.

—— The Code of 1650, being a compilation of the earliest laws of the General Court. Hartford, 1836.

—— The Book of the General Laws for the People within the Jurisdiction of Connecticut; collected out of the Records of the General Court. Folio, 1673. A fac-simile reprint from a copy of the original edition in the possession of Mr. Geo. Brinley. Hartford, 1865.

—— The Public Records of the Colony of, 1636–1780. Ed. by J. H. Trumbull and C. J. Hoadly. 17 vols. Hartford, 1850 ff. (Cited as Conn. Col. Rec.)

Convers, D. Marriage and Divorce in the United States. Philadelphia, 1889.

Cook, F. G. "The Marriage Celebration." Four articles, *Atlantic Monthly*, LXI, February–May, 1888. Boston, 1888.

Cooke, John Esten. "Virginia: A History of the People." In American Commonwealths. Boston, 1884.

Cooke, Parsons. The Marriage Question: or the lawfulness of marrying the sister of a deceased wife, considered. Boston, 1842.

Cowley, Charles. Browne's Divorce and its Consequences. 13th ed. Lowell, 1877.

—— Famous Divorces of All Ages. Lowell, 1878.

—— "Divorces and Divorce Laws of the Fathers of New England." *Albany Law Journal*, XX, 110–13, 131–33. Albany, 1879.

—— Our Divorce Courts: Their Origin and History; Why they are needed; How they are abused; and How they may be reformed. 2d ed. Lowell, 1880.

Croese, Gerard. Historia Quakeriana. 1st ed., Amsterdam, 1695; English ed., London, 1696.

Davis, Andrew McFarland. The Law of Adultery and Ignominious Punishments. Worcester, 1895.

—— Certain Additional Notes . . . . on . . . . Ignominious Punishments and the Massachusetts Currency. From the *Proceedings of the American Antiquarian Society*, April 26, 1899. Worcester, 1899.

Delaware. Acts of the General Assembly, 1752–1792. Folio.

——— Laws of the Government of New Castle, Kent, and Sussex, upon Delaware. By B. Franklin and D. Hall. Philadelphia, 1752.

Dexter, H. M. The Congregationalism of the Last Three Hundred Years, as Seen in its Literature. New York, 1880.

Dimock, Susan Whitney. Births, Marriages, and Deaths from the Records of the Town and Churches in Coventry, Connecticut, 1711–1844. New York, 1897.

"Domesticus." The Doctrine of Incest stated, with an examination of the question, whether a man may marry his deceased wife's sister. 2d ed. New York, 1827.

"Dorchester, Town Records of." *4th Report of Boston Record Commission.*

Doyle, J. A. English Colonies in America. 3 vols. New York, 1882–87.

Drake, S. A. The Making of New England, 1580–1643. New York; 1887.

——— Old Landmarks of Boston. Boston, 1889.

Drake, Samuel G. The History and Antiquities of the City of Boston. Boston, 1854.

Du Bois, W. E. Burghardt. "The Suppression of the African Slave-Trade." *Harvard Historical Studies*, I. New York, 1896.

Dunton, John. The Life and Errors. 2 vols. Westminster, 1818.

——— "Life and Errors [written 1686]." 2 *Massachusetts Historical Collections*, II. Boston, 1814.

——— "Letters Written from New England A. D., 1686." *Prince Society Publications.* With Notes and an Appendix by W. H. Whitmore. Boston, 1867.

Durfee, Thomas. Gleanings from the Judicial History of Rhode Island. Providence, 1883.

Earle, Alice Morse. "Old-Time Marriage Customs in New England." *Journal of American Folk-Lore*, VI, 97–102. Boston, 1893.

——— Customs and Fashions in Old New England. New York, 1894.

——— Colonial Days in Old New York. New York, 1896.

——— "Among Friends." *New England Magazine*, XIX, 18–23. Boston, 1898.

Edes, B. H. H. "Charlestown in the Provincial Period." In Memorial History of Boston, II. Boston, 1882–83.

Edwards, Jonathan. A Faithful Narrative of the Surprising Work of God in the Conversion, etc. With a Large Preface by Dr. Watts and Dr. Guyse. 2d ed. London, 1738.

Eggleston, Edward. "Courtship and Marriage in the Colonies." In Stedman and Hutchinson's *Library of American Literature*, IX, 523–27. New York, 1889.

Ellis, G. E. The Puritan Age in Massachusetts. Boston, 1888.

Essex Institute. Historical Collections. 37 vols. Salem, 1859–1901.

Evans, Hugh Davey. A Treatise on the Christian Doctrine of Marriage. New York, 1870.

Ewell, Marshall D. Cases on Domestic Relations [Leading Cases]. Student's ed. Boston, 1891.

Fernow, B. (editor). The Records of New Amsterdam. 7 vols. New York, 1897.

Fiske, John. Old Virginia and Her Neighbors. 2 vols. Boston, 1897.

Fowler, William C. "Historical Status of the Negro in Connecticut." Dawson's *Historical Magazine and Notes and Queries*, 3d series, III. Morrisiana, 1874.

Freeman, Frederick. The History of Cape Cod. 2 vols. Boston, 1869.

Free Remarks on Dr. Trumbull's Appeal to the public, relative to the unlawfulness of marrying a wife's sister. Norwich, 1810.

Friends, Philadelphia, Monthly Meeting of. Address on Marriage. Philadelphia, 1868.

Fulton, John. The Laws of Marriage: Containing the Hebrew Law, the Roman Law, the Law of the New Testament, and the Canon Law of the Universal Church, concerning the impediments of marriage and the dissolution of the marriage bond. New York, 1883.

Gale, John B. Affinity No Bar to Marriage. Troy, 1881.

—— Leviticus xviii and Marriage Between Affines. [Troy, 1886.]

Gemmill, J. A. The Practice of the Parliament of Canada upon Bills of Divorce, Including an Historical Sketch of Parliamentary Divorce. Toronto, 1889.

Georgia. Marbury and Crawford's Digest of the Laws, 1755–1800. Savannah, 1802.

—— Acts Passed by the General Assembly of the Colony of, 1755–74. Wormsloe, 1881.

Georgia Historical Society, Collections of. 4 vols. Savannah, 1840–78.

Gerard, James W. The Old Stadt Huys of New Amsterdam. Paper read before the New York Historical Society, June 15, 1875. New York, 1875.

Goddard, D. A. "The Press and Literature in the Provincial Period." In Memorial History of Boston, II.

Goodwin, J. A. The Pilgrim Republic. Boston, 1888.

Goodwin, Maud Wilder. The Colonial Cavalier or Southern Life before the Revolution. Boston, 1895.

Gordon, Thomas F. The History of Pennsylvania . . . . to 1775. Philadelphia, 1829.

Grant, Anne. Memoirs of an American Lady: with Sketches of Manners and Scenery in America as they existed previous to the Revolution. New York, 1809.

Green, George Washington. A Short History of Rhode Island. Providence, 1877.

Greenleaf, Simon. A Treatise on the Law of Evidence. 16th ed., by J. H. Wigmore. 3 vols. Boston, 1899.

Hallowell, Richard P. The Quaker Invasion of Massachusetts. 2d ed. Boston, 1883.

Hawks, F. L. History of North Carolina. 2 vols. Fayetteville, 1857–58.

Hawthorne, Nathaniel. Grandfather's Chair. Boston, 1893.

Hazard, Samuel. Annals of Pennsylvania. Philadelphia, 1850.

Hening, William Waller (editor). The Statutes at Large: Being a Collection of all the Laws of Virginia from the First Session of the Legislature in the Year 1619. 13 vols. Richmond, 1809–23.

Hepburn, Charles M. The Historical Development of Code Pleading in America and England. Cincinnati, 1897.

Hickox, G. A. Legal Disabilities of Married Women in Connecticut. Connecticut Woman's Suffrage Association, Tracts, No. 1. Hartford, 1871.

Hildreth, Richard. The History of the United States of America. 6 vols. New York, 1882.

Hill, D. G. (editor). The Records of Births, Marriages, and Deaths, and Intentions of Marriage in the Town of Dedham, 1635–1845. Dedham, 1886.

Historical Magazine and Notes and Queries Concerning the Antiquities, History, and Biography of America. 24 vols. Published in turn at Boston, New York, and Morrisiana, 1857–74.

Hoadly, C. J. See Connecticut Colonial Records.

Hoffman, M. Treatise upon the Estate and Rights of the Corporation of the City of New York as Proprietors. 2 vols. Revised ed. New York, 1862.

Hollister, G. H. The History of Connecticut. 2 vols. Hartford, 1857.

Howard, George Elliott. Local Constitutional History of the United States. Vol. I. Baltimore, 1889.

Howe, Daniel Waite. The Puritan Republic. Indianapolis, [1899].

Hutchinson, Thomas. The History of Massachusetts. From 1628–1774. 3 vols. Vol. I, Salem, 1795; Vol. II, Boston, 1795; Vol. III, London, 1828.

Irving, Washington. Knickerbocker's History of New York. Philadelphia, 1871.

James, Bartlett B. "The Labadist Colony in Maryland." *Johns Hopkins University Studies*, XVII. Baltimore, 1899.

Janeway, J. J. Unlawful Marriage. New York, 1844.

Jenkins, H. M. Historical Collections Relating to Gynedd (Montgomery County, Pa.). Philadelphia, 1884.

Jordan, Edith Monica. Some Aspects of Marriage and Courtship in Colonial New England. A thesis in the History Department, Stanford University, 1897.

Kalm, Peter. Travels in North America. Trans. by J. R. Forster. Warrington, 1770.

Kent, James. Commentaries on American Law. 14th ed. by J. M. Gould. 4 vols. Boston, 1896.

Kuczynski, Robert René. "The Registration Laws in the Colonies of Massachusetts Bay and New Plymouth." *Publications of the American Statistical Association*, September, 1900, VII, 65–73. Boston, 1901.

Lamb, Martha J. History of the City of New York. 2 vols. New York and Chicago, n. d.

Lauderdale Peerage Case. Webster, Sidney. Opinion on the Law of Marriage Prevailing in the Colony of New York in 1772. Given May 26, 1885. New York, 1885.

——— Fowler, Robert Ludlow. Letter and Opinion, May 11, 1885. New York, 1885.

——— Seward, Clarence A. Answers to the Interrogatories Propounded by Messrs. John C. Brodie and Sons, of Edinburgh, New York, June, 1885.

Law Reports. "Appeal Cases before the House of Lords and the Judicial Committee of the Privy Council, also Peerage Cases." X. Containing the Lauderdale Peerage Case. London, 1885.

Lechford, Thomas. "Plain Dealing or News from New England." Ed. by J. H. Trumbull. *Library of New England History*. IV. Boston, 1867.

——— "Plain Dealing: or Newes from New England." 3 *Massachusetts Historical Collections*, III, 55 ff.

——— Note-Book Kept by, in Boston, 1638–71. Cambridge, 1885.

Livingston, J. H. A Dissertation on the Marriage of a Man with his Sister-in-Law. New Brunswick, 1816.

Lodge, Henry Cabot. A Short History of the English Colonies in America. New York, 1882.

[MacClelland, Alexander]. The doctrine of incest stated, with an examination of the question whether a man may marry his deceased wife's sister. New York, 1827.

MacCorkle, William A. The Divine Law concerning Marriage. Boston, 1872.

McKenzie, A. "The Religious History of the Provincial Period." In Memorial History of Boston, II.

"Marriage Agreement, A." *Virginia Magazine of History and Biography*, IV, No. 1. Richmond, 1896.

"Marriage with a Deceased Wife's Sister Unlawful." *Church Quarterly Review*, XV, 404–30. London, 1887.

Marshall, William. An inquiry concerning the lawfulness of marriage between parties previously related by consanguinity or affinity, etc. New York, 1843.

Maryland, Acts of the Assembly, passed in the Province of, from 1692–1715. London, 1723.

Maryland, Archives of: Proceedings and Acts of the General Assembly, 1637–76, 2 vols. Proceedings of the Council, 1636–87/8, 2 vols. Judicial and Testamentary Business, 1637–50, 1 vol. Ed. by William Hand Browne. Baltimore, 1883–87.

Maryland, Laws of. Folio. By Thomas Bacon. Annapolis, 1765.

Maryland, Laws of, made since 1763. Annapolis, 1777, 1787.

Massachusetts. Records of the Court of Assistants. See Noble, John.

—— The Book of the General Lavves and Libertyes concerning the Inhabitants of the Massachusetts, collected out of the records of the General Court, for the several years wherein they were made and established. And now Revised . . . . 1649. Folio. Cambridge, 1660.

—— The General Laws and Liberties of the Massachusetts Colony: Revised & Re-printed by Order of the General Court Holden at Boston, May 15th, 1672. Edward Rawson, Secr. Folio. Cambridge, 1672.

—— Acts and Laws of her Majesties Province of the Massachusetts-Bay in New England, 1692–1714. Folio. Boston, 1714.

—— Acts and Laws of his Majesty's Province of the Massachusetts-Bay in New England. Folio. Boston, 1759.

—— Acts and Laws of his Majesty's Province of Massachusetts-Bay in New England, 1692–1765. Folio. Boston, 1769.

—— Acts and Resolves of the Province, VI–VIII, 1692–1780 (I–III of the Appendix). Boston, 1892–96.

Massachusetts Bay, Charters and General Laws of the Colony and Province of. Boston, 1814.

Massachusetts Bay Colony, Records of the Governor and Company of. Ed. by N. B. Shurtleff. 5 vols. Boston, 1853–54.

Massachusetts General Court (1841). House . . . . No. 7. Report of the special committee, to whom were referred petitions, praying for the repeal of so much of the Revised Statutes, as concerns the intermarriage of persons differing in complexion, etc.

——— House . . . . No. 28, 1839. Report on sundry petitions of women of various towns respecting distinction of color.

——— House . . . . No. 46. Report of the joint special committee to whom were referred petitions praying that so much of the Revised Statutes as relates to intermarriage between white persons, and negroes, mulattoes, or Indians, be erased; dated March 6, 1840.

Massachusetts. Legis. docs. Minority report of the committee on judiciary [by N. T. Leonard. Relative to Divorce. Feb. 18, 1843. Also an Act repealing certain laws relating to divorce]. Boston, 1843.

Massachusetts Historical Society, Collections of. 60 vols. Boston, 1792–1899.

——— *Proceedings of,* 1791–1900. 33 vols. Boston, 1879 ff.

Mather, Cotton. Magnalia Christi Americana: or, the Ecclesiastical History of New England. 2 vols. Hartford, 1820.

Mather, Increase, and others. The Answer of Several Ministers in and near Boston to that Case of Conscience, whether it is Lawful for a Man to Marry his Wives own Sister. Boston, 1695.

Matthews, Rev. Dr. Speech on the lawfulness of marrying a deceased wife's sister delivered before the general synod of the Reformed Dutch Church, June, 1843. New York, 1843.

Milledoler, Philip. Dissertation on Incestuous Marriages. New York, 1843.

Miller, N. D. Legal Status of Married Women in Pennsylvania. Read before the Social Science Association of Philadelphia, November 11, 1875. Reprinted from the *Pennsylvania Monthly* for December, 1875. Philadelphia, 1875.

Moore, George H. Notes on the History of Slavery in Massachusetts. New York, 1866.

——— Slave Marriages in Massachusetts. Dawson's *Historical Magazine and Notes and Queries,* 2d series, V.

Names of Persons for whom Marriage Licenses were issued by the Secretary of the Province of New York previous to 1784. Printed by order of Gideon J. Tucker, Sec. of State, with introduction by E. B. O'Callaghan. Albany, 1860.

New England. A Letter from New England, concerning the State of Religion there. Edinburgh, 1742.

Newhall, James R. Ye Great and General Court in Collonie Times. Lynn, 1897.

New Hampshire Provincial, Town, and State Papers. Documents and Records relating to the Province and State of New Hampshire. 12 vols. Concord, 1867–83.

New Hampshire. Acts and Laws passed by the General Court or Assembly of his Majesties Province of New-Hampshire in New-England, 1696–1725. Folio. Boston, 1726.

────── Acts and Laws of his Majesty's Province of New-Hampshire, in New England. Folio. Portsmouth, 1761 and 1771.

New Hampshire Historical Society, Collections of. Vols. I–VIII. Concord, 1824–66.

New Haven Colonial Records. 2 vols. Ed. by C. J. Hoadly. Hartford, 1857–58.

New Jersey, Documents relating to the Colony of, 1631–1776. Ed. by F. W. Ricord and W. Nelson. 19 vols. and Index. Newark, 1880 ff. (Cited from the binder's and half-title as "New Jersey Archives.")

────── The Grants, Concessions, and Original Constitutions of the Province of New Jersey. Ed. by A. Leaming and J. Spicer. 2d ed. Philadelphia, n. d.

────── Acts of the General Assembly of the Province, from the 2d year of Queen Anne to 25 George II. Folio. Woodbridge, 1752.

────── Acts of the General Assembly of the Province, 1702–1776. Ed. by S. Allinson. Folio. Burlington, 1776.

New York. Duke of York's Book of Lawes, under title of: "Laus Deo. East-Hampton Book of Laws. June y[e] 24th, 1665." In *Collections of the New York Historical Society* for the year 1809. New York, 1811. See Pennsylvania.

────── The Colonial Laws of. 5 vols. Albany, 1894.

────── Calendar of Historical Manuscripts. Ed. by O'Callaghan. Part I, "Dutch Manuscripts, 1630–64;" Albany, 1865. Part II, "English Manuscripts, 1664–1776;" Albany, 1866.

Nichols, T. L., and Mrs. Mary S. G. Marriage: its History, Character, and Results . . . . its Science and its Facts. New York, 1854.

Noble, John (editor). Records of the Court of Assistants of the Colony of Massachusetts Bay, 1630–1692. I, 1673–1692. Boston, 1901.

North Carolina, Colonial Records of. 10 vols. Ed. by W. L. Saunders. Raleigh, 1886–90.

────── Iredell-Martin's Public Acts of the General Assembly. Newbern, 1804.

────── Swan's Revisal (ed. 1852).

────── Davis' Revisal (ed. 1773).

O'Callaghan, E. B. Laws and Ordinances of New Netherland, 1638–1674. Albany, 1868.

Oliver, Peter. The Puritan Commonwealth. Boston, 1856.

Ostrander, S. M. A History of the City of Brooklyn and King's County. Ed. by A. Black. 2 vols. Brooklyn, 1894.

Palfrey, J G. History of New England. 5 vols. Boston, 1888–90.

Parsons, Theophilus. The Law of Contract. 8th ed. Ed. by Samuel Williston. 3 vols. Boston, 1893.

Penn, William. Select Works. 1 vol., Folio, London, 1771; 5 vols., 8vo, London, 1782.

—— A brief Account of the Rise and Progress of the People called Quakers. 12th ed. Manchester, 1834.

Pennsylvania and New York. Charter to William Penn, and Laws of the Province of Pennsylvania, 1682–1700, preceded by Duke of York's Laws in force [in Pa.] 1676–1682. Published under the direction of John Blair Linn; compiled and edited by Staughton George, Benjamin M. Nead, and Thomas McCamant. Harrisburg, 1879.

Pennsylvania, Laws of the Commonwealth of, 1700–1810. Philadelphia, 1810.

—— Carey and Bioren's Laws of the Commonwealth. 6 vols. Philadelphia, 1803.

—— Colonial Records of, 1664–1790: Minutes of the Provincial Council. 16 vols. Harrisburg, 1838–53.

Plymouth, Records of the Colony of. Ed. by Shurtleff and Pulsifer. 12 vols. Boston, 1855–61.

Prime, W. C. Along New England Roads. New York, 1892.

Reeve, Tapping. The Law of Husband and Wife, etc. 4th ed., by J. W. Eaton. Albany, 1888.

Rhode Island. The Proceedings of the First General Assembly of "The Incorporation of Providence Plantations" and the Code of Laws adopted by that Assembly in 1647. With Notes, historical and explanatory, by Willam R. Staples. Providence, 1847.

—— Laws and Acts of her Majesties Colony of Rhode Island and Providence Plantations made from the First Settlement in 1636 to 1705. Fac-simile of the MS. and a reprint of the Code of 1705. With an Historical Introduction by S. S. Rider. Providence, 1896.

—— The Charter and the Laws of his Majesties Colony of Rhode-Island and Providence Plantations in America, 1719. A fac-simile reprint, with a Bibliographical and Historical Introduction by S. S. Rider. Providence, 1895. Reprint of the Boston ed., 1719.

—— Acts and Laws of his Majesty's Colony of Rhode-Island, and Providence Plantations in America. Folio. Newport, 1730, 1745, 1752, and 1767.

Rhode Island. Supplementary Pages to the Digest of 1730 of the Acts and Laws of Rhode Island. Fac-simile reprint by S. S. Rider. Folio. Providence, [1898].

—— Acts and Laws of the English Colony of Rhode-Island and Providence-Plantations. . . . . passed since the Revision in June, 1767. Folio. Newport, 1772. Fac-simile reprint issued by Harry Gregory. Providence, 1893.

—— Records of the Colony of, 1636–1782. 10 vols. Edited by J. R. Bartlett. Providence, 1856–65.

"Rite of Marriage in New England." *Massachusetts Historical Society Proceedings*, 1858–60.

Rodgers, Rev. John. "A brief view of the state of religious liberty in the Colony of New York, 1773." 2 *Massachusetts Historical Collections*, I, 152. For the authorship, *ibid.*, II, 270.

"Salem, Town Records of, 1634–1659." Ed. by W. P. Upham. *Historical Collection of the Essex Institute*, IX.

Sanford, E. B. A History of Connecticut. Hartford, 1888.

Sargent, Lucius Manlius. Dealings with the Dead. 2 vols. Boston, 1856.

Schouler, James. A Treatise on Domestic Relations. 5th ed. Boston, 1895.

Scribner, C. H. A Treatise on the Law of Dower. 2d ed. 2 vols. Philadelphia, 1883.

Scudder, H. E. "Life in Boston in the Provincial Period." In Memorial History of Boston, II. Boston, 1882–83.

Sewall, Samuel. "Diary." *Collections of the Massachusetts Historical Society*, 5th series, V, VI, VII. Boston, 1878–80.

—— "Letter-Book." *Ibid.*, 6th series, I, II. Boston, 1886.

Sewel, William. The History of the Rise, Increase, and Progress of the Christian People called Quakers. Original Dutch ed., Amsterdam, 1717; 1st English ed., folio, London, 1722; later English eds.: London, 1725, folio; 1795, 2 vols., 8vo.

Shirley, J. M. "The Early Jurisprudence of New Hampshire." *Proceedings of the New Hampshire Historical Society*, 1876–84. Concord, 1885.

Shurtleff, N. B. A Topographical and Historical Description of Boston. 2d ed. Boston, 1872.

Smith, Samuel. History of the Colony of Nova Caesaria, or New Jersey. Burlington, 1765; reprinted, 1877.

Smith, Nathaniel, student in Physick. The Quakers Spiritual Court Proclaimed. London, 1668.

Snow, Caleb H. A History of Boston. Boston, 1824.

South Carolina. Brevard's Alphabetical Digest. 3 vols. Charleston, 1814.

South Carolina. Statutes at Large. Ed. by Cooper and McCord. 10 vols. Columbia, 1836–41.

Spotswood, Alexander. The Official Letters of. *Collections of the Virginia Historical Society*, new series, I, II. Richmond, 1882–85.

Steiner, B. C. "History of Slavery in Connecticut." *Johns Hopkins University Studies*, XI. Baltimore, 1893.

Stewart, David. Marriage and Divorce. San Francisco, 1887.

—— Husband and Wife. 2 vols. San Francisco, 1888.

Stiles, Henry R. History of the City of Brooklyn. 3 vols. Brooklyn, 1867–70.

—— Bundling: Its Origin, Progress, and Decline. Albany, 1871.

Stone, William L. History of New York City from the Discovery to the Present Day. New York, 1872.

Story, Joseph. Commentaries on the Conflict of Laws, Foreign and Domestic. 8th ed. by Melville M. Bigelow. Boston, 1883.

Strachey, William. For the Colony in Virginea Britannea: Lavves Diuine, Morall, and Martiall [Dale's Code]. In Force's Tracts, III. London, 1612.

Streeter, S. "Papers Relating to the Early History of Maryland." *Maryland Historical Society Publications*. Baltimore, 1876.

Thompson, Hannah. "Letters." *Pennsylvania Magazine of History and Biography*, XIV. Philadelphia, 1890.

Trumbull, B. Appeal to the Public, especially to the learned, with respect to the unlawfulness of divorces . . . . pleaded before the Consociation of . . . . New Haven . . . . 1785. New Haven, 1788.

—— Appeal to the Public relative to the Lawfulness of Marrying a Wife's Sister. N. p., 1810.

—— A Complete History of Connecticut, Civil and Ecclesiastical. 2 vols. New Haven, 1818.

Trumbull, J. H. See Connecticut Colonial Records.

—— The True Blue Laws of Connecticut and New Haven, and the False Blue Laws Forged by Peters. Hartford, 1876.

Underhill, Thomas. Hell broke loose: Or An History of the Quakers Both Old and New. Setting forth many of their Opinions and Practices. Published to antidote Christians against Formality in Religion and Apostasie. London, 1660.

Valentine, D. T. Manual of the Corporation of the City of New York. 1843 ff.

Vanderbilt, Gertrude Lefferts. The Social History of Flatbush and Manners and Customs of the Dutch Settlers in King's County. New York, 1899.

Veritas (pseud.). Remarks on the letter of Domesticus, containing the doctrine of incest stated. New York, 1827.

Vincent, Francis. A History of the State of Delaware from its First Settlement until the Present Time. Philadelphia, 1870.

Virginia, Colonial Records of. Richmond, 1874.

——— Acts of the Assembly, 1662–1715. London, 1727.

——— Acts of the Assembly. Williamsburg, 1769.

——— See Hening.

Waller, Henry D. History of the Town of Flushing, Long Island, New York. Flushing, 1899.

Washburn, Emory. "The Extinction of Slavery in Massachusetts (1857)." 4 *Massachusetts Historical Collections*, IV, and *Proceedings of the Massachusetts Historical Society*, 1855–58.

Watson, J. F. Annals and Occurrences of New York City and State. Philadelphia, 1846.

——— Annals of Philadelphia and Pennsylvania in the Olden Time. Enlarged . . . . by W. P. Hazard. 3 vols. Philadelphia, 1891.

Weeden, W. B. Economic and Social History of New England, 1620–1789. 2 vols. Boston, 1891.

Weeks, Stephen Beauregard. "The Religious Development in the Province of North Carolina." *Johns Hopkins University Studies*, X. Baltimore, 1892.

——— "Church and State in North Carolina." *Ibid.*, XI. Baltimore, 1893.

——— "Southern Quakers and Slavery." *Ibid.*, extra Vol., XV. Baltimore, 1896.

Weise, Arthur James. History of the City of Albany, New York. Albany, 1884.

Whitmore, W. H. The Colonial Laws of Massachusetts. Reprinted from the ed. of 1672, with the supplements through 1686. Boston, 1887.

——— The Colonial Laws of Massachusetts. Reprinted from the edition of 1660, with the supplements to 1672. Boston, 1889.

——— A Bibliographical Sketch of the Laws of the Massachusetts Colony from 1630 to 1686. Boston, 1890.

——— "The Inter-Charter Period." In Memorial History of Boston, II.

Winsor, Justin. Memorial History of Boston. 4 vols. Boston, 1882–83.

Winthrop, John. The History of New England from 1630–1649. Boston, 1853.

Woodruff, E. H. A Selection of Cases on Domestic Relations and the Law of Persons. New York, 1897.

Young, Alexander. Chronicles of the First Planters of the Colony of Massachusetts Bay from 1623–1636. Boston, 1846.
—— Chronicles of the Pilgrim Fathers of the Colony of Plymouth from 1602–1625. 2d ed. Boston, 1844.

IV. PROBLEMS OF MARRIAGE AND THE FAMILY

Abbott, B. V. Judge and Jury: A Popular Explanation of Leading Topics in the Law of the Land. New York, [1880].

Abbott, Frances M. "A Generation of College Women." *Forum*, XX, 377–84. New York, 1895.

—— "College Women and Matrimony." *Century*, LI, 796–98. New York, 1896.

Abbott, Samuel W. "Vital Statistics of Massachusetts: A Forty Years' Summary (1856–95). *28th Annual Report of the Massachusetts State Board of Health*, 711–829. Boston, 1897.

Acollas, Émile. Trois Leçons sur les principes philosophiques et juridiques du mariage. Geneva and Berne, 1871.

—— Le mariage. Paris, 1880.

Adalet. "Turkish Marriages Viewed from a Harem." *Nineteenth Century*, XXXII, 130–40. London, 1892.

Adam, Juliette. "The Dowries of Women in France." *North American Review*, CLII, 37–46. New York, 1891.

—— "The Place of Woman in Modern Life." *Fortnightly Review*, LVII, 522–29. London, 1892.

Adam, William. "Consanguinity in Marriage." *Ibid.*, II, 710–30; III, 74–88. London, 1865–66.

Adler, Felix. "The Ethics of Divorce." *Ethical Record*, II, 200–209; III, 1–7. Philadelphia, 1889–90.

Aftalion, Albert. La femme mariée, ses droits et ses intérêts pécuniaires. Paris, 1899.

Ager, Harry C. "Divorce and the Rights of Society." *American Journal of Politics*, III, 93–97. New York, 1893.

Agrippa, Heinrich Cornelius. See above, Part II.

Alcott, William A. The Moral Philosophy of Courtship and Marriage. 6th ed. Boston, 1860.

Alexander, W. Geschichte des weiblichen Geschlechts. Aus dem Englischen. Leipzig, 1780–81.

Allen, Grant. "Plain Words on the Woman Question." *Fortnightly Review*. LII, 448–58. London, 1889.

—— "Woman's Place in Nature." *Forum*, VII, 258–63. New York, 1889.

—— "The Girl of the Future." *Universal Review*, VII, 49. London, 1890.

Allen, Nathan. "Divorces in New England." *North American Review*, CXXX, 547–64. New York, 1880.

—— "The New England Family." *New Englander*, XLI, 137–59. New Haven, 1882.

—— Decadence of the Family. N. p.; n. d. (A broadside of three newspaper columns.)

Almy, C., and Fuller, Horace W. The Law of Married Women in Massachusetts. Boston, 1878.

Amat, Rt. Rev. Dr. Treatise on Matrimony According to the Doctrine and Discipline of the Catholic Church. San Francisco, 1864.

American Bar Association. Reports of the Committee on Jurisprudence and Law Reforms, to be Acted upon August 15, 1888, on Marriage and Divorce. N. p.; n. d.

American Statistical Association. Publications. Boston, 1888 ff.

Ames, Azel. Sex in Industry. A Plea for the Working Girl. Boston, 1875.

Ames, H. The Motives for and a New System of Divorce. An inaugural dissertation. Göttingen, 1891.

Andrews, Stephen P. Love, Marriage, and Divorce. New York, n. d.

Angstman, Charlotte Smith. "College Women and the New Science." *Popular Science Monthly*, LIII, 674–90. New York, 1898.

Ansell, Charles. Statistics of Families in the Upper and Professional Classes. National Life Assurance Society. London, 1874.

Anstruther, Eva. "Ladies' Clubs." *Nineteenth Century*, XLV, 598–611. London, 1899.

Anthony, P. L. The Marriage Relation, Polygamy and Concubinage, the Law of God and Public Utility. Little Rock, 1866.

Anthony, Susan B. "The Status of Woman, Past, Present, and Future." *Arena*, XVII, 901–8. Boston, 1897.

Arms, H. P. Intermarriage of the Deaf. Philadelphia, 1887.

Arndt, F. Der Frauen Anteil an die moderne Weltgeschichte. Leipzig, 1877.

Art of Governing a Wife, The, with Rules for Batchelors, to which is added an Essay against Unequal Marriages. London, 1747.

Assirelli, G. P. La famiglia e la società. Milan, 1887.

Astell, Mary. See above, Part II.

Atherton, Gertrude. "Divorce in the United States." *Contemporary Review*, LXII, 410–16. London, 1897.

Aubry. Le travail des femmes dans les ateliers, manufactures et magasins. Nancy, 1875.

Audlaw, Franz Freiherr von. Die Frauen in der Geschichte. 2 vols. Mayence, 1861.

Augspurg, Anita. Die ethische Seite der Frauenfrage. Minden and Leipzig, [1893].

Bacon, Leonard W. "Polygamy in New England." *Princeton Review*, new series, X, 39–57. New York, 1882.

—— "Divorce-Reform." *Ibid.*, new series, XII, 227–46. New York, 1883.

Baerenbach, Friedrich von. Die Socialwissenschaften. Leipzig, 1882.

Baier, J. Die Naturehe in ihrem Verhältnis zur paradiesischen, vorchristlichen und christlich-sakramentalen Ehe. Regensburg, 1886.

Bailly, Charles. Causes de l'affaiblissement de l'autorité paternelle et moyens de la relever suivi d'un idéal gouvernemental. Arbois, 1850.

Baltisch, F. Eigenthum und Viel-Kinderei, Haupt-quellen des Glücks und des Unglücks der Völker. Kiel, 1848.

Balzac, Honoré de. "Physiologie du mariage, ou méditations de philosophie éclectique sur le bonheur et le malheur conjugal." In Œuvres complètes. Paris, 1882.

Barclay, Thomas. "The New French Divorce Act." *Law Quarterly Review*, I, 355–64. London, 1885.

Barnes, Mary Clark. "The Science of Home Management." *North American Review*, CLXVII, 633–38. New York, 1898.

Barrows, W. "Marriage and Divorce in Civil Courts." *Congregational Review*, IX, 238–46. Boston, 1869.

Baudrillart, Henri. La famille et l'éducation en France dans leurs rapports avec l'état de la société. Paris, 1874.

Bebel, August. Die Frau und der Sozialismus. 31st ed. Stuttgart, 1900.

—— Woman in the Past, Present, and Future. Trans. from the German by H. B. Adams Walther. In the Bellamy Library, No. 15. London, 1894.

Bellangee, J. "Sexual Purity and the Double Standard." *Arena*, XI, 370–77. Boston, 1895.

Bennett, Edmund H. "National Divorce Legislation." *Forum*, II, 429–38. New York, 1887.

—— "Marriage Laws." *Ibid.*, III, 219–29. New York, 1887.

—— "Uniformity in Marriage and Divorce Laws." *American Law Register*, new series, XXXV, 221–31. Philadelphia, 1896.

Bentzon, Th. (Madame Blanc). "Family Life in America." *Forum*, XXI, 1–20. New York, 1896.

Berlin. Statistik der Ehescheidungen in der Stadt Berlin in den Jahren 1885 bis 1894. Berlin, n.d.

Bernardo, Domenico di. Il divorzio nella teoria e nella pratica. Palermo, 1875.

Bernasconi, B. F. Il divorzio nei rapparti colla natura umana. Casale, 1891.

Berriat-Saint-Prix, Jacques. Observations sur le divorce et l'adoption. Paris, 1833.

Bertheau, Charles. Essai sur les lois de la population. Paris, 1892.

Bertillon, Jacques. "Note pour l'étude statistique du divorce." Extrait des Annales de démographie internationale, IV, 457–80. Paris, [1880].

—— Étude démographique du divorce. Paris, 1883.

—— "Du sort des divorcés." Journal de la Société de statistique de Paris, XXIV. Paris, 1884.

—— "The Fate of the Divorced." Journal of the Statistical Society, XLVII, 519–26. London, 1884. (Trans. of the preceding.)

Besant, Anne. Marriage: As it was, as it is, and as it should be. N. p., n. d.

Betham-Edwards. "The Family Council in France." National Review, XXVIII, 47–58. London, 1896.

Bianchi, E. Il divorzio: considerazioni sul progetto di legge presentato al Parlamento Italiano. Pisa, 1879.

Billings, John S. "The Diminishing Birth-Rate in the United States." Forum, XV, 467–77. New York, 1893.

Bisland, Elizabeth. "The Modern Woman and Marriage." North American Review, CLX, 753–55. New York, 1895.

Bixby, J. T. "Marriage Becoming Less General, Why?" Nation, VI, 190, 191. New York, 1868.

Black, Clementina. "On Marriage: A Criticism." Fortnightly Review, XLVII, 586–94. London, 1890.

Blackburn, Helen. "Relation of Women to the State in Past Time." National Review, VIII, 392–99. London, 1886.

Blackburn, John. Marriage as Taught by the Socialists. A lecture delivered at Eagle-Street Chapel, London, January 22, 1840. With additions. London, n. d.

Blackwell, Elizabeth. The Human Element in Sex, being a Medical Inquiry into the Relation of Sexual Physiology to Christian Morality. New ed. London, 1894.

—— The Moral Education of the Young in Relation to Sex.

Blackwell, Emily. "The Industrial Position of Women." Popular Science Monthly, XXIII, 388–99. New York, 1883.

Blaikie, W. G. "The Family: Its Scriptural Ideal and its Modern Assailants." *Present Day Tracts*, No. 58. Religious Tract Society. London, [1889].

—— "Women's Battle in Great Britain." *North American Review*, CLXIII, 282–95. New York, 1896.

Blake, Lillie Devereux; Morais, Nina; Underwood, Sara A.; and Lozier, Clemence Sophia. "Dr. Hammond's Estimate of Woman." *North American Review*, CXXXVII, 495–519. New York, 1883.

Blake, Lillie Devereux. Woman's Place Today. New York, [1883].

Blanc, Madame (Th. Bentzon). The Condition of Woman in the United States. Trans. by Abby Langdon Alger. Boston, 1895.

Bobbio, Giovanni. Sulle origini e sul fondamento della famiglia. Studio filisofico-storico-giuridico. Torino, 1891.

Bodio, L. Separazioni personali di coniugi e i divorzi in Italia e in alcuni altri paesi. Rome, 1882.

Bonald, L. G. A. Du divorce considéré au 19e siècle relativement à l'état domestique et l'état public de société. Paris, 1801; 4th ed., 1839; 3d ed., in Œuvres, V, 1818.

Bonjean, Georges. Enfants révoltés et parents coupables. Paris, 1895.

Boone, T. Charles. The Marriage Looking Glass. London, 1848.

Bosse, R. Das Familienwesen oder Forschungen über seine Natur, Geschichte und Rechtsverhältnisse. Stuttgart and Tübingen, 1835.

Bothen, Heinrich Joachim. Zuverlässige Beschreibung des nunmehro ganz entdeckten herrenhutischen Ehe-Geheimnisses. 2 Theile. Frankfort and Berlin, 1751–52.

Bottet, Julien. La famille dans le passé et dans le présent. Amiens, 1892.

Botton, Max; Lebon, André; and Naquet, Alfred. Code annoté du divorce, contenant: le commentaire du livre 1, titre sixième du code civil revisé par le loi du 27 juillet, 1884. Paris, 1884.

Bouchotte, J. B. N. Observations sur l'accord de la raison et de la religion pour le rétablissement du divorce. Paris, 1790.

Bousset, Alice. Zwei Vorkämpferinnen für Frauenbildung: Luise Büchner, Marie Calm. Hamburg, 1893.

Bowes, John. The "Social Beasts"; or An Exposure of the Principles of Robert Owen, Esq., and the Socialists. Liverpool, 1840.

Boypsen, H. H. "Woman's Position in Pagan Times." *Forum*, XX, 311–16. New York, 1895.

Brackett, Anna Collender (editor). Woman and the Higher Education. New York, 1893.

Brackett, Anna Collender (editor). "Sex in Education." In her Education of American Girls, 368–91. New York, 1874.

Bradwell, J. B. Validity of Slave Marriages. Chicago, 1866. (Being the opinion in the case of Smith v. Rosenthal in the County Court of Cook County, Ill., September, 1866.)

Bramwell, Lord. "Marriage with a Deceased Wife's Sister." Nineteenth Century, XX, 403–15. London, 1886.

—— "Bishops and Sisters-in-Law." Ibid., XXI, 104–9. London, 1887.

Bran, H. A. "The Catholic Doctrine on Marriage." American Catholic Quarterly, VIII, 385–404. Philadelphia, 1883.

Bremner, C. S. "The Financial Dependence of Women." North American Review, CLVIII, 382–84. New York, 1894.

Bridel, Louis. La femme et le droit. Étude historique sur la condition des femmes. Paris, 1884.

—— Le droit des femmes et le mariage. Études critiques de législation comparée. Paris, 1893.

Brindley, John. The Marriage System of Socialism Freed from the Misrepresentations of Its Enemies; Being a Faithful Digest of Robert Owen's Lectures on the Marriage System of the New Moral World. Chester, 1840.

Brinkmann, Wilhelm. Bedeutung der Frau für die sittlichen Aufgaben der Familie. Berlin, 1892.

Brooks, W. K. "The Condition of Woman Zoölogically." Popular Science Monthly, XV, 145–55, 347–56. New York, 1879.

—— "Woman from the Standpoint of a Naturalist." Forum, XXII, 286–96. New York, 1896.

Brouardel, P. Le mariage: nullité, divorce. Paris, 1900.

Brown, Hugh Byron. Marriage and Divorce; A Criticism on M. Comte's Teachings on the Relation of the Sexes. New York, 1878.

Brown, W. K. Gunethics; or, the Ethical Status of Woman. New York, [1887].

Browne, Junius Henri. "To Marry or Not to Marry." Forum, VI, 432–42. New York, 1888.

—— "Are Women Companionable to Men?" Cosmopolitan, IV, 452–55. New York, 1888.

Brun, Samuel J. "Divorce Made Easy." North American Review, CLVII, 11–17. New York, 1893.

Bryce. "Marriage and Divorce Under Roman and English Law." In his Studies in History and Jurisprudence. New York and London, 1901.

Buchanan, Robert. "Is the Marriage Contract Eternal?" In his The Coming Terror, 259–85. 2d ed. London, 1891.

Büchner, Luise. Ueber weibliche Berufsarten. Darmstadt, 1872.

―――― Die Frauen und ihr Beruf. 5th ed. Leipzig, 1884.

Buckham, M. H. "The Relation of the Family to the State." *International Review*, XIII, 53–66. New York, 1882.

Burnett, G. W. "Matrimonial Domicile in Jurisdiction for Divorce." *Juridical Review*, VII, 251–59. Edinburgh, 1895.

Bushnell, Horace. "The Organic Unity of the Family." In his Christian Nurture, 90–122. New York, 1861.

Butte, Wilhelm. Die Biotomie des Menschen; oder die Wissenschaft der Natur-Eintheilungen des Lebens, als Mensch, als Mann und als Weib. Bonn, 1829.

Cadet, Ernest. Le mariage en France. Paris, 1870.

Caird, Mona. "Ideal Marriage." *Westminister Review*, CXXX, 617–36. London, 1888.

―――― "The Emancipation of the Family." *North American Review*, CL, 692–705; CLI, 22–37. New York, 1890.

―――― "A Defence of the So-Called 'Wild-Women.'" *Nineteenth Century*, XXXI, 811–29. London, 1892.

―――― The Morality of Marriage and Other Essays on the Status and Destiny of Women. London, 1897.

Camboulives, M. L'homme et la femme à tous les âges de la vie. Paris, 1890.

Cameron, Laura B. "How We Marry." *Westminster Review*, CXLV, 690–94. London, 1896.

Campbell, Helen. "Is American Domesticity Decreasing, and if so, Why?" *Arena*, XIX, 86 ff. Boston, 1898.

Carey, Edward. "The Matrimonial Market." *Forum*, XXI, 747–52. New York, 1896.

Carpenter, Edward. Das Weib und seine Stellung in der freien Gesellschaft. Trans. by H. B. Fischer. Leipzig, [1895?].

Caspari, Otto. Das Problem über die Ehe. Vom philosophischen, geschichtlichen und socialen Gesichtspunkte. Frankfort, 1899.

Cauderlier, G. Les lois de la population et leur application à la Belgique. Brussels, 1900.

Caverno, Charles. The Divorce Question. Examination of the Divorce Statistics of Illinois. Also Leake, Joseph B., Congressional Action on the Subject of Divorce. Chicago Congregational Club, 1884.

―――― "A Treatise on Divorce." *Social Science Series*, No. 2. Madison, 1889.

Cavilly, Georges de. La séparation de corps et le divorce à l'usage des gens du monde et la manière de s'en servir. Manuel des époux mal assortis. Paris, 1882.

Challamel, Jules. "Divorce in France." *Juridical Review*, II, 143–76. Edinburgh, 1890.

Chambré, A. St. John. "Of Divorce." *American Church Review*, XXXVIII, 17–30. New York, 1882.

Champion, Edme. "La révolution et la réforme de l'état civil." Extrait du numéro du 14 juin de *La Révolution*. Paris, 1887.

Chapman, Elizabeth Rachel. "Marriage Rejection and Marriage Reform." *Westminster Review*, CXXX, 358–77. London, 1888.

—————— "The Decline of Divorce." *Ibid.*, CXXXIII, 417–34. London, 1890.

—————— Marriage Questions in Modern Fiction, and Other Essays on Kindred Subjects. London, 1897.

Chauvin, Jeanne. Les professions accessibles aux femmes. Paris, 1892.

Chavassé, Jacques. Traité de l'excellence du mariage: de sa nécessité, et des moyens d'y vivre heureux. Ou l'on fait l'apologie des femmes; contre les calomnies des hommes. Paris, 1685.

Chester, Eliza. The Unmarried Woman. New York, 1892.

Child, G. W. "Marriages of Consanguinity." In Essays, 1869; also in *Westminster Review*, LXXX, 88–109. London, 1863.

[Chrestien, Michel]. Dissertation historique et dogmatique sur l'indissolubilité absolue du mariage, et le divorce. Paris, 1804.

"Christian Law of Marriage." *Church Quarterly Review*, XIX, 410–26. London, 1885.

Claflin, Tennie C. Constitutional Equality a Right of Woman; or, A consideration of the various relations which she sustains as a necessary part of the body of society and humanity. New York, 1871.

Clarke, Edward H. Sex in Education; or, A Fair Chance for the Girls. Boston, 1873.

Cohn, Gustav. Die deutsche Frauenbewegung. Berlin, 1896.

Colfavru, J. C. Du mariage et du contrat de mariage en Angleterre et aux États-Unis. Législation compareé de l'Angleterre, des États-Unis, et de la France. Paris, 1868.

—————— "La question du divorce devant les législateurs de la révolution." *Révolution française*, 3d year, No. 9, 769–78. Paris, 1884.

Colin-Campbell divorce. Ehescheidungsprocess—Colin-Campbell . . . . December, 1886. London, n. d.

Collet, Clara E. "Prospects of Marriage for Women." *Nineteenth Century*, XXXI, 537–52. London, 1892.

—————— "Official Statistics Bearing on the . . . . Employment of Women." *Journal of the Statistical Society*, LXI, 219–60. London, 1898.

Collins, W. S. "Marriage and Divorce in the United States." *Andover Review*, X, 602–16. Boston and New York, 1888.

Commons, John R. "The Family." Chap. x of "A Sociological View of Sovereignty." *American Journal of Sociology*, V, 683–89. Chicago, 1900.

Condorcet, M. J. A. N. Caritat, Marquis de. "Lettres d'un bourgeois de New Haven à un citoyen de Virginie, 1787." In Œuvres complètes, XII. Paris, 1804.

—— "Sur l'admission des femmes au droit de cité." *Journal de la Société de 1789*, July 3, 1790.

"Conflit des lois en matière du mariage et de divorce." *Revue de droit international*, XX, 344–48. Brussels and Leipzig, 1888.

Congregational churches. Report of the Committee on Marriage and Divorce: "The Church and the Family." N. p., n. d.

Contrat conjugal, ou loix du mariage, de la répudiation et du divorce. N. p., 1781; and Neuchatel, [1883].

Conway, Moncure Daniel. The Earthward Pilgrimage. London, 1870.

Cook, Frank Gaylord. "The Partiality of the Law to Married Women." *Atlantic Monthly*, LVIII, 311–17. Boston, 1886.

Cook, Joseph. "Marriage, with Preludes and Current Events." In Boston Monday Lectures. Boston, 1884.

Cook, Lady (née Claflin, Tennessee). "Short History of Marriage." *Westminster Review*, CXLI, 380–95. London, 1894.

Cooke, Rose Terry. "The Real Rights of Women." *North American Review*, CXLIX, 347–54. New York, 1889.

Cookson, Montague. "The Morality of Married Life." *Fortnightly Review*, XVIII, 397–412. London, 1872.

Coriveaud, A. Hygiène des familles. Paris, 1890.

Coudert, F. R. Divorce: Reply to M. Dumas. New York, 1880.

—— Marriage and Divorce Laws of Europe. New York, 1893.

Coulon, Henri. Le divorce et la séparation de corps. Paris, 1890.

—— De la réforme du mariage; modifications aux régimes matrimoniaux. Paris, 1900.

[Cox, Maria McIntosh]. Home Thoughts. New York, 1901.

Cox, S. S. "Mohammedan Marriages." *North American Review*, CXLIII, 1–16. New York, 1886.

Crafts, W. F. Practical Christian Sociology. New York, London, and Toronto, 1895.

Crawford, Mabel Sharman. "The Maltreatment of Wives." *Westminster Review*, CXXXIX, 292–303. London, 1893.

Crepaz, Adele. Die Gefahren der Frauen-Emancipation. Leipzig, 1892.

Crocker, Hannah Mather. Observations on the Real Rights of Women. Boston, 1818.

Croly, Jane Cunningham ("Jennie June"). History of the Woman's Club Movement in America. New York, [1898].

—— Women's Views of Divorce. New York, 1879.

Crum, F. S. "The Marriage Rate in Massachusetts." *Publications of American Statistical Association*, IV, 322–39. Boston, 1895.

—— "The Birth-Rate in Massachusetts." *Quarterly Journal of Economics*, XI, 248–65. Boston, 1897.

Crummell, Alexander. Marriage and Divorce. A Sermon, Liberia, March 10, 1864. Monrovia, 1864.

Daalen, H. B. van. Die Ehe und die geschlechtliche Stellung der Frau. Berlin, 1896.

Dall, Caroline H. Woman's Rights under the Law. Boston, 1861.

Daniel, Père. Le mariage chrétien et le Code Napoléon. Paris, 1870.

Darwin, George. Beneficial Restrictions to Liberty of Marriage." *Contemporary Review*, XXII, 412–26. London, 1873.

Davies, J. L. "Christianity and the Equality of the Sexes." *Ibid.*, XLVI, 224–34. London, 1884.

Davis, N. H. "Divorce." *International Review*, November-December, 1874. New York, 1874.

Debay, A. Die Philosophie des Ehelebens. Trans. from the 13th French ed. Berlin, 1895.

Deck, Louis. Syphilis et réglementation de la prostitution en Angleterre et aux Indes. Paris, 1898.

Decken, E. von der. Die gebildete Frau und die neue Zeit. Göttingen, 1897.

Defoe, Daniel. An Essay upon Projects. London, 1697.

—— See above, Part II.

Dendy, H. "Marriage in East London." *Contemporary Review*, LXV, 427–32. London, 1894.

—— Marriage in East London. Ed. J. B. Bosanquet. London, 1895.

Depeiges, J. De la procédure du divorce et de la séparation de corps. Commentaire de la loi du 18 avril, 1886. Extract from *Journal des avoués*. Paris, 1887.

Devas, C. S. Studies of Family Life. London and New York, 1886.

Devereaux, R. The Ascent of Woman. Boston, 1896.

Devine, E. T. "The Economic Function of Woman." *Annals of the American Academy*, V, 361–76. Philadelphia, 1895.

Didier, G. L. "Early Marriage." *Catholic World*, XVII, 839–44. New York, 1873.

Dike, Samuel W. "Facts as to Divorce in New England." In Christ and Modern Thought. Boston Monday Lectures, 1880–81. Boston, 1881.

—— "The Effect of Lax Divorce Legislation upon the Stability of American Institutions." *Journal of Social Science*, XIV, 152–63. Boston and New York, 1881.

—— "Some Aspects of the Divorce Question." *Princeton Review*, new series, XIII, 169–90. New York, 1884.

—— "The Religious Problem of the Country Town." *Andover Review*, II, 121–32; III, 38–46, 540–53; IV, 193–208. Boston, 1884–85.

—— Important Features of the Divorce Question for Pulpit Treatment. Montpelier, 1885.

—— What Christianity Has Done for the Family. Auburndale, n. d.

—— The Family in the History of Christianity. A lecture delivered before the American Institute of Christian Philosophy at Asbury Park, N. J., July 27, 1885. New York, 1886.

—— Perils to the Family. An address delivered before the Evangelical Alliance Conference at Washington, December 8, 1887. Auburndale, n. d.

—— "On Divorce." *Publications of the American Statistical Association*, I, 206–14. Boston, 1889.

—— "Statistics of Marriage and Divorce." *Political Science Quarterly*, IV, 592–614. New York, 1889.

—— "Sociological Notes" [on divorce legislation]. *Andover Review*, XI, 427–33. Boston, 1889.

—— "Problems of the Family." *Century*, XXXIX, 385–95. New York, 1890.

—— "Uniform Laws of Marriage and Divorce in the United States." *Arena*, II, 399–408. Boston, 1890.

—— "Sociology in the Higher Education of Woman." *Atlantic Monthly*, LXX, 668–76. Boston, 1892.

—— "The Condition and Needs of Statistics of Marriage and Divorce." *Publications of the American Statistical Association*, III, 513–18. Boston, 1893.

——, secretary. Reports of the National Divorce Reform League and of the National League for the Protection of the Family, 1886–1903. Montpelier and Boston, 1888.

—— Porter, Edward C.; and Palmer, Alice Freeman. The Church and the Home. A report to the General Association of Congregational Churches of Massachusetts. From the Minutes of the Association, 1893.

Dilke, Emilia F. S. "The Industrial Position of Women." *Fortnightly Review*, LIV, 499–508. London, 1893.

Discours qui a concouru à l'Institut National de France, sur cette question: Quelles doivent être, dans une république bien constituée, l'étendue et les limites du père de famille? Paris, an IX (1801).

Divorce. An Essay on Marriage; or, The Lawfulness of Divorce in Certain Case Considered. Addressed to the Feelings of Mankind. Philadelphia, 1788.

—— Ueber den einzig wahren Ehescheidungsgrund in der christlichen Kirche so wie in christlichen Staaten. Von einem Juristen. Bayreuth, 1838.

—— Reasons Why the Divorce Laws of Connecticut Should Be Changed. A paper read before a meeting of preachers at New Haven, January, 1868.

"Divorce and Remarriage." *Literary Digest*, XIX, 244, 245. New York, 1899.

Dix, Morgan. Lectures on the Two Estates; that of the Wedded in the Lord and that of the Single for the Kingdom of Heaven's Sake. New York, 1872.

Dixon, William Hepworth. Spiritual Wives. 2 vols. London, 1868.

Dohm, Hedwig. Der Jesuitismus im Hausstande. Ein Beitrag zur Frauenfrage. Berlin, 1873.

—— Wissenschaftliche Emanzipation der Frau. Berlin, 1874.

—— Der Frauen Natur und Recht. 2d ed. Berlin, n. d.

Dole, E. P. Talks about Law. Boston and New York, 1887.

Donaldson, James. "The Position of Women among the Early Christians." *Contemporary Review*, LVI, 433–51. London, 1889.

Donisthorpe, Wordsworth. "The Future of Marriage." *Fortnightly Review*, LI, 258–71. London, 1892.

Donle, Ludwig. Ueber internationale Eheschliessung mit besonderer Berücksichtigung der geltenden Codifikationen. Freiburg, 1892.

Doubleday, Thomas. The True Law of Population. London, 1842.

Dove, John. Miscellaneous Dissertations on Marriage, Celibacy, Covetousness, Virtue, etc. London, 1769.

Dow, Lorenzo. "Reflections on Matrimony." In his Polemical Works, 85–114. New York, 1814.

Dühren, Eugen. Das Geschlechtsleben in England mit besonderer Beziehung auf London. 2 vols. Charlottenburg and Berlin, 1901–3.

Dumas, Alexandre, the Younger. Man-Woman; or, The Temple, the Hearth, the Street. Trans. and ed. by George Vandenhoff. Philadelphia, 1873.

—— La question du divorce. Paris, 1879; 5th ed., 1880. (See Féval, Hornstein, Vidieu.)

—— Les femmes qui tuent et les femmes qui volent. Paris, 1880.

—— L'homme-femme; réponse à Henri d'Ideville. 30th ed. Paris, 1872. (See Ideville, Girardin, Kellen, "La femme-homme.")

Dumont, Arsène. "Essai sur le natalité en Massachusetts." *Journal de la société statistique de Paris*, XXXVIII, 332–53, 385–55; XXXIX, 64–69. Paris, 1897–98.

Dunning, R. The Christian Law of Marriage. New York, 1857.

Durkheim, Émile. "Introduction à la sociologie de la famille." *Annales de la Faculté des Lettres de Bordeaux*, 1888.

Durrieux, Alcée. Du divorce et de la séparation de corps depuis leur origine jusqu'à nos jours suivies d'un projet de loi sur la séparation de corps. Paris, 1881.

Dwight, Timothy. "Polygamy, Divorce." *Theology*, IV, 255–75. Middletown, 1818.

Dwinell, I. E. "Easy Divorce: Its Causes and Evils." *New Englander*, XLIII, 48–66. New Haven, 1884.

Eastman, William R. "Motherhood and Citizenship: Woman's Wisest Policy." *Forum*, XVIII, 609–21. New York, 1895.

Eberty, Gustav. "Geschichte der Bestrebungen für das Wohl der arbeitenden Frauen in England." *Arbeiterfreund*, 1865.

Edson, Cyrus. "American Life and Physical Deterioration [of Women]." *North American Review*, CLVII, 440–51. New York, 1893.

—— "The Evils of Early Marriages." *Ibid.*, CLVIII, 230–34. New York, 1894.

Ehebund, der, im Bereich der Kirche und des Staates. Zwickau, 1839.

Ehelicher Vertrag, oder Gesetze des Ehestands, der Verstossung und Ehescheidung. N. p., 1784.

Eichmann, A. E.; Harris, H. F.; and Turlay, W. W. "The Divorce Evil." *Arena*, XXIII, 88–102. Boston, 1900.

Ellis, J. Marriage and its Violation. New York, 1870.

"Emancipation of Women." *Westminster Review*, CII, 137–74. London, 1874.

Epenetus (pseud.). A friendly Conversation between two Christians, on the subject of Matrimony under the names of Inquisitor and Caution. London, 1818.

Equality of Sexes. De l'égalité des deux sexes. Discours physique et moral. Paris, 1673.

Ernst, George A. O. The Law of Married Women in Massachusetts. 2d ed. Boston, 1897.

Erxleben, Dorothea Christine. Gründlich Untersuchung der Ursachen, die das weibliche Geschlecht vom Studium abhalten, etc. Berlin, 1742.

——— Vernünftige Gedanken vom Studiren des schönen Geschlechts. Frankfort and Leipzig, 1749.

Essay on Marriage; or, the Lawfulness of Divorce in Certain Cases, considered. Philadelphia, 1788.

Eversley, William Pinder. The Law of the Domestic Relations. London, 1885.

Ewart, Felice. Die Emancipation in der Ehe. Briefe an einen Arzt. Hamburg and Leipzig, 1895.

Fairbanks, Lorenzo S. The Divorce Laws of Massachusetts. The Statute Analyzed and Explained. Boston, 1877.

Farine, Pierre. Guide du divorce, de la séparation de corps et de la séparation de biens. Paris, 1887.

Farr, William. "Influence of Marriage on the Mortality of the French People." *Transactions of the National Association for the Promotion of Social Science*, 1858, LVIII, 504–13. London, 1859.

——— Vital statistics. Ed. by Noel A. Humphreys. London, 1885.

Fay, Edward Allen. Marriages of the Deaf in America. Washington, 1898.

Felice, L. V. de. Il divorzio e la donna. Naples, 1893.

Femme-Homme, la. Mariage-adultère-divorce. Réponse d'une femme à M. Alexandre Dumas Fils. 3d ed. Paris, 1872.

Féré, Ch. La famille névropathique; théorie tératologique de l'hérédité et de la prédisposition morbide et de la dégénérescence. 2d ed. Paris, 1898.

Fernald, James C. The New Womanhood. New York, 1894.

Ferrero, G. "The Problem of Woman from the Bio-Sociological Point of View." *Monist*, IV, 261–74. Chicago, 1893–94.

Féval, Paul. Pas de divorce! Réponse à M. Alexandre Dumas. 11th ed. Paris, 1880.

Fiaux, Louis. La femme, le mariage, et le divorce. Étude de physiologie et de sociologie. Paris, 1880.

Fisher, Sydney G. The Cause of the Increase of Divorce. Philadelphia, 1890.

Flaischlen, G. "Le chapitre du divorce dans le protocole final de la conférence pour la codification du droit international privé." *Revue de droit international*, XXVII, 254–62. Brussels, 1895.

Floessel, Ernst. Die Schwiegermutter. Kulturgeschichtliche Beiträge. Dresden, 1890.

—— Volksbildung und Jugenderziehung. Leipzig, 1891.

Flower, B. O. "Early Environment in Home Life." *Arena*, XI,
483–93. Boston, 1894.

—— "Social Conditions as Feeders of Immorality." *Ibid.*,
XII, 399–412. Boston, 1895.

—— "Wellsprings of Immorality." *Ibid.*, XI, 56–70; XII, 337–
52. Boston, 1895.

—— "Prostitution within the Marriage Bond." *Ibid.*, XIII,
59–73. Boston, 1895.

Fournier, Alfred. Syphilis und Ehe. Trans. by P. Michelson.
Berlin, 1881.

France. Corps législatif. Conseil des anciens. Rapport fait par
Portalis sur la résolution du 29 prairial dernier, relatif au
divorce. Séance du 27 thermidor, an V (1797).

Frank, Louis. Essai sur la condition politique de la femme.
Paris, 1892.

Fränkel, Emil. Das jüdische Eherecht nach dem Reichscivilehe-
gesetz vom 6. Februar, 1875. Munich, 1891.

Franken, Constanze von. Katechismus der weiblichen Erwerbs-
und Berufsarten. Leipzig, 1898.

Franklin, B. F. Marriage and Divorce in Physical, Psychical,
Moral, and Social Relations, According to the Law Natural
and Revealed. New York, 1889.

Franklin, F. "The Marriage of Women College Graduates."
Nation, L, 330, 331. New York, 1890.

Fréchette, Annie Howells. "A Banner Divorce Country." *Century*,
LIX, 636–40. New York, 1900.

Fry, T. C. Social Policy for the Church, and Other Papers on
Social Subjects. London, 1893.

G . . . ., F. von. Ueber Ehesachen und insbesondere Ehescheidungen, uneheliche Vaterschaft, Stuprum und Bordelle. Minden, 1835.

Gabba, C. F. "Introduction of Divorce in Italy." *American
Church Review*, XXXIII, 111–38. New York, 1881.

—— Sur le conflit des loix regardant le mariage. London, 1887.

Gaertner, A. Im eignen Hause. Betrachtungen über Frauen-
thätigkeit auf dem socialen Gebiete. Berlin, 1891.

Galton, Francis. Inquiries into Human Faculty and its Development, 320–23. London, 1883.

Gamble, Eliza B. The Evolution of Woman. An Enquiry into the
Dogma of Her Inferiority to Man. New York, 1894.

Gardener, Helen H. Das Weib und ihre Stellung zur Religion
und Kirche. Trans. by W. Schaumburg. Leipzig, n. d.

Gardener, Helen H. "The Proposed National Law of Divorce." *Arena*, I, 413–22. Boston, 1890.

―――― "A Battle for Sound Morality, or the History of Recent Age-of-Consent Legislation in the United States." *Ibid.*, XIII, 353–71; XIV, 1–32, 205–20, 401–19. Boston, 1895.

―――― Robinson, C. H.; Rowen, J. E.; Gurley, Z. H.; Thompkins, A. C.; Lyons, Will H. "Opposing Views by Legislators on the Age of Consent." *Ibid.*, XIII, 209–25. Boston, 1895.

Gardner, Augustus K. Conjugal Sins. Revised ed. New York, n. d.

Gardner, G. E. "College Women and Matrimony." *Education*, January, 1900. Boston, 1900.

Garnett, L. M. J. The Women of Turkey and Their Folk-Lore. 2 vols. London, 1890–91.

Garrison, C. G. "Limits of Divorce." *Contemporary Review*, LXV, 285–92. London, 1894.

Gasparin, La Comtesse Agénor de. Le mariage au point de vue chrétien. 2d ed. 3 vols. Paris, 1844.

Gasparin, Agénor de. Die Familie, ihre Pflichten, ihre Freuden, und ihre Schmerzen. Deutsch von A. Scholz. 2 vols. Gütersloh, 1870.

Gates, Susa Young (a daughter of Brigham Young). "Family Life among the Mormons." *North American Review*, CL, 339–50. New York, 1890.

Gaume, J. Histoire de la société domestique . . . . ou influence du christianisme sur la famille. Paris, 1844.

Geddes, Patrick. Evolution of Sex and Sex in Education. Four lectures before the Twentieth Century Club, Education Department. Third season of lectures, 1899–1900.

Gibbons, James Cardinal; Potter, Henry C.; and Ingersoll, Robert G. "Is Divorce Wrong?" *North American Review*, CXLIX, 513–38. New York, 1889.

Giles, Alfred E. Marriage and Divorce. Boston, 1883.

Gioja, Melchiorre. Teoria civile e penale del divorzio. Milan, 1803.

Girardin, E. de. L'homme et la femme. Lettre à Dumas. 13th ed. Paris, 1872.

Giudici, Gaetano. Memoria sul divorzio. Milan. An. VI., Rep. (1798).

Gladstone, W. E.; Bradley, Joseph P.; and Dolph, Joseph N. "The Question of Divorce." *North American Review*, CXLIX, 641–52. New York, 1889.

Glock, W. Die christliche Ehe und ihre modernen Gegner. Karlsruhe and Leipzig, 1881.

Gneist, Rudolf. "Ueber gemeinschaftliche Schulen für Knaben und Mädchen und über die Universitätsbildung der Frauen nach den neueren Erfahrungen in den nordamerikanischen Freistaaten. *Arbeiterfreund*, 1874.

Godelle, M. C. Des principes fondamentaux de la famille moderne. Metz, 1869.

Godkin, E. L. "The Future of the Family." *Nation*, VII, 453, 454. New York, 1868.

—— "Marriage and Society." *Ibid.*, X, 332, 333. New York, 1870.

Godwin, William. Of Population, an enquiry concerning the power of increase in the numbers of mankind, being an answer to Mr. Malthus' essay on that subject. London, 1820.

Göhre, Paul. Drei Monate Fabrikarbeiter. Leipzig, 1891.

Goltz, Bogumis. Die Ehe und die Ehestands-Candidaten. Characteristik der Männer und Frauen. Berlin, n. d.

Goncourt, Edmond and Jules de. La femme au dix-huitième siècle. New ed. Paris, 1898.

Gorton, D. A. "Ethics of Marriage and Divorce." *National Quarterly Review*, XXXVII, 27–49. New York, 1878.

Graffenried, Clara de. "The Condition of Wage-Earning Women." *Forum*, XV, 68–82. New York, 1893.

Gray, G. Z. Husband and Wife. 2d ed. Boston, 1886.

Great Britain. Colonial Office. Marriage Law and Divorce Law (Foreign Countries and Colonies): Return giving an outline of marriage laws, and the state of the law on divorce. Part I, "Colonies" (except Canada). June 4, 1894. London, 1894.

—— Foreign Office. Miscellaneous, No. 2 (1894): Reports on the laws on marriage and divorce in foreign countries. Part II, "Foreign Countries." London, 1894.

—— Colonial Office. Marriage Law and Divorce Law (Foreign Countries and Colonies): Return giving an outline of marriage laws, and the state of the law on divorce. Part III, "Canada." August 22, 1894. London, 1894.

—— Home Office. Marriage Laws (United Kingdom): Return giving (1) a copy of the Report, dated July, 1868, of the Royal Commission on the Laws of Marriage; and (2) a summary of the enactments relating to marriage which have been passed since the 1st day of July, 1868. August 22, 1894. London, 1894.

—— Home Office. Matrimonial Causes Act, 1878 (Separation Orders): Return of the number of such orders, 1888–90, 1892–94. London, 1895.

—— Return of the Number of Divorces During the Last Ten Years. Part I, "Foreign Countries;" Part II, "British Colonies." Miscellaneous, No. 4. London, 1895.

Greeley, Horace; James, H.; and Andrews, S. P. Love, Marriage, Divorce, and the Sovereignty of the Individual; A Discussion. Ed. by S. P. Andrews. New York, 1853.

Greeley, Horace. "Marriage and Divorce. A Discussion Between Horace Greeley and Robert Dale Owen." In Recollections of a Busy Life, 571 ff. New York, 1869.

Greene, W. B. Critical Comments Upon . . . . Clarke's 'Sex in Education.' New York, 1874.

Grevin, Paul. L'égalité dans la famille. Douai, 1876.

[Grimke, Sarah M.]. Letters on the Equality of the Sexes. Boston, 1838.

Grimthorpe, Lord. "Marriage of Innocent Divorcees." *Nineteenth Century*, XXXVII, 325–36. London, 1895.

Gronlund, Laurence. The Co-operative Commonwealth in its Outlines. 3d ed. London, 1891.

Guérin, Jules. Reconnaissance des enfants naturels. Caen, 1864.

Guillaume, Baron. Le mariage en droit international privé, et le conférence de la Haye. Brussels, 1894.

Gumplowicz, Ludwig. Der Rassenkampf. Innsbruck, 1883.

——— "The Outlines of Sociology." Trans. by Frederick W. Moore. *Publications of the American Academy of Political and Social Science*. Philadelphia, 1899.

Günther, Carl. Das Recht der Frau auf Arbeit, eine sociologische Betrachtung. Berlin, 1899.

Günther, Reinhold. Weib und Sittlichkeit. Berlin, 1898.

Guyot, Yves. La prostitution. Paris, 1882.

Hahn, Alban von. Frauen-Berufe. Die Bühnenkünstlerin. 2d ed. Leipzig, 1899.

Hahn, August. Die Ehe nach ihrer Idee, und nach ihrer geschicht- lichen Entwicklung. Berlin, 1834.

Hahn, C. von. Vom Einflusse des Christenthums auf das Verhält- niss der Frauen. From the French. Munich, 1820.

Hall, A. C. The Christian Law Concerning Marriage and Divorce. 2d ed. Boston and New York, 1887.

Hamilton, Augusta. Marriage Rites, Customs, and Ceremonies of the Nations of the Universe. London, 1822.

Hamilton, Gail. New Atmosphere. Boston, 1868.

——— Woman's Worth and Worthlessness. A Complement to "New Atmosphere." New York, 1872.

Hansen, Jürgen. Ueber das Heirathen der Armen und das dabei betheiligte Recht der Commünen. Altona, 1832.

[Hardy, E. J.]. How to Be Happy Though Married; a Handbook to Marriage. New York, 1886, 1892.

Hare, W. H. Marriage and Divorce. Sioux Falls, 1893.

Harrison, Frederick. "The Emancipation of Women." *Fortnightly Review*, LVI, 437–52. London, 1891.

Harte, Richard. On the Laws and Customs Relating to Marriage. London, 1870.

Hartmann, Edward von. The Sexes Compared. Trans. by A. Kenner. London and New York, 1895.

Haushofer, M. "Die Ehefrage im deutschen Reich." In Existenzkampf der Frau. Berlin, 1895.

Hayden, William B. Ten Chapters on Marriage: Its Nature, Uses, Duties, and Final Issues. 2d ed. Boston, 1863.

Hayem, Armand. Le mariage. Paris, 1872.

Heaton, J. H. "The Chaos of Marriage and Divorce Laws." *New Review*, XI, 157–75, 304–8. London, 1894.

Heinzen, K. The Rights of Women and the Sexual Relations. Chicago, [1898].

Hencke, J. Ch. Völlig entdecktes Geheimnis der Natur sowohl in der Erzeugung des Menschen als auch in der willkührlichen Wahl des Geschlechts der Kinder. Braunschweig, 1786.

Henderson, Charles Richmond. Social Elements. New York, 1898.

Henne am Rhyn, Otto. Die Frau in der Kulturgeschichte. Berlin, 1892.

——— Die Schmach der modernen Kultur. Leipzig, n. d.

Hennequin. Du divorce. Paris, 1832.

Hennet. Du divorce. 3d ed. Paris, 1792.

Henrotin, Ellen M. "The Attitude of Women's Clubs toward Social Economics." *U. S. Department of Labor Bulletin*, No. 23, 501–45. Washington, 1899.

Héricourt, Madame d'. A Woman's Philosophy of Woman. New York, 1864.

Hermann, G. Sexualismus und Aetiologie. Leipzig, 1899.

Herstatt, W., and Kamp, O. Die hauswirthschaftliche Unterweisung der Landmädchen und Frauen in Deutschland und im Ausland. Wiesbaden, 1894.

Hertzberg, Nils. Der Beruf der Frau und ihre Stellung in der modernen Gesellschaft. Ed. by Werner. Leipzig, 1892.

Heydenreich, K. H. Mann und Weib. Ein Beytrag zur Philosophie über die Geschlechter. Leipzig, 1798.

Higginson, Thomas Wentworth. Common Sense about Women. Boston and New York, n. d.

Hill, Georgiana. Women in English Life from Mediæval to Modern Times. 2 vols. London, 1896.

[Hippel, T. G. von]. Die bürgerliche Verbesserung der Weiber. Berlin, 1792.

[Hippel, T. G. von]. Ueber die Ehe. 3d ed., Berlin, 1792; 4th ed., Frankfort and Leipzig, 1794.

——— Nachlass über weibliche Bildung. Berlin, 1801.

Hirsch, Hugo. Tabulated Digest of the Divorce Laws of the United States. [New York, 1888; new ed., 1901.]

Hirschel, J. J. Drei Fragen über die Civilehe. Mayence, 1878.

Hitchcock, Henry. "Modern Legislation Touching Marital Property Rights." *Journal of Social Science* (American Association), XIII, 12–35. Boston and New York, 1881.

Hobhouse, Emily. "Women Workers: How They Live and How They Wish to Live." *Nineteenth Century*, XLVII, 471–84. London, 1900.

Hoffmann, W. Die christliche Ehe. Berlin, 1860.

Hornstein, L'Abbé E. de. Le divorce. Réponse à M. Alexandre Dumas et à ceux qui préconisent cette doctrine antireligieuse et antisociale. Paris, 1880.

Howe, Julia Ward. Sex and Education. A Reply to . . . . Clarke's "Sex in Education." Boston, 1874.

Hughes, James L. "The Last Protest against Woman's Enfranchisement." *Arena*, 1894, 201–13. Boston, 1894. (Reply to Goldwin Smith.)

Hume, David. "Of Polygamy and Divorces." In his Essays, Moral, Political, and Literary, I, 231–39. London, 1875.

Hupel, August Wilhelm. Vom Zweck der Ehe. Ein Versuch, die Heurath der Castraten und die Trennung unglücklicher Ehen zu vertheidigen. Riga, 1771.

Hurd, P. R. "What Are the Scriptural Grounds of Divorce?" *New Englander and Yale Review*, XLV, 692–707. New Haven, 1886.

Hurtrel, Alice. La femme. Sa condition sociale depuis l'antiquité jusqu'à nos jours. Paris, 1887.

Hyacinthe, R. P. "De la société conjugale, base de la société domestique." *Revue des cours littéraires de la France et de l'étranger*. 4th year, No. 3, pp. 40–46, December 15, 1866.

Ichenhaeuser, Eliza. Die Ausnahmestellung Deutschlands in Sachen des Frauenstudiums. Berlin, 1897.

Ideville, Henri d'. L'homme qui tue et l'homme qui pardonne, précédé d'une lettre à M. Alexandre Dumas. Paris, 1872.

Inglis, James. Home, Marriage, and Family Relations in the Light of Scripture. Boston, 1865.

International Council of Women, Assembled by the National Woman Suffrage Association, Washington . . . . March 25 to April 1, 1888. Washington, 1888.

Italy. Ministero di Agricoltura, Industria e Commercio. Direzione della Statistica Generale. Le separazioni personali di coniugi e i divorzi in Italia e in alcuni altri paesi. Rome, 1882.

Ives, Alice E. "The Domestic Purse Strings." *Forum*, X, 106–14. New York, 1890.

James, Henry. "Is Marriage Holy?" *Atlantic Monthly*, XXV, 360–68. Boston, 1870.

Janes, E. "Divorce, Sociologically Considered." *New Englander and Yale Review*, LIV, 395–402. New Haven, 1891.

Janet, P. La famille: leçons de philosophie morale. 2d ed., Paris, 1877; 4th ed., 1890.

Janke, Heinrich. Die Uebervölkerung und ihre Abwehr. Leipzig, 1893.

Jannaris, A. N. "Mohammedan Marriage and Life." *Arena*, V, 160–77. Boston, 1892.

Jarrold, T. Dissertations on Man, Philosophical, Physiological, and Political, in Answer to Mr. Malthus's "Essay on the Principles of Population." London, 1806.

Jastrow, Hermann. Das Recht der Frau nach dem bürgerlichen Gesetzbuch. Dargestellt für die Frauen. Berlin, 1897.

Jay, William. An Essay on Marriage, or, the Duty of Christians to Marry Religiously. 2d ed. Bath, 1807.

Jeffrey, Jay. "Madam Necker on Divorce." *Edinburgh Review*, I, 486–95. Edinburgh, 1803.

Jessup, Henry Harris. The Women of the Arabs. With a chapter for children. Ed. by Robinson and Riley. New York, [1873].

Johnson, Helen Kendrick. Woman and the Republic. New York, 1897.

Johnson, Ovid F. Remarks upon Uniformity of State Legislation. Delivered before the Pennsylvania Board of Commissioners for the Promotion of Uniformity of Legislation in the United States, May 3, 1892.

Jones, J. H. Scientific Marriage, a Treatise Founded upon the Discoveries and Teachings of W. B. Powell. New York, 1889.

Jörg, G. C. G., and Tzschirner, H. G. Die Ehe aus dem Gesichtspunkte der Natur, der Moral, und der Kirche. Leipzig, 1819.

Josephi, Wilhelm. Ueber die Ehe und physische Erziehung. Göttingen, 1788.

Journal of Social Science, containing the Transactions of the American Association. New York, 1869–94.

Kappler, F. K. Das Recht der unehelichen Kinder nach französisch-badischem Recht und nach dem bürgerlichen Gesetzbuche. Dissertation. Freiburg, 1898.

Keidel, George C. (editor). The Évangile aux femmes. An Old-French Satire on Women. Baltimore, 1895.

Kellen, Tony. Was ist die Frau? Ideen und Paradoxe Alexander Dumas' des Jüngeren über die Frauen, die Liebe und die Ehe. Leipzig, 1892.

Keller, Benjamin F. "Divorce in France." *Publications of the American Statistical Association*, I, 469–73. Boston, 1889.

Kelly, Edmond. The French Law of Marriage, Marriage Contracts, and Divorce. 2d ed. revised by Oliver E. Bodington. London and New York, 1895.

Kimball, A. R. "Divorce as a State Industry." *Nation*, LIV, 334, 335. New York, 1892.

Kinney, A. The Conquest of Death [attained by the procreation of children]. New York, 1893.

Kitchener, Henry Thomas. Letters on Marriage, on the Causes of Matrimonial Infidelity, and on the Reciprocal Relations of the Sexes. 2 vols. London, 1812.

Klebs, Georg. Ueber das Verhältniss des männlichen und weiblichen Geschlechts in der Natur. Jena, 1894.

Klokow, J. Die Frau in der Geschichte. Leipzig, 1881.

Kolatschet, Adolf. Die Stellung der Frauen in Amerika. Vienna, 1864.

Kongress, der schweizerische. Bericht über die Verhandlungen des schweizerischen Kongresses für die Interessen der Frau abgehalten in Genf im September, 1896. Bern, 1897.

[Krug, Th. W.]. Philosophie der Ehe. Reutlingen, 1801.

Kuczynski, Robert René. "The Fecundity of the Native and Foreign Born Population of Massachusetts." *Quarterly Journal of Economics*, XVI, 1–36. Boston, 1902.

Kuhlenbeck, Ludwig. Reform der Ehe. Philosophische, kulturgeschichtliche und naturrechtliche Randbemerkungen zum 6ten Gebot. Leipzig, 1891.

Kuhnow, Anna. Gedanken und Erfahrungen über Frauenbildung und Frauenberuf. 2d ed. Leipzig, 1896.

Kunst mit Männern glücklich zu seyn. Ein Almanach für das Jahr 1801 nach Goethe, Lafontaine, Rousseau und Wieland. Berlin, 1801.

Kyle, J. H. Marriage and Divorce: Remarks in the Senate of the United States, February 3, 1892. Washington, 1892.

Lacombe, Paul. Le mariage libre. Paris, 1867.

Lagneau, Gustave. De l'influence de l'illégitimité sur la mortalité. Extract from *Annales d'hygiène et de médicine légale*. Paris, 1876.

——— Remarques démographiques sur le célibat en France. Paris, 1885.

Lallemand, Léon. Histoire des enfants abandonnés et délaissés. Paris, 1885.

——— La question des enfants abandonnés et délaissés au XIXième siècle. Paris, 1885.

Lanin, E. B. "Sexual Morality in Russia." *Fortnightly Review,* XLVIII, 372–97. London, 1890.

Lasaulx, Carl Joseph von. Uebereinstimmung der französischen Ehetrennungsgesetze, mit Gotteswort und dem Geiste der katholischen Kirche. N. p., 1816.

Lathrop, Noah. "The Holy Scriptures and Divorce." *Bibliotheca Sacra,* LVI, 266–77. Oberlin, 1899.

Laurent, Émile. Mariages consanguins et dégénérescences. Paris, 1895.

Lawrence, Hannah. The History of Woman in England, and Her Influence on Society and Literature. Vol. I, "To the Year 1200." London, 1843.

Lawrence, William Beach. "Étude de législation comparée et de droit international sur le mariage." *Revue de droit international,* II, 53–91, 243–87. Brussels, London, and Paris, 1870.

—— Disabilities of American Women Married Abroad. Foreign Treaties of the United States in Conflict with State Laws Relative to the Transmission of Real Estate to Aliens. New York, 1871.

—— Commentaire sur les éléments du droit international et sur l'histoire des progrès du droit des gens de Henry Wheaton. 4 vols. Leipzig, 1868–80.

Lea, John Walter. Christian Marriage: Its Open and Secret Enemies in England at the Present Time. London, 1881.

Leach, R. B., and Campbell, Vie H. "The Age of Consent." *Arena,* XII, 282–88. Boston, 1895.

Leake, Joseph B. Congressional Action on the Subject of Divorce. See Caverno.

Lecour, C. J. La prostitution à Paris et à Londres, 1789–1877. 3d ed. Paris, 1882.

Lee, Margaret. Divorce; or Faithful and Unfaithful. With a Review by W. E. Gladstone. New York, [1889]. (A novel against divorce.)

—— "Final Words on Divorce." *North American Review,* CL, 263, 264. New York, 1890.

Leffingwell, A. Illegitimacy and the Influence of Seasons upon Conduct. London, 1892.

Legouvé, Ernest. Histoire morale des femmes. 8th ed. Paris, n. d.

Legrand, L. Le mariage et les mœurs en France. Paris, 1879.

Lehr, Ernest. "D'un projet de règlement ou d'office international en matière de mariage." *Revue de droit international,* XVII, 151–60. Brussels and Leipzig, 1885.

—— Le mariage, le divorce et la séparation de corps dans les principaux pays civilisés. Paris, 1899.

Leo XIII. "Christian Marriage." In his The Pope and the People. 1895.

Le Play, F. L'organisation de la famille selon le vrai modèle signalé par l'histoire de toutes les races et de tous les temps. 4th ed. Tours and Paris, 1895.

Lewes, George Henry. "Marriage and Divorce." *Fortnightly Review*, XLIII, 640–53. London, 1885.

Leyser, Augustin von. Rechtliche Abhandlung von Schuldigkeit der Ehemänner ihren Frauen zu folgen. Wittenberg, 1742.

Lilly, W. S. "Ethics of Marriage." *Forum*, VIII, 504–14. New York, 1890.

Lindner, Friedrich. Die unehelichen Geburten als Socialphänomen. Eine Studie zur Statistik der Bevölkerungsbewegung im Königsreich Bayern. Dissertation zu Würzburg. Naumburg, 1899.

Lindwurm, Arnold. Ueber die Geschlechtsliebe im socialethischer Beziehung. Ein Beitrag zur Bevölkerungslehre. Leipzig, 1879.

Lingg, Karl Gustav. Die Civilehe. Augsburg, 1870.

Linton, E. Lynn. "The Revolt against Marriage." *Forum*, X, 585–95. New York, 1891.

——— "The Wild Women as Politicians; the Wild Women as Social Insurgents; and the Partisans of the Wild Women." *Nineteenth Century*, XXX, 79–88, 596–605; XXXI, 455–64. London, 1891–92. (See Caird.)

Lippmann, Frau. Die Frau im Kommunaldienst. Göttingen, 1896.

Little, W. J. K. "Marriage and Divorce: The Doctrine of the Church of England." *Contemporary Review*, LXVIII, 256–70. London, 1895.

Livermore, Mary A. What Shall We Do with Our Daughters? Boston, 1883.

——— "Co-operative Womanhood in the State." *North American Review*, CLIII, 283–295. New York, 1891.

Livermore, Mary A.; Barr, Amelia E.; Cooke, Rose Terry; Phelps, Elizabeth Stuart; and June, Jennie. "Women's Views of Divorce." *Ibid.*, CL, 110–35. New York, 1890.

Livezey, F. B. The Divorce Question. Ministers Seduce to Marriage. [Sykesville, 1896.]

Lockett, Jeannie. "Divorce Considered from a Woman's Point of View." *Westminster Review*, CXXXIII, 479–88. London, 1890.

Loeb, Isidor. The Legal Property Relations of Married Parties. A Study in Comparative Legislation. New York and London, 1900.

Lloyd, A Parlett. A Treatise on the Law of Divorce with the Causes for Which Divorce will be Granted in All the States and Territories. Boston and New York, 1887.

Loewenherz, Johanna. Prostitution oder Production, Eigenthum oder Ehe? Neuwied, n. d.

Loomis, H. "Divorce Legislation in Connecticut." *New Englander*, XXV, 436–53. New Haven, 1866.

Loti, P. "Woman in Japan." *Harper's Monthly*, LXXXII, 119–31. New York, 1890.

Lotze, Rudolph Hermann. Outlines of Practical Philosophy. Trans. and ed. by S. T. Ladd. Boston, 1885.

Lourbet, Jacques. La femme devant la science contemporaine. Paris, 1896.

Lucas, Hippolyte. La femme adultère. Extract from Les Français peints par lui-mêmes, III, 265–72. 1842.

Lusk, Hugh H. "Remarkable Success of Woman's Enfranchisement in New Zealand." *Forum*, XXIII, 173–83. New York, 1897.

Lyttelton, E. Training of the Young in Laws of Sex. London and New York, 1900.

M. "Marriage and Free Thought." *Fortnightly Review*, LVI, 259–78. London, 1891.

M. V. J. R. A. E. P. Traité de l'autorité des parents sur le mariage des enfants de famille. London, 1773.

Mahew, William H. "The Divorce Question." *New Church Review*, 518–28. Boston, 1896.

Maine. Registration Reports, 1892–1900. Augusta, 1894–1902.

Malcome, Howard. The Christian Rule of Marriage. Philadelphia, 1870.

Maleville, J. Du divorce et de la séparation de corps. Paris, 1801.

Malmesbury, Susan H. "The Future of Marriage." *Fortnightly Review*, LI, 272–82. London, 1892.

Man Superior to Woman; or, A Vindication of Man's Natural Right of Sovereign Authority over the Woman [A reply to Sophia]. London, 1739.

Mann, C. H. A Series of Five Sermons on Marriage. Giving Some of the Practical Bearings of the Teachings of Swedenborg's Work on "Conjugal Love." New York, 1882.

Mantegazza, Paul. Die Hygiene der Liebe. 3d ed., n. p., n. d.

Marconville, Jean de, Gentilhomme Percheron. De la bonté et mauvaisetie des femmes. Lyons, 1602.

Marduel, J. B. De l'autorité paternelle, de la piété filiale, et des atteintes portées à ces deux fondements de l'ordre social. 2 vols. Paris, 1828–32.

Marescalchi, Alfonso. Il divorzio e la instituzione sua in Italia. Rome, 1889.

Marr, Wilhelm. Der Mensch und die Ehe vor dem Richterstuhle der Sittlichkeit. Leipzig, 1848.

Marriage. An Essay on Marriage, in a Cautionary Epistle to a Young Gentleman. London, 1750.

—— Conjugal Love and Duty: A Discourse upon Hebrews xiii, 4. 4th ed. London, 1758.

—— The Advantages and Disadvantages of the Marriage State, Represented under the Similitude of a Dream. 5th ed. London, 1760.

—— Reflexions on Celibacy and Marriage, in Four Letters. London, 1771.

Marriage System of Socialism, Freed from the Misrepresentations of its Enemies. Chester, 1840.

Marsangy. Étude sur la moralité de la femme et de l'homme. Paris, 1890.

[Marshall, F.]. "Marriage." In his French Home Life, 311–50. New York, 1878.

Martin, E. S. "Marriage and Divorce." In his Windfalls of Observation. New York, 1893.

Martin, L. A. Histoire de la femme : sa condition politique, civile, morale et religieuse. 2 vols. Paris, 1862–63.

Martin, Victoria C. Woodhull. The Rapid Multiplication of the Unfit. London, 1891.

Massachusetts. Registration Reports, 1843–1899. Boston, 1843–1900.

Mathews, Shailer. "Christian Sociology: The Family." *American Journal of Sociology*, I, 457–72. Chicago, 1896.

Matteis, Luigi de. Matrimonio e divorzio secondo natura e religione, tradizione e storia—diritto e civiltá. Naples, 1885.

Maudsley, Henry. Sex in Mind and Education. New York, 1884.

Mayo-Smith, Richmond. Statistics and Sociology. New York and London, 1895.

Maxwell, Samuel. "National Divorce Legislation." *American Law Review*, XXI, 675–78. St. Louis, 1887.

Mazzoleni. La famiglia nei rapporti coll individuo e colla societá. Milan, 1870.

Meath, Earl of; Selden, Catherine; Edson, Cyrus; and Rickoff, Bertha Monroe. "The Women of Today." *North American Review*, CLVII, 423–55. New York, 1893.

Mémoire sur le mariage des protestants, en 1785. N. p., n. d.

Meriwether, Lee. "Is Divorce a Remedy?" *Westminster Review*, CXXXI, 676–85. London, 1889.

Merriman, D. Report of the Committee on Marriage and Divorce: Publications of the National Divorce Reform League. Special Issues of 1893, No. 2. Reprinted from the Minutes of the National Council [of the Congregational Churches], 1892.

Merrick, E. T. "Our Marriage and Divorce Laws." *Popular Science Monthly*, XXIII, 663–68. New York, 1883. (An examination of Gordon A. Stewart's article, June, 1883.)

Merz, E. H. Ueber Ehe und Ehescheidung. Leipzig, 1861.

Meyer, J., and Silbermann, J. "Die Frau im Handel und Gewerbe." In Gustav Dahm's Existenzkampf der Frau, Heft 7. Berlin, 1895.

Michelet, Jules. Woman (La Femme). Trans. from the last Paris ed. by J. W. Palmer. New York, 1860.

—— Love (L'Amour). Trans. from the 4th Paris ed. by J. W. Palmer. New York, 1870.

—— Le prêtre, la femme et la famille. Paris, 1890.

Michigan. Registration Reports, 1868–96. Lansing, 1868–98.

Milde, Natalie von. Goethe und Schiller und die Frauenfrage. Weimar, [1896].

—— Ist die Frauenbewegung natürlich? Hamburg, 1896.

Milhaud, Léon. De la protection des enfants sans famille. Enfants assistés et enfants moralement abandonnés. Paris, 1896.

Mill, John Stuart. On Liberty. London, 1859; first written, 1854.

—— The Subjection of Women. London, 1869; first written, 1861.

Mill, Mrs. John Stuart. "Enfranchisement of Women." *Westminster Review*, LV, 289–311; also in Dissertations and Discussions, III, 93–131. Boston, 1864.

Molinari, G. de. "The Decline of the French Population" [a translation]. *Journal of the Royal Statistical Society*, L, 183–97. London, 1887.

Monlezun, V. F. O. Essai sur la condition civile de la femme mariée à Rome et en France. Paris, 1878.

Monsabré, J. M. L. "Exposition du dogme catholique." V, "Mariage." In Conférences de Notre-Dame de Paris. Carême, 1887. 5th ed., Paris, 1895.

Mont, Emerich du. Das Weib. Philosophische Briefe über dessen Wesen und Verhältniss zum Manne. 2d ed. Leipzig, 1880.

Moqué, Alice L. "Educated Maternity." *Westminster Review*, CLIII, 53–60. London, 1900.

Morelli, Salvatore. La donna e la scienza, o la soluzione del problema sociale. Naples, 1869.

Morgan, Lady Sydney. Woman and Her Master. 2 vols. London, 1840.

Morgenstern, Lina.   Frauenarbeit in Deutschland.   2 Theile.   Berlin, n. d.

—— and others. "Die Stellung der Frau im Leben." *Deutsche Schriften für nationales Leben*, 1. Reihe, Heft 6.   Kiel and Leipzig, 1891.

Morillot, Léon.   De la condition des enfants nés hors mariage, etc.   Paris, 1865.

Morley, John.   "Condorcet's Plea for the Citizenship of Women." *Fortnightly Review*, XIII, 719–24.   London, 1870.

Morris, William, and Bax, Ernest Belfort.   Socialism: "Its Growth and Outcome."   London and New York, 1893.

Morrison, Frances.   The Influence of the Present Marriage System upon the Character and Interests of Females Contrasted with that Proposed by Robert Owen.   Manchester, 1838.

Moxom, Philip S.   "Final Words on Divorce."   *North American Review*, CL, 264–68.   New York, 1890.

Muirhead, J. H.   "Is the Family Declining?"   *International Journal of Ethics*, VII, 33–55.   Philadelphia, 1896.   (A reply to Charles H. Pearson's " Decline of the Family.")

Mulford, E.   "The Nation and the Family."   In his The Nation. New York, 1871.

Mülinen, Helene von.   Die Stellung der Frau zur socialen Aufgabe.   Bern, 1897.

Müller, Heinrich.   Ungerahtene Ehe | Oder | vornemste Ursachen | so heute den Ehestand zum Wehestand machen.   Frankfort, 1674.

Nadaillac, J. F. A. du P.   L'affaiblissement de la natalité en France, ses causes et ses conséquences.   2d ed.   Paris, 1886.

Naquet, Alfred.   Le divorce.   Paris, 1877.   2d ed.   1881.

—— "Divorce: From a French Point of View."   *North American Review*, CLV, 721–30.   New York, 1892.

National Divorce Reform League.   See Dike.

Naumann, Friedrich.   Christenthum und Familie.   Berlin, 1892.

Naville, Ernest.   La condition sociale des femmes.   Lausanne, 1891.

Necker, Albertine Adrienne.   Réflexions sur le divorce.   Paris, [1792?]; also Lausanne, 1794.

Neander, Th.   Zum Schutz der baltischen Frauen.   Ueber Frauen-Emancipation, Frauenberuf und Frauenideal.   2d ed.   Riga, 1893.

Nelson, William T.   A Treatise on the Law of Divorce and Annulment of Marriage.   2 vols.   Chicago, 1895.

Neubauer, Oberlandesgerichtsrath.   "Ehescheidung im Auslande." *ZVR.*, V–IX.   Stuttgart, 1884–91.

Neumann, H. Die unehelichen Kinder in Berlin. Jena, 1900.

New Jerusalem Church. General Convention. Report of the Committee on Religious Instruction on the Connection between Marriage and the Church in Man. Boston, 1863.

Newman, F. W. "Marriage Laws." In his Miscellanies, III, 222–251; from *Fraser's Magazine*, August, 1867. London, 1889.

Newsholme, Arthur. Vital Statistics. 3d ed. London, 1892.

Nichols, Thos. L., and Mrs. Mary S. Gove. Marriage, its History, Character, and Results. New York, 1854.

Nisbet, J. F. Marriage and Heredity. 2d ed. London, 1890.

Noble, Charles. A Compendium and Comparative View of the Thirty-eight State Laws of Marriage and Divorce in the United States [in 1882]. The Conflict and the Remedy. New York, 1882.

Noble, Lucy Gray. "Free Marriage." *Scribner's Monthly*, VI, 658–64. New York, 1873.

North, Thomas M. "Uniform Marriage and Divorce Laws." *North American Review*, CXLIV, 429–31. New York, 1887.

New Hampshire. Registration Reports, 1880–95. Manchester and Concord, 1881–96.

Notowitch, O. K. L'amour. Étude psycho-philosophique. Paris, 1896.

Nougarède, André. Essai sur l'histoire de la puissance paternelle. Paris, an IX (1801); 2d ed., 1814.

Odier, Pierre. Traité du contrat de mariage ou du régime des biens entre époux. 3 vols. Paris, 1847.

Oettingen, Alexander von. Die Moralstatistik in ihrer Bedeutung für eine christliche Socialethik. 2d ed. Erlangen, 1874.

—— Obligatorische und facultative Civilehe. Leipzig, 1881.

—— Zur Theorie und Praxis des Heiratens. Leipzig, n. d.

Ogden, R. "Divorce in South Dakota." *Nation*, LVI, 60, 61. New York, 1893.

Ogle, William. "On Marriage-Rates and Marriage-Ages, with Special Reference to the Growth of Population." *Journal of the Royal Statistical Society*, LIII, 253–80. London, 1890.

Olivecrona, K. d'. Le mariage des étrangers en Suède et des Suédois à l'étranger. Extract from *Journal du droit international privé*. Paris, 1883.

Olivi, Louis. "Du mariage en droit international privé." *Revue de droit international*, XV, 219–42, 357–85. Brussels and Leipzig, 1883.

Orelli, A. von. Die Familie im deutschen und schweizerischen Recht. Zurich, 1859.

Orléans, L'évêque d'. La femme chrétienne et française. 3d ed. Paris, 1868.

—— Le mariage chrétien. 3d ed. Paris, 1871.

Ormsby, George F. "Defective Alimony Decrees in Massachusetts." *Harvard Law Review*, IV, 25–34. Cambridge, 1891.

Orton, James. The Liberal Education of Women. New York and Chicago, 1873.

Ostrogorski, M. The Rights of Women. A Comparative Study in History and Legislation. London and New York, 1893.

Otto, Luise. Das Recht der Frauen auf Erwerb. Hamburg, 1868.

Owen, Robert. Letters on the Marriages of the Priesthood of the Old Immoral World, delivered in the year 1835, before the passing of the new marriage act. 4th ed. Leeds, 1840.

Owen, Robert Dale. "Marriage and Placement [in Hayti]." *Free Enquirer*, May 28, 1831. New York, 1831.

Ozanam, A. F. "Du divorce." In his Mélanges, I, 151–83. Paris, 1859.

Palmer, A. J. Divorce Abolished. Minneapolis, 1888.

Parent-Duchatelet, A. J. B. De la prostitution dans la ville de Paris. 2 vols. Paris, 1837.

Parkes, Bessie Rayner. Essays on Woman's Work. London, 1865.

Parsons, Benjamin. The Mental and Moral Dignity of Woman. 3d ed. London, 1846.

Peabody, Francis Greenwood. "The Teaching of Jesus Concerning the Family." In his Jesus Christ and the Social Question, chap. iii. New York and London, 1900.

Pearson, Charles Henry. "The Decline of the Family." In his National Life and Character: A Forecast, chap. v. London, 1893.

Pearson, Karl. The Ethic of Free Thought. London, 1888.

—— "Woman and Labor." *Fortnightly Review*, LXI, 561–77. London, 1894.

Peetermans, N., and Dumont, A. "Du mariage considéré dans ses rapports avec l'éducation physique des enfants." *Annales de la Société de Médecine de Gand*, 1841, 389–418.

Pelletan, Eugène. La famille: la mère. 5th ed. Paris, n. d.

Pennell, Elizabeth Robins. "A Century of Women's Rights." *Fortnightly Review*, XLVIII, 408–17. London, 1890.

Perthes, Fr. Matth. Die alte und die neue Lehre über Gesellschaft, Staat, Kirche, Schule, Ehe und Arbeit. 3d ed. Hamburg, 1849.

Phelps, E. J. "Divorce in the United States." *Forum*, VIII, 349–64. New York, 1889.

Phillimore, Robert. Thoughts on Divorce. London, 1844.

Phillimore, Robert. Commentaries upon International Law. 3d ed., 4 vols. London, 1879–89.

Phillips, Waldorf H. "The Divorce Question." *International Review*, XI, 139–52. New York, 1881.

Phillipps, Evelyn March. "The Working Lady in London." *Fortnightly Review*, LII, 192–203. London, 1892.

Pieraccini, Abbé. Il divorzio. Pisa, 1879. (A caricature.)

Pierstorff, Julius. Frauenfrage und Frauenbewegung. Göttingen, 1879.

Planta, P. C. von. Die Reconstruction der Familie und das Erbrecht. Chur, 1886.

Platt, Horace G. The Law as to the Property Rights of Married Women, as Contained in the Statutes and Decisions of California, Texas, and Nevada. San Francisco, 1885.

Pomeroy, H. Sterling. The Ethics of Marriage. With a Prefatory Note by Thomas Addis Emmet, M.D., and an Introduction by Rev. J. T. Duryea. New York, 1889.

Postlethwaite, H. L. "The Marriage Relations: Divorce." *Westminster Review*, CXXXIX, 394–401. London, 1893.

Potter, H. C. "The Message of Christ to the Family." In his Message of Christ to Manhood. Noble Lectures, 1898. Boston, 1899.

Potvin, T. S. "Should Marriages Be Indissoluble?" *New Englander and Yale Review*, LVI, 40–50. New Haven, 1892.

Powell, Aaron M.; Gardener, Helen H.; Willard, Frances E.; Lewis, A. H.; James, O. E.; Dromgoole, W. A.; Blackwell, Emily. "The Shame of America—The Age of Consent Laws in the United States." *Arena*, XI, 192–215. Boston, 1895.

Pratt, Orson, and Newman, J. P. Does the Bible Sanction Polygamy? A Discussion. 2d ed. With three sermons on the same subject by Smith, Pratt, and Cannon. Salt Lake City, 1876.

Previtti, L. Del divorzio. Florence, 1883.

Price, E. K. Discourse on the Family as an Element of Government. Philadelphia, 1864.

Proffatt, John. Woman before the Law. New York, 1874.

Proudhon, P. J. Amour et mariage. Brussels and Leipzig, n. d.

Quilter, Harry (editor). Is Marriage a Failure? Chicago and New York, 1889.

Radcliffe, Mary Anne. The Female Advocate, or an attempt to recover the Rights of Women from Male Usurpation. London, 1799.

Rankin, E. E. The Proper Attitude of our Ministers and Churches in Reference to the Divorce Laws of Connecticut. N. p., n. d.

Rattigan, H. A. B.   The Law of Divorce Applicable to Christians in India.   London, 1897.

Raume, Carl von.   Das Familienleben des niederen Volkes, unter Berücksichtigung der Lehren der Social-Demokratie.   Breslau, 1878.

Raumer, F. von.   "Uber die Ehe und Familie."   *Historisches Taschenbuch*, IV, 327–76.   Leipzig, 1833.

Rauschenbusch–Clough, Emma.   A Study of Mary Wollstonecraft and the Rights of Woman.   London, 1898.

Realf, James, Jr.   "The Sioux Falls Divorce Colony and Some Noted Colonists."   *Arena*, IV, 696–703.   Boston 1891.

Rebière, A.   Les femmes dans le science.   Paris, 1894.

Reclus, Élie.   Primitive Folk: Studies in Comparative Ethnology.   London, [1891].

Reibmayr, Albert.   Die Ehe Tuberkuloser und ihre Folgen.   Leipzig and Vienna, 1894.

Reports of the Conferences of State Boards of Commissioners for Promoting Uniformity of Legislation in the United States, 1892–1903.

Revue de droit international et de législation comparée.   29 vols.   Brussels and elsewhere, 1869–97.

Reynolds, J. P.   The Limiting of Childbearing among the Married.   Philadelphia, 1890.

Ribbe, Charles de.   Les familles et la société en France avant la Révolution.   4th ed.   2 vols.   Tours, 1879.

Richberg, J. C.   "Incongruity of the Divorce Laws of the United States, a Legal Tangle.   *Publications of the Michigan Political Science Association*, I, No. 4.   Ann Arbor, 1895.

Richter, Helene.   Marie Wollstonecraft.   Vienna, 1897.

Riehl, W. H.   Die Familie.   Stuttgart, 1855; 11th ed., 1897.

Rhode Island.   Registration Reports, 1853–1900.   Providence, 1854–1902.

Robinson, W. C.   "The Diagnostics of Divorce."   *Journal of Social Science* (American Association), XIV, 136–51.   Boston and New York, 1881.

Robÿns, Jules (compiler).   "Numero dei divorzi e separazioni in Belgio, Orlanda, e Francia."   *Annali di Statistica*, 2d series, XVII.   Rome, 1881.

Rodenbeck, Rudolf.   Die Ehe in besonderer Beziehung auf Ehescheidung, und Eheschliessung Geschiedener.   Gotha, 1882.

Romanes, George J.   "Mental Differences of Men and Women."   *Popular Science Monthly*, XXXI, 383–401.   New York, 1887.   The same in *Nineteenth Century*, XXI, 654–72.   London, 1887.

Rondelet, Antonin.   La vie dans le mariage.   Paris, 1885.

Ronga, Giovanni. Della condizione giuridica dei figli nati fuori di matrimonio. Turin, 1873.

Roskovány, Augustine de. Supplementa ad collectiones monumentorum et literaturae de matrimonio in ecclesia catholica. Nitriae, 1887.

Ross, Edward Alsworth. Social Control: A Survey of the Foundations of Order. New York and London, 1901.

Rubin, M., and Westergaard, H. Statistik der Ehen auf Grund der socialen Gliederung der Bevölkerung . . . . in Dänemark. Jena, 1890.

Russell, Alys. "Social Democracy and the Woman Question in Germany." In Bertrand Russell's German Social Democracy, 173–95. London, New York, and Bombay, 1896.

Ryan, Michael. Lectures on Population, Marriage, and Divorce, as Questions of State Medicine. London, 1831.

Ryan, Michael. The Philosophy of Marriage, in its Social, Moral, and Physical Relations. 3d ed. London, 1839.

St. Bon, Pacoret de. Les institutions de la famille dans le code civil italien. Grenoble, 1878.

Sacchi, A. Il divorzio in Italia. Rome, 1890.

Salmonson, M. From the Marriage License Window. Chicago, 1887.

Salter, William M. "The Future of the Family. A Lecture Delivered before the Society for Ethical Culture of Chicago, April 26, 1885." Religio-Philosophical Journal. Chicago.

Sandeman. The Honour of Marriage opposed to all Impurities. London, 1777.

Savage, Minot J. "Matrimony and the State." Forum, X, 115–123. New York, 1890.

Scheel, Hans von. "Frauenfrage und Frauenstudium." Jahrbücher für Nationalökonomie und Statistik, XXII, 1–16. Jena, 1874.

Scheube, H. Die Frauen des achtzehnten Jahrhunderts. Berlin, 1876.

Schindler, Solomon. "The Divorce Problem." Arena, I, 682–90. Boston, 1890.

Schkljarewsky, A. von. Unterscheidungs-Merkmale der männlichen und weiblichen Typen mit Bezug auf die Frage der höheren Frauenbildung. Trans. by Cäcilie Neudecker-Bortwicker. 2d ed. Würzburg, 1898.

Schmahl, Jeanne E. "La question de la femme." Nouvelle Revue, LXXXVI, 382–90. Paris, 1894.

——— "Le préjugé de sexe." Ibid., XCIII, 125–34. Paris, 1895.

Schoelcher, Victor. La famille, la propriété et le christianisme. Paris, 1875.

Scholz, Friedrich. Prostitution und Frauenbewegung. Leipzig, 1897.

Schönberg, Gustav. Die Frauenfrage. Basel, 1872.

Schopenhauer, Arthur. "Ueber die Weiber." In his Sämmtliche Wercke, II. Ed. by Frauenstadt. Leipzig, 1887.

—— "On Women." In Essays. Trans. by Mrs. Rudolf Dircks. London, 1897.

Schrank, J. Die amptlichen Vorschriften betr. die Prostitution in Wien, in ihrer administrativen, sanitären, und strafgerichtlichen Anwendung. Vienna, 1899.

Schreiner, Olive. "The Woman Question." Cosmopolitan, XXVIII, 45 ff., 182 ff. Irvington-on-the-Hudson, 1899.

—— "The Woman Movement of Our Day." Harper's Bazar, XXXVI, 3–8, 103–7, 222–27. New York, 1902.

Schulz-Dresden, Carl Theodor. Gefallene Mädchen und die Frauenforderung: "Gleiches moralisches Mass für beide Geschlechter." Berlin-Friedrichshagen, 1899.

Schultz, Alwin. Alltagsleben einer deutschen Frau zu Anfang des achtzehnten Jahrhunderts. Leipzig, 1890.

Schuyler, Eugene. "American Marriages Abroad." North American Review, CXLVIII, 424–34. New York, 1889.

Schwieriger-Lerchenfeld, A. Freiherr von. Das Frauenleben der Erde. Vienna, Pesth, and Leipzig, 1881.

Sears, C. E. Shakers. A Short Treatise on Marriage. Rochester, 1867.

Sedgwick, A. G. "Fraud in Divorce." Nation, XXXVI, 418, 419. New York, 1883.

Selden, C. P. "The Rule of the Mother." North American Review, CLXI, 637–40. New York, 1895.

Serrell, George. "The High-Church Doctrine as to Marriage and Divorce." Contemporary Review, LXVIII, 21–41. London, 1895.

Sewall, Samuel E. Legal condition of Women in Massachusetts. 4th ed. Boston, 1886.

Sewell, J. A. "Divorce and Remarriage." Westminster Review, CXLV, 182–92. London, 1896.

Sex-equality. De l'égalité des deux sexes, Discours physique et moral, où l'on voit l'importance de se défaire des préjugés. Paris, 1673.

Shinn, George W. Friendly Talks about Marriage. Boston, 1897.

Shinn, Millicent Washburn. "The Marriage Rate of College Women." Century Magazine, L, 946–48. New York, 1895.

Sidgwick, Mrs. Henry. Health Statistics of Women Students of Cambridge and Oxford and Their Sisters. Cambridge, 1890.

Sigourney, Mrs. L. H. Letters to Mothers. 6th ed. New York, 1846.

Simon, F. B. Die Gesundheitspflege des Weibes. 2d ed. Stuttgart, 1893.

Simon, J. and G. La femme du vingtième siècle. 21st ed. Paris, 1892.

Sincholle, A. Le mariage civil et le mariage religieux. Poitiers, 1876.

Small, Albion W., and Vincent, George E. An Introduction to the Study of Society. New York, Cincinnati, and Chicago, [1894].

Smith, Edgar Maurice. "Laws Governing the Age of Consent in Canada. A Comparison with Those of the United States." *Arena*, XIII, 88–91. Boston, 1895.

Smith, Eugene. "Conflict of State Laws,—the Evil and the Remedy." *Journal of Social Science* (American Association), XIX, 132–44. Boston and New York, 1885.

Smith, Mrs. E. O. Sanctity of Marriage. Woman's Rights Tracts, No. 5. Syracuse, 1853.

Smith, Goldwin. "The Place of Woman in the State." *Forum*, VIII, 515–30. New York, 1890.

Smith, Mary Roberts. "Education for Domestic Life." *Popular Science Monthly*, LIII, 521–25. New York, 1898.

——— "Statistics of College and Non-College Women." *Publications of American Statistical Association*, VII, 1–26. Boston, 1901.

Snider, Denton J. The Family. In his Social Institutions in their Origin, Growth, and Interconnection Psychologically Considered. St. Louis, 1901.

Snyder, William L. The Geography of Marriage; or Legal Perplexities of Marriage in the United States. New York, 1889.

——— The Problem of Uniform Legislation in the United States. Read before the American Bar Association, August 24, 1892. Reprinted from the *Transactions of the Association*.

Somerset, Lady Isabel. "The Welcome Child." *Arena*, XII, 42–49. Boston, 1895.

Sophia (pseud.). Woman not inferior to Man: or, A short and modest Vindication of the natural Right of the Fair-Sex to a Perfect Equality of Power, Dignity, and Esteem, with the Men. London, 1739; 2d ed., 1740.

——— Woman's Superior Excellency over Man: or, A Reply to . . . . *Man Superior to Woman*. London, 1740.

Spencer, Edgar A. Hints from a Lawyer. New York, 1888.

Spencer, Herbert. A Theory of Population Deduced from the Law of Animal Fertility. Republished from *Westminster Review*, LVII, 468–501. London, 1852.

Spencer, Herbert. "Justice." Part IV of the Principles of Ethics. New York, 1891.

Sprague, Henry H. Women under the Law of Massachusetts. Boston, 1884.

Stahl, F. J. "Die Familie." In his "Rechts- und Staatslehre auf der Grundlage christlicher Weltanschauung;" being Vol. II of his Philosophie des Rechts, 421–508. Heidelberg, 1854.

Stanley, Hiram M. "Our Civilization and the Marriage Problem." *Arena*, II, 94–100. Boston, 1890.

——— "Artificial Selection and the Marriage Problem." *Monist*, II, 51–55. Chicago, 1891.

Stanton, Elizabeth Cady. Address on the Divorce Bill, before the Judiciary Committee of the New York State Senate. Albany, 1861.

——— Address at the Decade Meeting on Marriage and Divorce. New York, 1871.

——— "Divorce versus Domestic Warfare." *Arena*, I, 560–69. Boston, 1890.

——— "Are Homogeneous Divorce Laws in All the States Desirable?" *North American Review*, CLXX, 405–9. New York, 1900.

——— Anthony, Susan B.; and Gage, Matilda Joslyn. History of Woman Suffrage. 3 vols. New York and Rochester, 1881–87.

Stanton, Theodore (editor). The Woman Question in Europe. A Series of Original Essays. New York, London, and Paris, 1884.

Stanwood, Edward. "National Jurisdiction over Marriage and Divorce as Affecting Polygamy in Utah." *Andover Review*, II, 66–78. Boston, 1884.

Statistik der Ehescheidungen in der Stadt Berlin in den Jahren 1885 bis 1894. Berlin, [1898?].

Stäudlin, Carl Friedrich. Geschichte der Vorstellungen und Lehren von der Ehe. Göttingen, 1826.

Stein, Lorenz von. Die Frau auf dem Gebiete der Nationalökonomie. Stuttgart, 1875; 6th ed., 1886.

——— Die Frau auf dem sozialen Gebiete. Stuttgart, 1880.

Stephen, Alfred. "The Law of Divorce. A Reply to Mr. Gladstone." *Contemporary Review*, LIX, 803–13. London, 1891.

Stephens, John. The Advantages which Man Derives from Woman. 3d ed. London, 1828.

Stetson, Charlotte Perkins. Women and Economics. A Study of the Economic Relation between Men and Women as a Factor in Social Evolution. 3d ed. Boston, 1900.

Stewart, Ethelbert. The Disintegration of the Families of the Workingmen. An Address, World's Fair Labor Congress, August 30, 1893. Chicago, 1893.

Stewart, Gordon A. "Our Marriage and Divorce Laws." *Popular Science Monthly*, XXIII, 224–37. New York, 1883.

Stimson, Frederic J. American Statute Law, I. Boston, 1886.

Stocquart, Émile. "Le mariage en droit international. Examen des législations des principaux pays d'Europe et d'Amérique." *Revue de droit international*, XIX, 581–608. Brussels and Leipzig, 1887.

—— "Marriage in Private International Law." *American Law Review*, XXIII. St. Louis, 1889.

—— "The New French Law of Divorce." *Ibid.*, XXVII, 1–13, 876–81. St. Louis, 1893.

Stölzel, A. Das Recht der väterlichen Gewalt in Preussen. Berlin, 1874.

Stopes, Charlotte Carmichael. British Free Women. Their Historical Privilege. London, 1894.

Story, Joseph. Conflict of Laws, Foreign and Domestic, in Regard to Contracts, Rights, and Remedies, and Especially in Regard to Marriages, Divorces, Wills, Successions, and Judgments. Boston, 1834.

Stow, Mrs. J. W. Probate Confiscation. 4th ed. San Francisco, 1879.

Strahan, S. A. K. Marriage and Disease. A Study of Heredity and the More Important Family Degenerations. London, 1892.

—— "The Struggle of the Sexes: Its Effect upon the Race." *Humanitarian*, III, 649–57.

Streitberg, Gisela von. Die falsche Moral im Leben des Weibes. Berlin and Leipzig, 1891.

—— Die Enterbten, Gefallenen und Verlorenen. Berlin and Leipzig, 1891.

Stürmer, Fritz. Moderner Eheschacher. Kulturstudien aus der Gegenwart. Leipzig, 1894.

Sullivan, Sir Edward. Woman the Predominant Partner. London, 1894.

Sulzer, Johann Georg. Anweisung zu Erziehung seiner Töchter. Zurich, 1781.

Swedenborg, Emanuel. Conjugal Love and Its Chaste Delights; also, Adulterous Love and its Sinful Pleasures. New ed. Trans. of the Amsterdam ed., 1768. London, 1862.

Switzerland. Bericht über die Verhandlungen des schweizerischen Kongresses für die Interessen der Frau abgehalten in Genf, im September, 1896. Bern, 1897.

Sybel, Heinrich von. Ueber die Emancipation der Frauen. Bonn, 1870.

Tait, William. Magdalenism. An Inquiry into the Extent, Causes, and Consequences of Prostitution in Edinburgh. 2d ed. Edinburgh, 1842.

Talmage, Thomas De Witt. The Marriage Ring. A series of discourses in Brooklyn Tabernacle. New York, 1886.

Teichmüller, G. Ueber die Frauenemancipation. Dorpat, 1877.

Thiersch, H. W. J. Ueber christliches Familienleben. 8th ed. Augsburg, 1889.

Thompson, William [and Mrs. Wheeler]. Appeal of one half of the Human Race, Women, against the Pretensions of the other half, Men, to retain them in political, and thence in civil and domestic slavery: in reply to a paragraph of Mr. [James] Mill's celebrated article on Government. London, 1825.

Thönes, Carl. Die christliche Anschauung der Ehe und ihre modernen Gegner. Leyden, 1881.

Thorald, A. W. On Marriage. New York, 1896.

Thoughts on the Propriety of preventing Marriages founded on Adultery. London, 1800.

Thulié, H. La femme: essai de sociologie physiologique. Paris, 1885.

Thwing, Charles F. "What Becomes of College Women?" *North American Review*, CLXI, 546-53. New York, 1895.

Tilton, Theodore. The Rights of Women. New York, 1871.

Tissot, J. Le mariage, la séparation et le divorce. Paris, 1868.

Tourneur, V. Quelques mots sur le divorce. Reims, 1848.

Trall, R. T. Sexual Physiology and Hygiene. Glasgow and London, 1897.

Transactions of the National Association for the Promotion of Social Science, 1857—. London, 1858-85.

[Tubermont, Guérin de]. Traité de contrats de mariage. Paris, 1708.

Turquan, V. "Résultats statistiques de cinq années de divorce." *L'économiste français*, October 26, 1889, 505-7. Paris, 1889.

Twining, Louisa. "Women as Public Servants." *Nineteenth Century*, XXVIII, 950-58. London, 1890.

Ussher, R. Neo-Malthusianism. An Enquiry into That System with Regard to its Economy and Morality. London, 1898.

Valerio, Agostino. Institutione d'ogni stato lodeuole delle donne christiane. Venice, 1575.

Van de Warter, E. "The Relations of Women to the Professions and Skilled Labor." *Popular Science Monthly*, VI, 454-70. New York, 1875.

Vanness, E. A Digest of the Laws of New York and New England, on Marriage, Dower, Divorce, etc. Hartford, 1877.

Varigny, C. de. The Women of the United States. New York, 1895.

Veblen, Thorstein. The Theory of the Leisure Class. An Economic Study in the Evolution of Institutions. New York and London, 1899.

Venables, Gilbert. "Civil and Religious Marriage." *National Review*, II, 437–43. London, 1883.

Vermont. Registration Reports, 1857–1896. Burlington and Montpelier, 1859–97.

Versuch über den wahren Begriff der Ehe und die Rechte bey deren Errichtung in den fürstl. Hessen-Casselischen Landen. Cassel, 1776.

Vidieu, Auguste. Famille et divorce. Paris, [1879].

Volkmar, F. N. Philosophie der Ehe. Halle, 1794.

Vortmann, T. Die Reform der Ehe. Zurich, 1894.

Vraye, Paul, and Gode, Georges. Le divorce et la séparation du corps. Paris, 1887.

Waddilove, A. "Shall Marriage Be Made Compulsorily a Civil Contract in the First Instance?" *Sessional Papers of the National Association for the Promotion of Social Science*, 1866.

Wade, John. Woman, Past and Present. London, 1859.

Walker, Alexander. Woman Physiologically Considered as to Mind, Morals, Marriage, Matrimonial Slavery, Infidelity, and Divorce. 2d ed. London, 1840.

—— Intermarriage. Birmingham, 1897.

Wallace, Alfred R. "Human Selection." *Fortnightly Review*, XLVIII, 325–37. London, 1890.

Walter, John. Christian Marriage: Its Open and Secret Enemies in England at the Present Day. London, 1881.

Walton, C. S. "The Status of the Wife in International Marriages." *American Law Review*, XXXI, 870 ff. St. Louis, 1897.

Ward, Lester F. Dynamic Sociology. 2 vols. New York, 1883.

—— "Our Better Halves." *Forum*, VI, 266–75. New York, 1888.

—— Pure Sociology. A Treatise on the Origin and Spontaneous Development of Society. New York and London, 1903.

Wardell-Yerburgh, O. P. (editor). Marriage Addresses and Marriage Hymns by Various Authors. London and New York, 1900.

Warner, Amos G. American Charities. A Study in Philanthropy and Economics. New York and Boston, 1894.

Watt, F. "Some Disused Roads to Marriage." *New Review*, XIV, 162 ff. London, 1896.

[Watterich?]. Die Ehe, populär wissenschaftlich dargestellt. Nordlingen, 1874.

Weber, J. K. Das in Deutschland, der Schweiz und Oesterreich geltende staatliche Eherecht. Augsburg, 1877.

Webster, Thomas. Woman Man's Equal. With an Introduction by Bishop Simpson. Cincinnati and New York, 1873.

Weil, Julius. Die Frauen im Recht. Juristische Untersuchungen am Damentisch. Berlin, 1872.

Weissbrodt, Karl. Die eheliche Pflicht. 6th ed. Berlin, 1899.

Welles, Charles Stuart. The New Marriage and Other Uniform Laws. New York and London, 1887.

Wells, Frank. Divorce in Massachusetts, 1863–1882. Extracts from the Forty-First Registration Report, 1882. [Boston, 1882.]

Wells, Kate Gannett. "Why More Girls Do Not Marry." North American Review, CLII, 175–81.

Wertheimer, Julius. "Homiculture." Nineteenth Century, XXIV, 390–92. London, 1898.

Westbrook, R. B. Marriage and Divorce. Philadelphia, 1883.

——— The Clerical Combination to Influence Civil Legislation on Marriage and Divorce. Philadelphia, 1887.

Wharton, F. A Treatise on the Conflict of Laws. 2d ed. Philadelphia, 1881.

Whitaker, Edward. "How the People Get Married." Gentleman's Magazine, new series, XXXIV, 394–404. London, 1885.

White, Frances Emily. "Woman's Place in Nature." Popular Science Monthly, VI, 292–301. New York, 1875.

Whitmore, H. J. "Statutory Restraints on the Marriage of Divorced Persons." Central Law Journal, LVII. St. Louis, 1903.

Whitney, Henry C. Marriage and Divorce—The Effects of Each on Personal Status and Property Rights Philadelphia, 1894.

Wilcox, Delos Franklin. Ethical Marriage. A Discussion of the Relations of Sex from the Standpoint of Social Duty. Ann Arbor, 1900.

Willcox, Walter F. "The Divorce Problem: A Study in Statistics." Columbia College Studies, I, No. 1. New York, 1891; 2d ed., 1897.

——— "A Study in Vital Statistics." Political Science Quarterly, VIII, 69–96. New York, Boston, and Chicago, 1893.

——— "The Marriage Rate in Michigan, 1870–1890." Publications of the American Statistical Association, IV, 1–11. Boston, 1895.

Wilpert, James von. Die Ehe der Zukunft. Leipzig, 1898.

Withington, Charles F. Consanguineous Marriages: Their Effect upon Offspring. Boston, 1885.

Wollstonecraft, Mary. Thoughts on the Education of Daughters with Reflections on Female Conduct in the More Important Duties of Life. London, 1787.

—— A Vindication of the Rights of Men, in a Letter to the Right Honourable Edmund Burke, Occasioned by His Reflections on the Revolution in France. London, 1790.

—— A Vindication of the Rights of Woman: With Strictures on Political and Moral Questions. London, 1792; new ed., by Mrs. Henry Fawcett, New York, 1890.

Woman's Influence. De l'influence des femmes dans l'ordre civil et politique. Eleuthéropolis, 1789.

Woman Question, Words of Weight on the. London, 1871.

"Woman's Rights Question Considered from a Biological Point of View." *Quarterly Journal of Science*, XV, 469–84. London, 1878.

Woman, An Essay on the Learning, Genius and Abilities of the Fair Sex, Proving Them Not Inferior to Man. 1774.

Women, the Social and Political Independence of. London, 1867.

Wood, Thomas D. Some Controlling Ideals of the Family Life of the Future. Reprinted from Proceedings of Fourth Lake Placid Conference on Home Economics. [New York, 1902.]

Woodhull, Victoria C. The Principles of Social Freedom. New York, 1874.

—— The Scare-Crows of Sexual Slavery. New York, 1874.

—— See Martin.

Wolf, Max. Die physische und sittliche Entartung des modernen Weibes. 4th ed. Dresden, 1894.

Woolsey, Theodore D. "Divorce." *New Englander*, XXVI, 88–113, 212–34, 482–505; XXVII, 12–44, 517–50, 764–89. New Haven, 1867–68.

—— "The Moral Statistics of the United States." *Journal of Social Science*, XIV, 129–35. Boston and New York, 1881.

—— Divorce and Divorce Legislation. 2d ed. New York, 1882.

—— and Jameson, John A. "Divorce." *North American Review*, CXXXVI, 305–25. New York, 1883.

Woolson, Abba Goold. Woman in American Society. Boston, 1873.

Wright, Carroll D., Commissioner. Marriage and Divorce in the United States, 1867–86. First Special Report of the Commissioner of Labor. Washington, 1889; revised, March 7, 1891; 2d ed., without change, 1897.

—— "Marriage and Divorce." *Christian Register*, LXX, 655–58; Boston, 1891; same in *Lend a Hand*, VII, Boston, 1891. Also extracts in *Arena*, V, 136–44, Boston, 1891.

Wright, Carroll D., Commissioner. "Census of Sex, Marriage, and Divorce." *Forum*, XVII, 484–96. New York, 1894.

—— "On Divorce." In Craft's Practical Christian Sociology. New York, London, and Toronto, 1895.

—— Outlines of Practical Sociology. New York, 1899.

Wright, Thomas. Womankind in Western Europe. London, 1869.

Yelverton, Theresa. "British Marriage Law and Practice." *Galaxy*, V, 197–205. New York, 1868.

Zamperini, Luigi. Il divorzio considerato nella teoria e nella pratica di D. di Bernardo. Verona, 1876.

Zane, Charles S. "The Death of Polygamy in Utah." *Forum*, XII, 368–75. New York, 1891.

Zeballos, Estanislao S. El matrimonio civil. Edicion privada. Buenos Aires, 1888.

Zmigrodski, Michael von. La question de la femme c'est la question de la mère. Paris, 1890.

Zuccarelli, A. Divorzio e scienza antropologica. Naples, 1893.

V. SESSION LAWS AND COLLECTED STATUTES USED IN CHAPTERS XVI–XVIII.

Alabama.—(1) Session Laws: annual, 1818–76; biennial, 1878–1903; (2) Collected Statutes: Toulmin's Digest, Tahawba, 1823; Aikin's Digest, Philadelphia, 1833; Clay's Digest, Tuskaloosa, 1843; Code, Montgomery, 1852, 1877; Code, Nashville, 1887; Code, 2 vols., Atlanta, 1897.

Alaska.—United States Statutes at Large, XXXI, XXXIII; Carter's Laws, Chicago, 1900.

Arizona.—(1) Session Laws: annual, 1864–68; biennial, 1871–1903; (2) Collected Statutes: Howell Code, Prescott, 1865; Bashford's Compiled Laws, including the Howell Code and the Session Laws, 1864–71, Albany, 1871; Revised Statutes, Prescott, 1887; Columbia, 1901.

Arkansas.—(1) Biennial Session Laws, 1840–1903; (2) Collected Statutes: Revised Statutes, Boston, 1838; Digest, Columbia, 1894.

California.—(1) Session Laws: annual Statutes, 1849–63; biennial Statutes, 1865–80; Amendments to the Codes, 1873/4–80; Statutes and Amendments to the Codes, 1881–1903; (2) Collected Statutes: Compiled Laws, 1850–53, Benicia, 1853; Hittell's General Laws, 1850-64, 4th ed., San Francisco, 1872; Civil Code, 2 vols., Sacramento, 1872; Political Code, 2 vols., Sacramento, 1872; Deering's Codes and Statutes, 4 vols., San Francisco, 1886; Pomeroy's Civil Code, San Francisco, 1901.

Colorado.— (1) Biennial Session Laws 1861–1903; (2) Collected Statutes: Revised Statutes, Central City, 1868; General Laws, Denver, 1877; General Statutes, Denver, 1883; Mills's Annotated Statutes, 3 vols., Chicago, 1891; Denver, 1897 (Vol. III).

Connecticut.—(1) Session Laws: annual to 1887; biennial, 1889–1903; (2) Collected Statutes: Acts and Laws, folio, New London, 1784; Hartford, 1786, 1805; Public Statute Laws, revisions of 1821, 1835, 1838, Hartford, 1821–39; Revised Statutes, Hartford, 1849; New Haven, 1854; General Statutes, New Haven, 1866, 1875; Hartford, 1887, 1902; Swift's System, 2 vols., Windham, 1795; Swift's Digest, 2 vols., New Haven, 1823, 1851.

Dakota.— (1) Session Laws: annual, 1862–75; biennial, 1877–89; (2) Collected Statutes: Levisee's Codes, St. Paul, 1884; Compiled Laws, Bismarck, 1887.

Delaware.—(1) Session Laws: annual to 1867; biennial, 1869–1903; (2) Collected Statutes: Laws, 1700–1813, Vols. I and II, New-Castle, 1797; Vols. III and IV, Wilmington, 1816; Revised Statutes, Dover, 1852; Wilmington, 1874, 1893.

District of Columbia.— Lovejoy's Compiled Statutes, Washington, 1894; Moore's Code, Washington, 1902.

Florida.— (1) Session Laws: annual, 1822–66; biennial 1868–1903; (2) Collected Statutes: Thompson's Manual or Digest, Boston, 1847; Bush's Digest, Tallahassee, 1872; McClellan's Digest, Tallahassee, 1881; Revised Statutes, Jacksonville, 1892.

Georgia.—(1) Annual Acts, 1822–1903; (2) Collected Statutes: Digest, Philadelphia, 1801; Clayton's Compilation, 1800–1810, Augusta, 1812; Lamar's Laws, 1810–19, Augusta, 1821, Dawson's Compilation, 1819–29, Milledgville, 1831; Foster's Digest, Philadelphia, 1831; Prince's Digest, 2d ed., Athens, 1837; Hotchkiss's Compilation, Savannah, 1845; Cobb's Analysis, New York, 1846; Cobb's Digest, 1851; Cobb's Compilation, New York, 1859; Code, Atlanta, 1867; Macon, 1873; Atlanta, 1882, 1896.

Hawaii.—United States Statutes at Large, XXXI; Civil Laws, Honolulu, 1897; Penal Laws, Honolulu, 1897.

Idaho.— (1) Session Laws: annual or biennial, 1864–1903; (2) Collected Statutes: Compiled and Revised Laws, Boise City, 1875; Revised Statutes, Boise City, 1887; Codes, 4 vols., Boise City, 1901.

Illinois.— (1) Session Laws: annual, 1821–55; biennial, 1857–1903; (2) Collected Statutes: Laws, Kaskaskia, 1818; Revised Code, Vandalia, 1827, 1833; Public and General Statutes, Chicago, 1839; Revised Statutes, 1845; Purple's Compilation, 2 vols., Chicago, 1856; Statutes, Chicago, 1864; Gross's Statutes, 3 vols., Springfield, 1872–74; Starr and Curtis's Annotated Statutes, 3 vols., Chicago, 1896; Jones and Addington's Supplements, 2 vols:, Chicago, 1902, 1903; Hurd's Revised Statutes, Chicago, 1898, 1899, 1901.

Indiana.—(1) Session Laws: annual or biennial, 1818–1903; (2) Collected Statutes: Laws, Corydon, 1818; Revised Laws, Corydon, 1824; Laws, Indianapolis, 1825; Revised Laws, Indianapolis, 1831; Revised Statutes, Indianapolis, 1838, 1843; General Laws, Indianapolis, 1849; Revised Statutes, 2 vols., Indianapolis, 1852; Horner's Revised Statutes, 2 vols., Chicago, 1896; Burns's Annotated Statutes, 3 vols., Indianapolis, 1901.

Indian Territory.—Carter's Annotated Statutes, St. Paul, 1899.

Iowa.—(1) Session Laws: annual, 1838-49; biennial, 1851–1902; (2) Collected Statutes: Revised Statutes, Iowa City, 1843; Code, Iowa City, 1851; Revision, Des Moines, 1860; Code, Des Moines, 1873; McClain's Annotated Codes and Statutes, with Supplement, 3 vols., Chicago, 1888–92; Annotated Code, Des Moines, 1897; Supplement, 1902.

Kansas.—(1) Session Laws: annual, 1857–77; biennial, 1879–1903; (2) Collected Statutes: Statutes, 1855; General Laws, Topeka, 1862; General Statutes, Lawrence, 1868; Dassler's General Statutes, 2 vols., St. Louis, 1876; Webb's General Statutes, Topeka, 1897; General Statutes, Topeka, 1901.

Kentucky.—(1) Annual or biennial Acts to 1902; (2) Collected Statutes: Littell's Statute Law, 5 vols., Frankfort, 1809–19; Humphrey's Compendium of the Common Law in Force in Kentucky, Lexington, 1822; Digest, 2 vols., Frankfort, 1834; Loughborough's Digest, Frankfort, 1842: Revised Statutes, Frankfort, 1852; Kentucky Statutes, Louisville, 1894, 1899, 1903.

Louisiana.—(1) Session Laws: annual, 1805-70; biennial, 1872–1902; (2) Collected Statutes: Acts . . . . of the Territory of Orleans (1804), New Orleans, 1805; *ibid.* (1806), New Orleans, 1807; Digest of the Civil Laws Now in Force in the Territory of Orleans [French and English], New Orleans, 1808; Laws of Las Siete Partidas, which are still in force in Louisiana, 2 vols., New Orleans, 1820; Code Civil de l'État de la Louisiane, 1825; Lislet's General Digest, 2 vols., New Orleans, 1828; Upton and Jennings's Civil Code, New Orleans, 1838; Revision, New Orleans, 1852; Civil Code, Baton Rouge, 1853; Revised Civil Code, New Orleans, 1870; Voorhies's Revised Statutes, New Orleans, 1876; Voorhies's Revised Laws, New Orleans, 1884; Revised Civil Code, New Orleans, 1888; Wolff's Revised Laws, New Orleans, 1897; Merrick's Revised Civil Code, 2 vols., New Orleans, 1900.

Maine.—(1) Public Acts or Acts and Resolves: annual, 1820–81; biennial, 1883–1903; (2) Collected Statutes: Laws, 2 vols., Brunswick, 1821; Vol. III, Portland, 1831; Smith's Laws, 1821–

34, Portland, 1834; Revised Statutes (1840), Augusta, 1841; 2d ed., Hallowell, 1847; Bangor, 1857; Portland, 1871, 1884; Freeman's Supplement to the Revised Statutes, 1885–95, Portland, 1895.

Maryland.— (1) Session Laws: annual to 1868; biennial, 1870–1902; (2) Collected Statutes: Laws Made Since 1763, folio, Annapolis, 1777; Laws, 1763–87, folio, Annapolis, 1787; Kilty's Laws, 2 vols., Annapolis, 1799; Scott and M'Cullough's Maryland Code, 2 vols., Baltimore, 1860; Poe's Maryland Code, Baltimore, 1888.

Massachusetts.— (1) Annual Acts and Resolves, 1780–1903; (2) Collected Statutes: Public General Laws, November 28, 1780, to February 16, 1816, 4 vols., Boston, 1807–16; Revised Statutes (1835), Boston, 1836; Supplement to the Revised Statutes, 1836–53, Boston, 1854; Supplement to the General Statutes, 2 vols., Boston, 1873–78; Public Statutes, Boston, 1882; Supplement to the Public Statutes, 1882–88, Boston, 1890; Public Laws, 2 vols. and Index, Boston, 1902; Crocker's Notes on the Public Statutes of Massachusetts, 2d ed., Boston, 1891.

Michigan.—(1) Session Laws: Annual Acts to 1851; biennial, 1853–1903; (2) Collected Statutes: Laws of the Territory, 4 vols., Lansing, 1871–84; Revised Statutes, Detroit, 1838, 1846; Howell's General Statutes, 3 vols., Chicago, 1882–90; Miller's Compiled Laws (1897), 3 vols., Lansing, 1899.

Minnesota.—(1) Session Laws: annual, 1849–79; biennial, 1881–1903: (2) Collected Statutes: Revised Statutes, St. Paul, 1851; General Statutes, St. Paul, 1866; *ibid.*, 2 vols., St. Paul, 1894.

Mississippi.—(1) Annual or biennial Session Laws to 1902; (2) Collected Statutes: Statutes of the Mississippi Territory, Natchez, 1816; Revised Code, Natchez, 1824; Digest, New York, 1839; Statutes, New Orleans, 1840; Hutchinson's Code, 1798–1848, Jackson, 1848; Revised Code, Jackson, 1857, 1880; Annotated Code, Nashville, 1892.

Missouri.—(1) Session Laws: annual, 1820–71; biennial, 1873–1903; (2) Collected Statutes: Revised Statutes, St. Louis, 1835; Laws . . . . of the District of Louisiana, of the Territory of Louisiana, of the Territory of Missouri, and of the State of Missouri to 1824, 2 vols., Jefferson City, 1842; Revised Statutes, St. Louis, 1845; *ibid.*, 2 vols., Jefferson City, 1856, 1879; Revised Laws, Jefferson City, 1889; Revised Statutes, 2 vols., Jefferson City, 1899.

Montana.—(1) Session Laws: annual, 1864–77; biennial, 1879–1903; (2) Collected Statutes: Compiled Statutes, Helena, 1888; Booth's Codes and Statutes, 4 vols., Butte, 1895; Sander's Codes and Statutes, Helena, 1895.

Nebraska.— (1) Session Laws, 1855–1903; (2) Collected Statutes: Statutes in Force August, 1867; Brown's General Statutes,

Lincoln, 1873; Brown's Compiled Statutes, Omaha, 1887; Laws, Resolutions, and Memorials, 1855–87, 3 vols., Lincoln, 1886–87, Brown and Wheeler's Compiled Statutes, Lincoln, 1891, 1893, 1899.

Nevada.—(1) Annual or biennial Session Laws, 1861–1903; (2) Cutting's Compiled Laws, 1861–1900, Carson City, 1900.

New Hampshire.—(1) Session Laws: annual to 1879; biennial, 1881–1903; (2) Collected Statutes: Laws, Portsmouth, 1797; Constitution and Laws, Dover, 1805; Laws, Exeter, 1815; Laws, Hopkinton, 1830; Revised Statutes (1842), Concord, 1843; Compiled Statutes, Concord, 1853; General Statutes, Manchester, 1867; General Laws, Manchester, 1878; Public Statutes, Concord, 1891, 1900.

New Jersey.—(1) Annual Acts, 1779–1903; (2) Collected Statutes: Patterson's Laws, Newark, 1800; Laws, Trenton, 1821; Elmer's Digest, Bridgeton, 1838; Statutes, Trenton, 1847; Nixon's Elmer's Digest, Philadelphia, 1855; Revised Statutes, Trenton, 1874; General Statutes, 3 vols., Jersey City, 1896.

New Mexico.—(1) Session Laws: annual, 1851–69; biennial, 1871–1903; (2) Collected Statutes: Revised Statutes, St. Louis, 1865; Compiled Laws, Santa Fé, 1885, 1897.

New York.—(1) Annual Laws to 1903; (2) Collected Statutes: Laws, 2 vols., folio, New York, 1789; Laws, 3 vols., New York and Albany, 1792–1800; Laws, 6 vols., Albany, 1802–12; Van Ness and Woodworth's Laws, 2 vols., Albany, 1813; Revised Statutes of 1827–28, 3 vols., Albany, 1829; Stover's Code of Civil Procedure, 3 vols., New York, 1892, 1902; Throop and Collin's Revised Statutes, 9th ed., 6 vols., New York, 1889–92; Birdseye's Revised Statutes, 3 vols., New York, 1896.

North Carolina.—(1) Session Laws: annual to 1877; biennial, 1879–1903; (2) Collected Statutes: Martin's Iredell's Public Acts, 1715–1803, 2 vols., Newbern, 1804; Haywood's Manual, Raleigh, 1819; Laws, 2 vols., Raleigh, 1821; Revised Statutes, 2 vols., Raleigh, 1837; Code, 2 vols., Raleigh, 1883.

North Dakota.—(1) Annual or biennial Session Laws, 1890–1903; (2) Revised Codes, Bismarck, 1895, 1899.

Ohio.—(1) Annual or biennial Session Laws, 1803–1903; (2) Collected Statutes: Chase's Statutes of Ohio and the Northwest, Territory, 1788–1833, 3 vols., Cincinnati, 1833–35; Swan's, Statutes, Cincinnati, 1854; Bates's Annotated Statutes, 3 vols., Cincinnati, 1897, 1903.

Oklahoma.—(1) Biennial Session Laws, 1895–1903; (2) Statutes, Guthrie, 1893; Wilson's Revised Annotated Statutes, Guthrie, 2 vols., 1903.

Oregon.—(1) Session Laws: annual, 1843–60; biennial, 1860–1903; (2) Collected Statutes: Deady and Lane's Organic and Other

General Laws, 1843 ff., n. p., 1874; Hill's Codes and General Laws, 2d ed., 2 vols., San Francisco, 1892; Bellinger and Cotton's Codes and Statutes, 2 vols., San Francisco, 1902.

Pennsylvania.—(1) Session Laws: annual, 1803–79; biennial, 1881–1903; (2) Collected Statutes: Acts of the Assembly, folio, Philadelphia, 1775; Dallas's Laws, 3 vols., folio, Philadelphia, 1793–97; Laws of the Commonwealth, 1700–1810, 4 vols., Philadelphia, 1810; Cary and Bioren's Laws, 8 vols., Philadelphia, 1803–8; Laws, from October, 1700, 10 vols., Philadelphia, 1822–44; Pepper and Lewis's Digest, 1700–1894, 2 vols., Philadelphia, 1896.

Porto Rico.—Revised Statutes and Codes, San Juan, 1902.

Rhode Island.—(1) Annual Laws or Acts to 1902; (2) Public Laws, Providence, 1798, 1822, 1844, 1882, 1896.

South Carolina.—(1) Annual Session Laws, 1790–1903; (2) Collected Statutes: Cooper and McCord's Statutes at Large, 10 vols., Columbia, 1837–41; Brevard's Alphabetical Digest, 3 vols., Charleston, 1814; Revised Statutes, Columbia, 1873, 1894; Code, 2 vols., Columbia, 1902.

South Dakota.—(1) Annual or biennial Session Laws, 1890–1903; (2) Grantham's Statutes, 2 vols., Chicago, 1899; Albany, 1901; Revised Codes, Pierre, 1903.

Tennessee.—(1) Session Laws: annual to 1873; biennial, 1875–1903; (2) Collected Statutes: Public Acts . . . . of North Carolina and Tennessee, 1715–1813, Nashville, 1815; Scott's Laws, 2 vols., Knoxville, 1821; Haywood and Cobb's Statute Laws, 2 vols., Knoxville, 1831; Caruther and Nicholson's Compilation, Nashville, 1836; Code, Nashville, 1858, 1884; Shannon's Annotated Code, Nashville, 1896.

Texas.—(1) Annual or biennial Session Laws, 1846–1901; (2) Collected Statutes: Ordinances and Decrees of the Consultation, Provisional Government of Texas and the Convention . . . . at Washington, March 1, 1836, Houston, 1838; Laws of the Republic, 9 vols., Houston, 1838–45; Dallam's Digest, Baltimore, 1845; Revised Statutes, Galveston, 1879; Revised Civil Statutes, 2 vols., St. Louis, 1888; Annotated Civil Statutes, Supplement, 1888–93, St. Louis, 1894; Sayles's Annotated Civil Statutes, 2 vols., St. Louis, 1897; Herron's Supplement, 1903; White's Penal Code, Austin, 1901.

Utah.—(1) Annual or biennial Session Laws, 1850–1903; (2) Collected Statutes: Acts, Resolutions, and Memorials, 1850–55, Great Salt Lake City, 1855; Compiled Laws, Salt Lake City, 1876, 1888; Revised Statutes, 1898.

Vermont.—(1) Session Laws: annual Laws or Acts and Resolves, 1787–1868; biennial, 1870–1902; (2) Collected Statutes: Slade's State Papers . . . . with Laws, 1779–86, Middlebury, 1823;

Laws, Rutland, 1798; Acts and Laws, Windsor, 1801; Laws, 2 vols., Randolph, 1808; Slade's Laws, Windsor, 1825; Revised Statutes, Burlington, 1840; Williams's Compiled Statutes, Burlington, 1851; General Statutes, 2d ed., 1870; Vermont Statutes (1894), Rutland, 1895.

Virginia.—(1) Acts of the Assembly: annual, 1807–79; biennial, 1881–1903; (2) Collected Statutes: Acts, Richmond, 1794, 1803, 1814; Revised Code, 2 vols., Richmond, 1819; Tate's Digest, Richmond, 1823; Supplement to Revised Code, Richmond, 1833; Tate's Digest, 2d ed., Richmond, 1841; Code, Richmond, 1849, 1860, 1868, 1873, 1887.

Washington.—(1) Session Laws: annual to 1869; biennial, 1871–1903; (2) Ballinger's Annotated Codes and Statutes, 2 vols., San Francisco, 1897.

West Virginia.—(1) Annual or biennial Acts, 1863–1903; (2) Collected Statutes: Kelly's Revised Statutes, 2 vols., St. Louis, 1878; Warth's Code, Charleston, 1887, 1891, 1900.

Wisconsin.—(1) Session Laws: annual, 1836–83; biennial, 1885–1903; (2) Revised Statutes, Southport, 1849, Chicago, 1858, 1872; Annotated Statutes, 2 vols., Chicago, 1889; Statutes, 2 vols., 1898.

Wyoming.—(1) Biennial Session Laws, 1869–1903; (2) Revised Statutes, Cheyenne, 1887; Laramie, 1899.

GENERAL INDICES

CASE INDEX

THE 147 Massachusetts cases of divorce and annulment, tabulated and discussed in chap. xv, are not included in this index.

Addison's case, ii, 106 n. 1.

Adkinson v. Adkinson (Thompson's *Laws of Pa.*, vii, 73–75), iii, 99.

Adler v. Adler (*San Francisco Law Journal*, July 16, 1900, p. 1), iii, 151.

Adriaens v. Adriaens (*N. Y. Col. MSS.*, x, 291, 293), ii, 376.

Alexander's case (*Laws of Md.*, 1805, chap. xxxiii), iii, 32.

Allen's case (*MSS. Court Files of Suffolk*, No. 3728), ii, 192 n. 1.

Almond v. Almond (4 Randolph, 662; 15 *Am. D.*, 781), ii, 369.

Andover v. Canton (13 *Mass.*, 551, 552), ii, 217 n. 3.

Andrews v. Page (3 Heiskell, 653–71), ii, 263; iii, 176.

Andriesen and Vosburgh, ii, 378.

Anonymous (9 C. E. Green, *Eq. Rep.*, 19), iii, 106 n. 7.

Askew v. Dupree (30 *Ga.*, 173), iii, 176.

Att'y Gen. v. Chatterton, i, 422 n. 1.

—— v. Mollineux, i, 422 n. 1.

Avery's case (*Doc. Rel. to Col. Hist. of N. Y.*, xii, 624, 625), ii, 290, 291.

Bailey v. S. (36 *Neb.*, 808–14), iii, 177.

Baldingh v. Baldingh (*N. Y. Col. MSS.*, viii, 415, 417, 419), ii, 376.

Bashaw v. S. (1 Yerger, 177–97), ii, 263; iii, 176.

Battersby's case, ii, 106 n. 1.

Baxter's case (*Conn. Col. Rec.*, i, 379), ii, 356.

Bayley and Rainer (*MSS. Records of Sup. Court of Jud.*, 1752–53, fol. 190), ii, 176.

Beale v. Row (*MSS. Records of Co. Court of Midd.*, iv, 218), ii, 202 n. 3.

Beamish v. Beamish (9 *House of Lords Cases*, 274–358), i, 289, 318–20.

Becke v. Bradwicke (*Mass. Col. Rec.*, i, 104), ii, 200, 201.

Beckwith v. Beckwith (*Conn. Col. Rec.*, i, 275), ii, 355, 356.

Beeck v. Verleth (*Records of New Amsterdam*, i, 159, 160, 164, 165, 173, 174; *Doc. Rel. to Col. Hist. of N. Y.*, xiv, 291), ii, 274–77.

Bell v. Bell (*Opinions U. S. Sup. Court*, No. 13, p. 551), iii, 207.

Bellingham's case, ii, 210, 211; iii, 173.

Belou v. Belou (*R. I. Col. Rec.*, ii, 543), ii, 364.

Benkert v. Benkert (32 *Cal.*, 467), iii, 137 n. 2.

Besems v. Nieuwland, ii, 281.

Beverlin v. Beverlin (29 *W. Va.*, 732–40), iii, 180, 182.

Beyer's case, i, 374 n. 5.

Blackburn v. Crawfords (3 Wall., 175), iii, 176.

Blake's case (*MSS. Court Files of Suffolk*, No. 531), ii, 159, 160.

Blanchard v. Lambert (43 *Ia.*, 228–32), ii, 470; iii, 177.

Bostwick v. Blades (4 *Am. Law Rec.*, 729), ii, 480 n. 6.

Bowman v. Bowman (24 *Ill. App.*, 165–78), iii, 177.

Boylan v. Deinzer (18 Stewart, 485), ii, 475 n. 1; iii, 106 n. 6.

Bruner v. Bruner (*Laws of Ind.*, 1842, 117), iii, 97.

Bullock v. Bullock (122 *Mass.*, 3), iii, 146 n. 2.

Bunting v. Lepingwell (2 Coke, *Reports*, 355–59), i, 289, 376 n. 2.

Burge v. Burge, ii, 349, 350.

Burr v. Burr (10 Paige, 20, 35), ii, 382 n. 2.

Boarman's case, ii, 210.

Brittanie and Latham (*Records of Court of Assistants*), ii, 170 n. 3.

Brook v. Brook (House of Lords, March, 1861), ii, 96 n. 5.

Brown v. Westbrook (27 *Ga.*, 102), ii, 376 n. 1.

Campbell v. Gullatt (43 *Ala.*, 57), iii, 176.

Carmichael v. S. (12 *Ohio*, 553–61), iii, 177.

Case v. Case (17 *Cal.*, 598), ii, 467 n. 1.

Caterall v. Caterall (1 Robinson, 580, 581), ii, 367 n. 2.

Caterall v. Sweetman (1 Robinson, 321), ii, 304 n. 4.

Chapman v. Chapman (16 *T. C. A.*, 384), iii, 176.

Cheney v. Arnold (15 *N. Y.*, 345), iii, 183.

Cheseldine v. Brewer (1 Har. and McH., 152), ii, 262 n. 5; iii, 180.

Chickering v. Chickering (*Acts and Laws*, 575, 576), iii, 5.

SUBJECT INDEX

Abercromby, John: on marriage with capture, i, 177 n. 1.

Abipones, i, 105; abhor close intermarriage, 126 n. 1; monogamy the rule, i, 143 n. 1; cohabitation with wives in turn, 145; liberty of choice, 212, 213; divorce, 232.

Abduction: pretended, i, 182–84; whether leading to free marriage among ancient Germans, 276 n. 2.

Adams, Charles Francis: on bundling, ii, 182 and n. 3, 184 and n. 4; confessions of pre-nuptial incontinence, 195–98; confessions in Groton church, 198 n. 2.

Adams, Henry: on status of early German woman, i, 257, 260, note; wedding ring, 279, 280.

Administration of marriage law: effective in early New England, ii, 126, 127, 143–51.

Admonition to the Parliament: quoted, i, 410; *Answer* to, 411.

Adoption: as means of social expansion, i, 13 and n. 3, 26 n. 2.

Adultery: according to scriptural teaching, ii, 19, 20; Jewish law, 20 n. 3, 99 n. 2; views of early Fathers, 24, 27; law of Theodosius II., 32; male, not recognized by early Roman law, 32 n. 3; nor by early Teutonic, 35 and n. 5; death penalty for, under Constantine, 32 n. 4; laws of Valentinian and Justinian, 32 n. 4; death penalty for, under early Teutonic law, 36, 37, 38; ground for separation under canon law, ii, 53; for divorce at Reformation, 62 and n. 2; death penalty favored by some reformers, 66, 67; punished by the *Reformatio legum,* 79; Samuel Johnson on, 106; under present English law, 110, 114, 115.

—— in the American colonies: death penalty for, ii, 169; this penalty enforced in Massachusetts, 169–71; punished by scarlet letter in Plymouth, 171, 172; also in New Hampshire, Connecticut, and Massachusetts, 172–76; espoused woman may commit, 180, 181; punishment for, in Virginia, ii, 236; New Netherland, 280; Pennsylvania, 319, 320 n. 6, 385, 386; early Massachusetts, male, not ground of divorce, 331, 345 and n. 1; same in Plymouth, 351; death penalty in New Haven, 352; how punished in Massachusetts, ii, 398 n 3.

Æthelberht, code of: allows one-sided divorce, ii, 39.

Affinity: forbidden degrees of, i, 129, 352 n. 1, 354 n. 5, 390, 391.

Afghanistan: wife-capture in, i, 160; wife-purchase, 197; sentiment of love, 248.

African aborigines: matrimonial institutions of, i, 33, 34, 107 n. 1; Starcke on, 46; marriage customs in Guinea, 83 n. 4; polyandry of Kafirs, 135 n. 2; rich indulge in polygyny, 146 n. 1; wife-capture rare, 159; symbol of rape, 172; coexistence of rape and purchase, 180; wife-purchase, 193, 194; free marriage, 214; divorce at pleasure, 226 and n. 3, 239; divorce in council, 241.

Agde, Council of: allows remarriage after divorce, ii, 39; did not originate spiritual divorce jurisdiction, 49 and nn. 2, 3.

Age of consent to carnal knowledge: in the various states and territories, iii, 195–203.

Age of consent to marriage: under canon law, i, 357–59; Swinburne on, 403 n. 1; in New York province, ii, 287; in the New England states, 395, 396; southern and southwestern states, 428, 429; middle and western states, 471, 472; reform needed, iii, 190, 191.

Age of parental consent to marriage: in the New England States, ii, 396, 397; southern and southwestern states, 429–33; middle and western states, 472, 473; reform needed, iii, 191.

Agnation: the Roman, i, 11, 12; extent of, according to Maine, 12; whether among Hebrews, 15–17; only element of, among early Aryans, 27, 28; relation of, to *patria potestas,* 30–32.

Ainos: wooing-gifts among, i, 218.

Alabama: marriage celebration in, ii, 417 n. 4; age of consent and of parental consent, 428, 429; license bond required when under age, 430; forbidden degrees, 433, 435; void or voidable marriages, 437, 438; miscegenation forbidden, 438; license system, 447; license bond, 448; return, 449; legislative divorce, iii, 39, 40; judicial divorce, 62–64; remarriage, 83; residence, 85; process, 89; common-law marriage, 176; age of consent to carnal knowledge, 200.

Alamanni: wife-purchase among, i, 264 and n. 3.

Alaska: marriage celebration in, ii, 463; witnesses, 465; definition, 470; age of consent to marriage, 471; forbidden degrees, 474; marriage certificate, 492; divorce, iii, 143, 144; remarriage, 149; residence, 157; courts silent as to common-law marriage, 182; age of consent to carnal knowledge, 202.

413

of father or guardian in the marriage contract, 276 n. 3; whether Anglo-Saxons married in their homes, 296, note; on marriage at church door, 299 n. 4; marriage celebration during the Commonwealth, i, 419 n. 2; on irregular marriages, 435, 436, notes, 443 n. 3, 447 n. 1; irregular royal marriage, 449 n. 3; Henry Fox's opposition to Hardwicke Act, 450 n. 1; clandestine marriages after Hardwicke Act, 459 n. 3; divorce among Anglo-Saxons, ii, 34 n. 1, 39 n. 5; number of irregular divorces in Middle Ages, 56 n. 2; traffic in, 58 n. 3; views of English reformers as to divorce, 72; *Reformatio legum*, 77 n. 4; Milton's low ideal of womanhood, 89, 91, 92; voidable marriages, 95 n. 4.

Jerome: on Roman divorce, ii, 18, note; indissolubility of marriage, 27; excuses Fabiola's remarriage after divorce, 28.

Jewell v. Jewell, iii, 178.

Jewish law: influence of, on the Puritans, ii, 130, 131, 152 and nn. 1, 2, 162, 169, 179, 199, 200, 217, 352. (*See* Hebrews, Hebraism.)

Jörs, P.: cited, ii, 16 n. 4.

Johnson, Samuel: on adultery, ii, 106 and n. 3.

Joint undivided families, i, 129.

Judicial separation under present English law, ii, 114, 115.

Judith: her marriage with Æthelwulf, i, 297 n. 1.

Julian: divorce law of, ii, 31.

Junius, F. A.: on the ring, i, 278 n. 3.

Juramentum de reconciliatione, ii, 51 n. 2.

Jury trial in divorce suits, iii, 28, 90, 158, 159.

Jus primae noctis: works on, i, 38; as evidence of promiscuity, 51 and n. 2, 52.

Jurisdiction, matrimonial, of the ecclesiastical courts: abuses of, i, 351-59, 412-14; ii, 56-59; rise of, in cases of divorce, 47-52. (*See* Canon law.)

Justin II.: on divorce, ii, 30.

Justinian: on divorce, ii, 30, 33.

Justin Martyr: on second marriage, ii, 25 n. 2.

Justice of the peace: celebrates marriage under law of 1653, i, 418; exercises matrimonial jurisdiction under, 420, 421-24.

—— marriage solemnized by, in New England colonies, ii, 127, 128; Rhode Island, 135 n. 1; Connecticut, 138 n. 3; Maryland colony, 240, 241, 242; North Carolina colony, 251, 252, 253, 255, 256; South Carolina colony, 261; Georgia, 262; New York province, 285-87, 291, 294, 307; New Jersey colony, 309-11; Pennsylvania, 320.

—— marriage solemnized by, in Massachusetts, ii, 389, 390; other New England states, 391; southern and southwestern

states, 412, 414, 415, 416, 417, 418, 421, 423; middle and western states, 454, 456, 457, 459, 460, 461, 462, 463-65; defects in the system of magisterial celebration, iii, 189, 190.

Juvenal: on divorce, ii, 18, note.

Kabinapek Indians: pairing season of, i, 99.

Kabyles: woman's right of "insurrection" among, i, 246 n. 1; effects of wife-purchase on divorce, 249 n. 1.

Kafirs: avoid marriage with persons living closely together, i, 128; Herero, polyandry among, i, 135 n. 2; polygyny among, when more women, 145; bride-price, 193; whether free marriage, 214, 216; free divorce, 227 and n. 2, 240; remarriage of woman after divorce, 245.

Kalm, Peter: on governor's license fees in New York province, ii, 297.

Kalmucks: forbidden degrees among, i, 126; symbol of rape, 168, 169 and n. 1, 172; exchange of gifts, 219.

Kames, Lord: quoted, i, 136 n. 3.

Kamtchadales: symbolical rape among, i, 166.

Kandhs: avoid marriage with members of the tribe, i, 128.

Kansas: marriage celebration in, ii, 464; definition, 470; age of consent to marriage, 472; forbidden degrees, 473-75; void and voidable marriages, 475-78; marriage of epileptic and imbecile restrained, 480; license, 488; return, 489 and n. 3, 491; state registration, 495; legislative divorce, iii, 98; judicial divorce, 127-29; remarriage, 148; residence, 156; common-law marriage, 177; age of consent to carnal knowledge, 201; divorce rate, 210.

Karems: effects of divorce on property among, i, 248.

Karlowa, O.: on *coemptio*, i, 199 n. 5.

Karok: bride-price among, i, 192.

Karo-Karo, of Sumatra: divorce among, i, 229.

Kasaph: betrothal by, i, 197.

Kautsky, Carl: on headship of woman in the family, i, 45; evolution of father-right and mother-right, 55; successive forms of marriage, 56-58; classificatory systems, 71.

Keith, Alexander: the marriage-broker, i, 443; his *Observations* quoted, 443, 444; his celebrations after passage of the marriage act, 459 n. 3.

Kemble, J. M.: on the penitentials, i, 326 n. 1.

Kent, James: on divorce in New York, ii, 383; his decision in Fenton v. Reed, iii, 175 and nn. 2, 3, 185.

Kentucky: celebration of marriage in, ii, 414; unauthorized celebration, 425; age of consent and of parental consent,

consent to carnal knowledge, 202; divorce rate, 210, 211.

Micronesians: punishment of adultery among, i, 106 n. 4; free courtship, 214.

Middlesex county, Mass.: cases of prenuptial incontinence, with confessions and penalties, ii, 189, 190, 193, 194.

Mielziner, M.: on Jewish marriage law, ii, 152 n. 2, 199 and n. 5; the Jewish "Get," ii, 13 n. 4.

Migration for divorce, iii, 205, 206.

Milford v. Worcester, iii, 178, 179.

Mill, J. S.: on marriage rate, iii, 213, 214; cited on individualism, 225 n. 1; on woman's callings, 241; effects of her subjection, 245 n. 2.

Mill, Mrs. J. S.: cited, iii, 239, note, 245, 247 n. 2.

Millenary Petition, i, 398, 414 n. 3, 415.

Milton, John: on Bucer, i, 411 n. 2; the corruption of the ecclesiastical courts, 414 n. 1; civil marriage, 433, 434; *porneia*, ii, 20 n. 1; characterizes Gratian and Peter Lombard, 52 n. 1; rejects divorce *a mensa*, 61 n. 2; use of allegorical method, 61 n. 3; analysis of his views on divorce, 85–92; his conception of wedlock realized in New England colonies, 127; divorce by mutual consent, iii, 251.

Minahassers of Celebes: free courtship among, i, 215.

Minnesota: marriage celebration in, ii, 462, 463, 465; witnesses, 265; unauthorized solemnization, 468; definition, 471; age of consent and of parental consent to marriage, 472, 473; forbidden degrees, 473–75; void or voidable marriages, 475–78; marriage of epileptic and imbecile restrained, 480; license, 486, 487; return, 489 and n. 3, 491; marriage certificate, 492; state registration, 495; legislative divorce, iii, 97; judicial divorce, 124, 125; remarriage, 148; residence, 155; soliciting divorce business forbidden, 160; common-law marriage, 177; age of consent to carnal knowledge, 201.

Ministers as celebrants of marriage: defects in the present laws regarding, iii, 186–89.

Miscegenation: forbidden in Maine and formerly in Rhode Island and Massachusetts, ii, 398, 399; in the southern and southwestern states, 438–40; middle and western states, 478, 479; law of Massachusetts colony on, 218; of Maryland colony, 244; North Carolina colony, 253.

Mishnah: on divorce, ii, 13 n. 4, 14.

Mississippi: marriage celebration in, ii, 417, 418; requisites for a legal marriage, 424; license essential to valid marriage, 425; marriage a civil contract, 427; age of parental consent, 429; forbidden degrees, 433, 434; void or voidable marriages, 435 n. 3, 436, 437; miscegenation forbidden, 438, 440; license system, 447;

license bond, 448; return 449, 450; legislative divorce, iii, 38, 39; judicial divorce, 64–66; remarriage, 83; residence, 85, 86; process, 89; rejects common-law marriage, 180, 181; age of consent to carnal knowledge, 200.

Missouri: marriage celebration in, ii, 417, 418; a civil contract, 427; age of parental consent, 429, 430; forbidden degrees, 433; void or voidable marriages, 435, 437; miscegenation forbidden, 438, 440; original triple system of banns, notice, or license, 443; present system, 447; certificate to married pair, 450; return, 449, 450; celebrant's record, 451; legislative divorce, iii, 38; judicial divorce, 66–68; remarriage, 82; residence, 87; process, 89; guilty wife forfeits dower, 94, 95; common-law marriage, 176; age of consent to carnal knowledge, 198.

Mohammedans. (*See* Islam, Arabs.)

Möllendorff, P. J. v.: on divorce in China, i, 236 and n. 1.

Moloch, the Carthaginian, i, 51.

Monogamic family: according to Morgan, i, 70; among animals, 96, 97; always the typical form, 150, 222, 223; iii, 224.

Monogamy: hetairistic, i, 56–58; among lower animals, 96, 97; the rule among Veddahs and American aborigines, 142, 143 and n. 1; among Mohammedans, 142; monogamy the typical form of sexual life, 150; iii, 224, 225.

Montana: marriage celebration in, ii, 464; witnesses, 465; marriage by declaration, 467; unauthorized solemnization, 468; requisites for legal marriage, 469; definition 471; age of consent and of parental consent to marriage, 472, 473; forbidden degrees, 473–75; void and voidable marriages, 475–78; license, 487, 488; return, 489 and n. 3, 491; marriage certificate, 492; legislative divorce, iii, 98; judicial divorce, 138, 139; remarriage, 149; residence, 156; notice, 158; soliciting divorce business forbidden, 160; courts silent as to common-law marriage, 182; age of consent to carnal knowledge, 202.

Moore, G. H.: on slavery in Massachusetts, ii, 217, 221, 222, 223, 224–26.

Morgan, H. D.: on *porneia*, ii, 20 n. 1.

Morgan, Lewis H.: his works, i, 34, 65 n. 4; works on, 36, 76 n. 3; his constructive theory analyzed, 65–70; criticism of his theory, 70–76; his *Systems of Consanguinity*, 66, 67; his five stages in evolution of the family and marriage, 67–70; on origin of aversion to close intermarriage, 122; on polygyny, 150.

Morganatic or "left-hand" marriages, i, 255, 256.

Morning-gift, i, 269 and n. 2.

Morocco: divorce in, i, 241, 243 n. 3, 244 n. 2.

Morong, i, 36.

New London, Conn.: wedding-feast at, ii, 142.

New Mexico: marriage celebration in, ii, 417 n. 4; marriage a civil contract, 427; age of consent and of parental consent, 428, 429; void or voidable marriages, 435 n. 3, 437, 438; favors marriage, 441; return, 449, 450; celebrant's record, 451; judicial divorce, iii, 74–76; remarriage, 82; residence, 87; notice, 88; courts silent as to common-law marriage, 181; age of consent to carnal knowledge, 200.

New Netherland: marriage laws of, influenced by those of Guelderland. ii, 268; civil matrimonial administration with religious celebration, 268, 269; Stuyvesant's letter on notice of intentions, 269; the first ordinance, 270; half-marriage after banns, 271; bundling, 271, 272; form of notice on the Delaware, 273; civil courts have jurisdiction, 273; case of Beeck and Verleth, 274–77; informal marriage de praesenti not valid, 277; case of Laers, 277, 278; cases of Fabricius and Doxy, 278, 279; adultery, 280; breach of promise, 281, 282; wills and contracts at second marriage, 282–84; divorce and arbitration, 376–82.

New York, the colony: bundling in, ii, 181; marriage law and custom in New Netherland, 267–84; under the Duke of York, 284; optional civil marriage, 285–87; registration, 288; wife-harboring punished, 288; remarriage after long absence, 289; case of self-marriage, 289, 290; Avery's offenses, 290, 291; complaints of marriages by justices, 291; Quaker marriages, 291–94; Dongan Act, 294–96; law and custom in the royal province, 296–300; question of law after 1691, 300, 301; Lauderdale Peerage case, 301–6; evidence of John Rodgers, 306–8; divorce in New Netherland, 376–82; divorce in royal province, 382–85.

—— the state: slave baptism and slave marriage, ii, 453; solemnization, 453; common-law marriage abolished, 454, 455; Indian marriages, 455; witnesses, 465; unauthorized solemnization, 468; definition, 471; age of consent to marriage, 472; forbidden degrees, 473–75; void and voidable marriages, 475–78; substitute for license system, 484, 485; return, 490, 491; marriage certificate and celebrant's record, 492; state registration, 495–97; divorce, iii, 101–5; remarriage, 102, 103, 104, 145; Van Voorhis v. Brintnall, 145; Smith v. Woodworth, 146; residence, 152, 153; notice, 158 n. 3; soliciting divorce business forbidden, 160; common-law marriage, 175; age of consent to carnal knowledge, 201; divorce rate, 216, 217.

New Zealand: wife-capture in, i, 159.

—— and Tasmania: divorce rate, iii, 211, note.

Nez-Percés: runaway bride among, regarded as a prostitute, i, 184 n. 2.

Niassers of Batu: no divorce among, i, 229.

Niblack, A. P.: quoted, i, 143 n. 1.

Nicaragua aborigines: divorce rare among, i, 247 n. 6.

Nicholas, Pope: his letter to the Bulgarians on marriage in church, i, 295 n. 6.

Nikâh al-mot'a marriage, i, 227 n. 1.

Nisbet, Judge: his decision in Head v. Head, ii, 375, 376; iii, 46–50.

Nisi: the decree in England, ii, 113, 114. (See Decree nisi.)

Niyoga, i, 84 and n. 2, 133.

Noble, John: his edition of assistants' records, ii, 332.

Nomenclatures: as basis of so-called systems of consanguinity, i, 70–73.

Norfolk's case, ii, 104, 105.

Northampton's case, ii, 80 and n. 4, 103.

North Carolina, the colony: struggle for free civil marriage in, ii, 247; first marriage law, 249, 250; liberty of Quakers, 250; vestries act, establishing ecclesiastical rites, 252; governor's license, 252; act of 1741, 252–54; law of 1766, 254–59; question of common-law marriage, iii, 172.

—— the state: celebration of marriage in, ii, 415; requisites for a legal marriage, 424; age of consent, 428, 429; age of parental consent, 429; forbidden degrees, 433, 434; void or voidable marriages, 455 n. 3, 437, 438; miscegenation forbidden, 439; survival of dual system of banns and license, 443; present license system, 447; return, 449; legislative divorce, iii, 36–38; judicial divorce, 57, 58; remarriage, 80, 81; residence, 86, 87; notice, 88; trial by jury, 90; alimony, property, and care of children, 91, 92–94; rejects common-law marriage, 180; age of consent to carnal knowledge, 200.

North Dakota: marriage celebration in, ii, 463, 464; witnesses, 465; unauthorized solemnization, 468; definition, 471; age of consent and of parental consent to marriage, 472, 473; forbidden degrees, 473–75; void and voidable marriages, 475–78; license, 488; return, 489 and n. 3, 491; divorce, iii, 142; remarriage, 149; residence, 156, 157; courts silent as to common-law marriage, 182; age of consent to carnal knowledge, 201.

Northwest Territory: marriage laws of, ii, 458, 459; divorce laws, iii, 113.

"Northumbrian Priests, Law of": denies remarriage after divorce, ii, 40.

Notice to defendant in divorce suits: in New England, iii, 25–27; southern and southwestern states, 88, 89; middle and western states, 158.

Nugent, Mr.: on the Hardwicke Act, i, 449, 452 n. 1, 453, 454 n. 1, 455 n. 1, 458.

Nullity: decree of, equivalent to divorce under the canon law, ii, 56–59.

Wooing gifts, i, 218, 219.

Woolsey, T. D.: on attempted divorce of Hipparete, ii, 12 n. 3; *porneia*, 20 n. 1; Jewish law of divorce, 20 n. 3; Paul's teaching regarding divorce, 21 n. 2; Hermas's views on divorce, 28 and n. 1; divorce by mutual consent under Christian emperors, 29, 30; Constantine's divorce law, 31; that of Theodosius II., 31, 32; adultery under Christian emperors, 32 n. 4; Luther's use of "desertion," 63 n. 1; Zurich ordinance of 1525, 64, 65; Luther's penalty for adultery, 67; Foljambe's case, 82 n. 2; voidable marriages, 94, 95; legislative divorce in the New England colonies, ii, 349 n. 2.

Wotjäken: proof-marriages among, i, 49 and n. 2; wife-lending among, 49, 50; prostitution of girls, 49 n. 1.

Wren, Bishop: his orders regarding the marriage celebration, i, 417 and n. 3.

Wright, Carroll D.: his report on marriage and divorce, iii, 205, 209, 210; quoted on migration for divorce, 206; judicial administration of divorce laws, 207; influence of legislation, 218; late marriages, 243; moral character of divorce, 252, 253.

Wright's case, ii, 191 n. 2.

Wundt, W.: cited, i, 98.

Würtemberg: ordinance of, ii, 68.

Wyandots: position of woman among, i, 45; polyandry prohibited among, 143 n. 1.

Wyatt, Walter: the Fleet parson, i, 442 n. 1.

Wyoming: marriage celebration in, ii, 464; witnesses, 465; unauthorized solemnization, 468; definition, 470; age of consent and of parental consent to marriage, 472, 473; forbidden degrees, 473–75; void and voidable marriages, 475–78; license, 487, 488; return, 489 and n. 3, 491; marriage certificate, 492; divorce, iii, 130, 131; remarriage, 148; residence, 157; notice, 158; courts silent as to common-law marriage, 182; age of consent to carnal knowledge, 201.

Yaméos: avoid marriage with persons of same community, i, 128.

Young, Ernest: denies *patria potestas*, among Germans, i, 260, note.

York: its marriage ritual, i, 284, 301, 303–8, 311.

Yucatan: pueblos in, i, 129; marriage by service, 186; husband's sole right of divorce, 231.

Yurok, of California: husband's sole right of divorce among, i, 231.

Zara: effects of divorce in, i, 242.

Zeitehen, i, 49 and n. 3, 235 n. 1.

Zimmer, H.: on Hindu wife-purchase, i, 197, 198 n. 1.

Zoepfl, H.: on Tacitus's account of the betrothal, 262 n. 2; canon-law betrothal, 293 n. 1; divorce among the early Germans, ii, 34 n. 1.

Zulus: bride-price among, i, 193, 194; love a check to divorce, 248.

Zwingli, Ulrich: his liberal views on divorce, ii, 64.